D0904479

Handbook of Consumer Finance Research

Handbook of Consumer Finance Research

Jing Jian Xiao, Ph.D.
Editor

 Springer

Jing Jian Xiao, Ph.D.
University of Rhode Island
Transition Center
2 Lower College Rd.
Kingston RI 02881
USA
jfei.editor@gmail.com

ISBN: 978-0-387-75733-9   e-ISBN: 978-0-387-75734-6

Library of Congress Control Number: 2007941873

Printed on acid-free paper

9 8 7 6 5 4 3 2 1

springer.com

Preface

For several reasons, American consumers are now facing many financial challenges. First, the social security system will likely be insolvent within the next 40 years. Second, private industries are moving from defined benefit pensions to defined contribution retirement plans. These trends require individual consumers to take more responsibility for their financial future. Another factor is the rising cost of higher education that many consumers now have to consider when planning their children's college education. In addition, easily accessible credit has pushed many consumers deep into debt, leading to record high individual bankruptcy filings, increased demand for credit counseling, and increased numbers of debt consolidations. These growing social issues recently prompted government and private organizations to sponsor joint efforts of financial education and research. Out of these developments grows the need for a book to summarize research findings and point out future directions. *Handbook of Consumer Finance Research* answers this call by addressing these social issues as well as directly helping consumer finance researchers, policy makers, educators, and practitioners to design, implement, and evaluate financial education and research initiatives.

Active, multidisciplinary researchers in consumer finance have contributed the chapters that provide a comprehensive overview of the current research. All chapters have received blind reviews by peers who are qualified researchers, some of whom are also chapter contributors. In each chapter, the author first critically reviews the research publications on the focused topic, then assesses the status of the research, and provides directions for future research. The authors were asked to search literature in multiple fields for the latest research in consumer finance, compile the findings, and present it in a manner accessible to people who are not specially trained in the field. In several chapters, the authors also present their original research.

The handbook is divided into four parts consisting of 25 chapters. Part I has six chapters that review research on basic concepts and theories in consumer finance such as risk tolerance, financial wellness, retirement savings, financial education, behavior theory application, and consumer economic socialization. Part II reviews consumer finance research in the Internet setting including e-banking, online insurance, and online shopping. The nine chapters in Part III describe consumer financial issues among special populations such as high school students, college students, older consumers, low-income consumers, family business owners, individual investors, and racial and ethnic minority consumers (Hispanic, African, and Asian Americans). Part IV discusses consumer financial issues on special topics such as healthcare, marriage, family communication, bankruptcy, workplace, regulation, and applied research.

The first of its kind to provide a comprehensive picture of consumer finance research, this book lays the foundation on which to develop more quality research in consumer finance. It helps to generate helpful information for financial educators, researchers, and policy makers to improve consumer financial well-being and quality of life. In addition, most contributors are professors who teach consumer finance and related courses at the university level making the material accessible to graduate and undergraduate students as well as professionals. Overall, it enriches the literature of consumer science, economics, finance, business, family studies, human development, and related fields.

Jing Jian Xiao
University of Rhode Island
Rhode Island, United States
August 2007

Acknowledgments

The following reviewers provided constructive blind reviews that helped greatly improve the quality of the book:

Myria Allen, Associate Professor, University of Arkansas
Joan Grey Anderson, Professor, University of Rhode Island
David Cordell, Associate Professor, Texas Tech University
Sharon Danes, Professor, University of Minnesota
Lucy Delgadillo, Assistant Professor, Utah State University
Sharon DeVaney, Professor, Purdue University
Jeff Dew, Research Associate, University of Virginia
Elizabeth Dolan, Associate Professor, University of New Hampshire
John Grable, Associate Professor, Kansas State University
Sherman Hanna, Professor, Ohio State University
Celia Hayhoe, Assistant Professor, Virginia Tech
George Haynes, Professor, Montana State University
Tahira Hira, Professor, Iowa State University
Joan Koonce, Associate Professor, University of Georgia
Yoon Lee, Associate Professor, Utah State University
Suzanne Lindamood, Research Attorney, Ohio Legislative Service Commission
Cäzilia Loibl, Assistant Professor, Ohio State University
Lewis Mandell, Professor, State University of New York at Buffalo
Rob Mayer, Professor, University of Utah
Yoko Mimura, Research Professional, University of Georgia
Barbara O'Neill, Professor, Rutgers University Cooperative Extension
Janice Prochaska, President and CEO, ProChange Behavior Systems
Kathryn Rettig, Professor, University of Minnesota
Peter Rose, Professor Emeritus, Texas A&M University
Tansel Yilmazer, Assistant Professor, Purdue University

Sharon Panulla at Springer provided helpful guidance, suggestions, and encouragement at all stages of the book production. Two other staffers at Springer, Anna Tobias and Jennifer Hadley, provided prompt and able assistance at various stages of the book.

When the book was planned and developed, I was the TCA Professor and Director of Take Charge America Institute for Consumer Financial Education and Research (TCAI) at the University of Arizona. I appreciate continuous support and encouragement from Soyeon Shim, the Director of the Norton School of Family and Consumer Science, University of Arizona. I also thank Mike Hall, Mike Sullivan, Peter Rose, and other TCAI board members for their support of the book idea. TCAI research council members, John Grable, George Haynes, Angela Lyons, and Peter Rose, contributed and/or reviewed chapters for the book.

Vicki Fitzsimmons, Brian Haroldson, and Sha Jin provided invaluable assistance at the final editing stage.

Contents

Part II   Internet and Consumer Finance

Part III   Consumer Finances of Special Populations

Part IV   Consumer Finance in Various Settings

Contributors

Fahzy Abdul-Rahman, Ph.D. Candidate, Department of Consumer Sciences, Ohio State University, 1787 Neil Avenue, Columbus, OH 43210, USA, abdul-rahman.4@osu.edu

Myria Watkins Allen, Ph.D., Associate Professor, Department of Communication, University of Arkansas, Fayetteville, AR 72701, USA, myria@uark.edu

Suzanne Bartholomae, Ph.D., Adjunct Assistant Professor, Department of Human Development and Family Science, Ohio State University, Columbus, OH 43210, USA, sbartholomae@ehe.ohio-state.edu

Ivan Beutler, Ph.D., Professor, School of Family Life, Brigham Young University, 2048 JFSB, Provo, UT 84602, USA, ivan_beutler@byu.edu

Cathy Faulcon Bowen, Ph.D., Associate Professor, Department of Agricultural and Extension Education, The Pennsylvania State University, 323 Agricultural Administration, University Park, PA 16802, USA, cbowen@psu.edu

Sharon A. Burns, Ph.D., CPA (Inactive), Executive Director of the Association for Financial Counseling and Planning Education, 1500 West Third Avenue, Suite 223, Columbus, OH 43212, USA, sburns@afcpe.org

Yi Cai, Ph.D., Assistant Professor, Department of Family and Consumer Sciences, California State University at Northridge, 18111 Nordhoff St., Northridge, CA 91330-8308, USA, yi.cai@csun.edu

Samuel Cheng-Chung Chen, Ph.D. Student, Department of Consumer Science, The Ohio State University, 2197 Lehner Rd., Columbus, OH 43224, USA, chensam11@gmail.com

Jinsook Erin Cho, Ph.D., Associate Professor of Design and Management, Parsons, New School University, 72 Fifth Avenue, Room 524, New York, NY 10011, USA, choje@newschool.edu

Brenda J. Cude, Ph.D., Professor, Department of Housing and Consumer Economics, University of Georgia, Dawson Hall, Athens, GA 30602, USA, bcude@uga.edu

Sharon M. Danes, Ph.D., Professor, Department of Family Social Science, University of Minnesota, 275F McNeal, 1985 Buford Avenue, St. Paul, MN 55108, USA, sdanes@umn.edu

Sharon A. DeVaney, Ph.D., Professor, Purdue University, 812 West State Street, West Lafayette, IN 47906-2060, USA, sdevaney@purdue.edu

Jeffrey Dew, Ph.D., Research Associate, The University of Virginia, Dawson's Row 2, Charlottesville, VA 22903, USA, jpd197@juno.com

Lori Dickson, Graduate Student, Department of English, Brigham Young University, USA, lori_d@byu.edu

Cynthia Needles Fletcher, Ph.D., Professor, Department of Human Development and Family Studies, Iowa State University, 4380 Palmer Building, Ames, IA 50011, USA, cynthia@iastate.edu

Jonathan J. Fox, Ph.D., Associate Professor, Department of Consumer Sciences, Ohio State University, Columbus, OH 43210, USA, fox.99@osu.edu

Steven Garasky, Ph.D., Associate Professor, Department of Human Development and Family Studies, Iowa State University, 4380 Palmer Building, Ames, IA 50011, USA, sgarasky@iastate.edu

John E. Grable, Ph.D., The Vera Mowery McAninch Professor of Human Development and Family Studies, Institute of Personal Financial Planning, School of Family Studies and Human Services, Kansas State University, 18 Justin Hall, Manhattan, KS 66506, USA, jgrable@ksu.edu

Sherman D. Hanna, Ph.D., Professor, Department of Consumer Science, The Ohio State University, 1787 Neil Avenue, Columbus, OH 43210, USA hanna.1@osu.edu

Deborah C. Haynes, Ph.D., Associate Professor, Department of Health and Human Development, Montana State University, 205B Herrick Hall, Bozeman, MT 59717, USA, dhaynes@montana.edu

George W. Haynes, Ph.D., Professor, Department of Agricultural Economics and Economics, Montana State University, 210E Linfield Hall, Bozeman, MT 59717, USA, haynes@montana.edu

Tahira K. Hira, Ph.D., Professor, Department of Human Development and Family Studies, Iowa State University, 1750 Beardshear Hall, Ames, IA 50011, USA, tkhira@iastate.edu

Sohyun Joo, Ph.D., Educational Consultant, Financial Planning Standards Board of Korea, 17th FL., Seongji Bldg., Dohwa 2-dong, Mapo-gu, Seoul 121-743, Korea, sjookwun@yahoo.com

Jinhee Kim, Ph.D., Associate Professor, University of Maryland, 1204 Marie Mount Hall, College Park, MD 20742, USA, jinkim@umd.edu

David A. Lander, J.D., Adjunct Professor, St. Louis University School of Law School, 3700 Lindell Blvd., St. Louis, MO 63108, USA, cdlander@charter.net

Jinkook Lee, Ph.D., Professor, Department of Consumer Sciences, Ohio State University, 1787 Neil Avenue, Columbus, OH 43210, USA, lee.42@osu.edu

Cäzilia Loibl, Ph.D., Assistant Professor, Department of Consumer Sciences, The Ohio State University, 1787 Neil Avenue, 265N Campbell Hall, Columbus, OH 43210, USA, loibl.3@osu.edu

Jean M. Lown, Ph.D., Professor, Utah State University, FCHD, 2905 Old Main Hall, Logan, UT 84322, USA, lown@cc.usu.edu

Angela C. Lyons, Ph.D., Associate Professor, University of Illinois at Urbana-Champaign, 440 Mumford Hall, 1301 West Gregory Drive, Urbana, IL 61801, USA, anglyons@uiuc.edu

Lewis Mandell, Ph.D., Professor, Department of Finance, State University of New York at Buffalo, 375 Jacobs Hall, University at Buffalo, Buffalo, NY 14260-4000, USA, lewm@Buffalo.edu

Robert N. Mayer, Ph.D., Professor, Department of Family and Consumer Studies, University of Utah, 225 S 1400 East, Salt Lake City, UT 84112, USA, robert.mayer@fcs.utah.edu

Robert B. Nielsen, Ph.D., Assistant Professor, Department of Housing and Consumer Economics, University of Georgia, 205 Dawson Hall, Athens, GA 30605, USA, rnielsen@uga.edu

Deanna L. Sharpe, Ph.D., Associate Professor, Personal Financial Planning Department, University of Missouri-Columbia, 239 Stanley Hall, Columbia, MO 65211, USA, sharped@missouri.edu

Kittichai Watchravesringkan, Ph.D., Assistant Professor, Department of Consumer, Apparel, and Retail Studies, University of North Carolina at Greensboro, PO Box 26170, Greensboro, NC 27402-6170, USA, k_watchr@uncg.edu

Jing Jian Xiao, Ph.D., Professor, Department of Human Development and Family Studies, University of Rhode Island, Transition Center, Kingston, RI 02881, USA xiao@uri.edu

Rui Yao, Ph.D., Assistant Professor, Department of Human Development, Consumer and Family Sciences, South Dakota State University, NFA 311, Box 2275A, Brookings, SD 57007, USA, rui_yao@yahoo.com

List of Figures

List of Tables

Part I
Concepts and Theories
of Consumer Finance

Chapter 1
Risk Tolerance

John E. Grable

Abstract This chapter provides an overview of the important role financial risk tolerance plays in shaping consumer financial decisions. A review of normative and descriptive models of risk tolerance is provided. Additional discussion regarding the measurement of risk tolerance is also presented. The chapter includes the presentation of a conceptual model of the principal factors affecting financial risk tolerance with recommendations designed to enhance the consumer finance field's knowledge of risk tolerance. The chapter concludes with a summary of additional research needed to better understand the multidimensional nature of risk tolerance.

The specific study of how a person's perceptions of risk influence behaviors has gained importance over the past two decades as consumers, investment advisers, researchers, and policy makers have come to face new and ever increasingly complex changes in the economic landscape. This is especially true in relation to the consumer finance field's examination and understanding of the role *financial risk tolerance* plays in shaping individual financial behaviors. One of the first definitions of risk tolerance appropriate for use by researchers interested in consumer and personal financial issues was proposed by Kogan and Wallach in 1964. They stated that risk tolerance is the willingness of an individual to engage in a behavior where there is a desirable goal but attainment of the goal is uncertain and accompanied by the possibility of loss. Okun (1976) described a key facet of risk tolerance as a person's perception of change and danger. According to Okun, "all risk-taking situations necessitate the evaluation of (a) the relative value of a given alternative and (b) the likelihood or probability of achieving it successfully" (p. 222). Weber, Blais, and Betz (2002) conceptualized a person's attitude toward taking financial risks to include risk perception and attitude toward perceived risk. Using their definitional framework, risk tolerance is "a person's standing on the continuum from risk aversion to risk seeking" (p. 264). Sometimes the term "risk preference" is used

J.E. Grable
Institute of Personal Financial Planning, School of Family Studies and Human Services, Kansas State University, Manhattan, KS 66506, USA
e-mail: jgrable@ksu.edu

J.J. Xiao, (ed.), *Handbook of Consumer Finance Research,*
© Springer 2008

to describe risk tolerance. Risk preference is a person's "tendency to be attracted or repelled by alternatives that he or she perceives as more risky over alternatives perceived as less risky" (Weber & Milliman, 1997). This definition decomposes risk tolerance into two parts: risk attitude and risk perception. Many personal and consumer finance researchers conceptualize risk tolerance as the maximum amount of uncertainty someone is willing to accept when making a financial decision or "the willingness to engage in behaviors in which the outcomes remain uncertain with the possibility of an identifiable negative outcome" (Irwin, 1993, p. 11).

Risk tolerance is an important factor that influences a wide range of personal financial decisions (Snelbecker, Roszkowski, & Cutler, 1990). Risk tolerance is an underlying factor within financial planning models, investment suitability analyses, and consumer decision frameworks. The debt versus savings decision individuals regularly make, the type of mortgage selected, and the use and management of credit cards are examples of situations where a person's financial risk tolerance can influence behavior (Campbell, 2006). Financial risk tolerance also affects the way people invest their resources for short- and long-term goals such as saving for a significant purchase and retirement. It is reasonable to expect that people with varying levels of risk tolerance should act differently when making investment decisions, with those having a high risk tolerance investing more aggressively.

Much of the early theoretical and empirical research conducted on the topic of risk tolerance involved testing and assessing individuals' perceptions and susceptibility to health, environmental, and physical risks (Csicsaky, 2001; MacCrimmon & Wehrung, 1986; Slovic, 2004) as evaluated through experimental economics methodologies (e.g., Bateman & Munro, 2005; Kahneman & Tversky, 1979). Outside of economics, the study of risk tolerance has been diverse. The earliest work on the recognition of risk and the willingness to engage in risky activities was concentrated in the area of consumer behavior (MacCrimmon & Wehrung, 1984). Researchers in the fields of finance (e.g., Cohn, Lewellen, Lease, & Schlarbaum, 1975; Markowitz, 1952; Siegel & Hoban, 1982), business (e.g., Fitzpatrick, 1983), natural hazards (e.g., Kunreuther, 1979), and natural and man-made disasters (e.g., Newman, 1972; Slovic, Fischhoff, & Lichtenstein, 1978) have also given attention to measuring risky situations and surveying propensities of individuals to take risks. Over the past quarter century there has been a growing movement to better understand risk tolerance from a household financial and psychological perspective (Dixon, Hayes, Rehfeldt, & Ebbs, 1998).

Researchers and theorists have attempted to explain risk tolerance, the likelihood of taking risks, and outcomes from risky actions through normative and descriptive models. Normative models describe how people ought to make decisions, whereas descriptive models attempt to explain how and why individuals actually make risk evaluations. The primary normative model is expected utility theory. Descriptive models, on the other hand, tend to be based on varied behavioral and/or psychosocial perspectives. Expected utility theory and a sampling of descriptive frameworks are reviewed below.

The Expected Utility Theory Framework

The use of expected utility theory (EUT) modeling is the primary approach used by researchers to describe how risk tolerance is conceptually linked with risk-taking behaviors. The conceptualization of EUT was advanced by Von Neumann and Morgenstern (1947). They argued that consumers should select choices with the highest expected outcomes. A consumer's utility function is typically assumed to resemble a constant relative risk aversion utility function (Hanna, Gutter, & Fan, 2001). "In the expected utility framework, risk preference is operationalized as risk attitudes that are descriptive labels for the shape of the utility function presumed to underlie a person's choices. Choice of a sure amount of money over a lottery with equal expected value would classify a person as risk averse" (Weber & Milliman, 1997, p. 124). Constant relative risk aversion is generally represented graphically so that as wealth increases marginal utility slowly increases but at an ever slowing rate. Low risk tolerance is represented with a concave utility function, whereas a convex utility function is representative of high risk tolerance. In its most basic form, EUT assumes that consumers are rational and that risk preferences remain constant. As such, a consumer should make the same choice (tradeoff) in terms of riskiness regardless of the situation or event.

Modern portfolio theory (MPT) was originally conceptualized by Markowitz (1952) as an extension of EUT to the analysis of investment portfolios. According to Mayo (2003), "The Markowitz model is premised on a risk-averse individual constructing a diversified portfolio that maximizes the individual's satisfaction (generally referred to as utility by economists) by maximizing portfolio returns for a given level of risk" (p. 170). Within MPT, investors develop risk and return trade-offs. Economists depict these trade-offs with indifference curves where investors prefer high returns with low risks. Trading off risks for returns is one way investors maximize utility. In general, MPT predicts that investors should only be willing to take additional risk if the return associated with the risk is high.

The shape of the utility function used within EUT and MPT frameworks is generally measured using a person's response to a series of hypothetical income gambles. For example, Hanna and Lindamood (2004, p. 37) asked a progression of questions similar to the following:

> "Suppose that you are about to retire, and have two choices for a pension:
> Pension A gives you an income equal to your pre-retirement income.
> Pension B has a 50 % chance your income will be double your pre-retirement income, and a 50 % chance that your income will be 20 % less than your pre-retirement income.
> You will have no other source of income during retirement, no chance of employment, and no other family income ever in the future.
> All incomes are after tax.
> Which pension would you choose?"

Using their approach, additional questions ask respondents to choose among different percentage changes in income. The result allows for the calculation of a person's relative risk aversion. Risk aversion, or the theoretical opposite—risk tolerance, can then be used to help explain household portfolio allocations. In its most basic form, risk tolerance is important within the context of EUT because only measures of risk tolerance based on hypothetical gambles have been directly linked to the theory. For example, Hanna and Chen (1997) showed that risk aversion has little impact for consumers investing for the long run, but does make a significant difference for those investing with shorter time horizons. The normative implication of this result is substantial. The long-run riskiness of stocks is less than commonly thought. Further, because wealth accumulation is positively associated with high return investments (e.g., stocks), it is important for everyone, even those with low risk tolerance, to invest a portion of investment assets in stocks. Individuals who eschew stocks and other high return investments must either be extremely thrifty today or run the risk of living in relative poverty in the future.

Behavioral Finance and Psychosocial Descriptive Frameworks

Even though EUT has traditionally been a favorite method for conceptualizing risk tolerance and risk-taking behaviors among economists, groups of researchers, primarily those housed in departments of psychology and behavioral sciences, have traditionally questioned the notion that risk tolerance can be represented within an economic utility framework (Olson, 2006). There is a growing body of evidence to suggest that the assumption that "risk is an immutable attribute of a decision alternative that is perceived the same way by different decision makers" (Weber, 1997, p. 129) may be incorrect. Consider the normative directive indicated by EUT that everyone saving for a long-term goal should invest in high return investments. Only a small part of the population follows this advice. Descriptive models attempt to explain why people often stray from this and other normatively appropriate behaviors.

The conflict between what consumers should do and what they actually do has been widely studied. Friedman and Savage (1948) were the first to challenge the standard utility function assumption by showing that few people have a constant risk aversion throughout the entire domain of wealth. They noted a paradox among consumers who purchase insurance but also gamble. Others have documented similar inconsistencies of behavior linked to differences in risk tolerance. One of the first to note such a paradox was Allais (1953). He asked individuals to choose a preference in each of two circumstances as shown in Table 1.1.

When offered the choice, nearly all individuals choose 1a over 1b; however, in the second situation most people choose 2b over 2a. This is a violation of the relative risk aversion assumption within economic utility theory. According to Schoemaker (1980), "The first preference implies, of course, that $U(1) > .1U(5) + .89U(1) + .01U(0)$ where the amounts are in millions. Combining terms, this simplifies to

Table 1.1 The Allais paradox.

	Choice 1a	Choice 1b
Situation one	$1 million for certain	$5 million with a probability of .1; $1 million with a probability of .89; and $0 with a probability of .01
	Choice 2a	Choice 2b
Situation two	$1 million with a probability of .11 and $0 with a probability of .89	$5 million with a probability of .1 and $0 with a probability of .9

$.11U(1) > .1U(5) + .01U(0)$. The second preference, however, implies exactly the opposite.... $1U(5) + .01U(0) > .11U(1)$" (p. 18). Similar evidence showing that a conflict between normative theory and actual behavior has been noted by Bell (1982), Coombs (1975), Ellsberg (1961), Kahneman and Tversky (1979), Loomes and Sugden (1982), Payne, Laughhunn, and Crum (1984), Shefrin and Statman (1985, 1993), Tversky (1969), and Tversky and Kahneman (1981). This growing body of empirical evidence has led to the development of a new sub-discipline within economics and finance—behavioral economics/finance (Kahneman & Tversky, 1979).

Kahneman and Tversky (1979) noted that "the magnitudes of potential loss and gain amounts, their chances of occurrence, and the exposure to potential loss contribute to the degree of threat (versus opportunity) in a risky situation" (p. 266). This observation led them to conclude that people are consistently more willing to take risks when certain losses are anticipated and to settle for sure gains when absolute rewards are expected. This insight is the fundamental tenet of prospect theory—a major behavioral finance theory (Statman, 1995; Tversky & Kahneman, 1981).

Although there have been a number of behavioral theories put forth as substitutes (e.g., regret theory, Ellsberg's paradox, satisficing theory), prospect theory (Kahneman & Tversky, 1979) continues to be the primary descriptive alternative to EUT. Within the prospect theory framework, value, rather than utility, is used to describe gains and losses. A value function, similar to a utility function, can be derived; however, "the value function for losses (the curve lying below the horizontal axis) is convex and relatively steep. In contrast, the value function for gains (above the horizontal axis) is concave and not quite so steep" (Plous, 1993, p. 95). One of the primary outcomes associated with prospect theory is that a person's risk tolerance will depend on how a situation or event is framed. Risks with sure gains are predicted to produce risk-averse behaviors, while risks with sure losses are expected to bring about risk-seeking preferences.

One argument critical of EUT, prospect theory, and behavioral frameworks is that each is consequential in nature. The underlying assumption in these frameworks is that individuals make decisions based on an assessment of consequences. A relatively new theory of risk tolerance and risk taking suggests that this assumption is incorrect. According to Loewenstein, Weber, Hsee, and Welch (2001), existing frameworks "posit that risky choice can be predicted by assuming that people assess the severity and likelihood of the possible outcomes of choice alternatives, albeit subjectively and possibly with bias or error, and integrate this information through some type of expectations-based calculus to arrive at a decision. Feelings triggered by the decision situation and imminent risky choice are seen as epiphenomenal—that is, not integral to the decision-making process" (p, 267). In response, Loewenstein and his associates proposed a "risk-as-feelings" theoretical perspective.

The risk-as-feelings hypothesis puts forward the notion that emotional reactions to risky situations often diverge from reasoned assessments. When this happens, emotional reactions directly influence behavior. Within the framework, emotional responses, such as worry, fear, dread, and anxiety influence judgments and choices. For example, people in good moods tend to view risky situations with less threat than individuals in a bad mood (Loewenstein et al., 2001; Olson, 2006). The risk-as-feelings framework is unique in terms of acknowledging the influences of cognitive and emotional factors on risk tolerance and risk-taking behaviors. The risk-as-feelings hypothesis offers a fresh approach to understanding both risk tolerance and risk-taking behaviors.

Risk Tolerance Measurement Issues

The formal assessment of risk tolerance can take on many forms (Roszkowski & Grable, 2005). In practice, risk tolerance tends to be measured and assessed using one of the six methods: (a) personal or professional judgment, (b) heuristics, (c) objectively, (d) single item questions, (e) risk scales, or (f) mixed measures.

Those that rely on personal or professional judgments have a tendency to use one of the four methods to assess the risk tolerance of other people. A judgment can be made based on the assumption that others have the same risk tolerance as the judge. It is also possible to perceive others as less risk tolerant. This is known as risk-as-value, where the judge perceives his or her own risk tolerance as being more desirable. An alternative is to predict that others have only slight differences in risk tolerance compared to the judge. The final approach involves relying on stereotypes to arrive at a judgment. Unfortunately, the literature on personal and professional judgment has not shown those that use this method to be particularly accurate (Roszkowski & Grable, 2005).

The use of heuristics is another way that some attempt to assess risk tolerance. A heuristic is a simplified rule that results in a mental shortcut to solve a problem. In terms of risk assessment, for instance, some people believe that, holding all other factors constant, males are more risk tolerant than females or that those that are self-employed tend to be more risk tolerant than others. Other risk-tolerance heuristic examples include associating general risk-taking behaviors with a willingness to take financial risks (e.g., skydiving to investing) and viewing occupational choice as a proxy for risk-taking preferences. The preponderance of research on the topic of heuristic validity suggests that very few heuristic rules can be used reliably.

The majority of risk-tolerance heuristics can lead to potentially serious miscalculations and incorrect categorizations of individuals into risk-tolerance groups (Grable, 2000; Grable & Lytton, 1998, 1999a).

Another technique that is sometimes used to describe a person's risk tolerance involves objectively assessing an individual's current investment approach and inferring risk tolerance from the observation. Using this method, someone who holds the majority of their investment assets in equities would be assumed to have a relatively high risk tolerance. Alternatively, someone who holds their investment assets in certificates of deposit would be classified as having a low risk tolerance. Researchers who use this approach measure relative risk aversion by looking at the ratio of risky assets to wealth (Riley & Chow, 1992). The validity of this assessment method has been questioned (Campbell, 2006; Cordell, 2001). Unless sufficient information is known prior to the judgment, this type of objective measure cannot account for the effect of outside influences, such as allocations based on the recommendations of advisors or friends and emotional biases at the time the portfolio allocation decision was made. Actual stock market results obtained by investors, compared to average market returns, suggest that objective measures are a weak substitute to scale measures. When compared to the markets, investors tend to underperform indices in both up and down markets (Barber & Odean, 2001; Odean, 1998). This implies that investors do not always actually invest in ways that match their true underlying risk tolerance.

Another approach for assessing risk tolerance involves the use of a valid and reliable scale. In some situations, however, a scale is either not available or requires too much time to administer. In these cases, single item questions are sometimes used to assess risk tolerance. One risk-tolerance question is widely used among those interested in consumer finance issues—the Survey of Consumer Finances (SCF) risk-tolerance item. The question is simple to use and assess, as shown below:

> Which of the following statements on this page comes closest to the amount of financial risk that you are willing to take when you save or make investments?
>
> 1. Take substantial financial risk expecting to earn substantial returns.
> 2. Take above-average financial risks expecting to earn above-average returns.
> 3. Take average financial risks expecting to earn average returns.
> 4. Not willing to take any financial risks.

This question is popular among researchers because it is one of the only risk-tolerance assessments asked in national surveys of consumers. This allows responses to the item to be compared to national averages. The downside associated with the use of this, or any other single item, is that it may not be a "good proxy for people's true risk aversion" (Chen & Finke, 1996, p. 94). Historical response patterns indicate that a large percent of those answering the question have no risk tolerance (Hanna and Lindamood, 2004). This skewed response pattern toward maximum risk aversion conflicts with actual risk-taking behaviors observed in everyday financial situations. Grable and Lytton (2001) also noted that the question does not fully represent the spectrum of financial risk tolerance. Instead, the item is most closely linked with investment choice attitudes.

Another method for assessing risk tolerance involves the use of a psychometrically designed scale (Roszkowski, Davey, & Grable, 2005). The history of risk scales can be traced back to the late 1950s. One of the earliest measures of risk tolerance was proposed by Atkinson (1957). Atkinson hypothesized that risk taking can be described by six factors: (a) assessment of the subjective probability of achieving success; (b) assessment of the subjective probability of failure; (c) the incentive value of success; (d) the incentive value of avoiding failure; (e) an achievement motive; and (f) the motive to avoid failure. Although Atkinson's work did not lead directly to a usable scale, his hypothesis laid the groundwork for the development of later scales that incorporated the multidimensional nature of risk.

A major advancement in the study of choice in risky situations occurred in the late 1950s and early 1960s. Wallach and Kogan (1959, 1961) developed the widely used Choice Dilemmas Questionnaire to measure risk preferences in everyday life situations. The original questionnaire required subjects to advise other individuals regarding 12 choices with two outcomes: a sure gain or a sure loss. An example of these questions includes the following: "Mr. A, an electrical engineer, has the choice of sticking with his present job at a modest, though adequate, salary or of moving on to another job offering more money but no long term security. Please advise Mr. A by deciding what probability of success would be sufficient to warrant choosing the risky alternative" (Wallach & Kogan, 1959, p. 558). These types of choice dilemmas were commonly used to measure risk-taking propensities for three decades. Beginning in the early 1980s, the choice dilemma approach came under increased attack for lack of validity and reliability.

The lack of consistency between and among distinctive choice dilemma questionnaires administered by different researchers was revealed as far back as 1962 by Slovic who concluded that choice dilemma measures lacked sufficient validity and reliability to be of much predictive use. Slovic came to this conclusion after examining all forms of the choice dilemma instrument, including dot estimation tests, word meanings tests for category width, life experiences inventories, multiple choice exams, recreational activity measures, job preference inventories, gambling assessments, and peer ratings. Kogan and Wallach (1964), the creators of the Choice Dilemmas Questionnaire, also found no evidence of general risk propensity across situations. Later researchers concluded that these findings were partially attributable to the one-dimensional type questions used in the instruments. MacCrimmon and Wehrung (1986) showed that one-dimensional questions (e.g., "how risk tolerant are you?") measure only a small part of the multidimensional nature of risk and that most people overestimate their risk preferences in these situations. MacCrimmon and Wehrung also concluded that "there is no particular reason to believe that a person who takes risks in one area of life is necessarily willing to take risks in all areas" (p. 51).

The development of more accurate risk-tolerance scales took a leap forward in the 1980s and 1990s. Researchers concluded that a scale must, at a minimum, gauge a person's attitude toward and behavior regarding the following dimensions:

(a) general risk-taking propensities, (b) gambles and speculations, (c) losses and gains, (d) experience or knowledge, (e) comfort, and (f) investing. Grable and Lytton (1999b) collapsed these diverse factors into three core risk-tolerance dimensions: (a) investment risk, (b) comfort and experience, and (c) speculation.

While there are few publicly available scales that have been designed to measure the multidimensional nature of risk tolerance, there have been a small number of attempts to measure risk attitudes using scaling methods (e.g., Barsky, Juster, Kimball, & Shapiro, 1997; Grable & Lytton, 1999b; Hanna and Lindamood, 2004; Roszkowski, 1999). One of the most reliable scales is the *Survey of Financial Risk Tolerance*© that was originally created by Roszkowski for The American College. The survey attempts to measure risk tolerance directly through a combination of closed- and open-ended questions. The survey includes 40 items. Some items require multiple responses, while others are phrased as multiple-choice questions. Roszkowski reported a reliability coefficient of 0.91 for this measure, which is exceptionally high. The validity of the items also appears high; however, there is no published data describing the survey's criterion (i.e., concurrent) validity. A publicly available alternative is a 13-item risk scale developed by Grable and Lytton (1999b). This multiple-choice question scale has been tested and shown to offer acceptable levels of validity and reliability (a = 0.75). A more traditional Likert-type scale was designed by Weber et al. (2002). The instrument, using a five-point likelihood agreement scale, is intended to be used to assess risk tolerance in five content areas, including investing versus gambling, health/safety, recreation, ethical, and social decisions. Alternative scales include experimental measures using hypothetical questions based on percentage changes in income. These scales are most often used to derive a person's relative risk aversion within EUT frameworks. Two of the most popular instruments were developed by Barsky et al. (1997) and Hanna and Lindamood (2004). In the case of the later measure, Hanna and Lindamood noted a statistically significant positive correlation between scale scores and risk-tolerance levels as measured with the SCF item.

The final method for assessing risk tolerance involves using a combination of the approaches listed above. Although there is scant research to support the idea that multiple measures may lead to more accurate descriptions of a person's risk tolerance, the logic of doing so is apparent. The concept of triangulation, where an answer to a complex question is derived from multiple perspectives (Lytton, Grable, & Klock, 2006), used in the social sciences indicates that a combination of approaches may produce meaningful results.

A Conceptual Model of the Factors Affecting Financial Risk Tolerance

An issue of particular importance to consumers, investment advisers, researchers, and policy makers involves understanding the factors associated with risk tolerance. Because a person's tolerance for risk has such a significant impact on the way individuals make decisions it is important to have a conceptual understanding of the factors that influence risk tolerance (Campbell, 2006). There are a number of demographic, socioeconomic, psychosocial, and other factors generally thought to be associated with financial risk tolerance. Table 1.2 summarizes consensus findings from the literature regarding the influence of certain individual characteristics on risk tolerance.

Based on relationships shown in Table 1.2 and additional risk-tolerance research conducted throughout the last two decades, it is possible to better understand, conceptually, how financial risk tolerance is influenced by personal and environmental factors. Figure 1.1 presents a conceptual model of the principal factors affecting financial risk tolerance. The model is an adaptation of an intervention model developed by Irwin (1993) who was among the first to develop a valid model showing the relationship between risk tolerance and risk-taking behaviors. Building upon a causal model of adolescent risk-taking behavior created by Irwin and Millstein (1986), Irwin determined that there are a number of predisposing factors that

Table 1.2 Factors associated with financial risk tolerance

Individual characteristic	Assumed to be more risk tolerant	Level of support in the literature[a]
Gender	Male	High
Age	Younger	Moderate
Marital status	Single	Moderate
Marital/gender interaction	Single male	High
Ethnicity	Non-Hispanic White	Moderate
Income	High	Moderate
Net worth	High	High
Financial satisfaction	High	High
Financial knowledge	High	High
Education	Bachelor's degree or higher	Moderate
Employment status	Employed full-time	Moderate
Occupation	Professional	Moderate
Income source	Business owner	High
Income variability	Stable and predictable	High
Household size	Large	Moderate
Homeownership	Owner	Low
Religiosity	Less religious	Moderate
Self-esteem	High	High
Locus of control	Internal	Low
Personality	Type A	High
Sensation seeking	High	High
Mood	Happy	High

Coding (approximate percent of reviewed articles supporting assumed relationship): high—80–100 %; moderate—50–79 %; low—0–49 %
[a]Statistics compiled from a review of 125 studies published between 1960 and 2006. Some studies dealt only with one or a few characteristics. In some cases, the number of studies was small (e.g., $n < 5$)

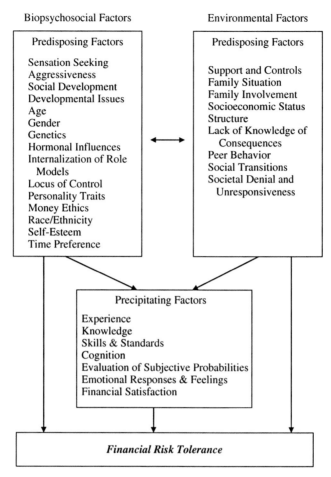

Fig. 1.1 Principal factors affecting financial risk tolerance. Adapted and modified from Irwin (1993)

influence both risk tolerance and risk taking. In general, Irwin's research showed that many of the demographic, socioeconomic, attitudinal, and psychological factors shown in Table 1.2, as well as other factors, can be used to better understand risk tolerance. The model presented here uses comparable terminology to that first suggested by Irwin (Fig. 1.1).

Similar to Irwin's (1993) model, the framework "highlights the importance of biopsychosocial factors which are primarily endogenous and environmental factors that are primarily exogenous" (p. 21). The model also delineates the role of predisposing and precipitating factors, both of which may lead to increased or decreased levels of risk tolerance, which, in turn, can cause a person to initiate, change, or terminate a risky behavior. Additionally, the model borrows language from Loewenstein et al. (2001) by showing that certain factors, such as cognition, emotion, and probability assessment, precipitate a person's willingness to take risks. A brief description of the primary factors in the model is presented below.

Biopsychosocial Factors

Biopsychosocial factors include beliefs, gender, sensation-seeking traits, aggressiveness, self-esteem, personality, locus of control, social development, developmental issues, age, genetics, hormonal influences, internationalization, money ethics, and ethnicity. According to Irwin (1993), "attitudes, perceptions, motivations, and intentions all predict the onset of behaviors" (p. 22). As suggested in Fig. 1.1, these biopsychosocial factors are predisposing characteristics, meaning that they are inherent traits or personality dimensions over which a person has little or no initial control.

Environmental Factors

Environmental factors are also predisposing factors, but they differ from biopsychosocial characteristics in one significant way; rather than being innate traits unique to a person or individual, these factors result from influences in the social environment. As suggested by Irwin (1993), "the protective role of supportive environment must be acknowledged" (p. 23). Examples of environmental factors include support and control, family situation, family involvement, socioeconomic status, structure, lack of knowledge of consequences, peer behavior, social transitions, and societal denial. Environmental and biopsychosocial factors are shown to interact with each other.

Precipitating Factors

As the model indicates, biopsychosocial and environmental factors are predisposing characteristics that influence an individual's tolerance for financial risk. Tolerance for financial risk plays a key role in a person's assessment of the risks and benefits associated with a course of action; however, before assessing and engaging in a risky financial behavior, individuals are often subject to precipitating factors. These are aspects of a person's life that impact the assessment of risk by influencing the decision-making process or causing a person to adjust their core level of risk tolerance prior to or when engaging in a behavior.

Lack of experience or knowledge and lack of skills are factors that influence both risk tolerance and risk taking (Campbell, 2006). For example, a person's risk tolerance may be very low when it comes to investing in stocks or stock mutual funds; however, when confronted with evidence from a salesperson or a neighbor who appears to be more knowledgeable and wealthy, the person may conclude that the risks associated with high risk investing are lower than they really are. The person in this example may make a risky purchase, even though this behavior runs counter to the person's true level of risk tolerance.

The use of predisposing and precipitating factors within a single framework offers a unique conceptual vantage point to better understand financial risk tolerance. Although many of the factors shown in Fig. 1.1 can be measured directly or through scaling methods, there have been few research attempts to predict a person's risk tolerance using predisposing and precipitating personal characteristics concurrently. A need exists, primarily from a descriptive rather than normative perspective, to evaluate financial risk tolerance using all or most of the factors shown in Fig. 1.1. Additionally, the following challenges remain in the development and application of this and other models of the principal factors affecting financial risk tolerance:

(a) Specification and standardization of predisposing and precipitating factor measures
(b) Further specification of possible modifiers and interaction effects with factors not specified in the current model
(c) Detailed specification of factor relationships through path analyses
(d) Standardization of "positive" and "negative" outcomes from risk-taking behavior
(e) Development of cohort and historical influence measures

Future Research Directions

Over the past two decades great strides in the consumer finance field's knowledge about risk tolerance have been made. These strides have led to a better understanding of the role risk tolerance plays when people make risky financial decisions; however, additional theoretical and empirical studies are needed. Such research can help elevate the field of consumer finance and the practice of financial planning from the use of hit-and-miss assessment techniques and qualitative assessments into a world of quantified practice standards. To borrow from Campbell (2006), a better understanding of risk tolerance may contribute to definitions of financial literacy as well as help explain why certain households maximize wealth accumulation over time while others do not.

Future research devoted to the fusing of financial risk-tolerance insights into useful tools for consumer finance researchers may require additional refinement of existing measures of predisposing and precipitating factors affecting risk tolerance and the development of new measures (Webley, 1995). Ultimately, two distinct, yet related, research programs are needed. The first program ought to be devoted to the testing of the relationships between and among predisposing factors, precipitating factors, and a person's tolerance for financial risk. The second program should be devoted to creating a standardized measure of financial risk tolerance. This second research agenda needs to build upon research conducted in the first program by creating scale items or multidimensional measures that incorporate the multifaceted nature of financial risk tolerance with known predispositions of individual decision makers. These two programs of study should eventually lead to a more comprehensive appreciation for and understanding of a person's overall tolerance for financial risk. This, in turn, will lead to a better understanding of how and why individuals engage in certain risky financial behaviors. Ultimately, a unified model of risk tolerance can emerge from such research.

Researchers interested in consumer finance issues, as they relate to risk tolerance, have much work to do in upcoming years to fully understand the normative and descriptive relationships between risk tolerance and financial behaviors. Future research directions include determining all of the following:

(a) How do individuals define risk tolerance in everyday financial situations?
(b) What factors influence a person's willingness to engage in everyday financial risk-taking behaviors?
(c) Does risk tolerance remain constant across domains and activities?
(d) Do experts define risk situations differently than non-experts?
(e) Does risk tolerance change over time?
(f) How do individuals evaluate risky actions?
(g) How does a person's nationality affect risk tolerance?
(h) Do people living in free-market economies act differently in terms of willingness to take risks than individuals who live in economically restricted nations?
(i) Does financial education influence risk tolerance?
(j) How do emotional responses influence risk tolerance?
(k) How do time preferences relate to risk tolerance?

The interconnection between financial risk tolerance and risk-taking behaviors, within the field of consumer finance, is one that offers many research opportunities in the future. Information from forthcoming studies will most certainly improve the lives of consumers and help researchers and policy makers better understand how and why people make risky choices.

References

Allais, M. (1953). Le comportement de l'homme rationel devant le risqué: Critique des potulats et axioms de le'ecole Americaine. *Econometrica, 21*, 503–546.

Atkinson, J. W. (1957). Motivational determinants of risk taking behavior. *Psychological Review, 64*, 359–372.

Barber, B. M., & Odean, T. (2001). Boys will be boys: Gender, overconfidence, and common stock investment. *The Quarterly Journal of Economics, 116*, 261–292.

Barsky, R. B., Juster, F. T., Kimball, M. S., & Shapiro, M. D. (1997). Preference parameters and behavioral heterogeneity: An experimental approach in the health and retirement study. *The Quarterly Journal of Economics, 5*, 537–579.

Bateman, I., & Munro, A. (2005). An experiment on risky choice amongst households. *The Economic Journal, 115*, C176–C189.

Bell, D. E. (1982). Regret in decision making under uncertainty. *Operations Research, 30*, 961–981.

Campbell, J. Y. (2006). Household finance. *Journal of Finance, 61*, 1553–1604.

Chen, P., & Finke, M. S. (1996). Negative net worth and the life cycle hypothesis. *Financial Counseling and Planning, 7*(1), 87–96.

Cohn, R. A., Lewellen, W. G., Lease, R. C., & Schlarbaum, G. G. (1975). Individual investor risk aversion and investment portfolio composition. *Journal of Finance, 30*, 605–620.

Coombs, C. H. (1975). Portfolio theory and the measurement of risk. In M. F. Kaplan & S. Schwartz (Eds.), *Human judgment and decision processes*. New York: Academic Press.

Cordell, D. M. (2001). RiskPACK: How to evaluate risk tolerance. *Journal of Financial Planning, 14*, 36–40.

Csicsaky, M. (2001). Health risk tolerance test and risk assessment. *Psychological Reports, 63*, 66–69.

Dixon, M. R., Hayes, L. J., Rehfeldt, R. A., & Ebbs, R. E. (1998). A possible adjusting procedure for studying outcomes of risk-taking. *Psychological Reports, 82,* 1047–1050.

Ellsberg, D. (1961). Risk, ambiguity and the savage axioms. *Quarterly Journal of Economics, 75,* 643–669.

Fitzpatrick, M. (1983). The definition and assessment of political risk in international business: A review of the literature. *Academy of Management Review, 8*, 249–254.

Friedman, M., & Savage, L. J. (1948). The utility analysis of choices involving risk. *Journal of Political Economy, 56*, 279–304.

Grable, J. E. (2000). Financial risk tolerance and additional factors which affect risk taking in everyday money matters. *Journal of Business and Psychology, 14*(4), 625–630.

Grable, J. E., & Lytton, R. H. (1998). Investor risk tolerance: Testing the efficacy of demographics as differentiating and classifying factors. *Financial Counseling and Planning, 9*(1), 61–74.

Grable, J. E., & Lytton, R. H. (1999a). Assessing financial risk tolerance: Do demographics, socioeconomic, and attitudinal factors work? *Family Economics and Resource Management Biennial, 3,* 80–88.

Grable, J. E., & Lytton, R. H. (1999b). Financial risk tolerance revisited: The development of a risk assessment instrument. *Financial Services Review, 8*, 163–181.

Grable, J. E., & Lytton, R. H. (2001). Assessing the concurrent validity of the SCF risk assessment item. *Financial Counseling and Planning, 12*(2), 43–52.

Hanna, S., & Chen, P. (1997). Subjective and objective risk tolerance: Implications for optimal portfolios. *Financial Counseling and Planning, 8*(2), 17–26.

Hanna, S. D., Gutter, M. S., & Fan, J. X. (2001). A measure of risk tolerance based on economic theory. *Financial Counseling and Planning, 12*(2), 53–60.

Hanna, S. D., & Lindamood, S. (2004). An improved measure of risk aversion. *Financial Counseling and Planning, 15* (2), 27–38.

Irwin, C. E. (1993). Adolescence and risk taking: How are they related? In N. J. Bell & R. W. Bell (Eds.), *Adolescent risk taking*. Newbury Park, CA: Sage.

Irwin, C. E., & Millstein, S. G. (1986). Biopsychosocial correlates of risk-taking behaviors during adolescence: Can the physician intervene? *Journal of Adolescent Health Care, 7*(Suppl), 82S–96S.

Kahneman, D., & Tversky, A. (1979). Prospect theory: An analysis of decision under risk. *Econometrica, 47*, 263–291.

Kogan, N., & Wallach, M. A. (1964). *Risk taking: A study in cognition and personality*. New York: Holt, Rinehart & Winston.

Kunreuther, H. (1979). The changing societal consequences of risks from natural hazards. *The Annals of the American Academy of Political and Social Sciences, 443*, 104–116.

Loewenstein, G. F., Weber, E. U., Hsee, C. K., & Welch, N. (2001). Risk as feelings. *Psychological Bulletin, 127*, 267–286.

Loomes, G., & Sugden, R. (1982). Regret theory: An alternative theory of rational choice under uncertainty. *The Economic Journal, 92*, 805–824.

Lytton, R. H., Grable, J. E., & Klock, D. D. (2006). *The process of financial planning: Developing a financial plan*. Erlanger, KY: National Underwriter.

MacCrimmon, K. R., & Wehrung, D. A. (1984). The risk-in-basket. *Journal of Business, 57*, 367–387.

MacCrimmon, K. R., & Wehrung, D. A. (1986). *Taking risks*. New York: The Free Press.

Markowitz, H. (1952). Portfolio selection. *Journal of Finance, 7*, 77–91.

Mayo, H. B. 2003. *Investments: An introduction* (7th ed.). Mason, OH: Thomson South-Western.

Newman, O. (1972). *Gambling: Hazard and reward*. Atlantic Highlands, NJ: Athlone Press/Humanities Press.

Odean, T. (1998). Are investors reluctant to realize their losses? *Journal of Finance, 53*, 1775–1798.

Okun, M. A. (1976). Adult age and cautiousness in decision. *Human Development, 19*, 220–233.

Olson, K. R. (2006). A literature review of social mood. *The Journal of Behavioral Finance, 7*, 193–203.

Payne, J. W., Laughhunn, D. J., & Crum, R. (1984). Multiattribute risky choice behavior: The editing of complex prospects. *Management Science, 11*, 1350–1361.

Plous, S. (1993). *The psychology of judgment and decision making*. New York: McGraw-Hill.

Riley, W. B., & Chow, K. V. (1992). Asset allocation and individual risk aversion. *Financial Analysts Journal, 48* (6), 32–37.

Roszkowski, M. J. (1999). Risk tolerance in financial decisions. In D. M. Cordell (Ed.), *Fundamentals of financial planning* (pp. 179–248). Bryn Mawr, PA: The American College.

Roszkowski, M. J., Davey, G., & Grable, J. E. (2005). Questioning the questionnaire method: Insights on measuring risk tolerance from psychology and psychometrics. *Journal of Financial Planning, 18*(4), 68–76.

Roszkowski, M. J., & Grable, J. (2005). Estimating risk tolerance: The degree of accuracy and the paramorphic representations of the estimate. *Financial Counseling and Planning, 16*(2), 29–47.

Schoemaker, P. J. H. (1980). *Experiments on decisions under risk: The expected utility hypothesis*. Boston: Martinus Nijhoff.

Shefrin, H., & Statman, M. (1985). The disposition to sell winners too early and ride loser too long: Theory and evidence. *The Journal of Finance, 40*, 777–792.

Shefrin, H., & Statman, M. (1993). Behavioral aspects of the design and marketing of financial products. *Financial Management, 22*(2), 123–134.

Siegel, F. W., & Hoban, J. P. (1982). Relative risk aversion revisited. *The Review of Economics and Statistics, 64*, 481–487.

Slovic, P. (1962). Convergent validation of risk taking measures. *Journal of Abnormal and Social Psychology, 65*, 68–71.

Slovic, P. (2004). *The perception of risk*. London: Earthscan.

Slovic, P., Fischhoff, B., & Lichtenstein, S. (1978). Accident probabilities and seat belt usage: A psychological perspective. *Accident Analysis and Prevention, 10*, 281–285.

Snelbecker, G. E., Roszkowski, M. J., & Cutler, N. E. (1990). Investors' risk tolerance and return aspirations, and financial advisors' interpretations: A conceptual model and exploratory data. *The Journal of Behavioral Economics, 19*, 377–393.

Statman, M. (1995, Fall). A behavioral framework for dollar-cost averaging. *The Journal of Portfolio Management*, 70–78.

Tversky, A. (1969). Intransitivity of preferences. *Psychological Review, 76*, 31–48.

Tversky, A., & Kahneman, D. (1981). The framing of decisions and the psychology of choice. *Science, 211*, 453–458.

Von Neumann, J., & Morgenstern, O. (1947). *Theory of games and economic behavior*. Princeton, NJ: Princeton University Press.

Wallach, M. A., & Kogan, N. (1959). Sex differences and judgment processes. *Journal of Personality, 27*, 555–564.

Wallach, M. A., & Kogan, N. (1961). Aspects of judgment and decision making: Interrelationships and changes with age. *Behavioral Science, 6*, 23–26.

Weber, E. U., Blais, A.-R., & Betz, N. E. (2002). A domain-specific risk-attitude scale: Measuring risk perceptions and risk behaviors. *Journal of Behavioral Decision Making, 15*, 263–290.

Weber, E. U., & Milliman, R. A. (1997). Perceived risk attitudes: Relating risk perceptions to risky choice. *Management Science, 43*, 123–144.

Webley, P. (1995). Accounts of accounts: En route to an economic psychology of personal finance. *Journal of Economic Psychology, 16,* 469–475.

Chapter 2
Personal Financial Wellness

Sohyun Joo

Abstract As the importance of financial health of individuals and families continues to grow, people often use the term "financial wellness" to mean the level of a person's financial health. Financial wellness is a comprehensive, multidimensional concept incorporating financial satisfaction, objective status of financial situation, financial attitudes, and behavior that cannot be assessed through one measure. This chapter discusses the concept and measurement of personal financial wellness and presents "Financial Wellness Diagram." Future research directions are also discussed.

Generally, well-being is defined as a state of being healthy, happy, and free from worry (Zimmerman, 1995). As the importance of financial health of individuals and families continues to grow, people often use the term "financial wellness" to mean the level of a person's financial health (search for "financial wellness" leads to thousands of websites, programs, and products). However, there is a lack of understanding of what is meant by personal financial wellness and no general measure of personal financial wellness exists (Baek & DeVaney, 2004; George, 1992; Hayhoe, 1990; Porter & Garman, 1993; Strumpel, 1976; Wilhelm & Varcoe, 1991).

Derived from the definition of general well-being, financial well-being could mean a state of being *financially* healthy, happy, and free from worry and this could be the concept that should be addressed. However, this chapter discusses the concept and measurement of "personal financial wellness" instead of financial well-being. Following discussion provides several reasons. First, in practice, financial wellness is a more concrete (rather than abstract) concept to work with: it is more functional (or empirical) rather than cognitive (or conceptual) concept. Second, financial wellness has multidisciplinary aspects. As suggested by Hansen, Rossberg, and Cramer (1994), as a primary interest to financial counselors, the concept of financial wellness has to incorporate multidisciplinary approach. Third, due to the wide usage of the word "wellness" in various health-related programs, the term "financial

S. Joo
Financial Planning Standards Board of Korea, 17th FL., Seongji Bldg, Dohwa 2-dong, Mapo-gu, Seoul 121–743, Korea
e-mail: sjookwun@yahoo.com

J.J. Xiao, (ed.), *Handbook of Consumer Finance Research,*
© Springer 2008

wellness" is easier to understand for general public. Fourth, the proposed measure of financial wellness in this chapter could provide practical tools for professionals.

Understanding and Defining Financial Wellness

To understand financial wellness, concepts that relate to financial wellness should be examined. This section reviews the meaning and measurement of financial wellness and related terms such as well-being, economic well-being, financial well-being, and material well-being.

Well-Being

The general consensus among researchers is that personal financial wellness is a sub-construct of overall well-being. Well-being means "non-instrumentally or ultimately good for a person" (plato.stanford.edu/entries/well-being), and well-being in an ordinary term is closely related with happiness or satisfaction. While well-being is used mostly with physical health, there are six interrelated domains that construct well-being: job, finances, house, health, leisure, and environmental satisfaction (Fletcher & Lorenz, 1985; van Praag, Frijters, & Ferrer-i-Carbonell, 2000).

Well-being is usually viewed as a subjective concept. Subjective well-being refers to "how people evaluate their lives and includes variables such as life and marital satisfaction, lack of depression and anxiety, and positive moods and emotions" (Diener, Suh, & Oishis, 1998, p. 25). Self-reported subjective well-being is a stable concept that can be measured reliably over time (Winter, Morris, & Gutkowska, 1999).

Zimmerman (1995) clarified the term "well-being" as "the state of being healthy, happy, and free from want; outcome of long-term socialization and developmental processes and concurrent environmental conditions and processes; composite of satisfactions in domains of marriage, job, leisure, family, and housing; degree to which basic needs are met" (p. 8). These concepts are now accepted as the general definitions of well-being.

Economic or Financial Well-Being

Economic and financial well-beings are often used interchangeably. Generally, financial well-being tends to include broader aspects of financial life, and economic well-being is most often used with income level (e.g., Breen, 1991; Hayhoe, 1990; Porter & Garman, 1993; Williams, 1993).

Breen (1991) viewed financial well-being as having sufficient income and assets, quality health and personal care, the right mix of products and services, as well as legal readiness and professional guidance. Williams (1993) theorized that economic well-being was a function of material and non-material aspects of one's financial situation. To identify economic well-being, she included money income, real or full income, agreement about distribution, and psychic income or perceived adequacy of income.

Material Well-Being

Material well-being is another concept that is used as a proxy of economic and financial well-beings. Family material well-being refers to the mix of goods, commodities, and services to which family members have access (Fergusson, Horwood, & Beautrais, 1981). Indicators of material well-being include ownership (home, car, television, etc.) and economizing behavior such as cutting down or reducing expenditures. Other examples of economizing strategies include postponed visits to a physician, money borrowed to meet everyday living costs, and reduced weekly shopping to save money.

Personal Financial Wellness

Personal financial wellness is a comprehensive, multidimensional concept incorporating financial satisfaction, objective status of financial situation, financial attitudes, and behavior that cannot be assessed through one measure (Joo, 1998).

Financial satisfaction is a key component of financial health. However, financial satisfaction does not necessarily mean good financial health. Sometimes, people can be satisfied with their financial situation, even though they have large debts. This is why an objective assessment of a person's financial situation is an important component of personal financial wellness. With an objective diagnosis, personal financial wellness can be measured reliably. In addition to subjective financial satisfaction and objective measures, individual perceptions (i.e., financial attitude) and financial behaviors are important components because these measure the potential of change in personal financial wellness. An individual's personal financial wellness can be said to be "high" (or a person is "well") when individuals are satisfied with their financial situations, their objective status is desirable, they have positive financial attitudes, and exhibit healthy financial behavior.

As indicated above, the concepts of personal financial wellness, economic well-being, and financial well-being are part of the broader concept of well-being. Much is known about well-being in general; however, little is known about personal financial wellness specifically. The following section presents some proxies of personal financial wellness.

Proxies of Financial Wellness

Proxies that can be used to measure financial wellness include money income, in-kind (non-money) income, wealth, consumption, financial behavior, financial satisfaction, financial attitudes, and financial ratios.

Money Income

Most research on economic well-being has used money income as a measure. Examples include family income, adjusted income, and per capita income (Bailey, 1987; Blinder, Kristol, & Cohen, 1980; Breen, 1991; Moon & Juster, 1995; Sabelhaus & Manchester, 1995; Weisbrod & Hansen, 1968; Williams, 1993). Money income represents potential access to resources.

Adjusted money income measures have also been used (e.g., Haveman & Wolfe, 1990; Minnesota, 1992; Radner, 1993; Smeeding, Torrey, & Rein, 1987; Van der Gaag & Smolensky, 1982). Van der Gaag and Smolensky used total household after tax income for measuring economic well-being. They adjusted income by the constant utility equivalence scale and named it "real household income."

Money income was also adjusted for differences in family size and composition (e.g., Luxembourg Income Study equivalence scale). Haveman and Wolfe (1990) and Radner (1993) used an equivalent income ratio, while the Minnesota (1992) used income-to-needs ratio.

Recently, researchers have recognized the potential weakness of money income as a measure of economic well-being. Weaknesses include the possibility that money income measures only a portion of the economic well-being of individuals, and income measures may create potential non-sampling errors. For example, Weinberg, Nelson, Roemer, and Welniak (1999) indicated that "Money income does not reflect the fact that some families receive part of their income in the form of non-cash benefits, such as food stamps, health benefits, rent-free or subsidized housing, and goods produced and consumed on the farm. In addition, money income does not reflect the fact that some people receive non-cash benefits as fringe benefits. In many surveys, there is a tendency for respondents to underreport their income" (p. 19).

In-Kind (Non-money) Income

Often non-money income has been used in addition to money income. Bailey (1987) used barter, fringe benefits, and other non-money income as indicators of well-being along with money income. Bailey included household production and use of values of owned durable goods as part of non-money income. Blau (1998) included intra-household resource allocation and gender division of house work as measures of standard of living, while Moon and Juster (1995) used the value of health insurance and lump-sum payments.

Wealth

Wealth is often used with other types of wellness measures, especially with income. Radner (1990) used income-wealth measures that include money income and stock of wealth. The stock of wealth is calculated from an annuitized value of wealth, and property income was excluded from the money income.

Consumption

A number of researchers (e.g., Blinder et al., 1980; Magrabi, Pennock, Poole, & Rachal, 1975) have used consumption, or consumer expenditure, as a proxy for both income and well-being. Magrabi and her associates (1975) used the value of consumption as a measure of economic well-being. Their measure included total net family income before taxes, the total number of rooms in residence, physical environment, telephone bills, food expenditure, entertainment expenditure, transportation expenditure, durable goods expenditure, and other non-durable goods expenditures.

Financial Behavior

Garman and Forgue (2006) argued that personal financial management can be an important component in the definition of financial well-being. As such, behavioral assessments of personal financial management have been used to measure financial well-being. Financial management includes (a) financial planning for long-term and short-term financial goals; (b) financial management of income and credit; (c) financial practices through the purchase of housing, insurance, automobile, and other durable and non-durable consumer goods and various services including banking, insurance, and investment; and (d) investment for the future (Garman & Forgue, 2006; Mathus, 1989).

Jeries and Allen (1986) argued that financial behavior reflects a person's economic well-being. They used financial adjustment (e.g., cut in living expenses, borrowing money, looking for another job) to measure possible financial hardship that reflected the economic well-being of individuals and families. Dickinson (1996) used the concept of financial empowerment, including financial knowledge, financial planning, credit management, debt management, investment, asset allocation, and retirement planning.

Financial Satisfaction

Overall satisfaction with one's financial situation is often used as a measure of financial well-being. According to Godwin (1994), there was no consensus on best measure of financial satisfaction. Some researchers have measured financial satisfaction with a single item, while others have used multiple-item measures. The pioneer work of developing a financial satisfaction measure was conducted by Cantril (1965). He developed a self-anchoring ladder scale. Researchers, such as Davis and Schumm (1987), Porter and Garman (1993), and Greenley, Greenberg, and Brown (1997), utilized a single-item scale to measure financial satisfaction by assessing the "overall satisfaction" of respondents.

Researchers like Lown and Ju (1992), Wilhelm, Varcoe, and Fridrich (1993), and Hira and Mugenda (1999) used multiple-item measures for financial satisfaction. Typically, financial satisfaction was measured with satisfaction on the level of income, money for family necessities, ability to handle financial emergencies, amount of money owed, level of savings, and money for future needs.

Financial Attitudes

A person's subjective perception of personal finances is used to measure financial well-being. Porter (1990) measured financial well-being using perceived attributes of financial domain. She defined the perceived attributes as "the value-related qualitative indicators of financial situation" (p. 23). Headey (1993) argued that the measure of overall economic well-being is not complete if looked at entirely from a psychological perspective or from an economic perspective. He argued that overall life satisfaction (i.e., well-being) must be assessed through the identification of personality, health, and social networks in addition to time use and satisfaction or dissatisfaction obtained from the used time. It is reasonable to hypothesize that his argument regarding the broad use of psychological, economic, and demographic measures also applies to the assessment of financial wellness. Cutler (1995) measured financial knowledge as one of the attitudinal measures of financial well-being. Hayhoe and Wilhelm (1998) assessed perceived economic well-being by asking respondents to subjectively assess a major area of financial concern, such as savings and amount of debt.

Financial Ratios

Financial ratios have also been used to measure an individual's financial well-being (DeVaney, 1994; DeVaney & Lytton, 1995; Greninger, Hampton, Kitt, & Achacoso, 1996). Certain financial ratios have been used as an assessment of the financial health of businesses for a long time. However, history of financial ratios as tools in the assessment of families' and individuals' financial wellness is relatively recent (Greninger et al., 1996).

DeVaney (1993) used financial ratios to examine the changes in the financial status of American households. She suggested that the following ratios apply to family financial well-being research: solvency ratio, investment asset/net worth ratio, liquidity ratio, annual consumer debt payments/disposable income ratio, annual shelter costs/total income ratio, and gross annual debt payments/disposable income ratio. DeVaney (1994) also developed guidelines for adequacy of the ratios that could be applied by families, educators, and advisors.

Greninger et al. (1996) identified and refined financial ratios using a Delphi study in the areas of liquidity, savings, asset allocation, inflation protection, tax burden, housing expenses, and insolvency. Based on the Delphi finding, they proposed a profile of financial well-being for the typical family and individual.

Financial Wellness Measurement

Personal financial wellness is a comprehensive, multidimensional concept incorporating objective and subjective components of well-being. Previous research showed that proxies for personal financial wellness (i.e., economic well-being, financial well-being, material well-being) were measured with one or a combination of constructs such as money income, non-money income, wealth, consumption, financial behavior, financial satisfaction, financial attitudes, and financial ratios. However, except for Joo (1998), no research in study measured personal financial wellness with the four comprehensive sub-concepts of financial wellness: financial satisfaction, financial behavior, financial attitudes, and objective status (such as income, wealth, consumption, and financial ratios).

Joo (1998) describes subjective perception scales, behavioral scales, objective scales, and overall satisfaction scales as follows:

> A subjective perception scale can measure subjective perception of personal finance. A subjective perception scale includes a respondent's perception of cash management, credit management, income adequacy, personal finance management, and consumer shopping skills.... A behavioral scale can measure behavioral assessment of personal financial management in cash management, credit management, income adequacy, personal financial management, and consumer shopping skills.... An objective scale can measure objective aspects of one's economic status. It can include some financial ratios and other economic data, such as income, assets, or savings. Certain financial ratios, such as consumer debt-service ratio, consumption-to-income ratio, liquidity ratio, housing expense ratio, annual debt-service ratio, debt-to-income ratio, solvency ratio, savings ratio, and investment assets-to-net worth ratio, can be included in objective scales of personal financial wellness.... An overall satisfaction scale of personal financial wellness can measure satisfaction with one's personal financial situation (p. 52).

A Study of Financial Wellness

This section presents findings from a study designed to further explore the meaning and measurement of personal financial wellness. A survey result with 216 randomly chosen financial counseling and planning professionals (educators, researchers, professors, and CFP® practitioners) is presented.

The Meaning of Personal Financial Wellness

Respondents were asked to provide their own definition of personal financial wellness. The answers were evaluated using a key word content analysis. Common key words included components of financial wellness as described in the literature. Examples include debt, credit, income, expenses, insurance, investment, asset, financial goals, knowledge, money, planning, saving, and stress. Descriptive words for financial wellness, such as enough, happy, healthy, health, need, satisfaction, security, well, and well-being, were also used in defining financial wellness.

Health

When respondents were asked to provide a definition of financial "wellness," they indicated that the word "health" was most appropriate. Response examples include

- "financial health of a family"
- "the level of health of a family's finances"
- "a state feeling of healthy, and stress-free regarding one's finances"
- "maintaining a state of financial health"

In addition, other respondents provided more detailed answers, such as

- "a healthy and prosperous financial environment that compliments and individuals lifestyle"
- "the degree to which an individual feels secure happy and healthy with their financial status"

Income and Saving

The second most common set of terms used to describe financial wellness included income and saving. Phrases to describe financial wellness include the following:

- "having enough income"
- "having sufficient income and assets to live the life you desire without having a significant debt ratio"
- "sufficient income and assets to support financial goals"

In most cases, respondents who used income and savings to describe financial wellness also offered more comprehensive definitions of the term. Examples include

- "a state of being in balance with plans for saving/investing/retirement in place. Income exceeds expenses, debt and funding future needs"
- "having enough income to meet ordinary and unexpected expenses/save 10 % of income/contributing to retirement plans/able to balance and prioritize needs and wants to meet goals"

Goal

Goal was the next most frequently used term to describe financial wellness. Respondents who used this word did so, most often, in conjunction with the following terms: investment, money, need, planning, retirement, and security. Other responses are listed below:

- "being aware of one's goals"
- "a sound plan, emergency fund established and living a productive financial life"
- "living within a spending and saving plan"

Other Terms

Respondents also mentioned credit management, asset, budgeting, controlling expenses, stress-free, and satisfied as being associated with a person's current financial situation, and as such, as components of financial wellness. Respondents who used these types of words defined financial wellness as

- "overall satisfaction with one's financial situation and behavior"
- "the management of money, banking, investments and credit that fosters good physical and mental health maintained by positive habits"
- "freedom from stress"
- "being sound of one's finances due to proper knowledge and management of all financial aspects of their life, household, business, etc."

Respondents also considered "well-being" or "financial well-being" as concepts similar to financial wellness. Respondents answered "how well someone is doing financially" as financial wellness.

The Measurement of Personal Financial Wellness

A key element of this study was to arrive at a consensus method for measuring personal financial wellness. A series of questions were asked to help arrive at a consensus. These questions included

(a) whether financial status of individuals should be measured in a subjective way, objective way, or both?
(b) whether the financial status should be measured with a single item or multiple items?
(c) whether income should be used to measure financial status, and if yes, what information should be gathered?
(d) whether debt should be used to measure financial status, and if yes, what information should be gathered?

The majority of the respondents (76.1 %) answered that the financial status of individuals should be measured both subjectively and objectively. Slightly more than 18 % of respondents answered that financial wellness should be measured using only objective factors, while only seven professionals answered that wellness should be measured using subjective tools.

When asked, "If the financial status of individuals is measured with 'income,' what information would you request from respondents?," 32 % of the professionals answered that they would want to know a client's "gross income." Eighteen percent of the respondents answered that they would inquire about "monthly take-home income (after-tax)," and 10 % of respondents answered that they would want to know a client's "discretionary income." Thirty-nine percent reported that they would request something else including gross weighted income, gross income, number of financial dependents, and money income.

When asked whether or not debt should be used to measure financial status, the majority of respondents (94 %) answered that they would gather "all debt" or "a percent of debt to income" if they thought financial status should be measured by "debt." Others responded that if the term debt were used, then other terms, such as net worth, cash flow, and annual percentage rate (APR), should also be used.

Results from the survey with professionals suggest that the definition of personal financial wellness is an active state of financial health, as exemplified by having a reasonable or low debt level, an active savings and/or retirement plan, and following a spending plan. Subjective evaluative terms related to financial wellness included high levels of financial satisfaction and low levels of financial stress. Results from this study indicate that financial wellness can be distinguished from the abstract concept of financial well-being by the sub-constructs of wellness as described in this study, namely financial satisfaction, financial behavior, financial attitudes, financial stress, and objective financial status (e.g., debt, savings, assets).

A Conceptual Framework of Personal Financial Wellness

This section presents a conceptual framework of personal financial wellness and its measurement. As shown in Fig. 2.1, personal financial wellness is one of the components of overall well-being. Personal financial wellness is an active and desirable status of financial health and includes four areas of sub-constructs.

The four sub-constructs of personal financial wellness include objective status, financial satisfaction, financial behavior, and subjective perception. Objective status refers to objective aspects of person's economic status, such as income, debt, net worth, and household wealth. Even though it certainly cannot buy the entire

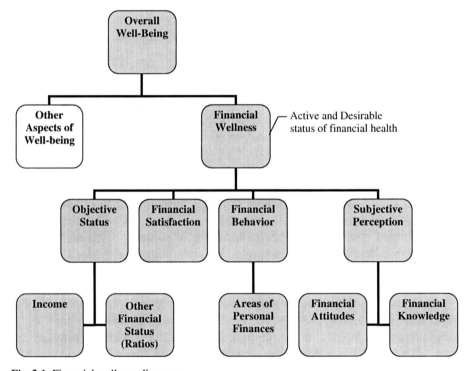

Fig. 2.1 Financial wellness diagram

happiness, income is one of the significant aspects of financial health. Objective status can be measured with various financial ratios as mentioned earlier.

Financial satisfaction is a significant sub-construct of personal financial wellness. It can be measured with one global item of overall financial satisfaction, or multiple items of financial satisfaction, such as satisfaction with income, amount of money for leisure, amount of savings, amount of emergency funds. Research has shown that single-item measurement can be equally representative as multiple items (Joo & Grable, 2004).

Financial behaviors include proper behavior with various personal finances topics. To become financially healthy, individuals need to exhibit desirable behaviors with cash management, credit and debt management, planning for various life cycle events (e.g., marriage, college planning, retirement, estate planning), and consumerism.

Finally, subjective perception is the driving force for savvy financial behaviors and becomes part of the fourth construct of personal financial wellness. Individuals' attitudes toward personal financial wellness on the various personal finance topics can lead to proper behaviors. Financial knowledge is also a significant component of subjective perception. As in the marketing theory of knowledge–attitude–behavior model, financial knowledge can influence financial attitudes and leads to better financial behavior, thus better financial wellness.

Future Research Directions

Financial counselors and other financial services professionals have a vested interest in better understanding the definition of financial wellness and the corresponding ways in which to measure this concept. This chapter is a first step in the process of enhancing the well-being of the individuals by better understanding as many of the factors that affect people in their daily financial lives. The fact that the results presented here are a first-step approach implies that more research is needed.

More in-depth multidisciplinary discussion of personal financial wellness is encouraged. The relationship between health wellness and financial wellness, especially, could lead to more practical guidance of developing workable financial wellness measurement. Researchers can use the proposed measurement from this chapter and further develop a systematic scaling method of personal financial wellness. A standardized way of scaling financial wellness for individuals and families in various life cycle stages will be very helpful for practitioners and educators. If this chapter helps guide future research endeavors, the ultimate purpose has been accomplished.

References

Back, E., & DeVaney, S. A. (2004). Assessing the baby boomers' financial wellness using financial ratios and a subjective measure. *Family and Consumer Sciences Research Journal, 32,* 321–348.

Bailey, A. W. (1987). Social and economic factors affecting the financial well-being of families. *Journal of Home Economics, Summer*, 14–18.

Blau, F. D. (1998). Trends in the well-being of American women, 1970–1995. *Journal of Economic Literature, 36*(1), 112–165.

Blinder, A. S., Kristol, I., & Cohen, W. J. (1980). The level and distribution of economic well-being. In M. Feldstein (Ed.), *The American economy in transition* (pp. 415–479). Chicago: University of Chicago Press.

Breen, R. F. (1991). The financially mature: What they want and how to help them get it. *Insurance Sales, 134*(9), 8–10.

Cantril, H. (1965). *The pattern of human concerns.* New Brunswick, NJ: Rutgers University Press.

Cutler, N. E. (1995, January). Three myths of risk-tolerance: What clients are not telling you. *Journal of the American Society of CLU & ChFC, 49*, 33–37.

Davis, E. P., & Schumm, W. R. (1987). Family financial satisfaction: The impact of reference point. *Home Economics Research Journal, 14*, 123–131.

DeVaney, S. A. (1993). Change in household financial ratios between 1983 and 1986: Were American households improving their financial status? *Financial Counseling and Planning, 4*, 31–46.

DeVaney, S. A. (1994). The usefulness of financial ratios as predictors of household insolvency: Two perspectives. *Financial Counseling and Planning, 5*, 5–24.

DeVaney, S. A., & Lytton, R. T. (1995). Household insolvency: A review of household debt repayment, delinquency and bankruptcy. *Financial Services Review, 4*, 137–156.

Dickinson, A. (1996). The financial well-being of women and the family. The *American Journal of Family Therapy, 24*(1), 65–73.

Diener, E., Suh, E., & Osihi, S. (1998). Recent studies on subjective well-being. *Indian Journal of Clinical Psychology, 24*, 25–41.

Fergusson, D. M., Horwood, L. J., & Beautrais, A. L. (1981). The measurement of family material well-being. *Journal of Marriage and the Family, 43*, 715–725.

Fletcher, C., & Lorenz, F. (1985) Social structural influences on the relationship between objective and subjective indicators of economic well-being. *Social Indicators Research, 16*, 333–345.

Garman, E. T., & Forgue, R. E. (2006). *Personal finance* (7th ed.). Boston: Houghton Mifflin Co.

George, L. K. (1992). Economic status and subjective well-being: A review of the literature and an agenda for future research. In N. E. Cutler, D. W. Gregg, & M. P. Lawton (Eds.), *Aging, money, and life satisfaction: Aspects of financial gerontology* (pp. 69–99). New York: Springer.

Godwin, D. D. (1994). Antecedents and consequences of newlyweds' cash flow management. *Financial Counseling and Planning, 5*, 161–190.

Greenley, J. R., Greenberg, J. S., & Brown, R. (1997). Measuring quality of life: A new and practical survey instrument. *Social Work, 42*, 244–254.

Greninger, S. A., Hampton, V. L., Kitt, K. A., & Achacoso, J. A. (1996). Ratios and benchmarks for measuring the financial well-being of families and individuals. *Financial Services Review, 5*(1), 57–70.

Hansen, J. C., Rossberg, R. H., & Cramer, S. H. (1994). *Counseling: Theory and practice.* Boston: Allyn and Bacon.

Haveman, R., & Wolfe, B. (1990). The economic well-being of the disabled. *Journal of Human Resources, 25*(1), 32–54.

Hayhoe, C. R. (1990). Theoretical model of perceived economic well-being. *Annual Proceedings of the Association for Financial Counseling and Planning Education*, 116–141.

Hayhoe, C. R., & Wilhelm, M. S. (1998). Modeling perceived economic well-being in a family setting: A gender perspective. *Financial Counseling and Planning, 9*(1), 21–34.

Headey, B. (1993). An economic model of subjective well-being: Integrating economic and psychological theories. *Social Indicators Research, 28*, 97–116.

Hira, T. K., & Mugenda, O. M. (1999). The relationships between self-worth and financial beliefs, behavior, and satisfaction. *Journal of Family and Consumer Sciences, 91*(4), 76–82.

Jeries, N., & Allen, C. M. (1986). Satisfaction/dissatisfaction with financial management among married students. *Proceedings of American Council on Consumer Interests Annual Conference*, 63–69.

Joo, S. (1998). *Personal financial wellness and worker job productivity.* Unpublished doctoral dissertation, Virginia Polytechnic Institute and State University, Blacksburg, VA.

Joo, S., & Grable, J. E. (2004). An exploratory framework of the determinants of financial satisfaction. *Journal of Family and Economic Issues, 25*(1), 25–50.

Lown, J. M., & Ju, I. (1992). A model of credit use and financial satisfaction. *Financial Counseling and Planning, 3,* 105–123.

Magrabi, F. M., Pennock, J. L., Poole, W. K., & Rachal, J. V. (1975). An index of economic welfare of rural families. *Journal of Consumer Research, 2*(3), 178–187.

Mathus, I. (1989). *Personal finance* (2nd ed.). Cincinnati, OH: South-Western Publishing Co.

Minnesota Extension Service. (1992). *Specialist research report: Economic well-being of non-institutionalized elderly with functional limitations.* Retrieved August 14, 2002, from http://www.cyfc.umn.edu/Documents/G/B/GB1013.html.

Moon, M., & Juster, F. T. (1995). Economic status measures in the health and retirement study. *Journal of Human Resources, 30*(health and retirement study supplement), S138–S157.

Porter, N. M. (1990). *Testing a model of financial well-being.* Unpublished doctoral dissertation, Virginia Polytechnic Institute and State University, Blacksburg, VA.

Porter, N. M., & Garman, E. T. (1993). Testing a conceptual model of financial well-being. *Financial Counseling and Planning, 4,* 135–164.

Radner, D. B. (1990). Assessing the economic status of the aged among nonaged using alternative income-wealth measures. *Social Security Bulletin, 53*(3), 2–14.

Radner, D. B. (1993). Economic well-being of the old: Family unit income and household wealth. *Social Security Bulletin, 56*(1), 3–19.

Sabelhaus, J., & Manchester, J. (1995). Baby boomers and their parents: How does their economic well-being compare in middle age? *Journal of Human Resources, 30,* 791–806.

Smeeding, T., Torrey, B. B., & Rein, M. (1987). Comparative well-being of children and elderly. *Contemporary Economic Policy, 5*(2), 52–72.

Strumpel, B. (Ed.). (1976). *Economic means for human needs.* Ann Arbor: MI: Institute for Social Research.

Van der Gaag, J., & Smolensky, E. (1982). Consumer expenditures and the evaluation of levels of living. *Review of Income and Wealth, 1,* 17–27.

van Praag, B. M. S., Frijters, P., Ferrer-i-Carbonell, A. (2000). *A structural model of well-being.* Tinbergen Institute Discussion Paper TI 2000-053/3. Retrieved August 12, 2002, from http://www.tinbergen.nl.

Weinberg, D. H., Nelson, C. T., Roemer, M. I., & Welniak, E. J. (1999). Economic well-being in the United States: How much improvement—fifty years of U.S. income data from the current population survey: Alternatives, trends, and quality. *American Economic Review, 89*(2), 18–22.

Weisbrod, B. A., & Hansen, W. L. (1968). An income-net worth approach to measuring economic welfare. *The American Economic Review, 58,* 1315–1329.

Wilhelm, M. S., & Varcoe, K. (1991). Assessment of financial well-being: Impact of objective economic indicators and money attitudes on financial satisfaction and financial progress. *Annual Proceedings of the Association for Financial Counseling and Planning Education,* 184–202.

Wilhelm, M. S., Varcoe, K., & Fridrich, A. H. (1993). Financial satisfaction and assessment of financial progress: Importance of money attitudes. *Financial Counseling and Planning, 4,* 181–198.

Williams, F. L. (1993). Financial counseling: Low-income or limited-income families. In V. S. Fitzsimmons (Ed.), *Economic changes: Challenges for financial counseling and planning professionals* (pp. 121–145). *Proceedings of the Association for Financial Counseling and Planning Education,* San Antonio, TX.

Winter, M., Morris, E. W., & Gutkowska, K. (1999). Constraints, domain conditions, and well-being: Evidence from Poland during the transition. *Journal of Consumer Affairs, 33,* 27–47.

Zimmerman, S. L. (1995). *Understanding family policy: Theories and applications* (2nd ed.). Thousand Oaks, CA: Sage.

Chapter 3
Retirement Savings

Sherman D. Hanna and Samuel Cheng-Chung Chen

Abstract The topic of retirement savings can be considered from a prescriptive (normative) approach, for which the primary question is how much should a household accumulate for retirement. The topic can also be considered from a descriptive (positive) approach, for which the most important question is whether households are saving enough for retirement. Because analyses using the descriptive approach depend on assumptions about whether households are saving enough for retirement, the two approaches are related. In this chapter we review concepts and literature related to both approaches. We conclude with a discussion of whether households in the United States are saving enough for retirement.

Prescriptions for Retirement Savings

Goal-Directed Planning

Robinson (2000) and Ho, Perdue, and Robinson (2006, p. 359) described goal-directed planning and provided a formula to describe the usual approach that financial planners and many households use to reach goals. Applying their concept to retirement planning, the fundamental equation for financial planning is based on the idea that the household should set its spending in each future period so that it will have enough wealth when it reaches retirement to meet its goal. The following formula shows what the household needs to accomplish:

$$W_n = W_0(1 + r)^n + \sum_{t=1}^{n}(E_t - C_t)(1 + r)^{n-t} \tag{3.1}$$

S.D. Hanna
Department of Consumer Science, The Ohio State University, 1787 Neil Avenue, Columbus, OH 43210, USA
e-mail: hanna.1@osu.edu

J.J. Xiao, (ed.), *Handbook of Consumer Finance Research,*
© Springer 2008

We discuss the formula in terms of annual periods, though it could be applied to monthly periods. W_n = wealth in terms of investment assets in the year n when the household reaches retirement, W_0 = initial investment assets, r = rate of return per year, t = year, n = number of years until retirement, E = net earnings in a year, C = consumption or spending in a year.

For instance, assume that a household wants to have its assets at retirement, W_n, equal to \$1,000,000. It currently has investments, W_0, equal to \$50,000. The rate of return it can obtain on investments, r, is equal to 6% per year. Retirement is n years away, where $n = 30$. The calculation of the amount needed to be saved out of earnings each year, $(E_t - C_t)$, can be easily done with a financial calculator, if the amount is assumed to be constant. If the amount to be saved each year is allowed to vary, a spreadsheet is needed for the calculation. If all amounts are in inflation-adjusted dollars and a constant amount is to be saved at the end of each year, $(E_t - C_t)$ is \$9,016.

The calculations are more complicated with amounts expressed in nominal dollars. If a household saves the same nominal amount each year, the inflation-adjusted amount to save each year would be much greater at younger ages than it would be at older ages when real income might be higher. Even if all amounts are expressed in inflation-adjusted dollars, the projected earnings might change with anticipated career advancement and changes in labor force participation of the household members. A spreadsheet can be used to find the amount to save each year, if there is a simplifying assumption, for instance, that the household should have constant spending each year before retirement. Some textbooks (e.g., Dalton, Dalton, Cangelosi, Guttery, & Wasserman, 2005, p. 686) suggest doing calculations in nominal amounts, but it is more reasonable to do all calculations in inflation-adjusted amounts and use inflation-adjusted rates of return.

The goal-directed approach does not provide us directly with how much should be saved each year for retirement, as a complete solution requires a specification of the retirement spending goal. For instance, a household might have a goal of having a particular standard of living in retirement, perhaps the same as before retirement. Given a particular retirement spending goal, it is easy to calculate the amount of retirement assets necessary to generate enough investment income to supplement other sources of retirement income, including social security, employer-provided defined benefit pensions, and employment income of household members. One important question is whether to purchase an immediate life annuity at retirement or to withdraw some amount from investment assets each year. An immediate life annuity is a contract from a financial company that agrees to pay a person a fixed amount per year as long as that person lives. The annuity can also be written for a couple or other type of household so that if one person dies, the surviving household members continue to receive some income.

If a life annuity is not purchased, there is a possibility that a retiree who lives much longer than average would eventually run out of investment assets, especially with high inflation and/or poor investment performance. A very conservative portfolio would be more likely to be depleted because of loss of purchasing power than a stock portfolio would because of investment losses (Ho et al., 2006, p. 416). A single person would need to accumulate about 14 times the initial annual amount to be withdrawn from the portfolio in order to have a very low chance of eventually running out of funds (Ho et al., 2006), which might be somewhat more than the amount needed for a variable life annuity (Clements, 2003).

Consider a worker expecting a Social Security pension of P dollars per year at retirement, at which time he would have a life expectancy of n years. The worker wants to spend C dollars per year in retirement and does not plan to work during retirement. If C is greater than P, the worker needs to generate $(C - P)$ dollars per year from investments during retirement. If money withdrawn from retirement investments is subject to income taxes, some adjustment is needed to account for that, but in the rest of our example we will ignore income taxes, which might be appropriate for someone who had invested in a Roth IRA for a long time. If the worker planned to purchase a life annuity and could obtain one with an inflation-adjusted rate of return of r, the amount he would need to accumulate by retirement would be equal to the present value of $(C - P)$ dollars per year for N years at an interest rate of r:

$$PV = (C - P)(1 - (1 + r)^{(-n)})/r \qquad (3.2)$$

Equation (3.2), based on receiving the annuity payments at the end of each year, would produce a PV of $609,460 for desired spending C of $50,000, Social Security pension P of $15,000, expected remaining lifetime n of 25 years, and an after tax inflation-adjusted interest rate r of 3 %. For the financial planning approach, the remaining calculations could be based on Eqn. (3.1), with W_n equal to the PV calculated from Eqn. (3.2). For instance, consider a 35-year-old worker with no accumulated retirement savings, with 30 years until retirement, who could obtain an inflation-adjusted rate of return of 6 % per year on investments, and would contribute the same amount per year in constant dollars. The amount at the end of each year to contribute would be:

$$A = r W_n/((1 + r)^n - 1)) \qquad (3.3)$$

For the assumptions listed above and the goal of accumulating $609,460 by the start of retirement, the worker would need to contribute $7,709 at the end of the first year, and then increase the annual contribution with inflation each year. At the end of 30 years the worker would have accumulated $609,460 in terms of purchasing power at age 35, so it would be possible to spend $50,000 per year during retirement.

In general, one should project what current investments and projected contributions to retirement investments will grow to by retirement and compare the projected accumulation to the amount needed to fill the gap between desired spending and the Social Security or other defined benefit pensions. There are many more complications to consider, including the fact that it is difficult to purchase an annuity that would provide a true payment that would adjust to inflation, but this example provides the essence of the calculations needed for advice to households. Households that can start investing 20–30 years from retirement should initially invest very aggressively in diversified mutual funds with stocks and perhaps real estate, and if they can avoid using retirement investments for other purposes should be able to accumulate enough for a comfortable retirement.

The assumptions made about pre-retirement consumption patterns are arbitrary without some additional assumptions. For instance, there is the well-known idea that because of the power of compounding, early saving is much more powerful than later saving. However, typically inflation-adjusted household income increases substantially with age until about age 50 and then decreases slightly until retirement. Therefore, it may be very difficult for a 25 year old to save and also achieve a desired current standard of living. Table 3.1 shows the pattern of U.S. household income in 2005 and the percent of income spent, by age. The pattern is based on a cross-section of U.S. households and therefore does not represent any particular household's pattern over time. It does suggest that households typically do not try to save a constant percent of income, but instead save a higher percent of income when income is high. The pattern is consistent with the life cycle savings model, discussed in the next section.

The Life Cycle Savings Model

Modigliani (1986) reviewed research that attempted to explain patterns of spending and saving, including Milton Friedman's permanent income model and the life cycle savings model. (Modigliani noted that he and Brumberg had an unpublished paper in 1954. Ando and Modigliani (1963) discussed implications for the macro-economy of the life cycle savings model. However, Modigliani's Nobel laureate acceptance speech (1986) is the clearest exposition by him of the life cycle savings model.) The life cycle savings model, though developed to try to explain household savings patterns, is a prescriptive theory that assumes a household will try to maximize expected lifetime utility from consumption. Modigliani (1986) noted that in the original, "stripped-down" version, a number of simplifying assumptions were made, including zero real interest rates. Given the assumptions, households would have the goal of having the same consumption each year, and assuming constant real income

Table 3.1 Household aftertax income and expenditures as percent of aftertax income, 2005

	Age of Householder						
	Under 25	25–34	35–44	45–54	55–64	65–74	>74
Income after taxes	27,120	53,257	69,619	71,442	61,068	43,976	27,924
Expenditures/aftertax income (%)	102	85	79	78	81	88	97

Calculated by authors based on data at bls.gov. Results of 2005 Consumer Expenditure Survey before retirement, a household should save the same percent of income each year and should accumulate enough investment assets so that it would be able to maintain the same consumption in retirement as it could have before retirement. There have been many extensions to the life cycle model, including some reviewed by Hanna, Fan, and Chang (1995), who noted that a 20 year old might not want to plan for as much consumption at age 80 as now, simply because the chance of being alive at age 80 might only be about 50 %. It may be rational for consumers to plan for somewhat lower consumption in retirement, especially in the later years of retirement.

Applying the Life Cycle Model to Retirement Planning

The life cycle model is concerned with maximizing utility from consumption over a lifetime, so some types of spending should be excluded from consideration, such as some employment-related expenses. Some types of consumption may be related to the household's leisure time, for instance, a household with limited vacation time might not be able to enjoy travel until retirement, so might want to plan for higher total consumption in retirement. Medical expenses typically are much higher in retirement, so a household might want to plan for higher total spending in retirement to maintain the quality of life. It seems plausible to assume that a household should plan to spend about the same per year after retirement as before retirement.

There are many complexities to applying the life cycle model to the analysis of the adequacy of retirement savings, but the standard approach is the one used by Engen, Gale, and Uccello (2005), who noted, "A household that is saving adequately is defined as one that is accumulating enough wealth to be able to smooth its marginal utility of consumption over time." The implications of this approach depend on various assumptions, but in general, we would expect that rational consumers will attempt to have consumption not change much from year to year, with some growth in inflation-adjusted consumption to take advantage of investment growth.

Sources of Retirement Income in the United States

Social Security

Social Security is a mandatory social insurance system operated by an agency of the federal government. It provides retirement, disability, and survivor benefits to almost all workers in the United States except for state and local governments that opted out of the federal system. Under the Social Security pension system, a worker can start receiving benefits as early as age 62, although benefits are reduced by 6.7 % per year for each year before the "normal" retirement age benefits are started. For workers born in 1960 or later, starting benefits at age 62 rather than the normal retirement age of 67 will result in a one-third cut in monthly benefits. Delaying benefits beyond the normal retirement age until age 70 will result in an 8 % increase for each year.

Social Security is funded by a payroll tax that is regressive to the extent that there is a limit on the amount of wages that are subject to the tax. In 2007, 6.2 % payroll tax used to fund the retirement, disability, and survivor benefit system was applied to the first $97,500 of a worker's wage, though the Medicare program's 1.45 % tax was applied to an unlimited range of wages. Social Security benefits have a progressive structure, in that very low wage workers have a high percent of wages replaced by benefits upon retirement or in the case of death or disability, and high-wage workers have low percent of wages replaced. For instance, a worker who made an wage of $10,000 and retires at age 65 in 2007 would receive a Social Security pension replacing over 56 % of his wage, but one who had a wage of $120,000 would have only 19 % replaced by the Social Security pension (based on calculations on the Quick Calculator at SocialSecurity.gov.)

Social Security provides the most important source of income for most elderly households in the United States. In the aggregate in 2004, Social Security provided 39 % of the income of households aged 65 and older, compared to 10 % from private pensions, 26 % from earnings, and 13 % from asset income (Social Security Administration, 2005). Butrica, Iams, and Smith (2003) estimated that at the median, Social Security would provide 57 % of the income of early baby boomer households at age 67. For lower income households, Social Security provides most retirement income, especially after there are no longer any earnings from employment. Scholz, Seshadri, and Khitatrakun (2006) estimated that for households in the bottom decile of lifetime earnings, Social Security provides almost all retirement resources.

Fears about the future of Social Security are frequently expressed in the popular press. The Social Security Trustees projected in 2005 that with no program changes, the combined Social Security Trust funds would be depleted in 2045, possibly leading to benefit cuts (Social Security Administration, 2005). However, even with such cuts, benefits in real terms for "medium-wage" workers in 2045 might be similar to benefits in 2005 for medium-wage workers. Because real wages would be much higher, the Social Security retirement benefit would replace a lower percent of final wages in 2045 than the same benefit replaced in 2005.

Defined Benefit Pensions

In the past, many employers offered defined benefit pensions (Costo, 2006), which are also referred to as formula pensions, because in many cases the level of benefits is determined by a formula involving the number of years worked and the average or final salary. Defined benefit pensions are seemingly unrelated to investment choices or performance, and one advantage from the worker's viewpoint is that no choices need to be made. The Pension Benefit Guarantee Corporation (PBGC) provides protection to most workers with defined benefit pension plans (U.S. Department of Labor, 2007). Only 21 % of all workers with private employers in 2006 had access to a defined benefit pension plan, and only 9 % of workers of employers with fewer than 100 employees had access to such plans (U.S. Department of Labor, 2006). Almost all (87 %) of government workers were eligible for an employer-sponsored pension plan (Herz, Meisenheimer, & Weinstein, 2000). Butrica et al. (2003) estimated that for the median 67-year-old household, defined benefit pension income accounts for 20 % of income for those born in the 1926–1935 period, and 13 % for those born in the 1936–1945 period, but will account for only 11 % of income for early baby boomer, born in the 1946–1955 period, and only 9 % of income for late baby boomers, those born in the 1956–1965 period.

Employer-Sponsored Defined Contribution Plans

Many employers offer defined contribution retirement plans, including 401(k) accounts, which typically require a worker to make a number of choices, including how much to contribute and how the worker's contributions and any employer contributions will be invested (U.S. Department of Labor, 2007). Of all workers with private employers in 2006, 54 % had access to a defined contribution pension plan and 70 % of workers of employers with 100 or more employees had access to such plans (U.S. Department of Labor, 2006). Butrica et al. (2003) projected that retirement accounts, including employer-sponsored defined contribution plans and individual retirement accounts, will only provide 7 % of retirement income for the median early baby boomer household at age 67. However, for some households, retirement accounts will be very important, as Hanna, Garman, and Yao (2003) estimated that for households with workers age 50–61 with defined contribution accounts, 79 % would have adequate resources at their planned retirement age to maintain their pre-retirement standard of living.

Household Savings, Including Individual Retirement Accounts

Most workers can contribute to an individual retirement account (IRA) and may be able to reduce their wages subject to federal income taxes by contributing to a traditional IRA. Many workers can make a non-deductible contribution to a Roth IRA, and there are other types of plans for individuals, such as the Simple IRA (Internal Revenue Service, 2006). For IRAs, investments grow with no income taxes imposed, but at retirement, all funds withdrawn from traditional IRAs are subject to federal income taxes, but no funds withdrawn from Roth IRAs are subject to federal income taxes. There are income limits for contributing to a Roth IRA.

Wages

In 2004, earnings accounted for 26 % of the aggregate income of elderly households (Social Security Administration, 2005). Labor force participation decreases as people get older, with men born in the 1921–1925 period having a 90 % participation rate for age 50–54, 56 % rate for age 60–64, 26 % rate for age 65–69, and 16 % rate for age 70–74 (Gendell, 2001). There have been only small changes in the labor force participation rates of older men since 1985, and some increases in the rates for older women (Gendell, 2001).

Empirical Studies on Retirement Adequacy

Overview

Are American households on track to achieve an adequate retirement? There have been a number of studies that analyzed large, national data sets to project whether the resources that working households would have at retirement, including Social Security, defined benefit pensions, and the income possible from accumulated assets, would provide a level of spending in retirement that would maintain the pre-retirement standard of living. There are a number of assumptions that need to be made, including when retirement will take place, whether household members will still be employed after retirement, the rate of return on investments, and what level of spending is adequate.

Table 3.2 summarizes selected studies of retirement adequacy. Moore and Mitchell (1997) had the most pessimistic estimates, with only 31 % of households having a high enough savings rate, assuming retirement at age 62. Ameriks (2000, 2001) projected that 52 % of households would have enough resources, as did Yuh, Montalto, and Hanna (1998) with an analysis of the 1995 Survey of Consumer Finances (SCF). Yao, Hanna, and Montalto (2003) used the same methods as Yuh, Montalto, et al. (1998) with the 1998 SCF and estimated that 56 % of households were on track to accumulate enough assets by retirement. Hanna et al. (2003) used a subset of households in the 2001 SCF with a worker aged 50–61 and the Yuh, Montalto, et al. (1998) methods, and estimated that 57 % of those households would accumulate enough assets by retirement. Butrica et al. (2003) used the MINTS data set and estimated that 60 % of baby boomer retirees would be able to replace at least 75 % of their pre-retirement earnings. Scholz et al. (2006) used a rigorous life cycle model and concluded that 80 % of households would achieve an optimal consumption level in retirement, and only a small proportion would fall substantially short of an optimal level. There are many differences in the assumption made in these studies, so the projected range of adequacy rates, from 31 to 80 %, resulted partly from differing assumptions, as well as different data sets. Many experts believe that the absolute level of consumption for retiree households will tend to improve in the future, but whether the level relative to the pre-retirement consumption level will improve in the future depends on the model assumptions.

Projecting the Rate of Return on Investments

For households with substantial retirement investments, the assumptions made about the rate of return will have an impact on the estimate of retirement adequacy. Yuh,

Table 3.2 Selected retirement adequacy studies

Author	Adequacy proportion and brief summary	Data set
Moore and Mitchell (1997)	31 % of households do not need to save more, based on retirement at 62; 40 % do not need to save more based on retirement at 65. The median couple household would have to save an additional 16 % of income for retirement at 62 or an additional 8 % of income for retirement at 65	1992 HRS
Yuh, Montalto, et al. (1998); Yuh, Hanna, et al. (1998)	52 % of households are on track to accumulate enough to maintain current predicted spending, assuming investment assets earn historical mean returns. However, based on pessimistic projection of investment returns, only 42 % are on track	1995 SCF
Ameriks (2000, 2001)	56 %. Based on 1998 SCF and financial planning software, 44 % fail at some time	1998 SCF
Yao et al. (2003)	56 % of households are on track to accumulate enough	1998 SCF
Hanna et al. (2003)	57 % of households are adequate. Projected retirement adequacy rate for households with a worker age 50–61 is 57 %. For households with a defined contribution plan, rate is 79 %	2001 SCF
Butrica et al. (2003)	65 % of current retirees, 56 % of near retirees, 55 % of early boomers, and 56 % of late boomers will replace 75 % or more of their lifetime earnings	1990–1999 MINT
Scholz et al. (2006)	80 % of American households are well prepared for retirement, based on a life cycle model, and small proportions fall substantially short of what they need	1992, 1994, 1996, 1998, 2002, 2004 HRS

HRS: Health and Retirement Study; MINT: Social Security Administration's Model of Income in the Near Term model; data from U.S. Census Bureau's Survey of Income and Program Participation (SIPP) for 1990–1993 matched to the Social Security Administration's earnings and benefit records through 1999; SCF: Survey of Consumer Finances

Hanna, and Montalto (1998) and other studies with the same methods used the historical inflation-adjusted geometric mean returns for large stocks, 7.0 %, for all stock investments, the long-term corporate bond return, 2.2 %, for bond investments, the small stock return, 9.2 %, for business investments, and 6.5 % for real estate investments.

Ameriks (2000, 2001) assumed that a household's rate of return corresponded to its risk tolerance, so that a household willing to take substantial risk had an inflation-adjusted return of 6.8 %, while a household willing to take average risk had a 4.4 % return. The HRS data sets do not provide as much detail as the SCF data sets about investments in mutual funds and retirement accounts. Scholz et al. (2006) assumed that portfolios had a return of 4 %. Moore and Mitchell (1997) assumed a 0.5 % real rate of return for cash equivalent assets such as savings accounts, 2.3 % for bonds, and 7.2 % for business assets and publicly traded stock investments. Butrica et al. (2006) did not state their assumptions about investment returns. The assumptions made about rates of return do not seem sufficiently different to account for much of the differences in retirement adequacy estimates.

Consumption Needs During Retirement

Scholz et al. (2006) assumed that consumption needs vary according to a life cycle model. Given their assumptions about the utility function and rate of return on investments, optimal consumption would be much lower during retirement than before retirement, especially for households with children at home. Mitchell and Moore (1998) and Moore and Mitchell (1997) use Palmer's (1992, 1994) approach, assuming that levels of post-retirement income should have minimum replacement rates of pre-retirement income to allow for taxes and savings. Yuh, Montalto, et al. (1998) conducted regressions on spending in the Consumer Expenditure Survey and used the estimated parameters to predict spending for households in the Survey of Consumer Finances data set. Yuh, Hanna, et al. (1998), Yao et al. (2003) and Hanna et al. (2003) all used the same approach. Butrica et al. (2003) estimated the percentage of wage-indexed shared lifetime earnings, and our interpretation in Table 3.2 is that the proportion of households in each cohort that had a replacement rate of 75 % or more was the proportion with adequacy. Ameriks (2000, 2001) estimated taxes, savings contributions, and debt payments, and therefore desired retirement spending was related to the estimate of pre-retirement income.

Conclusions

Roughly half of working households in the United States are not saving enough to be able to maintain their current spending after retirement. Scholz et al. (2006) obtained an estimate of 80 % of working households saving enough because of their assumptions that implied much lower optimal spending in retirement than before retirement. If Scholz et al. are correct, a large majority of households are behaving rationally, and no theoretical explanation other than the extended life cycle savings model is needed to explain household retirement savings behavior. If the more pessimistic studies are correct, then as Mitchell and Moore (1998) noted, it is important to ascertain why people do not behave rationally and what can be done to improve the situation. Mitchell and Moore discuss possible explanations, including lack of information and lack of self-control. Encouraging employers to have automatic enrollment in retirement plans and preset increases in contribution rates, as suggested by Thaler and Benartzi (2004) would improve the retirement situation for workers. Auto-enrollment plans started increasing after 2006 (Mincer, 2007). Workers who can start investing for retirement 20–30 years before retirement should be able to accumulate enough assets for retirement, and given the outlook for Social Security providing lower replacement rates, investing early for retirement seems prudent.

Future research on retirement adequacy should include careful estimation of spending needs in retirement, as that has been the weakest part of all retirement adequacy studies. More research on pre-retirement withdrawals from retirement accounts would provide more accurate estimates of future retirement adequacy. Normative portfolio studies should focus on more specific advice to workers saving for retirement as to optimal portfolio patterns for each level of risk aversion and for different levels of non-portfolio wealth.

References

Ameriks, J. (2000). Using retirement planning software to assess Americans' preparedness for retirement: An update. *Benefits Quarterly, Fourth Quarter,* 37–51.

Ameriks, J. (2001). Assessing retirement preparedness with planning software: 1998 update. *Benefits Quarterly, Fourth Quarter,* 44–53.

Ando, A., & Modigliani, F. (1963). The life-cycle hypothesis of saving. *American Economic Review, 53*(1), 55–74.

Butrica, B. A., Iams, H. M., & Smith, K. E. (2003). It's all relative: Understanding the retirement prospects of baby-boomers. Center for Retirement Research at Boston College, WRP 2003-21.

Clements, J. (2003, January 22). Buying annuities makes sense, but look out for these traps. *Wall Street Journal,* p. D1.

Costo, S. L. (2006). Trends in retirement plan coverage over the last decade. *Monthly Labor Review, 129*(2), 58–64.

Dalton, M. A., Dalton, J. F., Cangelosi, R. R., Guttery, R. S., & Wasserman, S. A. (2005) *Personal financial planning: Theory and practice.* St. Rose, LA: Kaplan Financial.

Engen, E. M., Gale, W. G., & Uccello, C. E. (2005). Lifetime earnings, Social Security benefits, and the adequacy of retirement wealth accumulation. *Social Security Bulletin, 66*(1), 38–57.

Gendell, M. (2001). Retirement age declines again in 1990s. *Monthly Labor Review, 124*(10), 12–21.

Hanna, S., Fan, X. J., & Y. R. Chang (1995). Optimal life cycle savings. *Financial Counseling and Planning, 6,* 1–15.

Hanna, S., Garman, E. T., & Yao, R. (2003). Projected retirement adequacy of workers age 50 to 61: Changes between 1998 and 2001. *Profit Sharing,* 1–40. Available: http://www.psca.org/DATA/retireAdeq/study2.pdf

Herz, D. E., Meisenheimer, J. R., & Weinstein, H. G. (2000). Health and retirement benefits: Data from two BLS surveys. *Monthly Labor Review, 123*(3), 3–20.

Ho, K., Perdue, G., & Robinson, C. (2006). *Personal financial planning.* Captus Press, Concord, Ontario, Canada.

Internal Revenue Service. (2006). *Individual retirement arrangements (IRAs)* (Publication 590). Retrieved March 23, 2007, from www.irs.gov/publications/p590/index.html.

Mincer, J. (2007, July 11). 'Auto-enroll' retirement plans take off. *Wall Street Journal,* p. D3.

Mitchell, O., & Moore, J. (1998). Can Americans afford to retire? New evidence on retirement saving adequacy. *The Journal of Risk and Insurance, 65,* 371–400.

Modigliani, F. (1986). Life cycle, thrift, and the wealth of nations. *American Economic Review, 76,* 297–313.

Moore, J. F., & Mitchell, O. S. (1997). *Projected retirement wealth and savings adequacy in the Health and Retirement Study* (NBER Working Paper 6240).

Palmer, B. A. (1992). Establishing retirement income objectives: The 1991 retire project. *Benefits Quarterly, Third Quarter,* 6–15.

Palmer, B. A. (1994). Retirement income replacement ratios: An update. *Benefits Quarterly, Second Quarter,* 59–75.

Robinson, C. (2000). *Conceptual frameworks for personal finance.* Available: http://www.captus.com/pfp/PFP-Research1.pdf.

Scholz, J., Seshadri, A., & Khitatrakun, S. (2006). Are Americans saving "optimally" for retirement? *Journal of Political Economy, 114,* 607–643.

Social Security Administration. (2005). *The distributional consequences of a "no-action" scenario: Updated results* (Policy Briefs, 2005-01).

Thaler, H. R., & Benartzi, S. (2004). Save more tomorrow^{TM}: Using behavioral economics to increase employee saving. *Journal of Political Economy, 112,* Part 2(1), 164–187.

U.S. Department of Labor (2006). *National compensation survey: Employee benefits in private industry in the United States, March 2006.* Retrieved July 5, 2007, from http://www.bls.gov/ncs/ebs/sp/ebsm0004.pdf.

U.S. Department of Labor (2007). *Retirement plans, benefits & savings.* Retrieved March 23, 2007, from http://www.dol.gov/dol/topic/retirement/index.htm.

Yao, R., Hanna, S. D., & Montalto, C. P. (2003). The capital accumulation ratio as an indicator of retirement adequacy. *Financial Counseling and Planning, 14*(2), 1–11.

Yuh, Y., Hanna, S. D., & Montalto, C. P. (1998). Mean and pessimistic projections of retirement adequacy. *Financial Services Review,* 9(3), 175–193.

Yuh, Y., Montalto, C. P., & Hanna, S. D. (1998). Are Americans prepared for retirement? *Financial Counseling and Planning, 9*(1), 1–12.

Chapter 4
Financial Education and Program Evaluation*

Jonathan J. Fox and Suzanne Bartholomae

Abstract This chapter provides an overview of the wide range of financial education programs aimed at improving Americans' financial literacy as well as a review of the current program evaluation evidence demonstrating the impact of financial education programs. We advocate for the adoption of a comprehensive framework for evaluation to assist those currently delivering, and planning to deliver, financial education while highlighting some of the key challenges. Jacobs's (*Evaluating family programs*, pp. 37–68, 1988) five-tier approach to program evaluation is described and outlined to provide a general framework to guide financial education evaluation.

Among Americans, burdensome consumer debt, low savings rates, and record bankruptcies are commonly considered the result of low financial literacy levels. As a result, both public and private initiatives have called on Americans to learn the basics of saving and investing for long-term financial independence, or otherwise to improve their level of financial literacy. Collectively, the scope and size of the financial education effort have been significant, although undoubtedly some initiatives are experiencing greater success than others.

To this end, we present an overview of the wide range of financial education programs aimed at improving Americans' financial literacy. Financial literacy denotes one's understanding and knowledge of financial concepts and is crucial to effective consumer financial decision making. Programs that educate to improve financial literacy "provide individuals with the knowledge, aptitude and skills base necessary to become questioning and informed consumers of financial services and manage their finances effectively" (Mason & Wilson, 2000, p. 5). Financial education can include any program that addresses the knowledge, attitudes, and/or behavior of an individual toward financial topics and concepts.

J.J. Fox
Department of Consumer Sciences, Ohio State University, Columbus, OH 43210, USA
e-mail: fox.99@osu.edu

*An earlier version of this manuscript appeared in *The Journal of Consumer Affairs*, Vol. 39, No. 1, 2005 ISSN 0022-0078, copyright 2005, by The American Council on Consumer Interests. Reprinted with permission from Blackwell Publishing. This version has been substantially updated and revised.

In this review, the overview of programs is followed by a short summary of the current evidence of the impact of financial education programs. We then outline a comprehensive framework for financial education evaluation. Our intention is to highlight some of the key challenges facing providers of financial education programs who wish to evaluate the effectiveness of their program. As a tool, we suggest a framework to guide the evaluation of financial education programs. Without question, the costs of deliberate program evaluation methods can be prohibitive for some education providers. However, the adoption of a more consistent and comprehensive framework to evaluation will better capitalize on economies of scope. Widespread adoption of a more consistent approach to program evaluation will facilitate program comparison and aid in identification of best practices in financial education. The critical link between formal knowledge and real economic outcomes is now well established (see Lusardi & Mitchell, 2007a, for a review). The next step is identifying the most effective and scalable programs in financial education.

Current Financial Education Programs

Over the past decade, there has been a dramatic increase in the development and delivery of financial education programs. In a 2004 Government Accountability Office report, the Comptroller General reported that "an estimated 20 different federal agencies operate about 30 different programs or initiatives related to financial literacy" (Government Accountability Office, 2004). A Fannie Mae Foundation report reviewed 90 financial education programs offered in the community and workplace. Of the 90 financial education programs, 65% were launched in the 1990s. Of these programs, three-fourths began in the late 1990s or in 2000 (Vitt et al., 2000). In Spring 2003, the Federal Reserve Bank of Cleveland reported on the financial education efforts in the Fourth District, which includes Ohio, eastern Kentucky, western Pennsylvania, and northern West Virginia. The study found almost half of the programs were 5 years old or less, whereas just over 10% of the programs had been around for 20 years or more (Hopley, 2003).

A host of public and private entities engage in personal financial education. Purveyors of financial education programs from the Fannie Mae report include (1) community organizations (29 programs), (2) Cooperative Extension Service (24 programs), (3) businesses (18 programs), (4) faith-based organizations (eight programs), (5) community colleges (seven programs), and (6) the U.S. Military (four programs) (Vitt et al., 2000). Of 164 community development corporations, social service agencies, local state and federal government agencies, faith-based organizations, foundations, and schools or universities responding to a Federal Reserve Bank of Cleveland survey, 32% delivered a financial education program, 12% funded a financial education program, and 2% did both (Hopley, 2003). Commercial banks commonly engage in financial education efforts. A recent study by the Consumer Bankers Association (2002) found that 66% of the 68 retail banks surveyed were conducting financial education programs.

Unified efforts to address financial literacy and education are being attempted with the Financial Literacy and Education Improvement Act, passed under Title V of the Fair and Accurate Credit Transactions Act of 2003. Specifically, the Financial Literacy and Education Commission was created. The commission is made up of 20 federal agencies with the goal of "coordinating federal efforts and developing a national strategy to promote financial literacy" (Government Accountability Office, 2004). In association with the financial literacy act, the Government Accountability Office was mandated to report recommendations to improve financial literacy and education efforts.

Several national financial education initiatives are underway, many spearheaded by federal agencies. For example, the National Partners for Financial Empowerment (NPFE) includes "consumer and community organizations, corporations, business organizations, federal, state and local governments, and nonprofit groups dedicated to helping improve personal finance skills" (National Partners for Financial Empowerment, 2000). Federal agencies serving as coalition partners include the U.S. Department of the Treasury, the U.S. Department of Labor, the Federal Reserve System, and the Securities and Exchange Commission. Increased interest in financial education culminated in the establishment of the Office of Financial Education by the Treasury Department, announced in May 2002. The mission of the office is "to provide Americans with the practical financial knowledge that enables them to make informed financial decisions and choices throughout various life stages" (U.S. Department of the Treasury, 2003).

National initiatives in financial education are also reflected in the economic research agenda. For example, both the Federal Reserve Board and the National Institute on Aging have recently targeted financial literacy through ongoing data collection efforts. The Federal Reserve's Survey of Consumers added a 28-item true–false knowledge quiz on financial management topics (e.g., savings, credit, mortgages; Hogarth & Hilgert, 2002). Similarly, the National Institute on Aging's Health and Retirement Survey added financial knowledge indicators in 2004 allowing researchers to demonstrate the strong ties between financial knowledge and family financial outcomes (Lusardi & Mitchell, 2007b).

The national financial education efforts vary by the setting, audience, and subject matter (Braunstein & Welch, 2002; Todd, 2002), with organizations and institutions frequently partnering to deliver financial education. These efforts can be organized into three categories based on themes or topics in personal finance. First, there are programs directed at improving financial literacy by broadly addressing personal finance topics, such as budgeting, saving, and credit management. Second, there are programs that give specific training in retirement and savings and are generally offered by employers. The third major category of programs addresses home buying and home ownership.

In the first category, there are several wide-ranging financial education initiatives aimed at school-age students. For example, among the banks responding to the Consumer Bankers Association (2002) survey, 87% supported youth financial education in grades K-12 in public schools. In a recent 5-year period, 50 organizations promoting children's financial education received 170 grants totaling $5.5 million

from the Chase Manhattan Foundation (Bank Works to Increase Kids' Financial
Literacy, 2001). The Jump$tart Coalition for Personal Financial Literacy is a public–
private partnership composed of more than 80 educator, corporate, and government organizations. Jump$tart's mission is to advance personal finance education
in schools, particularly through promoting the use of standards for grades K-12
(Jump$tart Colation for Personal Financial Literacy, 2002). The Jump$tart coalition
was the recipient of $1 million from the Chase Manhattan Foundation. The U.S.
Department of Education and Treasury partnered to give the Jump$tart coalition
$250,000 to further the collective initiative to incorporate personal finance educa-
tion into K-12 classrooms (U.S. Department of Education & U.S. Department of
Treasury, 2002).

General financial education initiatives also target broader audiences. For example, the Federal Deposit Insurance Corporation's (FDIC) Money Smart curriculum
targets adults with a 10-module curriculum covering basic financial topics such as
budgeting, saving, and credit management. The Money Smart Alliance Program
invites partners to become members and adopt the curriculum. The U.S. Department
of Defense (DoD) announced in February 2003 that the Money Smart curriculum
would be offered to 1.4 million servicemen and women at more than 3,000 military
installations around the globe (Federal Deposit Insurance Corporation, 2003a). Similarly, a month earlier, the Wachovia Corporation announced the first corporate-wide
implementation of Money Smart, hoping to reach 5,000 low- and moderate-income
individuals in 2003 in 11 states and the District of Columbia (Federal Deposit Insurance Corporation, 2003b). Project Money Smart is a financial education campaign
established in July 2000 by the Chicago Federal Reserve. Partnering with Consumer
Credit Counseling Service of Chicago and the Illinois Council on Economic Education, this social marketing initiative aims at promoting financial literacy through
public service announcements, a web site, brochures, and presentations (Moskow,
2000).

Several national campaigns, targeting specific financial goals, have been initiated
by organizations with the broader mission of improving financial literacy. In 1995,
the U.S. Department of Labor, along with the U.S. Department of the Treasury
and 65 public and private organizations, organized the American Savings Education Council (ASEC) "to educate Americans on all aspects of personal finance and
wealth development, including credit management, college savings, home purchase,
and retirement planning" (American Savings Education Council, 2000). The Securities and Exchange Commission, in partnership with almost 50 private and public
entities, encourages saving by way of their Facts on Saving and Investing Campaign
which began in 1998 (Vitt et al., 2000).

The U.S. Department of Agriculture (USDA) sponsored Money 2000, a
Cooperative Extension Service program intended to improve participants' finances
by increasing savings and/or reducing debt (O'Neill, Xiao, Bristow, Brennan, &
Kerbel, 2000). The USDA has now partnered with Consumer Federation of Amer-
ica in the America Saves initiative. America Saves, originally a partnership between
Consumer Federation of America Foundation and The Ford Foundation, started in
May 2001 and is "a nationwide campaign in which a broad coalition of nonprofit,

corporate, and government groups help individuals and families save and build wealth. Through information, advice, and encouragement, we assist those who wish to pay down debt, build an emergency fund, save for a home, save for an education, or save for retirement (America Saves, 2003).

The second category of financial education programs offers training in the areas of retirement planning and savings and usually consists of employer-sponsored programs. The Department of Labor and the NPFE encourage the provision of employer-sponsored financial education by providing "a forum for private-sector companies to come together with federal participation to bolster and greatly expand financial education in the workforce" (Vitt et al., 2000, p. 45). Whether through counseling, workshops, benefit fairs, or newsletters, approximately 75% of corporations surveyed in one study offered some form of financial education to employees during the 1990s (Todd, 2002). Of the 18 corporations sampled in the Fannie Mae study, all of the programs covered retirement planning, whereas 17 of the 18 covered investing and saving (Vitt et al., 2000). According to the Fannie Mae study, corporations offered programs continually or only once or twice annually, and the programs reached anywhere from 25 to 30,000 employees annually (Vitt et al., 2000).

Finally, the third category of financial education programming is anchored in home buying and home ownership programs. Home ownership programs often extend into training relevant to other financial goals, such as improving savings rates or decreasing debt (Braunstein & Welch, 2002; Todd, 2002). In 1993, over 1,000 organizations received funding from foundations to offer home ownership education programs (Todd, 2002). Among financial education initiatives, home ownership programs have the longest history, largely resulting from the 1968 Housing and Urban Development Act (Quercia & Wachter, 1996).

The energy and resources devoted to improving American financial literacy through financial education programs cannot be understated. As evidenced in the review above, there is no shortage of initiatives, campaigns, and partnerships undertaking financial education as a mission. With this fervor of financial education delivery, the important question and impending challenge to educators, researchers, and policy makers is discerning the effectiveness of these efforts.

The Impact of Financial Education

The common challenge facing organizations offering financial education is the need to show that their programs make a difference. For most, this comes from the evaluation component of the program. Evidence demonstrating the lasting effect of financial education programs appears to be inconsistent (Anthes & Most, 2000) and must be regarded with "cautious optimism" (Todd, 2002, p. 6).

Relative to many of the programs discussed previously, Vitt et al. (2000) discuss the prevalence of immediate program response measures and follow-up measures of program impact. Immediate program responses indicate participant satisfaction levels, and self-reported increases in knowledge and were part of 80 of the 90 programs studied by Vitt et al. (2000). Follow-up action measures, some of which presumably indicate how participants have applied what has been taught, were used in 58 of the 90 programs. The Fourth Federal Reserve District survey found over half (57%) of the programs tried to measure the immediate impact of financial education efforts and just under half (47%) conducted follow-up studies by surveying or meeting with program graduates at some point after program completion (Hopley, 2003). In a national sample of financial education providers, Lyons, Palmer, Jayarante, and Scherpf (2006) found that over 60% of educators conduct a program evaluation *most of the time* and 90% conduct an evaluation *some of the time*.

In an educational setting, the most visible assessment of learning outcomes is conducted by the Jump$tart Coalition for Personal Financial Literacy (Mandell, 2006). The national financial literacy examination is administered biennially. The most recent exam, administered in 2005–2006 to 5,775 high school seniors, found that students answered only 52.4% of basic personal finance questions correctly, up marginally from 52.3% in the 2003–2004 (Mandell, 2006). While slight improvements have been shown in financial literacy in recent years, none of the improvement can be linked to education programs or high school courses in personal finance. Surprisingly, the positive relationship between taking a personal finance course and test scores was not found in earlier years of the biennial survey, except for the 2003–2004 survey (Mandell, 2004). Even more disappointing, the 2005–2006 survey found that students who took a high school personal finance course tended to do worse on the test than students who did not take a course (Mandell, 2006). Many questions are raised by the inconsistent and weak relationship between taking a high school finance course and financial literacy among high school students.

The National Endowment for Financial Education High School Financial Planning Program (HSFPP) in 2003–2004 was evaluated both at the end of classroom curriculum use and 3 months after completion of the curriculum (National Endowment for Financial Education, 2004a, 2004b). As little as 10 hours of exposure to the curriculum showed a significant improvement in financial behavior and increased understanding of money management from the start of the curriculum and 3 months later. A similar NEFE evaluation was conducted in 1997–1998 and found increases in knowledge, self-efficacy, and savings rates (Danes, Huddleston-Casas, & Boyce, 1999).

Unfortunately, rigorous evaluation and reporting are not part of many programs currently offered in a school setting. The Consumer Bankers Association (2002) review of bank-sponsored K-12 financial education programs points out that only 56% of bank sponsors evaluate the programs in which they participate. Furthermore, only 21% of bank-sponsored programs used a more rigorous pre- and posttest method to identify program impact, and 35% of programs were deemed effective based only on the number of students completing the program (Consumer Bankers Association, 2002).

An alternative appraisal of the effect of general financial education programs in high schools, and perhaps the strongest evidence of impact to date, comes from a study of the effects of statewide curriculum mandates (Bernheim, Garrett, & Maki, 2001). By comparing those who attended schools in states with a current mandate for personal financial education to those who did not live in a "mandate state," Bernheim et al. (2001) find evidence of the positive effect of financial education state mandates on savings rates and net worth during peak earning years (age 35–49).

Examining both college and high school education, a study of university alumni shows minimal (even trending toward negative) impact of personal financial education delivered in high schools on learning outcomes (Peng, Bartholomae, Fox, & Cravener, 2007). For financial educators, Peng et al. do show more promising results for college level courses. Peng et al. argue that critical financial outcomes (namely credit card use and paying bills) are more apparent in the lives of college students than high school students, leading to stronger links between classroom information and personal financial practices.

In the college setting, limited evaluation has been conducted in terms of the effectiveness of college level financial education. Chen and Volpe (1998) surveyed students from 13 different campuses to study financial literacy levels and financial decision making. The authors highlighted the need for personal finance education among college students based on the failing median score on a financial knowledge test of 55.56%. Students' poor knowledge of personal financial management led to incorrect and expensive decisions in the areas of general knowledge, savings and borrowing, and investments. Perhaps the most significant contribution of the Chen and Volpe (1998) study was the finding that financial decisions were highly influenced by financial knowledge. Approximately 89% of students with higher levels of financial literacy made good spending decisions in a hypothetical situation, whereas only 68% of students with lower levels of financial knowledge made the correct choices. Bowen and Jones (2006) used a pretest–posttest design to determine the impact of an educational intervention regarding credit card and money attitudes among freshmen and sophomores. Based on a two-session intervention, there was a significant improvement in overall credit card knowledge score, and a majority of students changed, or planned to change, their credit card practices in a positive manner.

Relative to financial education in educational settings, studies of workplace financial education are more prevalent and somewhat more convincing (Todd, 2002). Improved savings rates have commonly been found to be the result of workplace financial education (Bernheim & Garett, 2003; Todd, 2002). Participation in and contributions to voluntary savings were higher among employees who participated in retirement seminars offered in the workplace, although the effect was stronger among nonhighly compensated workers than among highly compensated employees (Bayer et al., 1996). Nonetheless, Duflo & Saez (2003) conduct an experiment among University employees on the decision to participate in retirement information sessions. They conclude that social pressure and financial incentives outweigh the perceived value of the information itself. Bernheim and Garrett (2003) found median savings rates to be 22% higher for individuals whose employers offered financial education. This study accounted for saving that was separate from workplace saving and retirement plans. A major shortcoming of previous program evaluations has been not distinguishing between workplace (e.g., retirement plans) and household savings behavior (Todd, 2002).

Anderson, Uttley, and Kerbel (2006) tout the rare use of a pretest, posttest, long-term follow-up approach to evaluating the impact of financial education delivered in the workplace on 28 specific actions related to personal finances. For all actions ranging from writing down financial goals to assessing investment asset allocation, program participants report improvements. Perhaps the most significant contribution of the Anderson et al. study is the simplicity with which the outcomes were measured (action/no action) and analyzed (percent of participants taking action before and after education).

In a novel behavioral economics study, employees were introduced to Save More Tomorrow, a program requiring employees to commit to saving a portion of their future pay increase (Thaler & Bernatzi, 2001). The majority of program participants remained committed to the program through a third pay raise cycle, and the average savings rate increased from 3.5 to 11.6% over a 28-month period (Thaler & Bernatzi, 2001). Similarly, studies demonstrating the value of changing retirement plan default contribution rates (Duflo & Saez, 2003; Madrian & Shea, 2001) have demonstrated more significant impact on savings than information-/education-based opportunities (Duflo & Saez, 2003).

The evidence from targeted programs such as home ownership education or savings programs mostly supports the positive role of financial education. For example, Rutgers Cooperative Extension conducted a 6-month follow-up study of the monetary impact of Money 2000. Although the results were not compared with a control group, participants increased their savings by approximately $4,500 and reduced their debt by $2,600 (O'Neill, 2001).

Among Individual Development Account program participants, Shockey and Seiling (2004) use a pretest/posttest approach to program evaluation within a stages of change measure of program impact. From a community-based sample from four states (Hawaii, Indiana, Missouri, and Ohio), they show that financial education can be linked to improved confidence with finances which then can be linked to behavioral change (progression from just thinking about doing something to actually taking action). Notable in their approach is the use of a progression through stages as the key outcome of financial education, instead of learning or financial outcomes.

With respect to consumer debt, the effectiveness of counseling and education appears to be promising. A National Foundation for Credit Counseling report compared the credit performance over a 3-year period, 1997–2000, of individuals who received financial counseling to a matched group of noncounseled individuals (Elliehausen, Lundquist, & Staten, 2007). Compared to noncounseled borrowers, over half of counseled borrowers had improved bank card risk scores and the majority reduced the number of accounts, total debt, and delinquencies (Elliehausen et al., 2007). A study by Freddie Mac demonstrated the effectiveness of counseling mortgage holders. Borrowers who received counseling prior to home purchase, on average, had a 90-day mortgage delinquency rate that was 19% lower than noncounseled homeowners (Hirad & Zorn, 2001).

On the surface, a short financial management course required of Chapter 13 debtors appears to have a strong and positive impact. Course participants had a higher rate of plan completion compared to individuals who did not complete the debtor education program (Braucher, 2001). However, Braucher cautions that several other factors influenced plan completion, including "delaying full payment of attorneys fees for three years, permitting many low percentage, five-year plans, and use of wage orders to have debtors' employers pay the trustee directly" (p. 2). The additional factors meant it was impossible to attribute success solely to the debtor education program.

Addressing the issue of financial literacy and bankruptcy, one study used a quasi-experimental design to compare trained debtors (receiving a 3-hour financial education class), untrained debtors, and nondebtors in a New York sample (Wiener, Baron-Donovan, Gross, & Block-Lieb, 2005). After administering a pretest followed by a 3-month posttest, the impact of financial education showed a significant gain in credit card knowledge among trained debtors. Relative to untrained debtors and nondebtors, trained debtor knowledge was equivalent at the posttest, indicating to the authors that the trained debtor's knowledge "caught up" with the other two groups as a result of the training (Wiener et al., 2005, p. 358). Analysis of the three groups found that debtors demonstrated more negative attitudes toward frivolous spending relative to the other two groups, and less intention to buy than the nondebtors. Analysis of self-report behavior found improved use of credit cards, budgeting, bill paying, and use of predatory lenders for loans among the trained debtors.

In a community-based financial education program for women in Ohio, Fox and Bartholomae (2006) outline a multiyear evaluation. Though strong program impact is shown in perceived learning, more evidence is uncovered of diminishing returns to education as those who had attended previous financial education programs appear to gain less from continued education—even when targeted at women and their specific financial needs.

Programs focusing on the family and its collective financial literacy and education are rare, and evaluations equally so. Based in Australia, *EvenStart* is a 10-hour financial literacy program that educates parents about communicating with their children about money, as well as training with respect to their own money management, credit and debt, savings, and consumer issues. A qualitative study conducted on three program deliveries of *EvenStart* found positive outcomes associated with money management, savings, and the ability to discuss money with their children (Chodkiewicz, Betty, & Keiko, 2005). In an evaluation of financial workshops aimed at financial communication between parents and children, Lyons, Scherpf, and Roberts (2006) show a positive impact of education on the likelihood of using information presented for lower skill student. Surprisingly, given the intent of the workshops, little impact was shown on improved parent–child communication about finances.

The challenge to financial educators and evaluators remains in isolating the effects of financial counseling and education (Todd, 2002). The impact of many programs is frequently isolated to low-income, low-resource families (Braunstein & Welch, 2002), as evidenced in the study by Bayer et al. (1996). Isolation of effects is difficult because of the limited number of evaluations distinguishing among the mode of educational delivery. For example, the study of workplace financial education impact on savings rates by Bernheim and Garrett (2003) examined the effectiveness by lumping together several modes of delivery (e.g., seminars, consultations with a financial professional, and educational materials distributed by the employer). This combined approach limits our ability to determine what method produced what outcome.

Another challenge to educators and evaluators is identifying evidence regarding the appropriate duration of the program delivered. Participants in the American Dream Demonstration of Individual Development Accounts had an average of 12 hours of financial education. Evidence from this programming effort indicated that general financial education had a positive impact on savings levels for program participants (Schreiner, Clancy, & Sherraden, 2002). However, more detailed analysis demonstrated that a few hours of education increased savings, but 8–10 hours of education had no effect, demonstrating the need for more detailed evaluation research.

A more immediate challenge to educators is isolation of program impacts that are lasting. Participants self-select by attending programs; this forces evaluators to tease out this bias in their estimates of program impact (Duflo & Saez, 2003). Moreover, programs usually measure only immediate benefits, and evidence of the long-term benefits is still needed (Braunstein & Welch, 2002). Studies establishing a link between knowledge obtained from program training and experience or behaviors would also be constructive (Hogarth & Hilgert, 2002; Hopley, 2003). For example, preliminary evidence from the Survey of Consumers found a greater proportion (56%) of financially knowledgeable respondents had mutual funds in comparison to less knowledgeable consumers (25%) (Hogarth & Hilgert, 2002).

Guiding the Evaluation Process

Whether financial education focuses on community-sponsored general financial literacy programs, employer-sponsored retirement programs, or bank-sponsored home ownership programs, design, delivery, and evaluation have tended to occur in isolation. Efforts in designing and delivering financial education programs often take place without considering whether such efforts are effective and without integrating the evaluation component as part of design and delivery.

Meaningful program evaluation is an essential and integrated element of successful programs. Well-designed evaluations will "document individual program implementation and effectiveness, but also address collectively and cumulatively which programs work for whom, how, when, where, and why" (Weiss, 1988, p. 4). With a more systematic, consistent, and collaborative approach to program evaluation, stronger evidence of any link between financial education and targeted outcomes may emerge.

Most programs appear to be making some effort toward evaluation; however, there are few clear commonalities in the approach taken. Limited and inconsistent measurement inhibits our ability to understand how outcomes and effects are achieved by programs (Weiss, 1988). Some programs conduct informal evaluations (e.g., phone calls or self-evaluations), with program participants or instructors providing information. Other program evaluations involve more formal measurement methods such as surveys (Hopley, 2003). Measurement of program success is also inconsistent. For example, in the Fourth Federal Reserve District survey, program impact was most often measured by "tabulating numbers of home and car purchases, bank accounts opened, businesses started, and jobs obtained, debt reduction, fewer bankruptcies and foreclosures, improved credit reports and bringing mortgages current" (Hopley, 2003, p. 10). Outcome measures will vary significantly by the program goals, audience, and delivery method; thus, consistently defined measures present some difficulties.

In a broad assessment of current financial education evaluation efforts, Lyons, Palmer, et al. (2006) outline the practical challenges and significant costs of assessing programs. Based on focus group findings from 60 financial professionals and educators, Lyons et al. describe evaluation practices as secondary to program delivery, often being underfunded and delegated to educators with no evaluation expertise or experience. Moreover, evaluation efforts were not found to be driven by learning outcomes, and much debate remains on critical measures of program success. Most appropriately, Lyons et al. conclude that a thorough evaluation is neither possible nor recommended for all program providers. Evaluation funding and expertise is in short supply in most programming efforts. Targeted evaluation efforts to show program impact for selected programs, along with the establishment of national outcome and evaluation guidelines, were advocated.

Program evaluations generally fall into one of two categories, a process or formative evaluation and an impact or summative evaluation (Scriven, 1981). A formative evaluation collects information that provides feedback for educators and program organizers to make improvements in the program itself. Summative evaluation collects information on whether the program is making a difference in previously identified and desired outcome measures (Scriven, 1981). Summative evaluation information deals more with the issue at hand—whether or not financial education impacts financial behavior—as well as gathering evidence of program satisfaction, increased knowledge levels, or increased levels of confidence.

Given the wide range of impact evidence stemming from existing financial education programs it is not surprising that no single evaluation framework appears to be guiding financial educators. Defining an evaluation framework could help programmers "summarize and organize the essential elements of program evaluation, provide a common frame of reference for conducting evaluations, and clarify the steps in program evaluation" (Fisher, 2003, p. 23). An overarching framework for the evaluation of financial education programs would provide a guide or road map for collecting information about program development, delivery, effectiveness, and accountability. Widespread adoption of key elements in a common framework will not only make program evaluation less daunting for financial educators by providing a guide and frame of reference, but also contribute to consistency in data collection and clarity in program comparison.

Several program evaluation frameworks exist, and there is significant overlap among these frameworks (see Fisher, 2003, who advocates for an integration of several frameworks in the context of financial education). Below, we outline Jacobs's (1988) five-tiered approach to evaluation as a basic guide for organizations and agencies delivering financial education programs. Jacobs's (1988) approach to evaluation is commonly used in guiding family life education program evaluators (Hughes, 1994). The advantage of this framework is that it encourages evaluation to occur in each stage of programming, from conception to implementation to conclusion and follow-up. An additional benefit underlying this framework is the assumptions that evaluation (1) should be collected and analyzed in a systematic manner, (2) is an essential component of every program, (3) serves several functions, (4) has many audiences, and (5) should not detract from delivering a program (Weiss, 1988). Finally, the five-tiered approach is comprehensive in scope; it entails both formative and summative evaluations. Knox (2002) advocates that when planning and coordinating the impact evaluation process, the impact evaluation should be part of information drawn from a process that is both formative and summative.

The elements of a comprehensive program evaluation, as outlined by Jacobs (1988), can be summarized in five key steps: (1) preimplementation, (2) accountability, (3) program clarification, (4) progress toward objectives, and (5) program impact. The components of the model build upon one another, with each level requiring "greater efforts at data collection and tabulation, increased precision in program definition, and a greater commitment to the evaluation process" (Jacobs, 1988, p. 50). Program evaluators using this five-tiered approach can engage in several levels at once, and while it is stepwise, previous levels may need to be revisited (Jacobs, 1988). Immediately evident is the fact that evaluation is a graduated process, where identification of program impact comes only in the final stages of an involved, often costly, and comprehensive process. Table 4.1 outlines key stages and links each stage to applications in financial education.

In Jacobs's (1988) terminology, the preimplementation tier of an evaluation occurs during the initial organizational stages of a program and is more commonly known as needs assessment. Needs assessment allows those planning financial education programs to determine the targeted goals and plan an effective program. Vitt et al. (2000) report that only 22% of the 90 financial education programs reviewed conducted any formal needs assessment. In many instances, Vitt et al. (2000) found program organizers to have assumed the need for financial education so great that no further evidence was required. Testing financial literacy levels among the target group, and identifying any deficiencies, is an ideal approach to needs assessment for pure financial education. The recent Jump$tart Coalition studies are examples of establishing and identifying a national need for youth financial education through an ongoing literacy test (Mandell, 1998, 2001, 2002, 2006). The need for improved financial literacy is also frequently demonstrated with alarming rates of bankruptcy, high consumer debt levels, low savings rates, and other negative outcomes that may be the result of poor family financial management and low financial literacy levels.

The accountability tier of the evaluation consists of collecting information on the education and services provided, the cost of the program, and basic program participant information (Jacobs, 1988). The goal of this stage of the process is to document who has been reached by a program and in what way. Accountability is

Table 4.1 Five-tiered approach to program evaluation

Evaluation tier	What is the purpose of the evaluation?	Who will use the information collected from the evaluation?	What tasks should be undertaken by the program evaluator?	Application to a financial education program
Preimplementation—Information justifying a need for the program	To collect information that documents the need for the program within the community	Members of the community Potential funding agents	Outline characteristics of the program Conduct the needs assessment Adjust the program according to the needs assessment	Collect community-based financial statistics (e.g., debt delinquency, bankruptcy, and savings rates) Interview community leaders regarding causes and effects of financial illiteracy and/or financial troubles Locate local press coverage on financial topics, such as bankruptcy, financial stress Write a description of the financial education program (e.g., target audience, thoughts about changing literacy levels, details regarding program delivery, cost to program participant, who will deliver program, benefits of program)
Accountability—Information justifying program viability and utilization	To collect information about program users and program utilization	Funding agents Media sources Leaders in the community	Profile participant characteristics (e.g., background information) Describe program utilization data (e.g., numbers served by program) Estimate cost per unit of service (participant, course, class, etc.)	Provide descriptive profile of individuals who used the program (e.g., demographic information, personal finance data) Be able to report over a certain time frame (e.g., a year), how many individuals went through the program and at what cost

Table 4.1 (continued)

Evaluation tier	What is the purpose of the evaluation?	Who will use the information collected from the evaluation?	What tasks should be undertaken by the program evaluator?	Application to a financial education program
Program clarification—Information to finetune the program	To collect information used by program developers and personnel to improve the program	Participants of the program Implementers of the program (administration and staff)	Revisit and restate program goals, objectives, teaching methods (e.g., is the program reaching the original target audience or does the audience need to be redefined based on information from the previous evaluation stage) Explore program assumptions Gather information about how the program is administered and operated, who uses the program, which staff members deliver the program	Survey program participants about their satisfaction with the program (e.g., questions regarding satisfaction with the educational sessions, whether the financial education program met expectations) Staff feedback (e.g., program staff receives feedback from participants regarding future financial topics) Describe how the program operates (what topics are taught, who teaches it, who uses the program, what components do they use)
Progress toward objectives—Information demonstrating effectiveness	To collect information that documents the effectiveness of the program and to provide information that the program staff and administration can use to make program improvements	Participants of the program Implementers of the program (administration and staff) Funding agents—administrators, staff, evaluators, and developers of other programs	Formulate measurable indicators based on the short-term program objectives (e.g., what outcomes does the program wish to impact?) Combine several measurement strategies (e.g., measures that are program-specific and measures that are more general) Assess differential program effects based on participant characteristics (e.g., age, race)	Design and collect objective measures of program success (e.g., if desired program outcome is to increase financial literacy, administer a pre- and posttest of financial knowledge) Several behavioral indicators should also measure program outcome (e.g., participant reports activities to reduce debt during a 3-month period) Collect other types of data related to financial behavior (e.g., decision making, feelings of efficacy)

Table 4.1 (continued)

Evaluation tier	What is the purpose of the evaluation?	Who will use the information collected from the evaluation?	What tasks should be undertaken by the program evaluator?	Application to a financial education program
Program impact— Program information relative to the big picture	To provide information that contributes to an area of knowledge and/or evaluation and to document program effectiveness in comparison to other programs	Federal, state, and local policymakers Research community Academic community Potential funding agents Potential program adapters (including directors) Citizens of program and other communities	Determine method of data analysis Disseminate program and evaluation information Implement experimental or quasi-experimental methodologies (random assignments and/or control groups) to measure program effectiveness (short- and/or long-term) Continue to collect and compile data from program users and staff, about program utilization and implementation; efforts in this stage are contingent upon data collected at earlier stages	Analyze the indicators of success relative to the participants' characteristics (e.g., does financial literacy score vary by gender or age?) Publish findings of the effect of the financial education program Engage in advanced methodological data collection (e.g., implement random assignment of "treatment" of financial education program; construct a control group of individuals who do not participate in program) Evidence regarding the financial education program should (a) be tailored to specific audiences (e.g., community leaders versus funding agents), (b) be evaluated relative to other programs, (c) be critiqued in terms of strengths and weaknesses of study design and methodological design (e.g., measures and techniques)

Source: Jacobs (1988, pp. 52–55)

also important in determining whether the population in need of financial education has been served. It is also important to provide program data to funders, participants, and the community, with a larger goal of using amassed program utilization data to draw broader attention to the issue of financial literacy (Jacobs, 1988). Frequently, accountability in financial education programs is measured by collecting information during registration, an exit survey, or some other indication of participation. A prime example of the impact of accountability data is Consumer Federation of America's America Saves program in Cleveland. In a press release based on a program survey, an estimated 10,000 Cleveland residents were persuaded to save more, and 1,500 savers were officially enrolled for accounts, counseling, and/or workshops (Cleveland, 2002). Such significant and compelling figures can immediately signal positive community impact and begin building the case for the continuation and growth of the program.

The third tier, program clarification, is used to assess an ongoing program's strengths and weaknesses and to reassess program goals and objectives (Jacobs, 1988). Relative to other phases, program clarification contains more formative information for program organizers. In this stage of program evaluation, program planners review the mission, goals, objectives, and strategies being used in an overall effort to improve the service provided. After reviewing data from the preimplementation stage, programmers determine if the original target audience is being served and/or whether the definition of the target population needs to be broadened or narrowed. Additionally, information drawn from observations by program staff and participants is utilized to improve the program during this stage of evaluation (Jacobs, 1988). For classroom-delivered material, information used for program clarification is commonly derived from an exit survey of teacher ratings, overall satisfaction with the class, and increases in knowledge. In early stages of a program, open-ended comments of participants often guide program changes. A more rigorous method of providing evidence for program clarification would be through the use of a pre- and posttest, then linking high impact levels to best program practices. The National Endowment for Financial Education evaluation of the High School Financial Planning Program effectively uses this pre- and posttest approach to measure increases in financial knowledge, confidence, or intended improvements in financial behavior following the delivery of financial education (Danes et al., 1999).

In the progress-toward-objectives phase of evaluation, the focus moves to desired outcomes and the more summative measures. During this stage, program evaluators obtain objective measures of the impact of a program on participants. Information collected during this stage measures the effect of the program on the individual, whereas the accountability stage described earlier simply highlights program utilization (Jacobs, 1988). In most cases, it is unclear how to best measure progress-toward-objectives if the earlier three stages of evaluation are short-circuited. For example, workplace financial education programs frequently are designed with the clear intent of increasing rates of participation and savings among employees in qualified retirement plans. With such clear and measurable outcomes, it is not surprising that workplace financial education programs show the most consistent and compelling evidence of progress-toward-objectives (Braunstein & Welch, 2002;

Todd, 2002). The clearly defined targeted needs of the workers, along with ease in accountability by employers, make the measurement of progress-toward-objectives in workplace programs much easier than in other programs with more loosely defined goals and objectives.

The most common approach to gathering information on progress-toward-objectives is through some form of continued follow-up contact attempting to identify actions being taken that are in congruence with program goals. In the workplace, it is evident to the employer whether the employee decided to increase retirement contributions or to begin participation in a retirement program. In a high school financial literacy program, the outcome goals are typically more wide-ranging, participants are more difficult to track, and measuring progress-toward-objectives becomes a significant challenge. The differential effects of programs are examined during this stage, for example, whether a financial education program has a greater impact on males than on females. This type of information assists in the improvement of programs. An external evaluator is often contracted to conduct this evaluation stage, particularly when new program-specific measures need to be developed (Jacobs, 1988). Information from this stage of evaluation is important for programs planning to replicate and/or broaden their support (e.g., funders and stakeholders) because it provides the evidence needed to show effectiveness (Jacobs, 1988).

The goal of the final evaluation tier, program impact, builds on the progress-toward-objectives tier and entails the measurement of both short- and long-term impacts of a program (Jacobs, 1988). This stage of evaluation again reflects the goals and objectives of a program, making it difficult to compare programs that do not have the same focus and nearly impossible to identify the impact of programs with vaguely defined goals. At this stage, measurable levels of differences in treated and nontreated populations are reported. This stage of the process requires a formal experimental, or quasi-experimental, approach to analysis of those receiving some form of financial education and contrasting this group with a similar sample that has not participated in the financial education program (Jacobs, 1988). Only through such an experimental approach can the independent impact of the program itself be identified.

At this point, there is scarce evidence of such program impact in the financial education literature. Bernheim et al. (2001) provide one of the few examples of research contrasting a financially educated group with a noneducated group, showing the benefits of financial education mandates to be linked to the increased incidence of financial education in high schools, and then to higher savings rates and wealth accumulation. The differences between those receiving financial education and those who did not receive education were isolated to individuals who came from households where parents provided poor models of financial management (Bernheim et al., 2001). Similarly, Tennyson and Nguyen (2001) found higher scores for high school seniors on the Jump$tart personal financial literacy survey where specific financial education was mandated by states. While the above studies draw on national samples, the approach to program impact evaluation for localized programming efforts is decidedly more focused and straightforward.

Selection of a control group from the same population targeted in the needs assessment provides the necessary baseline for comparison. If the control group cannot be drawn from an identical population, then control variables measuring known determinants of the desired outcomes must be collected for both the treatment group and the control group. For example, if the desired outcome is increased personal savings, then information on income, wealth, household status, education, age, employment status, parenting practices, and financial goals needs to be collected and controlled for by evaluators in the program impact analysis. It is in this final stage where the independent impact of a financial education program is identified. At this point, there are too few examples of financial education evaluation research that have reached this fifth and conclusive tier. Because of this simple fact, definitive statements on the impact of financial education are premature.

Summary and Conclusions

The collective response by public and private organizations to the accepted and often demonstrated need for financial education has been impressive in size and scope. Such an investment in personal financial education comes with the expectation of demonstrated and significant benefits to program participants. Without reliable, valid, and relevant information collected from well-designed program evaluations, financial educators jeopardize their ability to provide effective recommendations for the direction of education policy.

Currently, financial education programs often omit evaluation as an integrated component of their program design. We have described and outlined a comprehensive evaluation framework in the hope that programs will make a commitment to the evaluation process (Table 4.1). Not only is Jacobs's five-tiered approach to program evaluation easy to understand but the framework has the advantage of offering great flexibility in its application. It is designed to address the needs of all financial education programs—those programs just getting off the ground, in the design and development stage, as well as programs that are well established and ready to measure effectiveness. The framework is flexible since it addresses a myriad of program goals and objectives regardless of the program's stage of development.

This program evaluation approach attempts to make good evaluation less difficult for educators and to provide a foundation to those who want to evaluate their program but are not sure how. It is our hope that sharing this framework will encourage educators to think about and integrate evaluation from program inception through eventual identification of program impacts. As mentioned, Jacobs's approach is comprehensive, in that it addresses programs regardless of the stage the program is in. This approach does not expect a program to cover all five stages in the initial offerings. The evaluation process will most likely evolve and grow with the program and the resources dedicated to the evaluation. The framework anticipates only programs with a long track record to have the ability to yield convincing evidence of program impact or progress toward objectives.

There are many benefits to be reaped by the financial educators who incorporate a well-designed program evaluation. Benefits of data collected through integrated and systematic financial education program evaluation include, but are not limited to, (1) sharing best practices, (2) improving effectiveness of existing programs, and (3) keeping the attention of community leaders, policy makers, and funding agents. Almost three-quarters of respondents in the Fourth District Federal Reserve survey indicated interest in attending a seminar that offered insight into the "best practices" of financial education (Hopley, 2003), evidencing the importance of sharing the successes and failures of financial education.

Still greater strides can be made in the arena of financial education programs, and evaluation in particular, if more systematic, consistent, and uniform data collection occurs. For many individuals involved in program delivery, the task of program evaluation may be daunting. We propose a comprehensive and integrated approach to planning and implementing a program evaluation so the process is not as overwhelming. By outlining the steps in the evaluation framework, program administrators can more easily identify the information that needs to be collected during each stage of the program and allocate resources accordingly. The information can be used to improve the program as well as to provide evidence for accountability and effectiveness. It is our hope that the framework will be adopted by financial educators so that we can begin to compile evidence of program impact which can be used to highlight flagship programs and inform future programming and policy.

Following Jacobs's (1988) model of evaluation, we describe the evaluation of financial education programs as an integrative part of the programming process, not an independent procedure used only to identify the benefits of undertaking the process. The assumptions underlying this framework are a strength, as they state that evaluation should be collected and analyzed in a systematic manner and as an essential component of every program (Jacobs, 1988). The evaluation process described herein, and recommended for all financial education programs, is interwoven with the programming itself, making good programming a part of good measurement, and vice versa. Through replication of this process within all types of financial education programs, we stand to significantly increase our understanding of the independent effect of financial education on desired financial outcomes.

References

America Saves. (2003). *Our goal*. Retrieved February 19, 2003, from http://www.americasaves.org/back_page/our_goal.cfm.

American Savings Education Council. (2000). *About ASEC*. Retrieved February 10, 2003, from http://www.asec.org/abtushm.htm.

Anderson, J. G., Uttley, C. M., & Kerbel, C. M. (2006). Outcomes of a workplace financial education program. *Journal of Consumer Education*, *23*, 37–49.

Anthes, W. L., & Most, B. W. (2000). Frozen in the headlights: The dynamics of women and money. *Journal of Financial Planning*, *13*(9), 130–142.

Bank Works to Increase Kids' Financial Literacy. (2001, February 19). Education USA, *43*, 8.

Bayer, P. J., Bernheim, B. D., & Scholz, J. K. (1996). *The effects of financial education in the workplace: Evidence from a survey of employers* (Working Paper 5655). Cambridge, MA: National Bureau of Economic Research.

Bernheim, B. D., & Garrett, D. M. (2003). The effects of financial education in the workplace: Evidence from a survey of households. *Journal of Public Economics, 87*(August), 1487–1519.

Bernheim, B. D., Garrett, D. M., & Maki, D. M. (2001). Education and saving: The long-term effects of high school financial curriculum mandates. *Journal of Public Economics, 80*(June), 436–466.

Bowen, C. F., & Jones, H. M. (2006). Empowering young adults to control their financial future. *Journal of Family and Consumer Science, 98*(1), 33–39.

Braucher, J. (2001). *Report on a study of debtors education in bankruptcy.* Retrieved July 13, 2003, from http://www.abiworld.org/ research/braucher.pdf.

Braunstein, S., & Welch, C. (2002). Financial literacy: An overview of practice, research, and policy. *Federal Reserve Bulletin, 88*(November), 445–458.

Chen, H., & Volpe, R. P. (1998). An analysis of personal financial literacy among college students. *Financial Services Review, 7*(2), 107–128.

Chodkiewicz, A., Betty, J., & Keiko, Y. (2005). Educating parents: The *EvenStart* Financial Literacy Program. *Literacy & Numeracy Studies, 14*(1), 33–46.

Cleveland Saves. (2002). *One-quarter of U.S. households are wealth poor.* Retrieved January 23, 2003, from http://www.clevelandsaves.org/back_page/wealth_poor.cfm.

Consumer Bankers Association. (2002). *CBA 2002 survey of bank-sponsored financial literacy programs.* Retrieved February 2, 2003, from http://www.cbanet.org/Issues/ Financial_Literacy/documents/2002%20Survey%20Overview.pdf.

Danes, S. M., Huddleston-Casas, C., & Boyce, L. (1999). Financial planning curriculum for teens: Impact evaluation. *Financial Counseling and Planning, 10*(1), 25–37.

Duflo, E., & Saez, E. (2003). The role of information and social interactions in retirement plan decisions: Evidence from a randomized experiment. *Quarterly Journal of Economics, 18*, 815–841.

Elliehausen, G., Lundquist, E. C., & Staten, M. E. (2007). The impact of credit counseling on subsequent borrower behavior. *Journal of Consumer Affairs, 41*, 1–28.

Federal Deposit Insurance Corporation. (2003a). *DOD joins FDIC's money smart alliance; Will deploy financial education program at military installations worldwide (MS-002–2003).* Retrieved February 4, 2003, from http://www.fdic.gov/consumers/consumer/ moneysmart/press/mspr0203.html.

Federal Deposit Insurance Corporation. (2003b). *FDIC and Wachovia corporation from first corporate-wise money smart alliance partnership (MS-001-2003).* Retrieved January 30, 2003, from http://www.fdic.gov/consumers/consumer/moneysmart/press/mspr0103.html.

Fisher, P. (2003). *Evaluating financial education: History, theory, and application.* Unpublished master's thesis, Ohio State University, Columbus, OH.

Fox, J. J., & Bartholomae, S. (2006). Considerations in financial education programming for women. *Journal of Consumer Education, 23*, 77–88.

Government Accountability Office. (2004). The federal government's role in improving financial literacy (GAO Publication No. 04-280). Washington, DC: U.S. Government Printing Office.

Hirad, A., & Zorn, P. M. (2001). *A little knowledge is a good thing: Empirical evidence of the effectiveness of pre-purchase homeownership counseling.* (Working Paper). McLean, VA: Freddie Mac.

Hogarth, J. M., & Hilgert, M. A. (2002). Financial knowledge, experience and learning preferences: Preliminary results from a new survey on financial literacy. Consumer interests annual, 48. Retrieved November 11, 2003, from http://www.consumerinterests.org/ public/articles/FinancialLiteracy-02.pdf.

Hopley, V. (2003). Financial education: What is it and what makes it so important? Community reinvestment report. Federal Reserve Bank of Cleveland (Spring), 1–12.

Hughes, R. (1994). A Framework for developing family life education programs. Family relations: *Interdisciplinary Journal of Applied Family Studies, 43*(1), 74–80.

Jacobs, F. H. (1988). The five-tiered approach to evaluation: Context and implementation. In Heather B. Weiss & Francine H. Jacobs (Eds.), *Evaluating family programs* (pp. 37–68). New York: Aldine DeGruyter.

Jump$tart Coalition for Personal Financial Literacy. (2002). *Jump$tart coalition homepage.* Retrieved February 1, 2003, from http://www.jumpstartcoalition.org.

Knox, A. B. (2002). *Evaluation for continuing education.* New York: Wiley.

Lusardi, A., & Mitchell, O. S. (2007a). Financial literacy and retirement preparedness: Evidence and implications for financial education. *Business Economics, 42,* 35–44.

Lusardi, A., & Mitchell, O. S. (2007b). Baby Boomer retirement security: The roles of planning, financial literacy, and housing wealth. *Journal of Monetary Economics, 54,* 205–224.

Lyons, A. C., Palmer, L., Jayaratne, K. S. U., & Scherpf, E. (2006). Are we making the grade? A national overview of financial education and program evaluation. *The Journal of Consumer Affairs, 40*(2), 208–235.

Lyons, A. C., Scherpf, E., & Roberts, H. (2006). Financial education and communication between parents and children. *Journal of Consumer Education, 23,* 64–76.

Madrian, B. C., & Shea, D. F. (2001). The power of suggestion: Inertia in 401(k) participation and savings behavior. *The Quarterly Journal of Economics. 116,* 1149–1187.

Mandell, L. (1998). *Our vulnerable youth: The financial literacy of American 12th graders.* Washington, DC: Jump$tart Coalition.

Mandell, L. (2001). *Improving financial literacy: What schools and parents can and cannot do.* Washington, DC: Jump$tart Coalition.

Mandell, L. (2002). *Financial literacy: A growing problem.* Washington, DC: Jump$tart Coalition.

Mandell, L. (2004). *Financial literacy: Are we improving?* Washington, DC: Jump$tart Coalition for Personal Financial Literacy.

Mandell, L. (2006). *Financial literacy: Improving education.* Washington, DC: Jump$tart Coalition for Personal Financial Literacy.

Mason, C. L. J., & Wilson, R. M. S. (2000). Conceptualizing financial literacy. Business school research series paper 2000:7, Loughborough University, London.

Moskow, M. H. (2000). *Project MoneySmart Kick-off* (*Federal Reserve Bank of Chicago Speeches*). Retrieved February 16, 2003, from http://www.chicagofed.org/newsandevents/speeches/2000/july272000.cfm.

National Endowment for Financial Education. (2004a). *Teens respond well to financial education, study shows.* Retrieved December 18, 2004, from http://www.nefe.org/pages/search.html.

National Endowment for Financial Education. (2004b). *Evaluation of HSFPP shows effectiveness in increasing teen financial knowledge. NEFE Digest.* Retrieved December 18, 2004, from http://www.nefe.org/pages/search.html.

National Partners for Financial Empowerment. (2000). *Mission: What is the national partners for financial empowerment?* Retrieved February 16, 2003, from http://www.npfe.org/index2.cfm.

O'Neill, B. (2001). *Money 2000^{TM} program impact report.* Retrieved February 4, 2003, from http://www.rec.rutgers.edu/money2000.

O'Neill, B., Xiao, J., Bristow, B., Brennan, P., & Kerbel, C. (2000). MONEY 2000: Feedback from and Impact on Participants. *Journal of Extension, 28*(December): http://www.joe.org.

Peng, T., Bartholomae, S., Fox, J. J., & Cravener, G. (2007). The impact of personal finance education delivered in high school and college courses. *Journal of Family and Economic Issues, 28*(2), 265–284.

Quercia, R. G., & Wachter, S. M. (1996). Homeownership counseling performance: How can it be measured? *Housing Policy Debate, 7*(1), 178.

Schreiner, M., Clancy, M., & Sherraden, M. (2002). *Saving performance in the American dream demonstration.* St. Louis, MO: Center for Social Development, Washington State University.

Scriven, M. S. (1981). *The logic of evaluation.* Inverness, CA: Edgepress.

Shockey, S. S., & Seiling, S. B. (2004). Moving into action: Application of the transtheoretical model of behavior change to financial education. *Financial Counseling and Planning, 15*(1), 41–52.

Tennyson, S., & Nguyen, C. C. (2001). State curriculum mandates and student knowledge of personal finance. *Journal of Consumer Affairs, 35*(Winter), 241–263.

Thaler, R. H., & Bernatzi, S. B. (2001). *Save more tomorrow: Using behavioral economics to increase employee savings* (Working Paper). University of California at Los Angeles.

Todd, R. M. (2002). Financial literacy education: A potential tool for reducing predatory lending? The region (Federal Reserve Bank of Minneapolis), *16*(December), 6–13.

U.S. Department of Education & U.S. Department of Treasury. (2002). Announce joint push for financial education. *Education Grants Alert, 12*(October), 1–3.

U.S. Department of the Treasury. (2003). *Office of Domestic Finance: Financial education.* Retrieved February 16, 2003, from http://www.ustreas.gov/offices/domestic-finance/financial-institution/fin_ed.html.

Vitt, L. A., Anderson, C., Kent, J., Lyter, D. M., Siegenthaler, J. K., & Ward, J. (2000). Personal finance and the rush to competence: Personal financial literacy in the U.S. A national field study commissioned and supported by The Fannie Mae Foundation, Institute for Socio-Financial Studies, Middleburg, VA.

Weiss, H. B. (1988). Family support and education programs: Working through ecological theories of human development. In Heather B. Weiss & Francine H. Jacobs (Eds.), *Evaluating family programs* (pp. 3–36). New York: Aldine DeGruyter.

Wiener, R. L., Baron-Donovan, C., Gross, K., & Block-Lieb, S. (2005). Debtor education, financial literacy, and pending bankruptcy legislation. *Behavioral Sciences and the Law, 23*, 347–366.

Chapter 5
Applying Behavior Theories to Financial Behavior

Jing Jian Xiao

Abstract This chapter discusses how two behavior theories can be applied to financial behavior research. The theory of planned behavior (TPB) is a motivational theory designed to predict and understand human behavior. The transtheoretical model of behavior change (TTM) is a multi-stage theory designed to guide people toward positive actions stage by stage. This chapter first discusses how to define financial behavior and then reviews the two theories and their applications to financial behavior. Finally, it discusses issues relevant to future research to better understand and predict financial behavior and to assist consumers to develop positive financial behaviors that improve their quality of life.

Financial educators not only impart financial knowledge to students but also encourage students to form positive financial behaviors to improve their quality of life (Hilgert, Hogarth, & Beverly 2003; Xiao, O'Neill, et al., 2004). In addition, positive financial behaviors contribute to financial satisfaction (Xiao, Sorhaindo, & Garman, 2006). To develop a behavior change focused educational program, researchers of consumer finance need to better understand how behaviors are formed and why and how to help consumers change undesirable financial behaviors and develop positive financial behaviors. There are many behavior theories in the social psychology literature. A literature review of behavior theories that apply to health behavior identified 12 theories and classified them into three categories: motivational, behavior enaction, and multi-stage theories (Armitage & Conner, 2000). This chapter describes two of them, the theory of planned behavior (TPB) and the transtheoretical model of behavior change (TTM). The purpose of the theory of planned behavior is to predict and understand human behavior (Ajzen, 1991), while the purpose of the transtheoretical model of change is to assist people in attaining positive behaviors and in changing negative behaviors (Prochaska, DiClemente, & Norcross, 1992). This chapter starts with a discussion of how to define financial behavior. Then it introduces the theory of planned behavior and the transtheoretical

J.J. Xiao
Department of Human Development and Family Studies, University of Rhode Island,
Transition Center, Kingston, RI 02881, USA
e-mail: xiao@uri.edu

model of change, their backgrounds, major constructs, frameworks, and accomplishments. In addition, it describes how these theories are applied to financial behaviors
and how future research can be improved to better understand and predict consumer
financial behavior, which generates helpful information for financial educators to
develop behavior change oriented education programs.

Defining Financial Behavior

Consumer economists have studied financial behavior for the last three decades.
Fitzsimmons, Hira, Bauer, and Hafstrom (1993) provided a good review of financial
behavior research from the 1970s to the early 1990s. In recent years, more studies
have focused on financial behaviors in various settings (for examples, see Hilgert
et al., 2003; Hogarth, Beverly, & Hilgert, 2003; Hogarth, Hilgert, & Schuchardt,
2002; Muske & Winter, 2001; O'Neill & Xiao, 2003; Xiao, 2006). In this section,
we discuss issues related to how financial behaviors are measured.

Financial behavior can be defined as any human behavior that is relevant to
money management. Common financial behaviors include cash, credit, and saving
behaviors. To appropriately define human behaviors or financial behaviors in particular in this chapter, we need to clarify following issues: (a) do we focus on behaviors
or outcomes, (b) should we focus on a single act or a behavior category, (c) how do
we measure the target behavior, and (d) should we use data from self-reports or
observations?

Behaviors Vs. Outcomes

Many financial education programs focus on increasing savings and reducing debts,
which are outcomes of positive financial behaviors. Behaviors are not outcomes
because they only contribute partly to the outcomes (Ajzen & Fishbein, 1980). Outcomes result from both a person's own behavior and other factors in many situations.
For example, a husband may want to increase his family savings, but it may not be
possible if his wife wants to spend all the income or if his child has a medical
emergency that requires spending all the income. However, behaviors should lead
to outcomes (Ajzen & Fishbein, 1980). For example, saving money regularly is
a behavior but increased savings is an outcome. Saving money regularly leads to
increased savings given other factors.

Single Acts Vs. Behavioral Categories

Behaviors can be observed by single acts or behavioral categories (Ajzen & Fishbein,
1980). A single act is a specific behavior that an individual performs. Using cash for
a grocery purchase is an example of a single action. For researchers, a single act

should be defined in a way that has inter-judge reliability: observers should agree upon the definition.

Many financial behaviors are defined by behavioral categories, or sets of single acts. For example, cash management is an abstract behavior which needs to be described by a set of single acts, such as reviewing monthly bills, recording monthly expenses, etc. When an abstract behavior is defined by a behavior category, the inter-judge reliability is more important. In some cases, single acts may or may not contribute to the target behavior category. For example, using cash for grocery purchases may represent a person's cash management behavior or just demonstrate this person's habit that has nothing to do with cash management.

Behavioral Elements

An appropriately defined behavior should have four essential elements: action, target, context, and time (Ajzen & Fishbein, 1980). Depending on the purpose of the research, the definition of the behavior should include specific details about these elements. For example, saving behavior (a behavioral category) can be a short-term or one-time action by saving a small amount of gift money in a savings account or a long-term commitment such as continuously contributing to 401(k) plans (contexts). Also, savings can be deposited in a savings account or invested in stock markets (targets). Saving behavior can be done regularly or occasionally (times).

Measurements of Behaviors

Behaviors can be measured in several ways (Ajzen & Fishbein, 1980). First, behavior can be measured as a binary variable, whether or not to perform the behavior. Second, it can be measured with multiple choices. For example, what is/are your payment method(s)?

— cash
— credit card
— check
— electronic deposit
— other

The third approach is to quantify the extent to which the behavior has been performed. For example, how much do you contribute to your 401(k) plan per month?

— 0
— $1–$200
— $201–$400
— > $400

Or, just ask the consumer how much you contribute to your 401(k) plan per month?

The fourth approach is to measure the frequency of performing the behavior. For example, how often do you use a credit card?

— almost daily
— a few times a week
— a few times a month
— a few times a year
— emergency only

The specific measurement approach to be used will depend on the target behavior in the research question. For example, if the purpose is to encourage workers to participate in 401(k) retirement saving plans, a binary variable, participate or not participate, will be adequate. But if the research question is to encourage workers to increase contributions to 401(k) plans, a multiple choice set with ranges of contributions or an actual contribution amount is required.

Self-Reports Vs. Observations

The ideal data collection approach to measure human behavior is through direct observations, but in reality, this rarely occurs (Ajzen & Fishbein, 1980). In many situations, direct observations are not possible and self-reports are used instead. Compared to direct observations, self-reports have the following advantages: they are necessary in many cases; they require less effort, time and money; and they can be used to collect information on specific targets, contexts, or times. It would be better if self-reported behaviors could be partially validated by actual, observed behavior in some way. For example, we may ask a consumer to report the behavior— have you missed your credit card debt payment for 60 or more days? And then we may use credit reports to verify the accuracy of this person's answer.

Understanding and Predicting Human Behaviors: Theory of Planned Behavior

Background on Theory of Planned Behavior

The theory of planned behavior is an extension of the theory of reasoned behavior (Ajzen, 1991). The theory of reasoned behavior was first introduced by Fishbein in 1967 and then defined, developed, and tested in the 1970s. It was summarized in a book by Fishbein and Ajzen (1975). The purpose of this theory is to predict and understand human behavior. According to the theory of reasoned behavior, a person's behavior is determined by her/his behavior intention. The intention is determined by this person's attitude toward the behavior, the subjective norm, and the relative importance between the attitude and the subjective norm. The development of the theory of reasoned behavior was motivated by the fact that existing attitude theories could not predict behavior (Ajzen & Fishbein, 1980). Later, the theory developer added to the model the perceived control to determine the behavior intention and behavior, and renamed the model as the theory of planned behavior (Ajzen, 1991).

The theory of planned behavior focuses on factors that determine individuals' actual behavioral choices (Fig. 5.1). According to this theory, three factors influence behavioral intentions: the positive or negative valence of attitudes about the target behavior, subjective norms, and perceived behavioral controls. In turn, behavioral intention influences one's behavior patterns (Ajzen, 1991; Ajzen & Fishbein, 1980). An attitude toward a behavior is recognized as a person's positive or negative evaluation of a relevant behavior and is composed of a person's salient beliefs regarding the perceived outcomes of performing a behavior. A subjective norm refers to a person's perception of whether significant referents approve or disapprove of a behavior. To capture non-volitional aspects of behavior, the theory of planned behavior incorporates an additional variable—perceived behavioral control, which is not typically associated with traditional attitude–behavioral models (e.g., Fishbein & Ajzen 1975). The perceived behavioral control describes the perceived difficulty level of performing the behavior—reflecting both past experience as well as anticipated barriers. As a general rule, the more favorable the attitude toward performing a behavior, the greater the perceived social approval, the easier the performance of the behavior is perceived to be, the stronger the behavioral intention. In turn, the greater the behavioral intention, the more likely the behavior will be performed. In addition, the perceived control may affect the behavior directly (Ajzen, 1991). The theory of planned behavior and its former version, the theory of reasoned behavior, have been applied in many subject areas such as weight loss, occupational orientation, family planning, consumer behavior, voting, alcoholism (Ajzen & Fishbein 1980), hunting (Hrubes, Ajzen, & Daigle, 2001), genetically modified food buying (Cook, Kerr, & Moore, 2002), technology adoption (Lynne, Casey, Hodges, & Rahmani, 1995), consumer complaining (East, 2000), online surveys (Bosnjak, Tuten, & Wittmann, 2005), etc. A comprehensive reference list of papers using the theory of reasoned behavior and the theory of planned behavior was compiled by Icek Ajzen and posted on his website (http://www-unix.oit.umass.edu/~aizen/index.html).

Several meta-analyses have been conducted to evaluate the efficacy of the theory of planned behavior and its former version, the theory of reasoned behavior.

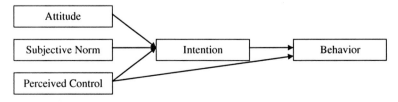

Fig. 5.1 The theory of planned behavior

A recent evaluation study that examined 185 independent studies indicates the theory in general is valid (Armitage & Conner, 2001). This evaluation research identified several issues relevant to the application of the theory. First, self-reports are not a reliable information source. If possible, researchers should use objective and observed variables to measure behavior. Second, perceived control is a concept different from self-efficacy, unlike the common assumption that they are the same measure with two different names. Compared to perceived control, self-efficacy is a better predictor of behavior. Third, there are alternative measures for intention, such as desire and self-prediction, in which intention and self-prediction are better predictors for behavior compared to desire. Fourth, subjective norm is a weak predictor of intention compared to two other variables, attitude and perceived control. Alternative categorizations are needed, such as moral and descriptive norms.

Its Applications to Financial Behavior

Several studies have applied the theory of planned behavior to consumer behavior in financial services such as investment decisions, mortgage use, and credit counseling. East (1993) applied the theory of planned behavior to investigate investment decisions with data from a sample of British consumers. The findings of three studies presented in the paper support the theory. Specifically, friends and relatives and easy access to funds strongly contributed to the investment decision. Bansal and Taylor (2002), using data from a sample of mortgage clients, applied the theory to customer service switching behavior. They examined whether interaction terms of several variables specified in the theory affect the behavior. They found that interactions between perceived control and intention, between perceived control and attitude, and between attitude and subjective norms significantly affected behavior intention. Using survey and account data from a sample of clients of a national consumer counseling agency, Xiao and Wu (2006) examined factors that are associated with consumer behavior in completing a debt management plan. They found that attitude toward the behavior and perceived control affected the actual behavior, but subjective norm did not. In addition, they found that satisfaction with the service also contributed to the actual behavior.

The theory of planned behavior is also applied to consumer behavior in the setting of e-commerce, such as online shopping and e-coupon use. Based on the theory of planned behavior, Lim and Dubinsky (2005) Lim decomposed belief constructs and included the interaction term of salient belief in the revised model. Based on data collected from a sample of college students, they found these new additional variables contribute to consumer online shopping intentions. A group of researchers applied the theory to consumer online purchase intentions (Shim, Easlick, Lotz, & Warrington, 2001). Based on data collected from a national sample of computer users, they found that intention to use the Internet for information search served as a mediating variable between antecedents, such as attitude, perceived control, and past experience, and the outcome variable, the online purchase intention. Attitude and past experience also directly contribute to the purchase intention. Fortin (2000) proposed a theoretical framework to explain consumer coupon and e-coupon behavior based on the theory of planned behavior. Kang, Hahn, Fortin, Hyun, and Eom (2006) compared the theory of reasoned behavior and the theory of planned behavior in the context of e-coupon use intentions and found that the theory of planned behavior explained the intention better.

Additionally, a group of researchers applied the theory of planned behavior to investigate how college students form financial behaviors such as cash, credit, and saving management. Based on their preliminary findings, all three antecedents of the behavior intention specified by the theory are associated with the intention and the intention contributes to the behavior (Shim, Xiao, Barber, & Lyons, 2007; Xiao, Shim, Barber, & Lyons, 2007).

Facilitating Behavior Change: Transtheoretical Model of Change (TTM)

Background of TTM

The transtheoretical model of behavior change (TTM) was developed in the 1970s by Prochaska and his colleagues (Prochaska, 1979; Prochaska et al., 1992). They formed the model by highlighting major psychological theories in a uniform framework for the purpose of helping people change their undesirable behaviors. "Transtheoretical" in the title means to transform theories into applications, which implies that this model was developed for the applied purpose of counseling. The model was first applied to cessation of smoking and then to a variety of other health-related behaviors, including alcohol abuse, drug abuse, high fat diet and weight control, psychological distress, and sun exposure (Prochaska, Redding, Harlow, Rossi, & Velicer, 1994). A few studies applied TTM to other areas, such as organizational change (Prochaska, 2000) and collaborative service delivery (Levesque, Prochaska, & Prochaska, 1999). More information about this model and its accomplishments can be found from the website of Pro-Change Behavior Systems: http://prochange.com/.

Major Constructs of TTM

Major constructs of TTM include stage of change, process of change, self-efficacy, and decisional balance. TTM identifies five stages of behavior change: precontemplation, contemplation, preparation, action, and maintenance. If a person is not willing to change in 6 months, s/he is in precontemplation. If a person is willing to change in 6 months, s/he is in contemplation. If s/he is willing to change in 30 days, s/he is in preparation. If s/he has started to change for less than 6 months, s/he is in action. If s/he has been changing for over 6 months but less than 18 months, s/he is in maintenance. If s/he has changed the behavior for more than 18 months, we consider her/his behavior has been changed. Some people may relapse to previous stages. At times, behavior change may take several cycles. TTM also identifies 10 processes of change, in which *processes* are strategies or interventions for facilitating the behavior change. Table 5.1 presents definitions of the change processes.

According to TTM, these strategies could be used more effectively if they are matched with appropriate stages of change. Figure 5.2 demonstrates the relationship between the stage of change and process of change.

Two indicators of success of behavior change are decisional balance and self-efficacy (or confidence). When people are at a later stage, they will perceive more benefits and fewer costs of behavior change, and they are more confident in avoiding the targeted, undesirable behavior when they face difficult situations.

Compared to other behavior change models, this model has the following unique features: (a) it integrates essentials of major psychological theories in a framework to offer more effective interventions; (b) it defines multiple stages of behavior change, which is different from an action paradigm, and has the potential to reach those both ready and not ready to change the targeted behavior; (c) it matches intervention strategies to different stages of behavior change, which makes it more effective compared to other intervention programs; and (d) it focuses on enhancing self-control (Prochaska, Redding, & Evers, 1996).

TTM is one of the multi-stage theories. Among five multi-stage theories reviewed by two psychologists, TTM is the one that most empirical studies support. Compared

Table 5.1 Change strategies and tactics that match change stages

Change stage	Change strategy	Change tactics
Precontemplation	Consciousness raising	Observations, interpretations, bibliotherapy
	Dramatic relief	Psychodrama, grieving losses, role playing
	Environmental reevaluation	Empathy training, documentaries
Contemplation	Self-reevaluation	Value clarification, imagery, corrective emotional experience
Preparation	Self-liberation	Decision-making therapy, New Year's resolution, logotherapy techniques, commitment enhancing techniques
Action/maintenance	Reinforcement management	Contingency contracts, overt and covert reinforcement, self-reward
	Helping relationships	Therapeutic alliance, social support, self-help groups
	Counter-conditioning	Relaxation, desensitization, assertion, positive self-statements
	Stimulus control	Restructuring one's environment, avoiding high-risk cues, fading techniques
All stages	Social liberation	Advocating for rights of repressed, empowering, policy interventions

Source: Prochaska, DiClemente, and Norcross (1992)

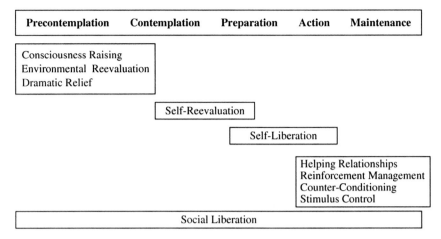

Fig. 5.2 Stages by processes of change (Pro-Change Behavior Systems, 2002)

to motivational theories, multi-stage theories are more sophisticated (Armitage & Conner, 2000). However, these authors raised several issues for multi-stage theories. These issues include: (a) psychologically, what actually happens at each stage, (b) do people go through each stage sequentially when they change their behaviors, and (c) are different stages really different in terms of determinants of the behavior change?

Its Applications to Financial Behavior

Application of TTM to financial behavior started in the last decade. Kerkman (1998) discussed how to use TTM in financial counseling and presented a case to demonstrate her approach. Bristow (1997) suggested that this model could be used to change people's financial behavior in Money 2000, a USDA Cooperative Extension program. Money 2000 was a successful financial education program, which was adopted by 29 states and reported a total dollar impact of almost $20 million (O'Neill, 2001). Based on data collected in 1998 among the program participants in New Jersey and New York, preliminary evidence indicated that certain processes of change were used more frequently by participants who reported behavioral changes (Xiao, O'Neill, et al., 2004). A group of researchers has applied TTM in the credit counseling setting to develop a measure to help consumers change behaviors to eliminate undesirable credit card debts (Xiao, Newman, Prochaska, Leon & Bassett, 2004; Xiao, Newman, et al., 2004). TTM was also applied in financial education programs for low-income consumers, and specific educational strategies under the framework of TTM were developed (Shockey & Seiling, 2004). In addition, TTM was used to provide advice for women on being better investors (Loibl & Hira, 2007).

Future Research Directions

This chapter briefly described two psychological theories on human behavior. The theory of planned behavior is used to understand and predict human behavior. The transtheoretical model of behavior change (TTM) is used to facilitate behavior change by providing stage-matched interventions. Studies that applied these theories to financial behavior have also been reviewed. Based on the literature review, the following suggestions for future research are provided to help better understand the formation and change of financial behaviors so that we can assist consumers in developing positive financial behaviors.

Researchers need to develop an inventory of financial behaviors that covers all aspects of behaviors relevant to consumer finance. In many existing studies, financial behaviors are defined for specific research purposes and many of them are not comprehensive. An inventory of financial behaviors with acceptable reliability and validity would be helpful for financial educators and researchers when they evaluate financial education programs and measure social impacts of the programs on people's behavior change and quality of life.

The two theories reviewed in this chapter have been applied to certain financial behaviors and certain populations, but they could be applied to more behaviors and more diverse populations. For example, many states have tax return sites to help low-income consumers to receive tax refunds. Another example is the *Go Direct* campaign launched by the U.S. Department of Treasury, which encourages electronic deposits of benefit checks issued by the U.S. Social Security Administration. Consumer economists could partner with government agencies and financial institutions to apply these theories to design effective education and outreach programs so these social initiatives would have greater impact.

TTM is considered a multi-stage theory whose advantages can help consumers change undesirable behaviors and form positive financial behaviors stage by stage. Strategies based on this theory could be developed to work with mass populations, emphasizing certain strategies for certain behavior change stages for greater social impact, and a cost-effective approach. Mass approaches also need to be personalized. An example would be online self-assessment tools that could reach millions of people but provide each user with a personalized response, based on their individual responses (O'Neill & Xiao, 2006).

The behavior theories reviewed in this chapter have been tested in numerous scientific studies and are well established. Consumer finance researchers could utilize the strategies, techniques, and tactics based on this line of research to generate practical information for financial educators and consumers.

Self-help websites based on these theories can be developed to help determined consumers change their undesirable financial behaviors themselves. Self-help manuals could also be developed for the same purpose. Use of these self-help websites and manuals could be monitored and studied to identify factors that are more effective than others in motivating and facilitating the behavior change.

One of the purposes of research on consumer financial behavior is to better understand factors that affect the formation and change of financial behaviors.

Specifically, financial educators are interested in knowing the role of financial education in behavior formation and change. In addition, financial educators need to know the important characteristics of financial education programs that will not only provide financial knowledge but also encourage consumers to form positive financial behaviors and change undesirable financial behaviors. Future research should generate information that has direct implications for financial educators to develop such education programs.

Future research also needs to examine how financial education, financial behavior, and quality of life are associated. The mission of many financial educators, especially those at land grant universities, is to improve people's quality of life by providing effective financial education. They hope the education will have a direct impact on these people's financial behaviors and eventually help improve the financial well-being of these people. Data on financial education, financial behavior, and quality of life could be collected to provide insights on this topic. Preliminary findings from a study on financial behavior of college students show that positive financial behaviors are associated with positive life outcomes (Shim et al., 2007; Xiao et al., 2007).

There are two issues that are not addressed by the behavior theories reviewed in this chapter: the structure of financial behaviors and interactions between financial behaviors. The first issue asks if there is a pattern when consumers adopt various financial behaviors. Some previous studies suggest the adoption of financial behaviors may have a hierarchical pattern and consumers adopt some financial behaviors before others. According to a study by Federal Reserve staff (Hilgert et al., 2003), it seems consumers adopt cash management behavior first, then credit behavior, and then saving and investing behavior. Studies on saving motives (Xiao & Noring, 1994) and financial asset shares (Xiao & Anderson, 1997) also show such a pattern. Is this pattern valid in general? If so, what is the theoretical foundation? The second issue is to ask if positive financial behaviors enhance each other. Do positive financial behaviors beget positive financial behaviors? If so, we may focus on promoting one particular financial behavior and hope the formation of that behavior will influence the formation of other positive financial behaviors. Some evidence shows that self-perceived financial behavior performance is associated with self-reported positive financial behavior (Xiao, et al., 2006). More theoretical and empirical studies are needed to address these issues.

Acknowledgments I thank Vicki Fitzsimmons, Barbara O'Neill and Janice Prochaska for their helpful suggestions and comments on earlier versions of this chapter.

References

Ajzen, I. (1991). The theory of planned behavior. *Organizational Behavior and Human Decision Processes*, 50, 179–211.
Ajzen & Fishbein, I., & Fishbein, M. (1980). *Understanding attitudes and predicting social behavior*. Englewood Cliffs, NJ: Prentice-Hall.

Armitage, C. J., & Conner, M. (2000). Social cognition models and health behavior: A structured review. *Psychology and Health, 15,* 173–189.

Armitage, C. J., & Conner, M. (2001). Efficacy of the theory of planned behavior: A meta-analytic review. *British Journal of Social Psychology, 40,* 471–499.

Bansal, H. S., & Taylor, S. F. (2002). Investigating interactive effects in the theory of planned behavior in a service-provider switching context. *Psychology & Marketing, 19,* 407–425.

Bosnjak, M., Tuten, T. L., & Wittmann, W. W. (2005). Unit (non)response in web-based access panel surveys: An extended planned-behavior approach. *Psychology & Marketing, 22,* 489–505.

Bristow, B. J. (1997). *Promoting financial well-being: Running a successful MONEY 2000 campaign.* Ithaca, NY: Cornell Cooperative Extension.

Cook, A. J., Kerr, G. N., & Moore, K. (2002). Attitudes and intentions towards purchasing GM food. *Journal of Economic Psychology, 23*(5), 557–572.

East, R. (1993). Investment decisions and the theory of planned behavior. *Journal of Economic Psychology, 14*(2), 337–375.

East, R. (2000). Complaining as planned behavior. *Psychology & Marketing, 17,* 1077–1095.

Fishbein, M., & Ajzen, I. (1975). *Belief, attitude, intention, and behavior: An introduction to theory and research.* Reading, MA: Addison-Wesley.

Fitzsimmons, V. S., Hira, T. K., Bauer, J. W., & Hafstrom, J. L. (1993). Financial management: Development of scales. *Journal of Family and Economic Issues, 14,* 257–273.

Fortin, D. R. (2000). Clipping coupons in cyberspace: A proposed model of behavior for deal-prone consumers. *Psychology & Marketing, 17,* 515–534.

Hilgert, M. A., Hogarth, J. M., & Beverly, S. G. (2003, July). Household financial management: The connection between knowledge and behavior. *Federal Reserve Bulletin, 89,* 309–322.

Hogarth, J. M., Beverly, S. G., & Hilgert, M. A. (2003). *Patterns of financial behaviors: Implications for community educators and policy makers.* Paper presented at Federal Reserve System Community Affairs Research Conference.

Hogarth, J. M., Hilgert, M. A., & Schuchardt, J. (2002). Money managers: The good, the bad, and the lost. *Proceedings of the Association of Financial Counselling and Planning Education,* 12–23.

Hrubes, D., Ajzen, I., & Daigle, J. (2001). Predicting hunting intentions and behavior: An application of the theory of planned behavior. *Leisure Sciences, 23,* 165–178.

Kang, H., Hahn, M., Fortin, D. R., Hyun, Y. J., & Eom, Y. (2006). Effects of perceived behavioral control on the consumer usage intention of e-coupons. *Psychology & Marketing, 23*(10), 841–864.

Kerkman, B. C. (1998). Motivation and stages of change in financial counseling: An application of a transtheoretical model from counseling psychology. *Financial Counseling and Planning, 9*(1), 13–20.

Levesque, D. A., Prochaska, J. M., & Prochaska, J. O. (1999). Stages of change and integrated service delivery. *Consulting Psychology Journal, 51,* 226–241.

Lim, H., & Dubinsky (2005), A. J. (2005). The theory of planned behavior in e-commerce: Making a case for interdependencies between salient beliefs. *Psychology & Marketing, 22,* 833–855.

Loibl, C., & Hira, T. K. (2007, March). New insights into advising female clients on investment decisions. *Journal of Financial Planning.* Retrieved July 20, 2007, from http://www.fpanet.org/journal/articles/2007_Issues/jfp0307-art9.cfm.

Lynne, G. D, Casey, C. F., Hodges, A., & Rahmani, M. (1995). Conservation technology adoption decisions and the theory of planned behavior. *Journal of Economic Psychology. 16*(4), 581–598.

Muske, G., & Winter, M. (2001). An in-depth look at family cash-flow management practices. *Journal of Family and Economic Issues, 22*(4), 353–372.

O'Neill, B. (2001). Updated MONEY 2000^{TM}: Impact data. Message to MONEY 2000^{TM} electronic mail group, MONEY2000-NATIONAL-L@cce.cornell.edu.

O'Neill, B., & Xiao, J. (2003). Financial fitness quiz: A tool for analyzing financial behavior. *Consumer Interest Annual, 49.* Retrieved November 18, 2007, from http://consumerinterests.org.

O'Neill, B., Xiao, J. J. (2006). Financial fitness quiz findings: Strengths, weaknesses, and disconnects. *Journal of Extension, 44*(1). Retrieved November 18, 2007, from http://www.joe.org.

Pro-Change Behavior Systems. (2002). *Mastering change: Counselors' guide to using the transtheoretical model with clients.* West Kingston, RI: Pro-Change Behavior Systems.

Prochaska, J. M. (2000). A transtheoretical model for assessing organizational change: A study of family service agencies' movement to time limited therapy. *Families in Society, 80*(1), 76–84.

Prochaska, J. O. (1979). Systems of psychotherapy: A transtheoretical analysis. Homewood, IL: Dorsey.

Prochaska, J. O., DiClemente, C. C., & Norcross, J. C. (1992). In search of how people change: Applications to addictive behaviors. *American Psychologist, 47*(9), 1102–1114.

Prochaska, J. O., Redding, C. A., & Evers, K. E. (1996). The transtheoretical model and stages of change. In K. Glanz, F. M. Lewis, & B. K. Rimer (Eds.), *Health behavior and health education: Theory, research, and practice* (2nd ed., pp. 60–84). San Francisco: Jossey-Bass.

Prochaska, J. O., Redding, C. A., Harlow, L. L., Rossi, J. S., & Velicer, W. F. (1994). The transtheoretical model of change and HIV prevention: A review. *Health Education Quarterly,* 21, 4.

Shim, S., Easlick, M. A., Lotz, S. L., & Warrington, P. (2001). An online prepurchase model: The role of intention to search. *Journal of Retailing, 77,* 397–416.

Shim, S., Xiao, J. J., Barber, B., & Lyons, A. (2007). *Pathways to success: A model of financial well-being of young adults.* (Working paper). Tucson, AZ: University of Arizona.

Shockey, S. S., & Seiling, S. B. (2004). Moving into action: Application of the transtheoretical model of behavior change to financial education. *Financial Counseling and Planning, 15*(1), 41–52.

Xiao, J. J., & Anderson, J. G. (1997). Hierarchical financial needs reflected by household financial asset shares. *Journal of Family and Economic Issues, 18*(4), 333–356.

Xiao, J. J., Newman, B. M., Prochaska, J. M., Leon, B., & Bassett, R. (2004). Voice of consumers in credit card debts: A qualitative approach. *Journal of Personal Finance, 3*(2), 56–74.

Xiao, J. J., Newman, B. M., Prochaska, J. M., Leon, B., Bassett, R., & Johnson, J. L. (2004). Applying the transtheoretical model of change to debt reducing behavior. *Financial Counseling and Planning, 15*(2), 89–100.

Xiao, J. J., & Noring, F. E. (1994). Perceived saving motives and hierarchical financial needs. *Financial Counseling and Planning.* 5, 25–44.

Xiao, J. J., O'Neill, B., Prochaska, J. M., Kerbal, C. M., Brennan, P., & Bristow, B. J. (2004). A consumer education program based on the transtheoretical model of change. *International Journal of Consumer Studies, 28*(1), 55–65.

Xiao, J. J., Shim, S., Barber, B., & Lyons, A. (2007). *Academic success and well-being of college students*: Financial behaviors matter (TCAI Report). Tucson, AZ: University of Arizona.

Xiao, J. J., Sorhaindo, B., & Garman, E. T. (2006). Financial behavior of consumers in credit counseling. *International Journal of Consumer Studies, 30*(2), 108–121.

Xiao, J. J., & Wu, J. (2006). Applying the theory of planned behavior to retain credit counseling clients. *Proceedings of the Association for Financial Counseling and Planning Education,* 91–100.

Chapter 6
Consumer Economic Socialization

Ivan Beutler and Lori Dickson

Abstract This chapter addresses the concept of consumer economic socialization as it has developed in the literature. Specifically, it covers the context in which the following have been studied: economic socialization; children and adolescents' developmental competencies in understanding and participating in economic and consumer processes; and major agents of economic socialization, including culture, media, schools, peers, and families. Needs for further research are also briefly discussed.

To function effectively in adult roles, youth need access to the fruits of economic activity. In modern society, these fruits are goods and services created through a long chain of productive processes. For example, with a cell phone call, a mother informs her son that she will arrive a little behind schedule. This simple call quiets his anxiety, but the economy behind the call is anything but simple. Built on decades of computer, satellite, and communications research and development, the cell phone industry is underwritten by huge capital investments and a sophisticated labor force of real people. Wages and goods and services are end results of this long chain of productive process. Employees depend on wages to procure goods and services. Wages are necessary but not sufficient for living well. The skillful dispatch of wages and other resources is an important part of the process of learning to function effectively in consumer roles. This process is called consumer economic socialization.

Inadequate consumer economic socialization comes at a cost, both to individual youth and the society in which they live. Failure to prepare for life's work means you will do some other work, likely with less satisfaction and purpose. Youth of each generation need to become socialized at a level commensurate with the resources accorded to them. It has been said that sellers in the market economy need only one eye, the eye trained on making the sale at the market price! But buyers need many eyes: for example, home buyers need one eye trained on structural soundness, one on

I. Beutler
School of Family Life, Brigham Young University, 2048 JFSB, Provo, UT 84602, USA
e-mail: ivan_beutler@byu.edu

the floor plan, one on decor, one on aesthetics, one on the asking price, and several eyes trained on location. It takes a thousand eyes to buy a home. The same can be said about socializing youth to be effective consumers. They need a thousand eyes! For this reason, consumer economic socialization literature has focused primarily on how children and adolescents become competent in consumer roles (Cram & Ng, 1999; John 1999; Lunt & Furnham, 1996; Webley & Young, 2006).

This chapter will outline the theoretical perspectives under which economic socialization has been studied; it will review literature on the developmental level of consumer and economic understanding among children and then among adolescents. Finally, it will examine the effect of specific socialization agents on youth.

Perspectives for Understanding Consumer Economic Socialization

Much of the research surrounding consumer economic socialization is conducted from a macroeconomic perspective, meaning that the economic cycle is seen as consisting primarily of production rather than consumption processes. In this view, consumption begins and ends with a purchase. However, consumption can be seen as an involved and elaborate process in and of itself—a process that is carried out in particular ways and that takes advantage of propinquous and value-oriented economies (Beutler, Owen, & Hefferan, 1988). Thus, the consumption processes of individual households are relevant to understanding how consumer economic socialization takes place. In these microenvironments, it is a matter of considerable consequence whether consumption processes are guided by prosocial values toward family, community, and personal growth (Kasser, Ryan, Zac, & Sameroff, 1995) or by materialistic values centered on visible financial success (Belk, 1988). At this level of economy, the value contexts in which persons are embedded makes a substantial difference in terms of their well-being, even at young ages (Kasser & Ryan, 1996).

Scholarship regarding consumer economic socialization has been developed by two main groups. *Psychologists* and a limited number of economists have considered how children learn about the adult world using concepts such as price, ownership, money, and savings. A second group of *consumer researchers*, including some family and consumer scientists and a larger group of marketing and communication scholars, have taken a more applied approach. Family and consumer scientists have focused on topics such as money values, socializing effects of families, financial aspirations, attitudes and behaviors, and financial education (e.g., Allen, Edwards, Hayhoe, & Leach, 2007; Bailey & Lown, 1993; Fox, Bartholomae, & Gutter, 2000; Furnham, 1984; Hibbert, Beutler, & Martin, 2004; Lachance, Legault, & Bujold, 2000; Mangleburg & Grewal, 1997; Masuo, Miroutu, Hanashiro, & Kim, 2004; Xiao, Noring, & Anderson, 1995). Marketing and communication scholars have documented a rising consumer sophistication among children, including their growing knowledge of product brands, advertising, decision making, and negotiating (John, 1999).

Both psychologists and consumer researchers have drawn on cognitive development literature (e.g., Leiser & Halmachi, 2006; Piaget, 1932) to provide their work with an organizing theme of age-related developmental stages. This type of research has provided descriptive information in answer to the question, "what are the stages?" in the cognitive process of gaining consumer competence (see Berti & Bombi, 1988; Furnham & Lewis, 1986; John, 1999 for reviews). The cognitive development model treats youth as "economic problem solvers" who learn to function in the adult world from inside their own heads. This developmental approach has proven useful, but it has also tended to overlook the question of *how* youth move between stages as they actively participate in the construction of their consumer reality (Duveen, 1994).

In response to this question, social psychologists have introduced social learning theory into the study of economic socialization. The social learning perspective is sensitive to the influence of culture and seeks to account for social interaction influences on children's development—political and social attitudes, historical customs, and values (Cram & Ng, 1999; Cummings & Taebel, 1978). From a very strict social learning perspective, some scholars (e.g., Duveen, 1994) have argued that youth do not solve encountered problems so much as they draw on ready-made solutions available within their society. Others have countered this argument, suggesting that youth actively participate in their own socialization through the scaffolding of basic economic principles such as ownership, money, and price (Cram & Ng, 1999).

Children's Consumer Socialization

Children's consumer behavior has long been the object of scholarly inquiry. Early attempts at research were focused on specific topics such as brand loyalty and conspicuous consumption (John, 1999). By the mid-1970s, the scholars began to address broader questions about children as consumers. At this time, the socialization research became known to the marketing community. As a result, public policy concerns about advertising to young children developed, and ironically, this interest surrounding the field promoted its further development (John, 1999). Now, over 25 years' worth of research is available on the consumer socialization of children. The majority of this research is developmental in nature; thus, a developmental understanding of children's socialization will be the focus of this section (Table 6.1).

Developmental Stages

Researchers have used various theoretical paradigms to explain the process of children's economic socialization. The majority have used some adaptation of Piaget's cognitive developmental model, meaning that they propose a series of hierarchical stages through which children progress as they become economically socialized. Berti and Bombi (1988), for example, have synthesized children's economic

Table 6.1 Children's consumer economic socialization: Recent studies

Developmental stage: level of understanding

Stage 1 none or beginning	Stage 2 isolated concepts	Stage 3 linking of concepts	Topics	References
No idea of the origin or source of money 1–4[a]	Money given by a bank or change given by a store clerk 5–6	Money as pay for work 7–8	The origin of money	Berti and Bombi (1979)
No awareness of payment needed NA[a]	Awareness that coins and bills have differing values NA	Can make correct change 13	Money and its value	Berti and Bombi (1979) Pollio and Gray (1973)
No grasp, transaction thought to be ritual based 6–8[a]	Realize shop owner buys inventory to sell, do not understand its for a profit 8–10	Able to integrate both systems and get difference between buying and selling prices 10–11	Prices & profit	Furth (1980) Jahoda (1981) Furnham and Cleare (1988)
	All scores improved with age, but had not maxed out by age 12 Money scores were higher than barter scores at each age (6–12) Demand-change scores exceeded supply-change at each age 6–8[a]		Supply & demand • money *vs.* barter • demand/supply change	Berti and Grivet (1990) Thompson and Siegler (2000) Leiser and Halachmi (2006)
Develop sense of possessiveness: "mine" noun-noun: "daddy-sock" 2	Over half of disputes are over possessions, these decreased with age 2–5	By age 11 understand private ownership and right of property transfer 10–12	Property ownership	Cram, Ng, and Jhaveri (1996)
Some common knowledge of socioeconomic situations 3–7	Socioeconomic knowledge more integrated, able to distinguish between personal and institutional relations 8–11	Nonconcrete and nonvisible processes become central focus, able to think hypothetically 12–17	Social meaning of economic status	Diez-Martinez and Ochoa (2006)

[a]Typical age.

development under each of Piaget's stages. However, researchers using Piaget's model often disagree over the number of stages that should be used and over children's level of understanding in each stage. This disagreement may be due to the different sample sizes and definitions of the stage boundaries used in their studies (Furnham, 1996). The recent trend in economic psychology has been to use three main phases to describe children's development, rather than all of Piaget's sub-stages. These general phases are "(1) no understanding, (2) understanding of some isolated concepts, and (3) linking of isolated concepts to achieve full understanding" (Furnham, 1996, p. 13–14).

Areas of Developmental Research

Most of the developmental research on economic socialization focuses on children's understanding of the adult economic world (Webley, 1996). Further, the majority of this research explores the content of children's economic knowledge rather than the process through which this knowledge is acquired (Furnham, 1996). Thus, children's understanding of money, possession, wealth and poverty, prices and profit, wages, and banking are well-studied topics. Other areas such as betting, taxes, interest rates, and recession are less studied, perhaps because children (and many adults) are not expected to understand these concepts (Furnham, 1996). The following is a sampling of some of these well-studied areas of children's economic understanding.

Money

Money is a vital part of economic transactions today, and most children are exposed to money at an early age. Although children may be able to complete transactions involving money, they do not necessarily understand the meaning of their actions (Furnham, 1996). Based on their work from several studies, Berti and Bombi (1979) identified six stages of children's understanding about money: "stage 1: no awareness of payment; stage 2: obligatory payment—no distinction between different kinds of money, and money can buy anything; stage 3: distinction between types of money—not all money is equivalent any more; stage 4: realization that money can be insufficient; stage 5: strict correspondence between money and objects—correct amount has to be given; stage 6: correct use of change" (p. 16–17). Making change is considered a difficult monetary concept, and children's ability to make change has also been studied by Pollio and Gray (1973). Among subjects that were of ages 7, 9, 11, and 13 and college aged, the 13-year olds were the youngest group in which every member was able to make change correctly.

Prices and Profit

Furth (1980) has outlined four stages in children's understanding of prices and profit: (1) no understanding of payment; (2) understanding customer payment but not shopkeeper payment; (3) understanding and relating payments made by both the customer and the shopkeeper; and (4) understanding all of these payments. Related to children's understanding of prices and profit is their understanding of banking. According to a study by Jahoda (1981), only one-fourth of his 14- and 16-year-old subjects understood that banks are profit-making organizations. Jahoda outlined a series of steps that children move through as they come to understand the concept of interest. These steps range from having no concept of interest to having a correct conception of why interest is charged on loans.

Supply and Demand

Berti and Grivet (1990) were some of the first researchers to explore children's understanding of supply and demand. Building on their research and the research of Leiser and Halachmi (2006) and Thompson and Siegler (2000) have differentiated between demand-change and supply-change problems and presented possible reasons why children score better on demand-change problems. One explanation for this phenomenon is that young children, especially preschoolers, follow the "more is more" principle. For example, a young child would assume that more people washing cars logically leads to more money being charged for each car washed. Positive correlations are understood before negative ones; thus, changes in demand would be easier for children to understand because when demand goes up, so does the price and vice versa.

Leiser and Halachmi (2006) built their research around this interesting dynamic. In a study, they gave children two scenarios accompanied by pictures. A sample scenario is as follows: there is a picture of Sarah with a pail and cars; the children are told that Sarah has decided to open a car wash. A second picture shows Sarah with several friends who have also decided to open car washes. The children are asked if the price of washing a car now will go up, go down, or stay the same. In order to test whether demand problems were easier for children or whether they were simply giving correct answers by following the "more is more" principle, Leiser and Halachmi (2006) asked an additional question in the experiment. By asking the children whether the buyer would be more (or less) pleased by the transaction, they were able to present a negative correlation: buyer satisfaction is negatively correlated with price. They found that even when this negative correlation was presented in a supply-change problem, demand-change problems were still easier for children to solve.

Property Ownership

Property ownership is a concept that is introduced to children soon after birth, and children's early sense of ownership is evident in their language development (Cram, Ng, & Jhaveri, 1996). Children develop the use of possessives early, around 24 months (Miller & Johnson-Laird, 1976); later, children are able to express possession with noun–noun or adjective–noun phrases (e.g., "daddy sock" and "his sock") (Cram et al., 1996, p. 111). Children learn about private ownership first through manipulation of objects in their environment and then through object disputes with peers; as they grow older, they increasingly react to the social meanings of objects (Cram et al., 1996). According to Cram et al. (1996), children understand private ownership and the right of property transfer by age 11.

Public ownership is much more difficult for children to grasp than private ownership because it is "embedded in an even more complex social institutional setting that is remote from the direct observation of young people" (Cram et al., 1996, p. 118). Cram et al. (1996) explained the process of coming to understand public and private ownership in Piagetian terms: as children encounter new information about ownership, they experience cognitive disequilibrium and must integrate the new information into their existing schema. These authors employed the idea of cognitive disequilibrium in a study that was designed to increase children's understanding of public ownership. Some researchers have examined the content of socialization messages about ownership. For example, Neo-Marxist researchers Cummings and Taebel (1978) have suggested that children are socialized to embrace capitalism; this in turn causes them to gradually develop a favorable attitude toward private ownership that is first fully apparent around the ninth grade.

The Social Meaning of Economic Status

The social meanings attached to economic status are fundamental to adult economic understanding. Occupation is one of the first areas where children differentiate between higher and lower economic status. In fact, children as young as $3\frac{1}{2}$ recognize that some jobs receive higher wages than others (Diez-Martinez & Ochoa, 2006). Diez-Martinez and Ochoa (2006), in a study of Mexican children, found that children expect different saving techniques of individuals that are in higher status and lower status professions. Cummings and Taebel (1978) note that America's educational system contributes to children's economic socialization by advocating capitalism. They argue that this perpetuates inequalities in economic status by directing children to consider the poor as weaker or less able.

From this review of literature, we can conclude that children's economic socialization occurs in a progressive fashion, with likely plateaus before each successive level of understanding. Acquired knowledge of economic principles is age-related, but there are clearly variations within any stages that are defined. The research just summarized on children's economic understanding is concerned with adult economic processes. However, Webley (1996) noted that children's economic socialization is not simply a function of their understanding of the adult world of economics. He emphasized the importance of the autonomous economic world that children create for themselves. Some of his research has been concerned with "swapping" during middle childhood as "an act with an economic form but a social function" (Webley, 1996, p. 154). Webley has also looked at other childhood economic systems, such as those involved in playing marbles, to suggest that children are actively involved in their own economic socialization. Both adult economic systems and children's autonomous economic systems are important aspects of economic socialization.

Adolescents' Consumer Socialization

Adolescence is a time of rapid change and growth when patterns and disciplines begin to be established for life. It is a time between childhood and adulthood to make preparations that enable the transition to adult roles. The drive for *emotional autonomy* starts early as adolescents begin to distinguish themselves psychologically from parents or others closest to them (Steinberg, 1996). Desire for independence is next manifested as *behavioral autonomy*, and finally in the late teens and emerging adult years, independence takes the form of "exploration in alternative possible life directions" (Arnett, 2000, p. 469). This drive for autonomy and identity development makes adolescence a key time for intentional and unintentional consumer socialization.

Adolescents are acknowledged as an important consumer group, both as independent consumers and because of their influence on adult consumption (Hoffmann & Tee, 2006). So, it is surprising that there is much less research on adolescents than on children when it comes to the process of consumer socialization. There is almost no literature on adolescents' developmental stages of economic understanding; however, their economic socialization is indirectly addressed in literature that deals with optimal socialization environments for adolescents.

Much work has been done on the socializing influences of parents, peers, and schools. Zimmer-Gembeck and Locke (2007) addressed this as they considered the influence of family and teachers on adolescent coping behavior. They found moderate evidence that the family is the primary place where coping strategies are socialized. In this way, parents also have influence over their adolescents' economic behaviors. For example, Furnham (1984) investigated parents' perceptions of this influence by asking about the effect of allowances on their adolescents' consumer behavior.

Adolescents who are exposed to less-desirable socialization environments have been shown to engage in more deviant and risk-taking behaviors (Fergusson, Vitaro, Wanner, & Brendgen, 2007; Lévy-Garboua, Lohéac, & Fayolle, 2006). Some of these problematic behaviors are tied to consumer behavior. For example, Delfabbro (2003) have addressed the issue of adolescent gambling. They found, in a sample of South Australian youth, that adolescents who engage in gambling behaviors are more likely to have family who view gambling as an appropriate and profitable enterprise. Because adolescents are particularly susceptible to some undesirable consumer-related behaviors, researchers are interested in determining the factors predicting involvement and those protecting against it.

It is clear from this research that less is known about specific developmental stages that adolescents pass through as they become economically socialized. Instead, scholars have focused on adolescence as a time of identity development and a time of susceptibility to negative socialization influences. Accordingly, most of these studies have examined adolescents' financial attitudes and behaviors in relation to risk-taking and deviant behavior.

Socializing Agents Affecting Children and Adolescents

Research on children and adolescents' general development toward economic socialization has just been reviewed. Now, specific socializing agents that influence youth will be discussed. These agents are external influences on youth's knowledge, values, and behaviors concerning money and other economic principles. Culture, media, schools, peers, and family are relevant socializing agents that will be discussed.

Culture

Culture is clearly an overarching influence on consumer socialization. One critique of using developmental theory to explain economic socialization is that it misses the influence of culture—it does not take experiential factors or external stimuli into consideration (Furnham, 1996). Researchers have found evidence that some children have an early understanding of economic concepts because of education or the social conditions they are living under. For example, Wosinki and Peitras (1990) found that Polish children had a better understanding of salary than other groups in their study. The researchers attributed these children's premature understanding of salary to the current economic crisis in their country.

Findings such as these have led researchers to conduct cultural and cross-cultural economic research. This research has confirmed similarities across youth of different nations in limited dimensions of economic socialization. For example, developmental commonalities in buying and selling have been reported between Chinese Malaysian children (Hong Kwan & Stacey, 1981), Glaswegian children (Jahoda, 1979), and Zimbabwe children (Jahoda, 1983). Ideas about the functioning of a bank in the Netherlands (Jahoda & Woerdenbagch, 1982) and in Hong Kong (Ng, 1983) produced similar patterns also, but with varying rates of understanding in regard to the more complex financial concepts.

Ownership, wealth, and poverty have also been examined cross-culturally (Berti, Bombi, & Lis, 1982; Leahy, 1981, Leahy; Ng & Cram, 1990; Ng & Jhaveri, 1988). These comparisons confirm similar levels of sequencing in children's economic socialization, but they also recognize many differences between countries and cultures, making the more subtle aspects of socialization difficult to adequately evaluate. Along with cross-cultural research, scholars have used methodology from fields outside the social sciences to examine economic socialization. For example, Wallendorf and Arnould (1988) have conducted an anthropological inquiry into object attachment in the United States and the Niger Republic.

Media

As mentioned earlier, most of the information on media as a socializing agent is written from the marketing perspective. John (1999) has created one of the most comprehensive developmental models of consumer socialization from the marketing perspective. John based her model on a review of 25 years of research reported in marketing and communication journals from 1974 to 1998. She conceptualized three stages of development that are shown to vary in developmental sophistication by age: *perceptual* (ages 3–7), *analytical* (ages 7–11), and *reflective* (ages 11–16). Each stage of a child's development is described in terms of *orientation, complexity,* and *perspective*, and each of these aspects becomes increasingly abstract, complex, and other-centered as children progress through the three stages. A simplified version of the conceptual model is illustrated in the upper portion of Table 6.2. Applied examples are shown in the lower portion of Table 6.2 based on John's review of literature.

Perceptual Stage

The perceptual stage (ages 3–7) is marked by a concrete orientation to objects in the marketplace. Children may recognize brand names but will have little understanding

Table 6.2 Consumer sophistication as stages of socialization: A marketing perspective

	Levels of Sophistication		
Three stages	Perceptual (3–7 ages)	Analytical (7–11 ages)	Reflective (11–16 ages)
Concepts:			
Orientation	Concrete	. . .	Abstract
Complexity	Unidimensional	. . .	Multidimensional
	Simple	. . .	Contingent ("If–then")
Perspective	Egocentric	. . .	Multiple perspective
	(own perspective)	. . .	(in social context)
Applied examples			
Knowledge regarding			
Advertising	• Believe ads are truthful, funny and interesting • Have a positive attitude toward ads		• Believe ads are biased and sometimes deceptive • Have a skeptical attitude toward ads
Products & brands	• Have some brand name recognition and limited symbolism savvy		• Have substantial brand name recognition and symbolism savvy
Knowledge & skill regarding shopping	• Understand sequence of basic shopping script events		• Shopping scripts complex and contingent
Information search	• Limited awareness of sources		• Contingent use of different sources
Product evaluation	• Based on perceptual attribute assessment		• Based on functional, perceptual and social attribute assessment
Decision & purchase Negotiation strategies	• Use of single attributes and limited repertoire of strategies		• Use of multiple attributes and full repertoire of strategies

Adapted from John (1999)

of their deeper symbolic meaning. The level of complexity at which they can understand market concepts is also low. Further, children in the perceptual stage approach consumer processes with an egocentric perspective. This impedes their ability to negotiate for objects they want because they are unable to simultaneously understand another's perspective as well as their own.

Analytical Stage

The analytical stage (ages 7–11) involves movement toward more analytical thought about concepts such as prices, advertising, and brands. Children in this stage begin to analyze such concepts on multiple dimensions. As a result, they are more flexible in their decision-making and purchasing strategies.

Reflective Stage

In the reflective stage (ages 11–16), children and adolescents build on their already-present understanding of the marketplace by developing a more complex knowledge of concepts such as pricing. These youth are able to evaluate advertising effectively because they are aware of other people's perspectives and motivations. Their interest in developing a personal identity and in fitting in by conforming make them keenly aware of the consumer environment. In this stage, there is substantial brand name recognition and understanding of consumption symbolism.

Ages associated with each stage are clearly only approximate. The age ranges within each stage are also fairly wide, so it is reasonable to expect variation in maturity within each stage as well. Consistent with a marketing perspective, this literature focuses on the point of purchase as the realm of primary importance in a child's consumer socialization.

Based on this information about children's consumer knowledge, the media and marketers have ample cause to focus their efforts on advertising to youth, who have a direct and indirect influence in the consumer marketplace. McNeal (1999) asserted that before children can walk, they have consumer clout that gradually grows until age 8 or 9, when they become bona fide consumers. At these ages, apparel is their fastest growing type of expenditure, not just money spent on treats as might be expected. Children's fastest growing source of income has become earnings, second in size only to allowances. American children now earn about one-third of their income doing chores around the house and completing other responsibilities deemed important by their parents. They spend about two-thirds of their $15 of average weekly income, accounting for an aggregate annual expenditure in the United States that approaches $28 billion annually. In addition, children directly influence over $187 billion of parents' annual purchases and indirectly influence at least another $300 billion annually (McNeal, 1999). These figures are astonishingly large, and from a marketing perspective, numbers alone provide sufficient reason to take advantage of children as consumers. As McNeal put it, "Satisfying kids is the most fundamental of all market efforts. It will keep a company in business in the fiercest of competition because it will keep kids coming back—for the rest of their lives" (p. 11).

In response to the marketing perspective, a smaller group of scholars takes the position that these children are the future and that their consumer potential should not be exploited. With the publishing of her book, *Born to buy*, Schor (2004) sounded a warning voice. She notes that marketing to children and adolescents under the guise of consumer socialization has promoted a consumer culture in America in which children aspire to be rich and believe that the brands they wear define their individual worth: "Children have become conduits from the consumer marketplace into the household, the link between advertisers and the family purse" (Schor, 2004, p. 11).

Schor (2004) conducted a survey of 300 fifth and sixth graders to examine children's involvement in the consumer marketplace. A consumer involvement scale was developed to measure involvement in the marketplace and to evaluate its effect on child well-being. Conclusions from in-depth interviews and data analysis affirmed that children who spend more time watching television and using other media become more enmeshed in the consumer culture. The study found that high consumer involvement was significantly associated with depression, anxiety, low self-esteem, and psychosomatic complaints in children. Higher levels of involvement also led to worsened relationships between parents and children. Thus, Schor asserted that children who are psychologically healthy will be worse off if they become involved in the consumer culture, and children with emotional problems will be helped if they distance themselves from marketers and media messages.

Schools

Much of the research on schools and economic socialization has been focused on understanding children and adolescents' deviant or risk-taking behavior. Lévy-Garboua et al. (2006) used a standard human capital model to understand the connection between education and risk-taking behavior. In this model, they treated risky behavior as disinvestment and education as joint human investment. This is a feasible approach because education leads to both increased productive capacity and a higher likelihood of avoiding risky behaviors that will diminish productive capacity (Webley & Young, 2006).

Peers

Peers are an acknowledged socializing influence, yet little research exists on the nature of their economic influence. Peer influence has been found to be particularly relevant when other socialization contexts, especially the family, are weak (John, 1999). Adolescents who are highly connected to parents and peers fare the best, while adolescents who report high levels of attachment to peers and low levels of attachment with parents are at most risk for psychosocial difficulties (Nada Raja, McGee, & Stanton, 1992). One of the key studies on the economic influence of peers was conducted by Bachmann, John, and Rao (1993). They found that peer influence affects children's attitude toward public luxuries but not private necessities.

Thus, they conclude that peer influence is tied to the understanding of consumption symbolism.

Family

A substantial body of literature exists on the family's role in the economic socialization of children (Rettig & Mortenson, 1986). Families operate as one of society's most salient economic socializing agents: they provide information networks, role models, environments conducive to human development, and grants and exchanges (Rettig, 1983). This section will review studies on the practice of giving allowances and on the family's role in transferring materialism, anxiety, the ability to delay gratification, and financially prudent behaviors to children.

Allowances

A modest body of literature exits around the practice of giving allowances to children. The consequences of this practice for the economic socialization of children are of considerable interest to scholars and parents alike. There is a pattern of prescriptive advice in the allowance literature that tends to be for or against certain allowance practices. However, as others have noted (e.g., Marshall, 1964; Meeks, 1998; Miller & Yung, 1990; Mortimer, Dennehy, Lee, & Finch, 1994), this advice tends to exceed the modest base of existing research which might have informed the matter.

Early efforts to systematically identify differences between allowance and nonallowance children met with limited success (Hollister, Rapp, & Goldsmith, 1986; Marshall, 1964; Marshall & Magruder, 1960). More recent work has sought to examine allowance practices in a broader economic socialization context. This approach has resulted in richer conceptual accounts of allowance arrangements, such as conditions of receipt, work obligations, dollar amounts transferred (Miller & Yung, 1990), allowance experience, cash versus credit buying (Abramovitch, Freedman, & Pliner, 1991), and effects of allowance use on intrinsic and extrinsic work values (Mortimer et al., 1994).

Miller and Yung (1990) identified two prominent allowance types used by parents today: one earned and the other entitled. An *earned allowance* consists of family money that is managed by a parent and transferred to a child on a regular basis. The transfer is typically contingent on the child's completion of chore assignments or compliance with other behaviors deemed appropriate by the parent. In contrast, an *entitled allowance* is characterized by a regular transfer of funds to the control of a child for his or her basic support. Conceptually, the earned and entitled-allowances have important differences. The earned allowance mirrors to a degree an employer–employee arrangement of wages in exchange for services rendered, and failure to comply with expectations typically results in decreased or discontinued payment (Feather, 1991; Furnham & Thomas, 1984). In contrast to the earned allowance, entitled allowances are not seen as payment for services rendered but as part of a family's obligation to share joint resources for needed living expenses (Feather,

1991; Miller & Yung, 1990). Entitlement transfers can be likened to government welfare payments that provide for the needs and desires of its members who are unable to support themselves.

Following the lead of Miller and Yung (1990), several authors have begun to move the allowance literature to a more conceptual level. They have theorized that entitled allowances may be preferable to earned allowances, since entitlement avoids the hierarchical character of paid employment. Entitlement also represents a greater degree of trust than having to work for money, and children may feel more responsible for the money they receive, make a greater effort to use it wisely, and become relatively more economically socialized (Abramovitch et al., 1991; Feather, 1991; Miller & Yung, 1990; Pliner, Freedman, Abramovitch, & Drake, 1996).

Although the literature has assumed that allowances are beneficial to children's economic socialization and that the type of allowance received is important, some authors have suggested otherwise. Pliner et al. (1996) found that children whose mothers had high economic expectations for them and who gave them warm, gentle guidance had similar behaviors to children who were given allowances. Thus, parental guidance and involvement in providing good socializing experiences—rather than type of allowance—may be the most important influences on children's economic socialization.

Children's Materialism

Several studies have found that parents influence children's level of materialism. The concept of materialism has been reviewed in the academic literature and described in terms of its primary features by Richins and Dawson (1992). One of the ways they describe materialism is as a value in which possessions and acquisitions are a central measure of a person's success and happiness in life. Kasser et al. (1995) found that the late adolescent children of nurturant mothers tended to be like their mothers in that they had nonmaterialistic and intrinsic values. In contrast, the children of cold and controlling mothers tended to be more materialistic. Adolescents and mothers from disadvantaged socioeconomic circumstances were found to be especially extrinsically oriented, which is a trait associated with materialism. A later study by Flouri (1999) examined adolescent materialism behavior for the effect of family influences. Again, a mother's materialism predicted her adolescent child's materialism. This research is beginning to demonstrate that families have an important socializing influence on their children by transmitting values such as materialism from one generation to the next.

Money Attitudes

A particularly interesting study (Allen et al., 2007) illustrates how anxiety and other negative money attitudes can be transferred within families. Building on the work of Anderson and Sabatelli (1990, 1992), two of the key variables were (1) the frequency with which college students had imagined-interactions (pretend talk) with their parents about money and (2) coalition communication, either parent to parent or parent to child, where at least one of the individuals is disconfirmed (shown disrespect and engaged in conflict as opposed to being shown respect, support, caring, and empathy).

Consistent with previous research findings, Allen et al. (2007) found that more frequent imagined interactions or *pretend talk* was highly correlated ($r = 0.68$) with unpleasantness. Students who engaged in frequent pretend talk seemed to be anticipating a future conversation with parents where there would be conflict and lack of respect. Thus, pretend talk may be a way of coping with anxiety, specifically anxiety resulting from power imbalance in family relationships and money matters. Student pretend talk was observed to be less pleasant in families where parents argued about money or in families with parent–child or parent–parent coalitions. Sixty-eight percent of those who argued about money were coalition families with a pattern of some members combining against another member. This study provides a lens to understand how at least some negative money attitudes are created and transferred from one generation to the next within the context of negative family relationships. It is also a call for more research to inform the topic of positive and negative money attitudes and familial relationships.

Delayed Gratification and Financial Prudence

Other studies have considered the family's influence on children's ability to delay gratification. In both the economic and the economic psychology literature, delayed gratification and self-control are frequently considered determinants of an individual's rate of saving (Wärnyard, 1999; Wood, 1998). Thus, delayed gratification has been suggested as an explanation for success or failure in meeting long-term financial goals (Angeletos, Laibson, Repettro, Tobacman, & Weinberg, 2001). Webley & Young (2006) tested this hypothesis using Dutch panel data. Results showed that two parental behaviors were positively correlated with children's saving behaviors: discussing financial matters with their children, and a having a conscientious and future-minded orientation. These parental behaviors had a weak but clear impact on children's economic behavior into adulthood.

Parents have also been found to influence children's adoption of financially prudent behaviors in early adulthood. In a study by Hibbert et al. (2004), financially prudent behaviors in the family of origin were considered in terms of college students' levels of financial strain and their debt avoidance behaviors. Students who reported higher frequencies of prudent behaviors in their family of origin tended to experience lower levels of financial strain. Their analysis concluded that parents had a modest but favorable influence on the financial well-being of the next generation to the extent that they modeled financial prudence (by living within their means, saving money, paying bills on time, and avoiding unnecessary debt).

Although the exact pathways through which families influence children's socialization are unclear, research has documented this influence in areas such as materialism, anxiety, ability to delay gratification, and financial prudence. Based on the limited research to date, it seems clear that families have an important role in the economic socialization of the next generation.

These socializing agents—culture, media, schools, peers, and family—are broad external influences on economic socialization. They work, along with children and adolescents' natural developmental tendencies, to create their unique understanding of the consumer marketplace and the economic world in which they live.

Conclusion

This chapter has reviewed the typical ages at which youth become developmentally capable of learning a variety of economic concepts. Future research should continue to build knowledge of the stages in which economic socialization occurs and the external factors that influence this development.

Over a lifetime, today's youth are likely to make allocation decisions that direct the use of several million dollars in the economy. How well youth make these allocations will depend to a considerable degree on their preparation to assume adult roles. Relatively few concepts critical to that preparation have been examined in the research to date, and those that have been examined apply mainly to children, some to adolescents, and fewer to emerging adults. Furthermore, existing research has focused on socialization through the transfer of cognitive knowledge. Far less research has been devoted to socialization through the transfer of values, attitudes, and aspirations. Hence, these content areas represent tremendous opportunities for further research.

Other content areas urgently need further research. One of these is the growing incidence of materialism and associated credit card misuse. College students are especially at risk (Roberts & Jones, 2001). They are members of a credit card generation and a growing consumer culture that avidly pursues goods and services for nonutilitarian reasons including status, envy provocation, and pleasure (Belk, 1988). These students have grown up in a credit card society where debt is used freely to facilitate consumer spending, contributing to a record number of bankruptcies. Students with high levels of consumer debt earn poorer grades, experience higher dropout rates, suffer higher rates of depression, and work more hours to pay bills. They also have poorer credit ratings, which result in decreased employment opportunities and decreased ability to secure student loan funding for graduate education. Hayhoe, Leach, Turner, Bruin, and Lawrence (2000) and a number of other scholars have concluded that beginning in junior high school, students need to receive instruction on responsible credit use.

Accordingly, socialization research is needed to inform existing financial education and to aid in the development of new curricula. Researchers and educators need to identify critical concepts to be taught and how and when to teach them. From childhood through the emerging adult years, children's preparation for adult economic responsibility needs to occur in ways that compliment their developmental readiness. Their preparation needs to begin early, but not in ways that rob them of their childhood. Parents and families have a comparative advantage as purveyors of knowledge in some areas; professionals and public institutions are more suited for others. The quest for what should be taught, how, when, and by whom raises tough questions which will require both qualitative and quantitative methods as well as survey and experimental approaches to gathering data.

Finally, researchers should recognize that economic socialization is not just about cognitive competence in the consumer economy; it is also about values, attitudes, aspirations, and experiences that enable youth to successfully assume adult roles (Lunt & Furnham, 1996). Youth will not become adults who make a net contribution to their community and economy if they are only consumers—their consumption needs to be carried out in ways that harmonize with and amplify their roles as involved and contributing citizens.

References

Abramovitch, R., Freedman, J. L., & Pliner, P. (1991). Children and money: Getting an allowance, credit versus cash, and knowledge of pricing. *Journal of Economic Psychology*, *12*, 27–45.

Allen, M. W., Edwards, R., Hayhoe, C. R., & Leach, L. (2007). Imagined interactions, family money management patterns and coalitions, and attitudes towards money and credit. *Journal of Family and Economic Issues*, *28*, 3–22.

Anderson, S. A., & Sabatelli, R. M. (1990). Differentiating differentiation and individuation: Conceptual and operating challenges. *The American Journal of Family Therapy*, *18*, 32–50.

Anderson, S. A., & Sabetelli, R. M. (1992). The differentiation in the family system scale (DIFS). *The American Journal of Family Therapy*, *20*, 77–89.

Angeletos, G.-M., Liabson, D., Repetto, A., Tobacman, J., & Weinburg, S. (2001). The hyperbolic buffer stock model: Calibration, simulation, and empirical evaluation. *Journal of Economic Perspectives*, *15*, 47–68.

Arnett, J. J. (2000). Emerging adulthood: A theory of development from the late teens through the twenties. *American Psychology*, *55*, 469–480.

Bachmann, G. R., John, D., & Rao, A. R. (1993). Children's susceptibility to peer group purchase influence: An exploratory investigation. In L. McAlister & M. L. Rothschild (Eds.), *Advances in consumer research*, (pp. 463–468, Vol. 20). Provo, UT: Association for Consumer Research.

Bailey, W. C., & Lown, J. M. (1993). A cross-cultural examination of the etiology of attitudes towards money. *Journal of Consumer Studies and Home Economics*, *17*, 391–402.

Belk, R. W. (1988). Third world consumer culture. *Research in Marketing*, *4*, 103–127.

Berti, A. E., & Bombi, A. S. (1979). Where does money come from? *Archivio di Psicologia*, *40*, 53–77.

Berti, A. E., & Bombi, A. S. (1988). *The child's construction of economics*. Cambridge, MA: Cambridge University Press; Paris: Editions de la Maison des Sciences de l'Homme.

Berti, A. E., Bombi, A. S., & Lis, A. (1982). The child's conceptions about means and of production and their owners. *European Journal of Social Psychology*, *12*, 221–239.

Berti, A. E., & Grivet, A. (1990). The development of economic reasoning in children from 8 to 13 years old: Price mechanism. *Contributi di Psicologia*, *3*, 37–47.

Beutler, I. F., Owen, A. J., & Hefferan, C. (1988). The boundary question in household production: A systems model approach. *Home Economics Research Journal*, *17*(4), 267–278.

Cram, F., & Ng, S. H. (1999). Consumer socialization. *Applied Psychology: An International Review*, *48*(3), 297–312.

Cram, F., Ng, S. H., & Jhaveri, N. (1996). Young people's understanding of private and public ownership. In P. Lunt & A. Furnham (Eds.), *Economic socialization: The economic beliefs and behaviors of young people* (pp. 110–1129). Cheltenham, UK: Edward Elgar.

Cummings, S., & Taebel, D. (1978). The economic socialization of children: A Neo-Marxist analysis. *Social Problems*, *26*(2), 198–210.

Delfabbro, P., & Thrupp, L. (2003). The social determinants of youth gambling in South Australian adolescents. *Journal of Adolescence, 26*, 313–330.

Diez-Martinez, E., & Ochoa, A. (2006). Occupational hierarchy as a device to study Mexican children's and adolescents' ideas about consumption and saving in adults. *Journal of Economic Psychology, 27*(1), 20–35.

Duveen, G. (1994). Review of Sonuga-Burke, E.J.S. and Webley, P. (1993), "Children's savings: A study of the development of economic behaviour", Hove, UK: Lawrence Erlbaum Associates. *Journal of Economic Psychology, 15*, 375–378.

Feather, N. T. (1991). Variables relating to the allocation of pocket money to children: Parental reasons and values. *Journal of Social Psychology, 30*, 221–234.

Fergusson, D. M., Vitaro, F., Wanner, B., & Brendgen, M. (2007). Protective and compensatory factors mitigating the influence of deviant friends on delinquent behaviors during early adolescence. *Journal of Adolescence, 30*, 33–50.

Flouri, E. (1999). An integrated model of consumer materialism: Can economic socialization and maternal values predict materialistic attitudes in adolescents? *Journal of Socio-Economics, 28*, 707–724.

Fox, J. J., Bartholomae, S., & Gutter, M. S. (2000). What do we know about financial socialization? *Consumer Interests Annual, 46*, 217.

Furnham, A. (1984). Many sides of the coin: The psychology of money usage. *Personality and Individual Differences, 5*(5), 501–509.

Furnham, A. (1996). The economic socialization of children. . In P. Lunt & A. Furnham (Eds.), *Economic socialization: The economic beliefs and behaviors of young people* (pp. 11–34). Cheltenham, UK: Edward Elgar.

Furnham, A., & Lewis, A. (1986). *The economic mind: The social psychology of economic behavior.* Great Britain: Harvester Press Publishing Group.

Furnham, A., & Thomas, P. (1984). Adults' perceptions of the economic socialization of children. *Journal of Adolescence, 7*, 217–231.

Furth, H. (1980). *The world of grown-ups.* New York: Elsevier.

Hayhoe, C. R., Leach, L. J., Turner, P. R., Bruin, M. J, & Lawrence, F. C. (2000). Differences in spending habits and credit card use of college students. *The Journal of Consumer Affairs. 34*(1), 113–133.

Hibbert, J. R., Beutler, I. F., & Martin, T. M. (2004). Financial prudence and next generation financial strain. *Journal of Financial Counseling and Planning, 15*(2), 9–16.

Hoffmann, R., & Tee, J. (2006). Adolescent–adult interactions and culture in the ultimatum game. *Journal of Economic Psychology, 27*(1), 98–116.

Hollister, J., Rapp, D., & Goldsmith, E. (1986). Monetary practices of sixth-grade students. *Child Study Journal, 16*, 183–190.

Hong Kwan, T., & Stacey, B. (1981). The understanding of socio-economic concepts in Malaysian Chinese school children. *Child Study Journal, 11*, 33–49.

Jahoda, G. (1979). The construction of economic reality by some Glaswegian children. *European Journal of Social Psychology, 9*, 115–127.

Jahoda, G. (1983). European "lag" in the development of an economic concept: A study in Zimbabwe. *British Journal of Developmental Psychology, 1*, 113–120.

Jahoda, G., & Woerdenbagch, A. (1982). The development of ideas about an economic institution: A cross-national replication. *British Journal of Social Psychology, 21*, 337–338.

Jahoda, M. (1981). Work, employment and unemployment: Values, theories and approaches in social research. *American Psychologist, 36*, 184–191.

John, D. (1999). Consumer socialization of children: A retrospective look at twenty-five years of research. *The Journal of Consumer Research, 26*(3), 183–213.

Kasser, T., & Ryan, R.M. (1996). Further examining the American dream: Differential correlates of intrinsic and extrinsic goals. *Personality and Social Psychology Bulletin, 22*, 280–287.

Kasser, T., Ryan, R. M., Zax, M., & Sameroff, A. J. (1995). The relations of material and social environments to late adolescents' materialistic and prosocial values. *Developmental Psychology, 31*(6), 907–914.

Lachance, M. J, Legault, F., & Bujold, N. (2000). Family structure, parent–child communication, and adolescent participation in family consumer tasks and decisions. *Family and Consumer Sciences Research Journal, 29*, 125–152.

Leahy, R. L. (1981). The development of the conception of economic inequality: Descriptions and comparisons of rich and poor people. *Child Development, 52*, 523–532.

Leahy, R. L. (1983). Development of the conception of economic inequality: II. Explanations, justifications, and concepts of social mobility and change. *Developmental Psychology, 19*, 111–125.

Leiser, D., & Halachmi, R. B. (2006). Children's understanding of market forces. *Journal of Economic Psychology, 27*(1), 6–19.

Lévy-Garboua, L., Lohéac Y., & Fayolle, B. (2006). Preference formation, school dissatisfaction and risky behavior of adolescents. *Journal of Economic Psychology, 27*(1), 165–183.

Lunt, P., & Furnham, A. (1996). *Economic socialization: The economic beliefs and behaviors of young people.* Cheltenham, UK: Edward Elgar.

Mangleburg, T. F., & Grewal, D. (1997). Socialization, gender, and adolescents' self-reports of their generalized use of product labels. *Journal of Consumer Affairs, 31*, 255–280.

Marshall, H. R. (1964). The relation of giving children an allowance to children's money knowledge and responsibility and to other practices of parents. *The Journal of Genetic Psychology, 104*, 35–51.

Marshall, H. R., & Magruder, L. (1960). Relations between parent money education practices and children's knowledge and use of money. *Child Development, 31*, 253–284.

Masuo, D. M., Miroutu, Y. L., Hanashiro, R., & Kim, J. H. (2004). College students' money beliefs and behaviors: An Asian perspective. *Journal of Family and Economic Issues, 25*, 469–481.

McNeal, J. U. (1999). *Kids market: Myths and realities.* Ithaca, NY: Paramount Market Publishing.

Meeks, C. B. (1998). Factors influencing adolescents' income and expenditures. *Journal of Family and Economic Issues, 19*(2), 131–150.

Miller, G. A., & Johnson-Laird, P. N. (1976). *Language and perception.* Cambridge, MA: Cambridge University Press.

Miller, J., & Yung, S. (1990). The role of allowances in adolescent socialization. *Youth Society, 22*(2), 137–159.

Mortimer, J. T., Dennehy, K., Lee, C., & Finch, M. D. (1994). Economic socialization in the American family: The prevalence, distribution and consequences of allowance arrangements. *Family Relations, 43*, 23–29.

Nada Raja, S., McGee, R., & Stanton, W. (1992). Perceived attachments to parents and peers and psychological well-being in adolescence. *Journal of Youth and Adolescence, 21*, 471–485.

Ng, S. H. (1983). Children's ideas about the bank and shops' profit: Developmental stages and the influence of cognitive contrasts and conflict. *Journal of Economic Psychology, 4*, 209–221.

Ng, S. H., & Cram, F. (1990). *Effects of cognitive conflict on children's understanding of public ownership.* Paper presented at the 22nd International Congress of Applied Psychology, Kyoto, Japan.

Ng, S. H., & Jhaveri, N. (1988). *Young people's understanding of economic inequality: An Indian–New Zealand comparison.* Paper presented at the XXIV International Congress of Psychology, Sydney, Australia.

Piaget, J. (1932). *The moral judgment of the child.* London: Routledge and Kegan Paul.

Pliner, P., Freedman, J., Abramovitch, R., & Drake, P. (1996). Children as consumers: In the laboratory and beyond. In P. Lunt & A. Furnham (Eds.), *Economic socialization: The economic beliefs and behaviors of young people* (pp. 11–34). Cheltenham, UK: Edward Elgar.

Pollio, H., & Gray, T. (1973). Change-making strategies in children and adults. *Journal of Psychology, 84*, 173–179.

Rettig, K. D. (1983). Family as economic socialization agent. *Illinois Teacher of Home Economics 27* (1), 5–7.

Rettig, K. D., & Mortenson, M. (1986). *Household production of financial management competence.* Paper prepared for the Human Resources Symposium, St. Louis, Missouri.

Richins, M. L., & Dawson, S. (1992). A consumer values orientation for materialism and its measurement: Scale development and validation. *The Journal of Consumer Research, 19*(3), 303–316.

Roberts, J. A., & Jones, E., (2001). Money attitudes, credit card use, and compulsive buying among American college students. *The Journal of Consumer Affairs, 35*, 213–240.

Schor, J. B. (2004). *Born to buy: The commercialized child and the new consumer culture.* New York: Scribner.

Steinberg, L. (1996). *Adolescence.* Dubuque, IA: McGraw-Hill.

Thompson, D. R., & Siegler, R. S. (2000). Buy low, sell high: The development of an informal theory of economics. *Child development, 71*, 660–677.

Wallendorf, M., & Arnould, E. J. (1988). "My favorite things": A cross-cultural inquiry into object attachment, possessiveness and social linkage. *The Journal of Consumer Research, 14*(4), 531–547.

Wärnyard, K. E. (1999). *The psychology of saving. A study on economic psychology.* Cheltenham, UK: Edward Elgar.

Webley, P. (1996). Playing the market: The autonomous economic world of children. In P. Lunt & A. Furnham (Eds.), *Economic socialization: The economic beliefs and behaviors of young people* (pp. 149–161). Cheltenham, UK: Edward Elgar.

Webley, P., & Nyhus, E. K. (2006). Parent's influence on children's future orientation and saving. *Journal of Economic Psychology, 27*(1), 140–164.

Webley, P., & Young, B. (2006). Forward. *Journal of Economic Psychology, 27*(1), 1–5.

Wood, M. (1998). Socio-economic status, delay of gratification, and impulse buying. *Journal of Economic Psychology, 19*, 295–320.

Wosinki, M., & Peitras, M. (1990). Economic socialization of Polish children in different macro-economics conditions. *Journal of Economic Psychology, 11*, 515–529.

Xiao, J. J., Noring, F. E., & Anderson, J. G. (1995). College students' attitudes towards credit cards. *Journal of Consumer Studies and Home Economics, 19*, 155–174.

Zimmer-Gembeck, M. J., & Locke, E. M. (2007). The socialization of adolescent coping behavior: Relationships with families and teachers. *Journal of adolescence, 30*, 1–16.

Part II
Internet and Consumer Finance

Chapter 7
E-banking

Jinkook Lee, Jinsook Erin Cho, and Fahzy Abdul-Rahman

Abstract Based on the 2004 Survey of Consumer Finances (SCF), this study identifies consumer segments left out in the adoption of e-banking technologies, such as ATMs, debit cards, direct deposits, and direct payments. While variations exist for each different type of e-banking technology, e-banking laggards tend to be older, less educated, divorced or separated, and less affluent. We also compare data from the 2004 SCF with data from 1995 to examine whether significant changes exist in the determinants of e-banking adoption over this 10-year period and report how the demographics of e-banking adoption have changed over time.

E-banking refers to the process or service that allows a bank customer to perform financial transactions via electronic media without necessarily requiring a visit to a brick-and-mortar banking institution, such as the use of an automated teller machine (ATM), debit card, direct deposit, direct payment, or some other form of funds transfer. These services offer consumers a great deal of convenience and save time when managing financial matters, and also lower costs by way of reduced service charges (Lee & Lee, 2000).

The first application of electronic banking took place in 1969, when Chemical Bank placed a cash dispenser at a branch in Queens, New York (Drennan, 2003). Subsequently, many other banks joined in to experiment with various forms of e-banking services. While some disappeared after the introduction stage (e.g., smart cards), some e-banking technologies blossomed over time (e.g., ATMs).

In the late 1990s, e-banking embraced a new wave of technology innovation, the Internet. Incorporation of the Internet improved the benefits of existing e-banking services. In particular, it greatly enhanced the consumer's ability to manage information. Financial transactions made by ATM, direct deposits and payments, and debit card transactions are recorded and verified instantly from a distant location via the Internet, which further reduces the need for brick-and-mortar banking institution visits. Now, e-banking is viewed as a sustainable innovation in its maturity stage, reaching to the late majority in the diffusion process.

J. Lee
Department of Consumer Sciences, Ohio State University, 1787 Neil Avenue, Columbus, OH 43210, USA
e-mail: lee.42@osu.edu

It is important to note, however, that there are still about 20 % of households in the United States that have not adopted even the most popular form of e-banking technology, ATM banking (Lee & Lee, 2000). Furthermore, from early 2000 to date, the size of non-adopters has grown steadily, rather than shrinking over time (Mester, 2006). It may be the case that these non-adopters opt not to use e-banking due to some rational risks associated with e-banking, such as privacy and security concerns. Or, a particular consumer segment is still left out of e-banking due to his/her disadvantageous social and economic position in society. If the latter is the case, efforts must be made to reach out and educate these consumers in order to help them enjoy the convenience and other benefits of e-banking services.

In this study, we investigate the demographic and social profile of e-banking non-adopters. In so doing, we use the 2004 Survey of Consumer Finances and focus on adoption rates of the most widely available of e-banking technologies: ATMs, debit cards, direct deposit and direct payment transactions. Further, this study compares the profiles of non-adopters between two periods that are 10 years apart (specifically, 1995 and 2004) and examines changes in terms of adoption rates of a particular technology as well as the characteristics of non-adopters.

Literature Review

The banking industry is on the forefront of adopting innovation, both to reduce the costs of bank operations and to improve services to customers. During the 1950s, when the computerization of business transactions was in its infancy, Bank of America initiated an effort to automate the banking system, which included ERMA (electronic recording method of accounting computer processing system) and MICR (magnetic ink character recognition) (Bellis, 2003). These systems computerized manual records as well as checks processing, account management, and electronically updated and posted checking accounts. Technology innovation in the banking industry further accelerated during the 1960s and 1970s, with particular focus on moving away from manual and paper recording to electronic and paperless transactions. Indeed, technology has transformed the way banks offer financial services to U.S. consumers.

However, consumers adoption of banking technologies had been rather slow up until about 10 years ago. While electronic banking has been available for some 35 years in various forms, it was only after the late 1990s that it became so clearly visible to consumers. Infact, a study by Lee and Lee (2000) with the Survey of Consumer Finances shows that even in 1995, consumer adoption of banking technologies was not to the extent that the industry had thought it would be and that those who adopt e-banking technologies still have the characteristics of innovators. From the late 1990s and forward, however, a U.S. consumer's usage of e-banking technology rose substantially. For example, according to *First Data Survey,* five out of every six ATM/debit cardholders surveyed used their ATM/debit card at least once in the 30 days prior to the survey in 2003, while about 80 % of U.S. consumers used at least one form of e-banking technology (Bucks, Kennickell, & Moore, 2006).

Direct deposit activities also increased drastically, thanks in part to the U.S. Department of Treasury's 1999 EFT initiative. In 2003, nearly four-fifths of Social Security recipients had their benefits deposited directly into their bank accounts and one-half of employees used direct deposit for their paychecks (McGrath, 2005).

Another significant form of e-banking technology that gained great popularity in recent times is online banking and online bill payment. By 2006, about 12 % of all U.S. checking account holders took care of their financial transactions each month with their mouse (Bielski, 2007); by 2010, about half of U.S. households will pay at least one bill online.

Adoption of E-banking Technologies

There have been two distinct theoretical approaches to understanding consumers' adoption of banking technologies. The first approach is to focus on consumer characteristics linked to the amount of time he/she takes to adopt or acquire innovation. The second approach is to examine consumer technology adoption by way of consumer predispositions, such as overall feelings, attitudes, perceptions, and/or intentions toward using a given technology.

The most influential research model that concerns the first approach is the diffusion of innovation (DI), a conceptual framework that is formalized by Rogers (1965). DI posits that innovations spread through society in an S-curve, as early adopters select the innovation first, followed by the majority, until a technology or innovation becomes common. DI is also a cumulative model in that the total number of people who accept innovation only increases over time. Bass (1969) further refines DI by conceptualizing the adoption of an innovation as the probability of adopting an innovation at any point in time. Thus, Bass' model recognizes the existence of non-adopters, even at the maturity stage of a new technology, while Rogers' model assumes that all consumers will eventually adopt the innovation as it moves through its product life cycle. The DI model also includes five characteristics of innovation that influence consumer acceptance. These are: relative advantage (i.e., the benefit of an innovation is greater than what it is replacing), compatibility (i.e., an innovation fits into a specific society), simplicity (i.e., an innovation is easy to understand and use), communicability (i.e., the benefit of using an innovation is visible and communicated), and trialability (i.e., an innovation can be tried before purchase). The extent to which innovation satisfies these five qualities determines the likelihood and also the speed of innovation. The DI framework is well incorporated into a present understanding of consumer bank technology acceptance (e.g., Dabholkar, 1996; Daniel, 1999; Howcroft, Hamilton, & Hewer, 2002; Lee & Lee, 2000; Lockett & Littler, 1997).

The most notable research model that concerns the second approach is the technology acceptance model (TAM). The TAM, which is proposed by Davis (1989), extends the theory of reasoned action (TRA) to the adoption of computers in the workplace. First, it assumes that the relationship between attitude toward behavior and behavioral intention is established in TRA. Thus, a prospective user's overall feelings or attitudes toward using a given technology-based system or procedure represents major determinants as to whether or not he/she will ultimately use the system (Davis, 1989). This model also incorporates the idea that ease of use and perceived technology usefulness are critical constructs that influence an individual's attitude toward using the innovative technology.

Recent empirical work related to diffusion of technological innovations expands use of the TAM model to include demographics (Gefen & Straub, 1997; Jayawardhena & Foley, 2000; Karjaluoto, Mattila, & Pento, 2002; Mick & Fournier, 1998; Taylor & Todd, 1995) and other perceptual variables, such as perceived risk (Cunningham, Gerlach, & Harper, 2005; Meuter, Ostrom, Roundtree, & Bitner, 2000), self-efficacy (Agarwal & Karahanna, 2000; Walker, Craig-Lees, Hecker, & Francis, 2002), and need for interaction (Dabholkar & Bagozzi, 2002).

Consumer Characteristics Associated with Adoption of E-banking Technology

Identifying consumer profiles associated with the adoption of technology is a central issue of studies that are based on the DI model more so than the TAM model. DI assumes that those who adopt technologies in the early stage of the life cycle differ from those who adopt it in its maturity stage in certain distinctive characteristics. For instance, those who adopt innovation in its introduction stage tend to be venturesome, gregarious, and have a high propensity for risk (Lassar, Manolis, & Lassar, 2005). These individuals also tend to have multiple sources of information. Further, Lee and Lee (2000) find that non-adopters of banking technology are less likely to have communication with professional information providers and to communicate with friends and family.

Demographics are also arguably related to technology adoption, although empirical results are somewhat mixed. The most prominent and consistent factors associated with technology adoption include income and education. High income and education increase the likelihood of technology adoption (Daniel, 1999; Jayawardhena & Foley, 2000; Karjaluoto et al. , 2002; Kolodinsky, Hogarth, & Hilgert, 2004; Lee & Lee, 2000; Lee, Lee, & Schumann, 2002). Specifically, with regard to banking technologies, consumers with above average income and at least some high school education are more likely to use e-banking services than those with below average income and less than a high school education (Kennickell & Kwast, 1997; Klee, 2006; Stavins, 2002; Taube, 1988).

The effects of education and income on technology adoption appear to hold true for international consumers as well. For instance, Mattilia, Karjaluoto, and Pento (2003) find that household income and education predict whether or not consumers in Finland adopt Internet banking. Also, Sathye (1999) indicates that educated and wealthy consumers are among those most likely to adopt Internet banking in Australia.

Studies also find that age is related to innovation adoption, as younger persons are generally more likely to adopt (Karjaluoto et al. , 2002; Lee et al. , 2002; Zeithaml & Gilly, 1987). We note, however, that the effect of age appears to vary across different types of banking technologies. For instance, respondents over the age of 65 are the least likely to adopt phone banking and PC banking. Those in their middle age are less likely to adopt PC banking, versus the youngest group of consumers, aged 35 and below. Studies also report that while elderly consumers were less likely to adopt ATM usage (Gilly & Zeithaml, 1985; Lee & Lee, 2000; Taube, 1988), they are more likely to use EFT (electronic fund transfer) than younger consumers (Lee & Lee, 2000).

The effect of gender is barely noticeable in terms of technology adoption in general (Kolodinsky et al., 2004; Taylor & Todd, 1995), although a few studies report that men tend to adopt computer-related technologies more often than women (Gefen & Straub, 1997). Some also argue that the effect of gender is mitigated by marital status. Since many married couples have jointly held banking accounts, e-banking adoption may be related to the combination of marital status and gender, with married couples more likely to adopt these innovations than either single males or single females (Kolodinsky et al., 2004).

Race is not often incorporated in adoption studies, and the few that examine the effect of race show mixed results. For instance, Lee and Lee (2000) report that for direct bill payments, minorities are less likely to have already adopted the technology than non-Hispanic whites. Kolodinsky et al. reports that minorities are more likely to adopt or intend to adopt banking technology, than whites.

The opposite descriptions of innovators delineate the general profile of non-adopters, or laggards. Specifically, laggards tend to be less educated and have lower incomes; they are rather isolated in terms of social networks and are less likely to communicate with professional information providers than innovators, such as reading magazines and/or third party experts that are expected to provide consumers with exposure to innovations (Dickerson & Gentry, 1983; Gatignon & Robertson, 1985; Gilly & Zeithaml, 1985; Kennedy, 1983; Lee & Lee, 2000; Midgley & Dowling, 1978; Zeithaml & Gilly, 1987).

As indicated, the aim of this study is to identify the characteristics of e-banking technology laggards, concerning ATM, debit card, direct deposit, and direct payment usage. We also examine whether and how the characteristics of non-adopters changes over the recent 10-year period. As technology moves through its diffusion curve, the profile of adopters/non-adopters tends to change. Specifically, the effects of variables that characterize innovators on adoption behaviors tend to lessen as the innovation diffuses into the larger population (Mester, 2006).

Methods

Data

We employ the 1995 and 2004 Surveys of Consumer Finance (SCF) for this study. The SCF is a triennial survey sponsored by the Federal Reserve Board with the cooperation of the Statistics of Income Division of the Internal Revenue Service

(Bucks et al. , 2006). It is designed to provide detailed information on U.S. families' balance sheets, their use of financial services, and demographics. For the 2004 SCF survey, 4,522 households were interviewed by the National Opinion Research Center at the University of Chicago between July and December. Likewise, 4,299 households were interviewed for the 1995 survey. This survey covers financial situations, demographic factors, financial attitudes, assets owned, labor participation, and liability conditions. Households are encouraged to refer to their financial documents and records to complete the survey.

The SCF collects information on the number of financial institutions with which a respondent (or the respondent's family member living in the same household) currently has accounts or loans or regularly does personal financial business. Financial institutions include banks, savings and loans, credit unions, brokerages, loan companies, and so forth, but not institutions where consumers only have credit cards or business accounts. In this study, only the respondents who are affiliated with at least one financial institution are included in the sample, since consumers who have no financial affiliation cannot make electronic financial transactions.

Dependent Variables

The probability of a consumer's adoption of e-banking technologies is employed as a set of separate, dependent variables. First, the dependent variables include a set of binary variables that indicate whether or not a respondent has adopted each of the four electronic banking technologies: ATMs, debit cards, direct deposit, and direct payment. We did so given that the effects of explanatory variables could vary across different types of electronic services. We note that, while significant and increasingly noticeable, Internet banking is not included in our data analysis, as the current data sets do not contain comprehensive information concerning consumers' online banking behaviors.

For bivariate analysis, we focus on examining the characteristics of households with financial institutions who have not adopted each of the four e-banking technologies (1=did not adopt, 0=adopted). For multivariate analysis, we study the characteristics of households with financial institutions who have not adopted each of the four e-banking technologies (1=adopt, 0=did not adopted).

Explanatory Variables

The following variables are included as explanatory variables: education, income, age, communication patterns, and other demographic variables, such as gender of household head, race, and martial status.

Education. To reduce potential multicollinearity with income and financial asset variables, as well as to examine potential non-linearity of educational impact, a set of dummy variables is included with high school graduates, or equivalent, as the base. Other categories include: less than high school education, some college, bachelor's degree, and graduate degree.

Income. To reduce heteroskedacity (unequal variance of the disturbances), the natural logarithm of the reconciled annual total household income before taxes is employed.

Age. The respondent's age is coded as a continuous variable.

Communication patterns. A set of two binary variables is employed to identify consumers' communication patterns in acquiring financial information: communication with professional information providers and personal sources (1=communicated, 0=did not communicate). Communication with professional information providers includes reading magazines and newspapers and consulting with financial planners, accountants, or bankers, while communication with personal sources includes consulting with family and friends.

Other Demographics. The following demographic variables are included: female-headed household, race–ethnicity, and marital status. For household head gender, male is used as the base. Respondents' race is categorized into Hispanics, blacks, other non-whites, and non-Hispanic whites (base). Marital status is a set of binary variables: divorced or separated, widowed, never married, and married or living with a partner (base). Table 7.1 presents a detailed description of the variables employed.

Table 7.1 Description of variables

Variables	Description
Adoption of innovation	
ATM	= 1 adopted ATM, 0 otherwise
Debit card	= 1 adopted debit card, 0 otherwise
Direct deposit	= 1 adopted direct deposit, 0 otherwise
Direct payment	= 1 adopted direct payment, 0 otherwise
Any of the above	= 1 adopted ATM, debit card, direct deposit, direct payment, or smart card, 0 otherwise
Education	
Less than high school	=1 if years of education < 12 and no GED, 0 otherwise
High school/GED	=1 if respondents report a high school diploma or passed GED, 0 otherwise; omitted category
Some college	=1 if years of education > 12 and ≤ 16 but no BS, 0 otherwise
Bachelor's degree	=1 if a college degree is earned, 0 otherwise
Graduate degree	=1 if years of education > 16, 0 otherwise
Income	Log of annual total household income
Age	Age of reference person
Communication with professional information providers	= 1 if reads books/magazines or consults with financial planners, bankers, accountants, or other experts, 0 otherwise
Communication with personal information providers	= 1 if talks with family or friends, 0 otherwise
Demographics	
Female-headed household	=1 if female head, 0 otherwise

Table 7.1 (continued)

Variables	Description
Race–ethnicity	
Hispanic	=1 if Hispanic, 0 otherwise
Black	=1 if black, 0 otherwise
Other non-white	=1 if other non-white, 0 otherwise
Non-Hispanic white	=1 if non-Hispanic white, 0 otherwise; omitted category
Martial status	
Divorced/separated	=1 if divorced or separated, 0 otherwise
Widowed	=1 if widowed, 0 otherwise
Never Married	=1 if single, never married, 0 otherwise
Married	=1 if married or living with partner, 0 otherwise; omitted category

Data Analysis

In order to analyze the extent of consumers' adoption of electronic banking technologies, we employ descriptive statistics, which examine the extent to which consumers adopt each of the four electronic banking technologies. To examine individual group differences, we conduct pair-wise tests and adopt Bonferroni adjustments to reduce the type 1 error.

To investigate the effects of potential determinants on consumers' adoption of financial innovation, we estimate the probability of consumers' adoption of each of the four e-banking technologies, using the 2004 SCF. Given that all of the dependent variables are binary, probit or logit analysis is appropriate. We thus employ logistic analyses. Using the RII (repeated imputed inference) technique, estimates are derived from all implicates, and the variability in the data due to missing values and imputation is incorporated in the estimation.

Then, we compare the determinants of adoption of e-banking in 2004 with those of 1995, using both 1995 and 2004 SCF. By estimating a full interaction model with the year of data collected (1995 versus 2004), we examine whether the effect of each explanatory variable on adoption changes from 1995 to 2004. In developing the full interaction model, we first create a year dummy, indicating in which year the data were collected, and create interaction terms between year dummy and the set of explanatory variables. T-test statistics for each parameter estimates of the interaction terms then indicates whether the effect of the explanatory variable is statistically different between the two time periods.

Results

The Extent of E-banking Technology

Table 7.2 summarizes the extent to which respondents adopt each e-banking technology in 2004, with a comparison to those in 1995. In 2004, the ATM is found to be the most diffused electronic service, followed by direct deposit. Debit cards and

Table 7.2 Non-adopters of electronic banking technologies (1995 and 2004 SCF)

	1995 (%)	2004 (%)
ATM	33.1	22.5
Debit card	80.8	38.1
Direct deposit	49.2	25.8
Direct payment	76.3	50.6

direct payment services come next. Still, 22.5 % of the respondents report not having used an ATM and about 25.8 % of respondents indicate never having used direct deposit service. For debit cards and direct payment, 38.1 and 50.6 % of respondents report not having used the technologies, respectively.

Demographics of Laggards

The demographic profiles of e-banking technology adopters and laggards are presented with bivariate statistics in Table 7.3. First, e-banking laggards tend to have a lower level of education as compared to adopters. This trend is consistent across all e-banking services, particularly with regard to direct payments. In the case of ATM usage, only about 12.9 % of consumers with bachelor's degrees had not adopted ATMs, whereas about 42.3 % of consumers with less than a high school education had not adopted ATMs. In fact, ad hoc tests of multiple pair-wise comparisons with Bonferroni adjustment reveal that, across different e-banking technologies, having at least some college education creates significant differences in consumer adoption of electronic financial services as compared to having a high school or equivalent education.

We also find that e-banking laggards are less likely to have communication with professional information providers. For example, 20.7 % consumers who had communicated with financial professionals had not adopted ATMs, whereas 26.5 % of consumers who had not communicated with financial professionals had not adopted ATMs. The differences are also significant for debit cards, direct deposit, direct payment, and smart card usage. Communication with friends or family members also shows a significant difference in consumers' adoption of most e-banking technologies, with the exception of debit card usage.

Electronic financial services laggards appear less affluent than adopters of all five financial innovations. For example, the mean and median annual household income of non-adopters of debit cards is $68,460 and $35,000, respectively, compared to $71,474 and $49,000 for adopters. Households with an annual income of less than $30,000 are significantly less likely to adopt electronic financial services in general.

Determinants of E-banking Adoption Varying Across Different Technologies

To identify the profile of laggards varying across different banking technologies, we employ logistic regressions. Table 7.4 summarizes the results.

Table 7.3 Non-adoption rate of five electronic banking technologies across demographic characteristics (2004 SCF)

Explanatory variables	ATM	Debit cards	Direct deposit	Direct payment
Education				
Less than high school	42.26	59.75	36.40	71.39
High school or equivalent	27.66	41.72	32.62	55.41
Some college	18.56	28.54	25.29	51.07
Bachelor's degree	12.85	29.80	18.40	40.29
Graduate degree	14.61	38.71	13.73	36.47
Chi-square statistics	717.90***	557.28***	614.35***	795.59***
Communication with professional information providers				
Yes	20.74	35.16	24.20	46.96
No	26.52	45.08	29.40	58.93
Chi-square statistics	122.42***	105.45***	41.16***	172.23***
Communication with personal sources				
Yes	17.85	35.57	21.38	43.74
No	23.42	38.65	26.65	51.93
Chi-square statistics	67.58***	0.92	46.23***	60.65***
Household income				
Less than $30,000	34.81	49.55	35.64	68.12
$30,000–$44,999	21.99	36.00	30.47	50.04
$45,000–$69,999	19.04	32.74	20.98	45.80
More than $70,000	10.76	29.87	14.77	33.62
Mean (adopters)	$76,955.24	$71,474.29	$76,421.23	$85,527.25
Mean (non-adopters)	$47,453.83	$68,459.40	$52,782.27	$55,452.74
Median (adopters)	$48,000	$49,000	$49,000	$54,000
Median (non-adopters)	$28,000	$35,000	$30,000	$33,000
F value	5.22*	9.79**	0.92	3.61
Age				
18–29	10.05	19.11	40.46	59.39
30–44	11.35	23.65	30.31	46.77
45–54	15.58	33.24	28.20	48.56
55 or older	40.60	60.02	14.31	51.04
Mean (adopters)	46.45	44.60	52.07	49.91
Mean (non-adopters)	61.58	58.37	43.46	49.79
Median (adopters)	45	43	50	48
Median (non-adopters)	64	58	43	48
F value	104.36***	44.84***	40.29***	0.29
Marital status				
Married/living with partner	19.56	34.49	24.97	46.88
Separated/divorced	16.76	35.65	18.14	45.55
Widowed	50.14	66.65	15.23	57.94
Never married	16.91	31.61	39.08	58.93
Chi-square statistics	703.82***	378.73***	367.74***	192.34***

Table 7.3 (continued)

Explanatory variables	ATM	Debit cards	Direct deposit	Direct payment
Race				
Non-Hispanic whites	23.18	39.68	22.84	47.10
Blacks	21.92	34.02	28.20	61.43
Hispanics	18.17	30.59	47.20	65.17
Others	19.71	37.59	28.16	49.80
Chi-square statistics	3.77	201.41***	445.68***	370.48***
Female-headed household				
Yes	27.63	41.03	27.60	57.87
No	20.52	37.03	25.06	47.76
Chi-square statistics	78.26***	26.89***	29.41***	184.89***

* < .05, ** < .01, *** < .001

Table 7.4 RII (repeated imputed inferences) results of logistic regression of adoption of electronic financial services (2004 SCF)

Explanatory/dependent variables	ATM	Debit card	Direct deposit	Direct payment
Intercept	2.894***	3.980***	−1.093***	−0.458
Education (high school graduate as base)				
Less than high school	−0.265	−0.593***	−0.258	−0.460**
Some college	0.247	0.409***	0.370**	0.115
Bachelor's degree	0.685***	0.306**	0.623***	0.443***
Graduate degree	0.843***	0.005	0.562***	0.532***
Income (Log)	0.074***	−0.120***	0.055*	0.024
Communication with professional information providers	0.174	0.230**	0.142	0.290***
Communication with personal sources	0.214	−0.018	0.105	0.084
Age	−0.053***	−0.050***	0.022***	−0.002
Race (white as base)				
Hispanic	0.075	0.245*	0.134	−0.341**
Black	0.052	0.231	−0.541***	−0.490***
Other	−0.250	−0.290	−0.216	−0.027
Marital status (married as base)				
Never married	0.373*	0.082	0.380**	0.089
Widowed	−0.098	−0.190	0.398*	0.016
Divorced/separated	−0.502**	−0.599***	−0.271*	−0.273*
Female-headed household	0.158	0.215*	−0.057	−0.179
−2 log likelihood	3841.66***	5246.50***	4736.70***	5816.35***
Degree of freedom	15	15	15	15

* < .05, ** < .01, *** < .001

For ATMs, the more educated a consumer, the more likely he/she is to adopt ATM usage. We also find that older consumers and divorced/separated consumers are less likely to adopt ATM usage. However, communication with a professional information provider and personal sources does not have any significant effect. As ATMs are an older technology, awareness is no longer an issue.

Concerning debit cards, we find that education of less than high school, old age, low income, and widowed, all have negative effects on the adoption of debit cards. On the other hand, at least some college education, communication with a professional source, Hispanic, and female household heads, all have significant and positive effects on debit card adoption.

For direct deposit, at least some college education, older, higher income, and marital status of never married and widowed, all have positive and significant effects on adoption. However, blacks and divorced respondents are significantly less likely to adopt direct deposit.

For direct payment, college and graduate degree education and communication with a professional information provider have positive and significant effect on adoption. Among the four banking technologies we examine, direct payment is the newest technology, which may still garner benefits from the advertisements of financial institutions. On the other hand, consumers who have education of less than high school, are Hispanic, black, and divorced/separated are less likely to adopt direct payment.

Changes in the Determinants of E-banking Adoption

To investigate specific changes in the determinants of consumers' e-banking adoption, a set of logistic regressions is conducted for different types of e-banking technologies both with 1994 and 2005 data sets. Results are presented in Tables 7.5–7.8.

First, Table 7.5 presents the differences in the determinants of ATM adoption from 1995 to 2004. We find that the more affluent the household, the more likely the use of ATMs in 2004, whereas household income is found not to be significantly associated with ATM adoption in 1995.

Table 7.6 presents the differences in consumers' adoption of debit cards. As can be seen, in 1995, household heads with graduate degrees are more likely to adopt debit card usage than high school graduates, but such difference disappears in 2004. Regarding income, we do not find any significant impact of income in 1995, but in 2004, income is negatively associated with adoption of debit cards, suggesting that the less affluent are more likely to adopt debit cards. Regarding race and ethnicity, we find that Hispanics are more likely to adopt debit cards than non-Hispanic whites in 2004, while adoption of debit cards does not show any difference between Hispanics and non-Hispanic whites. On the other hand, other racial and ethnic groups are less likely to adopt debit cards than non-Hispanic whites in 1995, but such difference disappears in 2004. Finally, we find that female-headed households are more

Table 7.5 Comparison of ATM adoption: 1995 versus 2004

Explanatory/year	1995	2004	$\beta_{1995} \neq \beta^a_{2004}$
Intercept	1.522***	2.894***	
Education (high school graduate as base)			
Less than high school	−0.267*	−0.265	0.1605
Some college	0.431***	0.247	−0.1868
Bachelor's degree	0.701***	0.685***	−0.0521
Graduate degree	0.996***	0.843***	−0.3009
Communication with professional information providers	0.337***	0.174	−0.1689
Communication with personal sources	0.062	0.214	0.2245
Age	−0.033***	−0.053***	−0.0146
Income (Log)	0.037	0.074*	0.1289***
Race (white as base)			
Hispanic	0.226	0.075	−0.0399
Black	0.011	0.052	0.2503
Other	−0.017	−0.250	−0.1086
Marital status (married as base)			
Never married	0.250	0.373*	0.2485
Widowed	−0.215	−0.098	0.0798
Divorced/separated	−0.393*	−0.502**	0.0887
Female-headed household	−0.051	0.158	0.2446

* $<.05$, ** $<.01$, *** $<.001$
[a] Chi-square statistics, testing interaction terms between independent variables × year

Table 7.6 Comparison of debit card adoption: 1995 versus 2004

Explanatory/year	1995	2004	$\beta_{1995} \neq \beta^a_{2004}$
Intercept	−1.067**	3.980***	
Education (high school graduate as base)			
Less than high school	−0.122	−0.593***	0.0664
Some college	0.449**	0.409***	0.2763
Bachelor's degree	0.531***	0.306*	−0.2167
Graduate degree	0.691***	0.005	−0.9061***
Communication with professional information providers	0.249*	0.230*	0.0627
Communication with personal sources	−0.118	−0.018	0.2881
Age	−0.027***	−0.050***	−0.0039
Income (Log)	0.036	−0.120***	0.1748***
Race (white as base)			
Hispanic	−0.051	0.245*	0.7813**
Black	0.546*	0.231	−0.0437
Other	−0.716*	−0.290	0.7492*

Table 7.6 (continued)

Marital status (married as base)			
Never married	0.022	0.082	0.2333
Widowed	−0.071	−0.190	−0.4268
Divorced/separated	−0.005	−0.599***	−0.0668
Female-headed household	−0.108	0.215*	0.7448**

* <.05, ** <.01, *** <.001

[a] Chi-square statistics, testing interaction terms between independent variables × year

likely to adopt debit cards than male-headed households in 2004, but such difference is not noted in 1995.

Regarding the adoption of direct deposits, we find that income is the only explanatory variable that shows different patterns of influence from 1995 to 2004 (Table 7.7). In 1995, income does not show any statistical significance in the adoption of direct deposits. However, in 2004, we find that high-income households are more likely to adopt direct deposits than households with less income. Age is the only factor that influences the adoption of direct payment differently from 1995 to 2004 (Table 7.8). While younger households are more likely to adopt direct payments than older households in 1995, such age effect disappears in 2004.

Table 7.7 Comparison of direct deposit adoption: 1995 versus 2004

Explanatory/year	1995	2004	$\beta_{1995} \neq \beta_{2004}^{a}$
Intercept	−1.317***	−1.093***	
Education (high school graduate as base)			
Less than high school	−0.392*	−0.258	0.1434
Some college	0.209*	0.370 **	0.2226
Bachelor's degree	0.434***	0.623***	0.1369
Graduate degree	0.663***	0.562***	−0.1706
Communication with professional information providers	0.119	0.142	0.0410
Communication with personal sources	0.107	0.105	−0.0004
Age	0.023***	0.022***	−0.0002
Income (Log)	−0.025	0.055*	0.0964***
Race (white as base)			
Hispanic	0.062	0.134	−0.0137
Black	−0.217	−0.541***	−0.4336
Other	−0.161	−0.216	−0.0867
Marital status (married as base)			
Never married	0.213	0.380*	0.2233
Widowed	0.293*	0.398*	−0.0571
Divorced/separated	−0.217	−0.271*	−0.0754
Female-headed household	0.178	−0.057	−0.1114

* <.05, ** <.01, *** <.001

[a] Chi-square statistics, testing interaction terms between independent variables × year

Table 7.8 Comparison of direct payment adoption: 1995 versus 2004

Explanatory/year	1995	2004	$\beta_{1995} \neq \beta_{2004}^{a}$
Intercept	−1.265***	−0.458	
Education (high school graduate as base)			
Less than high school	−0.244	−0.460**	−0.1632
Some college	0.164	0.115	−0.0849
Bachelor's degree	0.296*	0.443***	0.0266
Graduate degree	0.487***	0.532***	−0.1012
Communication with professional information providers	0.167*	0.290***	0.1613
Communication with personal sources	−0.008	0.084	0.0992
Age	−0.011***	−0.002	0.0125**
Income (Log)	0.049*	0.024	0.0319
Race (white as base)			
Hispanic	−0.656**	−0.341*	0.3320
Black	−0.621*	−0.490**	0.1749
Other	−0.069	−0.027	0.0716
Marital status (married as base)			
Never married	0.169	0.089	−0.0354
Widowed	−0.095	0.016	0.0166
Divorced/separated	−0.392*	−0.273*	0.2373
Female-headed household	−0.013	−0.179	−0.0594

[a] Chi-square statistics, testing interaction terms between independent variables × year
* <.05, ** <.01, *** <.001

Discussion and Implication

Based on the theoretical framework of innovations diffusion, we investigate consumer characteristics of e-banking technology laggards with data from the 1995 and 2004 Surveys of Consumer Finance (SCF). While some variations exist for different types of e-banking technology, e-banking laggards tend to be older, less educated, have less income, and divorced/separated than adopters of e-banking. The overall profiles of laggards did not change drastically between 1995 and 2004, although we find some differences in the effects of demographics on a specific type of e-banking technology between these two time periods. In the following section, we highlight these differences and offer implications of these findings.

First, we find that consumers with graduate degrees are more likely to adopt debit card usage than high school graduates in 1995, but such difference disappears in 2004. These results may reflect the fact that debit cards were relatively new in 1995 and those who had adopted it had one of the most significant characteristics of innovators, i.e., high education. As a debit card moves through the adoption curve, the impact of education on its adoption becomes less significant.

On the other hand, we find an insignificant impact on the use of debit cards in 1995, but in 2004, income is negatively associated with adoption of debit cards, suggesting that the less affluent are more likely to adopt debit cards. The negative impact of income on debit cards in 2004 may reflect the phenomenon that consumers with high household incomes prefer to use credit cards rather than debit cards. Unlike debit cards, credit cards offer certain incentives, such as frequent flyer miles or cash back bonuses, whose value increases with increasing usage. This may motivate high-income consumers to use credit cards over debit cards as their payment medium. In fact, Zinman (2005) finds that credit card usage is positively correlated with income and negatively correlated with the use of debit cards.

We also find a significant difference concerning the effect of income on the adoption of direct deposit between 1995 and 2004. In 1995, income does not show any statistical significance, but in 2004, high-income households are more likely to adopt direct deposits than low-income households. The benefits of direct deposit include not only convenience, but also the security and peace of mind that one can transfer money or checks without the worry of loss or postal delays. The security aspect of benefit is more appreciated by consumers who must transfer large amounts of money. Thus, it is reasonable to find that the use of direct deposit is positively related to household income. Also, a significant form of direct deposit is the deposit of one's salary, a service that is not widely available to temporary workers who tend to make less than full-time employees.

The differences in demographic characteristics between 1995 to 2004 are the least significant concerning the adoption of direct payment. In fact, age is the only factor whose effect is significantly different on direct payments between the two time periods. Specifically, we find that younger households are more likely to adopt direct payments than older households in 1995. However, in 2004 such age effect disappears. This may be due to the fact that, just like education, age is another factor consistently related to the adoption of innovation, whose effect lessens as the technology moves through the adoption curve. Also, direct bill payments are a banking technology that gains popularity as online banking becomes widely available. The effects of age on the adoption of bill payment may disappear as more and more older consumers join the Internet community.

In terms of race–ethnicity, in general, ethic minorities are less likely to adopt banking technology than whites. In particular, blacks are more likely to be laggards of direct deposits and direct payments than whites, even in 2004. However, we find that Hispanics, as opposed to whites, are more likely to adopt debit cards in 2004. We also find that the use of debit cards among Hispanics increases in 2004 compared to that of 1995. This may be due to the fact that compared to whites, Hispanics show stronger preferences for cash transactions over credit. Thus, the benefits of using debit cards may appeal more to Hispanics than to whites.

Regarding the effect of communication with a professional information provider, we find that communication with a professional information provider positively influences the adoption of debit cards and direct payments. At the same time, we find that communication with family and friends has no impact on the adoption of these technologies. This implies that financial institutions that wish to expand their customers' use of debit cards and direct payment are better off using their own sales forces or professional information providers to promote the usage of these technologies rather than relying on word-of-mouth promotion. In fact, communication with family and friends is not associated with the adoption of any e-banking technology. This may indicate that electronic banking technology is not likely to diffuse with word of mouth.

We note a couple of limitations to our study. First, the types of e-banking technology we investigate do not include online banking. This is largely due to the unavailability of data concerning online banking in the 1995 SCF data set. As a result, any inferences made with regard to online banking should be interpreted with caution. In fact, it would be an interesting future study to examine the consumer characteristics associated with online banking and to test whether and how these characteristics differ from those found with more traditional banking technologies. Second, our results are based on two-time observations of two independent consumer sets. The results should not be interpreted as the changes in the adoption behavior of a given individual over time. To reveal such information requires a panel study with observations at multiple time periods. To examine whether and why a particular consumer chooses to adopt or abandon a specific banking technology over time is another interesting avenue for future study.

References

Agarwal, R., & Karahanna, E. (2000). Time flies when you're having fun: Cognitive absorption and beliefs about information technology usage. *MIS Quarterly, 24*(4), 665–694.

Bass, F. M. (1969). A new product growth for model consumer durables. *Management Science, 15*(5), 215–227.

Bellis, M. (2003). *Inventors of the modern computer*. Retrieved January 10, 2007, from http://inventors.about.com/library/inventors/bl_ERMA_Computer.htm.

Bielski, L. (2007). Electronic bill pay usage heats up. *ABA Banking Journal, 99*(2), 53–56.

Bucks, B. K., Kennickell, A. B., & Moore, B. M. (2006). Recent changes in U.S. family finances: Evidence from the 2001 and 2004 Survey of Consumer Finances. *Federal Reserve Bulletin, 92*, A1–A38.

Cunningham, L. F., Gerlach, J., & Harper, M. D. (2005). Perceived risk and e-banking services: An analysis from the perspective of the consumer. *Journal of Financial Services Marketing, 10*(2), 165–179.

Dabholkar, P. A. (1996). Consumer evaluations of new technology-based self service options: An investigation of alternative models of service quality. *International Journal of Research in Marketing, 13*, 29–51.

Dabholkar, P. A., & Bagozzi, R. P. (2002). An attitudinal model of technology-based self service: Moderating effects of consumer traits and situational factors. *Journal of the Academy of Marketing Science, 30*(3), 184–201.

Daniel, E. (1999). Provision of electronic banking in the UK and the republic of Ireland. *International Journal of Bank Marketing, 17*(2), 72–82.

Davis, F. D. (1989). Perceived usefulness, perceived ease of use, and user acceptance of information technology. *MIS Quarterly, 13*(3), 319–339.

Dickerson, M. D., & Gentry, J. W. (1983). Characteristics of adopters and non-adopters of home computers. *Journal of Consumer Research, 10*(2), 225–235.

Drennan, B. (2003). *E-banking history*. Retrieved January 10, 2007, from http://www.drennangroup.com/history.html.

Gatignon, H., & Robertson, T. R. (1985). A propositional inventory for new diffusion research. *Journal of Consumer Research, 11*(4), 849–867.

Gefen, D., & Straub, D. W. (1997). Gender differences in the perception and use of E-mail: An extension to the technology acceptance model. *MIS Quarterly, 21*(4), 389–399.

Gilly, M. C., & Zeithaml, V. (1985). The elderly consumer and adoption of technologies. *Journal of Consumer Research, 12*(3), 353–357.

Howcroft, B., Hamilton, R., & Hewer, P. (2002). Consumer attitude and the usage and adoption of home-based banking in the United Kingdom. *International Journal of Bank Marketing, 20*(3), 111–121.

Jayawardhena, C., & Foley, P. (2000). Changes in the banking sector—The case of internet banking in the UK. *Internet Research, 10*(1), 19–31.

Karjaluoto, H., Mattila, M., & Pento, T. (2002). Factors underlying attitude formation towards online banking in Finland. *International Journal of Bank Marketing, 20*(6), 261–272.

Kennedy, A. (1983). Development, adoption and diffusion of new industrial products. *European Journal of Marketing, 17*(3), 31–87.

Kennickell, A. B., & Kwast, M. L. (1997). *Who uses electronic banking? Results from the 1995 Survey of Consumer Finances.* Paper presented at the Annual Meeting of the Western Economic Association, Seattle, WA.

Kim, B., Yilmazer, T., & Widdows, R. (2005). *The determinants of consumers' adoption of Internet banking.* Proceedings, Federal Reserve Bank of Boston.

Klee, E. (2006) *Families' use of payment instruments during a decade of change in the U.S. payment system.* Working Paper, Board of Governors of the Federal Reserve System.

Kolodinsky, J. M., Hogarth, J. M., & Hilgert, M. A. (2004). The adoption of electronic banking technologies by US consumers. *International Journal of Bank Marketing, 22*(4), 238–249.

Lassar, W. M., Manolis, C., & Lassar, S. S. (2005). The relationship between consumer innovativeness, personal characteristics, and online banking adoption. *International Journal of Bank Marketing, 23*(2), 176–200.

Lee, E., & Lee, J. (2000). Haven't adopted electronic financial services yet? The acceptance and diffusion of electronic banking technologies. *Financial Counseling and Planning, 11*(1), 49–61.

Lee, E., Lee, J., & Schumann, D. W. (2002). The influence of communication source and mode on consumer adoption of technological innovations. *Journal of Consumer Affairs, 36*(1), 1–27.

Lockett, A., & Littler, D. (1997). The adoption of direct banking services. *Journal of Marketing Management, 13*(8), 791–811.

Mattilia, M., Karjaluoto, H., & Pento, T. (2003). Internet banking adoption among mature customers: Early majority or laggards? *Journal of Services Marketing, 17*(5), 514–528.

McGrath, J. C. (2005). *Will online bill payment spell the demise of paper checks?* Payment Cards Center Discussion Paper 05-08, Federal Reserve Bank of Philadelphia.

Mester, L. J. (2006). Changes in the use of electronic means of payment: 1995–2004. *Business Review, Q2*, 26–30.

Meuter, M. L., Ostrom, A. L., Roundtree, R. I., & Bitner, M. J. (2000). Self-service technologies: Understanding customer satisfaction with technology-based service encounters. *Journal of Marketing, 64*(3), 50–64.

Mick, D. G., & Fournier, S. (1998). Paradoxes of technology: Consumer cognizance, emotions, and coping strategies. *Journal of Consumer Research, 25*(2), 123–43.

Midgley, D. F., & Dowling, G. R. (1978). Innovativeness: The concept and its measurement. *Journal of Consumer Research, 4*(4), 229–242.

Rogers, E. M. (1965). *Diffusion of innovations.* New York: The Free Press.

Sathye, M. (1999). Adoption of internet banking by Australian consumers: An empirical investigation. *International Journal of Bank Marketing, 17*(7), 324–334.

Stavins, J. (2002). Effect of consumer characteristics on the use of payment instruments. *New England Economic Review, 3*, 19–31.

Taube, P. M. (1988). The influence of selected factors on the frequency of atm usage. *Journal of Retail Banking, 10*(1), 47–52.

Taylor, S., & Todd, P. A. (1995). Understanding information technology usage: A test of competing models. *Information Systems Research, 6*(2), 144–176.

Walker, R. H., Craig-Lees, M., Hecker, R., & Francis, H. (2002). Technology-enabled service delivery: An investigation of reasons affecting customer adoption and rejection. *International Journal of Service Industry Management, 13*(1), 91–106.

Zeithaml, V. A., & Gilly, M. C. (1987). Characteristics affecting the acceptance of retailing technologies: A comparison of elderly and non-elderly consumers. *Journal of Retailing, 63*(1), 49–68.

Zinman, J. (2005). *Debit or credit?* Proceedings, Federal Reserve Bank of Boston.

Chapter 8
Online Insurance

Robert N. Mayer

Abstract While consumers increasingly use the Internet to borrow, manage, save, and invest their money, the growth of the Internet as a medium of transaction for insurance products has been slow. There are many reasons for the present situation, including resistance from insurance companies, intermediaries, and consumers. Paralleling the sluggish state of online insurance sales themselves, academic research on online insurance behavior has been slow in developing. Yet there may be as much to learn from studying a case of a market that failed to live up to its initial rosy predictions as from one that has.

The term "insurance" encompasses a wide variety of products. Some insurance, such as health insurance, is viewed as so essential that the governments of many countries provide it to all citizens. Other types of insurance, while not provided as a basic human right, are almost as necessary for functioning in an advanced, modern society. For example, most jurisdictions in the United States require motorists to purchase auto insurance, and financial institutions will not lend money for a home mortgage unless the property is covered by homeowner's insurance (and possibly even mortgage insurance). Life insurance, while voluntary, is commonly held, with over 54 million policies in effect in 2005 (American Council of Life Insurers, 2006). While far from necessities, some consumers buy more exotic types of insurance, such as pet insurance, special events insurance, and hole-in-one insurance. Taken as a whole, insurance purchases make up a substantial share of the overall consumer budget.

Variety in types of insurance is matched by diversity of the industry's channels of distribution. For many types of insurance, brokers and agents serve as intermediaries between insurance providers and customers, adding a "human touch" to an otherwise abstract financial service. The Internet provides an additional channel of distribution, or at least an adjunct to the more traditional ones. This chapter examines the role of the Internet in the sale of insurance to consumers. To date, this role

R.N. Mayer
Department of Family and Consumer Studies, University of Utah, 225 S 1400 East, Salt Lake City, UT 84112, USA
e-mail: robert.mayer@fcs.utah.edu

has been fairly limited if the Internet is judged as a stand-alone medium through which consumers initiate and conclude insurance transactions. When viewed as a consumer tool for acquiring information and as a seller tool for customer recruitment and retention, however, the Internet plays a more substantial part in the insurance industry.

This chapter is "consumer-focused," in the sense that it asks whether online insurance sales are likely to transform the insurance marketplace in a way that benefits consumers. Given that so many insurance sales have traditionally been made through intermediaries, however, it is also worthwhile to consider the impact of online sales on agents and brokers. Of the many markets within the broader insurance industry, this chapter spotlights developments in auto insurance and life insurance markets. Besides being widely held (Life Insurers Fact book, 2006; LIMRA, 2006), these are the two types of insurance for which it is most common for *individual* consumers to conduct prepurchase research, make purchases, and manage accounts online (Buchner, 2006).

The chapter unfolds as follows. The first section reviews the predictions that were made regarding the impact of the Internet on insurance sales and compares these predictions to the current state of affairs. The chapter's second section considers several explanations for the slow growth of online insurance markets. The third section examines forces that may yet turn the Internet into an important channel of distribution for insurance sales.

Insurance Channels of Distribution

Efforts to sell life and auto insurance online have taken place within an industry whose traditional channels of distribution are complex. There are several types of intermediaries in the insurance industry, and the names given to each type are not used with a high degree of precision and consistency. In particular, the terms "agent" and "broker" are often interchanged since both parties are technically independent of the companies whose insurance products they sell, both rely on various types of commissions for their compensation, and both try to establish long-term, one-on-one relationships with their customers. As used here, agents can represent either a single insurance carrier (a "captive agent") or multiple carriers (an "independent agent"). The agent's primary allegiance is to the insurance company or companies she/he represents, and the agent may discourage existing customers from switching carriers, even when it is in the customer's best interest to do so. Insurance brokers, like independent agents, work as intermediaries between multiple insurers and consumers. Unlike either captive or independent agents, though, a broker's primary allegiance and responsibility is to the customer, not one or more insurance carriers. Referring to the difference between agents and brokers, Mike Kreidler (2001), insurance commissioner for the state of Washington, wrote,

> Both agents and brokers should be responsive to their customer's needs. However, you should remember that the agent also represents the company or companies he or she is appointed by. The broker works for you.

Whereas a broker would seem to be the preferred intermediary from a consumer's point of view, brokers are relatively rare in the markets for individual insurance policies. Brokers are more commonly available for business purchasers of insurance, such as a delivery company that buys vehicle insurance for a large number of trucks.

The compensation mechanisms in the insurance industry vary for agents and brokers as well as among different types of insurance (e.g., life, health, auto, and home). As a general rule, though, these mechanisms have evolved in a fashion that aligns the financial interests of the insurance companies with those of the insurance agent or broker. Through the use of direct (typically, an up-front percentage of the insurance premium) and contingent commissions (e.g., for meeting certain volume or profitability goals), insurers reward agents and brokers for recruiting and retaining customers, especially customers who submit few claims. The Consumer Federation of America, an influential consumer organization specializing in financial matters, is critical of most insurance commissions, believing that they create potential conflicts of interest for agents and brokers and result in higher consumer prices (Hunter, 2005). The insurance industry defends these arrangements as beneficial to consumers, and some academic researchers agree (Berger, Cummins, & Weiss, 1997; Hoyt, Dumm, & Carson, 2006).

The Internet threatens to upset the traditional channels of distribution in the insurance industry. In other industries, notably airline travel and books, the Internet has served as a powerful force of disintermediation, that is, the removal of traditional layers in the chain of distribution. As the Internet boomed during the late 1990s, it appeared that the insurance industry, with its wide price differences among policies and its barriers to comparison shopping by consumers (Brown & Goolsbee, 2002; Dahlby & West, 1986), was also ripe for disintermediation. It was thought that aggregator sites offering policies from a variety of insurance carriers would lower prices, commoditize the insurance product, and put enormous pressure on agents to be more consumer-oriented (Garven, 2002).

For those who believed in the bright prospects of online insurance sales, there was supporting evidence. In 2000, a national consumer survey commissioned by QuickenInsurance and the Electronic Financial Services Council reported that one-quarter of Internet households were willing to use the web to shop around for and purchase insurance via an online marketplace or insurance carrier (Intuit, 2000). A 2001 study conducted by Gomez Inc. ("Gomez study," 2001) estimated that 30.3 % of the U.S. adult Internet users had sought information about property or casualty insurance online. The study also reported that the majority of online users were interested in at least managing their existing insurance policies with the help of the Internet. In early 2002, Celent estimated that 19 % of insurance buyers used the Internet for researching and shopping for insurance (although not necessarily making final transactions) and that their purchases accounted for 19 % of U.S. premiums on policies sold to individual consumers. The study predicted that this percentage would double by 2005, accounting for $200 billion in sales.

A few years later, in 2006, despite the slow growth of online insurance markets in the United States, predictions remained rosy, especially with respect to insurance markets outside of the United States. According to one report by Forrester Research, a marketing research and consulting firm, "online non-life insurance has grown spectacularly in the UK over the past five years . . . and we expect that rapid growth to continue for the next few years, with the number of online non-life insurance buyers growing from 7 million customers today to 11 million by 2011" (Ensor, 2006a). A companion report predicted that, led by auto insurance sales, the number of online non-life insurance buyers in Germany would grow from 2.2 million in 2005 to 3.7 million in 2011 (Ensor, 2006b).

Amid the optimism, there were cautionary voices. Some people doubted the whole enterprise of selling insurance online, believing that the Internet would always be subordinate to traditional, offline sales channels (Art et al. , 2001; Greenberg, 2002). Insurance agents, according to this point of view, were stubborn and resistant to change, and consumers did not really want to shop for insurance in their pajamas at 2 a.m. (Burger, 2006).

To date, the critics of online sales have been correct: a robust market for online insurance sales has failed to materialize. According to the insurance trade magazine *Insurance & Technology* (Burger, 2005), online sales of insurance were not slow to get started; "they've been pretty much a non-occurrence." Even if this description is overly harsh, what accounts for the slow growth of online insurance sales? Is it mostly attributable to the resistance of insurance companies and brokers, or are other factors at play as well (Clemons & Hitt, 2000; Eastman, Eastman, & Eastman, 2002)?

Reasons Behind the Slow Start

There is some evidence to support the view that the insurance industry—carriers and agents alike—did a poor job in their initial efforts to sell insurance online. Writing in 1999, consultant James Bukowski observed,

> The insurance industry has not adopted a comprehensive e-commerce strategy. You can find many sites that offer product and consumer information, agent locators, e-mail and even price indications. You will find almost none that offer full e-commerce capabilities.

In 2001, the consulting firm Booz Allen (2001) released a survey showing that insurance web sites lagged far behind those of other financial service companies in terms of functionality, especially providing consumers with the ability to manage their existing accounts online. The study also found that insurance companies were slow in responding to customer email. Goch (2002) noted that insurance web sites were failing to meet customer expectations in terms of quoting insurance prices, a deficiency that reflected the industry's antipathy toward price shopping by consumers.

Research conducted a few years later found that functionality was a continuing problem for insurance web sites. The Customer Respect Group conducted studies in 2005 and 2006 of 50 web sites representative of health care, life, and property and casualty insurers. Sites were graded along three dimensions: site usability, one-on-one communication with customers, and trust/privacy. In both years, the insurance industry as a whole scored considerably below the cross-industry average (C-IA). According to the 2006 report, the life insurance industry "achieved the dubious distinction of having the highest percentage of companies scoring 5.0 or below…a score [that] generally illustrates that a site fails to adequately respect the online user." The report was especially critical of the insurance industry's privacy practices:

> The Life Insurance group rated poorly for its willingness to share personal data. Two in three (66 %) state that they share personal data either with affiliates, business partners or third parties. This does not compare favorably with other industries surveyed in 2006, of which only 46 % share personal data. Furthermore, the majority (82 %) of life [insurance] companies that share data do not allow customers to opt-out; this compares with the C-IA of only 56 %. Likewise, only a third of the companies that use personal data for ongoing marketing allow users to opt-out (vs. 79 % for the C-IA). There is a continued low and disturbing level of transparency in the industry, with 26 % of companies not clear about data privacy policies. This is significantly worse than other industries, where the overall number of companies that are unclear is down to 8 %.

Poor performance by insurance web sites appears to be the case in Europe as well. In 2005, Forrester Research assessed 30 large European car insurance web sites. Their report concluded that "Europe's car insurance sites offer a poor [consumer] experience." Nearly half of the sites tested failed Forrester's web review standards (Ensor, 2005).

Whereas the studies conducted by Booz Allen, The Customer Respect Group, and Forrester question the usability and privacy practices of insurance web sites; two additional studies challenge the financial value to consumers of using these sites, especially ones promising to compare the prices of policies offered by multiple companies. A study conducted by the Consumer Federation of America in 2001 (Hunter & Hunt, 2001) found that only about a quarter of the comparison shopping sites were successful in identifying the least expensive term life insurance policy on the market. As a whole, the comparison sites were biased in favor of policies that carry commissions. Moreover, several sites that claimed or implied that they would present consumers with immediate and comparative rate quotes did not, serving instead as "lead generators" for insurance companies and intermediaries who would subsequently contact consumers by phone, mail, or email. Approximately a year later, an expanded follow-up study found that rate comparison sites had made no improvement in delivering the lowest-priced policies to online consumers (Mayer, Huh, & Cude, 2005). Nor were these sites particularly transparent to consumers, providing little information about the quality (breadth, currency) of their information or business relationships that might slant their purchase recommendations.

Although the insurance industry's initial steps may be described as clumsy and, in some cases, even duplicitous, the reasons for the industry's "failure to launch" may go further. They may stem as well from the inherent characteristics of insurance products and the nature of the insurance consumer.

Clemons and Hitt (2000) argue that the nature of the insurance product itself works against a rapid change in consumer purchasing habits. They write,

> Insurance is an event driven product (buy a car or house, change jobs, get married, and so forth) and the vast majority of customers renew their policies without a reconsideration of

the product, company, or agency. Even for the short-term products such as term life, at most 1/12 of the policies are up for renewal in any given year, and only a small fraction of these are actually "in play" (p. 28).

Some kinds of insurance do not seem susceptible to instant provision via the Internet of a large number of quotes from different companies. Every house, for instance, is different, so it would seem difficult to provide quotes for homeowners insurance. But one 2002 Chevy Silverado is like another, and term life insurance for a 45-year-old man in good health is a pretty standard product, right? Apparently not. Aggregator sites may want to offer consumers a range of price quotations for auto and life insurance, but there are many other factors to be considered in setting a price. If these sites want their quotations to accurately reflect a person's risk, they must ask consumers a large number of questions. At some point, the search process is no longer quick and easy. Moreover, even when aggregator sites collect a large amount of information about potential consumers, these sites cannot guarantee the rates that they quote will be supported by the companies they represent. Accurate insurance price quotes, even for relatively standardized products such as auto and life insurance, require a great deal of personalization.

Consumers, for their part, may not be all that interested in serving as their own insurance agents (Schwartz, 2004). According to insurance agency CEO Kevin McKenna (2006), writing in *Best's Review*, the aggregator-driven model of online insurance sales is flawed because it assumes that consumers want to shop around for the best deal and act as their own agent. "As direct marketers have learned over the years, offering the consumer a multitude of choices can lead to the consumer making no choice at all," according to McKenna. In a similar vein, Salvatore Castiglione, assistant deputy superintendent of the New York State Department of Insurance, commented,

> I think people are just naturally afraid of insurance, and they need to have that personal contact with a person—they just don't trust themselves to understand what they're buying on the Internet (Hoober, 2006, p. 4).

In addition to not wanting to make a complicated decision on their own, consumers may resist online insurance sales for an additional reason. Unlike shopping online for music CDs, clothing, or computers, shopping online for insurance involves providing a great deal of personally identifying information. In addition to only moderately sensitive personal information such as name, geographic address, phone number, and email address, insurance web sites may ask for a social security number, a date of birth, and intimate details about a person's health before offering online price quotes. Identity theft is real and well documented (Baum, 2006; Phan, 2005), and many consumers are hesitant to provide such sensitive and identifying personal information online. In a 2006 study, Buchner found that concerns about sharing personal information online ranked second behind "needed to speak to an agent" as a reason that people who shopped for insurance information online decided not to apply for a policy online.

State insurance regulators may have also slowed the growth of online insurance sales. Whether to guard their regulatory prerogatives or to prevent consumer fraud, some state regulators have hesitated to interpret licensing and signature require-ments in ways that encourage online insurance sales (Atkinson & Wilhelm, 2002; Kempler & Baxter, 2002). The National Association of Insurance Commissioners has taken the lead in trying to harmonize state rules in these areas, but most state insurance departments have adopted a hands-off, wait-and-see approach (Hoober, 2006).

In short, there may be a number of supply-side and consumer-side factors that explain the slow growth of insurance sales online. Despite these factors, however, there are pockets of success, and they may point to the unrealized potential—as well as the ultimate limits—of online insurance sales.

Signs of Life in the Online Insurance Industry

Two high-profile national advertising campaigns that aired on network television in the latter half of 2006 suggest insurance firms continue to believe that the online market is important. While auto insurer GEICO relied on its talking gecko and State Farm advertised that its "good neighbor" agents provide extraordinary customer service, Progressive Direct encouraged consumers to visit its web site and obtain car insurance quotes from multiple companies. Simultaneously, esurance.com was using a sexy, young female cartoon character named Erin to attract consumers to its web site for auto, home, renters, life, and health insurance. (Erin even has a fake blog on the site.)

Progressive Direct's offering of insurance quotes from multiple companies has blurred the lines among web sites operated by companies that rely primarily on agents (e.g., Allstate, State Farm, Mutual of Omaha, and John Hancock), insurers that rely predominantly on direct sales (e.g., GECIO), and aggregator sites such as InsWeb.com, Insure.com, Insurance.com, and AccuQuote.com that provide quotes from multiple insurers. Esurance further complicates the picture by providing links to both company and aggregator sites. When I entered my Utah zip code, for exam-ple, I was given the choice of AIG Auto Insurance and GEICO Direct for single price quotes or Comparison Market or Insurance Answer Center for comparison quotes. More comprehensive financial web sites such as Bankrate.com and Efinancial.com are also rewriting the distinctions within, the insurance industry, performing largely as aggregator sites for life, auto, and other types of insurance as well as other finan-cial products.

To which of these types of sites—company, aggregator, or hybrid—will the future of online insurance sales belong? Most analysts believe that the Internet will com-plement but be subordinate to personal selling in insurance markets. Consumers will use the Internet to educate themselves about insurance products, compare offerings, and even manage existing accounts. Katrina Burger (2005) writes, "The Web is providing an essential resource to distributors, customers, and carriers in terms of all kinds of product and market information, account status, pricing, and coverage options" (p. 1). But Burger (2006) also believes that consumers will continue to make the majority of their transactions by contacting a company representative or an insurance agent: "Distribution may be tech-enabled, but this is one area in which the human element will never vanish" (p. 1).

The empirical evidence is fairly clear about the continued dominance of offline channels. According to one study conducted for Yahoo (2005), people prefer by a ratio of about three to one accessing and managing their insurance offline rather than online. Still, about a fifth of respondents claimed that they made their insurance premium payment online. In a second study (Yahoo! 2006), 69 % of those surveyed said that they used both online and offline sources of information when researching insurance products. Again, those offline purchases exceeded online ones by a ratio of about three to one. The report authors concluded that the Internet was part of the "long and winding road to the [insurance] cash register."

A less guarded assessment is offered by comScore Networks (2006) based on 2005 data concerning auto insurance. The marketing research company's press release states that "consumers flocked online to research and purchase auto insurance in 2005." From 2004 to 2005, the number of insurance quotations submitted to consumers online increased by 24 % and the number of policies purchased via the Internet increased 29 %. Looked at from another perspective, the web site "abandonment rate" declined 51 %. The experience of agent insurers, direct insurers, and aggregator sites varied markedly, however. Whereas quotes initiated and submitted by agent insurer sites such as AllState and State Farm increased by 75 %, quotes submitted by direct insurers (e.g., GEICO) and aggregators (e.g., InsWeb) increased by only 23 and 11 % respectively.

Kevin McKenna (2006) offers a more nuanced and balanced assessment. He agrees that the online insurance market will be "carrier-driven" rather than "aggregator-driven," but the key lies in integrating the Internet with other channels of distribution, such as direct mail and email. McKenna believes that the Internet can be an especially powerful tool of lead generation for insurers and agents in a "Web-to-phone business model." He believes that this is particularly true for relatively simple insurance products, such as car and term life insurance. McKenna also views the Web as a potentially effective means of "customer remarketing," that is, using information collected via the Internet for appropriate cross-selling and up-selling. Finally, McKenna asserts that while Internet sales currently produce lower sales volumes compared to personal selling, they will eventually deliver higher sales margins.

Conclusions and Research Directions

The insurance industry appears to be an island in an ocean of disintermediation. While middlemen have been squeezed severely in industries such as computer hardware, photographic equipment, travel, books, and even investment brokerage, insurance carriers and agents have felt relatively little price pressure from the Internet.

The insurance industry's immunity to the price pressures of the Internet is attributable to features of insurance distribution, insurance products, and insurance consumers. Nevertheless, the slow growth of online insurance sales is surprising in light of the high degree of price dispersion within the industry and the resulting opportunities for well-informed consumers to save money. Many state departments of insurance provide consumers with rate comparisons for auto and homeowners insurers. These comparisons typically yield multiples of two or three times between the prices of the least and most expensive policies for the same coverage. Accordingly, consumers stand to gain a great deal from more intensive information search, especially the comparison of insurance quotes. The flipside of this situation is that insurers and agents have a strong incentive to preserve the status quo. So far, they have been largely successful.

Future research regarding online insurance purchases must move beyond the simple question of whether there is a future for this channel of distribution. Clearly there is such a future, as suggested by the relative success of online banking and investing, but substantial uncertainty remains regarding the specifics of the online insurance market. Will the aggregator sites survive or will their comparison quote function be taken over by sites like Progressive Direct and esurance? Given that consumers typically renew their insurance policies without a great deal of information search, will the Internet become primarily a tool for managing existing insurance accounts rather than competing for new ones?

Thinking beyond some of the more practical questions about the future of online insurance sales, future research can use the case of online insurance to investigate some more basic questions regarding online consumer behavior. For example, insurance provides compensation for potential financial losses rather than the possibility for financial gain? Is the Internet, a medium that already subjects its users to the risks of identity theft and invasion of privacy, better suited to purchases that exemplify the classic risk–reward relationship, such as investments, than to a more "conservative" product like insurance? As another example, many consumer purchases vary greatly across the life cycle, with insurance being one of these. Generally, people in the "single" and "newly married" phases of the family life cycle find insurance unattractive or unaffordable when compared to people in the various "full nest" and "empty nest" stages. Yet it is people who are in these earlier stages who tend to be most comfortable with buying online? Hence, is the sluggishness of online insurance sales best conceived as a one-time "cohort effect," that is, a temporary mismatch between the people most likely to want insurance products (older people) and those most likely to feel comfortable using the Internet for their insurance purchases (young people)? Or is there likely to be a continuing "age effect" whereby the same characteristics that make older people want insurance will also make them suspicious of purchasing it online?

In sum, the sale of online insurance has, so far at least, failed to live up to the bold predictions of its boosters. Whether the shortfall is temporary or long term, there is often as much to learn from consumer resistance and avoidance as there is from consumer acceptance and enthusiasm.

References

American Council of Life Insurers. (2006). *Life Insurers Fact Book: 2006.* Washington, DC: Author.

Art, M. M., Dynia, M. V., Silverhart, T. A., Jamison, K. S., Retzloff, C. D., & Drinkwater, M. (2001). *Our connected society: Finances and insurance online.* Windsor, CT: LIMRA.

Atkinson, R. D., & Wilhelm, T. G. (2002). *The best states for ecommerce.* Washington, DC: Progressive Policy Institute.

Baum, K. (2006, April 19). *Identity theft 2004.* Washington, DC: U.S. Department of Justice, Bureau of Justice Statistics.

Berger, A. N., Cummins, J. D., & Weiss, M. A. (1997). The coexistence of alternative distribution systems: The case for property-liability insurance. *Journal of Business, 70*(4), 515–546.

Booz Allen. (2001, August 22). *Booz Allen survey reveals gap between internet insurance offerings and customer needs.* Press Release. New York, NY.

Brown, J. R., & Goolsbee, A. (2002). Does the internet make markets more competitive? Evidence from the life insurance industry. *Journal of Political Economy, 110*(3), 481–507.

Buchner, A. (2006). *Marketing life insurance online.* New York: Jupiter Research.

Burger, K. (2005, June 15). Laggards no more. *Insurance & Technology,* S4.

Burger, K. (2006, February 15). Sold, not bought. *Insurance & Technology,* C3.

Celent. (2002). *Online insurance sales and marketing: Practices and profiles.* New York: Author.

Clemons, E. K., & Hitt, L. M. (2000). The internet and the future of financial services: Transparency, differential pricing and disintermediation (Working Paper). Philadelphia, PA: Wharton School of Business, University of Pennsylvania.

comScore Networks (2006, February 21). comScore reports 24% growth in auto insurance quotes and 29% growth in policies purchased online in 2005. Press Release. Reston, VA: Author.

The Customer Respect Group (2006, December 5). *50 life insurance companies ranked on how they treat online customers.* Ipswich, MA: Author.

Dahlby, B., & West, D. S. (1986). Price dispersion in an automobile insurance market. *Journal of Political Economy, 94*(2), 418–438.

Eastman, K. L., Eastman, J. K., & Eastman, A. D. (2002). Issues in marketing online insurance products: An exploratory look at agents' use, attitudes, and views of the impact of the internet. *Risk Management and Insurance Review, 5*(2), 117–134.

Ensor, B. (2005). *How to design better car insurance web sites.* Cambridge, MA: Forrester Research.

Ensor, B. (2006a). *UK online insurance dales forecast: 2006 to 2011.* Cambridge, MA: Forrester Research.

Ensor, B. (2006b). *German online insurance sales forecast: 2006 to 2011.* Cambridge, MA: Forrester Research.

Garven, J. R. (2002). On the implications of the internet for insurance markets and institutions. *Risk Management and Insurance Review, 5*(2), 105–116.

Goch, L. (2002, May). What works online: Some insurers have found the key to unlocking online sales. *Best's Review,* 24–34.

Gomez study identifies consumer adoption trends for p/c insurers (2001, May 21). *Insurance Journal.* Retrieved from http://www.insurancejournal.com/news/national/2001/05/21/13997.htm.

Greenberg, P. A. (2002, August 17). Online insurance: Who needs it? *E-Commerce Times,* Retrieved from http://www.ecommercetimes.com/story/opinion/12871.html.

Hoober, S. (2006, November). Insurance on the web: Humdrum sales never matched the hype. *The Regulator: Newsletter of the Insurance Regulatory Examiners Society,* 1–6.

Hoyt, R. E., Dumm, R. E., & Carson, J. M. (2006, May). *An examination of the role of insurance producers and compensation in the insurance industry.* Alexandria, VA: Independent Insurance Agents and Brokers of America.

Hunter, J. R. (2005, February 24). *The impact of commissions on prices and service quality for home and automobile insurance.* Washington, DC: Consumer Federation of America.

Hunter, J. R., & and Hunt, J. H. (2001). *Term life insurance on the internet: An evaluation of on-line quotes*. Washington, DC: Consumer Federation of America.

Intuit. (2000, April 19). *National consumer survey sees growing momentum for online insurance trend*. Press Release. Mountain View, CA: Author.

Kempler, C., & Baxter, K. H. (2002). State regulation of online insurance activities, *Electronic Banking Law & Commerce Report, September*, 1–5.

Kreidler, M. (2001, March). *How to pick an agent or broker*. Olympia, WA: Office of the Insurance Commissioner.

LIMRA. (2006). *Facts about life 2006*. Windsor, CT: Author.

Mayer, R. N., Huh, J., & Cude, B. J. (2005). Cues of credibility and price performance of life insurance web sites. *Journal of Consumer Affairs, 39*(1), 71–94.

Phan, D. (2005). *2005 identity fraud survey report*. Pleasanton, CA: Javelin Strategy & Research.

Schwartz, B. (2004). *The paradox of choice*. New York: Ecco Press.

Yahoo! (2005). *Selling money: The impact of the online channel on insurance*. Yahoo! Summit Series.

Yahoo! (2006). *Long & winding road: The route to the cash register*. Yahoo! Summit Series. Retrieved August 24, 2007, from http://www.iabuk.net/images/LongWinding Road_final_booklet_5_04_06_931.pdf.

Chapter 9
Online Shopping

Yi Cai and Brenda J. Cude

Abstract This chapter provides an overview of recent research related to online shopping and the conceptual frameworks that have guided that research. Specifically, the chapter addresses research related to who shops online and who does not, what attracts consumers to shop online, how and what consumers do when shopping online, and factors that might slow the growth in consumer online activities. The chapter reports on research related to the online shopping process, including consumer perceptions of privacy and security, as well as online information search. Directions for future research are suggested.

During the last two decades, the rapid diffusion of computer and information technologies throughout the business and consumer communities has resulted in dramatic changes. The application of the Internet to purchasing behavior is a notable change in the way buyers and sellers interact. According to the Pew Internet and American Life Project (2006), 73 % of Americans used the Internet in 2006, and about 70 % of adult Internet users made purchases online in 2005.

An efficient and flexible information search, communication, entertainment, education, and transaction tool, the Internet is key to a large and ever-growing array of online activities (see Fig. 9.1). Online shopping is a broadly defined activity that includes finding online retailers and products, searching for product information, selecting payment options, and communicating with other consumers and retailers as well as purchasing products or services. Thus, online shopping is one of the most important online activities. It has also made significant contributions to the economy, with an increasing percent of total retail sales from less than 1 % in 1999 to 3.3 % by the end of 2006 (Fig. 9.2). Total e-commerce sales were $108.7 billion in 2006, an increase of 23.5 % from 2005, compared with a 5.8 % increase for total retail sales from 2005 to 2006.

Y. Cai
Department of Family and Consumer Sciences, California State University at Northridge, 18111 Nordhoff St., Northridge, CA 91330-8308, USA
e-mail: yi.cai@csun.edu

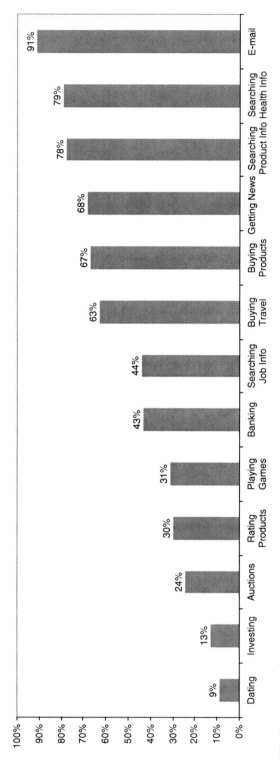

Fig. 9.1 Percent of American Internet users who report various activities
Source: Internet activities (Pew Internet and American Life Project, 2006)

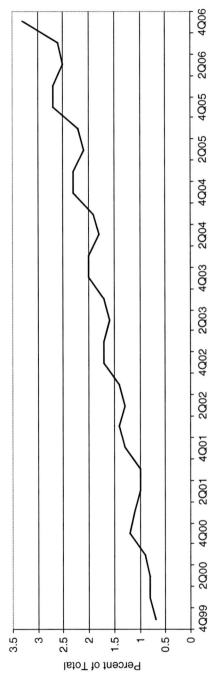

Fig. 9.2 Estimated quarterly e-commerce sales as a percent of total retail sales in the United States: Fourth quarter 1999 to fourth quarter 2006
Source: Quarterly retail e-commerce sales (U.S. Census Bureau, 2007)

This chapter reviews important research related to several aspects of online shopping. It begins with an overview of research related to consumer use of the Internet, including issues related to those with and without access. The next section examines research related to the online shopping channel and factors influencing consumers' acceptance of online shopping. The third section reviews research that examines the influence of the Internet on consumer decision-making, specifically online information search. A final section evaluates research related to the impact of consumer concerns about privacy and security in online transactions. The chapter concludes with comments regarding future research.

Consumers' Use of the Internet and Accessibility Issues

Understanding the Internet's potential to bring benefits to individuals at all levels is important. Researchers have shown that the Internet enables greater political participation (Polat, 2005), creates opportunities for community connectedness and sociability (Quan-Haase, Wellman, Witte, & Hampton, 2002), and enhances learning (Kazmer, 2005). The Internet also connects producers and marketers into a vast and logistical communication network that is more efficient than traditional channels. Davies, Pitt, Shapiro, and Watson (2005) summarized five technological forces that are relevant to e-commerce in general and highlighted its major benefits:

1. *Moore's law*: The exponential growth of computing power over time gives companies and consumers access to enormous processing power with relatively low cost.
2. *Metcalfe's law*: As the number of people using a service multiplies, the utility and efficiency of that service increases.
3. *Coasian economics*: The benefits of the Internet as a communication medium reduce the transaction costs for all concerned, especially customers. Coasian is a term based on economist Ronald Coase's (1937) study of transaction costs.
4. *The flock-of-birds phenomenon*: Birds flocking is a natural phenomenon and there are no "head" birds in charge. In the case of the Internet, there is indeed no one in charge; one person can interact with many on a global scale.
5. *The fish tank phenomenon*: With minimum entry barriers, the online marketplace contains many virtual "fish tanks" (websites) of varying sizes and content, enabling greater creativity on every level. The term was originally from *The Economist* ("The accidental superhighway," 1995). The phenomenon is named after the fact that in the early days of Internet, people used to put a video camera on top of their tropical fish tank, so that when surfers logged on to their site that is what they saw.

One implication of Davies et al.'s work is that as electronic technologies continue to grow in influence, consumers have the potential to benefit from e-commerce by taking more and more control of business transactions. However, an underlying assumption is that consumer participation in online activities in general and in e-commerce specifically will continue to grow exponentially. Therefore, it is important to learn who shops online and who does not and to investigate what attracts consumers to shop online, how and what they do when shopping online, and what factors might slow the growth in consumer online activities. Figures 9.3 and 9.4 illustrate the reasons Americans are and are not online.

Why Some Consumers Are Online and Others Are Not

In surveys, consumers cite a diversity of reasons for going online. For example, in a UCLA Center for Communication Policy (2003), the greatest proportion (19%) of Internet users said they started using the Internet for quick access to information, but the respondents also cited a host of other reasons (Fig. 9.3).

Despite the growth in the Internet's popularity, not everyone shops online. Some people are technological "have-nots," who do not have or want computers and/or Internet access. However, survey respondents are almost as likely to cite "no interest" as "no computer" as the reason for not being online (UCLA Center for Communication Policy, 2003) (Fig. 9.4).

Inequities in access to information and communication technology is a topic that popularized political and academic debates in the 1990s on the "digital divide." A series of influential surveys in both developing and developed countries (Georgia Institute of Technology, 1994, 1998; National Telecommunication and Information Administration, 1995, 1999; UCLA Center for Communication Policy, 2003; World Information Technology and Services Alliance, 2000) provided empirical support for the existence of a digital divide and helped to put the topic on scholarly and political agendas. Initially, many of the studies concluded that individuals' income, education, race, and/or ethnicity explained the gaps in access. Although Internet access spans every age range, access is highest among those aged 35 and under, with an access rate approaching 100%, compared with much lower access rates for those aged 56–65 (64%) and over age 65 (34%) (UCLA Center for Communication Policy, 2003). Those with lower educations and incomes as well as minority individuals have also been the "have-nots." More recent research reports that, at least in the United States, the gaps between those with and without Internet access are closing, especially the age and gender gaps (National Telecommunication and Information Administration, 1999; UCLA Center for Communication Policy, 2003). Recently, the digital divide has been redefined as an access to broadband issue, with rural and low-income areas having more limited access (Kruger, 2003; U.S. Department of Commerce, 2004).

In addition, recent work on Internet accessibility has advanced in two ways. First, organizations such as the World Bank (2006) and the World Information Technology and Services Alliance (2000) have looked more broadly at the role of the Internet in the global society. They developed several numerical e-readiness scores such as the Network Readiness Index (NRI) (Dutta & Mia, 2007). The

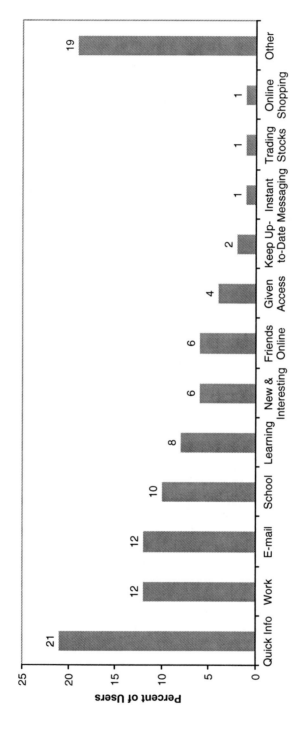

Fig. 9.3 Reasons Internet users started using the Internet
Source: The UCLA Internet report: Surveying the digital future (UCLA Center for Communication Policy, 2003)

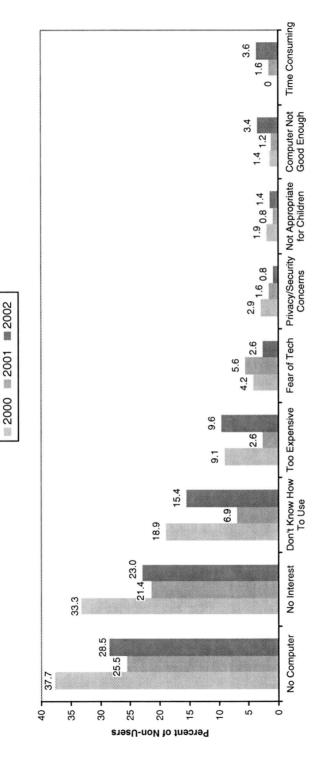

Fig. 9.4 Reasons Internet non-users do not go online
Source: The UCLA Internet report: Surveying the digital future (UCLA Center for Communication Policy, 2003)

indicators are useful because they reflect a specific definition of the digital divide and quantify it to facilitate comparison across nations. This approach moves the debate away from a reliance on physical and technological access (e.g., number of Internet users and use of online payment methods), which leads to a sharp but ambiguous dichotomy (Gunkel, 2003) that only pictures two clearly divided groups with a wide and difficult-to-bridge gap between them (Van Dijk, 2003). Moving beyond physical access redefines the digital divide issue by paying more attention to social, psychological, and cultural backgrounds (Hassani, 2006; Selwyn, 2006; Van Dijk, 2006).

A second development is the creation of a comprehensive model (Van Dijk, 2006) that incorporates different types of access such as motivational, material, skill, and usage access into a process rather than a single event of obtaining a particular technology (see Fig. 9.5).

Several key points can be drawn from this approach. First, it shows that access to digital technology does not necessarily equate with use; it appears that there are not only "have-nots" but also "want-nots." Second, digital technology skills have extended from managing hardware and software (instrumental skills) to a full range of skills including those required to search, select, and process information (informational skills) and to use digital sources to fulfill goals and improve one's status in society (strategic skills). Third, actual usage also is a multidimensional concept including usage time, application, and how active the user is. While Van Dijk designed the model to analyze the digital divide, it is also useful to examine specific online activities. For example, Rainie (2002) showed that about 74% of Internet users did not purchase gifts online during 2001 holiday season mainly because they did not want to risk using credit cards online. Thus, lack of motivational access to specific online activities may be a primary barrier that prevents some people (even those digital "haves") from actually using the technology.

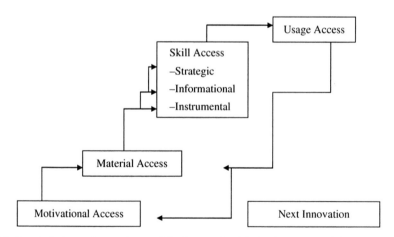

Fig. 9.5 A cumulative and recursive model of successive kinds of access to digital technologies
Source: Van Dijk (2006, p. 224)

In light of this comprehensive model, the factors explaining the digital divide and its specific implications (e.g., who does and does not shop online) can be physical, psychological, and social or cultural in nature. In addition to widely studied factors such as income, education, age, sex, and ethnicity, researchers can employ other variables such as personality, social and cultural networks and communities, social and professional institutions, and spatial mobility to redefine the digital divide. In Selwyn's (2006) qualitative study, the author found that Internet usage was influenced by more than material, temporal, or intellectual characteristics and was institutionally and organizationally mediated. Support for this idea can be found in other studies. Burke (2003) reported that the complexity of the familial relationship and household structure were crucial factors that influenced technology usage. For example, one may feel guilty spending time on the home computer at the expense of other members of the family.

Consumer Acceptance of Online Shopping

Although some people cannot or choose not to be online, it is almost unanimously accepted that the technology offers an opportunity for business transactions that cannot be ignored (Kraut et al., 2002). As a growing retail channel, the special characteristics and benefits as well as limitations of the Internet have been discussed extensively (Hoffman et al., 1996; Hoffman, Novak, & Chatterjee, 1996; Krantz, 1998).

The online shopping channel can be a valuable, interactive communication medium that facilitates flexible search, comparison shopping, and product and service evaluation. The attributes of the channel and their ability to match the users' purposes can facilitate usage.

Several theories have been used to explain how and why consumers choose to use the Internet. The media choice theory proposes that selection of media for a specific task is a function of the characteristics of the medium and the task (Fulk, Steinfeld, Schmitz, & Power, 1987). According to the theory, media can be differentiated by the degree of interactivity, communication richness, social presence, and vividness. Researchers have evaluated those characteristics and applied them to the choice of the Internet for shopping (Hoffman et al., 1996; Palmer, 1997). Hoffman et al. (1996) described the *flow experience* in a computer-mediated environment, which is characterized by interactivity, intrinsic enjoyment, and loss of self-consciousness and is self-reinforcing; the flow experience can be a determining factor in consumers' use of the Internet as a shopping channel. As the authors note, skills and focused attention are necessary antecedents for consumers to start the flow process on the Internet. Davis (1993) and O'Cass and Fenech (2003) used the technology acceptance model to explain the linkage between consumers' perceptions of the usefulness of the Internet and its ease of use with their acceptance and usage of online shopping.

Factors that Affect Consumers' Adoption and Use of Online Shopping

Although much has been written about the numerous advantages of e-commerce for both businesses and consumers, there is no guarantee that consumers will substitute the Internet for traditional shopping channels. Many factors may affect consumers' adoption and use of online shopping.

Numerous empirical studies have indicated that consumers' demographic and socioeconomic characteristics are influential in their use of the Internet for shopping. Researchers in the United States and other countries have found consistently that men, the more highly educated, and people in the higher income groups are more likely to buy online than are women, the less well educated, and lower income groups (Forsythe & Shi, 2003; Kau, Tang, & Ghose, 2003; Swinyard & Smith, 2003). Researchers have also found that consumers' Internet usage, such as Internet experience in years and frequency of Internet use, and access to high-speed Internet connections, have a positive effect on online buying and are highly correlated with socioeconomic characteristics such as income, education, and marital status (Swinyard & Smith, 2003). For example, surveys by the UCLA Center for Communication Policy (2003) indicate that very experienced Internet users are much more likely to buy books and travel online while new users are more likely to buy CDs and jewelry (Fig. 9.6).

Researchers have also found relationships between consumers' online shopping behaviors and their lifestyle and personality. For example, Casas, Zmud, and Bricka (2001) found that "time-starved" people tend to shop online more and people with an active "get-up-and-go" lifestyle and adventurous inclinations tend to shop offline. Consumers' attitudes toward online shopping, their shopping experience, and their shopping durations can also affect their adoption and use of online shopping although the relationships are not straightforward (Bellman, Lohse, & Johnson, 1999; Golob, 2003; Swinyard & Smith, 2003).

In addition, researchers have recognized the effects of product characteristics, for example, cost, tangibility, and degree of differentiation, on consumers' use of the Internet for information search and purchase (Alba et al., 1997; Peterson, Balasubramanian, & Bronnenberg, 1997). Consumers' purchases of specific products online can be attributed to a match or fit between the products' characteristics and those of the Internet. Rosen and Howard (2000) provided a model to assess the suitability of product categories to online retailing based on tactility, importance of customization, shipping costs, importance of instant satisfaction, and information intensity. Based on this suitability model, the authors gave the advantage to standardized or homogeneous products such as books, music, and video over differentiated or heterogeneous products. According to The State of Retailing Online 2007 report, for the first time in 2007, expenditures for clothes exceeded those for computers (Shop.org Research, 2007).

The product characteristics effect on online shopping is a typical case based on the transactional and distributive capabilities of the Internet. Coase's (1937)

Types of Products Purchased Online: New Users vs. Very Experienced Users

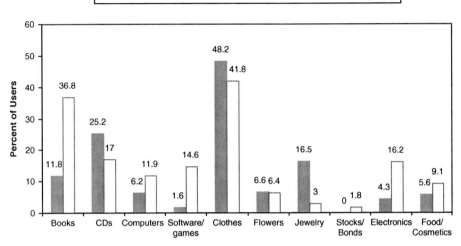

Types of Products Purchased Online: New Users vs. Very Experienced Users (Cont.)

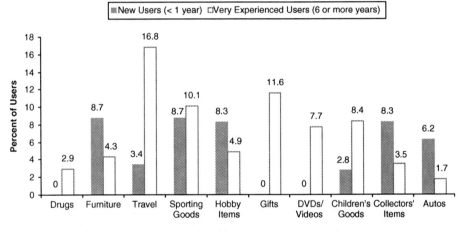

Fig. 9.6 Types of products purchased online: New vs. very experienced users
Source: The UCLA Internet report: Surveying the digital future (UCLA Center for Communication Policy, 2003)

transaction cost economics (TCE) argues that transaction costs are the major concern for coordinating the exchange of goods and services between suppliers and buyers. Liang and Huang (1998) employed the basic principle of TCE, that is, that consumers' choice of a transaction channel is guided by the objective of reducing transaction costs, to analyze consumers' acceptance of online shopping channels. The authors decomposed the transaction costs into seven categories: search cost, comparison cost, examination cost, negotiation cost, payment cost, delivery cost, and post-service cost. They concluded that Internet shopping lowers the search cost but raises the examination, payment, and post-service transaction costs.

Although Liang and Huang (1998) argued that product characteristics play a determinant role in consumer choice of retail channels and concluded that some products (e.g., books and flowers) are more suitable for marketing on the Web than others (e.g., shoes and toothpaste), they noticed that the effects of perceived transaction costs on the channel choice were mediated by consumers' experience. Indeed, a cost–benefit analysis may oversimplify the discussion of consumers' acceptance of online shopping channels by focusing on economic factors while overlooking some important social and personal factors.

Several researchers (see George, 2002; Suh & Han, 2003) have used the theory of planned behavior (TPB) (Azjen, 1991) as the basis for studies of online shopping behavior. According to the TPB, an individual's performance of a certain behavior is determined by his/her intent to perform that behavior; intent is influenced by attitudes toward the behavior, subjective norms about engaging in the behavior, and perceived behavioral control. Employing the TPB as a theoretical framework for consumers' acceptance and use of online shopping channels enables researchers to incorporate a variety of factors into the analyses. For example, George (2002) found that consumers' experiences, their concerns about privacy, and their perceptions of the trustworthiness of the Internet were associated with their Internet shopping behaviors. Other researchers also found that hedonic aspects of online shopping behaviors, such as perceived enjoyment and flexibility in navigation, play a role equal to the influence of utilitarian aspects of online shopping behaviors (Childers, Carr, Peck, & Carson, 2001). Investigation of a wider range of factors that influence consumers' acceptance and use of the Internet as a retail channel may provide insights to develop not only online marketing strategies but also new transaction media.

The Online Shopping Process and Information Search

Online shopping is not a single-stage behavior. When customers purchase a product, they must go through a process. A typical consumer decision process includes five stages: problem recognition, search, alternative evaluation, choice, and outcome evaluation. A mercantile model decomposes the consumer purchase process into three stages: purchase determination, purchase consumption, and post-purchase interaction (Kalakoto & Whinston, 1996). For an online purchase transaction, Liang and Huang (1998) defined a seven-step process: search, comparison, examination, negotiation, order and payment, delivery, and post-service.

Information Search: An Essential Step in the Online Shopping Process

A common feature of the above-mentioned decision models is that consumer information search behavior precedes all purchasing and choice behavior. Information search can be defined as a stage wherein consumers actively collect and integrate information from internal and external sources (Schmidt & Spreng, 1996). Consumer information search is one of the major consumer research topics in the area of online shopping and researchers have approached it from different perspectives, primarily psychology and economics. Numerous studies have addressed how many and what sources of information consumers use, the extent and duration of consumer information search, and types of information consumers search for (Lussier & Olshavsky, 1979; McColl-Kennedy & Fetter, 1999; Urbany, Dickson, & Kalapurakal, 1996).

According to Stigler's (1961) economics of information theory, a dominant paradigm in consumer information search research, consumers search until the perceived marginal benefits of search are equal to the perceived marginal costs. The theory assumes that consumers use an implicit cost–benefit analysis to choose a search strategy—what, when, where, and how much to search. Researchers have also incorporated other constructs, such as ability to search and motivation to search, into this cost–benefit framework (Schmidt & Spreng, 1996). Many factors can affect consumers' perceptions of search benefits and costs; the factors can be categorized into individual difference variables (e.g., demographic and socioeconomic characteristics), product type and product attributes, types of information sources used, and order of access (Srinivasan & Ratchford, 1991).

Information technology has brought the potential to influence almost all dimensions of consumers' information search behaviors, ranging from the amount of search, number and types of sources searched, and timing of search to the distribution and weighting of information gathered (Bakos & Brynjolfsson, 2000). One of the most important benefits of the Internet is the quantity and quality of information that the Internet can provide with minimal effort and cost. Burst Media reported in April 2006 that more than 50 % of U.S. adults in all income groups described the Internet as the primary source of information about products they plan to purchase (eMarketer, 2006). Alba et al. (1997) pointed out that a key difference between online and offline shopping is the ability of online consumers to obtain more information that facilitates better decision-making and makes the decision-making process more efficient. Empirical evidence indicates that consumers search more for information online than offline when they shop online (Ratchford, Lee, & Talukdar, 2003) and substitute online information sources for offline ones (Klein & Ford, 2003).

In theory, the amount, variety, efficiency, and interactivity of information available on the Internet promote consumers' online search. Using Stigler's (1961) theory as a framework, the attributes of online information search (relative to offline search) are intuitively associated with reduced costs (both time and cognitive costs) and increased benefits. Researchers consistently have found that search costs are lower in a virtual market than in a brick-and-mortar market (Bakos, 1997; Kulviwat, Guo, & Engchanil, 2004).

Despite its ability to provide vast amounts of information, some researchers have argued that the Internet may baffle consumers by offering too much information (Nachmias & Gilad, 2002). Indeed, the vast amount of information available online has no value unless, on the one hand, consumers have abilities and motivations to use them, and on the other, there are efficient mechanisms for identifying, retrieving, and organizing the information. In addition, the benefits of online information search are varied and uncertain. The commonly identified perceived benefits of online search include ease of use, effectiveness of search, user satisfaction (Kulviwat et al., 2004), reduced price paid (Bakos, 1997), greater product assortment and differentiation (Lynch & Ariely, 2000), and an enhanced experience (Zhang & Salverdry, 2001). However, it is difficult to conclude that the benefits of online search are necessarily greater than for offline search as the realized benefits are dependent largely on situational factors, personality factors, product attributes, and how effectively the consumer can use the technology.

In fact, the assumption that the costs of searching online (vs. offline) are lower can be challenged. Income has been commonly used as a proxy for information search costs (Klein & Ford, 2003), but it may be too broad a measure to accurately estimate online search costs without taking into consideration other factors. Another search cost is perceived risk, which should be assessed as a multidimensional variable including, for example, fear of technology, feelings of uncertainty and confusion, and privacy and security concerns. Thus, developing a valid, reliable, and complete measure of the costs of searching online presents significant challenges.

Beyond Economics of Information: Comprehensive Models of Information Search

Nevertheless, the basic idea of Stigler's (1961) theory, comparing the costs and benefits to determine the optimal amount of information search, makes it a parsimonious model to guide studies of online search. Combined with behavioral approaches such as the theory of planned behavior, the model provides a framework that can capture the process of consumer information search and the characteristics of the online environment. Shim, Eastlick, Lotz, and Warrington (2001) proposed a model of intention to search online using the theory of planned behavior. The model incorporated consumers' shopping attitudes, consumers' perceptions of the extent to which significant referents approve of Internet use for shopping (i.e., subjective norm), consumers' perceived behavioral control (e.g., computer skills, availability of transportation to travel), and consumers' past Internet purchase experiences as predictors for consumers' intentions to search.

Shim et al.'s (2001) model expanded the cost–benefit paradigm of information search by capturing non-economic factors, i.e., consumers' attitudes, perceptions, and behavioral aspects of online search. A more comprehensive model might incorporate not only consumer characteristics but also Internet characteristics (e.g., ease of use, interactivity, information format, and availability of intelligent agents such as shopping bots that visit a number of websites to identify information that matches a product profile provided by shoppers) and product characteristics (e.g., search goods, experience goods, and credence goods). For example, shopping bots can make comparison shopping more straightforward. However, using a shopping bot involves more than typing in a few keywords about a product and waiting for the results. Consumers must pre-articulate their needs, wants, and shopping goals to decide how to embed the use of this tool into their search and decide how to use the information it provides in their decision-making process.

It is important to address the possible interactions among consumer, Internet, and product characteristics and how those factors influence consumers' online information search. Research has shown that online consumer reviews have become an important source of information to consumers, especially as a complement to or even a substitute for other forms of business-to-consumer and offline word-of-mouth communication about product characteristics (McWilliam, 2000). However, Chevalier and Mayzlin (2002) identified three reasons to suspect that online consumer reviews might not be a good strategy for getting information: (1) consumers' incentives to take the time to provide reviews are not clear; (2) online venders can control the information displayed; (3) in the presence of consumer heterogeneity, reviews may have a bias toward the product evaluations. For example, one consumer may prefer a certain product or certain characteristics of a product, other consumers with different backgrounds, experiences, or preferences may not agree with him/her. Future research is worthwhile in this area.

Other researchers have argued that although the premise of Stigler's (1961) theory is parsimonious and logical, it must be qualified by a number of subtle and unrealistic assumptions (Peterson & Merino, 2003). One is the assumption of perfect information, i.e., that consumers have complete knowledge about the marginal costs and marginal benefits of search. Analytical and empirical studies have found that consumers tend not to follow this normative rule to search for information; they either stop searching when they reach some reference price or stop based on the total cost of search, not the marginal cost (Saad, 1996; Sonnemans, 1998). These results support Peterson and Merino's (2003) proposition that the Internet will not dramatically increase the amount of prepurchase information consumers acquire. In fact, considering the number of factors that influence consumer search behaviors and the difficulty of performing a cost–benefit analysis, consumers' decisions about the appropriate amount of search may be influenced less by economic factors online than offline. Future research is warranted in this area.

Consumers' actual purchase behaviors have been characterized as comprised of single or multiple steps with the overall shopping goal accomplished through enactment of one or more interrelated steps such as information search and purchase decision (Darden & Dorsch, 1990). While researchers consistently have modeled online information search behavior as an antecedent of the ultimate purchase decision (Klein, 1998; Shim et al., 2001), Shim et al. (2001) also found that consumers' intentions to search online mediated the relationships between consumers' intentions to purchase and several antecedent variables such as consumers' Internet purchase experiences. Perhaps in future research, online information search and the actual decision to purchase should not be viewed as independent processes.

Online Privacy and Security

In polls, American consumers have consistently expressed concerns about risks to their privacy when they shop online (Fig. 9.7). Many researchers have incorporated consumers' concerns about privacy and security issues into their online search and purchase models and interpreted the concerns as costs, risks, or obstacles for online search and purchase (Kulviwat et al., 2004; Kwon & Lee, 2003; Shim et al., 2001). Privacy and security concerns can also be related to issues such as consumer protection, online payment options, trustworthiness of online venders, information technologies, and online market efficiency.

The Internet has become a vast storage area for consumers' personal information, including both personally identifying information and financial information. Numerous public opinion polls and academic surveys (Georgia Institute of Technology, 1994, 1998; NUA, 1999; UCLA Center for Communication Policy, 2003) have assessed the salience of consumers' Internet privacy and security concerns. The primary reason for consumers' privacy and security concerns on the Internet is the tremendous amount of transaction-generated personal information that various websites collect, often in a completely invisible manner. Kang (1998) pointed out the uniqueness of online privacy and security issues associated with consumers' shopping experiences in the "real" world, where consumers are generally anonymous:

> In this alternate universe, you are invisibly stamped with a bar code as soon as you venture outside your home. . . . (The cyber mall) automatically records which stores you visit, which windows you peer into, in which order, and for how long. The specific stores collect even more detailed data when you enter their domain. Of course, whenever any item is actually purchased, the store as well as the credit, debit, or virtual cash company that

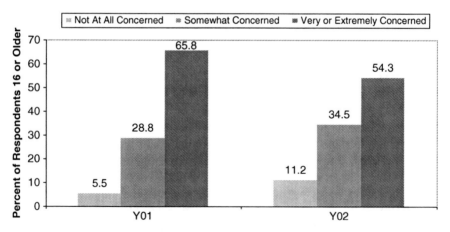

Fig. 9.7 American consumers' concerns about personal information when shopping online: 2001 and 2002
Source: The UCLA Internet report: Surveying the digital future (UCLA Center for Communication Policy, 2003)

provides payment through cyberspace take careful notes of what you bought (Kang, 1998, pp. 1198–1199).

Kang's example vividly illustrates that privacy and security concerns are a unique byproduct of e-commerce and explains why consumers continue to express concern. The development of efficient informational technologies such as "cookies," a personalization device used by websites to track visitors and their transactions, has made it easier for online venders to identify consumers' browsing and purchasing behaviors. Some consumers are simply unaware of cookies. Others know about them but are unwilling to block them because of the inconveniences that result. Blocking all cookies is the equivalent of telling supermarkets not to organize their aisles based on consumers' shopping behaviors or telling a storekeeper not to greet a repeat visitor. Online businesses face a delicate balance between meeting consumer demands for privacy protection and their desire for personalized treatment and thus a more efficient market.

Competing Views of Online Privacy and Security Protection

There are two competing views of how to handle consumers' perceptions of the privacy and security threats of the Internet: the self-regulatory framework proposed by the online industry and the legislative approach taken by consumer advocacy groups. A market concept of consumer privacy is the basis of the self-regulatory approach; it assumes that privacy, as a consumer property, is an expression of self and should remain free from government trespass (Zipperer & Collins, 1996). Within this framework, personal information is a commodity that consumers value highly. As a result, industry will seek to protect consumer information to gain their confidence and maximize profits.

Critics have challenged the industry argument that more complete information increases market efficiency and described the practices are socially problematic. Gandy (1993) explained how the data marketing industry identifies persons through commercial transactions, then classifies them into abstract, impersonal categories (such as race or sex), and finally, and most importantly, assesses groups using statistical models which claim to identify not only "good" customers, but also "risky" consumers who should be avoided.

Others have criticized the industry's self-regulatory efforts as inadequate. One effort, the Online Privacy Alliance (OPA), a coalition of more than 80 online companies and trade associations created in 1998, has produced Online Privacy Guidelines (Federal Trade Commission, 1999). Members of OPA agree to adopt and implement a posted privacy policy that provides a comprehensive notice of their information practices. In addition, the e-commerce industry has also created a voluntary enforcement mechanism, the use of privacy seals. TRUSTe and the Better Business Bureau Online (BBB Online) currently provide the seals, which are meant to certify that a website displaying a seal follows the certifying group's privacy guidelines. Miyazaki and Krishnamurthy (2002) and Rifon, LaRose, and Choi (2005) found that seals created favorable impressions among consumers about websites' privacy practices, while research by LaRose and Rifon (2006) suggested that the privacy practices of sites with seals were no better (and on some dimensions worse) than the practices of sites without seals.

Researchers and consumer advocacy groups have argued that the industry's self-regulatory efforts have failed to fully address fair information practices and, therefore, have done little to protect consumers (Electronic Privacy Information Center, 1998). On a theoretical level, self-regulation stresses the market value of consumer information but ignores the fact that fair information practices have other values, such as its role in promoting identity formation, free speech, and democracy, and therefore makes a faulty assumption about costs vs. benefits. Nehf (2003) has argued that a self-regulation approach is flawed because consumers find it difficult to value appropriately their privacy rights and to hold firms accountable for privacy breaches and thus may not incorporate privacy concerns into their decisions about sharing personal information.

On a practical level, online privacy notices typically are vaguely worded, technical, and legalistic, making them difficult for consumers to understand. Milne, Culnan, and Greene (2006) found that over time, the readability of online privacy notices has decreased while the notices have increased in length. Thus, consumers may not be able to assess accurately risks to their privacy in online transactions. The lack of uniformity among privacy notices and other protection mechanisms such as seals also increases consumers' costs of processing information. Perhaps most importantly, some websites may not post privacy policies at all. Miyazaki and Fernandez (2000) reviewed 381 websites and found that only 41.5 % provided any type of disclosure about privacy. Thus, consumers are likely to be in the dark about the information practices of most websites.

The extent to which consumers are willing to trade personal information for something else they value, such as discounts or convenience, is not well established. Industry groups have produced results emphasizing consumers' desire for personal treatment and willingness to reveal information about themselves (see, for example, Cyber Dialogue Survey, 1999). On the other hand, most academic research (Georgia Institute of Technology, 1998; Pew Internet and American Life Project, 2006; UCLA Center for Communication Policy, 2003) has shown that consumers are concerned about their online privacy, have become more concerned over time, and are not ready to trade privacy for convenience. However, the results come from a very simplistic approach (i.e., survey questions such as "Which of the following do you think is more important when you shop online: privacy or convenience?") which likely does not explain the complex relationship between privacy and other considerations. In addition, it is likely there are inconsistencies between consumers' attitudes and their behaviors when they use online services (Cai, Yang, & Cude, 2006), i.e., they do not do what they say they should. A more comprehensive approach to address the multiple aspects of consumers' online privacy concerns is warranted.

Online Shopping: By Consumers and for Consumers

Just as the invention of the horseless carriage and other technological developments improved people's lives, online shopping has overcome many of the physical limitations of brick-and-mortar stores. However, every technological development also creates problems for consumers. The challenge is to find a balance of costs and benefits that works for both retailers and consumers. There are many opportunities for future researchers to find ways to more accurately balance these costs and benefits as well as to understand how they influence consumers' use of the Internet.

Some of the areas highlighted in this chapter are as follows:

- Investigation of a wide range of factors that influence consumers' acceptance and use of the Internet as a retail channel and interactions among influential factors
- Development of a valid, reliable, and complete measure of the costs of online search
- The influence of economic vs. non-economic factors on the appropriate amount of online search
- Exploration of consumers' use of online reviews in purchase decisions
- A more comprehensive assessment of consumers' online privacy concerns and their influence on online shopping behaviors

Another area that is worthwhile for researchers to pursue is that of the online relationship between consumers and market agents such as department store sales persons and travel agents. As consumers' interactions with markets and market agents become easier and (potentially) less costly online compared to offline, do consumers see these relationships as less favorable, equal, or superior to relationships established offline? How willing are consumers to substitute online relationships for face-to-face relationships? What may be the costs and benefits from such substitutions?

Finally, Pitt, Berthon, Watson, and Zinkhan (2002) have written about the potential of the Internet to transform the balance of power in the market. As they state it, "Websites allow better informed consumers to interact, band together, become more aware of corporate shortcomings, and gain easier access to the legal system" (p. 7). A fruitful area for research is an investigation of why the Internet has not achieved its potential to increase consumer power in the market. Is it because the tools that consumers need are unavailable or too difficult to use? Is it because the tools are available but consumers have not used them to their advantage? Or are there other explanations?

References

Alba, J., Lynch, J., Weitz, B., Janiszewski, C., Lutz, R., Sawyer, A., & Wood, S. (1997). Interactive home shopping: Consumer, retailer, and manufacturer incentives to participate in electronic marketplaces. *Journal of Marketing, 61*, 38–53.

Azjen, I. (1991). The theory of planned behavior. *Organizational Behavior and Human Decision Processes, 50,* 179–211.

Bakos, J. Y. (1997). Reducing buyer search cost: Implications for electronic marketplaces. *Management Science, 43,* 1676–1692.

Bakos, J. Y., & Brynjolfsson, E. (2000). Bundling and competition on the Internet. *Marketing Science, 19*(1), 63–82.

Bellman, S., Lohse, G. L., & Johnson, E. J. (1999). Predictors of online buying behavior. *Communications of the Association for Computing Machinery, 42,* 32–38.

Burke, C. (2003). Women, guilt and home computers. In J. Turow & A. Kavanaugh (Eds.), *The wired homestead: An MIT sourcebook on the Internet and the family* (pp. 325–355). Cambridge, MA: MIT Press.

Cai, Y., Yang, Y., & Cude, B. (2006). *The inconsistency of U.S. consumers' opinion and use of online banking.* Manuscript submitted for publication.

Casas, J., Zmud, J., & Bricka, S. (2001, January). *Impact of shopping via Internet on travel for shopping purpose.* Paper presented at the 80th Annual Meeting of the Transportation Research Board, Washington, DC.

Chevalier, J. A., & Mayzlin, D. (2002). The effect of word of mouth on sales: Online book reviews. *Journal of Marketing Research, 39,* 345–354.

Childers, T. L., Carr, C. L., Peck, J., & Carson, S. (2001). Hedonic and utilitarian motivations for online retail shopping behavior. *Journal of Retailing, 77,* 511–535.

Coase, R. H. (1937). The nature of the firm. *Economica, 4,* 386–405.

Cyber Dialogue Survey. (1999). *Privacy vs. personalization.* Retrieved March, 2007, from http://www.egov.vic.gov.au/pdfs/wp-ic-1999-privacy2.pdf.

Darden, W. R., & Dorsch, M. J. (1990). An action strategy approach to examining shopping behavior. *Journal of Business Research, 21,* 289–308.

Davies, M., Pitt, L., Shapiro, D., & Watson, R. (2005). Betfair.com: Five technology forces revolutionize worldwide wagering. *European Management Journal, 23*(5), 533–541.

Davis, F. D. (1993). User acceptance of information technology: System characteristics, user perceptions and behavioral impacts. *International Journal of Man-Machine Studies, 38,* 475–487.

Dutta, S., & Mia, I. (2007). *Global information technology report 2006–2007: Connecting to the networked economy.* Hampshire, England: Palgrave Macmillan.

Electronic Privacy Information Center. (1998). *Surfer beware II: Notice is not enough.* Retrieved March, 2007, from http://www.epic.org/reports/surfer-beware2.html.

eMarketer. (2006, May 2). *When Americans buy . . . They go online first.* Retrieved March, 2007, from http://www.emarketer.com/Article.aspx?id=1003949.

Federal Trade Commission. (1999). *Self-regulation and online privacy: A report to Congress.* Retrieved August, 2004, from http://www.ftc.gov/opa/1999/9907/report1999.htm.

Forsythe, S., & Shi, B. (2003). Consumer patronage and risk perceptions in Internet shopping. *Journal of Business Research, 56,* 867–875.

Fulk, J., Steinfeld, C. W., Schmitz, J., & Power, G. J. (1987). A social information processing model of media use in organizations. *Communications Research, 14,* 520–552.

Gandy, O. (1993). *The panoptic sort: A political economy of personal information.* Boulder, CO: Westview Press.

George, J. F. (2002). Influences on the intent to make Internet purchases. *Internet Research: Electronic Networking Applications and Policy, 12*(2), 165–180.

Georgia Institute of Technology. (1994, 1998). *WWW user surveys.* Retrieved August, 2004, from http://www.cc.gatech.edu/gvu/user_surveys.

Golob, T. F. (2003). Structural equation modeling for travel behavior research. *Transportation Research B, 37,* 1–25.

Gunkel, D. (2003). Second thoughts: Toward a critique of the digital divide. *New Media & Society, 5*(4), 499–522.

Hassani, S. N. (2006). Locating digital divide at home, work, and everywhere else. *Poetics, 34,* 250–272.

Hoffman, D. L., & Novak, T. P. (1996). Marketing in the hypermedia computer-mediated environments: Conceptual foundations. *Journal of Marketing, 60*(3), 50–68.

Hoffman, D. L., Novak, T. P., & Chatterjee, P. (1996). Commercial scenarios for the web: Opportunities and challenges. *Journal of Computer Mediated Communications, 1*(3). Retrieved March, 2007, from http://jcmc.indiana.edu/vol1/issue3/hoffman.html.

Kalakoto, R., & Whinston, A. B. (1996). *Frontiers of electronic commerce*. Reading, MA: Addison-Wesley.

Kang, J. (1998). Information privacy in cyberspace transactions. *Stanford Law Review, 50*(4), 1193–1294.

Kau, A. K., Tang, Y. E., & Ghose, S. (2003). Typology of online shoppers. *The Journal of Consumer Marketing, 20*(2/3), 139–156.

Kazmer, M. M. (2005). Community-embedded learning. *Library Quarterly, 75*, 190–212.

Klein, L. R. (1998). Evaluating the potential of interactive media through a new lens: Search versus experience goods. *Journal of Business Research, 41*, 195–203.

Klein, L. R., & Ford, G. (2003). Consumer search for information in the digital age: An empirical study of prepurchase search for automobiles. *Journal of Interactive Marketing, 17*(3), 29–49.

Krantz, M. (1998, July 20). Click till you drop. *Time*, pp. 34–41.

Kraut, R., Kiesler, S., Boneva, B., Cummings, J., Helgeson, V., & Crawford, V. (2002). Internet paradox revisited. *Journal of Social Issues, 58*(1), 49–74.

Kruger, L. G. (2003, September 22). *Broadband Internet access and the digital divide: Federal Assistance Programs* (CRIS Report for Congress). Washington, DC: Congressional Research Service, The Library of Congress.

Kulviwat, S., Guo, C., & Engchanil, N. (2004). Determinants of online information search: A critical review and assessment. *Internet Research, 14*(3), 245–253.

Kwon, K.-N., & Lee, J. (2003). Concerns about payment security of Internet purchase: A perspective on current online shoppers. *Clothing and Textiles Research Journal, 21*(4), 174–184.

LaRose, R., & Rifon, N. (2006). Your privacy is assured—of being disturbed: Web sites with and without privacy seals. *New Media and Society, 12*(8), 1009–1029.

Liang, T. P., & Huang, J. S. (1998). An empirical study on consumer acceptance of products in electronic markets: A transaction cost model. *Decision Support Systems, 24*, 29–43.

Lussier, D., & Olshavsky, R. (1979). Task complexity and contingent processing in brand choice. *Journal of Consumer Research, 9*, 18–37.

Lynch, J. G., & Ariely, D. (2000). Wine online: Search costs affect competition on price, quality, and distribution. *Marketing Science, 19*(1), 83–103.

McColl-Kennedy, J. R., & Fetter, R. E. (1999). Dimensions of consumer search behavior in services. *The Journal of Services Marketing, 13*, 242–265.

McWilliam, G. (2000). Building strong brands through online communities. *MIT Sloan Management Review, 41*(3), 43–54.

Milne, G. R., Culnan, M. J., & Greene, H. (2006). A longitudinal assessment of online privacy notice readability. *Journal of Public Policy and Marketing, 25*(2), 238–249.

Miyazaki, A. D., & Fernandez, A. (2000). Internet privacy and security: An examination of online retailer disclosures. *Journal of Public Policy and Marketing, 19*(1), 54–61.

Miyazaki, A. D., & Krishnamurthy, S. (2002). Internet seals of approval: Effects on online privacy policies and consumer perceptions. *Journal of Consumer Affairs, 36*(1), 28–49.

Nachmias, R., & Gilad, A. (2002). Needle in a hyperstack: Searching for information on the World Wide Web. *Journal of Research on Technology in Education. 34*(4), 475–486.

National Telecommunication and Information Administration. (1995). *Falling through the net: A survey of the 'have-nots' in rural and urban America*. Retrieved March, 2007, from http://www.ntia.doc.gov/ntiahome/fallingthru.html.

National Telecommunication and Information Administration. (1999). *Falling through the net: Defining the digital divide*. Retrieved March, 2007, from http://www.ntia.doc.gov/ ntiahome/digitaldivide.

Nehf, J. (2003). Recognizing the societal value in information privacy. *Washington Law Review*, *78*, 1–92.

NUA Internet Surveys. (1999). *Jupiter Communications: Media coverage fuels consumer fears.* Retrieved August, 2004, from http://ww.nua.net/survey.

O'Cass, A., & Fenech, T. (2003). Web retailing adoption: Exploring the nature of Internet users Web retailing behavior. *Journal of Retailing and Consumer Services, 10*, 81–94.

Palmer, J. W. (1997). Electronic commerce in retailing: Differences across retail formats. *The Information Society, 13*, 75–91.

Peterson, R. A., Balasubramanian, S., & Bronnenberg, B. J. (1997). Exploring the implications of the Internet for consumer marketing. *Journal of Academy of Marketing Science, 25*(4), 329–346.

Peterson, R. A., & Merino, M. C. (2003). Consumer information search behavior and the Internet. *Psychology & Marketing, 20*(2), 99–121.

Pew Internet and American Life Project. (2006). *Internet activities.* Retrieved March, 2007, from http://www.pewinternet.org/trends/Internet_Activities_7.19.06.htm.

Pitt, L. F., Berthon, P. R., Watson, R. T., & Zinkhan, G. M. (2002). The Internet and the birth of real consumer power. *Business Horizons, July/August*, 7–14.

Polat, R. K. (2005). The Internet and political participation: Exploring the explanatory links. *European Journal of Communication, 20*, 435–459.

Quan-Haase, A., Wellman, B., Witte, J., & Hampton, K. N. (2002). Capitalizing on the net: Social contact, civic engagement, and sense of community. In B. Wellman & C. Haythornwaite (Eds.), *The Internet in everyday life* (pp. 291–325). Oxford: Blackwell.

Rainie, L. (2002). *Women surpass men as e-shoppers during the holidays* (Pew Internet and American Life Project). Retrieved March, 2007, from http://www.pewinternet.org/pdfs/PIP_Holiday_2001_Report.pdf.

Ratchford, B., Lee, M. S., & Talukdar, D. (2003). The impact of the Internet on information search for automobiles. *Journal of Marketing Research, 40*, 193–209.

Rifon, N. J., LaRose, R., & Choi, S. M. (2005, Winter). Your privacy is sealed: Effects of web privacy seals on trust and personal disclosures. *Journal of Consumer Affairs, 39*(2), 339–362.

Rosen, K. T., & Howard, A. L. (2000). E-retail: Gold rush or fool's gold? *California Management Review, 42*(3), 72–100.

Saad, G., & Russo, J. E. (1996). Stopping criteria in sequential choice. *Organizational Behavior and Human Decision Processes, 67*, 258–270.

Schmidt, J. B., & Spreng, R. A. (1996). A proposed model of external consumer information search. *Journal of Academy of Marketing Science, 24*, 246–256.

Selwyn, N. (2006). Digital division or digital decision? A study of non-users and low-users of computers. *Poetics, 34*, 273–292.

Shim, S., Eastlick, M. A., Lotz, S. L., & Warrington, P. (2001). An online prepurchase intentions model: The role of intention to search. *Journal of Retailing, 77*, 397–416.

Shop.org Research. (2007, May 14). *Online clothing sales surpass computers, according to Shop.Org/Forrester Research study.* Retrieved June, 2007, from http://www.shop.org/soro07/pr-051407.asp.

Sonnemans, J. (1998). Strategies of search. *Journal of Economic Behavior & Organization, 35*, 309–332.

Srinivasan, N., & Ratchford, B. (1991). An empirical test of a model of external search for automobiles. *Journal of Consumer Research, 18*(2), 233–242.

Stigler, G. J. (1961). The economics of information. *Journal of Political Economics, 29*, 213–225.

Suh, B., & Han, I. (2003). The impact of customer trust and perceived security control on the acceptance of electronic commerce. *International Journal of Electronic Commerce, 7*(3), 135–161.

Swinyard, W. R., & Smith, S. M. (2003). Why people (don't) shop online: A lifestyle study of the Internet consumer. *Psychology & Marketing, 20*, 567–597.

The accidental superhighway (1995, July 1). *The Economist*, p. S3.

UCLA Center for Communication Policy. (2003). The UCLA Internet Report: Surveying the Digital Future: Year Three. Retrieved March, 2007, from http://www.ccp.ucla.edu.

Urbany, J. E., Dickson, P. R., & Kalapurakal, R. (1996). Price search in the retail grocery market. *Journal of Marketing, 60*, 91–104.

U.S. Census Bureau. (2007). Quarterly retail e-commerce sales. Available at: http://www.census.gov/mrts/www/ecomm.html.

U.S. Department of Commerce. (2004, September). A nation online: Entering the broadband age. Washington, DC: Author.

Van Dijk, J. (2003). A framework for digital divide research. *Electronic Journal of Communication, 12(1)*. Retrieved March, 2007, from http://www.cios.org/www/ejc/v12n102.htm.

Van Dijk, J. (2006). Digital divide research, achievements and shortcomings. *Poetics, 34*, 221–235.

World Bank. (2000). The networking revolution: Opportunities and challenges for developing countries. Washington, DC: World Bank.

World Bank. (2006). Knowledge assessment methodology. Washington, DC: Author.

World Information Technology and Services Alliance. (2000). International survey of e-commerce. Arlington, VA: Author.

Zhang, H., & Salverdry, G. (2001). The implications of visualization ability and structure preview design for Web information search tasks. *International Journal of Human-Computer Interaction, 13*(1), 75–95.

Zipperer, R., & Collins, J. (1996). Privacy on the net. *Consumer Comments, 20*, 1–2.

Part III
Consumer Finances of Special Populations

Chapter 10
Financial Literacy of High School Students

Lewis Mandell

Abstract Five, large-scale, biennial national surveys of high school seniors from 1997 to 2006 have been used to measure the financial literacy of young American adults. The results show a low level of ability to make age-appropriate financial decisions in their own self-interests. Low baseline results in 1997 have further deteriorated with scores on the 31-question, multiple choice exam now hovering just over 50 %. Students from families with greater financial resources tend to be substantially more financially literate than those from families that are less well-off, thereby exacerbating the inequality of economic welfare among families. Moreover, high school classes in personal finance and money management have not proven to be effective in raising levels of financial literacy.

The Jump$tart Coalition for Personal Financial Literacy was formed in 1995 in response to a dichotomy seemingly lifted from the opening of Dickens's *A Tale of Two Cities*—it was both the best of times and the worst of times. On the positive side, real personal income in the United States had never been higher. On the downside, financial distress, measured by families filing for personal bankruptcy, had also never been higher. How could this be?

The early pioneers of what came to be known as the financial literacy movement came up with a hypothesis to explain this dichotomy. Deregulation of the nation's financial services industry over the previous 20 years had encouraged the proliferation of financial products, many of them innovative and complex. The virtual elimination of interest rate restrictions (on both deposits and consumer credit) allowed banks to extend credit (and credit cards) to a wider spectrum of consumers whose incomes and/or credit ratings had hitherto made them ineligible.

While most economists posited that variety and choice are good for consumers, it was also possible that many consumers lacked the ability to evaluate the new and complex financial instruments and make informed judgments in both choice of

L. Mandell
Department of Finance, State University of New York at Buffalo, 375 Jacobs Hall,
University at Buffalo, Buffalo, NY 14260–4000, USA
Email: lewm@buffalo.edu

instruments and extent of use that would be in their own best long-run interests. This ability was termed financial literacy.

The small group that became the Jump$tart Coalition shortly came to two additional conclusions. First, the problem was too large for any single organization to tackle and that a *consortium* of organizations with interest in financial literacy should be assembled. A second conclusion was that the current level of financial literacy should be measured as a baseline and that subsequent measures should be taken, at regular intervals, over time to measure progress in making Americans financially literate.

High school seniors were chosen as the population to measure for several reasons. First, they were adolescents on the verge of legal age for both the ownership of a variety of assets and the ability to obligate themselves to the repayment of debt. Second, they were in their last year of education whose form could be proscribed by adults acting on their behalf. Courses related to financial literacy *could* be mandated in high school, but not in college where students are allowed to choose their own course of study. Finally, from a pragmatic standpoint, the fledgling organization could not afford the cost of large-scale, detailed surveys of adults, involving paper and pencil tests of financial literacy. School-based administration of these tests was deemed to be an accurate and cost-efficient method of assessing financial literacy.

Other Studies of Financial Literacy

A number of surveys have shown that Americans of all ages lack the ability to make good financial choices (see Chen & Volpe, 1998; Volpe, Chen, & Liu, 2006, for a review). The lack of basic financial literacy has been shown to result in poor financial decision making. Nellie May's study of undergraduate college students in 2000 found that 25 % have four or more credit cards and about 10 % carried outstanding balances between $3,000 and $7,000 (Murray, 2002). Joo and Grable (2000) found that poor financial decisions also hurt productivity in the workplace. A 2001 Harris pole of graduating college seniors found that only 8 % believed that they were very knowledgeable about investing and financial planning in contrast to about half who believed they were not very or not at all knowledgeable.

For more than a decade, the Federal Reserve has focused on the importance of financial education and literacy in the functioning of the financial markets (see, for example, Braunstein & Welch, 2002; Greenspan, 2003, 2005; Hilgert, Hogarth, & Beverly, 2003).

Volpe et al. (2006) used a survey of corporate benefit administrators to identify important topics in personal finance and assess employee knowledge relating to these topics. Their survey identified basic personal finance as a critical area in which employee knowledge is deficient, particularly as it relates to retirement planning, investment and estate planning.

The Organization for Economic Co-operation and Development (2005) report *Improving Financial Literacy* found the lack of financial literacy to be widespread, affecting adults and/or high school students in Australia, Japan and Korea as well as the United States.

Jump$tart Surveys

In late 1997, the Jump$tart Coalition for Personal Financial Literacy conducted its first *Personal Financial Survey*. The results of this initial baseline survey were not reassuring. Just 10.2 % of the 1,532 high school seniors were able to answer at least three-quarters of the basic, age-relevant questions correctly. In fact, the average grade on the exam was a *failing* 57.3 %. (Mandell, 1998).

Given the results of this inauspicious start, the Jump$tart Coalition decided to administer a version of the *Personal Financial Survey* every 2 years to measure progress to the overall goal of universal financial literacy for all American high school graduates. Back in 1997, the Jump$tart founders optimistically forecast that by 2007, 10 years after the baseline measure, the *final* survey would document the achievement of this goal.

Results of Subsequent Surveys

In early 2000, a second nationwide survey was administered to 723 high school seniors. The results were substantially worse than those of the first survey, 2 years earlier (Mandell, 2001). During the academic year 2001–2002, the third nationwide survey was given to 4,024 twelfth graders. Overall results continued to decline from 51.9 % to a low of 50.2 % (Mandell, 2003).

The survey of 4,074 high school seniors completed in February 2004 showed the first improvement in overall scores since the surveys began in 1997. The mean rose by 2.1 percentage points from the low of 50.2 % achieved in 2000 to 52.3 %. While this result was better than the two previous surveys, it was still 4 percentage points below the baseline study of 1997, which itself has been characterized as a high flunk (Mandell, 2004). A record 5,775 twelfth grade students completed the Jump$tart survey by February 2006, achieving an average score of 52.4 %, a slight increase from 2004 (Mandell, 2006a).

The Sample

The Jump$tart survey uses a national sample of seniors in U.S. public high schools. The sample is stratified by state and clustered by school. The probability that a public high school within a state is chosen for inclusion in the sample is proportional to the number of seniors in that high school.

The universe used for school selection is all public high schools in the United States from the list provided online by the U.S. Department of Education. Since the cost of randomly selecting and testing students across every state would be prohibitive, students are clustered by high school so that the exam can be administered to entire classroom of students at one time.

The number of high school seniors sampled in each state is based on the number of public high school seniors in that state. The sampling interval is the proportion of all public high school seniors nationwide multiplied by the desired national sample size, adjusted for likely response rate. Within each state, every public high school is rank-ordered from smallest to largest by the number of twelfth grade students. Then, a random number between 1 and the sampling interval is chosen as the start number within each state. High school seniors are added up (from lowest to highest) and when the random start number is reached, that high school was chosen for inclusion in the sample. From that point on, the sampling interval is added to the cumulative number continually, until the largest high school is reached. Each time the random start plus a multiple of the sampling interval is reached, another high school is added to the sample. Each school that falls into the sample is contacted and asked if a specific class would take the Jump$tart survey.

To improve the probability that sampled school would participate in the survey, members of statewide Jump$tart Coalitions are asked to contact school principals to urge cooperation. As added incentive for the Jump$tart Coalitions, those states that want comparative state-specific results have been over-sampled (40 schools per state) since 2002 with the provision that state-specific results would be supplied if 10 or more schools within their state participated in the survey. As a result, the data used in the analysis must be weighted to insure that every school in the sample has a probability of selection proportionate to the size of its senior class size.

Letters are sent to the principals of the randomly selected schools, explaining the purpose of the study and asking for their cooperation. Principals who are personally known to members of the Jump$tart Coalition or of the state Coalitions were contacted by phone as well. They are asked to select a twelfth grade (non-honors) class in English or Social Studies (aside from economics) to participate in the survey. This was done to avoid biasing the results by specifically selecting classes in economics, business or related areas. To randomize the process further, principals were asked to select classes meeting closest to 10 a.m.

A small incentive is offered to help gain the cooperation of the schools. In 2006, the teacher who administered the survey was offered a $50 gift card from Staples to purchase school supplies. In earlier years, a small savings bond was used as an inducement. Some participating teachers decline this offer.

In 2006, 305 of the 1,733 sampled schools participated, a response rate of 17.6%. This was an increase from the response rate of 15.8% in 2004 but below both the 18.3% in the 2002 survey and 21.3% in the 2000 study; in addition, it was less than half of the 43.6% rate that had been achieved in 1997. Conversations with school officials indicate that while they have an interest in financial literacy, the intense pressure to achieve satisfactory scores on standardized national examinations has diverted energy and resources to core academic areas. In spite of varying response rates, however, the demographics of the five surveys were very similar, indicting that they were all reasonably representative of the population of twelfth graders in public schools.

The Survey Instrument

The survey instrument tends to consist of approximately 50 questions, of which 31 are the core financial literacy questions. All questions use a multiple choice format.

Prior to the first survey, members of the Jump$tart Coalition identified four key areas of coverage in their Personal Finance Standards. These areas were (1) income, (2) money management, (3) saving and investing and (4) spending and credit. The test questions attempted to cover the four key areas and their major subcategories. Wherever possible, questions were put into age- and life cycle-appropriate case studies to make them relevant to the students.

Test questions were largely identical to those used in previous years, except for ordering and cosmetic changes. To discourage teachers from teaching for the exam, the ordering of questions is changed in each survey, as is the ordering of answers to each of the questions. Furthermore, cosmetic changes are made in the questions, including changing the names of persons used in mini-case questions. In addition, regulatory and market changes over a period of several years have mandated substantive changes to some questions. For example, while credit reports could formerly be accessed without charge only if a consumer was denied credit, a new law was passed guaranteeing consumers access to their credit records, without charge, once each year. This forced the modification of the question relating to free access to credit records. While this changed the comparability of the questions somewhat, great care has been taken to minimize the impact of these necessary changes.

In an assessment of the reliability and validity of the 1997 and 2000 Jump$tart surveys, Lucey (2005) found that the surveys possess moderately high overall intercorrelation consistency as well as some degree of face and content validity. However, he found less support for their construct, congruent, and predictive validity and suggested further research into the degree to which the Jump$tart surveys measure financial understanding.

Financial Literacy by Category

Test Results by Demographics

Table 10.1 summarizes the results of the five studies by demographic variables. Recently, students from families with higher incomes have tended to do better than

Table 10.1 Test results by demographics

	1997 Mean score	2000 Mean score	2002 Mean score	2004 Mean score	2006 Mean score	2006 Proportion of students	2006 % C or better	2006 % Failing
	57.3%	51.9%	50.2%	52.3%	52.4%	100.0%	6.9%	62.0%
Parents' income								
Less than $20,000	55.2	46.3	45.7	49.5	48.5	8.0	2.9	74.2
$20,000–$39,999	58.2	52.0	50.7	51.3	50.8	17.0	5.6	67.3
$40,000–$79,999	59.6	57.2	52.3	54.1	53.7	29.1	8.1	57.5
$80,000 or more	59.0	55.0	52.7	55.9	55.6	27.0	10.5	52.0
Highest level of parents' education								
Neither finished H.S.	51.4	47.0	43.7	44.6	44.5	6.4	0.4	82.7
Completed H.S.	57.1	49.7	47.5	51.5	50.6	24.6	4.5	66.7
Some college	55.8	53.8	51.7	52.6	51.8	21.0	6.4	63.2
College grad or more	59.3	55.1	53.5	55.4	55.6	43.7	10.1	53.4
Sex								
Female	57.9	51.6	50.7	52.2	52.3	53.1	4.9	62.6
Male	56.9	52.2	49.8	52.4	52.6	46.6	9.3	60.8
Race								
White	60.9	54.5	53.7	55.5	55.0	71.3	8.9	54.6
African American	50.4	47.0	42.1	44.0	44.7	10.1	1.6	79.8
Hispanic American	55.1	45.3	44.8	48.3	46.8	8.6	2.0	79.6
Asian American	55.8	53.5	50.6	48.3	49.4	4.4	2.2	71.9
Native American	48.8	38.6	45.5	46.7	44.1	1.5	5.1	86.6

others on the exam. In 2006, for example, students whose parents' income totaled less than $20,000 per year had a mean score of 48.5% in contrast to an average of 55.6% for students whose parents' income was more than $80,000. In 2006, for the third consecutive survey, students from families with the highest incomes did better than all others and the differential appeared to be widening.

It is important to note that students from the highest income families did not always exhibit the highest rates of financial literacy. In the first two surveys (1997 and 2000), students from families in the $40,000–$79,999 income range did *better* than students in the top family income range. We attributed this to the notion that students from more affluent homes did not have to be as financially literate as their less affluent counterparts since they were almost universally college-bound and would probably be insulated from most financial responsibilities for at least four more years.

While we have no hard data to explain why students from the highest income families suddenly appear more financially literate than others, we feel that it is likely the result of a higher level of awareness of the importance of financial literacy by these wealthier and better-educated families.Based on conversations we have had with educators, early adopters of programs designed to address the problems of financial literacy appear to be the more affluent private and public high schools that are both more aware of the problem and less constrained by resource shortages than other schools.

Examination results are also strongly and monotonically related to parents' education. If neither parent completed high school, the average score in 2006 was 44.5 % rising to 55.6 % for those who had at least one parent who completed college. Also, while less than half of 1 % of those whose parents had less than a high school education scored a C or better on the exam (at least 75 %), 10.1 % of those in the highest education category did this well.

The surveys have found little difference in financial literacy by gender. In 2006, males did marginally better than females (52.6 versus 52.3 %) as they did in 2000 and 2004. However, in two of the five surveys (1997 and 2002), females did slightly better than males.

Performance differences were more closely related to race than any other background variable. White students have consistently outperformed all others while African Americans and Native Americans have tended to do least well. The difference of approximately 10 points in financial literacy scores representing close to a 20 % differential underscores one of the most important causes of racial inequality. Since racial groups with fewer financial resources also tend to have less ability to utilize these resources for their own best interests, overall economic well-being, which is a product of financial resources and financial literacy, is more poorly distributed than either component.

Students from the Midwest region of the United States did best on the exam with a mean score of 54.2 %. Those from the South did least well with a mean score of 49.9 %, a number unchanged from the previous survey.

Results by Aspirations

Students were asked about their educational plans and occupational aspirations as well as the full-time income they anticipated making from their first job. The results are shown in Table 10.2.

In 2006, nearly 71 % of students who participated in the survey planned to attend a 4-year college and more than half aspired to be professional workers (a sizeable proportion did not yet know what occupation they intended to undertake). Income expectations were varied, with 41.4 % expecting to begin work at $40,000 or more and an additional 20.4 % expecting to make between $30,000 and $40,000. This and previous surveys have found that educational aspiration is strongly and directly related to financial literacy while income expectation is also positively related, but not as strongly. This author concludes, in an earlier paper, that those with higher educational aspirations are relatively higher in literacy than in thriftiness (Mandell, 2005).

Table 10.2 Test results by aspirations

	1997 Mean score	2000 Mean score	2002 Mean score	2004 Mean score	2006 Mean score	2006 Proportion of students	2006 % C or better	2006 % Failing
	57.3 %	51.9 %	50.2 %	52.3 %	52.4 %	100.0 %	6.9 %	62.0 %
Educational Plans								
No further education	43.8	39.7	32.2	41.9	37.9	2.0	2.7	91.5
2-year or jr. college	53.8	43.3	46.4	48.0	47.5	14.7	1.7	76.6
4-year college	60.0	54.5	53.5	55.0	54.9	70.9	8.8	55.3
Planned occupation								
Manual work	45.5	38.7	39.4	40.0	41.0	2.7	1.4	87.9
Skilled trade	55.7	43.6	45.7	47.1	47.8	6.2	4.0	71.4
Service worker	54.4	41.3	43.3	49.0	49.5	10.6	5.6	67.4
Professional worker	59.6	55.0	53.1	55.2	54.9	50.3	8.9	54.9
Expected full-time income								
Under $15,000	47.4	40.6	39.0	45.1	42.5	2.8	1.4	82.2
$15,000–$19,999	53.3	41.7	46.6	48.8	46.4	6.1	2.4	78.8
$20,000–$29,999	58.5	53.4	50.3	51.3	51.6	13.5	5.7	63.7
$30,000 or more	59.5	54.4	52.6	53.8	53.9	20.4	6.9	58.8
$40,000 or more[a]				54.1	54.1	41.4	9.3	57.5

[a]$40,000 or more bracket was added in 2004

Results by Money Management Education

One of the strongest and most depressing findings from the Jump$tart surveys is that students who take a full-semester high school class in money management or personal finance are no more financially literate than students who have not taken such a course. Table 10.3 shows results from the four surveys (2000–2006) that

Table 10.3 Test results by money management education

	1997 Mean score	2000 Mean score	2002 Mean score	2004 Mean score	2006 Mean score	2006 Proportion of students	2006 % C or better	2006 % Failing
All students	57.3 %	51.9 %	50.2 %	52.3 %	52.4 %	100.0 %	6.9 %	62.0 %
Classes in H.S.[a]								
Entire course, money Mgt/personal finance		51.4	48.2	53.5	51.6	16.7	6.8	62.4
Portion of course, money Mgt/personal finance		52.9	49.8	52.7	53.4	29.3	7.3	59.7
Entire course, economics		51.0	49.8	53.0	53.2	38.1	7.8	59.9
Portion course, economics		52.1	51.1	53.2	53.0	27.4	7.9	60.0
Stock mkt game in class		55.1	52.4	55.8	55.0	27.7	10.0	55.0

[a]Percentages may total more than 100 %, with multiple responses possible

have included a question about courses related to financial literacy that the student may have taken. In three of the surveys, students who took a full-semester course in money management or personal finance actually did slightly *worse* than all students. In 2006, for example, 16.7 % of high school seniors who reported having had an entire course in money management or personal finance scored an average of 51.6 % on the exam in contrast to the average score of 52.4 % achieved by all students.

While the differences are not large enough to support a statistical conclusion that students who have had such a course are less financially literate than those who have not, there is no evidence to show that courses in money management or personal finance, as they are now taught, improve the financial literacy of their students.

It is also interesting to note that those students who had such a course at school were less likely than all students to achieve a C or better and were slightly more likely to have failed the exam.

It should be noted that evaluations of specific high school programs in financial literacy which used pre- and post-tests have found positive impact in both financial knowledge and financial behavior. An evaluation of the National Endowment for Financial Education's High School Financial Planning program, which could be taught in as little as 2 weeks or as long as a semester, found increased in knowledge and savings rates (Danes, 2004; Danes, Huddleston-Casas, & Boyce, 1999). Thus far, however, it has not been possible to test for specific part-semester programs as part of the Jump$tart surveys because of the number of such programs and the inability of students to recall the names of specific vendors.

Impact of State Mandates

In a well-known survey of Merrill-Lynch customers, Bernheim, Garrett, and Maki (2001) found that those who had attended high school in a state which mandated the teaching of personal finance tended in middle age to save a higher proportion of their incomes than others. However, in his analysis of the 1997 Jump$tart survey, Mandell (1998) found that students in states which mandated the teaching of consumer education or personal finance did not show higher mean financial literacy scores than those who lived in states where the mandates did not exist.

In further analysis of the 1997 Jump$tart data, Tennyson and Nguyen (2001) found no association between mandates and test scores when averaged over all forms of mandates. However, they did find that mandates requiring the teaching of a specific course were statistically associated with higher scores. This conforms to the findings of Mandell (2004) from a later Jump$tart survey of teachers, which are explained, in greater detail, immediately below.

Survey of Teachers and Schools

The, by now, well-publicized finding that high school classes in financial management or personal finance are ineffective in raising levels of financial literacy elicited a number of hypotheses to explain this phenomenon. The first hypothesis that students who took such classes were less likely to be academically talented and college-bound was disproved by 2002 data that showed no differences in the proportions of college-bound and non-college-bound students taking such a class.

A second hypothesis was that teachers of financial management or personal finance had little or no training in this field. A third hypothesis was that many students took the course as an elective rather than as a required course and did so because it was structured to be easier than required courses and, consequently, did not teach the material with equivalent rigor.

To address the second and third hypotheses, the 2004 Jump$tart survey added a separate survey of participating schools and received responses from 130 of the 252 schools that administered the Jump$tart survey (Mandell, 2004). While more than half (57.7 %) of schools offered a full-semester course in money management or personal finance, only 10.7 % required all students to take such a class. In addition, the course is not taken primarily by seniors who could presumably gain most from it since they are current or soon-to-be legal adults. In fact, the course was taken primarily by seniors in just 21.6 % of the schools which may account for low levels of recollection by the time they took the Jump$tart test in their senior year.

Teachers who taught full time courses in money management or personal finance tended to be well-educated in the area, professional and experienced. More than 90 % of schools used the same teachers to teach these full-semester courses year after year, and nearly two-thirds of these teachers have a graduate degree in business, consumer economics or related fields and nearly all have at least an undergraduate degree in the appropriate field.

Students who took a *required* course in money management or personal finance did better than all other students (54.2 %) on the financial literacy test. Unfortunately, just 6 % of all U.S. high school students are required to take such a course.

Success of Stock Market Games

One school-based educational program that is consistently related to higher financial literacy scores is playing a stock market game. Since first measured in the 2000 survey, students who play a stock market game in class do 3–4 percentage points better than all students, which translates to a 6–8 % increase in financial literacy. Although the reasons for the lone success of this activity are not clearly known, playing such an interactive game appears to stimulate interest in (at least) the investment-related aspects of personal finance.

What accounts for the failure of full-semester high school classes in money management to raise the financial literacy levels of our students? A number of interesting hypotheses have been advanced to explain this phenomenon. The success of investment games in raising financial literacy scores suggests that courses should be more interactive and fun, focusing on current real-world events. Some have suggested that many, if not most, of the subjects covered in a money management class are not relevant to high school students, and it is hard to hold their interest in subjects such as mortgages, investments and retirement. Still others have postulated that students remember little of what they learn in *any* class, once the final exams are completed, particularly if what they have learned is not reinforced by other classes that build on the subject matter.

Motivation to be Financially Literate

It is possible that courses in money management do not improve financial literacy because students do not realize just how important this material is to their futures. To test this hypothesis, three new questions were added to the 2006 Jump$tart survey to see how young adults felt about three issues:

1. The importance of one's own actions in avoiding financial distress;
2. The degree of discomfort caused by the financial inability to pay one's bills; and
3. The perceived difficulty of retiring without a pension (other than Social Security) or savings.

Greatest Cause of Financial Distress

Slightly more than two-thirds of the students attributed personal financial difficulty to the consumer's personal actions, largely to too much credit (28.9 %) and no financial plan (also 28.9 %). An additional 9.4 % felt that the greatest cause of financial difficulty was not enough savings.

Only 8.6 % of students felt that bad luck was the greatest cause of financial difficulty and those students had average financial literacy scores of 49.1 %. Another 24 % felt that the greatest cause was too little income, and their financial literacy average was 50.6 %. The best financial literacy scores were recorded by students who felt that the greatest cause of financial distress was buying too much on credit (56 %) and those who felt that it was due to the lack of a financial plan (53.8 %).

It appears that most students are aware of the primary causes of financial difficulty and that this knowledge, by itself, does not strongly motivate students to become financially literate.

How Bad Is Insolvency?

A second hypothesis related to motivation is that some young people may not regard financial distress and insolvency as being particularly bad or unusual in today's society. Perhaps everyone they know is also from an overconsuming, credit-dependent family and that they have adjusted to unpaid bills and calls from credit collectors.

Only 8.5 % of students, however, feel that it is not so bad if you cannot pay your bills. They tend to have very low financial literacy scores, averaging just 43.2 %.

Just 42.5 % of students feel that inability to pay bills is very bad, and their financial literacy scores are actually slightly lower than those who feel that it is pretty bad.

The conclusion here is that, aside from a small percentage of students, most feel that it is bad to be financially insolvent and the intensity of negative feelings toward this state is not a major driver of financial literacy.

Motivation to Retire Comfortably

Students were asked how hard it is to live in retirement entirely on Social Security. Once again, most students answered this question reasonably. Only 7.5 % responding that one could live well on Social Security, and their financial literacy scores were extremely low, just 39.9 %.

Half the students felt that it was tough to retire on Social Security alone, and they had the highest scores (56 %). An additional 42.3 % felt that people could get by on Social Security if they were willing to cut back on expenses and their average financial literacy score was 50.4 %.

Further analysis (Mandell & Klein, 2007) found that after controlling on all other variables, such as aspiration, that had a significant impact on financial literacy, the three motivational variables had a significant and positive relationship to financial literacy. This suggests that courses in money management and personal finance keep stressing to students the importance of being financially literate to insure their own futures.

Are Thrift and Financial Literacy Related?

Many financial problems of American consumers relate to low levels of personal saving and/or high levels of debt. Therefore, one desirable outcome of financial literacy would be an enhanced proclivity toward saving or thrift. Since 2004, a question has been added to the survey to enable us to see whether a relationship exists between self-evaluated levels of thrift and financial literacy scores.

Students were asked the following question:

Some people tend to be very thrifty, saving money whenever they have the chance, while others are very spending-oriented, buying whenever they can and even borrowing to consume more. How would you classify yourself?

(a) Very thrifty, saving money whenever I can
(b) Somewhat thrifty, often saving money
(c) Neither thrifty nor spending-oriented
(d) Somewhat spending-oriented, seldom saving money
(e) Very spending-oriented, hardly ever saving money.

In 2006, more than half the students thought of themselves as very or somewhat thrifty while only a quarter felt that they are somewhat or very spending-oriented. Thrift appears to have little or no relationship to financial literacy, however! Those who are very spending-oriented or very thrifty do worse on the test than others with more moderate savings behavior.

Results by Money Management Experience

All five Jump$tart surveys have clearly demonstrated that experience in managing one's finances does little if anything to raise a young person's overall level of financial literacy.

Credit Card Use

In 2006, 31.7% of high school seniors used a credit card. More than half of these students (presumably those over the age of 18) used their own card while about two-thirds used a card in the name of their parents. The overlap is due to the finding that 4.8% used both their own card and the card of their parents.

The 67.7% of students who did *not* use a credit card had an average score of 53.4% in contrast to 50.2% for those who used a credit card. The fact that non-credit card users were more financially literate than those who used credit cards is similar to results found in every survey except for 2000.

ATM Card Use

In 2004, for the first time, students were asked whether they used an ATM card and also whether they used it to make point of sale purchases directly as well as for obtaining cash. In 2006, 47.9% of students used an ATM card, a large increase from 42.4% in the 2004 survey. Nearly two-thirds of the ATM-using students employed the cards for direct purchases at point of sale as well as for obtaining cash.

Students who used an ATM card for both cash and purchases did better on the financial literacy test in both years than did those who used the card only for getting cash or who did not use it at all.

Paying for Car Insurance

The 2006 survey shows that nearly 80% of high school seniors have the use of an automobile and more than 60% of all seniors own their own cars. Of those who owned their own cars, nearly half paid (or helped pay) for their auto insurance. Students who owned their own car and paid for the insurance tended, over the five surveys, to be no more financially literate than those students who owned a car and had the insurance on it paid for by someone else.

Ownership of Financial Assets

Students with bank accounts do tend to be more financially literate than those without such accounts, although this could reflect differences in income. Sixty-four percent of students included in the 2006 survey owned no securities, either in their own name or in the name of their parents. There were few differences in literacy scores that were related to security ownership, whether in their names or in the names of their parents.

Employment History

Students who have also worked in the paid labor force have proven to be more financially literate than those who have not worked. This finding has been consistent in all Jump$tart surveys in which the question of work experience has been asked. This may relate to the finding by Alhabeeb (1999) that teenagers who are employed tend to spend more on consumption categories other than time-consumptive entertainment and transportation and, by inference, be more financially experienced than those teens who are not employed.

Parental Home Ownership

Most students (84.3 %) came from families that owned their own homes. These students had significantly higher scores in financial literacy (53.1 %) than did students whose parents rented their homes (48.5 %). This difference could well be related to the higher socioeconomic status of students from home-owning families.

Financial Literacy by Subject Category

Thus far, we have looked at overall test results by categories relating to various student characteristics and demographics. It is possible, however, that different types of students vary in their performance by subject category. To test this, we divide the questions into four categories of income, money management, savings and investing, and spending and scored the results of each subject. A subset of the spending questions relating to credit was broken out separately as well. In all surveys, students scored best on the income questions and worst in savings and investing.

Students in the highest-income category did better than others in *every* category in 2006, the first time that they had done so. This lends additional credibility to the hypothesis that families of students from higher income, better-educated families are starting to get serious about financial literacy. The difference between whites and African Americans was the largest in the income category, a difference of 13.3 percentage points.

Subject Expertise by Money Management Experience

It is reasonable to expect that money market experience in a particular area affects financial literacy in that area. For example, one might assume that students who use their own credit card would score higher in the credit area than other students. The results, though, show just the opposite, with students who *do not* use a credit card answering credit questions far more accurately than students who use credit cards. This finding has been consistent over time.

On the other hand, students with savings accounts (Savings Only or Savings and Checking) do better on the savings questions than do students without savings account, but they also tend to do better on all categories besides Income. The 2006 survey results tend to continue a trend showing more of a connection between experience and knowledge in related subject areas. The relationship is not yet, however, either strong or consistent.

Experience and Specific Knowledge

While experience in managing one's finances does little, if anything, to raise the overall level of financial literacy, certain types of experience have been shown to increase financial literacy related to that experience. In the 2006 survey, it was found, for example, that students who have never worked for pay are far less likely than those who have worked full- or part-time to know that income tax, Social Security and Medicare are deducted from an employee's paycheck.

In addition, those who own a car and pay for their own insurance are much more likely to know that collision insurance covers damage to a car than those who own a car and do not pay for their own insurance. Similarly, those who owned a car were more likely than other drivers to know that a car generally serves as collateral for a loan used to finance its purchase.

Along the same lines, students who own stocks or mutual funds, either in their own name or in their parents' name, are much more likely to know that an investment in stocks over an 18-year holding period is likely to earn a higher return than savings bonds, savings accounts or checking accounts. However, those who own stocks or mutual funds in their own names were slightly less likely to know this than those who own them in their parents' name casting doubt on the teaching value of owning stocks in one's own name (unaccompanied by other types of teaching).

Those whose folks are homeowners are more likely than the children of renters to know that money invested in the downpayment in a home is illiquid and may be difficult to access in the event of an emergency, but this difference may reflect the greater income of homeowners. Children of homeowners were also much more likely to know that a house financed with a fixed-rate mortgage is a good protection for sudden inflation.

Those who had a bank account were more likely to know that interest on savings accounts was taxable, but checking account holders (who presumably earned no interest on their accounts) was much more likely to know this than savings account holders. Those who used an ATM card were more likely than non-users to know that you cannot take money from *every* ATM without a fee.

Most surprising was the finding that students who did *not* have a credit card were more likely than credit card holders to know the consequences of paying only the minimum amount on credit card monthly statements. They were also more likely, than credit card users, to know that credit card companies often start young people with small credit lines to reduce their own risk of lending the money. Furthermore, the non-credit card users were more likely than users to know that banks share the credit history of borrowers with each other through credit reporting services and also to know that consumers can now check their credit records for free once a year. Finally, non-card users were also more likely to know what credit counseling services could and could not do for overextended borrowers. It should be noted, however, that among credit card users, those who held the card in their own name tended to be more knowledgeable about credit cards than those who used cards in the name of their parents. In some questions, they were more knowledgeable than students who did not use credit cards.

Just-in-Time Education

Given the lapse in time between a high school course in money management or personal finance and the bulk of financial decisions that must be made by young adults, it has been suggested that these courses focus exclusively on decisions that high school students are making currently or are likely to make in the near future. To see whether this is likely to be effective, 11 of the 31 Jump$tart questions which related to actual financial products used by some high school students (credit cards, bank accounts, auto insurance, etc.) were cross-tabulated by actual use of such products and by whether students had taken a high school course in money management or personal finance. Results showed that students who had taken such a course and who had actually purchased a financial product were no more knowledgeable about the financial product they had just purchased than those students who had not had a formal course of this type. This finding provides little support for a just-in-time focus that would concentrate on imminent financial decisions (Mandell, 2006c).

This does not imply that just-in-time education is not useful for adults who are about to make an important financial decision, particularly education delivered at the point of sale or that obtained by highly motivated consumers. It does however offer little support for changing the focus of courses offered at the high school level to become more relevant. The positive results experienced by students who play a real-time stock market game (with synthetic money) would point us more in the direction of high levels of interaction (and perhaps fun) than in immediate relevancy.

Parents and Allowances

Many parents are justifiably concerned that school-based education is doing little to prepare their children to handle finances efficiently. Attempts to teach by experience, such as giving children credit cards and stocks and mutual funds in their own name, have proven to be unsuccessful in promoting financial literacy, as previously mentioned. Two additional attempts at intergenerational transfer of financial prowess include the use of an allowance and the frank discussion of family finances.

Proponents of a regular allowance point to the budgetary skills generated by regular, but periodic infusions of income which necessarily engender disciplined spending to make the allowance last until it is received again. In the 2004 survey, however, it was found that students who received a regular allowance (that did not require the completion of chores to earn it) had a financial literacy score of just 50 % in contrast to those who received a regular allowance in return for chores (53.2 %) and even those who did not receive a regular allowance, receiving money only when they needed it (52.4 %). This was not the first such finding that giving an allowance to a child is not useful in improving a child's financial literacy. Nearly 50 years ago, it was found that the practice of giving an allowance does not deserve its present prominence in recommendations for money education (Marshall, 1960).

In addition, the 2000 survey found that students whose parents often discussed money matters with them did not score significantly better (52.6 %) than students whose parents sometimes (52.5 %) or rarely (52.4 %) discuss money matters with them (Mandell, 2001).

Financial Literacy and Financial Behavior

Improving financial literacy is merely an intermediate step in the overall societal goal of improving financial behavior. If financially literacy does not translate into useful and efficient financial decision making, little has been gained. The positive relationship between financial literacy and financial behavior has been shown among adults (Hilgert et al. , 2003).

In the 2006 Jump$tart survey, students who had checking accounts were asked whether they had ever bounced a check. Those who never bounced a check had financial literacy scores above 53 % while those who had bounced at least one check had financial literacy scores in the mid-40s, showing a positive association between financial literacy and beneficial financial behavior.

Financial Education and Financial Behavior

A separate study carried out by this author in 2005 followed a matched sample of students who graduated from a school system that taught a highly regarded course in personal financial management. Half the students took this course while the other half did not. Since the students came from the same environment and educational system, it provided an opportunity to examine the separable impact of the personal financial management course on subsequent financial behavior.

The study tracked students for 1–5 years after they graduated from high school, giving the subjects a mean age in the early twenties. The average personal financial literacy score, among all respondents, on the Jump$tart questions was 69.3 %. This was quite high by comparison to the national Jump$tart results of 52.3 % in 2004. However, there was virtually no difference between those who had taken the course who averaged 68.7 % and those who did not who averaged 69.9 %.

Students who had taken the course in personal financial management were not subsequently more savings-oriented than those who had not taken such a course. Nor did taking the course appear to have a consistent relationship to actual financial behavior. Those who had the course did do better in making credit card payments on time, balancing their checkbooks frequently and never worrying about debt. Those who did not have the course did better in paying off credit card balances, not bouncing checks, preparing their own taxes and having adequate savings and investments.

A regression analysis showed that neither having had the course nor having been out of high school longer had any significant effect on financial behavior. However, being a full-time college student or graduate had a positive and very significant impact on favorable financial behavior reinforcing the Jump$tart findings that aspiration seems to be the most important factor driving personal financial literacy (Mandell, 2006b).

Who Is Financially Literate?

Employing 2006 Jump$tart data, Mandell (2007a) analyzed those high school seniors who are financially literate. Using a cutoff score of 75 %, he found that the 6.9 % of the students who are, by this classification, financially literate are disproportionately white, male and the children of well-educated parents, all variables that are hard to change.

Summary and Future Research Directions

Virtually all studies of students completing high school conclude that our young adults are poorly prepared to make financial decisions in their own best interests. There is also agreement that financial literacy appears to be positively related to the possession of present and likely future financial resources, in that the most literate tend to be white, college-bound and the children of educated parents. Since financial well-being is a product of financial resources and the ability to utilize those resources most effectively, the inequality of financial well-being is probably greater than that of both income and wealth and represents a huge social problem.

The Jump$tart surveys, which track financial literacy over time, have found little improvement since 1997. There have been no comparable studies to contradict this finding. It is possible, however, that financial literacy measures something else, such as intelligence or academic ability, and it would be useful to measure these variables through reported SAT scores and grade point averages in order to isolate financial literacy from academic ability or accomplishment.

There is some disagreement on the impact of high school classes in consumer finances or personal money management on financial literacy. The Jump$tart surveys have consistently found no relationship between such full-semester classes and financial literacy. However, there is some (non-Jump$tart) evidence that programs that require less than a full semester may have a positive impact on both financial literacy and financial behavior. Research is needed to reconcile these findings.

Since only a small proportion of students taking a full-semester class in consumer finances or personal money management are seniors, it would be useful on future Jump$tart surveys to ask students who had taken such a class when they had taken it. It is possible that younger students find these materials to be less relevant to their lives and, consequently, less memorable.

Most evidence shows that higher financial literacy scores are associated with improved financial behavior. Therefore, if classes designed to improve financial literacy are ineffective, it would follow that they would be similarly ineffective in improving financial behavior. However, Bernheim's (2001) findings suggest that education may have a long-term effect on savings behavior that may not be noticeable in the short run, perhaps because students who are still in high school have little discretionary income to channel to savings. These findings are not inconsistent with those of Currie and Thomas (1995) who find positive long-term effects of the Head Start program which may not be apparent for nearly 20 years.

Similarly, there is mixed evidence concerning the effectiveness of educational mandates in this area. There seems to be agreement that specific courses, required of all students, will improve financial literacy somewhat. Research that focuses on best practices used by the most successful teachers would be very useful. However, there is no agreement on what should be taught, and the field of consumer education covers a wide range of subjects (see Alexander, 1979; Bannister & Monsma, 1982; Scott, 1990). The ? national standards suggest subjects that should be mastered by students in grades K-12, but widespread adoption of these standards may be some time off.

The positive results achieved by students who have played a stock market game suggest that effective teaching includes a high degree of interactivity as well as relevance and perhaps fun but these promising findings should be pursued.

A number of proposals have been advanced to improve the level of youth financial literacy. Some cite preliminary results (Mandell, 2007b) that show that financial learning among middle school students is most effective among sixth graders to propose that students be exposed to financial education in pre-high school grades. The National Association of State Boards of Education (2006) recommends making financial literacy and investor education a basic feature of education beginning in the first grade. A great deal of research is needed to find out the effectiveness of various methods of teaching younger students and the subjects (such as math) with which it could be best integrated.

Finally, those seeking ways to diminish inequality in the distribution of income, wealth and well-being as well as proponents of an ownership society have proposed substantial government grants to every new-born American to give young people a stake in our economy. Starting at the earliest possible grade, the teaching of personal finances would revolve around this personal investment account, which cannot be drawn down until age 18. The British adopted this policy 3 years ago, so results of utilizing this as a focal point for financial education will not be known for several more years.

References

Alexander, R. J. (1979). *State consumer education policy manual.* Denver, CO: Education Commission of the States.

Alhabeeb, M. J. (1999). Teens' consumption patterns: The impact of employment status and intensity. *Academy of Marketing Studies Journal, 2*(1), 45–54.

Bannister, R., & Monsma, C. (1982). *Classification of concepts in consumer education.* Cincinnati, OH: South-Western Publishing.

Bernheim, B. D., Garrett, D. M., & Maki, D. M. (2001). Education and saving: The long-term effects of high school financial curriculum mandates. *Journal of Public Economics, 80*(3), 435–465.

Braunstein, S., & Welch, C. (2002). Financial literacy: An overview of practice, research and policy. *Federal Reserve Bulletin, 87*(11) (November), 445–457.

Chen, H., & Volpe, R. P. (1998). An analysis of personal financial literacy among college students. *Financial Services Review, 7,* 107–128.

Currie, J., & Thomas, D. (1995). Does head start make a difference? *American Economic Review, 85*(3), 341–364.

Danes, S. M. (2004). Evaluation of the nefe high school financial planning program® 2003–2004. St. Paul, MN: University of Minnesota, Family Social Science Department.

Danes, S. M., Huddleston-Casas, C., & Boyce, L. (1999). Financial planning curriculum for teens: impact evaluation. *Financial Counseling and Planning, 10*(1), 25–37.

Greenspan, A. (2003). The importance of financial and economic literacy. *Social Education, 67*(2), 70–72.

Greenspan, A. (2005). The importance of financial education. *Social Education, 69*(2), 64–66.

Hilgert, M., Hogarth, J., & Beverly, S. (2003). Household financial management: The connection between knowledge and behavior. *Federal Reserve Bulletin, July,* 309–322.

Joo, S., & Grable, J. E. (2000). Improving employee productivity: The role of financial counseling and education. *Journal of Employment Counseling, 37,* 2–15.

Jump$tart Coalition for Personal Financial Literacy. (2007). *National standards in k-12 personal finance education with benchmarks, knowledge statements, and glossary,* Washington, DC: Author.

Lucey, T. A. (2005). Assessing the reliability and validity of the jump$tart survey of financial literacy. *Journal of Family and Economic Issues, 26*(2), 283–294.

Mandell, L. (1998). *Our vulnerable youth: The financial literacy of American 12th graders.* Washington, DC: Jumpstart Coalition.

Mandell, L. (2001). *Improving financial literacy: What schools and parents can and cannot do.* Washington, DC: Jumpstart Coalition.

Mandell, L. (2003). *Financial literacy, a growing problem: Results of the 2002 national Jump$tart survey.* Washington, DC: Jumpstart Coalition.

Mandell, L. (2004). *Financial literacy: Are we improving? Results of the 2004 national Jump$tart survey.* Washington, DC: Jumpstart Coalition.

Mandell, L. (2005, April). Financial literacy: Does it matter? (Working paper). Buffalo, NY: SUNY at Buffalo.

Mandell, L. (2006a). *Financial literacy: Improving education; Results of the 2006 national Jump$tart survey.* Washington, DC: Jumpstart Coalition.

Mandell, L. (2006b, January). The impact of financial literacy education on subsequent financial behavior (Working Paper). Buffalo, NY: SUNY at Buffalo.

Mandell, L. (2006c, January). Does just in time instruction improve financial literacy? *Credit Union Magazine, Savingteen Supplement,* 7–9.

Mandell, L. (2007a). Financial education in high school. In A. Lusardi (Ed.), *Improving the effectiveness of financial education and savings programs: Conference handbooks* (pp. 11–33). Cambridge, MA: NBER and Dartmouth College.

Mandell, L. (2007b, January). Teaching new dogs old tricks. *Savingteen,* 4–5.

Mandell, L., & Klein, L. S. (2007). Motivation and financial literacy. *Financial Services Review, 16*(2), 106–116.

Marshall, H. R., & Magruder, L. (1960). Relations between parent, money, education practices and children's use of money. *Child Development, 31,* 253–284.

Murray, D. (2002). How much do your kids know about credit? *Medical Economics, 77*(16), 58–66.

National Association of State Boards of Education. (2006). *Who owns our children?* Alexandria, VA: Author.

Organization for Economic Co-operation and Development. (2005). *Improving financial literacy: Analysis of issues and policies.* Paris: Author.

Scott, C. H. (1990). *1990 National survey: The status of consumer education in the United States schools, grades k-12.* Madison, NJ: National Coalition for Consumer Education.

Tennyson, S., & Nguyen, C. (2001). State curriculum mandates and student knowledge of personal finance. *The Journal of Consumer Affairs, 35*(2), 241–262.

Volpe, R. P., Chen, H., & Lui, S. (2006). An analysis of the importance of personal finance topics and the level of knowledge possessed by working adults. *Financial Services Review, 15*(1), 81–99.

Chapter 11
Risky Credit Card Behavior of College Students

Angela C. Lyons

Abstract This chapter provides an overview of the credit card practices of college students and identifies specific groups of students who are more likely to be at risk for mismanaging and misusing credit. It specifically highlights findings from one particular study that collected data from a large sample of college students on multiple campuses in the Midwest. In this chapter, educational recommendations are made to financial professionals, who are interested in using this research to develop and provide more effective financial education to college students. Also included is a discussion of emerging research related to college students' finances and directions for future research.

Across college campuses, there has been considerable debate about the heavy debt burdens that students are incurring. Trends in college pricing show that tuition and fee levels have been rising dramatically over the last 20 years (College Board, 2005a). Additional trends show that student aid has not kept pace with rising college costs (College Board, 2005b). With rising costs and financial aid packages falling short of covering these expenses, more and more students are turning to higher cost alternatives to finance their education (College Board, 2005b; Lyons, 2007a; The Education Resources Institute & The Institute for Higher Education Policy, 1998). These alternative forms of borrowing have included private educational loans, home equity loans and lines of credit, and even credit card debt. Private borrowing and home equity financing can be a sound financial decision, especially if interest rates on these loans are competitive with other college financing options. However, only in rare instances is credit card financing a rational option, because of higher interest rates and how quickly the interest compounds.

This chapter focuses on recent concerns that college students are accumulating large amounts of credit card debt at high interest rates, which in turn is placing them at risk for having large, and perhaps unmanageable, debt burdens when they graduate. To date, only a few studies provide empirical evidence to show that

A.C. Lyons
University of Illinois at Urbana-Champaign, 440 Mumford Hall, 1301 West Gregory Drive, Urbana, IL 61801, USA
e-mail: anglyons@uiuc.edu

students may, in fact, be turning to credit card debt to finance their education (e.g., Lyons, 2007a; Nellie Mae, 2005; The Education Resources Institute & The Institute for Higher Education Policy, 1998). For example, recent estimates from Nellie Mae (2005) suggest that 24 % of students may be using credit cards to pay for tuition, and over 70 % may be using them to pay for school supplies and textbooks. Additional research by Lyons (2007a) suggests that almost 50.0 % of students receiving financial assistance may be charging school-related items to their credit cards, because financial aid is not enough to cover their college costs. Yet, these percentages are only estimates. It is difficult to empirically document these claims, especially since they are self-reported and descriptive in nature.

Recent media reports have also suggested that college students are accruing too much credit card debt. Unfortunately, these reports have focused on anecdotal horror stories about students who have incurred excessively large amounts of debt – some of whom have even committed suicide (Norvilitis & Santa, 2002; Oleson, 2001). In response to this "growing problem," there have been a number of efforts made by college administrators and policy makers to limit students' access to credit such as preventing credit card solicitations on college campuses.

With the recent increase in the number of reports regarding college students' misuse or mismanagement of credit, researchers have begun to examine whether students are in fact incurring excessive amounts of credit card debt. In general, research that has examined the credit card usage and financial behaviors of college students has found that the vast majority of students are not accumulating large amounts of credit card debt (e.g., Joo, Grable, & Bagwell, 2003; Lawrence et al., 2003; Lyons, 2004, 2007a; Lyons & Andersen, 2002; Lyons & Hunt, 2003; Nellie Mae, 2005; The Education Resources Institute & The Institute for Higher Education Policy, 1998; United States Government Accountability Office, 2001). This has led some to question whether concerns over credit card usage on college campuses are warranted.

In 2003, the University of Illinois at Urbana-Champaign launched an online survey on 10 Midwest campuses to examine the credit usage and financial practices of college students (Lyons, 2007a). The main objectives of the study were to (1) identify and characterize those students who were most at risk for mismanaging and misusing credit cards; (2) identify some of the hidden consequences of financial mismanagement for students; and (3) provide insight into educational resources and services that could be developed to help students better manage their credit card debt and other finances. To date, this study provides one of the most comprehensive overviews of college students' credit behaviors. Most research in this area has used small convenience samples or data from individual college campuses. This study collected data from over 26,000 students on multiple campuses.

This chapter presents highlights from this research and uses this large data set to identify specific groups of students who are more likely than others to have difficulty managing their credit. The methodology used in this study is similar to that of Lyons (2004). However, traditional models of credit risk behavior are estimated that are able to take into account a large number of factors that Lyons (2004) and other researchers have not been able to control for simultaneously because of sampling and data limitations. The findings from this research provide insight into how financial professionals, educators, and campus administrators can develop and provide more effective financial education to students, especially those who are financially at risk. At the end of this chapter, some educational recommendations are made. Directions for future research are also included.

Literature Review

There is a large and growing body of literature related to the credit usage of college students. This research spans several disciplines including economics, sociology, and psychology. One line of research, in social and economic psychology, focuses on college students' attitudes, perceptions, and behaviors as they relate to spending habits, credit usage, and money in general (Hayhoe, 2002; Hayhoe, Leach, & Allen, 2005; Hayhoe, Leach, & Turner, 1999; Hayhoe, Leach, Turner, Bruin, & Lawrence, 2000; Joo et al., 2003; Kidwell, 2000; Norvilitis et al., 2006; Norvilitis, Szablicki, & Wilson, 2003; Pinto, Parente, & Palmer, 2001; Roberts & Jones, 2001; Xiao, Noring, & Anderson, 1995; Xiao, Shim, Barber, & Lyons, 2007). These studies specifically focus on the affective, cognitive, and behavioral components of students' attitudes about credit and how these attitudes relate to various student characteristics. In general, most of these studies have found that students have favorable attitudes toward consumer credit. Furthermore, those with more favorable attitudes toward credit have more favorable attitudes toward credit card use.

Another line of research has used applied economics to document demographic trends related to college students' ownership and usage of credit cards (e.g., Allen & Jover, 1997; Armstrong & Craven, 1993; Baum & O'Malley, 2003; Jamba-Joyner, Howard-Hamilton, & Mamarchew, 2000; Lawrence et al., 2003; Lyons, 2004, 2007a; Lyons, 2002; Lyons & Hunt, 2003; Mattson, Sahlhoff, Blackstone, Peden, & Nahm, 2004; Nellie Mae, 2005; The Education Resources Institute & The Institute for Higher Education Policy, 1998; United States Government Accountability Office, 2001; Xiao et al., 2007). Specifically, these studies provide numerous descriptive statistics on credit card ownership, how and when credit cards are acquired, number and types of credit cards held, average amounts owed, and purchase and repayment behaviors. In general, these studies have found that the majority of college students appear to be using credit cards responsibly and are not accumulating large amounts of debt. Key findings from these studies suggest that (1) approximately 75–80 % of college students have at least one credit card; (2) the vast majority obtain credit cards prior to college or during their freshman year; (3) over half of those with credit cards repay their balances in full each month; and (4) 15–25 % have balances over $1,000 and about 5–10 % have balances over $3,000.

Overall, the findings from this literature have been fairly consistent. However, the results still need to be interpreted with caution. The samples and methodologies used vary significantly across studies. For example, many of the studies are based on small sample sizes from particular campuses or individual classrooms. While some of these may be randomized samples, it is difficult to generalize the findings to the population of college students as a whole. Also, some of these studies are based on convenience samples from student loan providers or financial institutions. The statistics from these studies are based on samples of students who have taken out student loans or other types of credit and, thus, are more likely to borrow more in general.

Finally, it is important to note that many of these studies are primarily descriptive in nature, with most reporting only mean or median values for the populations sampled. This type of information provides an overview of the "average" state of students' credit card usage. However, it makes it difficult to specifically assess which students are accumulating large credit card balances and which students are having difficulty repaying those balances. Financial knowledge, attitudes, and behaviors are likely to vary across students with different demographic profiles. Thus, different groups of students are likely to have different financial needs. If researchers only focus on conducting analysis at the sample means, they may miss differences that exist for specific demographic groups.

A more recent line of research has used more rigorous analysis to profile students and examine the factors associated with credit card usage and credit risk. Some of these studies identify specific subgroups of students that are more likely to be "financially at risk" than others for misusing and mismanaging credit (e.g., Lyons, 2004, 2007a; Staten & Barron, 2002). These students are at risk of not being able to repay their debts after graduation, because of a lack of either financial experience or funds. For example, Staten and Barron (2002) used a pooled sample of active credit card accounts randomly selected from 15 general-purpose credit card issuers to look at how different marketing programs can affect college students' credit card balances, credit limits, and delinquency status. Lyons (2004, 2007a) used data collected from several college campuses in the Midwest to create a profile of "at-risk" students. She found that college students who were financially at risk for mismanaging and misusing credit were significantly more likely to be financially independent, to receive need-based financial aid, and to hold $1,000 or more in debt other than student loans and credit card debt. These students were also more likely to be female, black, and/or Hispanic. This chapter presents highlights from her recent work and provides direction for future research in this area.

Methodology

Probit models are estimated for four at-risk behaviors: (1) credit card balances of $1,000 or more, (2) delinquent on their credit card payments by 2 months or more, (3) reached the limit on their credit cards, and (4) only paid off their credit card balances some of the time or never (Lyons, 2004, 2007a). These measures of credit risk were constructed based on previous research which has consistently identified the misuse and/or mismanagement of credit by college students according to these four characteristics (e.g., Baum & O'Malley, 2003; Lyons, 2004, 2007a; The Education Resources Institute & The Institute for Higher Education Policy, 1998; United States Government Accountability Office, 2001). Each measure captures a slightly different aspect of financial risk (i.e., the amount of debt that is owed, the ability to make timely payments, future ability to borrow, and the ability to repay debts incurred).

For the first at-risk behavior, the relationship is assumed to be as follows:

$$\text{CCDEBT}_i^* = X_i'\beta_1 + \varepsilon_i \tag{11.1}$$

where $\text{CCDEBT}_i = 1$ iff $\text{CCDEBT}_i^* \geq 1,000$ and 0 otherwise for $i = \{1, \ldots, I\}$. CCDEBT_i is the discrete dependent variable that is equal to one if the ith student holds credit card balances of \$1,000 or more and zero otherwise. CCDEBT_i is determined by the continuous, latent variable CCDEBT_i^*, the actual amount of credit card debt held by the student. However, the total amount of credit card debt held is not observed. The data only consist of categorical information on the amount of credit card debt.

The factors that determine CCDEBT_i^*, and thus CCDEBT_i, are represented by the vector X_i. Included in X_i are factors that account for students' financial characteristics such as whether they receive financial aid, whether they have other types of debt such as a car loan, mortgage, or other private loan, when they obtained their first credit card, how they acquired the credit card they use the most, whether they are financially independent, and their monthly income. The vector X_i also controls for student demographics such as year in school, gender, race/ethnicity, marital status, grade point average, residential status, whether they are a first-generation college student, whether they rent an apartment, whether their parents own their home, and the population of their home town. Information on their level of financial knowledge and the likelihood that their financial situation will affect their ability to complete their college degree is also included. While previous studies have been able to include various combinations of these factors, this model is able to include a comprehensive set of variables given the richness of the data set.

Since the dependent variable is discrete choice, the probit method is used to estimate this model and obtain consistent estimates of the regressors. The error terms, ε_i, are assumed to be distributed standard normally with mean zero and variance σ_i equal to one. The probit method is also used to estimate the other three models and identify the factors that determine the probability that a student is (1) delinquent on their credit card payments by 2 months or more, (2) reaches the limit on their credit cards, and (3) only pays off their credit card balances some of the time or never. In all three cases, the likelihood function is estimated and consistent estimates of the regressors are obtained. Note that some of the regressors may be endogenous and dependent on other factors included in the model. Due to data limitations, it is not feasible to construct instruments to control for the possibility of endogeneity. Therefore, it is assumed that these values have been exogenously determined.

Data

An online survey was launched on 10 Midwest campuses in the spring of 2003 to examine the credit usage and financial practices of college students (Lyons, 2007a). The survey had a total of 52 questions and was divided into three sections: *current credit card usage and knowledge, financial education,* and *some information about you.* To comply with human subject guidelines on each campus, a special permission form explaining the intent of the survey was developed. Also, approval was obtained from campus administrators to send e-mails to all undergraduate students on each campus who had a registered e-mail account. The survey was posted on a secure server for a period of 30 days. A total of three mass e-mails were sent out to the students. The initial e-mail invited students to participate in the study and the other two e-mails were sent as reminders. Students who completed the survey were given the option to participate in a prize drawing. Winners were randomly selected from a pool of students who chose to submit their e-mail address to participate in the drawing. Because of the sensitive nature of some of the survey questions, extra precautions were taken to insure that no personal information was connected with students' names or e-mail addresses.

Approximately 168,000 undergraduate students from 10 Midwest campuses were invited to participate in the study. A total of 29,474 students responded to the survey, resulting in a response rate of approximately 17.6 %. However, 2,715 student observations (9.2 % of the sample) had to be dropped, primarily due to missing information. A few observations were also removed because students had either submitted their survey information multiple times or submitted blank surveys. In the end, the working sample for this study comprised 26,759 valid responses. Note that the response rate for this study is consistent with similar studies that have used online surveys to investigate the financial behaviors of college students. Response rates for other studies have typically ranged from 10 to 20 %, with most falling between 10 and 12 %. See Lyons (2007a) for more complete details on the sampling methods, survey design, and response rates. For more general information on conducting effective online surveys, see Lyons, Cude, Lawrence, and Gutter (2005).

Tables 11.1 and 11.2 provide an overview of the demographic and financial characteristics of the entire sample and of specific subgroups of students who were more likely to be at financial risk than others for misusing and/or mismanaging credit. For each table, the first set of columns presents the findings for the entire sample. The next three columns present the results for students with credit cards, students with credit cards and *no* at-risk characteristics, and students with credit cards and *at least one* at-risk characteristic. The remaining columns present information according to the four at-risk characteristics: credit card debt $\geq$ \$1, 000, delinquent on credit card payments, reached the limit on their credit cards, and only paid off credit card balances some of the time or never. Note that students who were classified as financially at risk may have had one or more of these characteristics.

Of the 26,759 students who comprised the working sample, 72.4 % reported having at least one credit card. Of these, 42.9 % indicated that they engaged in at least one of the four at-risk behaviors. About 42.1 % of at-risk students reported engaging in only one at-risk behavior (with the majority not paying off their balances in full each month), and 28.5 % reported engaging in two at-risk behaviors (primarily holding balances over \$1,000 and not paying off balances in full each month). Almost 19.9 % of at-risk students had three of the four at-risk characteristics, and only 9.5 % reported having all four characteristics.

Table 11.1 Demographic profile of college students by credit card usage and degree of financial risk

Variable (mean/percentage)	All students (N = 26,759)	Students with credit card (N = 19,375)	Not-at-risk with credit card (N = 11,062)	At-risk with credit card (N = 8,313)	Groups of at-risk students			
					Credit card debt≥ $1,000 (N = 4,217)	Delinquent on payments (N = 1,659)	Reached limit (N = 4,074)	Did not pay balance in full (N = 6,415)
Demographics								
Freshmen	23.6	17.3	21.9	11.1	3.6	6.8	11.4	9.5
Sophomore	22.0	20.5	23.4	16.5	10.9	13.4	17.6	15.0
Junior	25.0	27.3	25.9	29.3	30.7	30.6	29.6	29.6
Senior	29.4	34.9	28.8	43.1	54.7	49.3	41.5	45.9
Female	58.8	58.9	58.4	59.5	59.2	63.8	59.3	62.2
White	79.3	79.0	83.6	73.0	72.0	60.4	70.3	73.5
Black	4.8	4.4	1.3	8.4	9.8	17.6	10.0	9.9
Asian	9.0	9.8	10.2	9.2	8.0	9.8	9.8	7.3
Hispanic	4.1	4.0	2.5	6.1	6.7	8.0	6.1	6.3
Other race	2.8	2.8	2.5	3.3	3.6	4.2	3.8	3.1
Married	3.8	4.6	2.2	7.8	11.8	7.8	7.5	8.0
GPA (3.6–4.0)	28.5	28.4	33.9	21.1	20.2	13.7	19.4	18.8
GPA (3.0–3.5)	42.7	43.5	44.6	42.1	40.9	35.7	40.4	40.9
GPA (2.0–2.9)	27.3	26.9	20.6	35.2	37.6	48.0	38.1	38.5
GPA (< 2.0)	1.6	1.2	0.9	1.6	1.4	2.7	2.0	1.8
In-state resident	86.4	85.8	84.6	87.5	90.0	89.8	86.9	89.9
Out-of-state resident	10.9	11.3	13.0	9.2	7.5	7.1	9.2	7.9
International student	2.6	2.8	2.4	3.3	2.4	3.1	3.9	2.1

Table 11.1 (continued)

Variable (mean/percentage)	All students (N = 26,759)	Students with credit card (N = 19,375)	Not-at-risk with credit card (N = 11,062)	At-risk with credit card (N = 8,313)	Groups of at-risk students			
					Credit card debt ≥ $1,000 (N = 4,217)	Delinquent on payments (N = 1,659)	Reached limit (N = 4,074)	Did not pay balance in full (N = 6,415)
First-generation college student	22.9	23.3	20.0	27.7	31.4	32.6	28.4	29.1
Rents an apartment	44.4	49.8	45.5	55.6	62.5	60.2	55.9	57.3
Parents own home	89.0	89.4	92.7	85.1	83.5	78.2	83.8	84.1
Monthly income								
Income ($1–$249)	19.5	18.9	20.5	16.9	14.3	17.5	16.8	17.2
Income ($250–$499)	20.9	21.8	20.7	23.4	23.8	24.8	23.7	24.4
Income ($500–$749)	8.6	9.7	7.5	12.7	15.2	12.2	13.0	13.7
Income ($750–$999)	3.7	4.4	3.0	6.3	8.2	6.3	6.4	6.7
Income (≥ $1,000)	4.9	6.0	3.1	9.8	14.5	9.5	9.9	9.9
Regional information								
Rural area (pop under 2,500)	12.3	11.9	12.2	11.4	11.3	9.9	10.9	11.5
Town/city (pop 2,500–19,999)	30.5	30.3	30.6	29.9	30.2	28.8	29.2	30.2
City (pop 20,000–99,999)	35.0	35.5	37.1	33.2	32.3	30.4	33.8	33.5
City (pop 100,000 or more)	21.9	22.1	19.8	25.2	25.9	30.6	25.8	24.6
Personal finance course	27.2	27.9	29.6	25.8	25.2	22.9	24.5	25.0
Likelihood financial situation will affect completion of college degree…								
Likely	12.3	11.8	8.6	16.0	17.2	23.4	18.7	16.8
Somewhat likely	18.1	16.9	14.2	20.4	21.2	25.0	21.8	21.4
Not likely	69.5	71.3	77.1	63.5	61.4	51.5	59.4	61.7

"Students with credit card" represents students holding at least one credit card; "Not-at-risk with credit card" identifies students with a credit card but no at-risk behaviors; "At-risk with credit card" identifies students with a credit card and at least one at-risk behavior. The remaining columns classify students by specific at-risk behaviors and are conditional on holding a credit card. Note that the percentages may not sum to 100 due to rounding.

Table 11.2 Financial characteristics of college students by credit card usage and degree of financial risk

Variable (mean/percentage)	All students (N = 26,759)	Students with credit card (N = 19,375)	Not-at-risk with credit card (N = 11,062)	At-risk with credit card (N = 8,313)	Groups of at-risk students			
					Credit card debt≥ $1,000 (N = 4,217)	Delinquent on payments (N = 1,659)	Reached limit (N = 4,074)	Did not pay balance in full (N = 6,415)
Have a credit card(s)	72.4	100.0	100.0	100.0	100.0	100.0	100.0	100.0
Credit card usage								
4 or more credit cards	19.0	26.0	18.7	35.7	51.9	36.0	36.7	37.8
Credit card debt≥ $1,000	15.8	21.8	0.0	50.7	100.0	58.3	52.9	56.0
Credit card debt≥ $3,000	7.5	10.4	0.0	24.1	47.6	33.8	30.0	28.7
Delinquent on payments	6.2	8.6	0.0	20.0	22.9	100.0	28.5	21.4
Reached limit on credit cards	15.2	21.0	0.0	49.0	51.2	69.9	100.0	44.1
Did not pay balance in full	24.0	33.1	0.0	77.2	85.2	82.8	69.5	100.0
Credit card(s) obtained								
Before beginning college	36.4	49.6	53.9	43.8	41.8	35.4	43.4	40.9
First year of college	26.4	36.0	32.3	40.8	44.2	50.2	42.4	42.9
After first year of college	10.5	14.3	13.7	15.3	13.9	14.4	14.0	16.1
Credit card(s) acquired								
Through a mail application	25.1	34.4	30.4	39.9	47.0	39.5	39.8	40.9
At a bank/financial institution	20.8	28.3	32.6	22.6	16.7	18.3	22.9	21.0
From parents	10.7	14.6	19.1	8.7	3.5	3.9	7.0	7.7
Online	5.5	7.5	6.8	8.5	8.6	6.8	8.9	8.3
At a campus table	4.6	6.3	3.6	9.8	13.3	20.0	11.8	11.2
At a retail store	2.8	3.8	3.1	4.8	4.1	5.8	4.6	5.2
Over the phone	2.6	3.5	2.9	4.3	5.1	4.6	4.0	4.3
Other	1.0	1.4	1.4	1.3	1.7	1.1	0.9	1.3

Table 11.2 (continued)

Variable (mean/percentage)	All students (N = 26,759)	Students with credit card (N = 19,375)	Not-at-risk with credit card (N = 11,062)	At-risk with credit card (N = 8,313)	Groups of at-risk students			
					Credit card debt≥ $1,000 (N = 4,217)	Delinquent on payments (N = 1,659)	Reached limit (N = 4,074)	Did not pay balance in full (N = 6,415)
Financially independent	19.5	22.0	13.4	33.4	44.5	41.9	36.1	34.9
Financial assistance								
Receives financial aid	71.7	70.4	65.3	77.2	80.5	81.3	76.7	81.3
Federal student loans	48.2	48.8	38.4	62.7	68.7	70.2	63.4	69.1
Federal parent loans	10.1	10.0	8.3	12.3	12.6	11.9	11.9	13.7
Alternative or private loans	6.2	6.4	4.7	8.7	9.8	10.2	9.8	9.3
Federal work-study	11.6	11.2	8.9	14.3	15.6	19.7	14.8	15.6
Need-based grants	25.1	25.3	17.9	35.1	40.1	46.8	36.9	38.3
Scholarships	38.3	36.3	41.4	29.5	27.8	25.4	28.6	27.8
Tuition waiver	5.5	5.6	5.4	6.0	6.9	5.2	6.0	6.3
Financial aid≥ $10,000	18.1	20.0	12.4	30.1	38.3	37.6	32.8	33.8
Other debt								
Owes other debt	28.9	28.6	18.5	42.1	49.5	54.5	46.8	45.5
Car loan	11.3	13.1	7.7	20.3	27.9	20.3	20.9	22.4
Mortgage	2.3	2.8	1.4	4.7	7.1	4.0	4.2	4.9
Informal loan (family/friends)	8.2	7.7	6.0	9.9	10.6	14.7	12.1	10.2
Private loan from bank	3.2	3.5	1.7	5.9	8.0	7.9	7.0	6.5
Installment loan	1.9	2.2	0.6	4.3	6.6	5.1	5.1	4.8
Owes other debt≥ $1,000	16.0	16.9	10.0	26.1	34.8	31.3	29.2	28.4

"Students with credit card" represents students holding at least one credit card; "Not-at-risk with credit card" identifies students with a credit card but no at-risk behaviors; "At-risk with credit card" identifies students with a credit card and at least one at-risk behavior. The remaining columns classify students by Specific at-risk behaviors and are conditional on holding a credit card. Note that the percentages may not sum to 100 due to rounding.

Demographic Characteristics

Table 11.1 provides general demographic information. The first column reports the findings for the entire sample. With respect to year in school, 23.6 % of the students were freshmen, 22.0 % were sophomores, 25.0 % were juniors, and 29.4 % were seniors. In terms of gender and race/ethnicity, 58.8 % of the students were female, and 79.3 % were white, 4.8 % were black, 9.0 % were Asian, and 4.1 % were Hispanic. Only 3.8 % reported being married. With respect to academic performance, 71.2 % reported having a grade point average above 3.0. Further discussion of the sample can be found in Lyons (2007a).

The remaining columns in Table 11.1 focus on the demographics of students according to their financial risk status. Several findings are worth noting. First, students with credit cards who exhibited at-risk behaviors were more likely than students with credit cards who did not exhibit at-risk behaviors to be juniors or seniors, black or Hispanic, married, to have lower grade point averages, and/or to rent an apartment. In addition, they were more likely than other students to be the first person in their immediate family to attend college, to be financially independent from their parents, and to have higher monthly earnings. At-risk students also were more likely to report that their financial situation was "likely" or "somewhat likely" to affect their ability to complete their college degree. Finally, there is evidence to suggest that students who had taken a personal finance course in high school or college were somewhat less likely to be financially at risk.

Financial Characteristics

Table 11.2 presents the financial characteristics. Recall that 72.4 % of the total sample indicated that they held at least one credit card. The first column of Table 11.2 shows that 19.0 % also had four or more credit cards, 15.8 % reported that they owed $1,000 or more in credit card debt, and 7.5 % owed $3,000 or more. The majority of students (76.0 %) reported that they paid off their balances in full each month. However, 6.2 % were delinquent on their credit card payments by 2 months or more, and 15.2 % had reached the borrowing limit on their cards and were "maxed out." Students were also asked when they had acquired their first credit card and how they acquired the card they used the most. This information also is summarized in Table 11.2.

In comparing the entire sample to those with credit cards, Table 11.2 shows that financially at-risk students were more likely to hold four or more credit cards and owe more than $3,000 in credit card debt. At-risk students were also more likely to be delinquent on their payments and to have reached the borrowing limit on their cards. They were less likely to be paying off their balances in full each month. These findings should not be surprising since many of these characteristics were used to identify those who were financially at risk. Also, note that financially at-risk students were more likely to have acquired their cards through a mail application or at a campus table. They were less likely to have acquired their cards from their parents.

Financial risk also appears to be related to financial independence, whether a student is receiving financial aid, and other types of borrowing. Almost 20 % of students reported being financially independent from their parents (e.g., their parents were unable to claim them on their tax return). In addition, 71.7 % of students were receiving some type of financial aid to fund their college education, where financial aid included federal student loans, federal parent loans, alternative or private loans, federal work-study, need-based grants, scholarships, and/or tuition waivers. Approximately 18 % of students had financial aid loans that totaled $10,000 or more. Financially at-risk students were more likely than those not at risk to be receiving need-based financial aid in the form of federal loans, federal work-study, and/or need-based grants.

Some students also had other types of debt including car loans, mortgages, installment loans, informal loans from family/friends, and/or private loans from a financial institution. In general, 28.9 % of students indicated that they owed some type of other debt, with 16.0 % owing $10,000 or more in other debt. Not surprisingly, financially at-risk students were more likely to owe some type of other debt and to owe $10,000 or more in other debt.

Overall, this initial investigation of the data provides insight into which college students may be at greater financial risk than others for misusing and/or mismanaging consumer credit. The next step is to see if the regression results support the descriptive statistics.

Results

Probit models were estimated for the four at-risk behaviors. The results are presented in Table 11.3. Some researchers may be concerned that, among those who were not at risk, statistical differences may exist between those without credit cards and those with credit cards. For this reason, the models were estimated for only those students who reported having a credit card. Marginal effects were estimated at the sample means.

Probability of Having Credit Card Balances ≥ $1,000

Table 11.3 shows that students who received more in financial aid, owed more in other debt, and were financially independent from their parents were significantly more likely to hold $1,000 or more in credit card debt. Specifically, having $10,000 or more in financial aid increased a student's probability of owing $1,000 or more in credit card debt by 11.0 percentage points, while holding some type of other debt greater than or equal to $1,000 increased a student's probability by 9.9 percentage

Table 11.3 Probability college students are financially at risk (students with credit cards)

Variable	Credit card debt≥ $1,000		Delinquent on payments	
	Marginal effects	Standard errors	Marginal effects	Standard errors
Financial aid≥ $10,000	0.1102	(0.0080)***	0.0254	(0.0043)***
Other debt≥ $1,000	0.0986	(0.0087)***	0.0253	(0.0048)***
Financially independent	0.0765	(0.0082)***	0.0239	(0.0046)***
Obtained card before college	0.0829	(0.0083)***	0.0092	(0.0047)*
Obtained card first year in college	0.0854	(0.0091)***	0.0196	(0.0050)***
Acquired card in mail	0.1640	(0.0131)***	0.0467	(0.0080)***
Acquired card at bank	0.0379	(0.0126)***	0.0266	(0.0080)***
Acquired card at online	0.1680	(0.0203)***	0.0423	(0.0123)***
Acquired card at campus table	0.2643	(0.0225)***	0.1450	(0.0186)***
Acquired card at retail store	0.1112	(0.0235)***	0.0735	(0.0171)***
Acquired card at phone	0.2495	(0.0271)***	0.0676	(0.0170)***
Acquired card other	0.1507	(0.0352)***	0.0308	(0.0211)*
Freshman	−0.1532	(0.0057)***	−0.0412	(0.0038)***
Sophomore	−0.1071	(0.0059)***	−0.0279	(0.0037)***
Junior	−0.0413	(0.0059)***	−0.0108	(0.0034)***
Female	0.0218	(0.0056)***	0.0145	(0.0031)***
Black	0.1425	(0.0183)***	0.1110	(0.0130)***
Asian	0.0099	(0.0113)	0.0192	(0.0074)***
Hispanic	0.0890	(0.0168)***	0.0432	(0.0102)***
Married	0.0861	(0.0166)***	−0.0039	(0.0064)
GPA (3.0–3.5)	0.0459	(0.0072)***	0.0264	(0.0046)***
GPA (2.0–2.9)	0.1341	(0.0095)***	0.0847	(0.0070)***
GPA (<2.0)	0.2214	(0.0403)***	0.1958	(0.0330)***
Out-of-state resident	−0.0183	(0.0093)*	−0.0085	(0.0052)
International student	0.0288	(0.0214)	0.0016	(0.0103)
First-generation college student	0.0236	(0.0066)***	0.0054	(0.0036)
Rents an apartment	0.0317	(0.0064)***	0.0123	(0.0035)***
Parents own home	−0.0356	(0.0096)***	−0.0240	(0.0056)***
Income/month ($1–$249)	−0.0031	(0.0080)	−0.0038	(0.0043)
Income/month ($250–$499)	0.0365	(0.0081)***	0.0008	(0.0042)
Income/month ($500–$749)	0.0896	(0.0118)***	−0.0019	(0.0054)
Income/month ($750–$999)	0.0938	(0.0168)***	−0.0084	(0.0064)
Income/month (≥ $1,000)	0.1582	(0.0170)***	0.0010	(0.0068)
Town/city (pop 2,500–20,000)	−0.0431	(0.0085)***	−0.0173	(0.0046)***
City (pop 20,000–99,999)	−0.0165	(0.0075)**	−0.0120	(0.0039)***
City (pop 100,000 or more)	−0.0196	(0.0072)***	−0.0142	(0.0039)***
Personal finance course	−0.0161	(0.0060)***	−0.0102	(0.0033)***
Finances likely to affect degree	0.0387	(0.0095)***	0.0414	(0.0062)***
Finances somewhat likely to affect degree	0.0440	(0.0082)***	0.0325	(0.0052)***
Observations		19,477		19,477
R^2		0.2607		0.1944
Financial aid≥ $10,000	0.0950	(0.0082)***	0.1763	(0.0099)***
Other debt≥ $1,000	0.0958	(0.0091)***	0.1352	(0.0109)***
Financially independent	0.0626	(0.0084)***	0.0595	(0.0103)***

Table 11.3 (continued)

	Reached limit on credit cards		Did not pay balances in full	
	Marginal effects	Standard errors	Marginal effects	Standard errors
Obtained card before college	0.0362	(0.0089)***	0.0063	(0.0110)
Obtained card first year in college	0.0418	(0.0093)***	0.0507	(0.0113)***
Acquired card in mail	0.0889	(0.0114)***	0.0844	(0.0128)***
Acquired card at bank	0.0429	(0.0114)***	−0.0077	(0.0128)
Acquired card at online	0.1150	(0.0173)***	0.0887	(0.0183)***
Acquired card at campus table	0.1676	(0.0191)***	0.1796	(0.0205)***
Acquired card at retail store	0.0824	(0.0204)***	0.0954	(0.0230)***
Acquired card at phone	0.0904	(0.0216)***	0.1002	(0.0235)***
Acquired card other	−0.0194	(0.0267)	0.0021	(0.0321)
Freshman	−0.0191	(0.0105)*	−0.1137	(0.0118)***
Sophomore	−0.0020	(0.0089)	−0.0915	(0.0100)***
Junior	0.0055	(0.0074)	−0.0340	(0.0089)***
Female	0.0135	(0.0060)**	0.0610	(0.0074)***
Black	0.1587	(0.0179)***	0.3005	(0.0212)***
Asian	0.0180	(0.0118)	−0.0223	(0.0141)
Hispanic	0.0673	(0.0166)***	0.1420	(0.0203)***
Married	−0.0019	(0.0139)	0.0499	(0.0198)**
GPA (3.0–3.5)	0.0486	(0.0076)***	0.1008	(0.0092)***
GPA (2.0–2.9)	0.1300	(0.0095)***	0.2422	(0.0109)***
GPA (<2.0)	0.2386	(0.0350)***	0.3577	(0.0334)***
Out-of-state resident	−0.0042	(0.0101)	−0.0377	(0.0121)***
International student	0.1009	(0.0239)***	−0.0155	(0.0251)
First-generation college student	0.0010	(0.0068)	0.0170	(0.0086)**
Rents an apartment	0.0226	(0.0068)***	0.0450	(0.0085)***
Parents own home	−0.0370	(0.0098)***	−0.0691	(0.0127)***
Income/month ($1–$249)	0.0049	(0.0085)	0.0161	(0.0104)
Income/month ($250–$499)	0.0316	(0.0084)***	0.0638	(0.0103)***
Income/month ($500–$749)	0.0648	(0.0119)***	0.1281	(0.0142)***
Income/month ($750–$999)	0.0473	(0.0158)***	0.1077	(0.0199)***
Income/month (≥ $1,000)	0.0657	(0.0151)***	0.1238	(0.0184)***
Town/city (pop 2,500–20,000)	−0.0334	(0.0098)***	−0.0659	(0.0123)***
City (pop 20,000–99,999)	−0.0167	(0.0080)**	−0.0280	(0.0102)***
City (pop 100,000 or more)	−0.0064	(0.0079)	−0.0232	(0.0099)**
Personal finance course	−0.0248	(0.0063)***	−0.0433	(0.0078)***
Finances likely to affect degree	0.0655	(0.0100)***	0.0699	(0.0124)***
Finances somewhat likely to affect degree	0.0463	(0.0084)***	0.0739	(0.0104)***
Observations		19,477		19,477
R^2		0.1167		0.2006

Standard errors for the marginal effects are indicated by (·). Omitted categories include: obtained credit card after first year of college, acquired card from parents, senior, white, in-state resident, not working, rural area (pop<2,500), GPA (3.6–4.0), and finances not likely to affect degree. Ten campus dummies were also included in the models to control for individual campus effects.
*$p < 0.10$; **$p < 0.05$; ***$p < 0.01$

points. Being financially independent increased the probability by 7.7 percentage points.

Students who acquired their first credit card before college or during their first year at college were significantly more likely to be at risk than those who acquired it after their first year of college. Also, students who acquired the credit card they used the most from a source other than their parents were significantly more likely to have credit card balances of $1,000 or more. Those who acquired their credit card at a campus table or over the phone were most at risk. In particular, students who acquired their credit card at a campus table were 26.4 percentage points more likely to be at risk than those who acquired their card from their parents. Those who acquired a card over the phone were 25.0 percentage points more likely.

Other factors that significantly increased a student's probability of holding $1,000 or more in credit card debt included being a senior, female, black, Hispanic, married, renting an apartment, and being a first-generation college student. Those with lower grade point averages and higher earnings per month were also more likely to be at risk, as were those from hometowns that were located in rural areas with populations of less than 2,500. Of these, the factors that had the largest effects on credit card balances were being black, Hispanic, having a grade point average below 2.9, and a monthly income above $1,000. Specifically, black and Hispanic students were 14.3 and 8.9 percentage points more likely than whites to have credit card balances over $1,000, respectively. Those with grade point averages between 2.0 and 2.9 were 13.4 percentage points more likely than those with grade point averages above 3.5 to have credit card balances over $1,000, while those with grade point averages below 2.0 were 22.1 percentage points more likely. Being an out-of-state resident and having parents who owned their home significantly decreased the probability of having large credit card balances.

With respect to financial education, students who had taken a personal finance course were significantly less likely to be at risk for accumulating large credit card balances, but only by 1.6 percentage points. Not surprisingly, those who believed that their financial situation was likely to affect their ability to complete their college degree were more likely to be at risk.

Probability of Being Delinquent on Credit Card Payments

The results for the probit model for the probability a student was *delinquent on their credit card payments by 2 months or more* were fairly consistent with the findings from the previous model. However, the percentage point changes tended to be somewhat smaller. Yet, several factors continued to have a significantly large impact on the likelihood that a student was financially at risk. Students who acquired their first credit card at a campus table were 14.5 percentage points more likely to be delinquent than those who acquired their card from their parents. In addition, being Black significantly increased the likelihood of delinquency by 11.1 percentage points. A grade point average below 2.9 continued to result in significantly large effects. However, unlike the previous model, marital status, monthly income, and being a first-generation college student did not significantly affect the probability of delinquency.

Probability of Having Reached Limit on Credit Cards

The results for the probit model for the probability a student had *reached the limit on their credit cards* were also similar. The factors having the greatest impact continued to be being Black, having a lower grade point average, and having acquired a credit card at a campus table rather than from one's parents. Unlike the previous two models, the results for this model showed that international students were 10.1 percentage points more likely to have "maxed out" their credit cards than domestic students. This finding is perhaps not surprising since international students do not have as many financial options available to cover their education costs and daily living expenses. Interestingly, previous financial education had a larger effect on the probability a student had reached the limit on their credit cards than on whether they had accumulated large credit card balances or had been delinquent on their payments. Specifically, students who had taken a personal finance course were 2.5 percentage points less likely to have "maxed out" their credit cards.

Probability of Not Paying Balances in Full

The results from the final model for the probability a student *only paid off their credit card balances in full some of the time or never* were, not surprisingly, consistent with the previous models. However, the extent to which various factors affected financial risk was significantly larger. Students who had $10,000 or more in financial aid were 17.6 percentage points more likely to not repay their balances, and those who had $1,000 or more in other debt were 13.5 percentage points more likely. Being Black or Hispanic increased the probability of not repaying balances by 30.1 and 14.2 percentage points, respectively. As in the other models, students who acquired their cards at a campus table and those with lower grade point averages were significantly more likely to be at risk. Being female also increased the likelihood of not repaying balances by 6.1 percentage points. Financial education continued to have an effect and that effect was largest for this model. Students who had taken a personal finance course were 4.3 percentage points more likely to repay their credit card balances in full each month.

Discussion

The purpose of this chapter was to provide the reader with an overview of the credit practices of college students and identify specific groups of students who were more likely to carry higher credit card balances, be delinquent on their payments, max out their cards, and fail to repay balances in full each month. The findings from this study were similar to those found by previous researchers. The majority of students reported having credit cards (72.4 %), and most students appeared to be using them responsibly and were not accumulating large amounts of debt. Almost 16 % of the students sampled reported balances over $1,000 and 7.5 % reported balances over $3,000 compared to about 15–25 and 5–10 %, respectively, for other studies. In addition, over 75.0 % of students reported paying off their entire credit card balance each month—other studies have reported figures of between 50.0 and 60.0 %.

When the data were examined more closely, it was found that there were identifiable groups of students who were more likely than others to be at risk for misusing or mismanaging their credit. Specifically, at-risk students were more likely than those not at risk to be financially independent from their parents, to owe more in financial aid loans, and to owe other types of debt such as a car loan, mortgage, or other personal loan. They also were more likely to have lower grade point averages and to report higher earnings. Thus, at-risk students appear to be borrowing more in general. This finding suggests that rising college costs may be playing a key role in the rise of credit card usage on college campuses, and current levels of financial assistance may not be enough to cover these costs (College Board, 2005b; Lyons, 2007a; Nellie Mae, 2005). Those students most in need of financial assistance may be forced to work more hours per week and to turn to other forms of borrowing such as credit cards to complete their college degree. Those at greatest financial risk may be low- to middle-income students.

The results from this study also showed that how students acquire their credit cards has a significant effect on students' ability to manage their credit. Financially at-risk students were more likely than those not at risk to have acquired their first card prior to college or during their first year in college. They were also more likely to have acquired the card they used the most from a campus table, over the phone, or online rather than from their parents. These findings suggest that aggressive marketing practices by credit card companies to target college students may, in fact, be contributing to the rise in credit card debt on college campuses, putting some students at greater financial risk than others (The Education Resources & The Institute for Higher Education Institution, 1998; United States Government Accountability Office, 2001). Across the country, several colleges and universities have already limited credit card solicitations on their campuses while others have banned them altogether.

With respect to demographics, the findings from this report also revealed that financially at-risk students were more likely to be female, black, and/or Hispanic. It is interesting to note that these students belong to groups that have historically had difficulty obtaining credit (i.e., women, minorities, and low-income individuals). Of these three groups, black students were the most likely to be at risk, especially for having large debt burdens and mismanaging and misusing their credit cards. Given these findings, groups such as minorities and women may have specific financial education needs. Appropriate financial interventions may be needed to insure that these students are not at a financial disadvantage when they graduate.

Finally, this study showed that students who had taken, or were currently taking, a formal course in personal finance were significantly less likely to be at financial risk. While the percentage point impact of a personal finance course was less than that for some of the other factors, there is evidence that formal financial education may prevent some students from misusing and mismanaging their credit in the future. This finding is consistent with other studies that have investigated how the financial knowledge and practices students develop affect their overall financial well-being (Chen & Volpe, 1998; Lawrence, Cude, Lyons, Marks, & Machtmes, 2006; Lyons, 2004, 2004/2005, 2007a; Lyons & Hunt, 2003; Lyons, Scherpf, & Neelakantan, 2007; Lyons, Scherpf, & Roberts, 2006; Oleson, 2001; Palmer, Pinto, & Parente, 2001; Shim, Xiao, Barber, & Lyons, 2007; Weston, 2001; Xiao et al., 2007).

Implications for Financial Professionals and Campus Administrators

The findings from this study have important implications for financial professionals and campus administrators. Many campuses take a "one-size-fits-all" approach to providing financial education to college students. Some offer workshops and seminars on general financial education topics. Others go as far as to implement a general education requirement where all students must complete a personal finance course prior to graduation. However, we know now that there are identifiable subgroups of students that may be at greater financial risk than others, and these groups may benefit from more targeted financial education efforts. The key for campuses is to identify and implement the most appropriate interventions given their resource constraints so as to insure that these students are not at a financial disadvantage when they graduate and are able to make informed financial decisions.

Knowing which students are most likely to misuse or mismanage credit can be a critical step in helping financial professionals, educators, and campus administrators identify the appropriate financial interventions. However, in implementing these types of services, campus administrators face a number of challenges. Given the diverse needs of various groups of students, it is difficult to identify a single approach. In fact, for many campuses, "one size does not fit all" when it comes to financial education. Campuses often need to consider a variety of options.

Students who are most at risk may benefit from more one-on-one financial services to help them work out an individualized plan for their particular financial situation. However, one-on-one financial services, which are often tied to financial counseling and wellness centers, can be time and resource intensive. Moreover, campus offices, especially financial aid, may not be equipped or have the expertise to offer these services, especially to students who are experiencing serious financial difficulties. If campuses are faced with limited resources, they may want to consider forming partnerships with other campuses or local community organizations such as Cooperative Extension or Consumer Credit Counseling Services (CCCS). These non-profit organizations frequently help students with debt management and other financial issues. A number of opportunities exist for financial professionals and educators to help campus administrators provide financial education to college students. These partnerships have the potential to benefit students as well as faculty, staff, parents, and the entire community.

A number of studies provide specific recommendations to campus administrators and financial professionals on how they can develop targeted resources and services to help students better manage their finances. For a summary of these recommendations, see Lyons (2004, 2004/2005, 2007a), Mattson et al. (2004), Norvilitis and Santa Maria (2002), and Oleson (2001).

Also, the American Council on Consumer Interests (in partnership with the Federal Reserve Bank of New York, the Association for Financial Counseling and Planning Education, and Direct Selling Education Foundation) recently developed a financial education guide called *Get Financially Fit! A Financial Education Toolkit for College Campuses.* This step-by-step guide was designed to help campus administrators and financial professionals develop and implement successful financial education programs on college campuses. A series of steps helps them create tailored programs and services that best meet the needs of their students, taking into consideration available resources and expertise. A variety of best practices and examples of successful financial education efforts are included. There are also discussions on how to market financial education to students, identify potential partners, and look for opportunities to pool resources. Finally, tips are included on how to effectively assess whether particular programs are working (i.e., reaching the students they were designed to target).

The guide is supplemented by three student brochures that highlight basic personal finance concepts that college students need to know about savings, credit, budgeting, and consumer protection. Valuable tips on how they can get started with a financial plan are also included, along with links to key financial websites. The financial education toolkit and student brochures can be found at: http://www.consumerinterests.org.

Directions for Future Research

Overall, this chapter provides some interesting insight into college students' credit card behaviors, especially for those who are more likely to be financially at risk. However, there is still much work to be done before our understanding is complete. Research is already moving in new directions. Some researchers are now looking beyond general trends in credit card usage and are investigating the impact that credit usage has on the life successes of young adults (e.g., Lyons, 2004, 2007a, 2007b; Roberts, Golding, Towell, & Weinreb, 1999; Shim et al., 2007; Weston, 2001; Xiao et al., 2007). Factors that are being examined include campus retention rates, dropout rates, academic performance, employment and occupational outcomes, future financial security and access to credit, and physical and emotional well-being. Preliminary work is beginning to show that credit affects more than just students' finances—it permeates many aspects of their lives.

Additional research is taking a more holistic approach, examining how students develop their financial behaviors. Some of these studies have begun to empirically look at the role that parents, social networks, and formal financial education play in affecting the "financial socialization" of children and young adults (e.g., Lawrence et al., 2006; Lyons et al., 2006; Lyons et al., 2007; Palmer et al., 2001; Shim et al., 2007; Xiao et al., 2007). Preliminary research has shown that those who learn financial management skills at a younger age tend to do better financially than those who do not (Lawrence et al., 2006; Lyons et al., 2007). Shim et al. (2007) have taken this research one step further by developing, and empirically testing, a formal theoretical framework that explains the financial socialization of young adults and how the financial behaviors they develop affect a series of life outcomes related to overall life satisfaction. The proposed framework integrates three prominent psychological theories including lifespan development theory (Arnett, 2000), the theory of consumer socialization (John, 1999), and the theory of planned behavior (Ajzen, 1991).

Overall, this emerging body of research is still in its infancy stage. Little is known about how young adults develop specific financial behaviors and the relationship between those behaviors and various life outcomes such as academic performance, employment status, educational attainment, occupational choice, stress levels and health status, and interpersonal skills and relationships. As already mentioned, preliminary links have been found for some of these factors using descriptive analysis and cross-sectional data. However, these types of research questions are best addressed using more rigorous longitudinal analysis, which to date has not yet been done.

Also, as college costs continue to rise and students look for alternative way to finance their education, there are opportunities for researchers to examine several issues in the area of educational finance. For example, there is an immediate need to look at the relationships between traditional financial aid options and alternative financing options such as private education loans and credit card debt. Furthermore, if current trends in college education continue (College Board 2005a, 200b), the real financial issue facing students will not be the amount of credit card debt they have incurred, but rather the total amount they owe in student loans and private education loans. Thus, researchers may want to place more emphasis on addressing research questions related to educational finance in general.

Finally, financial education programs and services already exist on several college campuses, and more efforts are currently underway on other campuses to address the financial needs of students as well as faculty and staff. Research is needed to examine the long-term effects that these programs and services have on the ability of students to manage their finances and repay their debts. To date, researchers have not been able to adequately show whether financial education for college students is effective at changing their behaviors both before and after graduation.

Overall, there are numerous opportunities for researchers to explore the long-run consequences that credit usage, financial education, and other financial behaviors have on the life outcomes of young adults, especially those who may be particularly at risk. Longitudinal research that tracks students through their academic careers and into young adulthood is, perhaps, the most fruitful area for future research.

Researchers, students, financial professionals, educators, and campus administrators are encouraged to use this chapter as a foundation for future research and the development of future financial education programs and initiatives.

References

Ajzen, I. (1991). The theory of planned behavior. *Organizational Behavior and Human Decision Processes, 50*, 179–211.

Allen, J. L., & Jover, M. A. (1997). Credit card behavior of university students: Ethnic differences. *Consumer Interest Annual, 43*, 162–170.

Armstrong, C. J., & Craven, M. J. (1993). Credit card use and payment practices among college students. *Proceedings of the 6th Annual Conference of the Association for Financial Counseling and Planning Education*, pp. 148–159.

Arnett, J. J. (2000). Emerging adulthood: A theory of development from the late teens through the twenties. *American Psychologist, 55*(5), 469–480.

Baum, S., & O'Malley, M. (2003). *College on credit: How borrowers perceive their education debt. Results of the 2002 National Student Loan Survey.* Braintree, MA: Nellie Mae Corporation. Retrieved April 15, 2007, from http://www.nelliemae.com/library/nasls_2002.pdf.

Chen, H., & Volpe, R. P. (1998). An analysis of personal financial literacy among college students. *Financial Services Review, 7*(2), 107–128.

College Board. (2005a). *Trends in college pricing 2005.* Washington, DC: The Washington Office of the College Board.

College Board. (2005b). *Trends in student aid 2005.* Washington, DC: The Washington Office of the College Board.

Hayhoe, C. (2002). Comparison of affective credit attitude scores and credit use of college students at two points in time. *Journal of Family and Consumer Sciences, 94*(1), 71–77.

Hayhoe, C. R., Leach, L., & Allen, M. W. (2005). Credit cards held by college students. *Financial Counseling and Planning, 16*(1), 1–10.

Hayhoe, C., Leach, L., & Turner, P. (1999). Discriminating the number of credit cards held by college students using credit and money attitudes. *Journal of Economic Psychology, 20*(6), 643–656.

Hayhoe, C., Leach, L., Turner, P., Bruin, M., & Lawrence, F. (2000). Differences in spending habits and credit use of college students. *Journal of Consumer Affairs, 34*(1), 113–133.

Jamba-Joyner, L. A., Howard-Hamilton, M., & Mamarchew, H. (2000). College students and credit cards: Cause for concern. *NASFAA Journal of Student Financial Aid, 30*(3), 17–25.

John, D. R. (1999). Consumer socialization of children: A retrospective look at twenty-five years of research. *Journal of Consumer Research, 26*(3), 183–213.

Joo, S., Grable, J., & Bagwell, D. (2003). Credit card attitudes and behaviors of college students. *College Student Journal, 37*(3), 8–15.

Kidwell, B., & Turrisi, R. (2000). A cognitive analysis of credit card acquisition and college student financial development. *The Journal of College Students Development, 41*(6), 589–599.

Lawrence, F. C., Christofferson, R. C., Nester, S., Moser, B., Tucker, J. A., & Lyons, A. C. (2003). *Credit card usage of college students: Evidence from Louisiana State University* (Louisiana State University Agricultural Center, Research Information Sheet Number 107). Baton Rouge, LA: Louisiana State University. Retrieved July 30, 2007, from http://www.lsuagcenter.com/NR/rdonlyres/4D79415B-DA3E-43B4-9FF6-634F27D0D0°C/4106/RIS107CreditCard4.pdf.

Lawrence, F. C., Cude, B. J., Lyons, A. C., Marks, L., & Machtmes, K. (2006). College students' financial practices: A mixed methods analysis. *The Journal of Consumer Education, 23*, 13–26.

Lyons, A. C. (2004). A profile of financially at-risk college students. *The Journal of Consumer Affairs, 38*(1), 56–80.

Lyons, A. C. (2004/2005). A qualitative study on providing credit education to college students. *The Journal of Consumer Education, 22*, 9–18.

Lyons, A. C. (2007a). *Credit practices and financial education needs of Midwest college students.* Indianapolis, IN: Networks Financial Institute, Indiana State University.

Lyons, A. C. (2007b). *More than students' pocketbooks: The consequences of financial strain on college campuses* (Working Paper). Indianapolis, IN: Networks Financial Institute, Indiana State University.

Lyons, A. C., & Andersen, P. (2002). *Credit usage of college students: Evidence from the University of Illinois* (UIUC Office of Student Financial Aid Research Report). Urbana, IL: University of Illinois at Urbana-Champaign.

Lyons, A. C., Cude, B., Lawrence, F., & Gutter, M. (2005). Conducting research online: Challenges facing researchers in family and consumer sciences. *Family and Consumer Sciences Research Journal, 33*(4), 341–356.

Lyons, A. C., & Hunt, J. (2003). The credit practices and financial education needs of community college students. *Financial Counseling and Planning Journal, 14*(2), 63–74.

Lyons, A. C., Scherpf, E., & Neelakantan, U. (2007). *Intergenerational transfer of financial behaviors from parents to children.* (Working Paper). Indianapolis, IN: Networks Financial Institute, Indiana State University.

Lyons, A. C., Scherpf, E., & Roberts, H. (2006). Financial education and communication between parents and children. *The Journal of Consumer Education, 23*, 64–76.

Mattson, L., Sahlhoff, K., Blackstone, J., Peden, B., & Nahm, A.Y. (2004). Variables influencing credit card balances of students at a Midwestern university. *NASFAA Journal of Student Financial Aid, 34*(2), 7–18.

Nellie Mae. (2005). *Undergraduate students and credit cards in 2004: An analysis of usage rates and trends.* Braintree, MA: Nellie Mae. Retrieved July 30, 2007, from http://www.nelliemae.com/pdf/ccstudy_2005.pdf.

Norvilitis, J. M., Merwin, M. M., Osberg, T. M., Roehling, P. V., Young, P., & Kamas, M. M. (2006). Personality factors, money attitudes, financial knowledge, and credit-card debt in college students. *Journal of Applied Social Psychology, 36*(6), 1395–1413.

Norvilitis, J. M., & Santa Maria, P. (2002). Credit card debt on college campuses: Causes, consequences, and solutions. *College Student Journal, 36*(3), 357–364.

Norvilitis, J. M., Szablicki, P. B., & Wilson, S. D. (2003). Factors influencing levels of credit-card debt in college students. *Journal of Applied Social Psychology, 33*(5), 935–947.

Oleson, M. (2001). Student credit card debt in the 21st century: Options for financial aid administrators. *NASFAA Journal of Student Financial Aid, 31*(3), 35–44.

Palmer, T. S., Pinto, M. B., & Parente, D. H. (2001). College students' credit card debt and the role of parental involvement: Implications for public policy. *Journal of Public Policy & Marketing, 20*(1), 105–113.

Pinto, M. B., Parente, D. H., & Palmer, T. S. (2001). College student performance and credit card usage. *Journal of College Student Development, 42*(1), 49–58.

Roberts, J. A., & Jones, E. (2001). Money attitudes, credit card use, and compulsive buying among American college students. *The Journal of Consumer Affairs, 35*(2), 213–240.

Roberts, R., Golding, J., Towell, T., & Weinreb, I. (1999). The effects of economic circumstances on British students' mental and physical health. *Journal of American College Health, 48*(3), 103–109.

Shim, S., Xiao, J. J., Barber, B., & Lyons, A. (2007). *Pathways to life success: A model of financial well-being for young adults* (Working paper). Tucson, AZ: The University of Arizona, Take Charge America Institute for Consumer Financial Education and Research.

Staten, M. E., & Barron, J. M. (2002). *College student credit card usage* (Working Paper No. 65). Washington, DC: Credit Research Center, Georgetown University.

The Education Resources Institute & The Institute for Higher Education Policy. (1998). *Credit risk or credit worthy? College students and credit cards, a national survey.* Boston, MA: Author. Retrieved July 30, 2007, from http://www.ihep.org/Pubs/PDF/Credit.pdf.

United States Government Accountability Office. (2001). *Consumer finance: College students and credit cards* (GAO-01-773). Washington, DC: Author. Retrieved July 30, 2007, from http://www.gao.gov/new.items/d01773.pdf.

Weston, M. B. (2001). Creating a financial path to graduation. *Proceedings of the Association for Financial Counseling and Planning Education*, p. 131.

Xiao, J. J., Noring, F., & Anderson, J. (1995). College students' attitudes towards credit cards. *Journal of Consumer Studies and Home Economics*, *19*, 155–174.

Xiao, J. J., Shim, S., Barber, B., & Lyons, A. (2007). *Financial behaviors of college students: A pilot study* (Working paper). Tucson, AZ: The University of Arizona, Take Charge America Institute for Consumer Financial Education and Research.

Chapter 12
Financial Issues of Older Adults

Sharon A. DeVaney

Abstract This chapter highlights three important concerns regarding older adults. The concerns are (a) how to finance the increased number of years of retirement, (b) to provide for adequate health at the very old ages, and (c) that older women, especially minorities, are likely to be more economically disadvantaged than older men. To respond to the first and third concerns, older adults should consider working past the typical retirement age of 65 to increase retirement savings and delay the receipt of Social Security benefits to their full retirement age or age 70. To respond to the second concern, older adults should practice healthful behaviors.

In the United States, 65 years is the usual age for indicating who an elderly person is. However, some research on the older population begins with those who are only 50 years old. This chapter is focused on people who are aged 65 and over. When the discussion includes those who are younger than 65 years, it will be noted.

Another aspect of aging that is not clearly defined is the terminology that is most appropriate to use when referring to the older population. When the word "elderly," is used as a noun, it portrays older people in a negative perspective. In contrast, the use of the term "older adults," is more positive (Lee, 2007). Therefore, "older adults" will be used in this chapter to emphasize a positive approach to aging, and "elderly" will be used only as an adjective.

It is important to emphasize the positive aspects of aging. The movement to focus on the positive aspects of aging was highlighted by the MacArthur Group. This was a group of 16 scientists from multiple disciplines who began a series of studies on aging in 1984 (Rowe & Kahn, 1998). Their entire series of studies was based on the concept of "successful aging" which they believed was the confluence of three functions: decreasing the risk of disease and disease-related disability, maintaining physical and mental functioning, and being actively engaged with life. Therefore, the purpose of this chapter is to provide a summary of research on older adults and their financial concerns with the goal of promoting "successful aging."

S.A. DeVaney
Purdue University, 812 West State Street, West Lafayette, IN 47906-2060, USA
e-mail: sdevaney@purdue.edu

Demographics

In 1900, there were slightly more than 3 million Americans aged 65 and over. By 2000, the population of older Americans had swelled to 35 million. This meant that one of every eight Americans in 2000 was an older adult. By 2030, demographers estimate that one in five Americans will be an older adult, e.g., age 65 or older (Himes, 2004). There have been two major phases in the improvement of life expectancy during the last two centuries. The first was a reduction in infant mortality in the nineteenth and early twentieth centuries. The second phase is the more recent decrease in death rates among middle-aged and older people (Rowe & Kahn, 1998). Currently, more 65-year-olds are living to age 85, and more 85-year-olds are living into their nineties. The oldest old, those 85 and older, are the fastest growing segment of the population (Himes, 2004). The large increase in the number of older adults in the United States has led to two important issues. The issues are how to finance the increased number of years of retirement and how to provide for adequate health at the very old ages (Clark, Burkhauser, Moon, Quinn, & Smeeding, 2004).

Similar to the increase in diversity of the overall population of the United States, the elderly population is becoming more racially and ethnically diverse. In 2000, about 84 % of the elderly population was non-Hispanic white, 8 % was Black, 5 % was Hispanic, and 4 % of the elderly population was from other races. By 2050, the elderly population in the United States is expected to be 64 % non-Hispanic white, 12 % Black, 16 % Hispanic, and 7 % of other races (U.S. Bureau of the Census, 2001).

There are more women than men at every age among the elderly. In 2000, the number of men per 100 women was 82 among persons aged 65–74, 65 among those aged 75–84, and 41 among persons aged 85 and older (Clark et al., 2004). The economic status of older women depends on their marital status and their age cohort. The disparity in the number of men and women suggests that many women will grow older alone. In fact, the proportion of women aged 62 and over who will be divorced or never married is expected to reach 25 % by 2020. In comparison, the proportion of divorced or never married women in 1991 was 12 % (Clark et al., 2004).

Theoretical Framework

Although many theories from psychology and sociology are used to explain the changes that occur as people age, three theories from economics are important to the study of older adults and financial issues. The theories that attempt to explain how income and consumption vary over the life cycle include the life-cycle hypothesis, the permanent income hypothesis, and precautionary savings.

The life-cycle hypothesis of savings suggests that people try to maintain a relatively stable level of consumption over their lifetime (Ando & Modigliani, 1963).

In practice, this means that those who are younger borrow to meet consumption needs, those who are middle aged save a relatively large proportion of their earnings, and those who are older spend down their assets when their income is reduced in retirement. A strict interpretation of the life-cycle hypothesis suggests that people will spend all of their assets before the end of their life. In practice, this does not always happen.

The permanent income hypothesis suggests that people adjust their spending level to their perceived level of future income. Permanent income is believed to be what people can count on with confidence. Transitory income is believed to be income that is received accidentally or by chance; it is not expected to affect long-term consumption (Friedman, 1957).

Precautionary saving is aimed at providing against future drops in income. The precautionary savings model implies that older adults are cautious about spending down their assets. Their reluctance to spend down their assets is explained by their uncertainty about how long they will live, about the cost of health care in the future, and about the possibility of becoming impoverished (Carroll, 1997; Deaton, 1992).

Economic Status

Income

The median household income for households headed by a person aged 65 and older in 2005 was $26,036, while the median household income for households headed by a person under 65 in 2005 was twice as large, $52,287 (U.S. Bureau of the Census, 2006). The income distribution can also be examined by looking at income quintiles. In 2005, of all households, those in the lowest income quintile had incomes of $19,179 or less, while households in the highest quintile had incomes greater than $91,705. One-third (37.1 %) of all households in the lowest quintile were headed by a person aged 65 and over, while only 8.3 % of households headed by a person aged 65 and over were in the highest income quintile (U.S. Bureau of the Census, 2006).

Older Americans receive income from a wide variety of sources, including labor earnings, Social Security retirement benefits, employer-sponsored pensions, and interest on private savings. Among households aged 65 and over, over 90 % receive income from Social Security, about two-thirds receive income from assets, about 40 % receive income from pensions, and about one-fifth is from labor earnings (Clark et al., 2004).

For older adults in the lower income quintiles, Social Security is a primary source of income. Over 80 % of the income of households in the lowest two income quintiles is from Social Security. For older adults in the highest income quintile, labor earnings provide about one-third, assets provide one-fourth, and Social Security and pensions each provide about one-fifth of total household income (Clark et al., 2004).

Poverty

The official poverty definition is based on actual money income before taxes and does not include capital gains and non-cash benefits (Federal Interagency Forum on Aging Related Statistics, 2006). To determine who is poor, the U.S. Bureau of the Census compares family income with a set of poverty thresholds that vary by family size and composition and are updated annually for inflation.

The overall poverty rate in the United States in 2005 was 12.6% while the poverty rate for older persons was 10.1%. However, the threshold used to establish poverty status for older persons is about 10% lower than that for other age groups. The poverty threshold in 2005 was $9,367 and $11,815 for single persons and couples, respectively, who were aged 65 and older (U.S. Bureau of the Census, 2006). The percentage of the population who are in poverty increases as people age. In 2004, 9.4% of those aged 65–74 were living in poverty; 9.7% of those aged 75–84 and 12.6% aged 85 and over were living in poverty (Federal Interagency Forum on Aging Related Statistics, 2006).

Net Worth

Net worth (which is defined as total assets minus total liabilities) is another measure of economic status. Both the median and mean net worth of American households have a hump-shaped pattern that usually peaks between ages 55 and 64 (Bucks, Kennickell, & Moore, 2006). In 2004, median net worth for households with a head aged 55–64 was $248,700. For those aged 65–74, median net worth was $190,100, and for those aged 75 and older, median net worth was $163,100 (Bucks et al., 2006).

Liquid Assets

Liquid assets consist of cash or accounts that can be easily converted to cash. Financial advisors recommend that families should have 3–6 months of income in liquid assets as a reserve for emergencies (Johnson & Widdows, 1985). Using data from the 2004 Survey of Consumer Finances, Rodriguez-Flores and DeVaney (2007) compared emergency funds held by retirees, wage earners, and the self-employed. The researchers compared *subjective funds* (the amount the household thought they should have), *quick or liquid* emergency funds (saving, checking, and money market accounts), and *comprehensive* emergency funds (quick funds plus certificates of deposit, cash value of whole life insurance, and the market value of stocks, bonds, and mutual funds not held in retirement accounts). The analysis showed that retired and self-employed households held significantly larger amounts of emergency funds than wage earners. For example, wage-earner households had $15,367 in quick funds compared to $37,976 for retired households and $47,802 for self-employed households. This supports the theory of precautionary savings, suggesting that those who are concerned about uncertain income in the future (such as retirees and the self-employed) will save more for emergencies.

Non-financial Assets

The most commonly owned tangible assets (also known as non-financial assets) are homes and vehicles. It is not surprising that the majority of older adults own homes and vehicles. In 2004, 81.3 % of householders aged 65–74 years and 85.2 % of households aged 75 and older were homeowners. The median value of the primary residence was $150,000 for householders aged 65–74 and $125,000 for household-ers aged 75 and older. Vehicles were owned by 89.1 % of households aged 65–74 and by 76.9 % of households aged 75 and older. The median value of the vehicles owned by those aged 65–74 and aged 75 and older in 2004 was $12,400 and $8,400, respectively (Bucks et al., 2006). Hence, as people age, there is a slight reduction in homeownership and vehicle ownership.

Consumption

The Consumer Expenditure Survey (CES), sponsored by the Bureau of Labor Statis-tics, is the primary source of information on household consumption. Using data from the CES, Paulin (2000) investigated whether consumers who were older than 65 had different tastes, preferences, or physical needs than consumers who were younger than 65 by analyzing trends for several of the 13 major expenditure cat-egories. He found that older consumers purchased different amounts than younger consumers, but overall, the trend of expenditures was similar for older and younger consumers.

Using the Consumer Expenditure Survey, Abdel-Ghany and Sharpe (1997) com-pared spending by households aged 65–74 with those 75 and over. Housing was the largest expense for each age group. Transportation was the second largest expense for the 65–74 age group, while health care was the second largest expense for those aged 75 and over.

Abdel-Ghany and Sharpe (1997) also observed the following differences in spending. Households headed by college graduates spent more than those who did not complete high school on food away from home, alcohol and tobacco, ap-parel, entertainment, and personal care. Compared to White households, African-American households spent more on personal insurance and less on food away from home and entertainment. Compared to couples, unmarried female respondents spent more on apparel, but they spent less on food at home, food away from home, alcohol and tobacco, health care, and personal care. Unmarried male respondents spent more than couples on food away from home, entertainment, and personal insurance and less on food at home, health care, and personal care.

Butrica, Goldwyn, and Johnson (2005) examined spending by adults aged 65 and older using data from the 2000 Health and Retirement Study (HRS) and the 2001 Consumption and Activities Mail Survey of the HRS. Households aged 65–74 spent 33 % of their income on housing, 13 % on health care, 13 % on entertainment, 12 % on food, 12 % on transportation, 8 % on gifts, 6 % on other, and 3 % on clothing. Butrica and colleagues (2005) found that the share of housing expenses which was going to mortgages declined with age, but the share of housing expenses going to utilities and maintenance increased with age.

Debt

Using data from the 2001 Survey of Consumer Finances (SCF), Yilmazer and DeVaney (2005) examined how the holding of types and amount of debt changed over the life cycle. They hypothesized (a) that the likelihood of holding debt would decrease as age of the household head increased and (b) that the likelihood of holding most types of debt would be associated with lower financial assets. Their research supported both hypotheses. Also, their results showed that holding non-financial assets (such as vehicles, homes) had a positive effect on both the likelihood of holding secured debt and the amount of secured debt compared to total assets. Also, households headed by retired persons (compared to those headed by a working person) had lower levels of each type of debt ratio (mortgage debt/total assets, outstanding credit card balance/total assets, installment debt/total assets, and other debt/total assets).

Labor Force Participation

Many older adults continue to work after the typical retirement age. In fact, the two most significant changes in the U.S. labor market during the last half of the twentieth century were (a) the trend toward earlier retirement by older men and (b) increased levels of female labor force participation at all ages (Clark et al., 2004). However, the retirement trend for men has slowed since the mid-1980s, and labor force participation for both men and women has shown a slight upward trend since the mid-1980s. Data from the Current Population Surveys shows that the tendency to remain in the work force increased slightly for both men and women in 2005 (Federal Interagency Forum on Aging Related Statistics, 2006) compared to 2004. Continuing to work past typical retirement ages could help men and women to increase their current income and their retirement savings.

To predict which older adults were working, Bieker, DeVaney, and Chen (2001), analyzed data on household heads aged 65 and older from the 1998 Survey of Consumer Finances (SCF). Those who were employed were in good or excellent health and had asset income, while those who were not employed were more likely to be older, self-employed, and receiving Social Security benefits and pensions.

Unmarried women and married individuals with non-working spouses were less likely to be employed than a married individual with a working spouse.

Kim and DeVaney (2005) analyzed data from the Health and Retirement Study (HRS) to learn the differences in the selection of partial and full retirement. They found that *partial* retirees were more likely to be male, self-employed, with a college degree, and have a chronic health condition such as arthritis. *Full* retirees were more likely to be male, to hold defined benefit pensions or both defined benefit and defined contribution pensions, employee health insurance, and investment assets. Respondents were less likely to retire fully if they were in excellent or good health, self-employed, had debt, and if they had an advanced degree.

A study on retirement expectations of self-employed workers from the Health and Retirement Study (HRS) showed that 10 % planned to stop working altogether, 10 % said they would never stop, 16 % were considering a change in their job, and 63 % had no retirement plans (DeVaney & Kim, 2003). Among the self-employed with no retirement plans, 42 % were women, 26 % said their physical health was fair or poor, 22 % were minorities, and 19 % were not married. The "no retirement plans" group was the most likely to say they would make an intervivos transfer, suggesting that they had family members they needed to support. The results suggest that many older self-employed persons are financially vulnerable.

Housing

Housing usually becomes more important as people age. Retirees will have more time to spend at home and some prefer to change locations. Also, illness or disability can occur resulting in the need to make changes in the home or require a move. Robison and Moen (2000) proposed that older adults evaluated their expectations about future housing options using an array of choices clustered by risk or dependency. *Low* risk of dependency was defined as always living in or modifying one's current home. *Medium* risk was defined as living in a retirement community, purchasing long-term care insurance, or getting a reverse mortgage. *High* risk was defined as living with a family member, sharing a household with unrelated people, or living in a separate housing unit on a relative's property.

With data from the Cornell Retirement and Well-Being Study, Robison and Moen (2000) found that lower income, more years in the home, and volunteering increased the expectancy of remaining in the home (defined as low risk). Also, women were more likely to expect to remain in their homes than men. The medium-risk choices, moving to a retirement community and purchasing long-term-care insurance, were positively related to income. Also, unmarried persons were more likely than married persons to say they would move to a retirement community and/or purchase long-term care insurance. The choice of sharing a residence with a non-relative (defined as high risk) was an expectation of respondents who were in their fifties, males, unmarried persons, white persons, and those who owned their homes outright (versus holding a mortgage). Robison and Moen (2000) observed a trend away from depending on one's children for help; the trend cut across gender, income, age, and retirement status.

Health Care

Many retirees will no longer be covered by their employers' health insurance. Although older adults aged 65 and over are likely to be eligible for Medicare, they will need to make choices about Medicare options and to pay part of the cost of care. The various aspects of Medicare are explained in the following sections.

Medicare Parts A and B

Medicare is health insurance for people who are (a) aged 65 or older, (b) under age 65 with certain disabilities, and (c) any age with permanent kidney failure requiring dialysis or a kidney transplant. Medicare Part A helps cover inpatient care in hospitals. Most people automatically get Part A coverage because they or a spouse paid Medicare taxes while working.

Medicare Part B helps cover medical services such as doctors' services, outpatient care, and other medical care that Part A does not cover. Part B also covers some preventive services. Older adults must pay a monthly premium for Part B. Beginning January 1, 2007, the Part B premium will be based on modified adjusted gross income instead of being a flat amount (Centers for Medicare and Medicaid Services, 2006).

Medicare Part C

Medicare Advantage Plans (such as HMOs and PPOs) are health plan options that are approved by Medicare and run by private companies. They are part of the Medicare Program and are sometimes called Part C. Medicare pays an amount of money for the person's care every month to these private health plans, whether or not the person uses services (Centers for Medicare and Medicaid Services, 2006).

Medicare Part D

Beginning in 2006, Medicare offers prescription drug coverage for everyone with Medicare. This is called Part D. This coverage may help lower prescription drug costs and help protect against higher costs in the future. If a person joins a Medicare drug plan, he or she usually pays a monthly premium. Part D is optional. If a person decides not to enroll in a Medicare drug plan when they are first eligible, he may pay

a penalty if they choose to join later. These plans are run by insurance companies and other private companies approved by Medicare.

Each Medicare drug plan is different. When a person chooses a Medicare drug plan for the first time or switches to a different Medicare drug plan, he should compare the plans in his area and choose one that meets his costs and coverage needs. Information is available on the Internet at www.medicare.gov or by calling 1-800-633-4227 (Centers for Medicare and Medicaid Services, 2006). Although there has been a lot of research on out-of-pocket costs related to health care, the establishment of the drug plan indicates that a new stream of research will be needed.

Medigap

A Medigap policy is health insurance sold by private insurance companies to fill gaps in the Original Medicare Plan coverage. Medigap policies help pay a person's share (coinsurance, copayments, and deductibles) of the cost of Medicare-covered services. Generally, a person must have Medicare Parts A and B to buy a Medigap policy. In most states, people are able to choose from up to 12 different standardized Medigap policies (Medigap Plans A–L). Medigap policies must follow state and federal laws. A Medigap policy only works with the Original Medicare Plan. If a person joins a Medicare Advantage Plan (like a Health Maintenance Organization (HMO) or a Preferred Provider Organization (PPO)), the Medigap policy will not work (Centers for Medicare and Medicaid Services, 2006).

Medicaid

Medicaid offers help for low-income and low-wealth Americans of all ages. It is a joint federal/state program in which states have latitude in establishing eligibility and coverage. It supplements coverage for about one in every seven older adults (Clark et al., 2004). Research on family wealth transfer prior to becoming a Medicaid recipient has suggested that the amount transferred was modest, especially among nursing home residents (Lee, Kim, & Tanenbaum, 2006).

Long-Term Care

Long-term care refers to services that are needed for an extended period of time to cover poor health, disability, or frailty. Some services are more medical in nature, but many of the needs are supportive. Long-term care may be provided in nursing homes, assisted living facilities, adult day care, congregate meal service, or the home. In 2002, the funding sources for long-term care were Medicaid, 45 %; out of pocket, 23 %; Medicare, 14 %; private insurance, 11 %; other private, 4 %; and other public, 3 % (Clark et al., 2004).

A qualitative study to identify intentions for financing long-term care was conducted with a sample consisting of 16 couples (Stum, 2006). The study identified two decision-making styles: scrambling and advance planning. Scramblers were trying to make ends meet. They spoke of "hoping the kids would help" or relying on government resources if long-term care was needed. The advance planners were goal oriented and working to achieve financial security.

The possibility of self-funding long-term care was investigated by Lown and Palmer (2004). The advantage of self-funding is that the funds would be available for other expenses or inheritances. The disadvantage was that self-insuring would provide only one-third of the amount needed. Lown and Palmer (2004) suggested that a reverse annuity mortgage should also be considered as a technique to fund long-term care in addition to self-funding.

Long-Term Care Insurance

Another possibility for funding long-term care is the purchase of long-term care insurance (LTCI). The National Association of Insurance Commissioners (NAIC) has established rules for the sale of LTCI, but states also play an important role in regulating LTCI. Therefore, potential purchasers of LTCI should learn about the regulations in their state. The age of the insured at the time of purchase and the amount of risk that the insured is willing to accept are important determinants of the cost of the premium. LTCI buyers have the right to return their policies within 30 days of purchase. The insurer has the right to rescind the policy within the first 6 months if the insured person engaged in misrepresentation (Shilling, 2001).

Reverse Annuity Mortgages

Another possibility for funding long-term care or paying other expenses is a reverse annuity mortgage. Although reverse annuity mortgages have been available since 1982, their use until recently has been minimal. Half of all reverse mortgages ever issued have occurred in the last 2 years (Opdyke, 2006). In a reverse annuity mortgage, the property owner borrows against the value of a personal residence. The owner has three payment choices: a lump sum, monthly payments, or a credit line that can be accessed at any time. No interest is charged on the unused portion of the line of credit. The money borrowed is paid back to the bank with the accumulated interest when the owner dies, sells the home, or permanently moves out of the home (Weisman, 2004).

According to Shilling (2001), a reverse mortgage is a worthwhile strategy if any of the following conditions are present. The conditions are as follows: if there are no children to inherit or the children have homes of their own or the children have no intention of living in the area, or if it seems likely that a Medicaid application will be made in the near future (so transfers would create an unwieldy penalty period).

Economic Vulnerability of Older Women

As previously mentioned, women are more likely to be economically disadvantaged than men in old age (Clark et al., 2004). Women have longer life expectancies than men at every age. Older women who are widowed or divorced are less likely than older men to remarry. Women's labor force participation is frequently shorter than men's and less continuous. The interruption in work history to raise children or care for family members negatively affects pension income and Social Security benefits. Some of the issues related to the economic vulnerability of women are described in the next chapters.

Fan and Zick (2006) found that about-to-be-widowed households had increased miscellaneous expenditures and decreased expenditures for food at home, health care, transportation, and recreation in the 6 months before the spouse's death. The miscellaneous category includes funeral and burial expenses. Fan and Zick (2006) also found that total expenditures were about $10,000 more than after-tax income, suggesting that these households draw down their assets when a spouse dies.

Another study showed that older adults should communicate more openly about their financial status (Whirl & DeVaney, 2006) while both spouses are alive. Research based on in-depth interviews with widows and widowers showed that 95 % of widows wished they had been more interactive and inquisitive about family finances. Widows said they were "underprepared" to handle their financial affairs after the unexpected loss of their spouse. Men in the same study said they were satisfied with financial decisions made after the death of the spouse. However, women with children recovered more quickly, both emotionally and financially, after the death of a spouse than women without children. The recommendation to communicate more openly with family and friends about their finances may be applicable to the majority of older adults, whether married or single.

Suggestions for Future Research

Topics for research include (a) financing retirement needs assuming that retirees might live an additional 30 or 40 years after retiring and (b) financing long-term care assuming that one or more family members might need care for a lengthy period. Other topics of interest could focus on the needs of minorities and women although this should be included in how to finance a lengthy period of retirement or long-term care. A new area for research would be to examine satisfaction with Medicare Part D. Another area for research would be to investigate the financial scams that are perpetrated on older adults. Although the types of scams are similar to those used on other adults, the perpetrators who take advantage of older adults are aware that older adults may be lonely. Also older adults are less likely to realize that they are being victimized than young and middle-aged adults (Loonin & Renuart, 2006).

References

Abdel-Ghany, M., & Sharpe, D. L. (1997). Consumption patterns among the young–old and old–old. *The Journal of Consumer Affairs, 31*(1), 90–112.

Ando, A., & Modigliani, F. (1963). The life cycle hypothesis of saving: Aggregate implications and tests. *The American Economic Review, 53*(1), 55–84.

Bieker, R., DeVaney, S. A., & Chen, Z. (2001). Determinants of employment among older Americans. *Financial Counseling and Planning, 12*(2), 33–42.

Bucks, B. K., Kennickell, A. B., & Moore, K. B. (2006). Recent changes in U. S. family finances: Evidence from the 2001 and 2004 Survey of Consumer Finances. *Federal Reserve Bulletin,* A1–A38.

Butrica, B. A. Goldwyn, J. H., & Johnson, R. W. (2005). Understanding expenditure patterns in retirement (Working Paper 2005–03). Chestnut Hill, MA: Center for Retirement Research at Boston College.

Carroll, C. D. (1997). Buffer-stock saving and the life cycle/permanent income hypothesis. *Quarterly Journal of Economics, 112*(1), 1–55.

Centers for Medicare and Medicaid Services. (2006). *Medicare and you 2007 handbook.* Washington, DC: U.S. Department of Health & Human Services.

Clark, R. L., Burkhauser, R. V., Moon, M., Quinn, J. F., & Smeeding, T. M. (2004). *The economics of an aging society.* Malden, MA: Blackwell Publishing.

Deaton, A. (1992). *Understanding consumption.* Oxford: Oxford University Press.

DeVaney, S. A., & Kim, H. (2003). Older self-employed workers and planning for the future. *The Journal of Consumer Affairs, 37*(1) 101–120.

Fan, J. X., & Zick, C. D. (2006). Expenditure flows near widowhood. *Journal of Family and Economic Issues, 27*(2), 335–353.

Federal Interagency Forum on Aging Related Statistics. (2006). *Older Americans update 2006: Key indicators of well-being.* Hyattsville, MD: National Center for Health Statistics.

Friedman, M. (1957). *A theory of the consumption function.* Princeton, NJ: Princeton University Press.

Himes, C. L. (2004). *Elderly Americans. Annual Editions Aging* (16th ed.), pp. 2–6. Guilford, CT: McGraw-Hill/Dushkin.

Johnson, D. P., & Widdows, R. (1985). Emergency funds levels of households. *Consumer Interest Annual, 31,* 235–241.

Kim, H., & DeVaney, S. A. (2005). The selection of partial or full retirement by older workers. *Journal of Family and Economic Issues, 26*(3), 371–394.

Lee, J., Kim, H., & Tanenbaum, S. (2006). Medicaid and family wealth transfer. *The Gerontologist, 46*(1), 6–13.

Lee, S. A. (2007). 10 questions with noteworthy people: Dr. Gene Cohen on whether old dogs can learn new tricks. *Journal of Financial Planning, 20*(4) 20–23.

Loonin, D., & Renuart, E. (2006). *Life and debt: A survey of data addressing the debt loads of older persons and policy recommendations.* Washington, DC: National Consumer Law Center.

Lown, J. M., & Palmer, L. (2004). Long-term care insurance purchase: An alternative approach. *Financial Counseling and Planning, 15*(2), 1–11.

Opdyke, J. D. (2006, December 27). Making your house pay in retirement. *The Wall Street Journal,* D1–D2.

Paulin, G. D. (2000). Expenditure patterns of older Americans, 1984–1997. *Monthly Labor Review, 123*(5), 3–28.

Robison, J. T., & Moen, P. (2000). Future housing expectations in late midlife: The role of retirement, gender, and social integration. In K. Pillemer, P. Moen, E. Wethington, & N. Glasgow (Eds.), *Social integration in the second half of life* (pp. 158–189). Baltimore: The Johns Hopkins University Press.

Rodriguez-Flores, A., & DeVaney, S. A. (2007). The effect of employment status on households' emergency funds. *Journal of Personal Finance, 5*(4), 65–82.

Rowe, J. W., & Kahn, R. L. (1998). *Successful aging*. New York: Dell Publishing.

Shilling, D. (2001). *Financial planning for the older client* (5th ed.). Cincinnati, OH: The National Underwriter.

Stum, M. S. (2006). Financing long term care: Risk management intentions and behavior of couples. *Financial Counseling and Planning, 17*(2), 79–89.

U.S. Bureau of the Census. (2001). *Population projections of the United States by age, sex, race, Hispanic origin and nativity: 1999 to 2100.*

Weisman, S. (2004). *A guide to elder planning*. Upper Saddle River, NJ: Prentice Hall.

Whirl, S. P., & DeVaney, S. A. (2006). Communication strategies to help prepare for the unexpected loss of a spouse. *Journal of Personal Finance, 5*(3), 42–43.

Yilmazer, T., & DeVaney, S. A. (2005). Household debt over the life cycle. *Financial Services Review, 14*(4), 285–304.

Chapter 13
Consumer Finances of Low-Income Families

Steven Garasky, Robert B. Nielsen, and Cynthia Needles Fletcher

Abstract Serious challenges face families at the bottom of the economic ladder. The difficulties of balancing low incomes against expenditures are exacerbated by a lack of assets and insurance. We examine patterns of family asset ownership and health insurance coverage rates. A review of research focuses on selected dimensions of the financial environment of low-income families: the phenomena of the "unbanked," home ownership trends, credit use and predatory lending. In each of these areas, additional research is needed to identify ways to help families not only meet their needs, but also to accumulate assets that promote long-term economic well-being.

Serious challenges face families at the bottom of the economic ladder. Stagnant wages and increasingly restrictive public transfer programs have stifled income growth among low-income families. At the same time, in an effort to expand markets, those with marginal incomes have become the targets of marketing campaigns promoting middle-class lifestyles and extending credit to consumers traditionally viewed as unacceptably high-risk customers. Together, these forces are putting pressures on the finances of low-income consumers. The difficulties of balancing low incomes against expenditures are exacerbated by a lack of assets and insurance.

Limited access to earnings, other income, assets and health insurance coverage affects the ability of families to weather financial difficulties or generate income in ways other than by working. For example, middle- and high-income families can access savings when earnings are disrupted; low-income families may have to resort to short-term loans—often those available only from lenders in the fringe economy. Investment opportunities with greater returns often require minimum balances. Maintaining minimum investment levels is more difficult for families with limited incomes compared to families with greater resources. Having health insurance allows families to withstand financial shocks associated with expensive or unexpected

S. Garasky
Department of Human Development and Family Studies, Iowa State University, 4380 Palmer Building, Ames, IA 50011, USA
e-mail: sgarasky@iastate.edu

J.J. Xiao, (ed.), *Handbook of Consumer Finance Research,*
© Springer 2008

medical care needs. In short, the financial and insurance environment of low-income families may further hinder their ability to meet their basic needs.

Using data from the Survey of Income and Program Participation (SIPP), we examine patterns of asset ownership rates among low-income families compared to others. We define "low-income" as those in the bottom quintile of the income distribution. We also examine health insurance coverage rates among low-income individuals, again comparing them with those with higher incomes. This analysis is followed by a review of research evidence on selected dimensions of the financial environment of low-income families: the phenomena of being "unbanked," home ownership trends, credit use, predatory lending and access to public or private health insurance coverage. A discussion of future directions for research on the consumer finances of low-income families completes the chapter.

Consumer Finances of Low-Income Families: Current Evidence

The U.S. Census Bureau's Survey of Income and Program Participation (SIPP) is a leading source of data on social, demographic and economic trends over time. Researchers have relied on the SIPP for nearly three decades, in part, because it over-samples the low-income population. Descriptive information about families' use of basic financial services, ownership of physical assets and other financial investments in 2001 and 2003 is reported in Table 13.1. Data are from the 2001 SIPP panel, the most recent complete panel that is available. Families are categorized into quintiles according to annual total family income in 2001 and 2003. The discussion focuses on low-income families—those in the first (lowest) income quintile.

Expressed in 2003 dollars, median income for all families declined from $48,294 in 2001 to $46,320 in 2003. Real median annual family income also declined for families in the lowest quintile from $15,856 in 2001 to $15,442 in 2003. Median income in the second quintile fell as well from $31,788 to $31,537. These declines are in contrast to increases in median family income for the three highest-income quintiles between 2001 and 2003.

Low-income families face financial constraints—in terms of both assets and financial services utilization—that set them apart from middle- and upper-income families. For this analysis, family financial resources are grouped into three types: basic financial services, physical assets and investments. As shown in Table 13.1, the percentage of families with each of these resource types varies by income quintile. However, the contrast is greatest between families in the lowest income quintile compared to all others. Low-income families have fewer attachments to mainstream banking products and services. For example, in 2003 only 16% of the families in the lowest quintile had an interest-earning savings account. In contrast, 55% of families in the highest-income quintile had such accounts. The patterns of asset ownership changed little between 2001 and 2003.

Although the daily financial challenges faced by low-income families capture much of the attention of researchers and policy makers (e.g., Blank, Danziger, &

Table 13.1 Family financial resource ownership rates by annual income quintiles: 2001 and 2003

	2001						2003					
	All	Q1	Q2	Q3	Q4	Q5	All	Q1	Q2	Q3	Q4	Q5
Median annual income (2003 dollars)	48,294	15,856	31,788	48,287	69,201	111,998	46,320	15,442	31,537	48,580	70,239	113,777
Basic services												
Interest-earning savings	35.8	14.6	29.4	35.6	44.1	55.6	35.8	15.7	28.0	36.7	41.6	54.7
Interest-earning checking	53.3	27.1	43.8	55.9	65.4	74.5	52.5	26.4	44.6	53.7	63.7	71.3
Regular checking	31.6	23.0	32.0	35.6	34.5	33.1	31.8	23.4	32.2	33.8	36.6	32.1
Physical assets												
Own home	74.6	48.2	69.5	76.6	85.7	93.1	75.1	48.3	67.7	78.4	86.0	92.2
Rental property	6.8	2.3	4.9	6.4	7.7	12.5	5.8	2.4	4.1	5.7	6.4	9.8
Automobile	89.5	74.4	89.7	93.5	94.7	94.2	89.5	73.6	89.7	93.0	94.7	94.7
Investments												
Interest-earning assets at financial institutions[a]	64.0	34.1	55.6	66.9	76.4	87.0	64.1	34.0	56.3	66.1	75.3	85.4
Stock shares	24.5	6.8	15.3	21.6	30.1	48.8	21.2	6.6	12.4	18.0	24.8	42.4
Mutual fund shares	20.4	4.8	11.9	16.9	26.6	41.9	17.0	4.5	9.5	14.7	20.5	34.2
Savings bonds	13.0	3.9	8.2	12.1	16.9	24.0	11.5	2.9	7.0	10.2	15.2	21.3
IRA or Keogh	24.6	7.1	16.7	22.7	31.0	45.6	24.0	7.7	15.6	22.5	28.6	43.4
401(k) or Thrift Savings Plan (TSP)	30.9	7.1	17.6	28.7	43.9	57.2	30.8	6.7	17.9	27.7	41.7	57.3
Money market account	16.2	4.5	10.9	13.8	19.7	31.9	14.7	5.0	9.0	12.3	17.2	28.7
Government securities	1.3	0.3	0.9	1.0	1.6	2.6	1.1	0.4	0.7	1.0	1.0	2.1
Municipal or corporate bonds	3.3	0.8	2.4	2.9	3.8	6.7	2.7	1.1	1.4	2.5	2.7	5.7
Certificate of deposit	13.8	7.1	13.7	14.3	16.0	18.0	10.6	6.1	9.7	11.1	11.9	13.5
Other financial investments[b]	2.1	0.6	1.5	2.1	2.5	3.9	1.5	0.3	0.8	1.6	2.1	2.5

Source: Authors' calculations from 2001 Panel of the Survey of Income and Program Participation

Quintile upper limits for 2001 (in 2003 dollars) were: lowest quintile—$24,005; second quintile—$39,764; third quintile—$57,569; fourth quintile—$84,934.

Quintile upper limits for 2003 were: lowest quintile—$23,720; second quintile—$39,736; third quintile—$58,451; fourth quintile—$86,304

[a] Includes passbook savings accounts, certificates of deposit, money market deposit accounts, interest-earning accounts, U.S. government securities, and municipal or corporate bonds

[b] Includes mortgages held for sale of real estate, sale of business or property, investments in a non-corporate business, investments in a corporation, and other investments not reported in another category

Schoeni, 2006), there is also concern about the challenges these families face when attempting to accumulate assets for long-term goals such as acquiring a car, home or saving for retirement (McNichol & Springer, 2004; Neuberger, Greenstein, & Sweeney, 2005). Physical assets are less commonly held by low-income families than middle- and higher-income families. In 2001 and 2003, three-fourths (74%) of the low-income families owned a vehicle. Ownership rates among all other families were noticeably higher at 90% or above. Rates of home ownership also illustrate the asset accumulation challenges low-income families face. Home ownership is the primary asset among low-income families, yet less than half of these families in 2001 and 2003 reported owning homes. In addition, very few families with low incomes own longer-term financial products. For example, the percentage of the lowest-quintile families that hold stocks, mutual funds, municipal or corporate bonds or government securities is about half that of families in the second income quintile. The disparity in ownership rates of retirement-specific assets, such as IRAs, Keogh accounts and 401(k) or similar accounts, illustrates the difficulty of asset accumulation by low-income families. In both 2001 and 2003, only 7% of the lowest income families had 401(k) or similar accounts, compared to 57% of high-income families.

Although limited income and assets are threats to financial security, the lack of health insurance compounds the financial vulnerability of many low-income families. As shown in Table 13.2, members of high-income families are much more likely to have health insurance through an employer or union compared to those in low-income families (roughly 90 versus 60%) with little change in these trends between 2001 and 2003. However, the percentage of low-income people who relied on Medicaid increased from 2001 (35%) to 2003 (38%). Despite policies that attempt to expand coverage to members of low-income families, the ranks of the uninsured are filled by those with modest incomes. In 2003, 26% of people in low-income

Table 13.2 Individual health insurance coverage rates: 2001 and 2003

	2001[a]						2003[a]					
	All	Q1	Q2	Q3	Q4	Q5	All	Q1	Q2	Q3	Q4	Q5
Any private insurance	76.7	43.0	69.0	83.0	89.1	94.4	74.2	36.2	64.6	79.7	88.0	93.2
Employer or union provided	84.8	61.7	78.0	86.1	90.1	92.4	85.7	60.9	78.1	86.3	90.7	92.5
Privately purchased	9.8	20.7	15.2	9.1	6.6	5.7	9.7	24.2	15.4	9.2	6.0	5.7
Military coverage	2.1	3.3	2.5	2.6	2.1	1.1	2.4	3.0	3.2	3.1	2.2	1.5
Other	3.3	14.3	4.3	2.2	1.2	0.9	2.2	11.9	3.3	1.4	1.1	0.3
Medicaid[b]	11.4	34.9	13.8	6.0	3.8	1.7	12.3	37.9	15.3	8.0	4.1	2.0
Medicare	9.9	14.4	16.9	9.9	6.0	3.6	10.4	15.5	16.7	11.2	6.7	4.0
Uninsured	13.1	25.1	18.9	11.4	7.7	4.4	13.7	25.9	20.2	12.8	8.2	5.1

Source: Authors calculations from 2001 Panel of the Survey of Income and Program Participation
[a] Quintiles calculated based on individual's total family income in 2001 and 2003. Quintile upper limits for 2001 (in 2003 dollars) were: lowest quintile—$24,005; second quintile—$39,764; third quintile—$57,569; fourth quintile—$84,934. Quintile upper limits for 2003 were: lowest quintile—$23,720; second quintile—$39,736; third quintile—$58,451; fourth quintile—$86,304
[b] Includes coverage from Medicaid, State Children's Health Insurance Program (SCHIP), or other state-specific health insurance program

families were uninsured; only 5% of those in the highest-income quintile reported no health insurance coverage.

Research Evidence

Recent literature has provided new insights into low-income families' use of financial services and their success in accumulating assets as strategies for upward economic mobility. A series of studies has explored the phenomena of the "unbanked"—those who remain outside mainstream banking. Others have investigated the consequences of a lack of savings and how public policies create disincentives for low-income families to save. The role of home ownership in building financial security, the expansion of credit markets to low-income consumers and access to health insurance coverage have been other important topics explored by researchers within the last decade. The common theme throughout this literature is the need to build a stronger base of knowledge on which to design policies and programs to improve the economic well-being of those with very limited incomes.

The Unbanked

Having a bank account is the first step toward financial security (Beverly, McBride, & Schreiner, 2003; Hogarth, Anguelov, & Lee, 2004). Nevertheless, between 10 and 20% of all U.S. households are unbanked; they have neither a savings nor a checking account (Berry, 2004; Hurst, Luoh, & Stafford, 1998; Kennickell, Starr-McCluer, & Surette, 2000). Berry (2004) suggests, however, that the dichotomy between the banked and the unbanked is too rigid. In a survey of low-income consumers, Berry (2004) finds that among those currently without a bank account, about half had an account in the past, and 30% report some ongoing relationship with a bank. In addition, about half of those with a bank account also conduct some financial business with an alternative financial service (e.g., check-cashing business). Rates of being unbanked are higher for low-income families compared to higher-income families (Berry, 2004; Washington, 2006). Those without banking relationships are also more likely to be less educated, non-white, younger, unemployed, immigrants and renting rather than owning their residence (Berry, 2004; Hogarth et al., 2004; Rhine & Greene, 2006).

Many explanations have been given for low-income families being unbanked. Reasons include inadequate income, minimum balance requirements and service charges that are too high, the scarcity of bank branches in low-income and minority neighborhoods, inconvenient bank hours, credit problems, the availability of lower-cost services provided by alternative financial establishments, the desire to keep financial transactions "off the books" and not "deal with banks," language or cultural barriers for immigrants and a misunderstanding of the costs of choosing fringe banking providers (Berry, 2004; Hogarth & O'Donnell, 1999; Kennickell et al., 2000). As a result of these many barriers to mainstream financial services, the unbanked often seek out businesses in the fringe economy—those businesses that engage in financially predatory practices and charge excessive fees and prices for their goods and services (Caskey, 1994; Karger, 2005; Rhine, Greene, & Toussaint-Comeau, 2006). Also, there is some evidence that a consumer's decision to patronize alternative financial establishments is jointly made with the decision to be unbanked (Rhine et al., 2006).

The unbanked often have little or no money left for savings (Berry, 2004) and are less likely to own other financial assets, housing and vehicles (Carney & Gale, 2000). They also have fewer saving strategies compared to those who have bank accounts and rely on more informal strategies such as storing money with family members and friends (Beverly et al., 2003). Unbanked, low-income families are also unlikely to have a major credit card or a home mortgage. Instead, they rely on costly credit alternatives (Hogarth & O'Donnell, 1999) and are more likely to experience credit problems (Berry, 2004).

Savings and Asset Accumulation

It is well documented that low-income households hold little wealth (Bucks, Kennickell, & Moore, 2006; Cagetti & De Nardi, 2005; Haveman & Wolff, 2004; Hurst et al., 1998; Orzechowski & Sepielli, 2003; Sherraden, 1991) and that asset holdings are much less prevalent among low-income households compared to higher-income households (Haveman & Wolff, 2004; Huggett & Ventura, 2000; Orzechowski & Sepielli, 2003). For example, the bottom 60% of the nation in terms of income collectively possesses less than 5% of the nation's wealth (Boshara, 2005).

Building on the traditional concept of income poverty, Haveman and Wolff (2004) conceptualize "asset poverty" as an insufficiency of assets such that a household is not able to meet its basic needs as measured by the income poverty line for a period of 3 months. In 2001, one-fourth of American families had insufficient net worth to enable them to get by for 3 months at a poverty line level of living, and over one-third had insufficient liquid assets to support poverty level living for a 3-month period. Furthermore, Haveman and Wolff (2004) found using the asset poverty standard that 71% of non-elderly female heads with children were asset poor. In addition, during the years of rapid income growth from 1992 to 2001 when prosperity seemed to affect all groups, they found that asset poverty edged up slightly for the population as a whole. This is in contrast to the substantial decrease in income poverty over this period.

Differences in savings and assets between low- and high-income households have been attributed, at least in part, to social insurance and public assistance program availability and program eligibility rules (Hubbard, Skinner, & Zeldes, 1995; Huggett & Ventura, 2000; Kemp, 1991). Scholars (e.g., Hubbard et al., 1995) and policymakers (e.g., Kemp, 1991) asserted prior to the passage of the Personal Responsibility and Work Opportunity Reconciliation Act (PRWORA) of 1996 that assistance program asset limits deterred poor households from saving and accumulating assets. After more than three decades in which anti-poverty policy focused on income support, poverty analysts and advocates began in the 1990s to espouse strategies designed to help low-income households build wealth.

Asset accumulation strategies were viewed as a complement to the emphasis on work embodied in PRWORA (Blank, 2002). Saving and asset accumulation, however, only responded minimally to significant changes in incentives offered through the welfare reforms—suggesting that saving and asset limits are rarely binding for most low-income households (Hurst & Ziliak, 2006). Lifting limits on the value of a vehicle, however, did result in higher probabilities of low-income families owning a car (Hurst & Ziliak, 2006; Sullivan, 2006). Vehicle ownership has implications for economic outcomes of low-income families (Cervero, Sandoval, & Landis, 2002; Garasky, Fletcher, & Jensen, 2006; Ong, 2002). Automobiles serve an important role by providing easier access to employment opportunities, in addition to being one of the primary asset holdings among these families.

Home Ownership

Housing remains the primary store of wealth for most Americans (Belsky & Prakken, 2004). Home equity constituted roughly one-fifth of total household net wealth in 2001. Over two-thirds of U.S. households at that time owned a home with housing wealth broadly distributed across income levels. Median family net worth is over 30 times greater for home owners versus renters ($132,100 compared to $4,200 in 1998) (Kennickell et al., 2000). Home equity is especially important to lower-income households. According to Belsky and Prakken (2004), the median wealth of home owners with under $20,000 in income in 2001 was 81 times greater than the median wealth of renters with comparable incomes ($72,750 compared to $900).

Efforts to promote low-income home ownership have intensified in recent years (Belsky, Retsinas, & Duda, 2005). Low-income home ownership increased over the course of the 1990s and the early part of this decade as a result of expanded availability of mortgage credit to low-income borrowers. Home ownership is being actively promoted, in part, because it is seen as a way to help low-income households build assets. Belsky and colleagues (2005) contend that investing in a home is attractive because other investment alternatives do not allow households to leverage small amounts of money to acquire costly assets. Low-income families with only several thousands of dollars to invest can get a loan for as much as 95, 97 or even 100% of the value of the home they are purchasing. Homebuyers that put 10% down receive a 10% return on their investment for every 1% increase in the value of the home. In addition, part of their mortgage payment goes to paying down the principal on the loan. Over time, homebuyers build equity through loan repayment and also stand to benefit from any appreciation in the value of the home. Home ownership, however, can have shortcomings for low-income families. Lenders that base mortgage amounts on inflated home values or allow home owners to borrow at levels that are greater than 100% of home values leave families economically vulnerable to housing market downturns which may result in foreclosures, lost home equity and possible homelessness (Karger, 2005).

Credit Use and Predatory Lending

Lyons (2003) documents the expansion throughout the 1990s of borrowing opportunities to those traditionally constrained by credit markets—namely, low-income and minority families. Traditional lenders relaxed underwriting and offered new housing and consumer credit products; the industry embarked on aggressive marketing practices; and a new set of lenders targeted more marginal borrowers and offered more credit. As a result, the ability of all households to obtain their desired levels of debt increased. Among those experiencing the greatest gains in credit access were low-income families. Reflecting the growth of credit access, the share of low-income families with debt continued its upward trajectory in recent years, increasing 3.3 percentage points from 49.3% in 2001 to 52.6% in 2004 (Bucks et al., 2006). Lyons notes that this *democratization of credit* not only increased credit access, but may have also encouraged low-income families to live beyond their means.

Between 1983 and 1995, the fraction of poor households with a credit card more than doubled and the average balances held by the poor rose by almost as much as those of the non-poor (Bird, Hagstrom, & Wild, 1999). Similarly, lending to lower-income and minority households for home purchasing expanded, in part due to the growth of subprime and manufactured-home lending targeted toward these markets (Canner, Passmore, & Laderman, 1999). Karger (2005, p. 18) describes the "almost exponential growth" during the 1990s of subprime lending—described by the Federal Reserve Board as "extending credit to borrowers who exhibit characteristics indicating a significantly higher risk of default than traditional bank lending customers" (Board of Governors, 1999, p. 1). In addition, there was a compositional shift in wealth holdings. Households moved toward using their main home as a collateral source and increased non-collateralized debt, particularly for households with low equity positions in their home. As noted previously, this suggests that a sharp decline in house prices could now have a more adverse effect on consumer liquidity than was the case earlier (Hurst et al., 1998).

Access to Health Insurance Coverage

The vast majority of Americans receive health insurance coverage through a family member's insurance policy (DeNavas-Walt, Proctor, & Lee, 2006). A recent trend among employers, however, has been to reduce offers of insurance benefits to employees and their families due to rising costs (Glied, Lambrew, & Little, 2003; Kaiser Family Foundation & Health Research and Educational Trust, 2006). As fewer workers and their families obtain insurance coverage from their employers, the probability that individual family members will be without insurance increases (Nielsen & Garasky, forthcoming). Being uninsured affects one's ability to access medical care (Almeida, Dubay, & Ko, 2001), maintain personal health (Ayanian, Weissman, Schneider, Ginsburg, & Zaslavsky, 2000) and withstand the financial shocks that may arise from expensive or unexpected medical care needs (Wielawski, 2000).

In recent years, reduced benefits from employers and Medicaid expansions have contributed to an increase in the percentage of people who have public health insurance (Institute of Medicine, 2001). Medicaid and similar state-sponsored health insurance programs (e.g., State Children's Health Insurance Programs) have served as the primary health insurance safety net for those with low incomes who do not have access to employer-sponsored insurance. Without government-sponsored health insurance, an even larger percentage of Americans would be without health insurance (Dubay & Kenney, 2003; Kronick & Gilmer, 2002). Nevertheless, it is now relatively common for a low-income person's insurance status to change over time due to changes in their employment, changes in the employment of a family member, public assistance program participation and eligibility rules and having to choose between health insurance coverage and meeting other needs due to limited resources (i.e., coverage is unaffordable) (Czajka & Olsen, 2000; Kaiser Family Foundation, 2006; Short & Graefe, 2003; Swartz, Marcotte & McBride, 1993).

Future Directions

Two streams of future research are needed to better understand the consumer finances of low-income families. First, much remains unknown about *how* low-income families make consumer finance decisions. In recent years, journalists, sociologists, anthropologists and family scientists have begun to explore this important question using qualitative research methods (e.g., DeParle, 2004; Edin & Lein, 1997; Seccombe, 1999). Sherraden (2004) contends that ethnographic studies have provided some insights into the economic behavior of low-income and low-wealth households. For example, anecdotal evidence indicates that poor households do save, although not always in the same way or for the same purposes as middle-income households. Nevertheless, much remains to be understood about how low-income households save. More research is needed regarding the extent and nature of saving for low-income families. In addition, more needs to be learned about how the availability of reasonably priced financial services facilitates saving and wealth accumulation.

Low-income families may find financial decisions complicated and daunting (Berry, 2004; Beshears, Choi, Laibson, & Madrian, 2006; Gale, Gruber, & Orszag, 2006). As a result, they may procrastinate in making these decisions. Strategies to address this concern include simplifying investment decision-making by reducing the options that are available to potential investors and by having firms automatically enroll employees in savings plans. These approaches have the potential to increase participation in saving programs and increase contribution rates among current saving program participants (Beshears et al., 2006; Gale et al., 2006). Similarly, Duflo, Gale, Liebman, Orszag and Saez (2005) contend that the combination of clear and understandable programs, easily accessible savings vehicles and professional assistance could generate a significant increase in contributions to retirement accounts among middle- and low-income households. Additional research is needed to better understand the ability of low-income families to comprehend their saving options and to inform strategies such as these for increasing saving among low-income families by simplifying financial decision-making.

Second, there is a critical need to focus on research questions that have policy implications. Policymakers and educators have much to learn regarding assisting low-income families with their consumer finances. Current strategies to assist low-income families emphasize creating work incentives over providing cash assistance (Eissa & Nichols, 2005). The Earned Income Tax Credit (EITC) was begun in part to provide a work incentive to low-income individuals (Internal Revenue Service, 2007b). The EITC is a refundable federal income tax credit available to qualifying taxpayers who file a tax return. As an incentive to work, the credit amount increases with earnings at low levels of income, then decreases until it is phased out. Maximum credit amounts and eligible income ranges vary by household composition with largest benefits available to married couples with more than one qualifying child that file a joint tax return. In 2006 their maximum credit would have been $4,536 if they had an adjusted gross income (AGI) between $11,300 and $16,850, and $0 with an AGI of $38,348 or more (Internal Revenue Service, 2007b). Eligible income ranges and credit amounts have been revised several times since the program began in 1975 in order to expand the credit and eligibility (Ways & Means, 2004). Over time, the EITC has become the nation's largest cash transfer program for low- and moderate-income families (Blumenthal, Erard, & Ho, 2005). In 2006, 19.6 million individuals and families received credits totaling $36.6 billion (Internal Revenue Service, 2007a).

The EITC has been hailed as a success lifting more than 4 million people out of poverty each year (Blumenthal et al., 2005). Research also indicates that it has had numerous positive effects on families (Beverly, 2002) including increasing labor force participation and encouraging work (Neumark & Wascher, 2001). The EITC program, however, has shortcomings as well. While the EITC acts as a wage bonus to the lowest income workers, the credit phase-out may create a substantial marginal tax rate increase for families in the phase-out range and, thus, a disincentive to increase earnings. More specifically, after combining a reduced credit with additional federal and state income taxes and other payroll taxes, the effective marginal tax rate for families in the phase-out range can be over 50% (Bryan, 2005). Additionally, low participation rates among some groups and compliance issues—claimants receiving benefits for which they are not entitled—continue to plague the program (Blumenthal et al., 2005). Evidence suggests that knowledge about the program varies across subgroups indicating that additional outreach is needed to ensure greater participation among eligible individuals and families (Caputo, 2006; Phillips, 2001). Clearly, additional research is needed to enhance the effectiveness of the EITC program.

A number of research-based demonstration projects and small studies have been conducted in the past decade that provide some evidence into what policies and programs may be effective with low-income families. For example, government interventions intended to decrease the number of unbanked households have had mixed results. Washington (2006) found that legislation requiring banks to offer low-cost accounts decreased slightly the number of low-income minority unbanked households, but only with a substantial lag of 2–3 years. Caps on check-cashing fees led to a small, but more immediate, reduction in the number of unbanked among this population. Because price caps may lead to a reduction in the supply of check-cashing institutions, overall welfare effects are indeterminate. Regarding moving the unbanked into the financial mainstream, checking accounts may be more difficult to manage than other types of bank accounts (Hogarth et al., 2004). Therefore, it may be easier to reduce the number of unbanked households via more easy-to-manage accounts, such as savings accounts. Additional research about the unbanked would aid the design of banking programs and policies to meet low-income consumer finance needs.

Wiranowski (2003) contends that home-buying policies should not just focus on promoting low-income home ownership. All interested homebuyers—low-income individuals among them—should receive help so that they make choices that best suit them. Belsky and colleagues (2005) identify ways in which home ownership could be made even more beneficial for low-income families. These include getting low-income borrowers the lowest-cost credit for which they qualify, coaching them to improve their credit histories so that they can qualify for lower-cost credit and helping borrowers assess when it would be beneficial to refinance their mortgages. Belsky and his colleagues (2005) contend that achieving these goals will require financial education, help for low-income borrowers to save enough to have cash cushions against budget and income shocks and products that help them mitigate risks (e.g., house price declines and income disruptions). Each of these approaches to expanding home ownership among low-income families would benefit from additional research that examines potential costs and benefits, as well as strategies for implementation.

Sherraden (1991) proposed an institutional saving theory suggesting that low-income families can save with institutional supports. He conceptualized individual development accounts (IDAs) as a matched saving strategy for the poor to accumulate assets (Sherraden, 1991, 2000). IDAs are special savings accounts, started as early as birth, to be used for education, job training, home ownership, small business or other development purposes. IDAs can have multiple sources of matching deposits, including governments, corporations, foundations, community groups and individual donors. Today, over 40 states have initiated some type of IDA policy (Greenberg & Patel, 2006). A majority of states have IDAs in their state cash welfare plans, although funding levels vary widely (Boshara, 2005). The first large-scale evaluation of IDAs suggests that low-income families will contribute to IDAs and that IDAs can increase some forms of asset accumulation, but IDAs do not necessarily increase overall wealth (Boshara, 2005). Recent analyses of longitudinal data from this evaluation suggest that IDA participants have significant variations in savings patterns; married families are more successful in growing their IDAs; and contrary to previous findings, the matching rate and the financial education of participants are not significantly related to savings patterns (Han, 2006). Additional research is needed to confirm these findings and to identify ways to enhance saving via IDAs for groups of low-income families that may not be taking advantage of this opportunity.

Gale and colleagues (2006) suggest modifying income tax deduction rules to increase retirement saving. The conventional approach to subsidizing saving through 401(k) plans and traditional individual retirement arrangements (IRAs) provides tax deductions for contributions along with tax deferral on account earnings. This approach has not enticed low- and middle-income families to contribute very much to retirement accounts, in part because the value of these incentives is modest for families with low marginal income tax rates (Duflo et al., 2005). Gale and others (2006) propose eliminating tax incentives for IRA and 401(k) contributions and replacing them with a universal government-sponsored matching program. They argue that this would shift incentives toward increasing retirement savings among low- and moderate-income individuals. Results from a randomized experiment designed to test the effectiveness of offering matching incentives for IRA contributions at the time of tax preparation support this suggestion (Duflo et al., 2005). Additional studies are needed to further identify ways to increase long-term saving among low-income families using tax incentives.

In summary, low-income families face numerous barriers to meeting their basic needs that go beyond income. The evidence provided here suggests that they experience consumer finance obstacles in terms of interacting with banking and other financial institutions, saving and accumulating assets, purchasing a home, obtaining and using credit and accessing health insurance coverage. In each of these areas, additional research is needed in order to identify ways to help these families not only meet their consumer needs, but also accumulate assets that promote long-term economic well-being.

References

Almeida, R. A., Dubay, L. C., & Ko, G. (2001). Access to care and use of health services by low-income women. *Health Care Financing Review, 22*(4), 27–47.

Ayanian, J. Z., Weissman, J. S., Schneider, E. C., Ginsburg, J. A., & Zaslavsky, A. M. (2000). Unmet health needs of uninsured adults in the United States. *Journal of the American Medical Association, 284*(16), 2061–2069.

Belsky, E., & Prakken, J. (2004, December). *Housing wealth effects: Housing's impact on wealth accumulation, wealth distribution and consumer spending* (Joint Center for Housing Studies Working Paper W04-13). Cambridge, MA: Harvard University.

Belsky, E., Retsinas, N., & Duda, M. (2005, September). *The financial returns to low-income home ownership* (Joint Center for Housing Studies Working Paper W05-9). Cambridge, MA: Harvard University.

Berry, C. (2004, February). *To bank or not to bank? A survey of low-income households* (Joint Center for Housing Studies Working Paper BABC 04-3). Cambridge, MA: Harvard University.

Beshears, J., Choi, J., Laibson, D., &. Madrian, B. (2006, October). *Simplification and saving* (NBER Working Paper 12659). Cambridge, MA: National Bureau of Economic Research.

Beverly, S. (2002). What social workers need to know about the Earned Income Tax Credit. *Social Work, 47,* 259–266.

Beverly, S., McBride, A., & Schreiner, M. (2003). A framework of asset-accumulation stages and strategies. *Journal of Family and Economic Issues, 24,* 143–156.

Bird, E., Hagstrom, P., & Wild, R. (1999). Credit card debts of the poor: High and rising. *Journal of Policy Analysis and Management, 18,* 125–133.

Blank, R. (2002). Evaluating welfare reform in the United States. *Journal of Economic Literature, 40,* 1105–1166.

Blank, R. M., Danziger, S. H., & Schoeni, R. F. (2006). *Working and poor: How economic and policy changes are affecting low-wage workers.* New York: Russell Sage Foundation.

Blumenthal, M., Erard, B., & Ho, C. (2005). Participation and compliance with the Earned Income Tax Credit. *National Tax Journal, 58,* 189–213.

Board of Governors of the Federal Reserve System. (1999). *Interagency guidance on sub-prime lending.* Washington, DC: Government Printing Office.

Boshara, R. (2005, March). *Individual development accounts: Policies to build savings and assets for the poor* (Welfare Reform & Beyond, Policy Brief #32). Washington, DC: The Brookings Institute.

Bryan, J. (2005). Have the 1996 welfare reforms and expansion of the Earned Income Tax Credit eliminated the need for a basic income guarantee in the US? *Review of Social Economy, 63,* 595–611.

Bucks, B. K., Kennickell, A. B., & Moore, K. B. (2006). Recent changes in U.S. family finances: Evidence from the 2001 and 2004 Survey of Consumer Finances. *Federal Reserve Bulletin, 92,* 1–38.

Cagetti, M., & De Nardi, M. (2005). *Wealth inequality: Data and models* (Working Paper WP 2005–10). Chicago: Federal Reserve Bank.

Canner, G., Passmore, W., & Laderman, E. (1999). The role of specialized lenders in extending mortgages to lower-income and minority homebuyers. *Federal Reserve Bulletin, 85,* 709–723.

Caputo, R. (2006). The Earned Income Tax Credit: A study of eligible participants vs. non-participants. *Journal of Sociology and Social Welfare, 33,* 9–29.

Carney, S., & Gale, W.G. (2000, February). *Asset accumulation among low-income households.* Washington, DC: The Brookings Institute.

Caskey, J. (1994). *Fringe banking: Check-cashing outlets, pawnships, and the poor.* New York: Russell Sage Foundation.

Cervero, R., Sandoval, O., & Landis, J. (2002). Transportation as a stimulus of welfare-to-work: Private versus public mobility. *Journal of Planning Education and Research, 22,* 50–63.

Czajka, J. L., & Olsen, C. (2000). *The effects of trigger events on changes in children's health insurance coverage* (Report submitted to the Assistant Secretary for Planning and Evaluation). Washington, DC: Mathematica Policy Research, Inc.

DeNavas-Walt, C., Proctor, B. D., & Lee, C. H. (2006). *Income, poverty and health insurance coverage in the United States: 2005* (Current Population Report P60-231). Washington, DC: U.S. Census Bureau.

DeParle, J. (2004). *American dream: Three women, ten kids and a nation's drive to end welfare.* New York: Viking.

Dubay, L., & Kenney, G. (2003). Expanding public health insurance to parents: Effects on children's coverage under Medicaid. *Health Services Research, 38*(5), 1283–1301.

Duflo, E., Gale, W., Liebman, J., Orszag, P., & Saez, E. (2005, September). *Saving incentives for low- and middle-income families: Evidence from a field experiment with H&R Block* (NBER Working Paper 11680). Cambridge, MA: National Bureau of Economic Research.

Edin, K., & Lein, L. (1997). *Making ends meet.* New York: Russell Sage Foundation.

Eissa, N., & Nichols, A. (2005). Tax-transfer policy and labor market outcomes. *The American Economic Review, 95,* 88–93.

Gale, W., Gruber, J., & Orszag, P. (2006, April). *Improving opportunities and incentives for saving by middle- and low-income households* (Policy Brief 2006-02). Washington, DC: Brookings Institution.

Garasky, S., Fletcher, C. N., & Jensen, H. H. (2006). Transiting to work: The role of private transportation for low-income households. *Journal of Consumer Affairs, 40*(1), 64–89.

Glied, S. A., Lambrew, J. M., & Little, S. (2003). *The growing share of uninsured workers employed by large firms* (No. 672). New York City: The Commonwealth Fund.

Greenberg, M., & Patel, N. (2006, May). *Coordinating Individual Development Accounts and the Workforce Investment Act to increase access to postsecondary education and training* (Policy Report 06-09). St. Louis: Washington University, Center for Social Development.

Han, C. K. (2006). *Saving in Individual Development Accounts: Latent growth modeling.* (Working Paper No. 06-17). St. Louis: Washington University, Center for Social Development.

Haveman, R., & Wolff, E. (2004). The concept and measurement of asset poverty: Levels, trends and composition for the U.S., 1983–2001. *Journal of Economic Inequality, 2,* 145–169.

Hogarth, J., Anguelov, C., & Lee, J. (2004). Why don't households have a checking account? *Journal of Consumer Affairs, 38*(1), 1–34.

Hogarth, J. M., & O'Donnell, K. (1999). Banking relationship of lower-income families and the governmental trend toward electronic payment. *Federal Reserve Bulletin, 85,* 459–473.

Hubbard, R., Skinner, J., & Zeldes, S. (1995). Precautionary saving and social insurance. *The Journal of Political Economy, 103,* 360–399.

Huggett, M., & Ventura, G. (2000). Understanding why high income households save more than low income households. *Journal of Monetary Economics, 45,* 361–397.

Hurst, E., Luoh, M. C., & Stafford, F. P. (1998). The wealth dynamics of American families, 1984–1994. *Brookings Papers on Economic Activity, 1,* 267–337.

Hurst, E., & Ziliak, J. (2006). Do welfare asset limits affect household saving? Evidence from welfare reform. *Journal of Human Resources, 41,* 46–71.

Institute of Medicine. (2001). *Coverage matters: Insurance and health care.* Washington, DC: National Academy Press.

Internal Revenue Service, U.S. Department of the Treasury. (2007a). *Data book, 2006* (Publication 55B.) Washington, DC: U.S. Department of Treasury.

Internal Revenue Service, U.S. Department of the Treasury. (2007b). *Earned income tax credit (EITC): Overview.* Retrieved May 20, 2007, from http://www.irs.gov/individuals/article/0,,id=96406,00.html.

Kaiser Family Foundation. (2006). *The uninsured: A primer.* Menlo Park, CA: Kaiser Family Foundation.

Kaiser Family Foundation & Health Research and Educational Trust. (2006). *Employer health benefits: 2006 annual survey.* Menlo Park, CA and Chicago, IL: Kaiser Family Foundation and Health Research and Educational Trust.

Karger, H. (2005). *Shortchanged: Life and debt in the fringe economy.* San Francisco: Berrett-Koehler Publishers.

Kemp, J. (1991). *Testimony to the Joint Economic Committee Hearing on the war on poverty, November 19, 1991.* Washington, DC: Government Printing Office.

Kennickell, A. B., Starr-McCluer, M., & Surette, B. J. (2000). Recent changes in U.S. family finances: Results from the 1998 Survey of Consumer Finances. *Federal Reserve Bulletin, 86*(1), 1–29.

Kronick, R., & Gilmer, T. (2002). Insuring low-income adults: Does public coverage crowd out private? *Health Affairs, 21*(1), 225–239.

Lyons, A.C. (2003). How credit access has changed over time for U.S. households. *Journal of Consumer Affairs, 37*(2), 231–255.

McNichol, L., & Springer, J. (2004). *State policies to assist working-poor families.* Washington, DC: Center on Budget and Policy Priorities.

Neuberger, Z., Greenstein, R., & Sweeney, E.P. (2005). *Protecting low-income families' retirement savings: How retirement accounts are treated in means-tested programs and steps to remove barriers to retirement savings* (The Retirement Security Project. No. 2005-6). Retrieved May 20, 2007, from http://www.retirementsecurityproject.org.

Neumark, D., & Wascher, W. (2001). Using the EITC to help poor families: New evidence and a comparison with the minimum wage. *National Tax Journal, 54,* 281–318.

Nielsen, R. B., & Garasky, S. (forthcoming). Health insurance stability and health status: Do family-level coverage patterns matter? *Journal of Family Issues.*

Ong, P. M. (2002). Car ownership and welfare-to-work. *Journal of Policy Analysis and Management, 21*(2), 239–252.

Orzechowski, S., & Sepielli, P. (2003). *Net worth and asset ownership of households: 1998 and 2000* (Current Population Report P70-88). Washington, DC: U.S. Census Bureau.

Phillips, K. (2001). The Earned Income Tax Credit: Knowledge is money. *Political Science Quarterly, 116,* 413–424.

Rhine, S. L. W., & Greene, W.H. (2006). The determinants of being unbanked for U.S. immigrants. *Journal of Consumer Affairs, 40*(1), 21–40.

Rhine, S. L. W., Greene, W.H., & Toussaint-Comeau, M. (2006). The importance of check-cashing businesses to the unbanked: Racial/ethnic differences. *The Review of Economics and Statistics, 88*(1): 146–157.

Seccombe, K. (1999). *So you think I drive a Cadillac?* Boston: Allyn and Bacon.

Sherraden, M. (1991). *Assets and the poor: A new American Welfare Policy.* Armonk, NY: M.E. Sharpe.

Sherraden, M. (2000). From research to policy: Lessons from Individual Development Accounts. *Journal of Consumer Affairs, 34*(2), 159–181.

Sherraden, M. (2004). *Strategic Plan for CSD's Work in Asset Building: 2005-2010.* Retrieved May 20, 2007 from http://gwbweb.wustl.edu/csd/asset/index.htm.

Short, P. F., & Graefe, D. R. (2003). Battery-powered health insurance? Stability in coverage of the uninsured. *Health Affairs, 22*(6), 244–255.

Sullivan, J. (2006). Welfare reform, saving, and vehicle ownership: Do asset limits and vehicle exemptions matter? *Journal of Human Resources, 41,* 72–105.

Swartz, K., Marcotte, J., & McBride, T. D. (1993). Personal characteristics and spells without health insurance. *Inquiry, 30*(1), 64–77.

Washington, E. (2006). The impact of banking and fringe banking regulation on the number of unbanked Americans. *Journal of Human Resources, 41,* 106–137.

Ways and Means, U.S. House Committee on. (2004). *2004 Green Book: Background material and data on programs within the jurisdiction of the House Committee on Ways and Means.* Washington, DC: Government Printing Office.

Wielawski, I. (2000). Gouging the medically uninsured: A tale of two bills. *Health Affairs, 19*(5), 180–185.

Wiranowski, M. (2003, October). *Sustaining home ownership through education and counseling* (Fellowship for Emerging Leaders Working Paper Series). Cambridge, MA: Neighborhood Reinvestment Corporation and The Joint Center for Housing Studies of Harvard University.

Chapter 14
Management Issues of Business-Owning Families

George W. Haynes, Sharon M. Danes, and Deborah C. Haynes

Abstract This chapter summarizes the literature at the intersection of family and business for households owning a family business. While it may appear that these business-owning households earn higher income and accumulate more wealth, they face the challenges of managing the family/business interface. This chapter utilizes the Sustainable Family Business Model to carefully assesses two critically important dimensions: financial interface, where financial and human resources (typically labor) move between the family and business, and interpersonal relationships interface, where tensions between the family and business must be addressed for the family and business to survive and succeed.

Healthy communities depend on healthy family businesses. Healthy families depend on support from healthy businesses, and vice versa. These family businesses are the cornerstones of communities, creating earnings (wealth and income) for their owners and employees, donating to local organizations, providing civic leadership and making other important contributions. Nearly 20 % of all households in the United States have one or more members who are self-employed or own a business (Haynes & Ou, 2007). Nearly two-thirds of these business-owning households have an owner or manager in the household and one-third are self-employed individuals. Family businesses make substantial contributions to the U.S. economy by generating over 60 % of U.S. business revenue and providing jobs for over half of the non-agricultural labor force (Heck & Stafford, 2001).

The financial health of the household and business is inextricably intertwined for business-owning families. Any financial analysis of the business without careful consideration of the household is simply incomplete. Households owning businesses have a significantly higher probability of being high income and wealth than other households not owning a business (Haynes & Ou, 2007). While it may appear that these business-owning households are better off, they face the challenges of managing the family/business interface. The interface between the family and business has

G.W. Haynes
Department of Agricultural Economics and Economics, Montana State University, 210E Linfield Hall, Bozeman, MT 59717, USA
e-mail: haynes@montana.edu

J.J. Xiao, (ed.), *Handbook of Consumer Finance Research*,
© Springer 2008

two critically important dimensions: financial interface, where financial and human resources (typically labor) move between the family and business, and interpersonal relationships interface, where tensions between the family and business must be addressed for the family and business to survive. This chapter will focus on these financial and interpersonal relationship challenges faced by family businesses.

Family Impact on Business Performance

Families and businesses depend on the survival and success of one another in the family-owned business. A disruption in the family sphere is felt throughout the business and a disruption in the business sphere is felt throughout the family. There is clearly a "family effect" as suggested by Dyer (2006), and this "family effect" may be either positive or negative for the family business. Daily and Dollinger (1992) compared family owned and family-managed firms with professionally managed firms and concluded that family owned and family-managed firms appear to exhibit performance advantages. A more recent article by Anderson and Reeb (2003) supported these positive results by suggesting that family firms perform better than non-family firms. When children are in the household, household managers who work in the family business take more time to be with their children and are far less likely to outsource their child care than household mangers working outside of the family business (Haynes, Avery, & Hunts, 1999; Haynes et al., 1999; Heck, 1992). However, other authors have concluded that family firms are inherently inefficient because preferences are afforded to family members for key management and employment opportunities (Perrow, 1972) and because family conflicts interfere with the performance of the firm (Faccio, Lang, & Young, 2001). Other authors have suggested that no substantial differences in performance exist between family and non-family firms (Chrisman, Chua, & Litz, 2004).

The jury is out on whether family businesses perform better than non-family businesses because these analyses are dependent on how family businesses are defined (Dyer, 2006). The definition of family business used in this chapter does not include large publicly traded businesses, such as Ford or Wrigley's. Several definitions have been proposed for identifying a family business. In general, family business researchers define family businesses by the degree of ownership or management by family members, degree of family involvement, potential for generational transfer or multiple criteria (Handler, 1992). The most widespread criterion for defining family business is the degree of ownership or management by family members (Sharma, Chrisman, & Chua, 1997). Handler (1992) used family involvement to suggest that the family business is an organization in which family members influence major operation decisions and plans for succession. Dunn (1996) has suggested that the family must have a controlling interest in the business, while others have demanded that the business employ family members (Covin, 1994) to be classified as family firm. For those studying succession, the potential for generational transfer has been important in defining a family business (Astrachan & Kolenko, 1994; Fiegner, Brown, Prince, & File, 1994). Other researchers, such as the Family Business Group, have used multiple criteria to define a family household and family business. The Family Business Group defines the family as a group of people related by blood, marriage or adoption, who share a common dwelling. To qualify as family business, the owner-manager had to have been in business for at least a year, worked at least 6 hours per week year-round or a minimum of 312 hours per year in the business, been involved in its day-to-day management and resided with another family member (Winter, Fitzgerald, Heck, Haynes, & Danes, 1998).

While there are important conceptual considerations in defining a family business, there are important empirical considerations, too. Two major issues are critically important: (1) family business are often identified using business, rather than households lists; and (2) family business surveys always include an interview with the business manager, but rarely interview the household manager. Family businesses can be found by utilizing business lists, such as those provided by Dun and Bradstreet, Mass Mutual, local Chambers of Commerce and others, or by utilizing household lists. A majority of the family business studies have utilized business sampling frames, where business owners were asked if they were a family business or not (Anderson & Reeb, 2003; Daily & Dollinger, 1992; Feigener et al., 1994). In addition, major data collection efforts for small business researchers, such as the Survey of Small Business Finances, utilize business, rather than household, sampling frames. Business sampling frames miss small home-based businesses and nascent entrepreneurs that have not registered their business with Dun and Bradstreet, the local Chamber of Commerce or other organizations. Winter et al. (1998) were concerned that "using a single respondent to represent the business and the family may distort the reporting of what a family business is really like and how it operates and interacts with the owning family" (1998, p. 241). These concerns prompted the Family Business Group to focus on the interaction between family and business and collect data from a nationally representative sample of household and business managers in family business households, the National Family Business Survey.

Family and business economics/sociology/psychology merge at the intersection of the family and business. While it seems that the business economic concerns dominate any discussion of the economic health of the household, it is the interaction of family and business resources that impacts the performance of the family business. Undoubtedly, careful financial monitoring and analysis is required by the business to survive and succeed; however, any financial analysis of the business without a careful financial analysis of the family is useless. Personal finance professionals have an important role to play with family business owners to help the family maximize utility and the business to maximize profits. The intersection of the family and business is where relationship tension often resides and appropriate adjustment strategies are needed by both the family and the business to prevent these tensions from negatively impacting the family business. The next section examines a conceptual model to guide research in family business.

Conceptual Considerations—The Sustainable Family Business Model

The conceptual basis for this chapter resides in the Sustainable Family Business Model (Stafford, Duncan, Danes, & Winter, 1999). The conceptual model draws from family systems theory and behavioral theories of firm management, giving equal recognition to family and business systems and to the interplay between them in achieving mutual sustainability (Stafford et al., 1999). In contrast to traditional models of firm and entrepreneurial success, the Sustainable Family Business Model (SFBM) locates entrepreneurship and the firm within the social context of family (Fig. 14.1).

In the SFBM, the family and business have resources, constraints, processes and achievements that are largely independent of one another. The overall goal of SFBM is to identify the resources, constraints and processes that will lead to a sustainable family business. This model deviates from the classical economic model, where families efficiently pursue satisfaction or utility and businesses separately pursue profits (Lopez, 1986). In this model, family and business include resources, such as time and money, as well as interpersonal relationships, such as family support and affection, which are combined to pursue family business sustainability. The family system is a purposeful system, where resources and constraints are transformed through interpersonal and resource transactions into achievements, where the achievements are both subjective (for instance, achieving some level of satisfaction) and objective (for instance, earning income). The business system is also

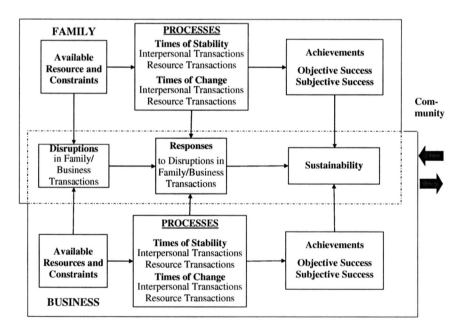

Fig. 14.1 The sustainable family business model
Source: Stafford, Duncan, Danes, and Winter (1999)

purposeful, where resources and constraints are converted into achievements, where achievements are measured by success in one's sense of "pleasure in providing a way of life" (Stafford et al., 1999, p. 205), business survival or success. The inherent conflicts, where the family pursues utility and the business pursues profits, are very challenging.

Both the family and business bring a stock of human, financial, social and cultural capital to the family business. Human capital is held in the form of skills, experience and education; financial capital is monetary resources, such as income, expenses, assets, liabilities and wealth; social capital is the networks of people associated with either entity; and cultural capital is the underpinnings of knowledge and basic values (Light, 2006). The transactions of the family produce stable households, good interpersonal relationships among family members, children and much more. Transactions of the business produce goods and services.

The intersection of family and business systems is most important when considering the intermingling of resources. Whether disruptions come from outside the family business, such as a change in public policy, or from inside, such as death, business and/or family managers must perceive, process and respond to that changing environment and reconstruct processes to ensure sustainability over time (Danes, Haberman, & McTavish, 2005). Resiliency is the owning family's adjustment of resources and interpersonal processes in response to disruptions (Danes, 2006). If families have built a stored capacity for resilience, when a disruption is encountered, the store of trust and creativity in problem solving can be more easily and quickly tapped and adapted to new situations (Danes, Rueter, Kwon, & Doherty, 2002). The degree of overlap between the family and business will determine how disruptions in one system impact the other, and the boundaries between the systems often become more permeable during disruptions. The goal is to achieve a sustainable family business system. Stafford et al. (1999) succinctly summarizes the importance of sustainability in the following:

> Sustainability results from the confluence of family success, business success and appropriate responses to disruptions. In other words, sustainability requires consideration of the family as well as the business. Sustainability also requires consideration of the ability of the family and business to cooperate in responding to disruptions in a way that does not impede the success of each (1999, p. 205).

Understanding the incidence of intermingling of resources is crucial in small business studies because intermingling obscures the financial records of either the family or the firm with potentially confusing and catastrophic results. For instance, when a family member takes cash from the business for personal use, profits of the business are understated. Or when the family utilizes a home equity mortgage to invest in business assets, assets for the business are overstated and liabilities are unstated (inflating the net worth of the business). In these instances, the family business may not know if it is profitable and may be jeopardizing its future. In addition, intermingling leads to inaccurate, and possibly deceptive, financial statements for the family business.

The SBFM provides the conceptual guidance for discussing financial intermingling and interpersonal relationships in the family business. The next two sections examine several studies addressing the intersection between the family and business systems.

Intermingling Between the Business and Family

The SFBM recognizes the overlap of family and business demands. While a substantial body of literature exists on how work affects family life and vice versa (Hollander & Elman, 1988; Netemeyer, Boles, & McMurrian, 1996; O'Driscoll, Ilgen, & Hildreth, 1992), much less is known about work and family when the family and work roles are closely related, such as in a family business. The intersection between the family and business is critical because it is here where the allocation of resources and resiliency of interpersonal relationships are tested.

Financial Intermingling at Family/Business Interface

Financial intermingling is an important topic for family businesses because "what is good for the business" may or may not be "good for the family." The financial intermingling literature has discussed several examples of intermingling: using family assets to secure business loans, using household income to meet business cash flow demands, borrowing money from the family for use in the business, borrowing money from the business for use in the family and using business income to meet cash flow demands in the family (Avery, Bostic, & Samolyk, 1998; Haynes, Walker, Rowe, & Hong, 1999); using personal savings and delayed or reduced compensation for business purposes (Freear, Sohl, & Wetzel, 1995); providing space and utilities (Winborg and Landstrom, 2001); using personal credit cards and home equity loans (Van Auken, 2003); and using family members as employees in the business (Heck & Walker, 1993), or vice versa.

In an important paper on the issue of intermingling of finances between the family and the business, Haynes, Walker, et al. (1999) found that substantial intermingling occurred between the family and the business. They used the 1997 National Family Business Survey (NFBS), a data set that included business characteristics, owner-manager characteristics and family characteristics, to determine the significant business and business manager characteristics associated with the likelihood of financial intermingling in family owned businesses. Business-to-family intermingling was more likely to occur when the family business manager was white than non-white; the location of the business was in a rural or small town than when the location was an urban area; the business borrowed money; and the business operated as a regular or subchapters corporation. Family-to-business intermingling was most likely to occur when the business manager was non-white than white; in a sole proprietorship than in other types of business formations; in more financially leveraged businesses; in family businesses with younger owners; and in family businesses whose owners have children aged 18 years or younger.

Other papers on the subject on financial intermingling include Haynes and Avery (1996), Muske, Fitzgerald, and Haynes (2003), and Yilmazer and Schrank (2006). Haynes and Avery (1996) used the Survey of Consumer Finances to investigate the debt structure of small businesses under the premise that personal and business debt was intertwined. They found that small business households comprise about 13 % of the population of households, but they account for nearly 37 % of the total debt held by households. One important hypothesis they suggested is that one would expect the total amount of debt held by a small business owner to be higher because the owner has the added burden of providing financial capital to the business. The implication of this debt structure is that the additional financial burden, in effect, provides a "hidden" avenue of financing of the small business because the responsibility for repaying the loan is ambiguously assigned to both the household and the business. Thus, this small-business financing source will be overlooked when looking at the traditional business data.

Muske et al. (2003) investigated the intermingling of family and business financial resources in copreneurial and non-copreneurial couples. They defined copreneurs as couples sharing a personal and a business relationship and suggested that such couples should have overlapping boundaries between family and business systems. Using the same data set as Haynes and Walker et al. (1999), Muske and his colleagues (2003) concluded that copreneurs were more likely to use the family's financial resources to assist the business than non-copreneurs. This suggests that copreneurs may effectively shift resources to support their chosen life style.

Yilmazer and Schrank (2006) used the Survey of Consumer Finances to compare the determinants of intermingling between family and non-family businesses. After determining that intermingling occurred in both family and non-family businesses, they showed that, once other business and household characteristics are controlled for, there was no significant difference between family and non-family businesses in the incidence of household-to-business and business-to-family intermingling. They concluded that the intermingling of household and business financial resources was likely influenced more by business characteristics and household wealth than by whether the business was classified as a family business or not.

Further work by Haynes (2007) extended the results of Haynes and his colleagues (1999) to Mexican- and Korean-American subgroups. Mexican-American family business managers were more likely to engage in financial intermingling than Korean-American business managers (76 % for Mexican-Americans and 57 % for Korean-Americans). While Mexican-Americans were substantially more likely to use family-to-business intermingling than Korean-Americans, only about 25 % of Mexican- and Korean-American business managers used any business-to-family intermingling. Interestingly, Mexican- and Korean-American business managers had very similar intermingling patterns as non-minority business managers.

Recent work by Haynes, Onochie, and Muske (2007) suggested that increases in the available cash in the business from higher gross sales or net profits bring more cash into the household, while only increases in the value of business (wealth) increase the amount of money spent on other household assets. Interestingly, these financial indicators of the businesses were not associated with measures of general well-being in the household. In a similar line of research, Zuiker et al. (2003) found that family businesses with more cash flow problems were more likely to inter-mingle finances than other family businesses without cash flow problems. In fact, Zuiker and her colleagues suggest that "if there was intermingling of resources from the family to the business, the odds were that the family business was experiencing business cash flow problems" (p. 75).

The financial resource intermingling is only one dimension of intermingling between the household and business. The next section examines the interpersonal transactions at the family/business interface as these families grapple with conflict and tension.

Interpersonal Transactions at Family/Business Interface

The previous section has focused on the financial relationships between the family and business; however, the transfer of resources between the spheres of influence (family and business) creates tension which must be mitigated for the family and business to survive and succeed. Certain (low or moderate) levels of tension acts as a creative mechanism and can increase the health, growth and success of both businesses and families, while higher levels of tension can have the opposite effect on those systems: reduced health and satisfaction, slower business growth and less success (Danes, 2006; Danes & Olson, 2003; Danes, Zuiker, Kean, & Arbuthnot, 1999; Kaye, 2002).

This family business tension is created by conflicts, which tend to fall into five ar-eas: justice conflict, role conflict, work/family conflict, identity conflict and succes-sion conflict. Justice conflicts arise over unfair compensation, quality of treatment or tensions surrounding the allocation of resources (Danes & Morgan, 2004). Role conflicts occur over confusion about roles related to performing a task or assigning decision-making authority. Work/family conflicts occur at the intersection of the family and business system when business work supercedes family needs over an extended length of time or when business managers have high demands in the fam-ily and business subsystems. Identity conflict arises as family members attempt to differentiate themselves from family expectations and establish their independence and autonomy. Succession conflicts are generally related to ownership issues.

Family business-owning couples report that conflicts related to work/family life balance and unfair distribution of resources (money, time, energy) between family and business systems create the greatest tensions (Danes & Morgan, 2004; Danes et al., 1999). Zuiker et al. (2003) found that family businesses reporting higher levels of tension over business issues and an additional child under the age of 18 in the household were more likely to have cash flow problems in both the family and the business. Olson et al. (2003) found that business success depended on fam-ily processes, such as how the family responded to conflict and disruptions, rather than on simply how the family business was managed. Olson et al. (2003) found that responses to disruptions explained 20 % of the variance in family business revenues. In addition, they found that reducing family tension, living in a two- or three-generation family, reallocating time from sleep to the business and hiring temporary help during hectic times increased business revenue. Clearly, the effect of family conflict and tension is significant for the family business.

Conflicts are often not easily resolved because family members are arguing about issues of deep concern, such as growth, power, management, inheritance or role definitions (Stewart & Danes, 2001). When these conflicts arise, it is the functional integrity of the business that helps the family navigate through conflict (Danes & Olson, 2003). If the family faces a number of events causing conflict or stress, it reduces the ability of the family system to mitigate (or buffer) tensions created by the business system (Danes et al., 1999; Rettig, Leichentritt, & Danes, 1999).

Women appear to be a more sensitive barometer of the functional integrity of the family (Danes & Olson, 2003). Women are more likely to raise more of the issues causing tension than men (Danes & Morgan, 2004; Danes & Morgan, 2004; Danes et al., 1999; Stewart & Danes, 2001). In addition, women seem to have a need to re-solve tensions and conflict to work effectively more than men (Fuss-Reineck, 1995; Stewart & Danes, 2001). Justice conflicts appear to concern women the most, while role conflict is the most significant concern for men (Danes, 2004; Danes & Mor-gan, 2004; Fitzgerald, Winter, Miller, & Paul, 2001). More recent work by Danes, Stafford, and Loy (2007) suggests that gender has a moderating effect on responses to disruptions. Interestingly, sleeping less to adjust to a disruption had a negative effect on gross revenue for males, but a large positive effect on the gross revenue for females.

Work by Miller, Fitzgerald, Winter, and Paul (1999) suggests that several ad-justment strategies are used to manage the interface between the family and busi-ness. When the business was very demanding, household managers adjusted to these demands by bringing business work home and skipping or putting off routine household tasks. Business managers were most likely to respond to the demands of the business by conducting business at home and getting less sleep. This research suggests that the boundary between the family and business is quite permeable, although family managers seem more likely to make significant adjustments than business managers.

Future Research

This chapter has summarized the literature at the intersection of family and business. It examined financial intermingling and interpersonal relationship tensions created at the intersection. Healthy businesses depend on support from healthy families, and vice versa, for the survival and success of family businesses. While this literature has addressed many critical issues associated with the intermingling of financial and non-financial resources, the question of whether intermingling increases the probability of survival and success of family businesses remains an open question.

The most significant challenge facing this line of research is the lack of ex-tensive panel data on family businesses. The analysis of family business survival and success requires extensive information on the health of both the family and business. Financial health could be measured by collecting information similar to the Survey of Consumer Finances on the family or household and Survey of Small Business Finances on the business. If a panel study could be designed to capture this detailed financial information over a long period of time, then the importance of financial intermingling could be more rigorously assessed. The interpersonal (non-financial) health could be measured by incorporating questions about family relationship health and resiliency into a larger panel study, where both family and business managers are interviewed. The National Family Business Survey has made a significant leap forward in gathering excellent information on family and business managers; however, the panel only covers two points in time, and only a limited amount of financial and resource information is collected.

The SFBM provides excellent conceptual guidance for the study of family business. The SFBM utilizes a systems approach to consider resources, constraints, processes and achievements for family and business. The financial modeling could be improved by integrating the work of Lopez (1986) in his study of agricultural households to more carefully identify how the family business fits into the utility function or set of constraints facing the household.

This line of research has proceeded forward by assuming that the family, very simply defined, impacts the business and how the business impacts the family. Dyer (2006) suggests that "definitions of family firms based strictly on percentages of ownership and management control—those most often used in current studies—will likely not differentiate the variable family effects and thus will not accurately predict nor explain differences in firm performance" (p. 270). Dyer (2006) has suggested a new typology based on agency costs and family assets and liabilities, which could enhance our understanding of the "family effect."

Identifying the most important outcome variable is challenging. While the effect of the family on the business is often measured in financial terms (such as sales and profits) or non-financial terms (such as conflict and tension), other measures of over-all household or family utility need consideration. This poses the opportunity for this research to consider concepts such as happiness as critical outcome measures for the household and business manager. Although measures of household and business manager happiness could be useful, we are really concerned about the happiness of the family (a much more substantive challenge empirically). We are interested in those business management practices that increase gross revenues but do not, at the same time, decrease the congruity between business and family. Including the notion of happiness in an analysis of the family business requires a reassessment of policy goals focused only on objective standards financial achievement. Healthy families and healthy businesses make substantive contributions to healthy communities.

The intersection between the family and business is a fertile area of research. Here are a few topics warranting further research:

- Influence of family resiliency on the financial success of the family business
- Impact of cultural differences on decisions to intermingling family and business resources

- Impact of family resiliency on the ability of the family firm to adapt to changes in public policy affecting the business
- Impact of business financial success on the objective and subjective success of the family
- Relationship between business and family success and perceptions of social responsibility in the community.

References

Anderson, R. C., & Reeb, D. M. (2003). Founding-family ownership and firm performance: Evidence from the S&P 500, *Journal of Finance*, *58*(3), 1301–1328.

Astrachan, J. H., & Kolenko, T. A. (1994). A neglected factor explaining family business success: Human resources practices. *Family Business Review*, *7*(3), 251–262.

Avery, R. W., Bostic, R. W., & Samolyk, K. A. (1998). The role of personal wealth in small business finance, *Journal of Banking and Finance, 22*(6–8), 1019–1061.

Chrisman, J. J., Chua, J. H., & Litz, R. A. (2004). Comparing the agency cost of family and non-family firms. *Entrepreneurship Theory and Practice*, *28*(4), 335–354.

Covin, T. J. (1994). Profiling preference for employment in family owned firms. *Family Business Review*, *7*(3), 287–296.

Daily, C. M., & Dollinger, M. J. (1992). An empirical examination of ownership structure in family and professionally managed firms, *Family Business Review*, *5*(2), 117–136.

Danes, S. M. (2006). Tensions within family business-owning couples over time. *Stress, Trauma and Crisis*, *9*(3–4), 227–246.

Danes, S. M., Haberman, H. R., & McTavish, D. (2005). Gendered discourse about family business. *Family Relations*, *54*, 116–130.

Danes, S. M., & Lee, Y. G. (2004). Tensions generated by business issues in farm business-owning couples. *Family Relations*, *53*, 357–366.

Danes, S. M., & Morgan, E. A. (2004). Family business owning couples: An EFT view into their unique conflict culture. *Contemporary Family Therapy*, *26*(3), 241–260.

Danes, S. M., & Olson, P. D. (2003). Women's role involvement in family businesses, business tensions, and business success. *Family Business Review*, *16*(1), 53–68.

Danes, S. M., Rueter, M. A., Kwon, H. K., & Doherty, W. (2002). Family FIRO model: An application to family business. *Family Business Review*, *15*, 31–43.

Danes, S. M., Stafford, K., & Loy, J. T. (2007). Family business performance: The effects of gender and management. *Journal of Business Research*, *60*(10), 1058–1069.

Danes, S. M., Zuiker, V. S., Kean, R., & Arbuthnot, J. (1999). Predictors of family business tensions and goal achievement. *Family Business Review, 12*, 241–252.

Dunn, B. (1996). Family enterprises in the UK: A special sector? *Family Business Review*, *9*(2), 139–156.

Dyer, W. G., Jr. (2006). Examining the "family effect" on firm performance. Family Business Review, 19(4), 253–273.

Faccio, M., Lang, L. P. H., & Young, L. (2001). Dividends and expropriation, *American Economic Review*, *91*, 54–78.

Fiegner, M. K., Brown, B. M., Prince, R. A., & File, K. M. (1994). A comparison of successor development in family and nonfamily businesses. *Family Business Review*, *7*(4), 313–329.

Fitzgerald, M. A., Winter, M., Miller, N., & Paul, J. (2001). Adjustment strategies in the family business: Implications of gender and management role. *Journal of Family and Economic Issues*, *22*, 265–291.

Freear, J., Sohl, J., & Wetzel, J. (1995). *Who bankrolls software entrepreneurs?* Babson College Frontiers of Entrepreneurship Research, 1995. Retrieved June 15, 2007, from http://www.babson.edu/entrep/fer/papers95/freear.htm.

Fuss-Reineck, M. E. (1995). *Home to business and business to home: Role carryover between spouses in family businesses.* Unpublished doctoral dissertation, University of Minnesota, St. Paul, MN.

Handler, S. C. (1992). Methodological issues and considerations in studying family business. *Family Business Review, 5*(3), 257–276.

Haynes, D. C., Avery, R. J., & Hunts, H. H. (1999). The decision to outsource child care in households engaged n a family business. *Family Business Review, 12*(3), 269–281.

Haynes, D. C., & Haynes, G. W. (1999). Family businesses: A unique blending of family and work. *Journal of Family and Consumer Sciences, 91*(1), 122–124.

Haynes, G. W., & Avery, R. J. (1996). Family businesses: Can the family and business finances be separated. *Journal of Entrepreneurial and Small Business Finance, 5*(1), 61–74.

Haynes, G. W., Onochie, J., Lee, M., Puryear, A., Rogoff, E., & Heck, R. K. Z. (2007, January). *Financial intermingling in Korean- and Mexican-American small businesses.* Paper presented at the meeting of United States Association of Small Business and Entrepreneurship, Orlando, FL.

Haynes, G. W., Onochie, J., & Muske, G. (2007). Is what's good for business, good for the family: A financial assessment. *Journal of Family and Economic Issues, 28*(3), 395–409.

Haynes, G. W., & Ou, C. (2007). Income and wealth: How did households owning small businesses fare from 1989 to 2004. Monograph for the U.S. Small Business Administration.

Haynes, G. W., Walker, R., Rowe, B. R., & Hong, G. S. (1999). The intermingling of business and family finances in family-owned businesses. *Family Business Review, 12*(3), 225–239.

Heck, R. K. Z. (1992). The effects of children on the major dimensions of home-based employment. *Journal of Family and Economic Issues, 13*, 315–346.

Heck, R. K. Z., & Stafford, K. (2001). The vital institution of family business: Economic benefits hidden in plain sight. In G. K. McCann & N. Upton (Eds.), *Destroying myths and creating value in family business* (pp. 9–17). Deland, FL: Stetson University.

Heck, R. K. Z., & Walker, R. (1993). Family-owned home businesses, their employees and unpaid helpers. *Family Business Review, 6*, 397–416.

Hollander, B., & Elman, N. (1988). Family owned businesses: An emerging field of inquiry. *Family Business Review, 1*(2), 145–185.

Kaye, K. (2002). Penetrating the cycle of sustained conflict. In E. E. Aronoff, J. H. Astrachan, & J. L. Ward (Eds.), *Family and business sourcebook II* (pp. 355–370). Marietta, GA: Business Resources.

Light, I. (2006, October). Presentation on entrepreneurship, 2003 and 2005 National Minority Business Owners Survey Conference, Lawrence N. Field Center for Entrepreneurship, Baruch College, New York

Lopez, R. (1986). Structural models of the farm household that allow for interdependent utility and profit maximization decisions. In I. Singh, L. Squire, & J. Staus (Eds). *Agricultural household models: Extensions, applications and policy* (pp. 306–325). Baltimore and London: The Johns Hopkins University Press.

Miller, N. J., Fitzgerald, M. A., Winter, M., & Paul, J. (1999). Exploring the overlap of family and business demands: Household and family business managers' adjustment strategies. *Family Business Review, 12*(3), 253–268.

Muske, G., Fitzgerald, M. A., & Haynes, G. (2003). The intermingling of financial resources among copreneurial couples. *17th Annual U. S. Association for Small Business and Entrepreneurship Conference Proceedings* (CD-ROM). Madison, WI: USASBE.

Netemeyer, R. G., Boles, J. S., & McMurrian, R. (1996). Development and validation of work–family conflict and family–work conflict scales. *Journal of Applied Psychology, 81*(4), 400–410.

O'Driscoll, M. P., Ilgen, D. R., & Hildreth, K. (1992). Time devoted to job and off-job activities, interrole conflict and affective experiences. *Journal of Applied Psychology, 77*, 272–279.

Olson, P. D., Zuiker, V. S., Danes, S. M., Stafford, K., Heck, R. K. Z., & Duncan, K. A. (2003). The impact of the family and business on family business sustainability. *Journal of Business Venturing, 18*(5), 639–666.

Perrow, C. (1972). *Complex organizations: A critical essay*. Glenview, IL: Scott, Foresman.

Rettig, K. D., Leichentritt, R. D., & Danes, S. M. (1999). The effects of resources, decision making and decision implementing on perceived family well-being in adjusting to an economic stressor. *Journal of Family and Economic Issues, 20*(1), 5–34.

Sharma, P., Chrisman, J. J., & Chua, J. H. (1997). Strategic management of the family business: Past research and future challenges. *Family Business Review, 10*(1), 1–33.

Stafford, K., Duncan, K. A., Danes, S. M., & Winter, M. (1999). A research model of sustainable family business. *Family Business Review, 12*(3), 197–208.

Stewart, C. C., & Danes, S. M. (2001). The relationship between inclusion and control in resort family businesses: A developmental approach to conflict. *Journal of Family and Economic Issues, 22*(3), 293–320.

Van Auken, H. (2003). An empirical investigation of bootstrap financing among small firms. *Journal of Small Business Strategy, 14*(3), 22–36.

Winborg, J., & Landstrom, H. (2001). Financial bootstrapping in small businesses: Examining small business managers' resource acquisition behaviors. *Journal of Business Venturing, 16*(3), 235–254.

Winter, M., Fitzgerald, M. A., Heck, R. K. Z., Haynes, G. W., & Danes, S. M. (1998). Revisiting the study of family businesses: Methodological challenges, dilemmas and alternative approaches. *Family Business Review, 11*(3), 239–252.

Yilmazer, T., & Schrank, H. (2006). Financial intermingling in small family businesses, *Journal of Business Venturing, 21*(5), 726–751.

Zuiker, V. S., Lee, Y. G., Olson, P. D., Danes, S. M., VanGuilder-Dik, A. N., & Katras, M. J. (2003). The influence of business, family, and resource intermingling characteristics in predicting cash flow problems in family-owned businesses. *Financial Counseling and Planning, 13*(2), 1–17.

Chapter 15
Gender Differences in Investment Behavior

Tahira K. Hira and Cäzilia Loibl

Abstract The objectives of this chapter are to identify significant personal and environmental factors that influence investment behavior and to specify the investment decision-making process, particularly with respect to female investors. It is expected that the results presented here will help readers to consider new approaches to investment education. Specifically, this chapter aims to: (a) explore differences between men and women in a variety of financial behaviors, investment decision-making process; (b) identify patterns of investment involvement and learning preferences; and (c) determine socio-economic and behavior factors that explain gender differences in specific investment behavior (portfolio diversification).

Despite a narrowing of the gender differences in education, income, and wealth over time, the measures of long-term financial security for women are still at lower levels compared to men (U.S. Department of Labor, 2003). In general, women invest less money and invest their money in less risky investments compared to men. Some explanations for this behavior include lower earnings, lower financial knowledge, lower comfort levels with math, or smaller retirement benefits (National, 2000). Women may also differ from men in their access to information, as well as the ability or inclination to use available information (Bajtelsmit & Bernasek, 1996). Although women have become more interested in, and better informed about, investments (OppenheimerFunds Distributor, 2004), the NASD Investor Literacy Research stresses that women still miss basic market knowledge (Applied Research & Consulting LLC, 2003), have lower levels of math comfort (Hayes & Kelly, 1998), prefer traditional print media to software or the Internet to gather financial information (Loibl & Hira, 2004), and favor stable, easy-to-manage investments (National Center for Women and Retirement Research, 1998).

In addition, the knowledge quiz of the National Association of Securities Dealers (NASD) Investor Literacy study points out women's continuing lack of basic investment knowledge (Applied Research & Consulting LLC, 2003). In another

T.K. Hira
President's Office, Iowa State University, 1750 Beardshear Hall, Ames, IA 50011, USA
e-mail: tkhira@iastate.edu

recent survey, a large number of baby boomer women claimed that they "do not understand" investment accounts (49 %), 401(k)s (33 %), or individual retirement accounts (36 %) (Prudential Financial, 2005). More specifically, comparing, for instance, a 48-year-old, college-educated female investor with an annual income of $72,640 to a male investor with the same demographics, the gender differential accounts for an increase of about 10 % in predicted investor competence for the male investor (Graham, Harvey, & Huang, 2004).

One of the difficulties encountered in examining gender differences in investing is the scarcity of gender-specific and comparable data with sufficient control variables. Bajtelsmit and Bernasek (1996) stated that future researchers should investigate more thoroughly the cause of gender differences, particularly with respect to understanding the decision-making process and potential teachable moments, as well as key topics and educational strategies that are suitable for adult female learners. The following study was designed to investigate some of these differences.

Literature Review

According to several studies, women are more risk averse than men in investment decisions (Bernasek & Shwiff, 2001; Hinz, McCarthy, & Turner, 1997; Jianakoplos & Bernasek, 1998; Powell & Ansic, 1997). The empirical research indicates that women favor stable, easy-to-manage investments (Merrill Lynch Investment Managers, 2005; OppenheimerFunds Distributor, 2004; Prudential Financial, 2005), generally investing less in securities and being more conservative investors (National, 2000). An extremely low risk tolerance in long-term investing may prevent female clients from accumulating adequate retirement funds and reaching other longer-term financial goals. Investors with a low risk tolerance may experience opportunity losses by not investing in stocks, while investors with an extremely high risk tolerance may incur unnecessary losses in wealth (Graham, Stendardi, Myers, & Graham, 2002; Yao & Hanna, 2005).

Even in a marriage, wives are generally much less willing to take risks as investors than husbands, which indicates that the risk tolerance levels of both husband and wife should be considered in assessing a married couple's risk tolerance (Hanna & Lindamood, 2005). When viewing the married couple as a unit, the risk level of the combined husband–wife portfolio is between the risk levels of the two individual portfolios (Powell & Ansic, 1997). Wives' dominance has been shown to be highest in egalitarian partnerships, with automatic and wife-dominated decisions reported more frequently compared to in traditional partnerships (Meier, Kirchler, & Christian-Hubert, 1999). In socially equal partnerships, wives appear to adapt to the dominance wielded by their husbands in savings and investment decisions. In addition, spouses with higher expertise than their partners have been found to exert more dominance in the decision-making process (Meier et al., 1999). In 2004, baby boomer women revealed that joint decisions dominate IRAs (62 % versus 33 % solely) and investment accounts (49 % versus 39 % solely), reporting that they alone are responsible for investment decision-making related to 401(k) accounts (41 % versus 39 % joint) (Prudential Financial, 2005).

That women appear to be less risk tolerant investors is closely related to the finding that women are less confident in their investment decision-making. Men tend to feel more competent in financial matters (Beyer & Bowden, 1997) than women, and men also tend to be more overconfident about their financial decision-making abilities (Barber & Odean, 2001). For example, men trade stocks more frequently than women, and the performance of men is hurt more by excessive trading than is the performance of women, with this difference being the greatest between single men and women. Married couples influence one another's investment decisions, thereby reducing the effects of gender differences in overconfidence (Barber & Odean, 2001).

The self-serving attribution bias is greater among men than among women, with men tending to emphasize their successes rather than their investment failures (Beyer & Bowden, 1997; Deaux & Farris, 1977; Meehan & Overton, 1986). Men are also more likely to spend more time and money on security analysis. Men make more transactions, rely less on their brokers, anticipate higher possible returns, and believe that returns are more highly predictable than women (Lewellen, Lease, & Schlarbaum, 1977). Both men and women expect their own portfolios to outperform the market, but men expect to outperform by a greater margin than do women (Barber & Odean, 2001).

Gender differences in investor self-confidence may be linked with a person's ability to acknowledge the lack of clear and unambiguous feedback from the financial markets. When feedback is immediate and unmistakable, women's confidence equals that of men, but feedback in the stock market, for instance, is ambiguous, which seems to influence women's opinion of their abilities as investors. Women's confidence in investment decisions is significantly lower than that of men when controlling for professional background and ability, as well as when the expected outcomes of the different investments are equivalent (Estes & Hosseini, 1988). However, women seem to have recently gained greater confidence. According to a 2005 study, women are more likely than men to say that they do a "very good job" of managing their investments (34 % versus 25 %). In addition, women are more likely than men to describe themselves as "very successful" investors (19 % versus 14 %) (Merrill Lynch Investment Managers, 2005).

Researchers have found that financial perceptions, spending behaviors, and satisfaction with the financial situation are significantly influenced by gender (Hira & Mugenda, 2000) and that women invest less in securities and are more conservative investors (National, 2000). According to Charles Schwab's (2004) quarterly investment indicators, men maintain an average of 2.5 holdings in investment accounts more than female investors. Women's tendency to put more thought into investment decisions results in a lower trade rate and, in turn, a higher rate of return (Barber & Odean, 2001).

However, Graham et al. (2002) argued that women's reluctance to take investment risk and lower investment confidence lead to lower investment returns, smaller retirement funds, and lower retirement income. Sundén & Surette (1998) emphasized the role of demographic variables, such as marital status, in combination with occupational choice and full-time status, in impacting women's investment behavior. Dwyer, Gilkeson, and List (2002) found that the impact of gender is significantly weakened when knowledge disparities of financial markets and investments disappear.

Although there is a large body of literature on gender differences in a variety of areas, the examination of differences in investment decision-making and behavior is a relatively new avenue for researchers. Furthermore, to date, the research has not produced a clear understanding of the underlying causes of gender differences in investment behavior. The overall objectives of this study was to select a sample of highly educated and high-income household to detail gender differences in investments behavior in general and to specifically explore how men and women differed in handling financial tasks, assets ownership, risk tolerance level, investment preferences, investment actions steps taken in the past 12 months and planned for the next 6 months, patterns of involvement in investing, learning preferences, and gender differences. This study also identifies factors that influence one's investment behavior and if they differ by gender.

Method

Sample Design

The Iowa State University Center for Survey Statistics and Methodology (Center) was contracted to provide sampling, instrument design, and data collection and analysis services. A national randomized sample of 7500 telephone numbers was purchased from Survey Sampling International. However, given the natural disasters in Louisiana, Mississippi, and Florida (Hurricanes Katrina and Rita) coincided with the onset of data collection (October 17, 2006), the households selected in those areas were either deleted from the sample (Louisiana, Mississippi, and surrounding areas) or were contacted later in the study (Florida). The sample was selected using a targeted randomly selected national white pages sample. The goal was to contact households, determine if the household met the study criteria (minimum annual household income of $75,000), and then identify and interview the household adult most knowledgeable about investing. While a white pages sample does not include non-published numbers or most cell phone numbers, it nevertheless efficiently provides a good cross-section of households across the continental United States. Both non-published numbers and cell phone numbers result in a higher-than-average refusal rate, and attempting to call cell phones adds the complication of varying minute/payment packages.

Data Collection

The Center was responsible for recruitment, training, and supervision of telephone interviewers. Center professional staff and the principal investigator collaborated in presenting the training sessions for 21 telephone interviewers (center employees including student employees). Interviewers were trained in appropriate techniques for screening households, identifying selected respondents, and for the interviewing process itself. Question-by-question specifications for each survey item were reviewed with staff as part of the training protocol. A manual with interviewing procedures and question-by-question specifications was developed and used both for training and for reference throughout the interviewing process. Project training was conducted on October 3 and interviewers then participated in practice sessions until the beginning of data collection on October 17, 2005. Data collection ended on February 24, 2006. All interviewing was done in the Center's computer lab under the direct supervision of project staff. The interviews were 15–20 min in length. Interviewers were monitored at random intervals as a quality control measure, and the CATI software was programmed to include edit checks to detect illegal values or logic errors as responses were entered into the computer during the interview. A total of 911 interviews were completed by trained interviewers, producing a 22 % response rate.

Sample Characteristics

A majority of the respondents was white (84 %); male (65 %); married (90 %); and, on average, 48 years old. More men (92 %) were married than women (86 %); and majority (76 %) had at least a Bachelor's degree. Similarly, a majority of the respondents was employed full-time (75 %); and a much larger percentage of men than women were fully employed (m: 84 %, w: 60 %). Slightly less than half (41 %) of the respondents held professional positions, such as engineers, physicians, attorneys, teachers, and architects. Slightly more than a quarter (26 %) indicated that they held managerial positions such as financial analysts, accountants, executives, educational administrators, and managers. The percentage of women employed in the professional occupational category (45 %) was slightly higher than that of men (39 %). Average household annual income for majority of the respondents (73 %) was between $75,000 and $150,000. However, 14 % of the respondents were in the highest income category, earning more than $200,000 annually. The total asset values varied from a low of $5,000 to a high of $20 million, representing a wide spread. The mean value of total assets was higher among men ($1,192,039) than women ($1,037,746). A significantly larger percentage of men (31 %) than women (23 %) reported total household assets over $1 million.

Results

Gender Differences in Investment Behavior of High-Income Households

Handling of Routine Money Management Tasks

Slightly under half of the respondents (48 %) indicated that they themselves handle routine money management tasks, with a slightly larger percentage of women

(60 %) than men (42 %) reporting that they handle daily money management tasks. Almost twice as many men (31 %) than women (17 %) reported that their spouse or partner handled daily money management tasks, and an almost equal percentage of men (27 %) and women (24 %) reported sharing daily money management tasks. A majority of the respondents (80 %) reported that they had saved or invested money in every one of the 6 months prior to the interview. A large majority of the respondents had savings accounts (93 %) and employer-sponsored retirement accounts (87 %). A larger percentage of women than men were likely to report having savings accounts (m: 92 %; w: 94.7 %), certificates of deposit (m: 31 %; w: 4 %), annuities (m: 28 %; w: 34 %), and life insurance with cash value (m: 64 %; w: 70 %). On the other hand, a much larger percentage of men reported having an IRA/Keogh plan (m: 74 %; w: 67 %).

Investment Decision-Making Responsibility

The majority of respondents indicated that investment decisions were made jointly with their spouses (57 %). A much larger percentage of women (66 %) than men (52 %) said that they make investment decisions with their partners, and a much smaller percentage of women (15 %) than men (35 %) make investment decisions on their own. A majority of the respondents (80 %) owned stocks or stock mutual funds. Similar proportions of women and men (49 %) reported investing in the less volatile money market mutual funds; however, a slightly larger proportion of women than men invested in government savings bonds/bond mutual funds (w: 52 %; m: 50 %). On the other hand, more men than women invested in volatile stocks/stock mutual funds (m: 82 %; w: 76 %) or corporate bonds/bond mutual funds (m: 35 %; w: 25 %)

Risk Tolerance Level, Investment Attitudes and Investor Confidence

A review of the investment literature clearly shows that one of the significant determinants of investment behavior is risk tolerance level. In our effort to better understand the behavior of this sample, we included a question to determine risk tolerance levels. Most respondents (46 %) were willing to take average risk for average returns and a smaller percentage (39 %) indicated that they were willing to take above-average risk for an above-average return. The willingness to take specific levels of risk in anticipation of specific levels of return varied significantly between men and women. A majority of the women (69 %) indicated that they preferred to take no, below-average, or average risks with their investments, while slightly over half of the men (51 %) indicated that they prefer to take above-average or substantial risk to make above-average and substantial returns on their investments.

The majority of the men and women found investing to be a satisfying (80 %) but time-consuming (74 %) experience. However, more men than women indicated that they found investing exciting (m: 70 %, w: 62 %) or satisfying (m: 81 %, w: 78 %). Generally speaking, women find investing less exciting and satisfying and investment decisions to be more stressful, difficult, and time-consuming than men.

More women than men stressed the time-related and mental efforts of investment decision-making. Only about half of the women described themselves as being confident (w: 50 %, m: 70 %) or knowledgeable about investing (w: 50 %, m: 70 %), or indicated that they review and compare their investment performance with market benchmarks on a regular basis (w: 49 %, m: 66 %). While women perceived themselves as having less investment control than men, the difference was less than 10 percentage points with respect to having a consistent investment strategy, being satisfied with current investment allocation, investing regularly, and having started investing early in life. Overall, women were less confident in their investing abilities.

Investment Actions Steps Taken and Planned

To gain better understanding of the preparation and process that goes into making an investment decision, we inquired about investment action steps taken by participants over the 12 months prior to the interviews and the steps planned for the next 6 months. Participants were asked to think about whether, over the past 12 months, they had: (a) increased the amount they invested, (b) reviewed their investment performance, (c) changed their investment mix, (d) consulted with a financial advisor, or (e) learned about a new investment concept or product. Men seem to be more actively engaged investors compared to women, with a larger percentage of men (58 %) than women (51 %) indicating that they changed the amounts they invested during the previous year. Similarly, a slightly larger percentage of men (61 %) than women (44 %) indicated that they altered asset allocations over the previous 12 months. However, a larger percentage of women (55 %) than men (50 %) reported to have consulted with financial advisors over the previous 12 months.

A large majority (over 90 %) of respondents planned to review the performance of their investments and to consult with an advisor. However, fewer participants indicated that they planned to reallocate funds (32 %) or increase the invested amounts (44 %). A slightly larger percentage of women (52 %) than men (50 %) indicated that they planned to consult with a financial advisor. On the other hand, a larger percentage of men (45 %) than women (43 %) said that they will change the amount of sums they plan to invest during the next 6 months. Similarly, a larger percentage of men reported that they plan to change their asset allocation during the next 6 months (m: 36.1 %; w: 26 %). These results indicate that, overall, more men than women planned to be actively engaged in investment activities in the following 6 months.

Actions Before Investment Selection and After Below Expectations Performance

Participants in this study were asked to identify the actions they take before selecting an investment as well as when an investment does not perform according to their expectations. The majority of respondents (78 %) indicated that they consider the level of risk they are willing to take before making any specific investment decisions. However, men reported a greater willingness to take above-average or substantial risk when choosing investments. Most participants also reported that before making an investment they determine what returns they would like to get (63 %), check the current financial market conditions (62 %), and consider a variety of investment options (59 %). Differences between men and women in these areas were not very prominent.

When investments did not perform according to expectations, about half of the respondents in this study preferred to wait it out; however, more women than men were willing to wait it out (w: 55 %; m: 48 %). A much smaller percentage of respondents said that they would consult with a financial advisor, with women again being more likely than men to consult with a financial advisor when an investment does not produce the desired results (w: 36 %; m: 28 %).

Patterns of Involvement in Investing and Investor Learning Preferences

Patterns of Investment Involvement

Over half of the respondents (60 %) indicated that their involvement in savings and investments gradually increased over the years and was not a result of any specific event, with more men than women reporting gradual change (m: 66 %, w: 60 %). Slightly less than a third reported that their involvement remained the same over time, and less than 10 % of respondents decreased their involvement in saving and investing over the years. The proportion of women indicating increased involvement was slightly lower than that of men (w: 54 %, m: 63 %). One-third of the men and about 40 % of the women reported increases in their investment involvement due to a specific event.

Participants who indicated that change in their involvement in saving and investing was caused by specific life events were asked to identify whether those specific life events included marriage, divorce, having children, retirement, death, sudden financial gain, or something else. About 20 % of both men and women reported marriage as the largest single event that altered their involvement in saving and investing. However, a much larger percentage of women reported divorce as an event that brought significant change in their involvement in saving and investing (w: 11 %, m: 1 %). A larger percentage of women also reported changes in their investment behavior in response to the arrival of children (m: 12 %, w: 18 %) or the death of a family member (m: 3 %, w: 11 %). On the other hand, more men than women reported retirement (m: 14 %, w: 6 %) and sudden financial gain (m: 14 %, w: 8 %) as agents of change for their saving and investment behavior.

Investor Learning Preferences

A majority of participants indicated that they enjoy learning new things about investing (87 %), preferably by talking with knowledgeable people one-on-one (87 %) or by doing research to gather detailed information (75 %). More women than men described themselves as wanting to know all of the details in fine print when learning something new about investing (w: 79 %, m: 73 %). Women were more likely than men to prefer instructor-based learning about investing (w: 64 %, m: 53 %), and more men than women preferred self-directed learning (m: 79 %, w: 69 %).

Variables Influencing Investment Behavior and Differences by Gender

In this section, we explore the relationships between a number of important variables such as: investor socialization, future orientation, investor involvement, investment regularity, household income, assets and debts, and the relative impact of these variables on an important aspect of investment behavior: diversification in individual portfolio choice. In Table 15.1, we present differences in the means and standard deviations of various investment and socio-economic variables. Details about the measures of these variables are presented in Appendix. A quick review of the results shows that men and women in our study had similar socio-economic background; differences in their race, marital status, family size, education, income, assets, and obligations were not statistically significant. Similarly, no significant differences were found in various beliefs and behaviors such as investor consciousness, investor involvement, and investment regularity.

Age was the only socio-economic characteristic where significant differences were noted between men and women, the average age for women was 46.69 years whereas the average age for men was only 49.0 years. Men and women also differed in few aspects of their financial socialization. For example, women had higher score on socialization scale than men; women's mean socialization score was 4.3 whereas for men it was 4.1. On the other hand men scored higher (mean score: men 23.7, women 23.1) on future orientation and had more diversified portfolios than women, mean number of investment types for men (2.15) was higher than women (1.99).

Portfolio Diversification

Investor behavior regarding the important principle of diversification in individual portfolio choice was further investigated by exploring the relation between various investment behaviors and the portfolio diversification index. Results of the Pearson correlation exploring these relationships for men, women, and the whole sample are presented in Table 15.2. Most of the variables included in the analyses are significantly associated with the portfolio diversification level of the respondent. An individual's socialization, future orientation, investor involvement, investment regularity, the annual household income, and the respondents' total assets are strongly associated with portfolio diversification. Exception being the relationship between total assets and portfolio diversification index for women. However, the relationship between the total obligations and the portfolio diversification index was negative and marginally significant; for all respondents it was −0.0068, for women −0.025, and for men −0.087; and all were significant at $p < 0.10$.

Table 15.1 Mean and standard deviation of sample characteristics

Variable	Ranges	All respondents	Women	Men	F-statistics
Investor socialization	1–6	4.19 (0.780)	4.30 (0.768)	4.14 (0.781)	9.404**
Future orientation	13–30	23.51 (3.265)	23.17 (3.295)	23.69 (3.237)	5.286*
Investor consciousness	9–25	17.71 (2.932)	17.87 (2.729)	17.63 (3.036)	n.s.
Investor involvement	5–25	18.67 (3.809)	18.50 (3.736)	18.75 (3.849)	n.s.
Investment regularity	1–4	3.60 (0.888)	3.56 (0.911)	3.62 (0.875)	n.s.
Portfolio diversification	0–4	2.10 (1.223)	1.99 (1.229)	2.15 (1.217)	3.212^{m}
Annual household income	1–14	6.29 (4.307)	6.25 (4.401)	6.32 (4.260)	n.s.
Total assets	20,000 to 20m	1.139m (1.478m)	1.038m (1.547m)	1.192m (1.439m)	n.s.
Total obligations	0–2.5m	0.232m (0.224m)	0.246m (0.219m)	0.224m (0.226m)	n.s.
Age	25–85	48.21 (10.678)	46.69 (10.519)	49.03 (10.683)	9.986**
Gender (men=1)	0–1	0.65 (0.478)	–	–	
Race (white=1)	0–1	0.84 (0.369)	0.81 (0.397)	0.86 (0.352)	n.s.
Marital status (married=1)	0–1	0.90 (0.306)	0.86 (0.348)	0.92 (0.279)	n.s.
Family size	1–8	3.42 (1.313)	3.42 (1.334)	3.42 (1.302)	n.s.
Education (B.Sc. plus=1)	0–1	0.76 (0.426)	0.73 (0.442)	0.78 (0.417)	n.s.
N		911	320	591	

$^{m} p < 0.10, * p < 0.05, ** p < 0.005$

Table 15.2 Pearson correlation coefficients between the portfolio diversification index and investment behavior

	Investor socialization	Future orientation	Investor involvement	Investment regularity	Household income	Total assets
All respondents	0.123**	0.197**	0.236**	0.146**	0.277**	0.222**
Women	0.197**	0.176**	0.255**	0.199**	0.295**	n.s.
Men	0.095*	0.202**	0.225**	0.116**	0.267**	0.297**

Only significant coefficients shown; $** p < 0.01$ level; $* p < 0.05$ level (two-tailed)

Determinants of Portfolio Diversification

OLS regression analyses were conducted to investigate whether the investor involvement index and other disposition variables can predict portfolio behavior in a multivariate analysis (Table 15.3). We have analyzed the portfolio diversification index measured by the variety of household assets reported by the respondents (see Appendix for details) for the full sample, as well as for women and men, respectively.

Table 15.3 OLS regression for predicting portfolio diversification

Variable	All Beta	Standard error	Women Beta	Standard error	Men Beta	Standard error
(Constant)	−0.754	0.836	−1.028	1.410	−1.002	1.041
Age	−0.001	0.027	−0.039	0.046	0.024	0.033
Gender	−0.034	0.089				
Race	0.053	0.055	−0.028	0.115	0.067	0.063
Marital status	−0.040	0.049	−0.003	0.083	−0.022	0.064
Family size	0.022	0.036	0.084	0.063	0.006	0.045
High education	0.038	0.090	0.123	0.171	−0.029	0.108
Low education	−0.050	0.172	0.052	0.323	−0.127	0.204
Investor socialization	0.166**	0.054	0.300**	0.098	0.134*	0.065
Future orientation	0.036**	0.014	0.047 ^{m}	0.024	0.026	0.017
Investor consciousness	−0.023	0.015	−0.014	0.029	−0.025	0.017
Investor involvement	0.050***	0.012	0.061**	0.021	0.048**	0.014
Investment regularity	0.063	0.051	0.053	0.094	0.077	0.060
Annual household income	0.051***	0.011	0.061**	0.019	0.043**	0.014
Total assets	0.000[1]	0.000	0.000[1]	0.000	0.000[1]	0.000
Total obligations	0.000[1]	0.000	0.000[1]	0.000	0.000[1]	0.000
	711		199		452	
R^2	16.2	0.000	21.9	0.000	19.5	0.000

$^m p < 0.10$, $^* p < 0.05$, $^{**} p < 0.005$, $^{***} p < 0.001$; Middle Education was omitted; 1—Unstandardized coefficient is very close to zero

We find household income and investor involvement to be the most important predictors of portfolio diversification for the combined sample. Apart from this, women and men differ on a variety of variables in their portfolio diversification as presented in italics in Table 15.3. In particular, total assets and future orientation play less significant roles for women's portfolio diversification compared to men's. On the other hand, socialization influences seem to be less relevant for male investors than for female investors. Investment experience, that is, higher household income and deeper investor involvement, appears to define individual portfolio choices (variable measures are presented in the Appendix).

Discussion

While both women and men were involved in money management tasks, women more frequently reported being responsible for these tasks and men were more likely to be in charge of investment-related activities. Other researchers have reported similar findings (Lindamood & Hanna, 2005; Meier et al., 1999). Men were more likely to make adjustments to their investments, either by increasing the amount or by altering the investment mix. Women, however, were more likely to seek the advice of a financial professional.

Women were more likely than men to have visited a financial planner and were also more likely than men to plan a consultation with a financial planner within the upcoming 6 months. While women preferred to get investment information from financial advisors, men were more likely to learn about investments on their own. These results are consistent with what was reported in our study on financial learning at the workplace (Loibl & Hira, 2006). Contrary to a recent study on sources of economic information (Blinder & Krueger, 2004) where television was the number one source of information, television played a minor role for the investment information gathering in this study.

Both women and men reported that evaluating risk was their foremost criterion when making an investment decision. Other considerations included investment returns, market conditions, other options, and investment goals. Consistent with findings reported by Yao and Hanna (2005), men preferred above-average or substantial risk and women preferred average or below-average risk. When an investment did not produce expected returns, men were more likely than women to make investment changes, which echoed the earlier finding that, in response to an investment review, men were more likely than women to adjust their investments. These findings affirm the notion of male overconfidence in stock investments reported by Barber and Odean (2001).

More than half of the respondents reported that their involvement in saving and investment increased over the years in a gradual process. Women were more likely than men to change investment involvement in response to an important life event. Women reported changing their investment involvement at higher rates than men in response to the arrival of children or the death of a family member, while men reported retirement and sudden gain as more common agents of change. The largest gap between women and men occurred in the financial significance of divorce. For women, divorce was second only to marriage and children, which ranked equally, as a cause of financial involvement.

The measures of perceived behavioral control captured people's confidence in their abilities to perform the behavior under investigation. Only about half of the women, considerably less than the men, described themselves as being confident or knowledgeable about investing or regularly reviewing and comparing their investment performance with market benchmarks. This finding is in line with the literature in the field stating that women investors exhibit, in general, lower investment confidence, and a rather conservative record of investment behaviors. Correlation results show that there is a significant relationship between portfolio diversification on the one hand and investment socialization, future orientation, investor involvement, investment regularity, household income, and assets on the other hand. The regression results reinforce these findings. We learned that socio-demographic characteristics are not significant in explaining the portfolio diversification. Three economic variables (income, assets, and debts) and four socio-psychological variables (investment socialization, future orientation, investor involvement, and investment regularity) are significant in explaining the portfolio diversification. One exception is that total assets were significant in explaining portfolio diversification for the whole sample and the group of men, but not for women.

Learning preferences varied greatly by gender, and women found investing to be less exciting and satisfying, as well as more stressful, difficult, and time-consuming compared to men. The styles in which men and women preferred to learn about investments also varied greatly. Women preferred instructor-based learning while men preferred self-directed learning. The single most preferred means of learning about investment for both men and women was to consult with a knowledgeable person, such as a financial advisor. While both ranked consultation with a financial advisor as important, women and men varied in how they felt about them. Women were more likely to describe financial advisors as sources of information and careful listeners; men were more likely to describe financial advisors as exerting too much pressure and charging too much for their services.

Implications and Future Directions

In view of the discussion above, there are some dominant themes that begin to emerge from this analysis. These dominant themes provide the basis for further analysis and guidance in developing recommendations for general financial education materials and an investment education program for women. It is clear that such materials and programs must be grounded in the everyday realities of the lives of the female learner. In other words, the materials and programs need to be relevant, realistic, and of interest to the women. An investment education program for women also needs to provide investment strategies that are responsive to their concerns and is appreciative of the high demands they experience in their everyday lives. The educational materials must prepare women to be both critical of the available financial investments instruments and aware of their social roles (e.g., family, culture, and media) in shaping their confidence and influencing their decisions about money matters and investments.

It is important to explore why women see daily money management as their responsibility. Also, there is a need to understand why women are less focused on or interested in long-term money management. Women prefer less risk than men when it comes to money matters, so it is important to explore what they perceive as risk. What does it mean to experience no risk, below-average risk, or average risk when it comes to money matters and investments? Women are less confident than men about their financial futures, about their knowledge of retirement needs, and about their present financial situations. Specific educational materials and consulting efforts are needed to identify areas and issues concerning money and investments that women are least confident about. In addition, it is important to find ways to increase confidence among female clients, perhaps by increasing their direct involvement in investing.

Curricular implications should include assessment strategies for poorly performing investments and strategies for responding to these investments in a timely and responsible manner. Women are more dependent than men on their spouses for financial security, which is an issue that needs to be further explored. Women find investing to be more stressful and less exciting than men. Why and what do women find so stressful about investing? Perhaps it related to their perception of risk and their knowledge of the markets and securities.

This study focuses on a relatively narrow time frame, it does not assess the dynamics of the gender-connected investment behavior process. In particular, it leaves open the question as to whether positive change is currently underway in improving investment decision processes and investment outcomes for women. This study sheds light on some dimensions of the investment decision-making process and leaves other dimensions open for future inquiry. However, for future researchers it is critical that they pursue some of this inquiry over a longer period of time.

Acknowledgments The authors gratefully acknowledge the support this project has received from the FINRA Investor Education Foundation.

Appendix

Investor Socialization

Responses to the first three items were measured on a three-point scale where 1=never, 2=sometimes, and 3=often:

- When you were growing up, how often did your parents talk with you about how to handle money?
- When you were growing up, how often did your parents talk with you about the importance of saving money for the future?
- When you were growing up, how often did your parents display concern or worry about money matters?
- When you were growing up, who influenced you the most in your understanding of how to handle money? Responses to this question were measured on a three-point scale: no one=1; father, mother, or another adult=2; both mother and father=3
- When you were growing up, how financially secure did you feel that your family was? And responses were measured on a five-point scale: 1–5: varying from not at all secure=1 to very secure = 5
- Do you recall any specific learning events or experiences when you were growing up that shaped the way you think about money? Responses included: No=0, Yes=1.

Future Orientation

Responses to the following questions were measured on a five-point scale where 1=strongly disagree and 5=strongly agree:

- I am responsible for my own financial well-being.
- I like to plan for my financial future.
- It is important to set clear financial goals with time lines and dollar amounts.
- I get irritated with people who don't plan ahead and save or invest for their own future.
- I have a clear idea of what my financial needs will be during retirement.
- I am confident that I will have a financially secure future.

Investor Consciousness (Personality)

Responses to the following questions were measured on a five-point scale, where 1=strongly disagree and 5=strongly agree:

- Investing is exciting
- Investing is stressful
- Investing is satisfying
- Investing is difficult
- Investing is time-consuming

Investor Involvement

Responses to the question "Before you make specific investment decisions, how often do you first . . .

- Review your overall investment goals?
- Consider the level of risk you are willing to take?
- Determine what return you'd like to get from the investment?
- Consider a variety of investment options?
- Check the current financial market conditions?"

Responses to the above items were measured on a five-point scale: 1=never and 5=always.

Investment Regularity

Responses to the question "Thinking of the past 6 months, how many of those months did you put money into some type of investment or savings account?" Responses were measured on a five-point scale: 1=none; 2=1 or 2 months; 3=3–5 months, 4=all 6 months.

Portfolio Diversification

Portfolio diversification was measured (now=0, yes=1) by the variety of household assets reported by the respondents:

- Government savings bonds or bond mutual funds
- Corporate bonds or bond mutual funds
- Stock mutual funds
- Money market mutual funds

Total Household Income

Current household income from all sources, such as employment, social security, investments, and interest for all members, was reported by selecting one of the 14 income categories ranging from a low of $75,000–$80,000, to a high of over $200,000 a year.

Total Household Assets

Participants reported an estimate of the total overall value of their household assets, including financial assets, the home, and other real estate owned by the respondents.

Total Household Obligations

All participants provided an estimate of the total value of their financial obligations, including any mortgages, loans, or credit card debt.

References

Applied Research & Consulting LLC. (2003). *NASD investor literacy research*. Retrieved September 10, 2005, from http://www.nasdr.com/pdf-text/surveyexecsum.pdf.

Bajtelsmit, V. L., & Bernasek, A. (1996). Why do women invest differently than men? *Financial Counseling and Planning, 7,* 1–10.

Barber, B., & Odean, T. (2001). Boys will be boys: Gender, overconfidence, and common stock investment. *The Quarterly Journal of Economics, 116*(1), 261–292.

Bernasek, A., & Shwiff, S. (2001). Gender, risk, and retirement. *Journal of Economic Issues, 35*(2), 345–356.

Beyer, S., & Bowden, E. M. (1997). Gender differences in self-perceptions: Convergent evidence from three measures of accuracy and bias. *Personality and Social Psychology, 23*(2), 157–172.

Blinder, A. S., & Krueger, A. B. (2004). What does the public know about economic policy, and how does it know it? *Brookings Papers on Economic Activity* (1), 327–387.

Charles Schwab & Co., I. (2004). Schwab self-directed brokerage account indicators: Retrieved on September 21, 2005, from http://corporateservices.schwab.com/retirement_plan_services/sdba_indicators_html.

Deaux, K., & Farris, E. (1977). Attributing causes for one's own performance: The effects of sex, norms, and outcome. *Journal of Research in Personality, 11*, 59–72.

Dwyer, P. D., Gilkeson, J. H., & List, J. A. (2002). Gender differences in revealed risk taking: Evidence from mutual fund investors. *Economics Letters, 76*(2), 151–158.

Estes, R., & Hosseini, J. (1988). The gender gap on Wall Street: An empirical analysis of confidence in investment decision making. *The Journal of Psychology, 122*(6), 577–590.

Graham, J. F., Stendardi Jr., E. J., Myers, J. K., & Graham, M. J. (2002). Gender differences in investment strategies: An information processing perspective. *The International Journal of Bank Marketing, 20*(1), 17–27.

Graham, J. R., Harvey, C. R., & Huang, H. (2004). Investor competence, trading frequency, and home bias. *AFA 2006 Boston Meetings* (Unpublished presentation). Retrieved September 10, 2005, from http://ssrn.com/abstract=620801.

Hanna, S. D., & Lindamood, S. (2005, October). *Risk tolerance of married couples*. Paper presented at the Academy of Financial Services Annual Meeting, Chicago IL.

Hayes, C. L., & Kelly, K. (1998). *Money makeovers: How women can control their financial destiny*. New York: Doubleday.

Hinz, R. P., McCarthy, D. D., & Turner, J. A. (1997). Are women conservative investors? Gender differences in participant-directed pension investments. In M. S. Gordon, O. S. Mitchell, & M. M. Twinney (Eds.), *Positioning pensions for the twenty-first century* (pp. 91–103). Philadelphia: University of Pennsylvania Press.

Hira, T. K., & Mugenda, O. (2000). Gender differences in financial perceptions, behaviors and satisfaction. *Journal of Financial Planning, 13*(2), 86–92.

Jianakoplos, N. A., & Bernasek, A. (1998). Are women more risk averse? *Economic Inquiry, 36*, 620–630.

Lewellen, W. G., Lease, R. C., & Schlarbaum, G. G. (1977). Patterns of investment strategy and behavior among individual investors. *Journal of Business, 50*(3) 296–333.

Lindamood, S., & Hanna, S. D. (2005, October). *Determinants of the wife being the financially knowledgeable spouse*. Paper presented at the Academy of Financial Services Annual Conference, Chicago, IL.

Loibl, C., & Hira, T. K. (2004, October). *The effect of financial conversation on financial learning and its outcomes*. Paper presented at Academy of Financial Services Annual Conference, Chicago, IL.

Loibl, C., & Hira, T. K. (2006). A workplace and gender-related perspective on financial planning information sources and knowledge outcomes. *Financial Services Review, 15*(1), 21–42.

Meehan, A. M., & Overton, W. F. (1986). Gender differences in expectancies for success and performance on Piagetian Spatial Tasks. *Merrill-Palmer Quarterly, 32*, 427–441.

Meier, K., Kirchler, E., & Christian-Hubert, A. (1999). Savings and investment decisions within private households: Spouses' dominance in decisions on various forms of investment. *Journal of Economic Psychology, 20*, 499–519.

Merrill Lynch Investment Managers. (2005). *When it comes to investing, gender a strong influence on behavior*. Retrieved September 10, 2005, from http://www.ml.com/media/47547.pdf.

National Center for Women and Retirement Research. (1998, July 15). *Dreyfus research reveals investor's concerns* (Press Release). New York: National Center for Women and Retirement Research.

National Endowment for Financial Education. (2000). *Frozen in the headlights: The dynamics of women and money*. Retrieved September 10, 2005, from http://www.nefe.org/pages/ dynamic-swhitepaper.html.

OppenheimerFunds Distributor, I. (2004). *Women & investing—10 years later*. Retrieved September 10, 2005, from http://www.oppenheimerfunds.com.

Powell, M., & Ansic, D. (1997). Gender differences in risk behavior in financial decision-making: An experimental analysis. *Journal of Economic Psychology, 18*, 605–628.

Prudential Financial. (2005). *Prudential Financial's study on the financial experience and behaviors among women 2004–2005.* Retrieved September 10, 2005, from www.prudential. com/media/managed/WomanBro2004_Complete.pdf.

Sundén, A., & Surette, B. J. (1998). Gender differences in the allocation of assets in retirement savings plans. *American Economic Review, 88*(2), 207–211.

U.S. Department of Labor. (2003). *Highlights of women's earnings in 2002.* Washington, DC: U.S. Department of Labor.

Yao, R., & Hanna, S. D. (2005). The effect of gender and marital status on financial risk tolerance. *Journal of Personal Finance, 4*(1), 66–85.

Chapter 16
Financial Behavior of Hispanic Americans

Kittichai Watchravesringkan

Abstract The United States is a multicultural country with increasingly high numbers of bankruptcies, credit problems, and low savings and investment rates. In particular, the Hispanic population is one group of ethnic minority consumers whose financial practices may become critical with regard to these increasing financial problems due to certain characteristics this group possesses (e.g., low educational attainment). This chapter first reviews relevant research related to Hispanic consumers' finances. Then this chapter reports findings from an original study of Hispanic college students. Using in-depth interviews, the study explores the role that consumer socialization agents play in influencing Hispanic students' financial behaviors. The informants for this study indicated that socialization agents play an important role in the acquisition and development of financial skills throughout their lives.

The United States is rapidly becoming a culture of indebtedness. High numbers of bankruptcies, credit problems, and low savings and investment rates in the United States have fueled public and private sectors to call for the development of educational means to teach these consumers about financial principles. Such programs are necessary partly because of consumers' inadequate levels of financial literacy that can pose serious long-term negative societal consequences. In addition, healthy financial situations have tremendous implications for individuals' psychological well-being and life satisfaction. The majority of studies regarding the effect of traditional socioeconomic and psychological factors and consequences of financial management have focused on the dominant U.S. racial population, i.e., Caucasians (e.g., Bowen & Lago, 1997; Medina & Chau, 1998; Zhou & Su, 2000). Therefore, research on ethnic minority consumers in general, and on Hispanic consumers in particular, has been extremely limited.

The United States is a multicultural country where the population of ethnic minorities, particularly Hispanics, is becoming more visible. The Hispanic population

K. Watchravesringkan
University of North Carolina at Greensboro, Department of Consumer, Apparel, and Retail Studies, PO Box 26170, Greensboro, NC 27402-6170, USA
e-mail: k_watchr@uncg.edu

J.J. Xiao, (ed.), *Handbook of Consumer Finance Research,*
© Springer 2008

is the largest and most rapidly growing ethnic minority in the United States with promising levels of spending power that contribute to the nation's economy (U.S. Census Bureau, 2000). However, certain characteristics of this segment (e.g., their low educational attainment as compared to other ethnic minorities, their reluctance to engage in long-term financial management) may be critical for their financial practices. Given this context, there is a need to understand Hispanics' financial management behaviors and collectively educate them in order to help them improve their financial literacy levels.

The present chapter reviews relevant research related to Hispanic consumers' finances. This chapter also reports on a current study that has been undertaken to understand the role of consumer socialization agents in Hispanic Americans' financial behaviors. Finally, this chapter closes by offering potential future research directions.

Overall Characteristics of Hispanics

"Hispanic" is a generic term used to refer to "a person of Mexican, Puerto Rican, Cuban, Central or other Spanish/Hispanic culture of origin" (Humphreys, 2004, p. 7). Rather than referring to a particular group, Hispanic is used as an ethnic category; therefore, persons of Hispanic origin may be of any race. As their culture varies with their country of origin, reliance on the Spanish language "often is the uniting factor" (Humphreys, 2004, p. 7). The Hispanic population in the United States continues to grow in size and prominence, making them the largest minority group in the United States. Hispanics represented 2.5 % of the country's population in 2000 as compared to only 4.5 % in 1970; they have more than $686 billion in current spending power (Browne, 2006; U.S. Census Bureau, 2000). The Hispanic segment is growing six times faster than the non-Hispanic sector; consequently, Hispanics are expected to account for almost 15 % of the total U.S. population in 2010 (Arriola, 2003). Hispanic families are larger than white and African–American families, with 3.71 family members versus 2.97 and 3.31, respectively (U.S. Census Bureau, 2000). In addition to the already high number of Hispanics living in the western and southwest regions, this group is expected to grow at an exponential rate in other regions such as the south, midwest, and northeast, thereby distributing Hispanics generally throughout the nation. As such, the significant growth and spread of the Hispanic population across the United States has affected the nation's politics and economy and has redefined many aspects of American society (Korgaonkar, Karson, & Lund, 2000).

Despite their shared Spanish language, Hispanics are not homogeneous. Of the 35.3 million Hispanics in the United States, 66 % are Mexicans, 14.5 % are Central and South Americans, 9 % are Puerto Ricans, 4 % are Cubans, and 6.5 % are from other Spanish-speaking countries (U.S. Census of the Population, 2000). Although these subgroups differ considerably in terms of cultures, values, linguistic elements, demographics, and socioeconomic information, many researchers have studied Hispanics as a single segment when it comes to comparing their consumption behaviors with those of non-Hispanics (Bowen & Lago, 1997; Medina & Chau, 1998; Medina, Saegert, & Gresham, 1996; Plath & Stevenson, 2005; Stevenson & Plath, 2006).

Several studies have reported that Hispanics tend to have strong ties with their families, their community, and their shared ethnic group (Contreras, Kerns, & Neal-Barnett, 2002). Wilkinson (1987) found that Hispanics value a functional dominance role in men and more traditional roles in women; they reinforce sex-role distinctions through child-rearing practices, exhibit strong kinship bonds, and maintain a dedicated focus on their children. They are likely to be associated with higher degrees of dependence, conformity, and family influence (Bellinger & Valencia, 1982; Penaloza & Gilly, 1986), as well as influence by others (Marin & Triandis, 1985). Thus, family plays an important role in influencing the social and cognitive performance of Hispanic children through adolescence (Solis, 1995), as well as influencing their adaptation to U.S. life (Parke, 2004). Hispanic child-rearing practices encourage the development of a self-identity embedded strongly within the family context (Parke, 2004).

Zinn and Wells (2000) reported that Hispanics possess a larger family size as compared to other ethnic groups (3.71 members for Hispanics versus 3.31 for African–Americans and 2.97 for whites) (U.S. Census Bureau, 2000) and members of the same family are likely to reside in the same community (Farr & Wilson-Figueroa, 1997). In addition, Hispanics are less likely to be geographically mobile than whites (Contreras et al., 2002).

Financial Issues Facing Hispanics

Money Management

Bowen and Lago (1997) conducted a comprehensive review of literature on money management (e.g., budgeting, use of credit, and saving and investing) in families of African–American and Hispanic ethnic backgrounds. Among these ethnic families with limited incomes, Bowen and Lago found significant money management differences. For example, Mullis and Schnittgrund (1982) reported that when asked whether they have used a method of budgeting for families and/or have tracked all expenses, Hispanics displayed the lowest frequency of positive response as compared to other ethnic groups (i.e., whites and blacks). Fan and Zuiker (1994) also found that Hispanic families tended to allocate more of their budget to food at home, shelter, fuel and utilities, and apparel than non-Hispanic white (NHW) families. Related to saving, Schnittgrund and Baker (1983) reported that 44 % of Hispanics reported regularly saving money.

With respect to credit management, a study by Schnittgrund and Baker (1983) found that 81 % of Hispanic respondents reported that they had used credit. In addition, Hogarth, Swanson, and Selgelken (1993) stated that Hispanics tended to express negative attitudes toward credit; however, these Hispanic consumers also acknowledged the importance of credit. Hogarth et al. further mentioned that their level of credit knowledge and understanding varied. Later, Medina and Chau (1998) examined the credit card usage behaviors of college-educated Hispanic Americans and non-Hispanic whites and reported that there are no significant differences related to credit card usage behaviors for banks, store, and gas credit cards between these two groups. However, they found that Hispanic Americans exhibited a larger percentage of ownership of retail store and gas credit cards than non-Hispanic whites. These results may imply that Hispanics tend to be more loyal toward retailers than non-Hispanic whites (Wilkes & Valencia, 1985). Medina and Chau (1998) further explained that Hispanics may emphasize "borrowing rather than convenience and that retail credit card borrowing might be at the center of this behavior" (p. 443). A recent report on profiling financially at-risk college students (those who carry credit card balances of at least $1,000, are delinquent on their card payments by at least 2 months, have spent their maximum credit limits and have not paid off their credit card balances) revealed that Hispanic students were more likely to encounter difficulties in making credit card payments (Lyons, 2004).

Medina et al. (1996) also conducted a cross-cultural comparison of Mexican Americans and Caucasians on their attitudes toward money, using modified version scales (MAS). They found that Mexican Americans scored significantly lower than Caucasians in terms of the quality dimension of MAS, suggesting that purchasing high-ticket items is not a predominant behavior among Mexican Americans because they may not believe that high price is a signal of high quality. Furthermore, they found that Mexican Americans scored significantly lower than their Caucasian counterparts related to the retention/time dimension of MAS, suggesting that Mexican Americans are less likely to place high value on the use and administration of money for future planning (Yamauchi & Templer, 1982). In addition, Hanna and Lindamood (2007) reported that after controlling for financial behavior problems (e.g., late payments, bankruptcy, overspending, and negative net worth) and household characteristics, Hispanics are more likely to be credit constrained than whites. They are more likely to be denied when applying for credit, such as for mortgages, which consequently leads to their inability to accumulate wealth and reach their financial objectives.

Financial Investment Behaviors

Data from the 1998 Survey of Consumer Finances (SCF) indicate that, in general, Hispanics' financial portfolios tend to be smaller and grow at a slower rate than NHW families (Plath & Stevenson, 2005; Stevenson & Plath, 2006). For example, the researchers found that Hispanics were less likely to invest in life insurance than NHWs even though life insurance helps to sustain and support the integrity of the family. They also found that Hispanics tended to invest less in real estate even though such tangible assets provide an immediate benefit to family members. Furthermore, Plath and Stevenson found that Hispanics are less likely to invest in retirement and other vacation properties as compared to NHWs.

However, the survey also found that Hispanics were more likely to seek other types of investments such as federal bank accounts and near-term savings related to liquidity (such as saving bonds) than their NHW counterparts. This may be because Hispanics tend to be skeptical of advertising claims that consequently leads them to be less likely to accept new products and services (Medina et al., 1996). Therefore, Hispanics are likely to be loyal to branded products as a mechanism of risk reduction in buying products (Hoyer & Desphande, 1982; Penaloza, 1994). In addition, Plath and Stevenson (2005) further reported that Hispanics were more likely to invest and/or save money for short-term purposes such as education as compared to their NHW counterparts. Medina et al. (1996) explained that Hispanics are more likely to have present-oriented attitudes and are less likely to delay gratification as well as future acquisition planning. Plath and Stevenson (2005) further found that Hispanics' savings deposit levels increased as their income levels rose. Interestingly, they stated that educational attainment level does not reflect the stock investment practices of Hispanic households. That is, regardless of their level of educational attainment, Hispanic households are unlikely to invest in common and corporate stocks.

Attitudes Toward Unbanked Accounts Among Hispanics

Recently, Rhine, Greene, and Toussaint-Comeau (2006) surveyed Hispanic families in Chicago and reported that it is not uncommon for these families to make a joint decision toward unbanked accounts and to patronize check-cashing businesses. Activities that these Hispanic consumers conducted with check-cashing businesses include, but are not limited to, cashing checks, purchasing money orders, using money wire transfer services, and paying local utility bills. Although check-cashing business services seem convenient, many Hispanic Americans are not aware of the advantages of relying on mainstream financial institutions for these services (e.g., establishing credit worthiness, accumulating assets, building wealth, and reducing risks associated with holding uninsured cash reserves). However, Rhine et al. (2006) found that among Hispanics, cost-related reasons (i.e., not having enough money to open an account, not writing enough checks, and viewing the fees and/or minimum balances needed to maintain accounts as too high) are of great concern. These participants also reported other reasons not to have a checking account: they want to keep records private and they do not like to deal with or do not trust banks. The high degree of distrust toward mainstream financial institutions displayed by Hispanics may stem from "a distrust of nonkin . . . that is often said to hamper Mexican–Americans in dealing with their problems" (Chandler, 1979, p. 156).

A Study of Hispanic College Students

Guided by the theory of consumer socialization, the purpose of the current research is to improve our understanding of Hispanic American college students' financial behaviors. Consumer socialization refers to the process by which young consumers develop consumer-related skills, knowledge, values, and attitudes throughout their different life stages via the influence of socialization agents, such as family and peers (Moschis, 1981; Ward, 1974). Consumer socialization may help us better understand this ethnic segment because Hispanics' identification with their family, community, and ethnic group is very important in terms of social and cognitive performance (Contreras et al., 2002; Solis, 1995). The current study not only explores the underlying motivations of Hispanic American college students' financial behaviors but also explores how their financial behaviors are formed. Specifically, the current research attempts to answer two research questions: (1) how do Hispanic American college students develop and acquire their financial skills? and (2) what kinds of values (which may affect their financial management) do these Hispanic American students believe they should possess and/or not possess? In this chapter, consumer financial management behaviors refer to categories of cash-flow management, credit management, saving, and investment (Hilgert, Hogarth, & Beverly, 2003; Xiao, Sorhaindo, & Garman, 2006).

In addition, Hispanic American college students are chosen for the current study for several reasons. Labeled by the media as "Generation Debt," college students in general have been experiencing financial burdens caused by tuition hikes, countless credit card solicitations, a lack of financial literacy, and the acceptance of debt as a normal aspect of a modern consumer society; altogether, these factors imply that students are financially at risk (Lea & Webley, 1995; Lyons, 2004; Matz, 2005). While financial burdens have contributed to poor academic performance, college withdrawal, and short- versus long-term psychological problems, Hispanics tend to display low rates of college educational attainment that is partly caused by financial limitations and a lack of financial support (Castillo & Hill, 2004). Next, studies have reported that Hispanic students are more likely to be financially at risk than other racial or ethnic groups (Bowen & Lago, 1997; Lyons, 2004). In addition, many Hispanics who attend college are first-generation college students (Strange, 2000; Wawrzynski & Sedlacek, 2003) who will eventually contribute to our nation's economic prosperity. In addition, researchers report that Hispanic adolescents tend to view education as a means to improve their lives and avoid the difficult lives of their parents (Lopez, 2001; Portes & Rumbaut, 2001). Finally, it is important to explore the roles socialization agents (e.g., family, peers) play and the influence of values on their financial management.

Methodology

Due to the exploratory nature of the current study, this study was undertaken through a series of in-depth interviews with Hispanic American college students who attend a mid-size Southern college to gain a deeper understanding of their development and acquisition of financial skills and what kinds of values which may affect their financial management they believe they should or should not possess.

These informants were recruited using a convenience sample from General Educational Courses and a snowball sampling technique to ensure varieties in terms of major, e.g., Music, Art, Sociology, Retail Studies, Apparel Design, Marketing, Finances, etc. To enhance the participation rate, monetary incentives were given to those who participated in the study. As a result, 11 informants aged between 20 and 25 years old (four males and seven females) were interviewed: one Nicaraguan, two Guatemalans, one Puerto Rican, two Columbians, two Chileans, and three Mexicans. Although this number may seem small, it exceeds the number suggested by McCracken (1988) as sufficient for generating themes in this type of qualitative research.

The interviews with these informants began with "grand-tour" questions (see McCracken, 1988) related to their demographic information and their experiences about financial management. The in-depth interview was kept as loosely structured as possible to allow informants to express their own experiences in their own ways and at their own pace. The questions asked included the following: How do you manage your finances? Are you currently satisfied with the way you handle your finances? How do you learn to develop financial skills? What kind of values that may impact your financial management do you believe that you should or should not have? Each interview lasted approximately 60–70 min and was audiotaped. In addition, these informants were either first-generation students who came to the United States at an early age or second-generation Hispanic Americans born in the United States.

Upon completion of each interview, interview data was transcribed word by word. The researcher began analysis of the data by reading and interpreting the interview texts for coded key phrases (Marshall & Rossman, 1999; McCracken, 1988). When all the interviews were completed, these coded key phrases were compared and contrasted across all interviews in an attempt to generate categories that represented significant themes in the responses (Rubin & Rubin, 1995). The researcher periodically submitted his interpretations to his colleague, who challenged interpretations that may involve personal biases and suggested proposed alternatives (cf. Wallendorf, 1989). The researcher also submitted selected conclusions to the informants to obtain their responses. Although some of the informants' responses tended to be skeptical, most of them agreed with the interpretations.

Principal Emergent Themes

Development and Acquisition of Financial Skills: The Role of Socialization Agents

All informants indicated that they learned to acquire and develop financial skills such as saving, investing, managing credit card usage, and budgeting from their parents at an early age. Interestingly, while almost all informants mentioned that they learned the value of money and learned to manage finances from their father, these informants also attributed having learned bad financial skills (e.g., saving, credit card usage) from their mother. For example, Maria (all informant's names are pseudonyms) stated that

I remember when I was young, I had a piggy bank.... then when I grew up, I learned the importance of money from my dad...he's worked so hard to buy his own house. He's always told us save your money, do what you can to make money...I learned a lot from my dad...related to financial skills...my mom?.... One thing I know that my mom is not good with saying no to credit cards...seeing her get all these credit cards and wishing she would have never gotten them makes me feel like "okay, I don't want to do that."

Nadia added

The concept of saving is really important to me. I know that I am young and I have like my whole life to save, but I still think that you should start early.... My parents always tell me to save, save, and save, especially my father.

Christina also mentioned that

My dad always tells me that I have my mom's side of financial spending. It's poor spending behaviors. I don't save. I learned my credit card spending and not saving from my Mom. She has credit card debt. However, my dad also has his credit cards, but he's not in debt. He always saves up his money...and he saves it for a long time.

When asked about how siblings influence their financial behaviors, Jada stated that

I saw my sister made mistakes with the credit card. She was in debt for a really long time...that was a pain for her so I don't want to get into that situation...I also learned a lot of my brother, like the whole car situation. He got himself in debt with a new car. So I knew not to do that...he said, "I'll never...if I could go back I wouldn't have done that."

Similarly, Isabel noted

My older sister seems to have some trouble with money, especially with her credit cards. She suggests, "You should not apply for a credit card. You shouldn't do that...look at me, see it's like taken me years to pay off this debt and you know...you get caught up with this stuff. That was a mistake. However, if you have to, be careful. You can end up with lots of debts before even you graduate."

Most of the informants mentioned that their peers have had an impact on their financial behaviors to a certain degree. However, most of them mentioned that they themselves are the ones in charge of their finances.

My friends have somewhat influenced on my spending...and the use of credit card...and how I use money...however, the bottom line is.... learn to say no to them and to yourself. [Christina]

I always save money...I don't own any credit cards...I am frugal and...thrifty...my friends see me as a role model...they sometimes seek help...or advice from me on how to save...or budget money...when I go out with my friends, I always see them...swipe their parents' credit cards like crazy. Despite what you see your friends spending...you have to control yourself...not to follow...that kind of bad spending habits...like eating out all the time. [Sarina]

Some of the informants mentioned that the media seems to play an important role in obtaining financial skills and knowledge. For example, Jose mentioned that

I learn from media, like watching TV...like regular news or...CNBC...or CNN...to obtain some financial skills.... such as credit card usage. Those are good places to start.... I learn what an annual percentage rate is.... the Internet also a good place to learn. You can teach yourself, if you want to learn.

I like watching [Suze Orman's] show.... she does talk a lot on how to be smart with your money... I learn a lot from her show... like what credit history means.... and how having bad credit can impact your life... like to finance a house or buying a car, or something. [Miguel]

Interestingly, the religious community seemed to play an important role in these students' finances.

I used to go to church a lot.... church is big in our family. I learned... through religion, just money shouldn't be a priority.... you shouldn't let money take over your beliefs and values.... Religion taught me, don't become... greedy... don't buy it if you can't afford it. I worry about money a lot. But I guess in the past year, I leave it to God's hands... don't worry so much because he'll worry for you. God will help you get through it. [Maria]

Values Affecting Financial Management

A common theme that emerged was the type of values that one should possess. Many of these informants believed that being goal-driven, hardworking, rational spenders with a sense of integrity would help them manage their finances effectively.

I believe that... definitely working hard, and continual working hard will help one... to be satisfied... and feel secure about their own finances... I used to have two jobs when I was in high school and I saved a lot. I also believe that being rational when spending... being smart... don't live beyond what you can afford. [Jada]

Just kind of thinking long term, like the kind of things that you want in the future... set your future goals and work toward them... you don't want to have tons and tons of debt or you don't want to have horrible credit. Being goal-oriented always push me to work harder because eventually I would like to buy a house or a condo. I work well with having goals. [Sarina]

You have to be smart with your money. I have only a store card, I don't have other cards, well except a debit card. And I have a thousand dollars credit limit on it. I never use more than a hundred dollars on it. I always pay it off in the next bill or so. I usually don't carry balance to the next bill. [Jose]

I think integrity is a big one. If you are borrowing money from someone or from a financial institution such as a bank, you need to pay [it] back. It is important to pay them back. Because that will help maintain a good relationship... and will allow for more opportunities to borrow money in the future should they arise. [Juan]

Some informants mentioned "bad" values which they believe one should not possess because such values seemed to contribute to unhealthy finances.

I believe that being materialistic is bad. Although I don't consider myself to be very materialistic, being materialistic can be bad for you... may cause you to be in debt. Because you are spending money on things that you might not even use... unnecessary items that you could have used for something else that you really do need. [Christina]

Materialism is bad. People should not have... some people get caught up in having the best of the best. Big names, big flashy things... I want more and more and more and never stop... I think sometimes people get too caught up in it and don't realize that maybe it's hurting their lives... by the time that they realize, it's a bit too late. It takes time to fix this. [Miguel]

> Valuing appearances too much may hurt you ... like consumer vanity ... I think. Because I tend to spend too much on cosmetic products and I can't resist these products. It does not matter what the price is, 'cause I am gonna buy it. I know that I am always around my friends who love pretty things ... You know we are girls. ... I also love watching celebrities and ... um ... I know sometimes I try to be them ... buying expensive make-up that I can't afford ... so I put on my credit card. [Gina]

Interestingly, most of the informants mentioned that educational values were values one should have, especially drawn from financial courses that they needed to have in order to prepare them for college.

> I [didn't] have any classes related to finances when I was in high school. ... when I got into a college, I didn't know how to deal with credit cards. It is easy to obtain one. Once you have one, you are hooked. ... this is really bad ... I also believe that having knowledge related to financial portfolio would help me prepare my future. My parents talk to me about CD, bonds, and stocks; however, I feel that I have very little knowledge related to this issue. And I am now thinking that I need to know more. [Pedro]

> I think that it would be interesting if school provides classes about. ... how to manage finances ... or what is CD accounts, bonds ... what are these things. I know I would definitely enroll in this class. [Nadia]

However, many of these informants mentioned the benefit of being knowledgeable about finances.

> Being knowledgeable about the amount of money that you are spending ... can help you manage your finances effectively. Like ... when you starting out, write out a budget ... just be realistic, you can't go out and spend like ... a thousand dollars on your credit card a month. 'Cause that's gonna come back and bite you at the end. So you just set out a budget and figure out how ... much money you have that's expendable ... you just can't live beyond your means. [Sarina]

Conclusion

Given the recent financial problems facing today's American society, the current study explores the financial behaviors of Hispanic American college students. The results drawn from this qualitative study should be interpreted with caution as the sample of Hispanic American college students was rather small. Although results from the current study may not be generalizable to the entire Hispanic American college population, they seem to reveal interesting findings related to the influence of socialization agents on their formation of financial behaviors.

By and large, the informants' responses seemed to answer the two major research questions. First, it does appear that all socialization agents play an important role to a certain degree in aiding these Hispanic Americans in learning and developing financial skills throughout their life. The results also show that these financial skills are cognitively developed and socially learned as individuals engage in the socialization process throughout their different life-cycle stages (Moschis, 1981, 1987). Almost all informants mentioned that they learned and developed their financial behaviors from their parents. However, fathers and mothers seemed to influence children's financial perspectives differently (Parke, 2004; Solis, 1995). That is, those who live with both parents tended to learn financial skills from their father. The father plays an important role related to knowledge of financial portfolios (e.g., stocks, bonds, and CDs). Interestingly, the role of religion and the Catholic ideology seems to have an impact on how these informants learn and cope with their financial situations (Contreras et al., 2002). However, the Catholic ideology seems to have a limited influence on their financial behaviors, as only one informant mentioned Catholicism specifically. Although some of the informants mentioned that they are very religious, the role of the religious seems almost insignificant in influencing their financial management. Peer influence is also somewhat significant among these informants with respect to the acquisition and development of their financial knowledge (Hoyer & Desphande, 1982; Singh, Kwon, & Pereira, 2003). These informants tend to have their own perspectives related to financial management, even though some of them accept that their peers have influenced their finances. In addition, the results of the current study are somewhat in line with Singh et al.'s (2003) study, suggesting that these informants were likely to learn how to manage their finances through media such as TV and the Internet.

Related to the second research question, it is interesting to note that while most of these informants mentioned that having "good" values (such as being driven by goals, working hard, having a sense of integrity, and being a rational spender) could contribute to healthy finances, possessing "bad" values such as materialism and vanity could, in turn, contribute to unhealthy finances. Such values are directly or indirectly learned and are acquired through interactions with socialization agents (Bush, Smith, & Martin, 1999), which in turn have proved to guide and influence their financial behaviors (Shim, Warrington, & Goldsberry, 1999). Interestingly, while these informants tend to acquire "good" values in managing healthy finances from their family, they tend to acquire "bad" values from outside their family (e.g., peers, media).

It is also interesting to note that those with business majors (e.g., Jose, Miguel, Isabel who participated in the current study) are likely to be more knowledgeable about their financial skills as compared to those with other majors, i.e., art, sociology, and music (e.g., Nadia, Christina, Juan who participated in the current study). Those with business majors were also willing to learn about financial portfolios (e.g., investments in stocks and bonds) either through taking classes, researching online, or learning from acquaintances.

In sum, the current study provides an initial step to help gain a deeper understanding of Hispanic American college students' financial behaviors by exploring the role of socialization agents and the impact of values on financial management. The results may aid academic administrators, financial counselors, and consumer educators in gaining a greater understanding of this particular college segment and finding means to develop effective outreach programs geared toward this growing segment.

General Discussion and Future Directions

This section presents general discussion related to the Hispanic population and their financial behaviors. In this chapter, there have been several attempts to argue that consumer finance educators need to consider the financial characteristics of the Hispanic population, particularly Hispanic American college-aged individuals, and hopefully find a means to assist in educating them about good financial heath. Understanding the descriptive information associated with Hispanic Americans' financial portfolios (e.g., near-term investment) and socioeconomic information may be insufficient for offering them effective educational/intervention programs. A clear understanding of the underlying motivations associated with socialization agents may empower education programs geared toward this ethnic minority. In addition, there are limited studies related to Hispanic consumers' financial behaviors and most of them tend to rely on secondary data. Thus, informal and qualitative approaches may be a good way to start to learn about how Hispanic consumers manage their finances. Learning about financial management from Hispanic college-aged individuals may help us to better understand how this ethnic minority manages finances because obtaining such information from Hispanics in general seems to be rather difficult as many display low levels of trust toward researchers or a reluctance to participate in the studies.

However, some contend that different educational/intervention programs may be warranted for Hispanics versus Hispanic Americans. This is an area that needs to be examined since there seems to be a gap in the literature when investigating Hispanic financial behaviors. In addition, the Hispanic population is very heterogeneous, comprised of different nationalities (e.g., Cuban, Columbian, Chilean, and Mexican). While Hispanics share a common language, they may be very different in terms of their values, cultures, attitudes, and behaviors. Therefore, examining within-group differences related to underlying motivations in conjunction with their financial behaviors may provide interesting results. Such results may help us to determine whether Hispanic ethnic groups should be assisted and/or marketed separately. That is, providing only one type of educational/intervention program may be ineffective for this ethnic group, if that is the case.

Lastly, it may be interesting to examine the impact of different parental child-rearing styles in influencing financial behaviors. Since studies (e.g., Parke, 2004; Parke & O'Neil, 1999) related to parental child-rearing styles have reported that parents play different roles (as instructors, educators, consultants, coaches, and supervisors), it might be interesting to examine the relationship between the aspects of financial behaviors (e.g., investment, saving) and the roles that parents can serve (e.g., consultant, coach) in managing their finances and when such relationships develop.

Acknowledgments The author expresses his sincere appreciation to the Take Charge America Institute (TCAI) at the University of Arizona for providing financial support for the original study presented in this chapter.

References

Arriola, R. (2003). U.S. Hispanic market has immense potential for card issuers. *U.S. Banker, 64*.

Bellinger, D., & Valencia, H. (1982). Understanding the Hispanic market. *Business Horizons, 25*, 47–50.

Bowen, C. F., & Lago, D. J. (1997). Money management in families: A review of the literature with a racial, ethnic, and limited income perspective. *Advancing the Consumer Interest, 9*, 9–15.

Browne, M. (2006, January 1). Ready to spend. *Convenience Store News, 42*, 67–68.

Bush, A. J., Smith, R., & Martin, C. (1999). The influence of consumer socialization variables on attitude toward advertising: A comparison of African–Americans and Caucasians. *Journal of Advertising, 28*, 13–24.

Castillo, L. G., & Hill, R. D. (2004). Predictors of distress in Chicana college students. *Journal of Multicultural Counseling and Development, 32*, 261–248.

Chandler, C. R. (1979). Traditionalism in a modern setting: A comparison of Anglo- and Mexican–American value orientations. *Human Organization, 38*, 153–159.

Contreras, J. M., Kerns, K. A., & Neal-Barnett, A. M. (2002). *Latino children and families in the United States.* Westport, CT: Praeger.

Fan, J. X., & Zuiker, V. S. (1994). Budget allocation patterns of Hispanic versus non-Hispanic white households. *Consumer Interests Annual, 40*, 89–96.

Farr, K. A., & Wilson-Figueroa, M. (1997). Talking about health and health care: Experiences and perceptions of Latino women in a farm working community. *Women's Health, 25*, 23–40.

Hanna, S. D., & Lindamood, S. (2007). *Credit constraints: The role of race/ethnic group.* Paper presented at the American Council on Consumer Interest Conference, St. Louis, Missouri.

Hilgert, M. A., Hogarth, J. M., & Beverly, S. G. (2003). Household financial management: The connection between knowledge and behaviour. *Federal Reserve Bulletin, 89*, 309–322.

Hogarth, J., Swanson, J., & Selgelken, J. B. (1993). *Results from focus group interviews conducted as part of the needs assessment for building an understanding of credit services.* Unpublished manuscript, Cornell University.

Hoyer, W., & Desphande, R. (1982). Cross-cultural influences on buyer behavior: The impact of Hispanic ethnicity. In B. J. Walker (Ed.), *Marketing educators' proceedings* (pp. 89–92). Chicago, IL: American Marketing Association.

Humphreys, J. M. (2004). The multicultural economy 2004: America's minority buying power, Georgia business and economic conditions 2004. *Selig Center for Economic Growth, Terry College of Business, The University of Georgia, 64*, 1–27.

Korgaonkar, P. K., Karson, E. J., & Lund, D. (2000). Hispanic and direct marketing advertising. *Journal of Consumer Marketing, 17*, 137–157.

Lea, S. E. G., & Webley, P. (1995). Psychological factors in consumer debt: Money management, economic socialization, and credit use. *Journal of Economic Psychology, 16*(4), 681–702.

Lopez, G. (2001). The value of hard work: Lessons on parent involvement from an (im)migrant household. *Harvard Educational Review, 71*, 416–437.

Lyons, A. (2004). A profile of financially at-risk college students. *The Journal of Consumer Affairs, 38*, 56–80.

Marin, G., & Triandis, H. C. (1985). Allocentrism as important characteristics of the behavior of Latin Americans and Hispanics. In R. Diaz-Guerrero (Ed.), *Cross-cultural and national studies in social psychology* (pp. 85–104). Atlanta, GA: Elsevier.

Marshall, C., & Rossman, G. B. (1999). *Designing qualitative research* (3rd ed.). Thousand Oaks, CA: Sage.

Matz, D. (2005, July 25). "Generation debt" hurts more than just students. *Credit Union Journal, 9*(29), 4–4.

McCracken, G. (1988). *The long interview.* Newbury Park, CA: Sage.

Medina, J. F., & Chau, C.-T. (1998). Credit card usage behavior between Anglos and Hispanics. *Hispanic Journal of Behavioral Sciences, 20*, 429–447.

Medina, J. F., Saegert, J., & Gresham, A. (1996). Comparison of Mexican–American and Anglo-American attitudes toward money. *Journal of Consumer Affairs, 30*, 124–145.

Moschis, G. P. (1981). Patterns of consumer learning. *Journal of Academy of Marketing Science, 9*, 110–117.

Moschis, G. P. (1987). *Consumer socialization: A life cycle perspective*. Lexington, MA: Lexington Books.

Mullis, R. J., & Schnittgrund, K. P. (1982). Budget behavior: Variance over the life cycle of low income families. *Journal of Consumer Studies and Home Economics, 6*, 113–120.

Parke, R. D. (2004). Development in the family. *Annual Review Psychology, 55*, 365–399.

Parke, R. D., & O'Neil, R. (1999). Social relationships across contexts: Family–peer linkages. In W. A. Collins & B. Laursen (Eds.), *Minnesota symposium on child psychology* (pp. 211–239). Hillsdale, NJ: Erlbaum.

Penaloza, L. (1994). Atravesando fronteras/border crossing: A critical ethnographic exploration of the consumer acculturation of Mexican immigrants. *Journal of Consumer Research, 21*, 32–54.

Penaloza, L., & Gilly, M. C. (1986). The Hispanic family: Consumer research issues. *Psychology and Marketing, 3*, 291–304.

Plath, D. A., & Stevenson, T. H. (2005). Financial services consumption behavior across Hispanic American consumers. *Journal of Business Research, 58*, 1089–1099.

Portes, A., & Rumbaut, R. (2001). *Legacies: The story of the immigrant second generation.* Berkley, CA: University of California Press.

Rhine, S. L., Greene, W. H., & Toussaint-Comeau, M. (2006). The importance of check-cashing business to the unbanked: Racial/ethnic differences. *The Review of Economics and Statistics, 88*, 146–157.

Rubin, H. J., & Rubin, I. S. (1995). What did you hear? Data analysis. In H. J. Rubin & I. S. Rubin (Eds.), *Qualitative interviewing: The art of hearing data* (pp. 226–256). Thousand Oaks, CA: Sage.

Schnittgrund, K., & Baker, G. (1983). Financial management of low income urban families. *Journal of Consumer Studies and Home Economics, 7*, 261–270.

Singh, N., Kwon, I.-W., & Pereira, A. (2003). Cross-cultural consumer socialization: An exploratory study of socialization influences across three ethnic groups. *Psychology and Marketing, 20*, 867–881.

Shim, S., Warrington, P., & Glodsberry, E. (1999). A personal value-based model of college students' attitudes and expected choice behavior regarding retailing careers. *Family and Consumer Sciences Research Journal, 28*, 28–52.

Solis, J. (1995). Diversity of Latino families. In R. Zambrana (Ed.), *Understanding Latino families: Scholarship, policy, and practices* (pp. 62–80). London: Sage.

Stevenson, D. A., & Plath, T. H. (2006). Marketing financial services to Hispanic American consumers: A portfolio-centric analysis. *Journal of Services Marketing, 20*, 37–50.

Strange, A. (2000). Predictors of college adjustment and success: Similarities and differences among Southeast-Asian–American, Hispanic, and White students. *Education, 120*, 731–741.

U.S. Census Bureau (2000). *Educational attainment in the United States: 2003.* Retrieved May 25, 2006, from http://www.census.gov/prod/2003pubs/c2kbr-24.pdf.

U.S. Census of the Population (2000). *Census 2000: Hispanics in the U.S.A.* Retrieved May 25, 2006, from http://www.census.gov/mso/www/pres_lib/hisorig/sld001htm.

Wallendorf, M., & Belk, R. W. (1989). Assessing trustworthiness in naturalistic consumer research. In E. C. Hirschman (Ed.). *Interpretive consumer research* (pp. 69–84). Provo, UT: Association for Consumer Research.

Ward, S. (1974). Consumer socialization. *Journal of Consumer Research, 1*, 1–14.

Wawrzynski, M. R., & Sedlacek, W. E. (2003). Race and gender differences in transfer student experience. *Journal of College Student Development, 44*, 489–501.

Wilkes, R. E., & Valencia, H. (1985). A note on generic purchaser generalizations and subcultural variations. *Journal of Marketing, 49*, 114–120.

Wilkinson, D. (1987). Ethnicity. In S. Steinmetz & M. B. Sussman (Eds.), *Handbook of marriage and the family* (pp. 345–405): New York: Plenum Press.

Xiao, J. J., Sorhaindo, B., & Garman, E. T. (2006). Financial behaviours of consumers in credit counseling. *International Journal of Consumer Studies*, *30*, 108–121.

Yamauchi, K. T., & Templer, D. I. (1982). The development of a money attitude scale. *Journal of Personality Assessment*, *46*, 522–528.

Zinn, M. B., & Wells, B. (2000). Diversity within Latino families: New lessons from family social science. In D. H. Demo, K. Allen, & M. Fine (Eds.), *Handbook of family diversity* (pp. 252–273). New York: Oxford University Press.

Zhou, L. & Su, H.-J. (2000). Predicting college student debt: An exploratory study on sociodemographic, economic, attitudinal, and behavioral determinants. *Proceedings of the Association for Financial Counseling and Planning Education*, 133–140.

Chapter 17
Money Matters of African Americans

Cathy Faulcon Bowen

Abstract This chapter highlights studies involving African Americans and money matters. Four themes are covered: money knowledge, wealth, spending choices, and retirement. Albeit slow, as a group African Americans or Blacks are making progress on the journey to financial security. Like the rest of the nation, financial knowledge could be improved. Their participation in the stock market has increased, yet it still trails the participation rates of other racial groups. Their spending power is expected to rise with their increased education level. They are as confident as all American workers about their retirement security although their savings and other preparations could be improved.

In recent decades, there has been increased interest in how individuals in the United States manage money. In part, this interest may be attributed to the awareness of the nation's financial illiteracy. Numerous reports continually provide evidence about Americans' ignorance of basic money matters and societal trends such as increased bankruptcy filings that substantiate these reports (American Bankruptcy Institute, 2007). Our governing bodies and federal agencies have acknowledged the need to improve the financial education of all Americans. A few states have even mandated a personal finance course as a high school graduation requirement (National Council on Economic Education, 2005) or established an Office of Financial Education (Commonwealth of Pennsylvania, Governor's Office, Executive Order, 2004) to help coordinate and encourage financial education efforts among public and private organizations. The most recent bankruptcy law (Bankruptcy Abuse Prevention and Consumer Protection Act, effective October 2005) even mandates that filers complete a personal finance course (a minimum of 2 hours in length) on basic money matters before the bankruptcy process is complete. Finally, in 2002, the U.S. Treasury established an Office of Financial Education. This office orchestrates the work of The Financial Literacy and Education Commission, which is comprised of 20 government departments or entities with programs and projects in personal

C.F. Bowen
Department of Agricultural and Extension Education, The Pennsylvania State University, 323 Agricultural Administration, University Park, PA 16802, USA
e-mail: cbowen@psu.edu

finance. In short, there is a grave need to improve the financial literacy of all Americans and multiple efforts are being made to satisfy this need.

Although the general population received a failing grade in overall knowledge about personal finances, African Americans, the third largest segment of the U.S. population (U.S. Census Bureau, 2006), appear to be underperforming even more, thereby putting their financial security at risk. Researchers and marketers have noticed this deficit and have conducted studies to describe and explain their money management knowledge, attitude, and behaviors. Although African Americans may have been included in many studies about money matters, this chapter is limited to those reports that included a substantial number in the sample or population studied.

Four themes surfaced in the literature review: knowledge about money, wealth, spending patterns, and retirement. While there are other topics, most of the empirical work reported since 1995 addressed these themes and are used to organize this chapter.

Bowen, Lago, and Furry (1997) provided an earlier review of the literature that addressed money management from a racial, ethnic, and limited income perspective. Most of the reports in that review were based on primary data collected by researchers. Conversely, the majority of the works reported here, especially reports focused on wealth, is based on analysis conducted using large data sets (e.g., Survey of Consumer Finance, Panel Study of Income Dynamics, and Health and Retirement Study) collected by governmental agencies or yearly surveys conducted by organizations that study personal finance behaviors.

Knowledge

High School Students

Studies focused on financial knowledge have been segmented via life stages with most focused on teens or young adults. Since 1997, the Jump$tart Coalition for Personal Finance has surveyed high school 12th graders on consumer and financial issues they are likely to face as young adults (credit, banking, saving). These young adults are literally months away from living alone or away from home. Since the initial survey, respondents have never received a passing grade (70 % or higher). In fact, the score was on a steady decline until 2004 when the mean score for all students moved from 50.2 in 2002 to 50.3 in 2004. The 2006 mean score for all students continued the upward trend, albeit slight, to 52.4 (Mandell, 2006a). Moreover, for each year except 2000, African American teens' mean score was the lowest when compared to the mean scores of Whites and Hispanics. Yet, while still receiving a failing score each year, White students' average score was the highest above the mean for all students.

In 2004 and 2006, Operation Hope commissioned a separate analysis of African American students involved in the Jump$tart survey (Mandell, 2004, 2006b). The 2004 findings suggested that the financial literacy of African American students was not related to family income. African American students in families with annual incomes under $20,000 had scores that were 87 % of their White counterparts, whereas, African American students in families earning $80,000 or more had scores that were only 76 % of their White counterparts. Nevertheless, the 2006 results showed the opposite, with African American teens from families making $80,000 or more earning scores that were 88.6 % of White students, which suggested a closing of the gap between these groups of teens. An examination of the 2004 and 2006 relative scores of all African Americans measured as a percent of the scores of Whites on income, money management savings, and spending revealed slight gains by African Americans on income (78 % vs. 80 %) and savings (76 % vs. 82 %). However, the spending score remained the same (84 %) and there was a slight decrease in the money management score (78.3 % vs. 77.3 %). The 2006 study suggests that African American teens might be missing opportunities to develop money management skills because a lower proportion of them worked part-time during the summer (74 % vs. 85 %), had bank accounts (69 % vs. 85 %), had taken a money management class (44 % vs. 48 %), or played the stock market game (23 % vs. 30 %) compared to White students. Meanwhile, the same proportions of African American and White students indicated having investments (35 %).

While many educational programs are in place to teach teens about money, almost none in the literature focused specifically on African Americans. Slaughter (2006) conducted a qualitative study of 49 African American students to explore their experiences with money matters and to test the effectiveness of a web-based personal finance program (*Practical Money Skills*) on the teens' money knowledge. Interviews with half of the teens revealed that they understood the importance of saving money and the consequences of poor financial decisions and reported learning these lessons by observing their parents or having discussions with them. None of the students attended a high school that required a personal finance class. In addition, comparison of the pre-test and post-test scores on the nine financial areas included in the web-based curriculum revealed that the lowest gain (6.2 %) was achieved in the area of *Banking Services* and the highest gain in the area of the *Influences of Advertising* (21.78 %).

College Students

Reports focusing on African American college students have examined overall financial knowledge or selected financial behaviors. Murphy (2005) reported the results of an exploratory study involving 277 undergraduates attending a historically black college/university (HBCU). The purpose of this study was to assess the influence of race, gender, age, major, and parental educational level on the financial knowledge of students. Seventy-seven percent of the students were Black. The mean financial knowledge score was 30 % or 3 out of 10 questions answered correctly. Non-Blacks had more accurate knowledge than Blacks and typically scored above the mean. Business majors had a higher level of financial knowledge and students whose parents were more educated had higher knowledge scores.

Grable and Joo (2006) extracted Blacks and non-Hispanic White students from a 2001 study conducted by Henry, Weber, and Yarbrough (2001) to examine their money management behaviors and financial outcomes. These researchers found that Black students held more credit card debt than non-Hispanic White students and reported higher levels of financial stress. Compared to the non-Hispanic White students, Black students in this study tended to be slightly younger and not employed.

Perry and Morris (2005) examined the relationship between consumer knowledge, income, and locus of control on financial behavior. The percentage of each race (African American, Asian American, Latino/Hispanic, and White) in the sample of 10,977 was not reported. However, the sample was restricted to families with incomes of $75,000 or less, thereby increasing the likelihood of greater proportions of African Americans and Hispanic respondents than Asian Americans and Whites who tend to have higher incomes. This sample of consumers between the ages of 20–40 was drawn from the 1999 Freddie Mac Consumer Credit Survey. The Perry and Morris findings support the premise that consumers' propensity to save, budget, and control spending depends somewhat on consumers' level of perceived control over life outcomes, their knowledge, and financial resources. However, their findings were inconclusive regarding race/ethnicity moderating the relationship between (a) locus of control and responsible financial management behaviors (i.e., control spending, pay bills on time, plan for their financial future, save money, and provide for their family), (b) income and responsible financial management, and (c) financial knowledge and responsible financial management behavior. These researchers found that only African Americans and Hispanic/Latino externals (locus of control) and low-income African Americans were more likely to engage in financial management behaviors than their White counterparts. Finally, African Americans' interaction with financial knowledge was not significant suggesting that the effect of financial knowledge on this group was no different than it was for Whites.

General Population

Lusardi (2005) studied the financial education and savings behavior of Blacks and Hispanic households using data from the 1992 wave of the Health and Retirement Study and the 2002 National Survey of Latinos. This researcher concluded that seminars have some effect on the savings behavior of individuals with the lowest levels of wealth and education, and that programs offered by the government or employers should focus on basic financial planning targeted to specific needs of minority groups.

Still other reports discussed the progress of African American women and their need for education about personal finances. A survey by Peter D. Hart Research Associates (2001) for the Fannie Mae Foundation states that 74 % of African American women say they have it easier financially compared to their mothers or grandmothers. Yet, 50 % feel somewhat or not at all comfortable with their knowledge of retirement planning, 51 % have the same feeling about managing debt, 45 % are not confident about their knowledge of credit ratings, and 57 % are not comfortable with the home buying process.

Knowledge about saving and investing is critical for financial security. Although African Americans have some knowledge about these two areas, it may be superficial. Nearly half (46 %) of African Americans describe their personal knowledge of investing or saving for retirement as general, while another third (32 %) said that they have limited knowledge and 13 % described their knowledge as nil. Only 9 % described their knowledge as comprehensive (Employee Benefit Research Institute, 2003). A similar finding was reported in the 2004 Ariel/Schwab survey when the majority of African American and White investors failed a ten-item investment quiz (Ariel Mutual Funds/Charles Schwab & Co. Inc., 2006). While there is room for improvement on knowledge about saving and investing, the 2007 results suggests that African Americans may be overly confident about their ability to manage retirement income so it lasts throughout life. Sixty-three (63 %) agreed that people did not need to be sophisticated investors to manage their savings in retirement (Employee Benefit Research Institute, 2007).

Several media reports have suggested that African Americans should increase their knowledge about personal finances (Jarrett, 2002; Parker, 2004; Reed Business Information, 2006). However, none of these reports included empirical evidence to support this suggestion.

Wealth

Regardless of the study or the way wealth is measured, the general consensus is that African American wealth is lagging woefully behind that of Whites in the United States and that African American participation in the stock market or ownership of stocks is very low. Researchers have studied this issue from various angles and nearly all have used large data sets collected by governmental agencies.

Chiteji and Stafford (1999) and Keister (2004) examined the effect of family structure on Blacks' assets. Chiteji and Stafford analyzed 1999 Panel Study of Income Dynamics (PSID) data for 1,933 households aged 25–54 to determine if parental asset ownership affected their offspring's assets during adulthood. For the parents, Chiteji and Stafford found that non-Blacks held bank accounts with balances three times higher than the balances that Blacks held in banks and Blacks stock holdings per family were less than one-fifth the holdings of non-Black households. The proportion of young families that held stocks was greater for those whose parents owned stock than for families whose parents did not own stocks. Gittleman and Wolff (2004) also analyzed PSID data from 1984, 1989, and 1994. They found that Whites had greater wealth compared to African Americans and that inheritances played a larger role in their wealth accumulation.

Keister (2004) used the National Longitudinal Survey of Youth 1979 cohort (ages 14–21) to examine the relationship between family background and racial differences in adult wealth ownership. The data for the report came from the 1985–1998 collection when the 1979 cohort was aged 21–38. The sample included 3,053 respondents. Keister found that: (a) as the number of siblings increased, adult wealth decreased; (b) family disruption (divorce or separation) decreased adult wealth; (c) Blacks and Hispanics are less likely than Whites to own homes and stocks; (d) Whites were more likely to begin buying homes and financial assets earlier in life; and (e) having highly educated parents increased adult wealth. In sum, Keister's results suggested that the persistent racial divide in wealth ownership is at least partially traceable to family processes during childhood. Work by Gutter, Fox, and Montalto (1999) which focused on racial differences in investor decision making reported that family situations impacted ownership of risky assets. They found that the presence of children increased the likelihood of ownership of risky assets and that household size negatively impacted risky asset ownership. Other studies provide conflicting findings on the reasons for the disparity between African Americans' and Whites' risky asset ownership. Gutter and Fontes (2006) concluded that the disparity may be attributable to differences in information exposure and barriers to investment markets. Conversely, Coleman (2003) reports that after including household net worth as an independent variable, African Americans did not express a lower degree of risk aversion nor did they hold a significantly lower percentage of risky assets.

A report by Kochhar (2004) for the Pew Hispanic Center, *The Wealth of Hispanic Households, 1996–2002,* contains comparative data on African Americans' wealth standing. The report was based on data in the Survey of Income and Program Participation (SIPP). According to this report, in 2002, of the top three segments of the U.S. population, Black households had the lowest median net worth (total assets minus debt) of $5,988. Hispanic households had a median net worth of $7,932 while White households had a median net worth of $88,651. Between 1999 and 2001, the net worth of Hispanic and Black households fell by 27 % each while the net worth of White households increased by 2 %. Finally, homes represented the largest portion of net worth for Blacks (63 %) and Hispanics (61 %). For Whites, homes represented only 39 % of their net worth. Other researchers (Choudhury, 2001/2002; Smith, 1995; Straight, 2002) have reported similar findings regarding the proportion of Black wealth represented by real estate.

Several studies have documented the lack of African American participation in the stock market and its likely contribution to the unequal wealth of African Americans and Whites (Altonji & Doraszelski, 2005; Brimmer, 1988; Choudhury, 2001/2002; Keister, 2000, 2004; Kochhar, 2004). African American participation in the stock market may not be reflected in individual stock ownership.

Straight (2002) compared the asset accumulation differences of races using the 1995 and 1998 Survey of Consumer Finance data and found that the net worth of Black families rose by 33 % during this period while the net worth of White families rose by 16 %. Furthermore, in 1995, higher-income Black families had three times more ($22,461 vs. $7,487) in thrift-type plans than White families. Of that amount, Black families had a higher proportion invested in stocks (57 % compared to 11 % for White families). Thrift plans were defined as 401(k), 403(b), thrift savings, and supplemental retirement plans. By 1998, Black families had increased the amount in these types of plans to $27,000 while White families had reduced amounts to

$6,000. Even with these reduced amounts, White families had 63 % invested in stocks compared to Black families' 50 %. Straight concluded that a difference in allocation of assets between Blacks and Whites is much closer when groups are matched on similar socioeconomic characteristics.

The annual Black Investor Survey conducted since 1998 by Ariel Mutual Funds and Charles Schwab and Company (2006) presented findings that disagree with those of Straight. This random survey questioned 500 Black and 500 White households with incomes above $50,000 about their savings and investment attitudes and behaviors. The 2006 report indicated that Black participation in the stock market is trending downward from a high of 74 % in 2004 to 64 % in 2006. Conversely, the percentage of Whites with stock investments remains unchanged (83 %) since the first year of the study in 1998.

DeVaney, Anong, and Yang (2007) analyzed the 2005 SCF. They found that Black families were less likely to own homes, investment accounts, and retirement accounts compared to White families. Furthermore, the value of these assets owned by Blacks was of less value than the value of assets owned by Whites. Variables that influenced the likelihood of owning assets and the value of the assets were education, income, and contact with more than one financial institution. The study's sample consisted of 481 Black families and 3,468 White families.

Plath and Stevenson (2000) used the 1998 Survey of Consumer Finances (SCF) data to examine the financial characteristics of U.S. households to provide financial planners with information on the preferences of African Americans for financial products. Their findings support the work of others regarding low stock ownerships and high preference for insurance and real estate.

Choudhury (2001/2002) used the 1992 Health and Retirement Study data to analyze the wealth held by White, Black, and Hispanic households and to understand their savings behavior. This researcher's findings suggest that at every income level, Blacks were unlikely to hold risky, high-yielding assets. Choudhury concluded that not participating in the stock market results in slower wealth accumulation, and a variety of reasons may be contributors to Blacks' lack of participation. Yao, Gutter, and Hanna (2005) also reported that Blacks are less likely than Whites to state that they are willing to take some risks in investments.

Using PSID data and models to correct some of the shortcomings of other methods used to study wealth, Altonji and Doraszelski (2005) were able to explain all or nearly the entire wealth gap for Whites but only a fraction of the wealth gap for Blacks. Altonji and Doraszelski concluded that the differences in savings behavior and/or rates of return play an important role in the wealth gap between Whites and Blacks.

Once again the Health and Retirement Study data were used to study the wealth of racial groups. Smith (1995) reported that lower incomes, poorer health, and the definitions of wealth that exclude Social Security and employer pensions are factors which contribute to the wealth disparity. Smith concluded that disparities in wealth are due partly because of differences in inheritances and bequests across generations. Blau and Graham (1990) surmised the same although they used the National Longitudinal Surveys for young men (1976) and young women (1978).

The Survey of Consumer Finance data were used by Badu, Daniels, and Salandro (1999) and Keister (2000) to study wealth and race. Badu et al. analyzed the 1992 data and found that Black households were significantly more risk averse or have less tolerance for risk in their choices of assets. In addition, Black household heads under age 35 relied heavily on credit cards, which in turn affected future net worth. Silva and Epstein (2005) work supported this finding. They reported that nearly 60 % of African Americans held a credit card in 2001 and nearly 84 % of those holding cards revolved the balance. Keister's work (2000) was guided by the question, "What accounts for persistent racial differences in wealth ownership?" She used data from the 1960–1995 SCF. After separating the effects of asset ownership from the effects of racial differences in family wealth history, earnings, education, marital behavior, and fertility, Keister found a reduced wealth inequality but not a complete removal. This researcher concluded that racial differences in wealth ownership are influenced by many factors. However, the way families save is an important factor in wealth.

Spending Power and Choices

The African American population has been recognized as a source of additional profits and subsequently has garnered the attention of marketers (New York Life, 2006; Target Market News, 2005). For example, Nielsen Media Research created an African American Advisory Council (2006, November 6) to provide advice on how to reach this population via television. According to the 2000 U.S. Census, 35 million African Americans represented 12 % of the U.S. population. Collectively, this population segment is showing signs of increasing buying power. For example, in 2000 their median household income was $27,910, purportedly at the time the highest ever. By 2006, the median income had reached $30,134. Target Market News (2005) estimated that Blacks earned $679 billion in 2004. Humphreys (2006) and the Selig Center projected that the nation's Black buying power will rise from the $318 billion in 1990 to $1.1 trillion by 2011—a 237 % increase in 22 years! Fueling this increase will be more job opportunities and increased educational attainment.

As buying power increases, studies which document African American spending continuously report that compared to other ethnic groups, Black consumers outspend others on apparel, food at home, beverages, vehicles, telephone services, transportation, electricity, and natural gas (Fontes & Fan, 2006; Humphreys, 1998, 2006; Target Market News, 2003). The top five areas for expenditures in descending order for 2004 and 2005 were housing, food, vehicles, clothing, and health care (Target Market News, 2005, 2007).

In terms of low-expense categories, Blacks spend a lower percentage of their income on personal insurance, pensions, eating out, household furnishings, and health care (Humphreys, 1998, 2006). Humphreys and Target Market News findings regarding health care spending conflict.

Outspending other racial groups on vehicles may be due to the higher annual percentage rates African Americans pay for auto loans. The Consumer Federation of

America (2006, 2007) reported that African Americans typically paid 2 percentage points more for auto loans than other Americans. Data for these reports were drawn from the 2005 Opinion Research Corporation and the 2004 Survey of Consumer Finances.

Fan and Lewis (1999), using a combination of data sources [Consumer Expenditure Survey (1980–1992); Consumer Price Index (1980–1992); and ACCRA Cost of Living Index (1990)] studied the budget allocation patterns of African Americans. While their findings were similar to the results reported by previous researchers, i.e., African Americans, compared to other households (Asian Americans, Hispanic Americans, or Caucasian Americans), spent significantly less on food away from home, entertainment, health care, and tobacco products and spent more on apparel and utilities. This work added a unique contribution to the literature. Specifically, it provides data showing that there are different preferences within an ethnic group. For example, low-income African Americans allocate their budget differently than higher-income African Americans, thereby causing readers to question generic statements regarding African Americans spending patterns. Low-income African Americans spent less on transportation and education but more on food at home than low-income Caucasians. However, in the case of education, higher-income African Americans spent more than higher-income Caucasians. The difference in many expense categories was smaller between higher-income Caucasians and higher-income African Americans than the differences between lower-income Caucasians and lower-income African Americans.

Retirement

Most Americans are not taking the retirement financial planning process seriously. While 70 % are setting aside something for retirement, only 42 % indicated that they have estimated or calculated the amount of money they will need at retirement (Helman, Copeland, & VanDerhei, 2006). Those who are close to retirement may feel that this would be a useless activity because Social Security will be their only or primary source of income. Such is the case for African Americans aged 65 and older. Eighty-eight percent had income from Social Security and only 19 % had income from private pensions or annuities. Likewise, only 29 % had income from personal assets (Beedon & Wu, 2003).

The Minority Retirement Confidence Survey (MRCS) has been conducted for selected years (1998, 1999, 2001, 2003, and 2007), as a part of the annual Retirement Confidence Survey for the Employee Benefits Retirement Institute (EBRI). The 2007 report indicates that African Americans appear to be as confident as all Americans that they will have enough money to live comfortably in retirement. In 1998, 63 % indicated that they were somewhat or very confident about their retirement savings being adequate. That confidence steadily climbed to 67 % in 1999 and 65 % in 2000. Confidence levels dropped in 2001 (54 %) and 2003 (57 %) before rebounding to 71 % in 2007. Over roughly the same time period, 1998–2003, the proportion of African Americans who had personally saved something for retirement increased from 49 to 62%. The 2007 report shows a drastic drop in the proportion (48%) of consumers who indicate they have saved for retirement (Helman, VanDerhei, & Copeland, 2007). The increased personal savings might be a contributing factor to the increased confidence that they will have enough money to live contentedly in retirement.

African Americans are significantly more dependent on employer pensions than Whites. Two-thirds of employed Blacks work for employers that have a traditional pension plan (i.e., government), compared to about half of the employed Whites. Type of employer (non-government vs. government) is likely to influence African Americans' belief that government and corporations have a major responsibility for Americans having a comfortable retirement. African Americans may also be banking on real estate to help fund their retirement. More Blacks than Whites own real estate other than their home (42% vs. 33%) and of these, more Blacks than Whites (58% vs. 48%) indicated that they expect their properties to help fund their retirement (Ariel/Schwab, 2006). Other studies have documented African Americans' preference for real estate and low-risk investments (Brimmer, 1988) over other investments.

Hingorani (2001) studied 200 College of Business students at a historical Black college/university to determine their understanding of the stock market which could impact future decisions related to retirement planning. Of the students surveyed, only 14% believed that they understood the stock market well. Hingorani asserted that universities should prepare students for financial vulnerabilities and provide them an opportunity to obtain the knowledge to make accurate decisions for their well-being.

Concluding Comments/Future Research

There is a growing collection of reports about the financial knowledge, attitude, and behavior of African Americans. Of note is the interest that marketers have in this societal segment (Phoenix Marketing International, 2006; Plath & Stevenson, 2000; Reed Business Information, 2006; Sherman, 1997) because of their projected increasing buying power. Most of the works cited above were concerned with the wealth disparity between Whites and African Americans, followed by retirement related issues, spending patterns, and lastly, their knowledge about money matters. In addition, many of the studies cited were conducted using large data sets collected for a governmental entity.

Because most of the above reports were prepared using existing data sets, it prompts the question of why there were so few smaller scale studies. Possible reasons might include: (a) difficulty in reaching African Americans audiences; (b) unwillingness of this audience to talk about money issues with non-family members; and (c) studies with small samples and focused on ethnic minorities may be more difficult to get published.

Several reports on the wealth gap between African Americans and Whites sug-
gested a lack of participation in the stock market was a primary reason (Altonji
& Doraszelski, 2005; Brimmer, 1988; Choudhury, 2001/2002; Keister, 2000, 2004;
Kochhar, 2004). Conley (2000) suggested that the disparity could be due to African
Americans' philanthropy, i.e., giving away wealth rather than retaining it. While
African Americans may be saving and investing money, the propensity for the low-
risk instruments will guarantee lower returns and lower wealth accumulation, and
less wealth to transfer to the next generation. Lack of estate planning to transfer
wealth so the tax bite is minimized may be another reason less wealth is transferred
among African Americans.

Researchers (Chiteji & Stafford, 1999) have made the connection between
parental tendency to buy stocks and their offspring subsequently buying stocks,
thereby, giving credence to the expression "an apple does not fall too far from the
tree." Thus, to increase African Americans participation in the stock market beyond
their employer retirement plans, additional targeted educational efforts may be necessary. Investors are often warned not to invest in things they do not understand and
it appears that African Americans are doing just that by selecting real estate and
lower risk, easier to understand investments.

Future Research

Given the lack of reports based on primary data, researchers might conduct smaller
scale studies that could provide additional insights about African Americans' knowledge, behavior, and attitudes regarding money. Qualitative studies might also provide more in-depth information that cannot be gathered from large survey studies.

While previous research always serves as a starting point for future research,
researchers are encouraged to view African Americans and money with new lenses
that are not completely colored by the work of previous research and always compared against other ethnic groups. Decades of social imbalance and starting from a
negative position will require decades of steady climbing to illustrate any consistent positive results. At the same time improvements are being made, negative or
unfavorable cycles continue to fester in some areas. African Americans are making
progress on their journey to financial security but the journey will likely be slow
unless there is a major societal jolt or traumatic event that reshapes attitudes and
behaviors overnight.

In-depth examination of the spending patterns of African Americans beyond
the dollar amounts spent on various categories (e.g., food, clothing, personal care)
might be useful. Why are amounts in certain categories above or below amounts
spent by other groups? Are they paying too much for certain products because:
(a) they are charged higher annual percentage rates as reported for car loans by
Consumer Federation of America (2006, 2007), (b) they do not comparison-shop
for products/services, or (c) the services or products they are buying require more
time to produce and therefore more money to acquire (e.g., haircut, hair permanents,
larger clothes). One survey of Black homes' television spending reported that urban

African American cable subscribers on average pay $4 more for cable, $2 more for digital cable, and $5 more for satellite service (Reed Business Information, 2006).

Faculty members employed in educational institutions with concentrated enrollments of African Americans have a captive audience and could begin work in this area. For example, freshman could be engaged in studies upon entrance in community colleges and universities and followed for subsequent years. Researchers could study the impact of financial education workshops and classes on the students' financial behavior while in college and after they graduate. In addition, graduates' offspring could be studied to see if their knowledge, attitudes, and behaviors related to money differed from the offspring of African Americans who did not participate in financial education classes and workshops.

High schools with concentrated populations of African American students might also be targeted for research studies. These studies could be designed to increase general financial knowledge or focus on a specific area such as understanding how the stock market works or they could focus on basic financial education topics needed for daily survival. The financial education needs of geographical areas may vary and could be determined with a careful needs assessment.

The teaching techniques used to help new African American investors understand stocks could be a factor in increasing their participation in the stock market. Research might focus on providing those answers. What impact does the method of instruction have on learners' behavior, attitude, and knowledge about stocks and participation in the stock market? Is there greater participation in the stock market (a) if the instructor or financial advisor is closer to the age of the learner, (b) if assistance is provided in selecting and monitoring the first stock purchased, (c) if learners have access to a live trading room during the educational sessions, or (d) a combination of the above factors? Finally, does the age one is exposed to buying stocks impact their participation in the stock market (i.e., do African Americans who learn about stocks as teens have a higher participation rate in the stock market than those who learn as adults?)

None of the reports examined explored the financial education in African American children/students lower than high school. Things learned early in life require less effort to perform on a routine basis. In short, they become habits that we perform without giving much thought to the actions. Some of the foundation money concepts can be established early in life (e.g., saving, spending within means). This appears to be an untapped area of study. Studies could be conducted with African American children who are consistently exposed to literature or books with financial concepts.

Attitudes are shaped because of repeated exposures over a period of time. Thus, it will take years of concentrated and purposeful efforts to reshape the attitudes, knowledge, and behaviors related to managing money.

The journey on the road to financial security is likely to be easier or less traumatic if financial education starts early in life. African Americans, like other segments of the population, are focusing on the realities of becoming financially secure. Efforts, such as the 1890 Family and Consumer Sciences Distance Education Instructional Alliance (n.d.) work on the family financial certificate program, should increase the number of Black professionals with expertise in personal finance planning and education who will work with African Americans.

Appendix: Data Sets Defined

The Consumer Expenditure Survey (CES) program consists of two surveys collected for the Bureau of Labor Statistics by the Census Bureau (quarterly interview survey and the diary survey) to provide information on the buying habits of Americans.

The Current Population Survey (CPS) is a monthly survey of about 60,000 households conducted by the Bureau of the Census for the Bureau of Labor Statistics.

The Health and Retirement Study (HRS) surveys more than 22,000 Americans over the age of 50 every 2 years. The study paints an emerging portrait of an aging America's physical and mental health, insurance coverage, financial status, family support systems, labor market status, and retirement planning.

The Panel Study of Income Dynamics (PSID) is a longitudinal study of a representative sample of U.S. individuals and the family units in which they reside. It emphasizes aspects of economic and demographic behavior and includes sociological and psychological measures.

The Survey of Consumer Finances (SCF) is sponsored by the Federal Reserve Board. This triennia (every 3 years) survey collects information concerning household financial characteristics and behavior. The survey is believed to be the best source of information about family finances in the United States. The survey collects information from approximately 4,500 respondents.

The Survey of Income and Program Participation (SIPP) collects source and amount of income, labor force information, program participation and eligibility data, and demographic characteristics to measure the effectiveness of existing government programs.

References

1890 Family and Consumer Sciences Distance Education Instructional Alliance (n.d.). Retrieved June 15, 2007, from http://www.ncat.edu/~wjflemin/1890a.ppt.

Altonji, J. G., & Doraszelski, U. (2005). The role of permanent income and demographics in black/white differences in wealth. *The Journal of Human Resources 40*(1), 1–30.

American Bankruptcy Institute. (2007). *Annual business and non-business filings by year (1980–2005)*. Retrieved March 25, 2007, from http://www.abiworld.org.

Ariel Mutual Funds/Charles Schwab & Co. Inc. (2006). *Black investor survey: Saving and investing among higher income African-American and white Americans.* Retrieved November 15, from http://www.arielcapital.com/content/view/643/1173/.

Badu, Y. A., Daniels, K. N., & Salandro, D. P. (1999). An empirical analysis of differences in black and white asset and liability combinations. *Financial Services Review 8*, 129–147.

Beedon, L., & Wu, K. B. (2003). Social security and African Americans: Some facts. Retrieved November 16, 2006, from http://www.aarp.org.

Blau, F. D., & Graham, J. W. (1990). Black–white differences in wealth and asset composition. *The Quarterly Journal of Economics, 105*(2), 321–339.

Bowen, C. F., Lago, D., & Furry, M. M. (1997). Money management in families: A review of the literature with a racial, ethnic, and limited income perspective. *Advancing the Consumer Interest, 9*(2), 32–42.

Brimmer, A. F. (1988). Income, wealth, and investment behavior in the black community. *The American Economic Review, 78*(2), 151–155.

Chiteji, N. S., & Stafford, F. P. (1999). Portfolio choices of parents and their children as young adults: Asset accumulation by African-American families. *The American Economic Review, 89*(2), 377–380.

Choudhury, S. (2001/2002). Racial and ethnic differences in wealth and asset choices. *Social Security Bulletin, 64*(4), 1–15.

Coleman, S. (2003). Risk tolerance and the investment behavior of Black and Hispanic heads of household. *Financial Counseling and Planning, 14*(2), 43–51.

Commonwealth of Pennsylvania, Governor's Office, Executive Order. (2004). *Financial Education and Literacy.*

Conley, D. (2000). The racial wealth gap: Origins and implications for philanthropy in the African American Community. *Nonprofit and Voluntary Sector Quarterly, 29*(4), 530–540.

Consumer Federation of America. (2006, February 15). *African Americans pay higher auto loan rates but can take steps to reduce this expense.* Retrieved May 21, 2007, from http://www.consumerfed.org/pdfs/African_American_Auto_Financing_Rates_021506.pdf.

Consumer Federation of America. (2007, May 7). *African Americans pay higher auto loan rates but can take steps to reduce this expense.* Retrieved May 21, 2007, from http://www.consumerfed.org/pdfs/Auto_Loan_Press_Release_5-7-07.pdf.

DeVaney, S. A., Anong, S. T., & Yang (2007). Asset ownership by Black and White families. *Financial Counseling and Planning, 18*(1), 33–45.

Employee Benefit Research Institute (2003). *The 2003 minority retirement confidence survey summary of findings.* Retrieved January 9, 2007, from http://www.ebri.org/.

Employee Benefit Research Institute. (2007). 2007 Minority retirement confidence survey fact sheet. *Managing money in retirement.* Retrieved June 19, 2007, from http://www.ebri.org/.

Fan, J. E., & Lewis, J. E. (1999). Budget allocation patterns of African Americans. *The Journal of Consumer Affairs, 33*(1), 134–164.

Fontes, A., & Fan, J. X. (2006). The effects of ethnic identity on household budget allocation to status conveying goods. *Journal of Family Economic Issues, 27*, 643–663.

Gittleman, M., & Wolff, E. N. (2004). Racial differences in patterns of wealth accumulation. *The Journal of Human Resources 39*(1), 193–227.

Grable, J. E., & Joo, S. (2006) Student racial differences in credit card debt and financial behaviors and stress. *College Student Journal, Mobile, 40*(2), 400–409.

Gutter, M. S., & Fontes, A. (2006). Racial differences in risky asset ownership: A two-stage model of the investment decision-making process. *Financial Counseling and Planning, 17*(2), 64–78.

Gutter, M. S., Fox, J. J., & Montalto, C. P. (1999). Racial differences in investor decision making. *Financial Services Review, 8*, 149–162.

Hart, P. (2001). *African-American women and personal finances.* Retrieved November 11, 2006, from http://www.knowledgeplex.org/kp/report/report/relfiles/aawpf_summary.pdf.

Helman, R., Copeland, C., & VanDerhei, J. (2006). *Will more of us be working forever? The 2006 Retirement Confidence Survey* (Issue Brief, 292). Employee Benefit Research Institute.

Helman, R., VanDerhei, J., & Copeland, C. (2007). *Minority workers remain confident about retirement despite lagging preparations and false expectations* (Issue Brief, 306). Employee Benefit Research Institute.

Henry, R. A., Weber, J. G., & Yarbrough, D. (2001). Money management practices of college students. *College Student Journal, 4*, 244–247.

Hingorani, V. L. (2001). Defined contribution pension plans: Are African-Americans being prepared for the changing world of personal finance. *2001 Proceedings of thee Decisions of Science Institute*, San Francisco, CA. Retrieved January 3, 2007, from http://www.sbaer.uca.edu/Research/2001/DSI/pdffiles/PAPERS/Volume1/pt3/0421.pdf.

Humphreys, J. M. (1998). African-American buying power by place of residence: 1990–1999. *Georgia Business and Economic Conditions, 58*(4), 1–15.

Humphreys, J. M. (2006). The multicultural economy 2006. *Georgia Business and Economic Conditions, 66*(3), 1–15.

Jarrett, R. (2002). Changing the color of wealth. *Black Issues in Higher Education, 19*(10), 60.

Keister, L. A. (2000). Race and wealth inequality: The impact of racial differences in asset ownership on the distribution of household wealth. *Social Science Research, 29*, 477–502.

Keister, L. A. (2004). Race, family structure, and wealth: The effect of childhood family on adult asset ownership. *Sociological Perspectives, 47*(2), 161–187.

Kochhar, R. (2004). *The wealth of Hispanic households: 1996 to 2002*. Washington, DC: Pew Hispanic Center.

Lusardi, A. (2005). *Financial education and the saving behavior of African-American and Hispanic households*. Retrieved November 11, 2006, from http://www.dartmouth.edu/~alusardi/Papers/Financial %20Education_sep05.pdf.

Mandell, L. (2004). *The state of financial literacy of young African-American adults in America*. Retrieved January 9, 2007, from http://www.operationhope.org/fileupload/File/ TheStateofFinancialLiteracyReport.pdf.

Mandell, L. (2006a) *Financial literacy: Improving education*. Jump$tart Coalition for Personal Financial Literacy.

Mandell, L. (2006b). *The financial literacy of young African-American adults: Results of the 2006 Jump$tart survey*. Retrieved November 11, 2006, from http://www.operationhope.org/ fileupload/File/TheStateofFinancialLiteracy2006.pdf.

Murphy, A. J. (2005). Money, money, money: An exploratory study on the financial literacy of black college students. *College Student Journal, 39*(3), 478–488.

National Council on Economic Education. (2005). *Survey of the states: Economic and personal finance education in our nation's schools in 2004*. Retrieved November 10, 2006, from http://www.ncee.net/about/survey2004/NCEESurvey2004web.pdf.

New York Life Insurance and Annuity Company. (2006). *African American wealth: Powerful trends and new opportunities*. Retrieved October 26, 2006, from http://www.newyorklife.com/cda/0,3254,13767,00.html.

Nielsen Media Research. (2006). *Nielsen Media Research establishes African American Advisory Council*. Retrieved December 12, 2006, from http://www.nielson media.com.

Parker, A. (2004, October 1). National Urban League launches campaign to teach youths financial strategies. *Knight Ridder Tribune Business News*, p. 1.

Perry, V., & Morris, M. (2005). Who is in control? The role of self-perception, knowledge, and income in explaining consumer financial behavior. *The Journal of Consumer Affairs, 39*(2), 299–313.

Phoenix Marketing International. (2006). *Affluent African Americans shown to be wealthier than the overall affluent market*. Retrieved October 26, 2006, from http://www.phoenixmi.com/about/news/multicultural/2006072001.phtml.

Plath, D. A., & Stevenson, T. H. (2000). Financial services and African American market: What every financial planner should know. *Financial Services Review, 94*, 343–359.

Reed. W. (2006, September 28–October 4). Financial literacy for blacks. *Westside Gazette* (Ft. Lauderdale, FL), 5B.

Reed Business Information. (2006). *Survey tracks black homes' TV spending*. Retrieved October 26, 2006, from http://www.multichannel.com/article/CA6347285.html.

Sherman, Z. (1997). *Paradoxes in African-American consumption: An examination of marketing strategies and black identity*. Retrieved October 26, 2006, from http://www.ithaca.edu/ icjournal/ 01_africanamerican.pdf.

Silva, J., & Epstein, R. (2005). *Costly credit: African Americans and Latinos in debt* (Briefing Paper). New York: Demos.

Slaughter, H. B. (2006). *Financial illiteracy: An American epidemic: A qualitative study on the effectiveness of Web-based financial literacy technology training on African-American high school students in Pittsburgh, Pennsylvania.* Unpublished doctoral dissertation, Robert Morris University, Pittsburgh, PA.

Smith, J. P. (1995). Racial and ethnic differences in wealth in the health and retirement study. *The Journal of Human Resources, 30,* S158–S183.

Straight, R. L. (2002). Wealth: Asset-accumulation differences by race: SCF data, 1995 and 1998. *The American Economic Review, 92*(2), 330–334.

Target Market News. (2003). *New buying power report shows blacks still outspend other ethnic segments.* Retrieved November 16, 2006, from http://www.targetmarketnews.com/ Buying%20Power%20report%2003.htm.

Target Market News. (2005). *Latest 'buying power' report shows black consumers spending more on home life.* Retrieved March 5, 2007, from http://targetmarketnews.com.

Target Market News. (2007). *Black stats.* Retrieved June 21, 2007, from http://www. targetmarketnews.com/.

U.S. Census Bureau. (2006). *Nation's population one-third minority.* Retrieved January 8, 2007, from http://www.census.gov/Press-Release/www/releases/archieves/population/006808.html.

Yao, R., Gutter, M. S., & Hanna, S. (2005). The financial risk tolerance of Blacks, Hispanics and Whites. *Financial Counseling and Planning, 16*(1), 51–62.

Chapter 18
Financial Behaviors of Asian Americans

Rui Yao

Abstract The Asian American population in the United States has been increasing. Research has been done on the economic well-being of this minority group but is far from being adequate. It was generally found that Asian Americans have higher education and more wealth. This group was even labeled, by some researchers, as the "model minority." Was it more education that brought wealth to them or was it more hours worked? Some preliminary research has been done to answer this question. This chapter serves the purpose to summarize past research on Asian American consumer finances and point out direction for future research.

The United States is a multiethnic nation. Asians currently living in the U.S., which refer to Asian Americans in this chapter, are one part of the society. According to the American Community Survey, 14.9 million individuals reported themselves as Asian alone or combined with other races in 2006, accounting for 4.98% of the total U.S. population (299.4 million in 2006). This Asian population increased 3.18% from 2005 to 2006, which was the second fastest growing population after the Hispanic population (3.38% over the same period) (U.S. Census Bureau, 2007a). The median household income of Asians alone in 2006 ($63,642) were higher than national averages ($48,451) (Webster & Bishaw, 2007).

Compared to the total U.S. population, according to the 2005 American Community Survey, Asian Americans are better educated, with 49.1% of age 25 and older having a bachelor's degree or higher level of education, much higher than the 27.2% for the total population. They are more likely to work at management and professional levels. The proportion of civilian-employed single-race Asians, aged 16 and older, who work in management, professional, and related occupations was 47.0% in 2005 (vs. 34.1% of the total U.S. population) (U.S. Census Bureau, 2007b). However, they are less likely to own a home (59.1 vs. 66.9% of the total U.S. population); their married-couple families have a slightly higher poverty rate

R. Yao
Department of Human Development, Consumer and Family Sciences, South Dakota State University, NFA 311, Box 2275A, Brookings, SD 57007, USA
e-mail: rui_yao@yahoo.com

(6.9 vs. 5.0% of the total U.S. population) (U.S. Census Bureau, 2007b). There seems to be fairly large differences among different groups in this population. Who are those making a decent level of income? Who are in poverty? Why are they in poverty? What factors are associated with their economic well-being? What impact does their well-being have on U.S. economics as a whole?

A vast volume of research has been done on consumer finance; however, research that includes Asian Americans appears to be inadequate. One reason may be that few national datasets provide detailed information on consumer finances that differentiate Asian Americans from other race/ethnicity groups. Also adding to the scarcity of research on Asian Americans in the United States may be the lack of the passion of academia for investigating the financial well-being of Asian Americans due to the small population of this group. There is evidence in the literature that Asian Americans have been ignored or combined with other race/ethnicity groups (e.g., Bryant, 1986; Getter, 2006; Han, 2004; Hogarth, Anguelov, & Lee, 2004; Hunt, 2004; Olney, 1998; Wolff, 1998).

In this chapter, Asian American will be defined first, followed by an introduction of national datasets that include Asian Americans to highlight datasets available to be employed in the study of Asian American consumer finances. Then an array of research that has been done on the general financial well-being of Asian Americans, their financial attitudes and behavior, income and expenditures, debt management, and housing issues related to this racial group in the United States will be introduced. Finally, a summary of the research will be presented and future research directions will be discussed.

The Terms "Asian Americans" and "Hispanics/Latinos"

Legally, Asian Americans are U.S. citizens with an Asian background (e.g., their grandparents were immigrants from Asia). First-generation immigrants who live in the U.S. but are not American citizens (i.e., they have other nationalities) technically do not fall into this category. However, during any data collecting process, it is possible that people with an Asian heritage, whether a U.S. citizen or not, identify themselves as "Asian." Therefore, unless respondents offer to disclose their nationality, it is almost impossible for any data collector to distinguish Asians in America (i.e., immigrants from Asian countries who are currently living in the United States) from Americans with an Asian background (i.e., Asian Americans).

The U.S. Census counts all people regardless of their citizenship or immigration status. In its 2000 survey, the Census asked respondents to select one or more of the race categories listed in the questionnaire. The categories included American Indian or Alaska Native, Asian, Black or African American, Native Hawaiian or other Pacific Islander, and White (http://www.census.gov/population/www/socdemo/race/racefactcb.html). According to the U.S. Census Bureau, Asians in the U.S. include those residing in the U.S. who report an origin from an Asian country. Asians may either be Hispanic or non-Hispanic. Data on Asians may be reported as "alone" or "in-combination" (U.S. Census Bureau, 2007c). This definition is used in this chapter to refer to Asian Americans.

Hispanic/Latino is not a separate race but rather an ethnicity. In this chapter, Hispanics/Latinos refer to those who, in various surveys, identified themselves only as Hispanics/Latinos. All other people are categorized, in this chapter, according to the race that they selected as their primary race.

National Datasets That Include Asian Americans

Most national datasets include information on respondents' race/ethnicity information. However, many of them group Asians with other races such as American Indians, Alaska Natives, and Native Hawaiian/Pacific Islanders. The group sometimes is called "other race." These "other" people, of course, are not homogeneous. Even a few datasets do distinguish Asians from other groups; the sample sizes of Asian Americans remain small. The downside of having a small sample is that Asian Americans are likely to be grouped into another race category, and the results are not likely to be very meaningful.

Another problem with the race categorization deals with the interracial marriage. It is possible that someone is born into a family that has more than one racial/ethnic background. It is completely up to the respondents in any data collecting process to report their primary, if not limited to only one, race/ethnicity. For example, someone with a White father and a Black mother could identify himself as either White or Black. Let us further assume he is born into a family with mostly Black relatives; he identifies himself as Black. The influence of his White father and relatives of other races is ignored in the studies conducted by researchers using this dataset. If this person married someone with an Asian heritage, he will still identify himself as a Black; therefore, the influence of his wife is overlooked. Strictly speaking, if this person is the head of the household, the household should be referred to as a household headed by a Black person.

Major datasets that are used by researchers in the consumer finances field are briefly introduced below. However, readers should keep in mind that the race/ethnicity categorization is never a clear-cut process. It is possible for one individual to have multiple racial/ethnic identities. Due to the data limitations, researchers in this field have focused on people's self-identification of race/ethnicity.

The Current Population Survey (*CPS*) (www.census.gov/cps/) is a monthly survey of about 50,000 households that provides data, at the national level, on the social, economic, and demographic characteristics of the U.S. population. The survey is jointly sponsored by the Census Bureau and the Bureau of Labor Statistics. The survey shows the federal government's monthly unemployment statistics and other estimates of labor force characteristics. One of its supplements, the March Annual Demographic Supplement, is currently the official source of estimates of income and poverty in the United States. The CPS does not collect household asset-holding information except for their home ownership, nor does it collect data on household expenditures. Household liabilities are not collected in details either. A variety of demographic characteristics including age, gender, race, marital status, educational attainment, and health are recorded in the survey along with employment status and earnings. In this dataset, an individual could be recorded as one race only (e.g., White, Black, Asian) or a mixture of difference race/ethnicity backgrounds.

The Consumer Expenditure Survey (*CES*) (www.bls.gov/cex/) data are collected by the Census Bureau for the Bureau of Labor Statistics. The data provide information on the buying habits of consumers in the United States. The two independent surveys (the quarterly Interview Survey and the weekly Diary Survey) utilize different household samples and collect different data. The Interview Survey includes monthly expenditures such as housing and entertainment, while the Diary Survey includes weekly expenditures on items such as food and beverages. Respondents are categorized as Whites, Blacks, Asian, and other races.

The Survey of Income and Program Participation (*SIPP*) (www.sipp.census. gov/sipp/) is a monthly survey, sponsored by the U.S. Census Bureau, which collects cross-sectional and longitudinal data on the source and amount of household income, labor force participation, and general demographic characteristics. The survey is a continuous series of national panels that serves to show the distribution of income and other measures of economic well-being. The SIPP records a detailed list of real and financial assets and liabilities of households and their expenditures such as the out-of-pocket costs of medical care, shelter costs, and child support payments. Respondent's race/ethnicity is collected in the survey to be one of the following: White, Black, American Indian/Aleut/Eskimo, Asian/Pacific Islander, and other.

The National Longitudinal Surveys (*NLS*) (www.bls.gov/nls/) are a set of surveys, sponsored by the U.S. Department of Labor, focused on gathering information on individual respondents' labor market participation at different points in time. These surveys collect race information by asking respondents to identify themselves into one or more race/ethnicity groups including White, Black/African American, Asian, native Hawaiian/Pacific Islander, American Indian/Alaska Native, another self-specified race, and Hispanic/Latino.

The Survey of Consumer Finances (*SCF*) (www.federalreserve.gov/PUBS/oss/ oss2/scfindex.html) is sponsored by the Federal Reserve Board with the cooperation of the Department of Treasury. This survey is a national survey conducted every 3 years to record a detailed inventory of household financial assets and their liabilities. It also presents information on household demographic and economic characteristics, their expectations, and attitudes. Respondents are selected randomly to represent the national population. Respondents' race/ethnicity background is collected in the survey. The question asks the respondents to select one of the following race/ethnicity categories that they feel best describe themselves: White, Black or African-American, Hispanic or Latino, Asian, American Indian or Alaska Native, Hawaiian Native or other Pacific Islander, or other race.

Asian is one of the choices. However, in the public dataset, Asian, American Indian, Alaska Native, and Native Hawaiian/Pacific Islander are combined into the "other" category. Researchers who use this dataset have not been able to

differentiate Asian Americans from respondents with other racial/ethnic backgrounds (e.g.,Bucks, Kennickell, & Moore, 2006; Zhong & Xiao, 1995).

For couple households, the SCF provides race/ethnicity information only on the respondent, who is the more knowledgeable person about family finances. Researchers who employ this dataset in their studies do not know whether the respondent and the spouse or partner are of the same race/ethnicity.

The Health and Retirement Study (HRS) (hrsonline.isr.umich.edu/), sponsored by the National Institute on Aging, is a biannual longitudinal survey that provides the economic well-being (e.g., income and net worth, retirement plans and perspectives, and housing) as well as health and other information of individual respondents over age 50. The HRS survey contains a race question that asks respondents to select a race/ethnicity that they consider themselves to belong. The race/ethnicity groups include White/Caucasian, Black/African American, and other (including American Indian, Alaskan Native, Asian, and Pacific Islander).

Asian is one of the choices. However, in the public released datasets, the race variable is masked. The Asian group is combined with American, Alaskan Native, and Pacific Islander groups into one "other" category. Researchers who employ this dataset, too, are unable to study characteristics that apply to the Asian American group in particular (e.g., Smith, 1995).

The American Community Survey (ACS) (www.census.gov/acs/www/) is a nationwide survey designed to provide communities a fresh look at how they are changing. It will replace the decennial long form in future censuses and is a critical element in the Census Bureau's reengineered 2010 census. The American Community Survey will provide estimates of demographic, housing, social, and economic characteristics every year for all states, as well as for all cities, counties, metropolitan areas, and population groups of 65,000 people or more. For smaller areas, it will take three to five years to accumulate sufficient sample to produce data for areas as small as census tracts. The 2006 data set is available for public use, which has three race variables and one Hispanic origin variable. In the questionnaire, when race is asked, seven options are listed for Asians: Asian Indian, Chinese, Filipino, Japanese, Korean, Vietnamese, and Other Asian.

Financial Well-Being

Researchers have paid attention to income, wealth, and poverty of Asian Americans. Some studies concluded that Asian Americans are wealthier while others claimed that these households either have more wealth or tend to be more likely to live in poverty. Cobb-Clark and Hildebrand (2006) employed six SIPP datasets to study the wealth and asset holdings of U.S. households. They found that immigrants from European and Asian countries have substantially more wealth than average immigrant households. The Census data consistently shows that Asian American households vary widely in their well-being. They occupy the extremes of wealth and poverty. Using the 1990 Census of Population and Housing dataset, Kwon,

Zuiker, and Bauer (2004) examined factors that are associated with Asian immigrant household poverty status. The authors found that households that had a higher human capital level and experienced acculturation were less likely to live below the poverty threshold. The latter study mentioned an interesting point that acculturation made a difference in the well-being among Asian immigrant households.

Education is likely to be related to level of earnings. Previous literature noticed this relationship and investigated the earning differentials between Asian Americans and other races. However, findings showed the reason for Asian Americans to earn a higher level of income may be that they work longer hours than otherwise similar Whites. Chiswick (1983) compared the employment and earnings of American-born Asian men with different origins and between them as a whole group and American-born Whites. The author found that among American-born male adults, those who had a Chinese or Japanese origin were more educated and received higher earnings than those who had a Filipino origin; men with an Asian background in general were more educated and earned more than Whites. The 1970 Census of Population data, used in this analysis, included only males aged between 25 and 64 who were born in the United States, worked at least 1 week in 1969, and identified themselves to be White or have a Chinese, Japanese, or Filipino origin. Earning was defined as wages, salaries, and self-employment income; and employment was represented by the number of weeks worked in 1969. Geographic area and demographic variables other than race were controlled for in the analysis as well as human capital. Men with a Japanese background earned significantly less than Whites, and Japanese-origin men worked significantly longer than their White counterparts. Men who had a Filipino origin earned significantly less and worked significantly fewer hours than White men. These results indicated that working harder may be the reason why certain racial/ethnic groups earned more or less than otherwise similar Whites.

Financial Attitudes and Behaviors

Research has shown that the majority of Asian Americans (62 %) have personal savings for retirement, similar to Whites (66 %) and higher than Hispanics and Blacks (EBRI, 2001). Asian Americans also are the most confident ones to believe that they are adequately planning for retirement (EBRI, 2002). Springstead and Wilson (2000) compared participation rates in IRAs, 401(k)s, and the TSP. They concluded that Asian Americans were more likely to participate in tax-deferred savings accounts than White Americans. Household financial well-being is dependent on attitude toward financial issues and financial behaviors. Examples of research on Asian Americans' money beliefs, banking status, emergency fund savings, and personal investments are discussed below.

Using the Money Beliefs and Behaviors Scale developed by Furnham (1984), Masuo, Malroutu, Hanashiro, and Kim (2004) compared money beliefs and behaviors of college students in Korea and Japan and college students in the United States with Japanese or Korean background. The authors asked the participants to complete a questionnaire. The comparison revealed that Korean and Japanese college students had significantly different money beliefs from their U.S. counterparts. College students in Korea and Japan were found to firmly believe that money could solve all problems. Asian American college students were more likely to prefer to use cash rather than credit cards, to keep personal the details of their financial status, and to feel guilty about spending money on necessities even when they could afford to do so. These findings are very important, in that they suggest although Asian students and Asian American students share similar cultures, they display different money attitudes and money behaviors. Therefore, acculturation may be the reason for this difference. Another example of research that showed the effect of acculturation is the work done by Rhine and Greene (2006). The authors found that immigrants who had lived in the United States for a longer period of time are less likely to be unbanked than those who came to the country recently.

Using the 1992–1993 Consumer Expenditure Survey, Hong and Kao (1997) examined the emergency fund adequacy of Asian American households. The authors concluded that more Asian Americans held adequate emergency funds than were non-Hispanic Whites, African Americans, and Hispanics. Therefore, the race variable did appear to have played a role in the different emergency funds adequacy among households. However, the research done by Carol, Rhee, and Rhee (1999) failed to find evidence that showed the impact of culture on savings behavior, using the 1980 and 1990 Census data in their study. The authors argued that the immigrants' savings patterns did not necessarily represent savings patterns in their countries of origin. This statement indicated that acculturation may have been the reason why immigrants and people in their countries of origin may display different savings behavior. Another example of research that did not find a significant difference in financial behaviors is the study done by Perry and Morris (2005). The authors studied the relationship between responsible financial management behavior and locus of control, income, and financial knowledge using the 1999 Freddie Mac Consumer Credit Survey data. The authors found that compared with otherwise similar Whites, Asian Americans did not seem to behave significantly differently in terms of controlling expenditures, paying bills on time, planning for financial future, saving, and providing for themselves and their family.

Income and Expenditure

Lots of research results showed that Asian Americans, compared to average Americans, have higher earnings. However, some researchers argued that it is the education level and longer work hours that made a difference. Barringer, Takeuchi, and Xenos (1990) found that most Asian Americans are better educated than Whites, Blacks, and Hispanics. However, after controlling for other variables, only Japanese Americans' income came near to that of Whites. Higher education of Asian Americans did not lead to income equity with Whites. Portes and Zhou (1996), using the 5% 1980 Public Use Microdata Sample from the U.S. Census, found that self-employment had a positive effect on the logged average earnings of respondents with Chinese or Korean backgrounds and a negative effect on the logged earnings of those with Japanese background and Whites. They argued that Japanese immigrants and Whites had higher average earnings than other groups. Interestingly, the authors also found that self-employment had a negative effect on the logged hourly earnings of all groups except Korean immigrants. This indicated that the positive effect of average earnings of Chinese immigrants was merely the increased number of hours involved in their self-employment work. Sharpe and Abdel-Ghany (2006) employed the 2000 Census data and compared the determinants of income level of six Asian groups in the United States, Whites and Blacks. Results demonstrated that human capital investment and structural barriers explained the income differentials among these groups. Compared with otherwise similar Whites, Chinese, Filipinos, Korean, and Vietnamese immigrant households had significantly less household income; and Japanese households had significantly more. All Asian American household groups had significantly more household income than their otherwise similar Black counterparts. The authors argued that higher education is the key to increase household income and fluency in English determines access to higher education. The authors employed Asian Indians and Vietnamese as an example, which demonstrated that possibly due to the fluency in English, Asian Indians did not have a significantly lower household income than their White counterparts, whereas the poor English fluency of Vietnamese contributed to their low income levels.

Researchers have also been interested in expenditure patterns of minority households. They agreed that even after controlling for other variables, Asian Americans did display a different expenditure pattern. Compared with otherwise similar Whites, Asian American households were found to spend more on education (Fan, 1997) and housing (Fontes & Fan, 2006); however, they spend less on fuel, utilities, household equipment, alcohol, and tobacco products (Fan, 1997). Using the 1980–1992 Consumer Expenditure Survey, the 1980–1992 Consumer Price Index, and the 1990 Cost of Living Index, Fan and Koonce-Lewis (1999) compared budget allocation patterns of African Americans to that of Asian Americans, Caucasian Americans, and Hispanic Americans. Results showed, compared to African Americans, Asian Americans spent more on food away from home, entertainment, shelter, transportation, and health care and less on apparel, fuel, and utilities.

Debt Management

Debt status and management of Asian Americans were not substantially investigated by researchers. Baum and O'Malley (2003) conducted a Nellie Mae survey of student loan borrowers in repayment. The authors examined the impact of debt burdens on student loan borrowers in repayment who had at least one federal student loan in 2002. It was found that although Asian American students did not have significantly higher or lower undergraduate debt or total debt than White students, they did feel less burdened with their educational debt. Compared with students from other races, Asian American students were the least likely to state a willingness to opt for lower payments even if it means that they would have to pay more in the long run. Whether Asian American students have better debt management skills than students with other racial/ethnicity backgrounds, as may be indicated by the above results, cannot be concluded because it was also found in the research that Asian American students had the highest current earnings among all students.

By randomly sending an online survey in fall 2001 to a total of 2,650 undergraduate students, graduate students, and professional students at the University of Illinois, Lyons (2004) summarized data of college students who were financially at risk. White students and Asian students did not show a difference in their likelihood to have a credit card debt of $1,000 or more, to not pay their credit card balance in full, or to make late payments. The author also did analyses with only those who had at least one credit card. Results were the same except that Asian and Hispanic students were more likely to not pay their credit card balance in full than otherwise similar White students.

The survey instrument was not included in this research. Therefore, it is not known whether students could specify that they did not own any credit card but still could answer questions related to credit card management such as paying balance in full. If so, the reason why Asian students with or without a credit card were not significantly different in paying their balance in full may be because some Asian students who did not own a credit card indicated that they paid credit card balance in full in the survey. More research needs to be done to explore the reasons why Asian American students were less likely than White students to pay credit card balance in full, whether it is due to a lack of knowledge on debt management, over spending, poorer economic well-being, or some other reasons. Regardless of the reasons, more education needs to be designed to target the debt management skills of Asian American students.

Housing Issues

According to a report of the Asian Real Estate Association of America (AREAA) (2007), the homeownership rate for Asian Americans was 53 % in 2000, which was lower than that of the total population 65 %. By 2005, Asian American homeownership increased considerably to 59 %, still 6 percentage points lower than that of the total population (67 %). AREAA found that in 18 metropolitan areas, 25 % or more of Asian American households were linguistically isolated, which may be one of the reasons why these households are less likely than the total population to own a home. Language barriers can be one of the factors that affect household ability to understand the mortgage loan terms as well as the housing market as a whole.

Researchers have attributed the racial differences in mortgage lending to the cultural affinity (Calomiris, Kahn, & Longhofer, 1994; Hunter & Walker, 1996). If this affinity affects mortgage lending, White loan officers will be more lenient toward White applicants and minority applicants will benefit from their affinity with minority loan officers. On the contrary, Black, Collins, and Cyree (1997) found some evidence that Black-owned banks rejected a higher proportion of Black mortgage loan applicants than White-owned banks.

Whether minority (Black, Hispanic, & Asian) bank workforce was more likely to approve minority borrowers for mortgage loans was examined by Kim and Squires (1998). The analyses were done in five major metropolitan areas: Atlanta, Boston, Denver, Milwaukee, and San Francisco. The three datasets used included the 1993 EEO-1 report, the 1993 Home Mortgage Disclosure Act report, and the 1990 Census. The authors controlled for the median single-family housing value of the census tract in which the property was located, the rate of families in poverty, the applicant's household income, the amount of the loan, the number of mortgage applications submitted to the institution, and total employment of the institution. The race effect on the probability that the mortgage loan application was approved was examined. Their findings illustrated that in the financial institutions, Asians and Blacks were hired to work at lower levels than if they worked elsewhere. When controlled for everything else listed above, mortgage loan applications filed by Asians were the most likely to be approved in all cities except Atlanta, which was represented by a large Black population. The controlled results confirmed the cultural affinity hypothesis that the racial composition of the workforce at the administrative and professional levels did have a significant effect on the probability of the mortgage application being approved. However, the employment of Asian workers did not have a significant impact on the likelihood of mortgage loan applications filed by Asians to be approved.

Researchers agreed that renters bear a greater housing cost burden than homeowners, especially for lower income households (Apgar, Dispasquale, Cummings, & McArdle, 1990; Schwenk, 1991). Chi and Laquartra (1998) employed the 1987 American Housing Surveys and analyzed factors that affected this housing cost burden. Their results showed that Asian American households were more likely than otherwise similar non-Hispanic White households to have a higher risk of excessive housing costs, even after controlling for housing tenure. The authors argued that this result might be due to the possibility that Asian American households tend to view their home as an investment.

Coulson (1999), Painter, Gabriel, and Myers (2001), and Krivo and Kaufman (2004) compared home ownership rates between Asian Americans and other ethnic groups. Their findings consistently showed that Asian Americans were less likely than their White counterparts to own a home. These studies, however, did not differentiate among Asian American groups. Coulson (1999) employed the March 1996 Current Population Survey and investigated factors that affected the low home ownership rates of immigrant and non-immigrant Asian Americans, given their higher income and education levels. Their findings demonstrated that being an immigrant substantially lowered Asian American households' probability of owning a home. However, this effect became less important over time. Youth in the families and the high rate of residence in areas with high value to rent ratios also negatively affected these households' home ownership. Painter et al. (2001) employed the 1980 and 1990 Census data to examine the relationship between home ownership and factors such as race and immigration status. The authors found that Asian Americans were as likely to own a home as otherwise similar Whites and that the immigrant status did not lead to a lower likelihood for Asian Americans to become a homeowner.

Some studies differentiated among Asian American groups. Borjas (2002) used the 1990 Census data to analyze the national origin differentials in homeownership rates. He found that after controlling for socioeconomic characteristics and metropolitan area-fixed effects, immigrants from China, India, Korea, and Philippines were less likely to own a home than natives. Using the 1990 Census data, Painter, Yang, and Yu (2003) examined the differences in home ownership rates among Asian American groups. Contrary to the findings by Borjas, these authors found that most Asian American groups were as likely as otherwise similar Whites to own a home. However, Chinese American households were significantly more likely to own a home than other groups.

Conclusions and Future Research Directions

This chapter serves the purpose of providing a preliminary summary of the research done on Asian American consumer finances. The population of Asian Americans is growing. The phrase "Asian Americans" is an umbrella term for this greatly diversified group. First of all, Asian Americans are from many Asian countries such as China, Japan, Korea, Philippines, Vietnam, Cambodia, Thailand, Laos, India, and Pakistan. Although previously believed to share similar cultures in "Confucian Dynamism" (Hofstede & Bond, 1988), each of these Asian American groups is unique in language, life style, and cultural values and beliefs (Kim, Yang, Atkinson, Wolfe, & Hong, 2001). Socioeconomic levels also vary widely among these Asian American ethnic groups. According to Reeves and Bennett (2004), the median family income for Asian Americans ranges from $70,849 for Japanese Americans to $32,384 for Hmong Americans. Similarly, the education attainment varies greatly among these groups: 63.9 % of Asian Indians 25 years or older held a bachelor's or higher degree in 2000, whereas 7.5 % of Hmong Americans had such a degree. There are also great differences in the occupation of Asian American groups. Of those aged 16 or older, 59.9 % Asian Indians were in the management, professional, and related positions, while only 13.4 % Laotian Americans were in these same occupations.

Past literature has served the field of consumer finances by recognizing the existing differences in financial well-being of households with various racial/ethnic backgrounds. However, without in-depth discussions of the reasons behind the visible race/ethnicity, readers could be directed to believe that race/ethnicity is a factor that affects household financial well-being. This is, to some extent, misleading. The differences in consumer finances that are claimed, by some researchers, to be race/ethnicity related may be due to other factors that are hidden behind the race/ethnicity variable. It is erroneous to claim that a household is likely to be wealthier or poorer because it belongs to a certain race/ethnicity group. Cultures and beliefs that are associated with race/ethnicity are more likely to affect an individual's financial behavior, which have direct impact on his/her economic well-being.

Immigration status (regardless of race/ethnicity background), although difficult to determine using survey instruments, may also affect household financial attitude and behavior. Imagine a young person with a temporary work visa who is not sure whether he will be able to stay in the United States is included in a research survey on consumer finances. Due to the uncertainty of the future and the possible short investment horizon, this person is very likely to show a risk tolerance level and risk behavior that are far more conservative than he would have preferred had he known he would stay in the United States for a much longer time (e.g., 30 years). Unlike first-generation immigrants who were born and raised in another culture, later-generation immigrants may feel more acquainted with American values and beliefs. Therefore, households led by these people may have different money attitudes and behavior that directly affect their economic well-being. The results found in Masuo et al. (2004) indicated that the degree of affinity to a certain culture, rather than race/ethnicity itself, influences money attitudes and beliefs of young immigrants. The study done by Kwon et al. (2004) provided evidence to this claim by stating that the degree of acculturation affected Asian immigrant household economic well-being.

Some researchers believe that Asian Americans, with their above-average socioeconomic success, are a model minority (e.g., Peterson, 1971) because they are not underrepresented in educational and occupational achievements and economic success. However, other researchers argue that this group does face economic discrimination (e.g., Wong, 1982). The Asian American population, currently inadequately studied by academia and the industries, is growing faster than the overall population (Bernstein, 2004). The nation cannot afford to ignore the great purchasing power and enormous needs in financial services that Asian Americans represent and must address the diverse needs of Asian Americans. The future of cultural-sensitive services will depend not only on the knowledge of this culturally diversified group but also on the direction of research studies in the field of consumer finances. Past research did not show success in finding the real factors that directly affect the well-being among racial/ethnic groups. Future research should focus more on the factors behind the veil of race/ethnicity and strive to better serve minority communities and help improve their economic well-being.

References

Apgar, W. C., Jr., Dispasquale, D., Cummings, J., & McArdle, N. (1990). *The state of the nation's housing 1990*. Cambridge, MA: Joint Center for Housing Studies, Harvard University.

Asian Real Estate Association of America. (2007, June). *Following the path to Asian American home ownership*. Retrieved August 1, 2007, from http://www.areaa.org/cms/AREAA_UCLA_2007b.pdf.

Barnes, J. S., & Bennett, C. E. (2002). *The Asian population: 2000*. Washington, DC: U.S. Census Bureau.

Barringer, H. R., Takeuchi, D. T., & Xenos, P. (1990). Education, occupation prestige, and income of Asian Americans. *Sociology of Education, 63*(1), 27–43.

Baum, S., & O'Malley, M. (2003). College on credit: How borrowers perceive their education debt. *NASFAA Journal of Student Financial Aid, 33*(3), 7–19.

Bernstein, R. (2004). Hispanic and Asian Americans increasing faster than overall population. Retrieved January 19, 2007, from http://www.census.gov/Press-Release/www/releases/archives/race/001839.html.

Black, H. M., Collins, C., & Cyree, K. (1997). Do Black-owned banks discriminate against Black borrowers? *Journal of Real Estate Finance and Economics, 11*, 189–204.

Borjas, G. J. (2002). Homeownership in the immigrant population. *Journal of Urban Economics, 52*(3), 448–476.

Bryant, W. K. (1986). Assets and debts in a consumer portfolio. *Journal of Consumer Affairs, 20*(1), 19–35.

Bucks, B. K., Kennickell, A. B., & Moore, K. B. (2006). Recent changes in U.S. family finances: Evidence from the 2001 and 2004 Survey of Consumer Finances. *Federal Reserve Bulletin*. Retrieved November 11, 2006, from http://www.federalreserve.gov/pubs/ bulletin/2006/financesurvey.pdf.

Calomiris, C. W., Kahn, C. M., & Longhofer, S. D. (1994). Housing finance intervention and private incentives: Helping minorities and the poor. *Journal of Money, Credit and Banking, 26*(3), 634–674.

Carol, C. D., Rhee, B., & Rhee, C. (1999). Does cultural origin affect saving behavior? Evidence from immigrants. *Economic Development and Cultural Change, 48*, 33–50.

Chi, P. S. K., & Laquatra, J. (1998). Profiles of housing cost burden in the United States. *Journal of Family and Economic Issues, 19*(2), 175–193.

Chiswick, B. R. (1983). An analysis of the earnings and employment of Asian-American men. *Journal of Labor Economics, 1*(2), 197–214.

Cobb-Clark, D. A., & Hildebrand, A. A. (2006). The wealth and asset holdings of U.S.-born and foreign-born households: Evidence from SIPP data. *Review of Income and Wealth, 52*(1), 17–42.

Coulson, N. E. (1999). Why are Hispanic- and Asian-American home-ownership rates so low?: Immigration and other factors. *Journal of Urban Economics, 45*(2), 209–227.

Employee Benefit Research Institute. (2001). *Retirement planning, savings, & expectations among ethnic groups*. Retrieved January 19, 2007, from http://www.ebri.org/rcs/1998/rcs-expectations.pdf.

Employee Benefit Research Institute. (2002). *Minority groups express concerns about saving and retirement planning*. Retrieved January 19, 2007, from http://www.ebri.org/prrel/pr564.pdf.

Fan, J. X. (1997). Expenditure patterns of Asian American: Evidence from the U.S. Consumer Expenditure Survey, 1980–1992. *Family and Consumer Science Research Journal, 25*(4), 339–368.

Fan, J. X., & Koonce-Lewis, J. (1999). Budget allocation patterns of African Americans. *Journal of Consumer Affairs, 33*(1), 134–164.

Fontes, A., & Fan, J. X. (2006). The effects of ethnic identity on household budget allocation to status conveying goods. *Journal of Family and Economic Issues, 27*, 643–663.

Furnham, A. (1984). Many sides of the coin: The psychology of money usage. *Personality and Individual Differences, 5*, 95–103.

Getter, D. E. (2006). Consumer credit risk and pricing. *Journal of Consumer Affairs, 40*(1), 41–63.

Han, S. (2004). Discrimination in lending: Theory and evidence. *Journal of Real Estate Finance and Economics, 29*(1), 5–46.

Hofstede, G., & Bond, M. H. (1988). The Confucius connection: From cultural roots to economic growth. *Organizational Dynamics, 16*, 5–21.

Hogarth, J. M., Anguelov, C. E., & Lee, J. (2004). Why don't households have a checking account? *Journal of Consumer Affairs, 38*(1), 1–34.

Hong, G., & Kao, Y. E. (1997). Emergency fund adequacy of Asian Americans. *Journal of Family and Economic Issues, 18*(2), 127–145.

Hunt, M. O. (2004). Race/ethnicity and beliefs about wealth and poverty. *Social Science Quarterly, 85*(3), 827–853.

Hunter, W. C., & Walker, M. B. (1996). The cultural affinity hypothesis and mortgage lending decisions. *Journal of Real Estate Finance and Economics, 13*, 57–70.

Kim, B. S. K., Yang, P. H., Atkinson, D. R., Wolfe, M. M., & Hong, S. (2001). Cultural value similarities and differences among Asian American Ethnic Groups. *Cultural Diversity and Ethnic Minority Psychology, 7*(4), 343–361.

Kim, S., & Squires, G. D. (1998). The color of money and the people who lend it. *Journal of Housing Research, 9*(2), 271–284.

Krivo, L. J., & Kaufman, R. L. (2004). Housing and wealth inequality: Racial-ethnic differences in home equity in the United States. *Demography, 41*(3), 585–605.

Kwon, H., Zuiker, V. S., & Bauer, J. W. (2004). Factors associated with the poverty status of Asian immigrant householders by citizenship status. *Journal of Family and Economic Issues, 25*(1), 101–120.

Lyons, A. C. (2004). A profile of financially at-risk college students. *Journal of Consumer Affairs, 38*(1), 56–80.

Masuo, D. M., Malroutu, Y. L., Hanashiro, R., & Kim, J. H. (2004). College students' money beliefs and behaviors: An Asian perspective. *Journal of Family and Economic Issues, 25*(4), 469–481.

Olney, M. L. (1998). When your world is not enough: Race, collateral, and household credit. *Journal of Economic History, 58*(2), 408–431.

Painter, G., Gabriel, S. A., & Myers, D. (2001). Race, immigrant status, and housing tenure choice, *Journal of Urban Economics, 49*(1), 150–167.

Painter, G., Yang, L., & Yu, Z. (2003). Heterogeneity in Asian American home-ownership: The impact of household endowments and immigrant status. *Urban Studies, 40*(3), 505–530.

Perry, V. G., & Morris, M. D. (2005). Who is in control? The role of self-perception, knowledge, and income in explaining consumer financial behavior. *Journal of Consumer Affairs, 39*(2), 299–313.

Peterson, W. (1971). *Japanese Americans: Oppression and success.* New York: Random House.

Portes, A., & Zhou, M. (1996). Self-employment and earnings of immigrants. *American Sociological Review, 61*(2), 219–230.

Reeves, T., & Bennett, C. E. (2004). We the people: Asians in the United States. Washington, DC: U.S. Census Bureau.

Rhine, S. L. W., & Greene, W. H. (2006). The determinants of being unbanked for U.S. immigrants. *Journal of Consumer Affairs, 40*(1), 21–40.

Schwenk, N. E. (1991). Trends in housing. *Family Economics Review, 4*(1), 14–19.

Sharpe, D. L., & Abdel-Ghany, M. (2006). Determinants of income differentials: Comparing Asians with Whites and Blacks. *Journal of Family and Economic Issues, 27*(4), 588–600.

Smith, J. P. (1995). Racial and ethnic differences in wealth in the Health and Retirement Study. *Journal of Human Resources, 30,* 158–183.

Springstead, G. R., & Wilson, T. M. (2000). Participation in voluntary individual savings accounts: An analysis of IRAs, 401(k)s, and TSP. *Social Security Bulletin,63*(1), 34–39.

U.S. Census Bureau. (2007a, May 17). *Minority population tops 100 million.* (News release). Washington, DC: Author.

U.S. Census Bureau. (2007b, March 1). *Facts for features: Asian/Pacific American heritage month: May 2007.* (News release). Washington, DC: Author.

U.S. Census Bureau. (2007c). *The American Community – Asians: 2004.* Washington, DC: Author.

Webster, B. H., & Bishaw, A. (2007). *Income, earnings, and poverty data from the 2006 American Community Survey.* (ACS-08). Washington, DC: U.S. Census Bureau.

Wolff, E. N. (1998). Recent trends in the size distribution of household wealth. *Journal of Economic Perspectives, 12*(3), 131–150.

Wong, M. G. (1982). The cost of being Chinese, Japanese, and Filipino in the United States: 1960, 1970, 1976. *Pacific Sociological Review, 25,* 59–78.

Zhong, L. X., & Xiao, J. J. (1995). Determinants of family bond and stock holdings. *Financial Counseling and Planning, 6,* 107–114.

Part IV
Consumer Finance in Various Settings

Chapter 19
Consumer Financial Issues in Health Care

Deanna L. Sharpe

Abstract While government officials, health care providers, and insurers debate the cause and cure of high and rising health care costs, consumers face the daunting task of making critical health care decisions for themselves and family members in a complex market. This chapter describes the characteristics of and key players in that market. Reasons given in the academic and popular press for high and rising health care costs are evaluated. Effectiveness of insurance in keeping health care attainable and affordable for consumers is explored. The chapter concludes with suggestions for future research.

In 2004, the United States spent close to $2 trillion dollars on health care, or about $6,280 per person. From 2003 to 2004, total national health care spending increased 7.9%, over three times the rate of inflation (Smith, Cowan, Heffler, & Catlin, 2006). Health care spending is expected to increase at the same rate over the next decade, reaching $4 trillion dollars by 2015 (Borger et al., 2006).

No industrialized nation spends more on health care, including those that provide health insurance to all citizens (National Coalition on Health Care, 2004). The United States spends 244% more per capita on health care than the United Kingdom, 180% more than Canada (Blue Cross Blue Shield Association, 2006). Currently, 16% of U.S. Gross Domestic Product (GDP) is devoted to health care. It is the largest sector of domestic spending; almost 1.25 times larger than food or housing, 2.5 times larger than national defense (Bureau of Economic Analysis, 2005; Smith et al., 2006). Despite a recent modest decline in the growth of health care costs, by 2015, it is expected that $1 of every $5 of domestic spending will be allocated to health care (Borger et al., 2006).

Some argue that this high amount of spending on health care is not a problem. It simply reflects the fact that, as a prosperous nation, we can afford to spend more on health care (Pauly, 2003). The market is meeting the demand for more care,

D.L. Sharpe
Personal Financial Planning Department, University of Missouri-Columbia, 239 Stanley Hall, Columbia, MO 65211, USA
e-mail: sharped@missouri.edu

J.J. Xiao, (ed.), *Handbook of Consumer Finance Research,*
© Springer 2008

better care, and use of more costly technical equipment for medical diagnosis and treatment. This seems to be a minority view, however (Bodenheimer, 2005a).

Many watching the health care market are uneasy. They observe health care costs rising at an average annual rate of 9.9% since 1970, about 2.5 percentage points faster than domestic GDP, and seriously question the sustainability of such growth (Kaiser Family Foundation, 2006a). They foresee the demands that the large Baby Boom generation will make on Medicare and Medicaid and wonder about the long-term viability of these public health care programs (Auerbach, Gale, Orszag, & Potter, 2003). They worry that more federal and state dollars allocated to health care will mean fewer dollars available for other necessary goods and services such as education, police and fire protection (Davis, Anderson, Rowland, & Steinberg, 1990). This result is mitigated by the transfer of funds from the young (where dependency ratios are declining) to old (where dependency ratios are increasing), however.

"Crowding out" already appears to be happening at the household level. Participants in the 2006 Employee Benefit Research Institute Health Confidence Survey reported that, despite having health care coverage, rising health care costs forced cut backs in other household budget items. Over one-third had reduced retirement savings, up from 25% just 2 years earlier. Half (53%) had reduced other savings. For some, health care bills made it difficult to pay for other basic necessities (36%, up from 25% in 2004) and other bills (37%, up from 30% 2004) (Employee Benefit Research Institute, 2006).

While policy makers, health care providers, and insurers debate the cause and cure of high and rising health care costs, consumers face the daunting task of making critical health care decisions for themselves and family members in a complex market. This chapter describes the characteristics of and key players in that market. Reasons given in the academic and popular press for high and rising health care costs are evaluated. Effectiveness of insurance in keeping health care attainable and affordable for consumers is explored. The chapter concludes with suggestions for future research.

Market for Health Care

Characteristics of Health Care

Health care is a multifaceted consumer good. It has qualities of a public good. Society benefits when health care maintains worker productivity and reduces spread of communicable disease (Smith, Beaglehole, Woodward, & Drager, 2003). It also has qualities of a private good. Our health status directly affects the quality of our lives, so we purchase health care to benefit ourselves. In addition, each of us is personally responsible for making lifestyle choices that either enhance or detract from good health (Gillett, 1998).

Economists consider health care to be an aspect of human capital, an investment that we make in ourselves to enhance our productivity. In a now classic article,

Michael Grossman (1972) introduced the idea that "good health" can be likened to a durable capital good that produces "healthy time." Recognizing the public and private benefits of good health, Grossman noted that healthy time is desirable because it makes the person who possesses it more productive in work, in the market, and at home. With good health, leisure activities can be enjoyed to a greater extent and a person's overall quality of life is improved as well.

Economists also view health care as a normal good (Newhouse, 1992). As our resources increase, we want more or better health care. It is generally not controversial for an individual to purchase as much health care as desired as long as that individuals pays his or her own medical bill. When government or insurance companies pay some or all of health care costs, however, constraints are imposed. The government-sponsored health care programs—Medicaid for the low-income or Medicare for older Americans—provide a limited amount of basic health care only to those meeting strict eligibility standards. Cost controls for private insurance take various forms such as refusing payment for certain types of treatments or limiting access to specialists.

Health care consumers are often at a disadvantage. In marketing terms, health care is a "high credence" consumer item (Sharma & Patterson, 1999). Unlike the market for consumer durables such as automobiles or microwaves, objective, unbiased assessments of quality are not readily available. Local markets may offer few choices of health care providers and comparison of service quality is difficult. No objective ranking of hospital quality exists nor are doctor's error rates public information. Most consumers interacting with medical personnel or purchasing medical treatment or equipment lack the technical knowledge necessary to judge the quality of what they receive even after purchase (Darby & Karni, 1973; Sharma & Patterson, 1999). Consequently, consumers must place a high level of trust, or credence, in the health care provider. This trust may be misplaced, however. A recent survey by the Commonwealth Fund of approximately 6,000 sick adults in Australia, Canada, New Zealand, the United States, the United Kingdom, and Germany found that one-third of U.S. respondents had experienced a medical or medication mistake or lab error, a higher proportion than any other country in the survey (Schoen et al., 2005).

Sectors of the Health Care Market

The health care market operates in the public and the private sectors. Medicaid and Medicare are government-funded health insurance programs. Medicaid is a social welfare program for low-income individuals and families of all ages. It is jointly funded by state and federal dollars, and managed at the state level. Medicare is an entitlement program for those aged 65 and older. It is funded and administered by the federal government.

Public health care spending was 45 % of national health expenditures in 2005; the remainder was private spending (Centers for Medicaid and Medicare Services, 2007). For fiscal year 2007, the $205 billion and $387 billion allocated to Medicaid and Medicare, respectively, represent a little over one-fifth of projected federal budget outlays (Office of Management and Budget, 2007).

Dynamics of the Health Care Market

The health care market has several players: policy makers, purchasers, insurers, providers, and suppliers. Policy makers establish and enforce the laws and regulations that govern exchange in the health care market. Individuals, employers, and governments purchase health care services or health insurance. Insurers collect money from health insurance purchasers to reimburse health care providers when claims are made. Health care providers use the money they receive to pay suppliers for such things as medical equipment, medical supplies, and pharmaceuticals (Bodenheimer, 2005a).

Competing interests exist. Payments made by purchasers and insurers constitute revenue to health care providers and suppliers. Not surprisingly, purchasers and insurers favor finding ways to reduce costs, whereas providers and suppliers resist cost containment. Bodenheimer (2005a) calls this conflict the "fundamental battle in the health care economy" (p. 848). Internal "skirmishes" create additional tensions. Insurance companies would like to reduce payments to providers, but want more money from purchasers. Pharmaceutical makers demand a high price to maintain their profits, but hospitals negotiate for a low price to keep their costs down. If an insurance provider caps reimbursement to a physician group, primary care physicians may disagree with specialists regarding distribution of the check (Bodenheimer, 2005a). According to economic theory, competition should drive costs down, but in the health care market, it has not.

Why Health Care Costs Are High

Various reasons for high and increasing health care costs have been proposed. Some explanations focus on factors outside the health care market. Economic growth and an aging population are cases in point. The economic growth argument is simple. Richer nations can afford more health care. Thus, it should be no surprise that as the GDP of a country increases, the dollar amount allocated to health care grows as well. Indeed, if the overall economy is growing, spending more on health care need not result in less spent on other sectors of the economy (Chernew, Hirth, & Cutler, 2003; Pauly, 2003). Critics of this view note that the ratio of per capita health expenditures to per capita GDP in the United States far exceeds that of other industrialized countries (Reinhardt, Hussey, & Anderson, 2002). Consequently, an expanding economy is not a sufficient explanation for rising health care costs in the United States (Bodenheimer, 2005a).

Population aging has been offered as another potential reason for rising health care costs. It seems to be a plausible explanation. Over the past several decades, growth in the population aged 65 and older has outpaced growth of younger age groups (He, Sengupta, Velkoff, & DeBarros, 2005). Per capita health expenditures for persons over age 75 are five times higher than those for persons age 25–34 (Reinhardt, 2003). It seems reasonable, then, that countries with an older population would spend more on health care than countries with a younger population. But, research indicates an aging population accounts for less than 7 % of the growth in health care expenditures (Reinhardt, 2003). In multivariate analysis of cross-sectional, cross-national data, no significant relationship has been found between the proportion of aged in a nation and national health expenditures (Gruber & Wise, 2002; Richardson, 1999).

Factors within the health care market such as excessive administrative costs, market power of health care providers, and absence of effective cost-containment measures have also been blamed for raising health care costs (Bodenheimer, 2005a, 2005b). Some evidence exists to support this claim. A 2002 study found administrative costs in private insurance were about four times larger than administrative costs in public health care programs such as federal and state Medicaid programs (12.8 % vs. 3 %, respectively). Advertising and marketing expenses constituted much of this difference (Levit, Smith, Cowan, Sensenig, & Catlin, 2004). Bodenheimer (2005b) notes that integration of financing and service delivery, whether in public or private plans, reduces administrative costs.

Health care providers in the United States have more market power (i.e., ability to raise prices without losing business) than health care purchasers. Bodenheimer (2005c) traces this differential to hospital and physician control of the Blue Cross Blue Shield organizations that initially offered health insurance in the United States. Lucrative reimbursement formulas for hospitals and physicians were established in these initial health care plans and later replicated in Medicare. International comparisons indicate that U.S. physicians are paid more than their non-U.S. counterparts for performing similar services. Reinhardt et al. (2002) report that average physician income in the United States is 5.5 times larger than average employee income; in Sweden and the United Kingdom, the ratio is 1.5. But they also caution that such comparisons should be made with care. Although the OECD defines physician income as "average professional earnings net of deductible practice expenditure, before taxes," the calculation of "professional earnings" can vary by country.

Evidence from other countries suggests that capping health care spending can control growth in medical costs. In Germany and Canada, increases in physician fees are connected to the quantity of physician services. If physicians increase visits or procedures, the payment per each item is reduced so that an annual expenditure cap is not exceeded. The United Kingdom uses a globally budgeted system where monies for all services are budgeted in advance. The United States uses a similar approach with Veterans Affairs hospitals. Critics of cost controls express concern that budgets might not allow purchase of high-quality care, the decision making processes among all players are complex, and special interests can dominate (Bodenheimer, 2005b).

Rising prescription drug costs have also been implicated as a reason for higher medical costs. In 2005, $200.7 billion was spent on prescription drugs, almost five times more than the $40.3 billion spent in 1990. At 10 % in 2005, prescription drugs costs comprise a smaller share of national health care spending than hospital (31 %) or physician services (21 %) (Kaiser Family Foundation, 2007). But, these costs have grown rapidly. Between 1994 and 2003, annual increases in prescription drug costs were in double digits, peaking at 18 % in 1999 before trending back down to 6 % in 2005 (Kaiser Family Foundation, 2007). The cost of new drugs drives much of these increases in cost.

Why are new prescription drugs costly? Market structure plays a role. The Federal Food and Drug Administration (FDA) must approve all prescription drugs before they can be sold. Conducting the research to develop a new drug and verifying that it meets the FDA's high standards for efficacy and safety is a time consuming and costly process. To give drug companies an incentive to undertake this process, the FDA gives them an opportunity to recoup their costs by allowing them to have a time-limited monopoly on sale of a new drug. Thus, the initial price of new drugs is high. When the time-limited monopoly ends, less-expensive generic copies of the drug may be sold, tending to drive down market price by giving consumers a lower-cost alternative.

The number of generic competitors seems to matter. An FDA study on "Generic Competition and Drug Prices" found that the average generic to brand name price fell to 94 % when one generic competitor was present (U.S. Food and Drug Administration, 2006). It dropped to almost half of that (52 %) when a second competitor entered the market. With 15 or more competitors, the average relative price fell below 15 %. Apparently, there is considerable producer surplus in the prescription drug market.

Argument exists regarding the cost/benefit trade-offs of new drugs. According to Kleinke (2001), production and use of new prescription drugs generates a fundamental shift in health care delivery, substituting "consumption of medical products" for traditional physician and other medical services (p. 43). He asserts that cost-containment measures would restrict important medical advances. New drug prices, although high, represent improved health care options for consumers and may be less costly overall than other forms of treatment. Zhang and Soumerai (2007) counter that current research offers no conclusive evidence that those new drugs actually do provide lower costs and better quality outcomes for consumers. Much of the debate centers on issues of data quality and research design. Advocates of either point of view would agree that more studies and better studies on the economic benefit of new drugs needs to be conducted.

Prescription drug utilization levels have also influenced national health care spending on prescription medication. Between 1994 and 2005, the number of prescriptions filled grew almost eight times faster than the U.S. population (71 % vs. 9 %) (Kaiser Family Foundation, 2007). Aging of the population may have been a contributing factor. Seniors account for a large part of the prescription drug market. Although they comprise about 13 % of the population, they account for 34 % of all prescriptions dispenses and 42 % of prescription drug expenditures (Families USA, 2000; Rubin, Koelln, & Speas, 1995). Advertising of drug companies directly to the public may be another contributing factor via a shift in consumer demand for the advertised medications.

Economists and policy analysts generally point to technological innovation as the prime driver of the high and increasing cost of health care (Newhouse, 1992). As an example, technological innovations in the treatment of heart attacks have lessened the need for invasive surgery and have sped patient recovery. But, use of these innovations requires more capital (specialized labs), labor (specialized physician training and caregiver time to oversee patient recovery), and expenses related to teaching physicians how to use the new technology (Bodenheimer, 2005b).

Spread of technology is quicker and cost per unit of service is higher in the United States than in other developed nations (Reinhardt et al., 2002). This difference has been attributed to generous insurance payments made to physicians and hospitals that use new technology (Gelijns & Rosenberg, 1994). The supply push from physicians or demand pull from health care consumers wanting to use the new technology is another factor (Organization for Economic Cooperation and Development, 2004). To mitigate the threat of malpractice suits, physicians may choose to err on the side of using more rather than less technology in diagnosis and treatment procedures. Typically, it is third party payers in the form of health insurance companies that bear most of the cost of such procedures. Thus, health care consumers that do not bear the full cost of using technology may have little motivation to economize. In this type of environment, incentive for overuse of technology exists.

Several agencies in the United States assess the cost and benefit of technological innovation, including the Medicare Coverage Advisory Committee, the Veterans Affairs hospital system, and the Technology Evaluation Center of the Blue Cross/Blue Shield Association (Garber, 2001). Influence of the scientific reports from these agencies is limited to the interests of health insurance providers, however. Results from a study of large insurers indicated that manufacturers and early adopters of medical technology had considerable influence over health care coverage decisions whereas health care consumers had very little say (Chernew, Jacobson, Hofer, Aaronson, & Fendrick, 2004).

Role of Health Insurance in Reduction of Health Care Costs

Health insurance plans have evolved over time in response to demand for ways to help consumers lower their out-of-pocket costs for health care and to provide protection against potentially catastrophic financial loss due to treatment of illness, injury, or disability. In 1965, amendments to the Social Security Act established two federal health insurance programs, Medicaid for the low-income and Medicare for those over age 65. Others must turn to the private market to obtain health insurance. Employer-sponsored group insurance plans typically have lower premiums and fewer barriers to entry as compared with private insurance plans. In addition, employers often subsidize premium costs, in part or in full, as an employee benefit. Thus, it is not too surprising that for the past decade, 6 in 10 Americans under age 65 have obtained their health coverage through an employer-sponsored insurance plan, whereas less than 8 % have purchased private insurance (Fronstin, 2006).

Types of health insurance have changed over time. Currently, consumers or employee benefit administrators can choose from fee-for-service, managed care or high deductible "consumer-driven" health care plans. Cost containment is a goal of each type of health insurance. The incentive and payment structures used to achieve that end differ, however.

Fee-for-Service

Prior to the 1980s, employer-sponsored health plans were typically fee-for-service plans (Kaiser Family Foundation, 2006a). With these plans, consumers pay a fee for a service rendered and then apply for reimbursement of covered costs. Fee-for-service-type plans include basic health care, major medical, and comprehensive medical coverage. Basic health care typically pays for hospital, surgical, and physician costs with little or no deductible. But, covered expenses are quite limited. Major medical insurance covers a broader array of medical services or helps to pay for high cost services up to a maximum limit (usually set at $1 million). Consumers in a major medical insurance plan share costs in the form of annual deductibles (an amount paid out-of-pocket before insurance pays), and co-insurance (a percentage of health care costs paid by the insured up to a so-called "stop-loss" limit, above which the insurance company will pay 100 % of the cost). Comprehensive health care is similar to major medical, but deductibles are usually smaller and a broader range of inpatient and outpatient services are covered.

Managed Care

In the 1970s, concern for rising health care costs and equitable access to health care services led to the development of managed care plans (Gruber, Shadle, & Polich, 1988). Health Maintenance Organizations (HMO) were the first such plans. Preferred Provider Organizations (PPO) and Point of Service (POS) plans soon followed.

Managed care plans endeavor to control costs by contracting directly with health care providers and controlling access to health care services. Health care providers receive financial incentives for keeping costs down. Preventive care such as annual exams, immunizations, and diagnostic tests are emphasized. Low co-pays (typically $5–$20) encourage consumers to obtain treatment before health conditions worsen and more costly intervention is required.

HMOs, PPOs, and POSs have different coverage limitations. HMOs are more restrictive. To have their health costs covered, consumers must use a health care provider that has contracted with the HMO. A referral must be obtained from a primary care physician before a specialist can be seen. PPO plans allow consumers to use health care professionals who have not contracted with the PPO plan; however, consumers will share a larger portion of the cost of care if they do so. A POS plan resembles a PPO, but the participating physicians are part of an HMO, so coverage is often more comprehensive than in a PPO. Also, co-pays in a POS are typically lower than in a PPO.

The cost reductions associated with managed care plans spurred a rapid transfer out of fee-for-service plans among employers. In 1988, 73 % of workers had fee-for-service plans. After that enrollment in fee-for-service plans dropped dramatically, representing only 3 % of employer-sponsored health plans by 2005. Initially, HMO-type plans drew the greatest interest of employee benefit administrators. Between 1988 and 1996, the market share of HMOs virtually doubled, rising from 16 to 31 %. Enrollment peaked in 1996 and then slowly declined to about one-fifth of the employer-sponsored health care market in 2005.

Ironically, the HMO design features that contributed to cost reductions also generated consumer dissatisfaction. After analyzing the results of 79 different studies of HMO quality, Miller and Luft 2002 concluded that success in cost containment had come at the price of limited access to health care services and reduction in health care quality. Policy pricing was also an issue, but in different ways in the public and private sector. Riley, Tudor, Chiang, and Ingber (2006) cite instances of government overpayment of Medicare HMOs in the mid-1990s. In the private market, HMO firms waged fierce price wars in an attempt to expand their enrollment base. For many firms, the lowered premiums failed to cover operating costs, resulting in substantial financial losses (Gruber et al., 1988).

Current Distribution and Price of Employer-Sponsored Health Care Plans

The proportion of employers offering the Preferred Provider Organization (PPO) form of managed care has steadily grown, perhaps due to the greater degree of choice given to health care consumers as compared with HMO plans. Among workers with an employer-provided health care plan in 2005, three out of five had a PPO. About one-fifth had HMO coverage, 15 % had a Point of Service Plan (POS), and 3 % had a fee-for-service plan (Kaiser Family Foundation, 2006a).

A recent survey of employer-sponsored health benefits indicates that the average annual employer premium contribution of $8,850 for PPO plans is 8 % higher than an HMO plan and 12 % higher than a POS plan. Worker contributions to a PPO vary by plan coverage. On average, workers with a PPO family plan pay a bit less annually than they would with other types of plans ($2,915 for a PPO plan vs. $3,079 for an HMO plan or $3,226 for a POS plan). Conversely, single employees on average pay a little more per year ($636 for a PPO plan vs. $590 for an HMO plan or $634 for a POS plan) (Kaiser Family Foundation, 2006a).

Consumer-Driven Health Care

Consumer-driven health care plans are a recent entrant into the employer-sponsored health insurance market. Rather than contain costs by limiting consumer choice, these plans broaden consumer choice and financial responsibility. A large proportion of the health care cost is borne by the consumer, creating a financial incentive to select lower cost and perhaps higher quality services. The plans give consumers information to help them make knowledgeable choices in the management of their health (Rosenthal & Milstein, 2004).

Plan specifics vary. With health reimbursement accounts (HRAs), employees draw on an account funded by their employer to pay for health care. When the account is depleted, the employee pays out-of-pocket until a high deductible (typically $1,000 for an individual, $2,000 for a family) is met. At that point, the plan becomes a traditional major medical plan. If the employer allows, unused funds may be carried forward to the next year. HRAs are not portable from one employer to another and can only be used for health-related expenses. Employees cannot contribute to HRAs (Gabel, Whitmore, Rice, & LoSasso, 2004). Health Savings Accounts (HSAs) are comparable to HRAs except both employers and employees may contribute to an HSA (MacDonald, Fronstin, & Mahon, 2005).

With either "personalized" or "customized-package plans," employees use web-based tools to select health services. Personalized choice plans give employees broad discretion in selecting individual physicians and hospitals and in designing their own network and benefit plans. Customized-package plans limit employee choices to a predetermined list of network options and benefit packages. Typically, employees are offered only one carrier's products. In both types of plans, employers pay a fixed amount toward purchase of selected services. Employees pay the remaining cost. Currently, only a few employers offer personalized plans. Customized-package health plans are found in the small and midsize employer market (Gabel et al., 2004).

Research on initial consumer-driven health care plans suggests that outcomes may differ from what plan designers intended. Compared with those who have comprehensive health insurance, consumers with high deductible plans are more likely to economize on health care services. But, they are also more likely to delay or avoid necessary care. Plan structure has not shielded consumers from bearing a financial burden for health care. A recent study found that 42 % of consumers with a high deductible health plan spent 5 % or more of their income on health-related expenses as compared with 12 % of consumers with a comprehensive medical plan (MacDonald et al., 2005).

A critical flaw of these plans, however, may be their heavy dependence on informed consumer choice. The high credence qualities of health care make choice difficult. Consumers must possess a clear understanding of their own health risks or those of family members. They also must invest time and effort in understanding the implications of various plan options. Effective choices require a certain level of technical knowledge. Not all consumers are willing or able to make the effort. In a recent survey of U.S. residents, only one-third of respondents were confident that they could select their health insurance on their own, even though they felt comfortable talking with their doctors about their own health (MacDonald et al., 2005).

The Uninsured

Health insurance is not attainable or affordable to all. In 1998, the proportion of the U.S. population without health insurance coverage peaked at 16.3 % (DeNavas-Walt, Proctor, & Lee, 2006). After 2 years of modest decline, the proportion of uninsured rose again, reaching almost 16 % in 2005. The proportion of uninsured among workers is almost 3 percentage points higher (18.7 %) (DeNavas-Walt et al., 2006).

Two dominant factors in the increase in uninsured are decline in the number of employers offering health care coverage and the rising cost-share expected from employees. Between 2000 and 2006, the proportion of all firms offering health benefits dropped from 69 to 61 % (Schoen et al., 2005). Largest declines in offer rates have occurred for non-union low-wage firms that employ less than 200 workers (Schoen et al., 2005). In a recent survey by the Kaiser Family Foundation (2006b), high cost was the reason that almost three out of four firms gave for not offering health insurance. High cost is also a reason that employees may opt out of offered coverage. In 2001, 36 % of employees with single coverage paid $200 or less in monthly premiums. In 2006, only 3 % of workers had premiums that low. Almost three in four (72 %) paid monthly premiums over $300 and 22 % paid more than $400. Most of those with family coverage in 2001 paid less than $650 per month (76 %). In 2006, only 7 % had rates at that level. Half were paying more than $950 (Kaiser Family Foundation, 2006a).

The rising number of uninsured working age adults and children is a social concern. Uninsured poor can rely on Medicaid. Among the non-poor, health needs can go unmet or worsen to the point that emergency care is necessary (Ayanian, Weissman, Schneider, Ginsburg, & Zaslavsky, 2000; Krebs-Carter & Holahan, 2000). Unpaid hospital bills are passed on to those with insurance in the form of higher costs. Uninsured children have less access to health care, a problem that exacerbates the health problems of special-needs children (Newacheck, McManus, Fox, Hung, & Halfon, 2000; Olson, Suk-fong, & Newacheck, 2005). Inadequate treatment for illness or chronic conditions (e.g., asthma) can affect a child's ability to learn and days in school, which in turn affects future economic productivity.

Push for National Health Care

Frustrations with the expenses of fee-for-service plans, limitations of managed care plans, the significant consumer issues associated with consumer-driven health care plans, and the number of uninsured have encouraged consideration of national health care. Advocates assert basic health care is a right, not a commodity to be purchased only by those who have the means (Geyman, 2003; Woolhandler & Himmerstein, 2002).

National health care would require a fundamental restructuring of the health care finance and delivery system. In place of the current mix of health insurance programs, government would administer payments for health care services. The private sector would deliver those services. Medical decisions would remain in the hands of physicians and patients. Consumers could freely obtain health care services from qualified medical personnel. Access to health care would be universal (Physician's Working Group, 2003).

Debate over national health care is strong and the issue not likely to be quickly resolved. A central concern is that funding national health care would require a substantial increase in tax dollars. After careful analysis of health care funding, Woolhandler and Himmerstein (2002) counter that almost 6 of every 10 dollars in health care finance already come from tax dollars. What is needed is not more tax, but a redistribution of the taxes already collected.

Future Research Directions

Health care is vital. There is no debate about that. Much difference of opinion exists, however, regarding the extent to which rising health care costs should be a concern, what drives these rising costs, how health care resources should be allocated, the need for reform in the health care market, and the direction such reform should take. Before purposeful dialogue on these topics can occur, quality research is needed to sort out myth and popular ideas from fact, to evaluate effects of existing policy, and to explore possible impact of policy changes. Thoughtful contributions to the health care discussion are needed from a variety of subject matter experts.

Family and consumer economists can contribute expertise on a number of health care issues. A few examples will be noted here. First, better understanding of the dynamics of consumer choice in the health care market is needed. Economic theory underlying consumer-driven health care proposes that consumers use information to make optimal decisions. Observation of consumers in these plans indicates that, to the contrary, consumers are not always willing or able to process health care information and, faced with high deductibles, they forgo needed health care. Both outcomes, it could be argued, are not optimal for the consumer. What disconnects exist between the incentive structure perceived by consumers and the one intended by policy makers? What changes in information delivery might help the consumer better understand and use highly technical and complex health information? What alternate forms of cost sharing might lessen the financial anxiety of consumers while retaining incentives for cost reduction?

Second, families are primary caregivers for the ill and infirm. What are the short- and long-term financial outcomes of caring for a disabled family member in the home? Existing research suggests trade-offs can be high. For example, in a study of the financial issues associated with having a child with autism, families reported draining retirement savings, taking on debt, and moving precariously close to bankruptcy to fund high out-of-pocket behavior therapy costs that insurance would not cover (Sharpe & Baker, 2007). Leiter, Krauss, Anderson, and Wells (2004) found that women with a severely disabled child under age 18 cut back labor hours or left employment to care for their child. What effect does this nonmarket production have on health care costs, both in the household and for society? When women leave market work for care giving, what is the impact on the family's access to health care or ability to save for long-term goals? How does the focus of time and money resources on a disabled child affect the human capital development of the child and of siblings?

Suppose it is a parent or grandparent rather than a child that is disabled or unable to care for themselves? How might outcomes differ? Is care given for love or money? There is some evidence that adult caregivers' employment decisions are influenced by their own financial and health status as well as the health status of an impaired elderly relative (White-Means, 1992). White-Means and Hong (2000) found that the potential for receiving a bequest influenced adult children's decisions regarding leaving the labor market to care for an aging family member and time or money transfers between the adult child and the aging elder.

Third, Hispanic, Asian, and other ethnic population groups in the United States are increasing in number. This growing diversity raises questions about similarities and differences in health care usage and expenditures by race and ethnic group. To what extent might minority populations prefer folk remedies to a clinical model of health care? How would such choices affect public health? How do language differences affect access to and usage of health care? To what extent do population sub-groups have specialized care needs?

Fourth, how might public and private resources be reallocated to create more equitable access to health care for all age groups? Even with Medicare, older individuals have high out-of-pocket costs for health care. Between 1980 and 1997, real out-of-pocket spending by seniors on health care increased by 81 %. For the same time period, senior's real expenditures on prescription drugs rose 169 %, while the budget share allocated to prescription drugs increased 34 % (Fan, Sharpe, & Hong, 2003). Population aging will strain resources to meet existing entitlements. At the same time, in 2005, 19 % of children in poverty and 18 % of workers are without health insurance (DeNavas-Walt et al., 2006). What factors are driving reductions in health care benefits to current and retired employees? To what extent and under what conditions are HSAs or HRAs in high-deductible plans an effective substitute for employer-funded health care?

Finally, in an era of increased cost sharing, a clearer picture of the dynamic relationship between health and wealth is needed. Despite research on this issue, evidence regarding direction of causation remains inconclusive. Socio-economic status and health are clearly linked (Williams, 1990). But, what are the driving factors? Research has established that persons with higher debt-to-income ratios also have poor physical health and self-reported levels of health (Drentea & Lavrakas, 2000). Financial stress is a significant contributor to workplace absenteeism, which further reduces economic resources (Jacobson et al., 1996). Some recent work suggests that poor health may be a more important contributor to financial stress than financial stress contributes to poor health (Lyons & Yilmazer, 2005). Do the healthy earn more and amass more wealth (McClellan, 1998) or can the wealthy purchase more and better health care (Ettner, 1996; Smith, 1999), or is a third factor at work such as preference for future vs. current consumption (Barsky, Juster, Kimbal, & Shapiro, 1997)?

In summary, consumer health care issues center on access, affordability, information quality, choice, equitable distribution across age, gender, racial and ethnic groups, and the role of health in accumulation of wealth. By the very nature of the case, demand for good health, and hence quality health care, is virtually unlimited. To lose health is to lose life itself. But, resources to obtain that health have limits. Rising health care costs have begun to force some significant trade-offs for individuals, households, and society at large. Current and coming demographic changes force more open consideration of cost sharing between the private and public sectors, employers and employees, and older and younger generations. To engage in meaningful, productive dialogue on these and other health-related issues, information obtained from further unbiased, scientific research is essential.

References

Auerbach, A. J., Gale, W. G., Orszag, P., & Potter, S. R. (2003). *Budget blues: Fiscal outlook and options for reform.* Washington, DC: The Urban Institute. Retrieved February 2, 2007, from http://www.urban.org/url.cfm?ID=310778.

Ayanian, J. Z., Weissman, J. S., Schneider, E. C., Ginsburg, J. A., & Zaslavsky, A. M. (2000) Unmet health needs of uninsured adults in the United States. *Journal of the American Medical Society, 284,* 2061–2069.

Barsky, R. B., Juster, F. T., Kimbal, M. S., & Shapiro, M. D. (1997). Preference parameters and behavioral heterogeneity: An experimental approach in the health and retirement Study. *Quarterly Journal of Economics, 112*(2), 537–579.

Blue Cross Blue Shield Association. (2006). *Medical cost reference guide.* Retrieved January 29, 2007, from http://www.bcbs.com/betterknowledge/mcrg/MCRG.pdf.

Bodenheimer, T. (2005a). High and rising health care costs. Part 1: Seeking an explanation. *Annals of Internal Medicine, 142*(10), 847–854.

Bodenheimer, T. (2005b). High and rising health care costs. Part 2: Technologic innovations. *Annals of Internal Medicine, 142*(11), 932–937.

Bodenheimer, T. (2005c). High and rising health care costs. Part 3: The role of health care providers. *Annals of Internal Medicine, 142*(12), 998–1002.

Borger, C., Smith, S., Truffer, C., Keehan, S., Sisko, A., Poisal, J., & Clemens, M. K. (2006) Health spending projections through 2015: Changes on the horizon. *Health Affairs, 25*(2), W61–W73.

Bureau of Economic Analysis. (2005). *Gross domestic product and related measures: Level and change from the preceding period.* Retrieved January 31, 2007, from http://www.bea.gov/bea/newsrelarchive/2005/gdp205p.xls.

Centers for Medicaid and Medicare Services [CMS]. (2007). *National health expenditure tables.* Retrieved February 2, 2007, from http://www.cms.hhs.gov/NationalHealthExpendData/downloads/tables.pdf.

Chernew, M. E., Hirth, R. A., & Cutler, D. M. (2003). Increased spending on health care: How much can the United States afford? *Health Affairs, 22,* 15–25.

Chernew, M. E., Jacobson, P. D., Hofer, T. P, Aaronson, K. D., & Fendrick, A. M. (2004). Barriers to constraining health care cost growth. *Health Affairs, 23*, 122–128.

Darby, M. R., & Karni, E. R. (1973). Free competition and optimal amount of fraud. *Journal of Law and Economics, 16*, 67–86.

Davis, K., Anderson, G. F., Rowland, D., & Steinberg, E. P. (1990). *Health care cost containment.* Baltimore: Johns Hopkins University Press.

DeNavas-Walt, C, Proctor, B. D., & Lee, C. H. (2006). *Income, poverty, health insurance coverage in the United States: 2005* (Publication P60-231). Washington, DC: U.S. Census Bureau.

Drentea, P., & Lavrakas, P. J. (2000). Over the limit: The association among health, race and debt. *Social Science & Medicine, 50*, 517–529.

Employee Benefit Research Institute. (2006). 2006 Health Confidence Survey: Dissatisfaction with health care system doubles since 1998. *EBRI Notes, 27*(11), 1–11.

Ettner, S. (1996). New evidence on the relationship between income and wealth. *Journal of Health Economics, 15*, 67–85.

Families USA. (2000). Cost overdoses: Growth in drug spending for the elderly, 1992–2010. Washington, DC: Families USA.

Fan, J. X., Sharpe, D. L., & Hong, S. (2003). Health care and prescription drug spending by seniors. *Monthly Labor Review, 126*(3), 16–26.

Fronstin, P. (2006) *Sources of health insurance and characteristics of the uninsured: Analysis of the March 2006 Current Population Survey* (EBRI Issue Brief no. 298).

Gabel, J. R., Whitmore, H., Rice, T., & LoSasso, A. T. (2004) Employer's contradictory views about consumer-driven health care: Results from a national survey. *Health Affairs Web Exclusive.* Retrieved January 31, 2007, from http://content.healthaffairs.org/cgi/reprint/hlthaff.w4.210v1.pdf.

Garber, A. M. (2001). Evidence-based coverage policy. *Health Affairs, 20*, 62–82.

Gelijns, A., & Rosenberg, N. (1994). The dynamics of technological change in medicine. *Health Affairs, 13*, 28–46.

Geyman, J. P. (2003). Myths as barriers to health care reform in the United States. *International Journal of Health Services, 333*(2), 315–329.

Gillett, G. (1998) As others see us: A view from abroad—justice and health care in a caring society. *British Medical Journal, 317*(7150): 53–54.

Grossman, M. (1972). On the concept of human capital and the demand for wealth. *Journal of Political Economy, 80*(2), 323–355.

Gruber, J., & Wise, D. (2002). *An international perspective on policies of aging societies.* In S. H. Altman & D. I. Shactman (Eds.), *Policies for an aging society* (pp. 34–62). Baltimore: Johns Hopkins University Press.

Gruber, L. R., Shadle, M., & Polich, C. L. (1988). From movement to industry: The growth of HMOs. *Health Affairs, 7*(3), 197–208.

He, W., Sengupta, M., Velkoff, V. A., & DeBarros, K. A. (2005). *65+ in the United States: 2005.* Washington, DC: U. S. Census Bureau.

Jacobson, B. H., Aldana, S. G., Goetzel, R. Z., Vardell, K. D., Adams, T. B., & Pietras, R. J. (1996). The relationship between perceived stress and self-reported illness-related absenteeism. *American Journal of Health Promotion, 11*(1), 54–61.

Kaiser Family Foundation. (2006a). *Employer health benefits: 2006 summary of findings.* Washington, DC: Kaiser Family Foundation.

Kaiser Family Foundation. (2006b). *Comparing projected growth health care expenditures and the economy.* Retrieved January 30, 2007, from http://www.kff.org/insurance/snapshot/chcm050206oth2.cfm.

Kaiser Family Foundation. (2007). *Prescription drug trends.* Washington, DC: Kaiser Family Foundation.

Kleinke, J. D. (2001) The price of progress: Prescription drugs in the health care market. *Health Affairs, 20*(5), 43–60.

Krebs-Carter, M., & Holahan, J. (2000). *State strategies for covering uninsured adults* (Discussion paper 00-02). Washington, DC: The Urban Institute. Retrieved January 31, 2007, from http://www.urban.org/UploadedPDF/discussion00-02.pdf.

Leiter, V., Krauss, M. W., Anderson, B., & Wells, N. (2004). The consequences of caring: Effects of mothering child with special needs. *Journal of Family Issues, 25*(3), 379–403.

Levit, K., Smith, C., Cowan, C., Sensenig, A., & Catlin, A. (2004) Health spending rebound continues in 2002. *Health Affairs, 23,*147–159.

Lyons, A. C., & Yilmazer, T. (2005) Financial strain and health: Evidence from the Survey of Consumer Finances. *Southern Economic Journal, 71*(4), 873–890.

MacDonald, J., Fronstin, P., & Mahon, M. (2005). *Consumer-driven health plan participants less satisfied then those with comprehensive insurance.* Washington, DC: EBRI.

McClellan, M. (1998). Health events, health insurance, and labor supply: Evidence from the Health and retirement survey. In D. A. Wise (Ed.), *Frontiers in the economics of aging* (pp. 301–346). Chicago: University of Chicago Press.

Miller, R. H., & Luft, H. S. (2002) HMO plan performance update: An analysis of the literature 1997–2001. *Health Affairs, 24*(1), 63–86.

National Coalition on Health Care [NCHC]. (2004). *Facts on health care costs.* Retrieved January 29, 2007, from http://www.nchc.org/facts/cost.shtml.

Newacheck, P. W., McManus, M., Fox, H. B., Hung, Y., & Halfon, N. (2000). Access to health care for children with special health care needs. *Pediatrics, 105*(4 part 1), 760–766.

Newhouse, J. P. (1992). Medical care costs: How much welfare loss? *Journal of Economic Perspectives, 6*(3), 3–21.

Office of Management and Budget. (2007). *Table S-11 budget summary by category.* Retrieved February 2, 2007, from http://www.whitehouse.gov/omb/budget/fy2007/tables.html.

Olson, L. M., Suk-fong, S. T., & Newacheck, P. W. (2005). Children in the United States with discontinuous health insurance coverage. *New England Journal of Medicine, 353*(4), 382–391.

Organization for Economic Cooperation and Development. (2004). *A disease-based comparison of health systems.* Retrieved January 31, 2007, from http://www.oecd.org.

Pauly, M. V. (2003). Should we be worried about high real medical spending growth in the United States? *Health Affairs Web Exclusive,* W3-15–W3-27. Retrieved January 31, 2007, from http://content.healthaffairs.org/cgi/reprint/hlthaff.w3.15v1?ck=nck.

Physician's Working Group for Single-Payer National Health Insurance. (2003). Proposal of the Physician's Working Group for Single-Payer National Health Insurance. *Journal of the American Medical Association, 290*(6), 798–805.

Reinhardt, U. E. (2003). Does the aging of the population really drive the demand for health care? *Health Affairs, 22,* 27–39.

Reinhardt, U. E., Hussey, P. S., & Anderson, G. F. (2002). Cross-national comparisons of health systems using OECD data. *Health Affairs, 21,* 169–181.

Richardson, J., & Robertson, I. (1999) Ageing and the cost of health services (Working paper no. 90). Sydney: Centre for Health Program Evaluation.

Riley, G., Tudor, C., Chiang, Y. P., & Ingber, M. (2006) Health status of Medicare enrollees in HMOs and fee-for-service in 1994. *Health Care Financing Review, 17*(4), 65–76.

Rosenthal, M., & Milstein, A. (2004) Consumer-driven plans: What's offered? Who chooses? *Health Services Research, 39*(4), 1055–1070.

Rubin, R. M., Koelln, K., & Speas, R. K. (1995). Out-of-pocket health expenditures by elderly households: Change over the 1980s. *Journal of Gerontology: Social Sciences, 50*B(5), S291–S300.

Schoen, C., Osborn, R., Huyuh, P. T., Doty, M., Zapert, K., Peugh, J., & Davis, K. (2005) Taking the pulse of health care systems: Experiences of patients with health problems in six countries. *Health Affairs Web Exclusive,* W5-509–W5-525. Retrieved January 31, 2007, from http://content.healthaffairs.org/cgi/reprint/hlthaff.w5.509v3.

Sharma, N., & Patterson, P. G. (1999). The impact of communication effectiveness and service quality on relationship commitment in consumer, professional services. *Journal of Services Marketing*, *13*(2), 151–171.

Sharpe, D. L., & Baker, D. L. (2007). Financial issues associated with having a child with autism. *Journal of Family and Economic Issues, 28,* 247–264.

Smith, C., Cowan, C., Heffler, S., & Catlin, A., (2006) National health spending in 2004. *Health Affairs 25*(1), 186–196.

Smith, J. P. (1999). Healthy bodies and thick wallets: The dual relation between health and economic status. *Journal of Economic Perspectives*, *13*(2), 145–166.

Smith, R. D., Beaglehole, R., Woodward, D., & Drager, N. (Eds.) (2003). *Global public goods for health: A health economic and public health perspective.* Oxford: Oxford University Press.

U.S. Food and Drug Administration. (2006). *Generic competition and drug prices.* Retrieved June 4, 2007, from http://www.fda.gov/cder/ogd/generic_competition.htm.

White-Means, S. I. (1992). Allocation of labor to informal home health production: Health care for frail elderly, if time permits. *Journal of Consumer Affairs*, *26*(1), 69–89.

White-Means, S. I., & Hong, G. S. (2000). Out-of-pocket health care expenditure patterns and financial burden across the life cycle stages. *Journal of Consumer Affairs*, *34*(2), 291–313.

Williams, D. R. (1990). Socio-economic differentials in health: A review and redirection. *Social Psychology Quarterly*, *53*(2), 81–99.

Woolhandler, S., & Himmerstein, D. U. (2002). Paying for national health care and not getting it. *Health Affairs*, *21*(4), 88–98.

Zhang, Y., & Soumerai, S. B. (2007). Do newer prescription drugs pay for themselves? A reassessment of the evidence. *Health Affairs*, *26*(1), 880–886.

Chapter 20
Marriage and Finance

Jeffrey Dew

Abstract This chapter reviews interdisciplinary research concerning the association between marriage and personal finances. The first section of the chapter discusses financial practices within marriage and the financial differences between married couples and other family types. The second section reviews the research on the ability of financial factors to predict marital formation, satisfaction/conflict, and dissolution. The chapter also suggests future research avenues.

Scholars have repeatedly noted the lack of information on how families handle money. In her seminal work on meanings of money, Zelizer (1994, p. 43) wrote, "In terms of evidence, to study money in the family is to enter largely uncharted territory. . . . we know less about money matters than about family violence or even marital sex." A decade later, scholars are still calling for more research on how families utilize their money (Daly, 2003; Israelsen & Hatch, 2005). The relationship between finances and marriage is actually reciprocal. That is, financial issues predict marital processes and outcomes just as marriage predicts financial behavior. Considering the many legal stipulations and social norms surrounding both marriage and financial matters, it is not surprising that this relationship is bidirectional.

Understanding the reciprocal relationship between marriage and finances benefits practitioners as well as theorists. Financial planners may benefit from understanding how married couples' financial needs differ from single individuals' needs. The relationship between finances and marriage is also important for premarital educators and marital therapists (Poduska & Allred, 1990) because couples seeking marital therapy often have elevated levels of financial problems and conflicts over finances (Aniol & Snyder, 1997). Finally, the relationship between marriage and finances is relevant to policy. Welfare reform, passed in 1996 and reauthorized in 2006, allows states to use federal money to encourage and strengthen marriage among low-income individuals as an antipoverty strategy.

This chapter reviews recent, and some classic, research on the relationship between marriage and finances from multiple disciplines. First, the meaning of

J. Dew
The University of Virginia, Dawson's Row 2, Charlottesville, VA 22903, USA
e-mail: jpd197@juno.com

J.J. Xiao, (ed.), *Handbook of Consumer Finance Research*,
© Springer 2008

marriage for financial behaviors is reviewed. Second, the ability of different financial issues to predict marital formation, quality, and dissolution is evaluated. Suggestions for future research are made throughout the review.

Marriage and Financial Practices

Financial Management in Marriage

Scholars know little about how marriage shapes financial practices. For the most part, research has analyzed differences between married couples' and single individuals' financial behavior. For example, married couples are more likely than cohabiting couples to pool their income (Heimdal & Houseknecht, 2003), and married couples also pool their savings (Fletschner & Klawitter, 2005). Further, married couples accumulate more assets and utilize consumer debt more than single individuals do (Fan, 2000; Hao, 1996; Lupton & Smith, 2003). Interestingly, marriage has no bearing on financial risk tolerance, although having children does negatively predict financial risk tolerance (Chaulk, Johnson, & Bulcroft, 2003). Beyond these simple descriptive differences, little is known about the meaning of marriage for financial behaviors.

Many research questions regarding marriage and financial behaviors remain unanswered. For example, scholars have only recently described income and asset pooling among married couples. The reasons for pooling have yet to be investigated. Scholars also do not know whether individuals consolidate their debt when they marry, and the patterns of married couples' joint debt assumption are unknown.

Research has also generally overlooked issues in family consumption—an activity that consumes much of family's time (Daly, 2003). For example, cohabiting parents spend more than married parents on alcohol and tobacco (DeLeire & Kalil, 2005), but other consumption differences are unknown. For example, what financial instruments (e.g., cash, credit cards, etc.) do different family types tend to use to make large purchases? How much information do married couples gather before they make purchases? Additionally, few descriptions of marital status differences in the uses of various investment instruments exist.

Beyond describing the differences in financial behavior between married couples and other families, the mechanisms that lead to these differences also need uncovering. That is, research needs to investigate why married couples and single individuals enact differing financial behaviors. Selection, the tendency for individuals with different characteristics to make different union choices, is likely to be one explanation since individuals that are financially stable are more likely to marry (Clarkberg, 1999; Oppenheimer, 2003; Xie, Raymo, Goyette, & Thornton, 2003). Financially stable individuals may use their money differently from individuals who financially struggle. Thus, differences in financial behaviors may already be in place before individuals marry and may have nothing to do with the marriage itself.

Scholars have identified other reasons than selection for behavioral differences between married and single individuals. Following marriage, both men and women reduce the frequency and intensity of risky behaviors (e.g., drinking) (Waite & Gallagher, 2000). Thus, on average, the norms of marriage seem to elicit safe and conventional behaviors in married individuals. Likewise, marriage may encourage couples to utilizing their money more responsibly. Additionally, following marriage, individuals have to balance using money to maximize their own well-being with the well-being of the family. This may lead to different financial behaviors than the individual would have engaged in before they were married. These mechanisms (selection, conventionalization, etc.) need to be tested, though.

Income and Wealth Accumulation Differences

One area that has received a fair amount of attention is the income and wealth differences between married couples and others. Even though marriage is no longer necessary to economically advance, married individuals are economically better off than their single counterparts, on average (Waite & Gallagher, 2000). The mechanisms behind the financial advantage of marriage are only beginning to be examined.

Married couples generally have higher incomes than single individuals. Married couples have the highest median income of all family forms and, with the exception of single male households, have the highest per adult capita incomes (DeNavas-Walt, Proctor, & Lee, 2006). Further, the likelihood that an individual will ever attain an "affluent" income in their lifetime (e.g., 10 times the poverty level) is strongly enhanced by marriage (Hirschl, Altobelli, & Rank, 2003). Additionally, only 5 % of married couples live below the poverty line when compared with 28 % of single women and 13 % of single men (DeNavas-Walt et al., 2006). Beyond income-based definitions of poverty, marriage also decreases other types of economic hardships, even among low-income individuals (Lerman, 2002).

Scholars have put forth many explanations for the income advantage of marriage. Married couples often have access to two incomes, whereas noncohabiting singles have only one income (Greenwood, Guner, & Knowles, 2003). Married couples also benefit from economies of scale where two individuals can live with fewer expenses if they live together instead of apart. Individuals with better earnings/earnings potential also marry more than individuals with poorer economic prospects (Clarkberg, 1999; Oppenheimer, 2003; Xie et al., 2003). Very little research has analyzed whether these factors account for the income differences between married couples and single individuals, though.

Marriage and wealth also relate. In cross-sectional estimates, married couples have more assets than single, divorced, or cohabiting individuals (Waite & Gallagher, 2000). Further, married couples accumulate more assets over time, on average (Hao, 1996; Zagorsky, 2003a). Divorce devastates adults' financial net-worth, but remarriage often makes up the lost wealth (Wilmoth & Koso, 2002; Zagorsky, 2003b).

The same mechanisms that explain the income advantage for married couples (two-earners, economies of scale, specialization) are also frequently cited in bringing about the asset advantage. Interestingly, although cohabiting couples have many of the same advantages as married couples have, union duration does not predict asset accumulation for cohabiting couples, whereas union duration and assets are positively related for married couples (Hao, 1996). Further, longitudinal data shows that per person, married individuals accumulate 77 % more assets annually than single individuals (Zagorsky, 2003b). Consequently, marriage likely enables couples to accumulate assets for reasons other than simply having two earners and benefiting from economies of scale.

Selection is one explanation for married couples' wealth advantages. Due to social norms (Smock, Manning, & Porter, 2005), the type of union that couples choose is often related to the economic characteristics of the partners. Individuals with stable economic characteristics tend to marry each other, whereas economically disadvantaged individuals will cohabit and delay marriage until they have attained a measure of economic stability (Oppenheimer, 2003; Smock et al., 2005). Although selection may produce wealth differences, married couples still have considerably more assets (and save at higher rates) than other families even after statistically controlling for economic factors and for the number of earners in the home (Lupton & Smith, 2003; Schmidt & Sevak, 2006).

Other explanations may account for the wealth differences that exist between family types. Marriage entails social norms of permanence and public expressions of commitment that may increase trust and allow married couples to feel more comfortable investing in their marriage (Cherlin, 2004; Pollak, 1985). Support for this notion of marriage conferring a higher level of trust than cohabitation is the fact that married couples are far more likely than cohabiting couples to pool their incomes (Heimdal & Houseknecht, 2003). Income pooling allows couples to live less expensive because of economies of scale. By pooling financial assets, married couples will also have access to more interest income than they would if they held their assets separately. Further, if marriage allows individuals to trust their partner more than other types of unions, it would allow spouses to acquire investment properties (homes, real estate) with less risk. Relatedly, trust allows couples to hold volatile (yet profitable) investments for a long time period thus mitigating some market risk. Interestingly, young married individuals do not have more wealth than unmarried individuals, perhaps indicating that the marital advantage of wealth takes many years to materialize (Schmidt & Sevak, 2006).

Social norms surrounding marriage may also encourage wealth accumulation. As noted above, marriage may "conventionalize" individuals so that they may feel obligated to save and invest some of their income instead of using it all. Further, the "marital script" also explicitly includes financial investments such as home buying, saving for children's college funds, and retirement (Townsend, 2002; Waite & Gallagher, 2000). All of these investments require decades of regular financial inputs. Consequently, marriage—with its norms of lifelong commitment—is ideally suited to achieving these financial goals.

Another explanation for wealth differences is that married couples receive greater social (e.g., economic) support than cohabiting couples or other types of families. By definition, a married individual has access to the resources of more kin than singles have. Further, married couples with children receive more economic transfers from their families than cohabiting couples and single mothers, and these transfers positively predict wealth levels (Hao, 1996). Interestingly, when the analysis is restricted to young adults, married couples and cohabiting couples do not differ on likelihood of receiving financial transfers from family (Eggebeen, 2005). It may be that marital childbearing may elicit more financial support from families than simply just marrying. At any rate, these higher levels of transfers to married couples with children may partially account for the wealth advantage of married couples.

Prospective longitudinal studies would provide better tests of the mechanisms that link income, wealth, and marriage. Prospective studies would assess individuals' wealth and income before and after marital unions. Thus, for example, evidence of economic differences between individuals that precede union formation might help settle questions of whether marriage influences financial behavior or whether financial differences exist prior to marriage.

Marriage, Gender, and Control of Money

Marriage often changes an individual's relationship with money. Whereas before marriage an individual is in full control of his or her money, following marriage income has to be allocated among various family members (Lundberg & Pollak, 1996). Neoclassical economic models assume that marriages are single economic units with all members acting to maximize the utility of the unit (Blau, Ferber, & Winkler, 2001). Neoclassical economic theory further assumes that this maximization occurs without any problems "either because there is a consensus on preferences within the family or because decisions are made by an altruistic family head and accepted by all other members." (Blau et al., 2001, p. 49). Although most married couples pool their finances, in line with the unitary view of neoclassical economic theory, recent research has questioned the other basic neoclassical economic assumptions.

First, recent studies have challenged the ideas of common preferences in marriage. If wives and husbands shared preferences regarding consumption and savings behaviors, marital arguments regarding money would not arise. However, finances continue to be problematic for some couples (Amato & Rogers, 1997; Aniol & Snyder, 1997; Schramm, Marshall, Harris, & Lee, 2005; Zagorsky, 2003a). Further, when wives control the finances, expenditures on women's and children's goods increases and child well-being increases (Lundberg & Pollak, 1996; Thomas, 1990). These differences should not occur under the common preference model.

Historical analyses have also thrown much doubt on the idea of husbands serving as an altruistic family head. Primary historical sources show that even as recently as the 1930s, husbands certainly were not altruistic heads nor were many wives happy with the husbands' distribution of their husbands wage. In the early twentieth century, wives had to beg their husbands to share his wages so that she could have adequate funds to run the home (Zelizer, 1994). Some wives had to resort to "sexual blackmail" or "stealing from their husbands" when he gave her less than was needed to run the home.

Finally, women and men may not even view finances the same way. In nationally representative longitudinal samples, husbands and wives differed on their estimates of family income, assets, and debt (Zagorsky, 2003a). Husbands reported more income and assets than wives did, whereas wives reported more debts. These differences were significant. For example, 50 % of the spouses reported a 35 % or greater difference in their assets. If husbands and wives do not even have a shared understanding of their current finances, it is unlikely that they will be able to have common preferences on the allocation of their income and wealth.

Despite the proliferation of theoretical models that allow husbands and wives to have their own preferences and to negotiate over the intrahousehold allocations of resources (see Lundberg & Pollak, 1996, for a review), few recent studies have analyzed how husbands and wives actually distribute and manage money within the home. The topic of marital financial management and decision making enjoyed a vogue during the 1970s and 1980s among financial planners and gender scholars (e.g., Blumstein & Schwartz, 1984; Davis, 1976; Spiro, 1983). Recent research on the how couples communicate about, and manage financial issues and decisions is rarer, though exceptions do exist. In an investigation of marital power, for example, one study showed that the higher the share of the total family income that wives' contributed, the more involved they were in managing the families' finances (Bernasek & Bajtelsmit, 2002). Another recent study investigated interaction behavior between wives and husbands as they tried to persuade each other in different purchasing situations (Su, Fern, & Ye, 2003).

The intersection between gender, marriage, and finances merits more scholarly attention. Research could consider how social norms of gender and marriage influence husbands' and wives' financial behaviors and feelings of power within the marriage. An interesting example is an analysis of the conditions that lead to different portfolio profiles in wives' defined contribution plans. Wives whose husbands are less educated, older, or earn less than they do tend to have less risky (and hence less profitable) portfolios, whereas wives' characteristics do not predict husbands' investment strategies (Lyons & Yilmazer, 2004). Considerable work also remains to be done by communication researchers and financial planners, on the ways that husbands and wives work together (or separately) to manage financial issues. Particularly needed to advance this area of research is income, savings, and consumption data that is measured on the spouse level and that is combined with marital data such as gender role identities and couples' feelings of fairness in handling the finances.

Financial Considerations in Marital Processes and Outcomes

Not only does marriage predict individuals' financial practices but recent research also affirms that individuals' financial practices predict various aspects of marriage including marital formation, marital satisfaction and quality, marital distress, and divorce. Though these relationships are widely believed to exist, some scholars have asserted that they are untested (Andersen, 2005; Kerkmann, Lee, Lown, & Allgood, 2000). Examining the literature across disciplines, however, shows that empirical studies have tested the associations between finances and marital outcomes, and that finances do indeed predict marriage outcomes.

Finances and Union Formation

Interestingly, a paradox emerges when finances and the likelihood of marriage are considered. On the one hand, marriage is no longer economically necessary, whereas in the not-to-distant past marriage increased the likelihood of economic survival for both men and women. This change has especially influenced women; increasing job opportunities for women have made remaining single economically feasible. The ability for women to support themselves following a divorce has also increased over the past 30 years (McKeever & Wolfinger, 2001). Based on this shift, one would suspect a decline in the relationship between economic stability and the likelihood of marriage. With only one exception (Sassler & Goldscheider, 2004), though, recent research shows that financial considerations are still quite relevant to the decision to marry.

Economic factors are certainly not the only consideration the decision to marry but they are important and seem to govern the timing of marriage. Marriage, because of its increasing decline, has become a symbol of "status that one builds up to", the "capstone of adult personal life" rather than the "foundation" (Cherlin, 2004, p. 855). The social norms surrounding marriage thus specify that individuals and couples should be economically stable before marriage (Cherlin, 2004; Smock et al., 2005). The economic stability/potential of a prospective partner is difficult for young adults to assess, however, and individuals will postpone marriage when they are uncertain about the economic viability of their union (Oppenheimer, 1988).

Recent studies have linked economic uncertainty and marital timing. Men's earnings, employment status, occupational potential, and education are positively associated with marital formation and negatively associated with age at marriage (Clarkberg, 1999; Oppenheimer, 2003; Smock & Manning, 1997; Xie et al., 2003). Further, individuals with less financial stability use cohabitation as a union strategy until they achieve desired levels of financial stability so they can marry (Oppenheimer, 2003; Smock & Manning, 1997). Interestingly, even though men have begun to value prospective wives' earning capabilities more (Buss, Shackelford, Kirkpatrick, & Larsen, 2001), women's earning capabilities have not been shown to make a difference in the transition to marriage. Thus, marriage formation is still strongly associated with men's economic well-being. Male economic stability seems to signal that a marriage will be economically secure and afford a measure of prosperity (Edin, 2001; Oppenheimer, 2003).

Despite the extensive literature that links economic stability to union formation, many questions remain unanswered. For example, research has not really gone beyond education, employment, and earnings to determine whether other financial issues serve as signals of economic stability and influence marital timing. For example, assets, consumer debt, and student debt during early adulthood may influence marital timing and union formation (Dew, 2007b).

Further, research has not examined whether individuals evaluate potential spouses' ability to manage the money that they earn. Although the ability to procure money is important, the ability to manage that money is equally important for financial and marital stability. For example, marital arguments over finances and/or divorce often results when one spouse perceives that the other spouse is mishandling money (Amato & Rogers, 1997; Aniol & Snyder, 1997). Studies have not shown whether individuals evaluate a potential spouse's ability to manage money, however.

Finances and Marital Quality

Scholars have also analyzed how different financial aspects of marriage relate to couples' marital experiences. For example, scholars have long recognized that economic pressure may add to couples' marital distress. The family stress model of economic pressure and marital distress shows that negative economic events, such as not being able to pay bills, losing a job, or cutting back in consumption are associated with increases in spouses' negative affective states (Conger, Ge, & Lorenz, 1994). Increases in depression and hostility are then linked to negative marital behaviors such as arguments, withdrawal of spousal support, and discussions of divorce (Conger, Rueter, & Elder, 1999; Vinokur, Price, & Caplan, 1996). Researchers have tested the family stress model using longitudinal data and multiple methods, across cultures, and in nationally representative samples (U.S.) and have shown that it is a good model of the links between nonnormative economic stressors and marital distress (Conger et al., 1990; Dew, 2007a; Kinnunen & Pulkkinen, 1998; Kwon, Rueter, Lee, Koh, & Ok, 2003).

Moving away from nonnormative economic stressors, researchers have begun to analyze how "mundane" financial issues such as savings behaviors, the use of consumer debt, and money management behaviors relate to reports of marital quality. These studies have found that the mechanisms that allow financial issues to predict marital quality extend beyond feelings of economic pressure. For example, married couples' consumer debt predicts changes in marital conflict even after controlling for the elements of the family stress model (Dew, 2007a). Additionally, married couples that share financial decision-making power are more satisfied than couples who do not share the decision-making power, and married couples are more likely to be dissatisfied when they do not pool their finances (Kurdek, 1991; Schaninger & Buss, 1986). Much work remains to be done in studying the relationship between "everyday" financial behaviors and couples marital quality.

Because financial needs change over time (Baek & Hong, 2004; Xiao, 1996), research has also examined how financial issues might relate to marriage at different points in the life course. Not surprisingly, financial need and anxiety has been found to be greatest in early adulthood (Drentea, 2000; Mirowsky & Ross, 1999). Further, recently married couples report that consumer debt and changes in consumer debt are associated with problems such as declines in marital satisfaction (Dew, 2008; Schramm et al., 2005). Also, when recently married couples perceive that they manage money effectively, they are more satisfied with their marriage (Kerkmann et al., 2000).

Interestingly, by the time that couples retire, few financial issues are related to marital distress. In a qualitative analysis, only 11 % of retirement-aged couples indicated that financial issues were problematic (Henry, Miller, & Giarrusso, 2005). Further, although financial issues such as mortgage debt, consumer debt, and income-to-needs ratios indirectly predict couples' marital distress, they do not seem to matter for couples that have been retired for many years (Dew, 2006). Given the impending retirement of the large "baby boom" cohort, further studies of how financial issues relate to marriage are relevant. Such studies would be especially pertinent since some researchers have claimed that much of the baby boom cohort has not saved enough for retirement and has more mortgage debt than any previous cohort (Kutza, 2005; Masnick, Di, & Belsky, 2005).

Future research into the relationship between finances and marital quality might profitably examine the links between individual spouse's characteristics, marital dynamics, and broader contextual issues (e.g., local economies). Couples' finances and their marital quality are subject to the influence of forces from these three areas. An example of research that blends two of these three areas is a study that showed that individual spouses' materialism predicts perceptions of economic difficulties which are associated with decreased marital satisfaction (Dean, Carroll, & Yang, 2007). Interestingly, spouses' materialism predicts perceptions of economic difficulties more than household income. Studies that blend variables from multiple areas have the potential to increase understanding of the relationship between finances and marital quality.

Finances and Divorce

Since financial issues predict both marital formation and quality, it is not surprising that they also been linked to marital dissolution. Two major topics within this area are the association between assets and divorce and the relationship between financial disagreements and divorce.

Scholars have known about the negative association between financial assets and divorce for decades (Levinger, 1965; Locke, 1951). Assets are such a strong predictor of future divorce that they reduce the relationship between income and divorce to nonsignificance (Dew, 2005; Galligan & Bahr, 1978). Only one study has failed to find a relationship between financial assets and future divorce. This study simultaneously considered assets and various relationship dynamics as predictors of divorce. Assets did not predict divorce with relationship dynamics in the model (Sanchez & Gager, 2000). This study provides interesting clues to the mechanisms that may explain the relationship between assets and divorce. In an interesting twist, one recent study found that assets negatively predict divorce except for husbands and wives who earn the same amount and have poor marital quality (Finke & Pierce, 2006). These scholars asserted that these couples who know they are about to divorce start to accumulate assets so that they will have a higher standard of living following the divorce.

Scholars have offered many theories to explain this relationship. In social exchange theory, assets may be an attraction to the marriage. That is, assets may enhance individuals' experience of marriage, may increase marital satisfaction, and may make divorce less likely (Levinger, 1976). Commitment theorists assert that assets are barriers to divorce rather than attraction to the marriage. These theorists argue that assets can keep spouses together who would otherwise divorce because they do not want to split their assets and live at a lower standard of living (Booth, Johnson, White, & Edwards, 1986; Johnson, 1991; Johnson, Caughlin, & Huston, 1999). In other words, assets raise the cost of divorce. Scholars are just beginning to test these explanatory mechanisms against each other, and to extend the literature by testing whether the association between assets and divorce differs by gender, and whether the relationship is spurious (Dew, 2005).

Another way that financial issues purportedly relate to divorce is through spouses' disagreements about family finances. Studies that examine married couples prospectively (e.g., prior to the divorce) find that disagreements over finances strongly predict of divorce. Prospective longitudinal data from both convenience samples and nationally representative samples show that variables such as arguing over finances, or feeling that one's spouse handles money foolishly, predicts future divorce—sometimes even predicting divorce 15 years later (Amato & Rogers, 1997; Terling-Watt, 2001). In these studies, financial disagreements more than doubled the likelihood that a couple would divorce (Amato & Rogers, 1997). Only extramarital affairs and drug/alcohol abuse more strongly predicted divorce than financial disagreements do, and financial disagreements are one of the few predictors of divorce that applied to both husbands and wives (Amato & Rogers, 1997; Terling-Watt, 2001). Further, when spouses feel that financial decision-making power is shared equally, and when they have a similar view of their finances, the likelihood of divorce declines (Schaninger & Buss, 1986; Zagorsky, 2003a).

Both marriage and consumer finance practitioners might benefit from continued research in this area. Aniol and Snyder's (1997) study showed that couples who seek financial counseling often have elevated levels of marital problems and vice versa. It might be interesting to design treatment studies and evaluate whether financial counseling has a side-benefit of improving marriage. Research has shown that financially troubled couples who implemented their financial counselors' advice report improvements in their health (O'Neill, Sorhaindo, Xiao, & Garman, 2005), and filing bankruptcy helped some couples avoid divorce in a qualitative study (Thorne, 2001). These findings suggest that couples who receive financial counseling may experience improvements in their marriage and avoid divorce.

Conclusion

Although Zelizer's (1994) assertion—that scholars have very little evidence of a relationship between marriage and finances—is less true now, this reciprocal relationship still merits considerable research. This review has shown that the vantage points of many disciplines help contribute to this undertaking. Practitioners that deal with the relationship between financial behavior and marital issues are underrepresented in this area of research. Including their unique perspectives would benefit scholars' understanding. Further, a more detailed understanding of married couples' financial practices is needed. For example, married couples' consumption, pooling, and current details of their decision-making processes are warranted. Another research area that needs strengthening is investigating the mechanisms behind family structure differences and financial well-being. Finally, understanding the relationship between individual spouses' attitudes and histories, couples' marriages, and the contexts in which their marriages are situated would greatly add to the literature. To accomplish these goals, new types of data are needed that blend detailed financial behavior and attitude questions with items on spouses' marital history and quality. As researchers more thoroughly test how marriages and finances relate, practitioners and scholars will be better equipped to understand an issue central to married couples' daily lives.

References

Amato, P. R., & Rogers, S. J. (1997). A longitudinal study of marital problems and subsequent divorce. *Journal of Marriage and the Family, 59,* 612–624.

Andersen, J. D. (2005). Financial problems and divorce: Do demographic characteristics strengthen the relationship? *Journal of Divorce and Remarriage, 43,* 149–161.

Aniol, J. C., & Snyder, D. K. (1997). Differential assessment of financial and relationship distress: Implications for couple therapy. *Journal of Marital and Family Therapy, 23,* 347–352.

Baek, E., & Hong, G.-S. (2004). Effects of family life-cycle stages on consumer debts. *Journal of Family and Economic Issues, 25,* 359–385.

Bernasek, A., & Bajtelsmit, V. L. (2002). Predictors of women's involvement in household financial decision-making. *Financial Counseling and Planning, 13,* 39–47.

Blau, F. D., Ferber, M. A., & Winkler, A. E. (2001). *The economics of women, men, and work* (4th ed.). Upper Saddle River, NJ: Prentice Hall.

Blumstein, P., & Schwartz, P. (1984). *American couples.* New York: Pocket Books.

Booth, A., Johnson, D. R., White, L. K., & Edwards, J. N. (1986). Divorce and marital instability over the life course. *Journal of Family Issues, 7,* 421–442.

Buss, D. M., Shackelford, T. K., Kirkpatrick, L. A., & Larsen, R. J. (2001). A half century of mate preferences: The cultural evolution of values. *Journal of Marriage and Family, 63,* 491–503.

Chaulk, B., Johnson, P. J., & Bulcroft, R. (2003). Effects of marriage and children on financial risk tolerance: A synthesis of family development and prospect theory. *Journal of Family and Economic Issues, 24,* 257–279.

Cherlin, A. J. (2004). The deinstitutionalization of American marriage. *Journal of Marriage and Family, 66,* 848–861.

Clarkberg, M. (1999). The price of partnering: The role of economic well-being in young adults' first union experiences. *Social Forces, 77,* 945–968.

Conger, R. D., Elder, G. H., Jr., Lorenz, F. O., Conger, K. J., Simons, R. L., Whitbeck, L. B., et al. (1990). Linking economic hardship to marital quality and instability. *Journal of Marriage and the Family, 52,* 643–656.

Conger, R. D., Ge, X. J., & Lorenz, F. O. (1994). Economic stress and marital relations. In J. R. D. Conger & G. H. Elder (Ed.), *Families in troubled times,* 187–203. New York: Aldine de Gruyter.

Conger, R. D., Rueter, M. A., & Elder, G. H., Jr. (1999). Couple resilience to economic pressure. *Journal of Personality and Social Psychology, 76,* 54–71.

Daly, K. J. (2003). Family theory and the theories families live by. *Journal of Marriage and Family*, *65*, 771–784.

Davis, H. L. (1976). Decision making within the household. *The Journal of Consumer Research*, *2*, 241–260.

Dean, L. R., Carroll, J. S., & Yang, C. (2007). Materialism, perceived financial problems, and marital satisfaction. *Family and Consumer Sciences Research Journal*, *35*, 260–281.

DeLeire, T., & Kalil, A. (2005). How do cohabiting couples with children spend their money? *Journal of Marriage and Family*, *67*, 286–295.

DeNavas-Walt, C., Proctor, B. D., & Lee, C. H. (2006). Income, poverty, and health insurance coverage in the United States: 2005. Retrieved January 10, 2007, from http://www.census.gov/prod/2006pubs/p60-231.pdf

Dew, J. P. (2005). *The meaning of assets in marriage.* Paper presented at the annual conference of National Council of Family Relations, Phoenix, AZ.

Dew, J. P. (2006). *Financial issues and marital distress during the retirement transition.* Paper presented at the annual conference of the National Council of Family Relations, Minneapolis, MN.

Dew, J. P. (2007a). Two sides of the same coin? The differing roles of assets and consumer debt in marriage. *Journal of Family and Economic Issues*, *28*, 89–104.

Dew, J. P. (2007b). *The role of student debt, consumer debt, and assets in union transitions during early adulthood.* Paper presented at the annual conference of the Population Association of America, New York.

Dew, J. P. (2008). The relationship between debt change and marital satisfaction change in recently married couples. *Family Relations, 57*, 60–71.

Drentea, P. (2000). Age, debt, and anxiety. *Journal of Health and Social Behavior*, *41*, 437–450.

Edin, K. (2001). What do low-income single-mothers say about marriage? *Social Problems*, *47*, 112–133.

Eggebeen, D. J. (2005). Cohabitation and exchanges of support. *Social Forces*, *83*, 1097–1110.

Fan, J. X. (2000). Linking consumer debt and consumer expenditures: Do borrowers spend money differently? *Family and Consumer Sciences Research Journal*, *28*, 358–401.

Finke, M. S., & Pierce, N. L. (2006). Precautionary savings behavior of maritally stressed couples. *Family and Consumer Sciences Research Journal*, *34*, 223–240.

Fletschner, D., & Klawitter, M. (2005). *Yours, mine, and ours: How married couples hold their savings.* Paper presented at the annual conference of the Association for Public Policy Analysis and Management, Washington, DC.

Galligan, R. J., & Bahr, S. J. (1978). Economic well-being and marital stability: Implications for income maintenance programs. *Journal of Marriage and the Family*, *40*, 283–290.

Greenwood, J., Guner, N., & Knowles, J. A. (2003). More on marriage, fertility, and the distribution of income. *International Economic Review*, *44*, 827–862.

Hao, L. (1996). Family structure, private transfers, and the economic well-being of families with children. *Social Forces*, *75*, 269–292.

Heimdal, K. R., & Houseknecht, S. K. (2003). Cohabiting and married couples' income organization: Approaches in Sweden and in the United States. *Journal of Marriage and Family*, *65*, 525–538.

Henry, R. G., Miller, R. B., & Giarrusso, R. (2005). Difficulties, disagreements, and disappointments in late-life marriages. *International Journal of Aging and Human Development*, *61*, 243–264.

Hirschl, T. A., Altobelli, J., & Rank, M. R. (2003). Does marriage increase the odds of affluence? Exploring the life course probabilities. *Journal of Marriage and Family*, *65*, 927–938.

Israelsen, C. L., & Hatch, S. (2005). Proactive research: Where art thou? *Financial Counseling and Planning*, *16*.

Johnson, M. P. (1991). Commitment to personal relationships. In W. H. Jones & D. W. Perlman (Eds.), *Advances in personal relationships* (pp. 117–143, Vol. 3). London: Jessica Kingsly.

Johnson, M. P., Caughlin, J. P., & Huston, T. L. (1999). The tripartite nature of marital commitment: Personal, moral, and structural reasons to stay married. *Journal of Marriage and the Family, 61*, 160–177.

Kerkmann, B. C., Lee, T. R., Lown, J. M., & Allgood, S. M. (2000). Financial management, financial problems, and marital satisfaction among recently married university students. *Financial Counseling and Planning, 11*, 55–64.

Kinnunen, U., & Pulkkinen, L. (1998). Linking economic stress to marital quality among Finnish marital couples. *Journal of Family Issues, 19*, 705–724.

Kurdek, L. A. (1991). Predictors of increases in marital distress in newlywed couples: A 3-year prospective longitudinal study. *Developmental Psychology, 27*, 627–636.

Kutza, E. A. (2005). The intersection of economics and family status in late life. Implications for the future. *Marriage & Family Review, 37*, 9–26.

Kwon, H.-K., Rueter, M. A., Lee, M.-S., Koh, S., & Ok, S. W. (2003). Marital relationships following the Korean economic crisis: Applying the family stress model. *Journal of Marriage and Family, 65*, 316–325.

Lerman, R. I. (2002). How do marriage, cohabitation, and single parenthood affect the material hardships of families with children? Retrieved January 10, 2007, from http://www.census.gov/prod/2006pubs/p60-231.pdf

Levinger, G. (1965). Marital cohesiveness and dissolution: An integrative review. *Journal of Marriage and Family, 27*, 19–28.

Levinger, G. (1976). A socio-psychological perspective on marital dissolution. *Journal of Social Issues, 32*, 21–47.

Locke, H. J. (1951). *Predicting adjustment in marriage: A comparison of a divorced and a happily married group.* New York: Henry Holt.

Lundberg, S., & Pollak, R. A. (1996). Bargaining and distribution in marriage. *The Journal of Economic Perspectives, 10*, 139–158.

Lupton, J., & Smith, J. (2003). Marriage, assets, and savings. In S. Grossbard-Shechtman (Ed.), *Marriage and the economy: Theory and evidence from advanced industrial societies* (pp. 129–152). Cambridge, UK: Cambridge University Press.

Lyons, A. C., & Yilmazer, T. (2004). How does marriage affect the allocation of assets in women's defined contribution plans? Retrieved January 11, 2007, from http://escholarship.bc.edu/cgi/viewcontent.cgi?article=1011&context=retirement_papers

Masnick, G. S., Di, Z. X., & Belsky, E. S. (2005). *Emerging cohort trends in housing debt and home equity.* Paper presented at the Population Association of America, Philadelphia, PA.

McKeever, M., & Wolfinger, N. H. (2001). Reexamining the economic costs of marital disruption for women. *Social Science Quarterly, 82*, 202–217.

Mirowsky, J., & Ross, C. E. (1999). Economic hardship across the life course. *American Sociological Review, 64*, 548–569.

O'Neill, B., Sorhaindo, B., Xiao, J. J., & Garman, E. T. (2005). Financially distressed consumers: Their financial practices, financial well-being, and health. *Financial Counseling and Planning, 16*, 73–87.

Oppenheimer, V. K. (1988). A theory of marriage timing. *The American Journal of Sociology, 94*, 563–591.

Oppenheimer, V. K. (2003). Cohabiting and marriage during young men's career-development process. *Demography, 40*, 127–149.

Poduska, B. E., & Allred, G. H. (1990). Family finances: The missing link in MFT training. *The American Journal of Family Therapy, 18*, 161–168.

Pollak, R. A. (1985). A transaction cost approach to families and households. *Journal of Economic Literature, 23*, 581–608.

Sanchez, L., & Gager, C. T. (2000). Hard living, perceived entitlement to a great marriage, and marital dissolution. *Journal of Marriage and the Family, 62*, 708–722.

Sassler, S., & Goldscheider, F. (2004). Revisiting Jane Austen's theory of marriage timing: Changes in union formation among American men in the late 20th century. *Journal of Family Issues, 25*, 139–166.

Schaninger, C. M., & Buss, W. C. (1986). A longitudinal comparison of consumption and finance handling between happily married and divorced couples. *Journal of Marriage and the Family*, *48*, 129–136.

Schmidt, L., & Sevak, P. (2006). Gender, marriage, and asset accumulation in the United States. *Feminist Economics*, *12*, 139–166.

Schramm, D. G., Marshall, J. P., Harris, V. W., & Lee, T. R. (2005). After "I Do": The newlywed transition. *Marriage and Family Review*, *38*, 45–67.

Smock, P. J., & Manning, W. D. (1997). Cohabiting partners' economic circumstances and marriage. *Demography*, *34*, 331–341.

Smock, P. J., Manning, W. D., & Porter, M. (2005). "Everything's there except money": How money shapes decisions to marry among cohabitors. *Journal of Marriage and Family*, *67*, 680–696.

Spiro, R. L. (1983). Persuasion in family decision-making. *The Journal of Consumer Research*, *9*, 393–402.

Su, C., Fern, E. F., & Ye, K. (2003). A temporal dynamic model of spousal family purchase-decision behavior. *Journal of Marketing Research*, *40*, 268–281.

Terling-Watt, T. (2001). Explaining divorce: An examination of the relationship between marital characteristics and divorce. *Journal of Divorce and Remarriage*, *35*(3/4), 125–145.

Thomas, D. (1990). Intra-household resource allocation: An inferential approach. *The Journal of Human Resources*, *25*, 635–664.

Thorne, D. K. (2001). *Personal bankruptcy through the eyes of the stigmatized: Insight into issues of shame, gender, and marital discord*. Unpublished PhD Dissertation, Washington State University.

Townsend, N. W. (2002). *The package deal: Marriage, work, and fatherhood in men's lives*. Philadelphia, PA: Temple University Press.

Vinokur, A. D., Price, R. H., & Caplan, R. D. (1996). Hard times and hurtful partners: How financial strain affects depression and relationship satisfaction of unemployed persons and their spouses. *Journal of Personality and Social Psychology*, *71*, 166–179.

Waite, L. J., & Gallagher, M. (2000). *The case for marriage: Why married people are happier, healthier, and better off financially*. New York: Doubleday.

Wilmoth, J., & Koso, G. (2002). Does marital history matter? Marital status and wealth outcomes among preretirment adults. *Journal of Marriage and Family*, *64*, 254–268.

Xiao, J. J. (1996). Effects of family income and life cycle stages on financial asset ownership. *Financial Counseling and Planning*, *7*, 21–30.

Xie, Y., Raymo, J. M., Goyette, K., & Thornton, A. (2003). Economic potential and entry into marriage and cohabitation. *Demography*, *40*, 351–367.

Zagorsky, J. L. (2003a). Husbands' and wives' view of the family finances. *Journal of Socio-Economics*, *32*, 127–146.

Zagorsky, J. L. (2003b). Marriage and divorce's impact on wealth. *Journal of Sociology*, *41*, 406–424.

Zelizer, V. A. (1994). *The social meaning of money*. New York: Basic Books.

Chapter 21
Consumer Finance and Parent-Child Communication

Myria Watkins Allen

Abstract Most research investigating parent–child communication about consumer finance has focused on consumer socialization and been based on the family communication patterns theory. Five additional theories are suggested for guiding consumer finance researchers as they seek to better understand the complexity of parent–child conversations: communication privacy management theory, relational dialectics theory, relational communication theory, emotional regulation theory, and communication accommodation theory. As families face increasingly complex financial circumstances and decisions, increasingly complex research exploring parent–child communication is needed.

Parental communication is important in terms of educating young people about issues such as budgeting, saving, investing, and preparing for retirement, equipping them with useful and effective consumer skills, and helping them avoid and/or manage problematic financial issues such as excessive credit card debt. Yet family financial conversations are more complex than simply educating young people and often occur within families as they seek to complete important financial tasks (e.g., managing debt, making investments, preparing for retirement, funding family goals, meeting the monthly financial obligations). Financial conversations may also involve relational issues such as power, secrecy, conflict, and control. The scholarly literature largely fails to address the complexity of these conversations. In this chapter the existing research is summarized, useful communication theories are identified, and additional research directions are offered. Opportunities abound for cutting edge research and for the application of communication theories to the area of consumer finance.

To date, researchers focusing on interpersonal communication have generally overlooked economic issues except for some studies of marital communication (e.g., Nwoye, 2000; Schaninger & Buss, 1986). Consumer finance research has focused almost exclusively on the scope of parental influence on children's consumption-related

M.W. Allen
Department of Communication, University of Arkansas, Fayetteville, AR 72701, USA
e-mail: myria@uark.edu

knowledge, attitudes, and behaviors, how parenting style influences a child's learning of consumer skills, and how parents react to child-directed marketing activity. Most consumer finance research has explored the structure (e.g., parenting styles) or the frequency or extent of family communication about consumption (see Bakir, Rose, & Shoham, 2005; Viswanathan, Childers, & Moore, 2000, for brief reviews of the literature). Little explanatory or predictive research exists on additional topics such as parent–child communication about finances, money management, and consumer debt (Hira, 1997; Moore-Shay & Berchmans, 1996).

In order to limit the scope of the review, this chapter focuses specifically on parent–child communication. Initially, the research discussing the role of parental communication on the socialization of young consumers is reviewed. This is followed by research exploring other types of financial conversations between parents and children. The chapter concludes with a discussion of five additional communication theories proposed as especially useful in enhancing our understanding of the complexity of parent–child communication about finance-related issues.

Parent–Child Communication and Consumer Socialization

The Consumer Socialization Model

For almost 25 years researchers have sought to better understand issues related to the consumer socialization of children (see John, 1999, for a review of this research). Consumer socialization is "the process by which young people acquire skills, knowledge, and attitudes relevant to their functioning in the marketplace" (Ward, 1980, p. 380). In the late 1970s Moschis and his colleagues (e.g., Moore & Moschis, 1981; Moschis & Churchill, 1978; Moschis et al., 1986; Moschis & Moore, 1984) began investigating the socializing role of communication on consumer behaviors. Previously few researchers had explored the socializing effects of interpersonal communication on young people's consumer behaviors (Moschis, 1985) focusing instead on mass media's role. Like most early consumer socialization research, Moschi's (1985) work was grounded within the cognitive development and social learning theories, and he classified socialization outcomes in terms of cognitive, affective, and behavioral concepts using stages in the consumer decision-making process (Moschi, 1987). The consumer socialization model he developed placed the child as the center of a nexus of socializing agents, including family members, peers, schools, employers, and the media.

Parents remain the most widely researched socialization agents and their influence appears to be the most pervasive, long lasting, and important (Caruana & Vassallo, 2003; Martin & Bush, 2000; Moschis, Prahasto, & Mitchell, 1986). Parental consumer socialization instruction generally involves (1) modeling consumer behaviors, (2) making rules about children's consumer behaviors, and (3) engaging in direct discussions about purchasing decisions, money, credit, and related topics. Using Mochis' consumer socialization model, recent scholars (e.g., Bush, Smith, & Martin, 1999; Lachance, Legault, & Bujold, 2000; Viswanathan et al.,

2000) have studied various consumption-related issues, often focusing on how parents control children's access to or help them understand mass media advertising content (e.g., Bakir et al., 2005; Buijzen & Valkenburg, 2003, 2005).

The Application of Family Communication Patterns Theory

Moschi's earliest research asked children simply to identify how frequently they talked with their parents about specific consumer-related issues. A refinement occurred when he and his colleagues begin integrating family communication patterns (FCP) theory (see Koerner & Fitzpatrick, 2006, for an overview of the theory) into their research. FCP researchers contend two different family orientations exist for how parents seek to achieve agreement within families: a "concept" orientation encouraging debate, rational discussion, and creative thinking and a "socio" orientation encouraging conformist thinking and emphasizing family harmony and acceptance of authority. The children of concept-oriented parents are more likely to purchase goods rationally rather than buying due to social needs, display more discontent with the products they purchase, and develop and articulate an independent consumption perspective (Moschis, 1985, 1987). Children raised in a concept-oriented communication environment in the United States (Caruana & Vassallo, 2003; Foxman, Tansuhaj, & Ekstrom, 1989) and in Japan (Rose, Boush, & Shoham, 2002) are more likely to influence their family's purchasing decisions. Those raised by socio-oriented parents are more likely to grow up to depend more on mass media content and peer conversation for consumer information (Moschis, 1985, 1987) and participate less in family decision-making and information seeking about consumption behaviors (Carlson, Grossbart, & Walsh, 1990; Moschis et al., 1986).

In the interpersonal communication literature, the original FCP theory was refined as researchers came to understand that the two orientations interact consistently. As a result, four family types were identified: pluralistic, laissez-faire, consensual, and protective (see Koerner & Fitzpatrick, 2006, for a description). Some recent consumer socialization literature has been based on the fourfold typology (e.g., Caruana & Vassallo, 2003; Chan & McNeal, 2003).

The sex of the parent also became an important factor in the consumer socialization research. Carlson and colleagues (e.g., Carlson et al., 1990; Carlson & Walsh, 1994) explored the role of FCP between mothers and their children on consumer socialization because "mothers are assumed to play primary roles in intergenerational influence processes" (Carlson & Walsh, p. 27). Recent research continues to explore the socializing influence of the communication received from the mother (e.g., Mandrik, Fern, & Bao, 2005).

The Role of Antecedent Variables

Antecedent variables (e.g., age, gender, number of parents) also affect how parents and children talk about consumer-related issues (Moschis, 1985). Girls are more likely to receive purposeful training (e.g., parent-guided purchasing events), as are upper-SES children. Discussions are more conceptual in single-parent homes, where adolescents are more likely to participate in family consumer tasks (Lachance et al., 2000). Parents who engaged in discussions and tasks with their children are more likely to involve them in consumer decisions. However, consumer communication between the parent and the child can moderate the effects of family structure (i.e., single parent, dual parent) on adolescents' participation in family consumer activities.

Other Financial Topics Discussed

Some descriptive research exists that identifies financial topics directly discussed between parents and their children (e.g., American Savings Education Council, 2001). Parents in the American Savings Education Council's (AESC) national survey reported involving their pre-teen and teen children in discussions about paying for education (72 % had), how to track expenses (56 % had), how to make a budget (52 % had), and about different kinds of investments (40 % had). However, Bowen (1996) found parents and children differed in the money management topics they remembered discussing. Parents mentioned talking with their children about savings most frequently followed by budgeting, allowances, and checking. Teens most frequently mentioned talking with their parents about budgeting followed by checking, savings, and allowances.

In a descriptive study, Allen et al. (2002) interviewed 103 college students about the range of financial topics they discussed with their parents, the overall conversational climate of such discussions, the relationship between the financial discussions and parent–child conflict, the guidelines parents set for their continued financial assistance, how students ask for money and how parents respond, the financial advice they receive from parents, and the extent to which gender differences exist in family financial discussions. The researchers found that in comparison to men, females indicated their parents were open and approachable during financial conversations, they received more advice about when to use their credit cards, and they were more likely to negatively compare their budgeting skills to their parents (Allen et al., 2002). Males were more likely to receive advice on budgeting and to indicate financial issues within the family were forbidden topics.

When investigating how willing college students are to talk with their parents about how many credit cards they had (or their spending habits), how much debt they had, and the types of things they charged on their credit cards (or spent money on), Edwards, Allen, and Hayhoe (2007) found young men were less open in their conversations and less likely to discuss their finances with their parents. However, a better predictor of such conversations was a college student's level of financial dependence on his/her parents. Those college students, regardless of gender, who were least likely to discuss their financial situation with their parents were more obsessed with money, regarded it as a source of power and status, perceived the likelihood of more inequity in their future pay, and tended not to budget or save their money.

Several researchers have focused on the long-term implications of parent–child financial conversations in contexts other than consumer socialization. Clarke, Heaton, Israelsen, and Eggett (2005) assessed the extent to which parents modeled and taught adult financial roles to their children and whether or not the young people implemented the lessons learned upon reaching early adulthood. They found fathers modeled financial tasks more frequently than mothers but that young adults felt more financially prepared if their mother had modeled the financial tasks and the adolescent had practiced the tasks. Less emphasis was placed during parent–child conversations on the financial tasks needed by young adults than those needed during the teen years.

Some recent research has focused on family communication and credit; however, more such research is badly needed given national data on rising consumer debt. Pinto, Parente, and Mansfield (2005) investigated the relative importance of four socialization agents (parents, peers, media, and schools) on college students' credit use habits, finding a significant negative relationship between the amount of credit information learned from parents and students' credit use. A college student is more open in his/her discussions with parents about credit card use when the family's overall communication environment is open, when he/she is dependent on parents for advice and information regarding credit cards, has lower levels of credit card debt, and experiences less tension about talking with his/her parents about credit (Edwards et al., 2004).

Recently Allen and her colleagues (e.g., Allen, Edwards, & Hayhoe, 2007; Hayhoe, Leach, Allen, & Edwards, 2005) focused on the relevance of imagined interactions to family financial discussions. Rosenblatt and Meyer (1986) developed the idea of imagined interaction based on Mead's (1934) concept of internal dialogue. Rosenblatt and Meyer proposed that imagined interactions are similar to actual interactions in that imagined interactions involve significant others and may be rambling or coherent, brief or lengthy. In an imagined interaction, a social actor forms a mental representation (verbal, visual, or a combination of verbal and visual) of a conversation and this mental representation may precede, follow, or even occur simultaneously with actual interaction (Honeycutt, 2003). Imagined interactions function primarily to rehearse or review conversation and can also help people cope with stressful situations.

Allen et al. (2007) argued that if a young person has unpleasant imagined interactions with parents regarding money management and credit issues, this may keep the teen from turning to his/her parents for advice or assistance with financial problems. Imagined interaction frequency and pleasantness are related to college students' attitudes toward credit and their money beliefs and behaviors, are influenced by patterns of family economic behavior (Allen et al., 2007), and have been linked to the number of credit cards students have (Hayhoe et al., 2005). Counselors can use imagined interactions to help parents and teens rehearse more productive conversational strategies when talking about financial issues.

Future Research Directions

Several communication theories have been identified in the previous sections (i.e., family communication patterns, imagined interactions). Although this chapter focuses primarily on logical–empirical theories, there are some excellent interpretive theories which can inform our understanding of family communication about financial issues (e.g., symbolic convergence theory, narrative performance theory). Only one interpretive study involving family communication and consumer socialization was identified for this review. As an alternative "to the positivistic paradigm that dominates family buying behavior research" Buttle (1994, p. 76) applied the co-ordinated management of meaning theory (CMM) to gain insight into the communication structures and processes multiple members in one family used to make consumer-related decisions regarding the family vacation. This was the first, and last, known application of CMM to consumer research.

The next section discusses five additional theories that hold promise for future research into consumer finance and family communication (i.e., communication privacy management theory, relational dialectics theory, relational communication theory, emotional regulation theory, communication accommodation theory). For additional information on these and other communication theories recommended sources include *Engaging Theories in Family Communication* (Braithwaite & Baxter, 2006) and the special issue of the *Journal of Family Communication* (2006) devoted to exploring ways to advance family communication theories and methods.

Why do some families fail to discuss financial issues even when such discussions can help children learn to make good financial decisions (Olson & DeFrain, 2003)? "Family taboos on talking about money can leave children mystified about it, irrationally fearful, or ignorant of it. These people may end up living in a dangerous economic fog, hoping that money will always (somehow) come and always (magically) be enough" (Spayde, 2003, p. 58). The communication privacy management theory (Petronio, 2002; Petronio & Caughlin, 2006; Petronio, Jones, & Morr, 2003) provides a useful framework for understanding the rules families construct and negotiate about what and how financial topics can be discussed within and outside (e.g., with financial professionals) the immediate family unit. The theory details the turbulence that can result when family privacy rules are broken. Researchers can investigate (1) the content of the privacy rules existing within families experiencing serious financial problems and (2) how young people are socialized into family privacy rules which cause them not to seek assistance when it is needed. This theory might also be used to better understand the potential for family violence and/or estrangement when privacy rules regarding the discussion of financial issues are violated.

Olson et al. (1983) found that the most common family stressor concerned finances, and adolescents' use of spending money was identified as a major conflict area between parents and adolescents. In addition to the communication privacy management theory, several additional theories (i.e., relational dialectics theory, relational communication theory) provide insights into the communication-related aspects of problematic family financial discussions. Relational dialectics theory discusses how within any relationship interdependent, competing, and mutually contradictory pressures occur that influence the content and tone of communication (Baxter, 1990, 2006). Edwards et al. (2004) discussed two dialectical tensions (i.e., openness–closedness and dependence–independence) college students experience as they decide whether or not and what to tell their parents about their credit card usage and spending behaviors. Relational dialectics theory is especially useful to researchers interested in studying the changing content, tone, and importance of family financial conversations as children mature and begin distancing themselves emotionally and financially from their parents.

Like FCP, the focus of relational communication theory is on relational types and the outcomes of these patterns. Primarily used to identify communication patterns and tactics occurring within dyads, the theory can also help account for larger family units and for the expression of emotions. Researchers and practitioners interested in exploring family communication behaviors that communicate respect or disrespect, or that relate to conflict and control issues, will find this theory useful. Transcripts of family conversations regarding problematic financial issues can be analyzed to identify control and domination messages occurring within the family and then help family members identify ways to communicate more productively. This theory provides an alternative lens to FCP theory that allows researchers to investigate why parental communication empowers children in some families to learn how to make wise financial decisions but disempowers children in other families.

Often the nonverbal messages conveyed during a financial conversation can be more important than the actual words exchanged. Raver and Spagnola (2002) found that if a mother is highly negative in how she expresses her emotions within the context of economic hardship, her children are less accurate at identifying and expressing emotions and more likely to generate irrelevant/incomplete solutions to maternal sadness. Given the interest in intergenerational consumer finance research, the emotional regulation theory (see Cupach & Olson, 2006) is useful in understanding how parents' unproductive emotional responses to financial issues can be passed on through family communication behaviors. In preparing this review, no other research was identified that investigated the emotional messages conveyed during parent–child discussions even though many financial decisions may be more influenced by emotion than by logic.

Finally, cultural differences exist in the meanings of money (Falicov, 2001) and in money management behaviors. Communication accommodation theory (see Harwood, Soliz, & Lin, 2006) is useful when exploring the communication occurring within interethnic families and intergenerationally. Specifically, the theory looks at how diverse communicators converge and diverge in their conversational style, interpret each other's meanings, attempt to control the conversation, and manage the discourse (e.g., topic selection, face management). Discourse management is a useful way to look at how money is talked about within ethnically diverse families since such conversations influence the attitudes family members hold regarding financial topics. Given the growth of the Hispanic population and their purchasing power in the United States, it is surprising no studies were identified that explored Hispanic parent–child financial conversations. This theory could be used by financial counselors interested in communicating more successfully with ethnically diverse clients. Also, the theory would be useful in investigating cross-generational financial conversations (e.g., children–grandparents).

In addition to broadening the theoretical frameworks used in discussing consumer finance and family communication, future researchers might consider their sampling unit and measures used. Limited research on consumer finance related issues has focused on single-parent homes and only one study (i.e., Cotte & Wood, 2004) was identified that looked at the influence of communication between siblings. Even within the same family, different relationships exist between the dyads. Both John (1999) and Palan (1998) called for future research at the dyadic level and several recent studies have done so (e.g., Bakir et al., 2005). Allen et al. (2007) measured the perceived communication climate within family dyads and then aggregated these dyads into various family coalitions which were then related to college students' willingness to discuss money and credit issues with their parents, their attitudes toward money and credit, and the frequency of their imagined interactions with parents about money and credit issues.

Over time, the measurement instruments and approaches used have been refined. However, Viswanathan et al. (2000) attributed the relative lack of consumer socialization research to the lack of adequate research instruments, contending that most researchers investigating consumer socialization have used either a 6-item or 12-item scale originally developed by Moschis. Generally, consumption interaction has been the single indicator for family communication (Palan, 1998). Palan's study was the first to specifically investigate the relationship between consumption-specific family communication and the overall quality of the communication environment within the family. Viswanathan et al. developed and validated scales for assessing adult children's perceptions of the parental transmission of consumer-related preferences, consumer skills, and consumer attitudes. Edwards et al. (2004) developed an instrument for measuring the relational dialectics (openness–closedness, independence–autonomy) involved when parent–college students discuss financial issues.

Several criticisms can be made regarding the current state of the literature. The most obvious criticism is that the theoretical base guiding most research is very narrow. The consumer socialization model and the family communication patterns theory remain the primary theoretical foundations, although the FCP research has been criticized (see Palan, 1998). Although there are multiple opportunities for scholars to "conduct meaningful theoretical and applied research" investigating consumer socialization (John, 1999, p. 207), research is critically needed to address other topics occurring within parent–child financial conversations. Other criticisms include that little research has explored the father's role in any depth, few researchers have focused on the long-term implications of parent–child communication on the financial behaviors and attitudes of young adults, few studies address how parents help their teens practice financial skills, and researchers have largely overlooked dysfunctional or problematic financial conversations between parents and children.

References

Allen, M. W., Amason, P., Warren, R. B., Lin, L., Dubbs, K., & Copeland, K. (2002). *Financial discussion within the family: Conversational climate, discussants, topics, and advice.* Paper presented at the National Communication Association's annual meeting, New Orleans, LA.

Allen, M. W., Edwards, R., & Hayhoe, C. (2007). Imagined interactions, family money management patterns and coalitions, and attitudes toward money and credit. *Journal of Family and Economic Issues, 28,* 3–22.

American Savings Education Council. (2001). *2001 parents, youth and money survey.* Retrieved January 30, 2002, from http://www.asec.org/2001pym/highlite.htm.

Bakir, A., Rose, G. M., & Shoham, A. (2005). Consumption communication and parental control of children's television viewing: A multi-rater approach. *Journal of Marketing Theory and Practice, 13,* 47–58.

Baxter, L. A. (1990). Dialectical contradictions in relationship development. *Journal of Personal and Social Relationships, 7,* 69–88.

Baxter, L. A. (2006). Relational dialectics theory: Multivocal dialogues of family communication. In D. O. Braithwaite & L. A. Baxter (Eds.), *Emerging theories in family communication: Multiple perspectives* (pp. 130–145). Thousand Oaks, CA: Sage.

Bowen, C. (1996). Informal money management education: Perceptions of teens and parents. *Consumer Interests Annual, 42,* 233–234.

Braithwaite, D. O., & Baxter, L. A. (Eds.) (2006), *Engaging theories in family communication: Multiple perspectives.* Newbury Park, CA: Sage.

Buijzen, M., & Valkenburg, P. M. (2003). The unintended effects of television advertising: A parent–child survey. *Communication Research, 30,* 483–503.

Buijzen, M., & Valkenburg, P. M. (2005). Parental mediation of undesired advertising effects. *Journal of Broadcasting & Electronic Media, 49,* 153–165.

Bush, A. J., Smith, R., & Martin, C. A. (1999). The influence of consumer socialization variables on attitude toward advertising: A comparison of African-Americans and Caucasians. *Journal of Advertising, 28,* 13–24.

Buttle, F. (1994). The co-ordinated management of meaning: A case exemplar of a new consumer research technology. *European Journal of Marketing, 28,* 76–100.

Carlson, L., Grossbart, S., & Walsh, A. (1990). Mothers' communication orientation and consumer socialization tendencies. *Journal of Advertising, 19,* 27–39.

Carlson, L., & Walsh, A. (1994). Family communication patterns and marketplace motivations, attitudes, and behaviors of children and mothers. *Journal of Consumer Affairs, 28,* 25–54.

Caruana, A., & Vassallo, R. (2003). Children's perceptions of their influence over purchases: The role of parental communication patterns. *The Journal of Consumer Marketing, 20,* 55–66.

Chan, K., & McNeal, J. U. (2003). Parent–child communications about consumption and advertising in China. *The Journal of Consumer Marketing, 20,* 317–334.

Clarke, M. C., Heaton, M. B., Israelsen, C. L., & Eggett, D. L. (2005). The acquisition of family financial roles and responsibilities. *Family and Consumer Sciences Research Journal, 33,* 321–340.

Cotte, J., & Wood, S. L. (2004). Families and innovative consumer behavior: A triadic analysis of sibling and parental influence. *Journal of Consumer Research, 31,* 78–86.

Cupach, W. R., & Olson, L. N. (2006). Emotion regulation theory: A lens for viewing family conflict and violence. In D. O. Braithwaite & L. A. Baxter (Eds.), *Engaging theories in family communication: Multiple perspectives* (pp. 213–228). Newbury Park, CA: Sage.

Edwards, R., Allen, M. W., Brewster, B., Hayhoe, C., Leach, L., & Waldhart, E. (2004). *Family communication about credit card use by college students.* Paper presented the annual meeting of the International Communication Association, New Orleans, LA.

Edwards, R., Allen, M. W., & Hayhoe, C. (2007). Financial attitudes and family communication about students' finances: The role of sex differences. *Communication Reports, 20,* 2, 90–100.

Falicov, C. J. (2001). The cultural meanings of money: The case of Latinos and Anglo-Americans. *The American Behavioral Scientist, 45,* 313–328.

Foxman, E. R., Tansuhaj, P. S., & Ekstrom, K. M. (1989). Adolescents' influence in family purchase decisions: A socialization perspective. *Journal of Business Research, 18*, 159–173.

Harwood, J., Soliz, J., & Lin, M. (2006). Communication accommodation theory: An intergroup approach to family relationships. In D. O. Braithwaite & L. A. Baxter (Eds.), *Engaging theories in family communication: Multiple perspectives* (pp. 19–34). Newbury Park, CA: Sage.

Hayhoe, C. R., Leach, L., Allen, M. W., & Edwards, R. (2005). Distinguishing the number of credit cards held by college students employing credit and money attitudes and imagined interactions. *Financial Counseling & Planning, 16*, 1–10.

Hira, T. K. (1997). Financial attitudes, beliefs and behaviors: Differences by age. *Journal of Consumer Studies and Home Economics, 21*, 271–290.

Honeycutt, J. M. (2003). *Imagined interactions: Daydreaming about communication.* Cresskill, NJ: Hampton Press.

John, D. R. (1999). Consumer socialization of children: A retrospective look at twenty-five years of research. *Journal of Consumer Research, 26*, 183–213.

Koerner, A. F., & Fitzpatrick, M. A. (2006). Family communication patterns theory: A social cognitive approach. In D. O. Braithwaite & L. A. Baxter (Eds.), *Engaging theories in family communication: Multiple perspectives* (pp. 50–65). Newbury Park, CA: Sage.

Lachance, M. J., Legault, F., & Bujold, N. (2000). Family structure, parent–child communication, and adolescent participation in family consumer tasks and decisions. *Family and Consumer Sciences Research Journal, 29*, 125–152.

Mandrik, C. A., Fern, E. F., & Bao, Y. (2005). Intergenerational influence: Roles of conformity to peers and communication effectiveness. *Psychology & Marketing, 10*, 813–832.

Martin, C., & Bush, A. (2000). Do role models influence teenagers' purchase intentions and behavior? *Journal of Consumer Marketing, 17*, 441–454.

Mead, G. H. (1934). *Mind, self and society.* Chicago: University of Chicago.

Moore, R. L., & Moschis, G. P. (1981). The role of family communication in consumer learning. *Journal of Communication, 31*, 42–51.

Moore-Shay, E. S., & Berchmans, B. M. (1996). The role of the family environment in the development of shared consumption values: An intergenerational study. *Advances in Consumer Research, 23*, 484–490.

Moschis, G. P. (1985). The role of family communication in consumer socialization of children and adolescents. *Journal of Consumer Research, 11*, 898–913.

Moschis, G. P. (1987). *Consumer socialization: A life-cycle perspective.* Lexington, MA: Lexington Books.

Moschis, G. P., & Churchill Jr., G. A. (1978). Consumer socialization: A theoretical and empirical analysis. *Journal of Marketing Research, 15*, 599–610.

Moschis, G. P., & Mitchell, L. G. (1986). Television advertising and interpersonal influences on teenagers' participation in family consumer decisions. *Advances in Consumer Research, 13*, 181–185.

Moschis, G. P., & Moore, R. L. (1984). Anticipatory consumer socialization. *Journal of the Academy of Marketing Science, 12*, 109–123.

Moschis, G. P., Prahasto, A. E., & Mitchell, L. G. (1986). Family communication influences on the development of consumer behavior: Some additional findings. *Advances in Consumer Research, 13*, 365–369.

Nwoye, A. (2000). A framework for intervention in marital conflicts over family finances: A view from Africa. *The American Journal of Family Therapy, 28*, 1, 75–87.

Olson, D. H., & DeFrain, J. (2003). *Marriages and families: Intimacy, diversity, and strength* (4th ed.). Boston, MA: McGraw-Hill.

Olson, D. H., McCubbin, H. I., Barnes, H. L., Larsen, A. S., Muxen, M. J., & Wilson, M. A. (1983). *Families: What makes them work?* Beverly Hills, CA: Sage.

Palan, K. M. (1998). Relationships between family communication and consumer activities of adolescents: An exploratory study. *Academy of Marketing Science Journal, 26*, 338–349.

Petronio, S. (2002). *Boundaries of privacy: Dialectics of disclosure.* Albany: State University of New York Press.

Petronio, S., & Caughlin, J. P. (2006). Communication privacy management theory: Understanding families. In D. O. Braithwaite & L. A. Baxter (Eds.), *Engaging theories in family communication: Multiple perspectives* (pp. 35–49). Newbury Park, CA: Sage.

Petronio, S., Jones, S., & Morr, M. C. (2003). Family privacy dilemmas: Managing communication boundaries within family groups. In L. R. Frey (Ed.), *Group communication in context: Studies of bonafide groups* (2nd ed., pp. 23–55). Mahwah, NJ: Erlbaum.

Pinto, M. B., Parente, D. H., & Mansfield, P. N. (2005). Information learned from socialization agents: Its relationship to credit card use. *Family and Consumer Sciences Research Journal, 33*, 357–367.

Raver, C. C., & Spagnola, M. (2002). "When my mommy was angry, I was speechless": Children's perceptions of maternal emotional expressiveness within the context of economic hardship. *Marriage & Family Review, 34*, 63–75.

Rose, G. M., Boush, D., & Shoham, A. (2002). Family communication and children's purchasing influence: A cross-national examination. *Journal of Business Research, 11*, 867–873.

Rosenblatt, P. C., & Meyer, C. (1986). Imagined interactions and the family. *Family Relations, 35*, 319–324.

Schaninger, C. M., & Buss, W. C. (1986). A longitudinal comparison of consumption and finance handling between happily married and divorced couples. *Journal of Marriage and the Family, 48*, 129–136.

Spayde, J. (2003, July/August). Making friends with your finances. *Utne Reader*, 57–60.

Viswanathan, M., Childers, T. L., & Moore, E. S. (2000). The measurement of intergenerational communication and influence on consumption: Development, validation, and cross-cultural comparison of the IGEN scale. *Academy of Marketing Science, 28*, 406–425.

Ward, S. (1980). Consumer socialization. In H. H. Kasarjian & T. S. Robertson (Eds.), *Perspectives in consumer behavior* (pp. 380–396). Glenville, IL: Scott, Foresman.

Chapter 22
Consumer Bankruptcy

Jean M. Lown

Abstract This chapter presents background information on consumer bankruptcy and a brief introduction to bankruptcy procedures. Differing perspectives on the reasons for the growth in filings are discussed. In addition, the new bankruptcy law is evaluated from the perspective of consumer interests.

Consumer bankruptcy rates soared over the past 25 years from 250,000 filings in 1979 to 1.5 million in 2004, although the most dramatic increases were concentrated in the period from 1985 to 1997 (Tabb, 2006, 2007). In an attempt to staunch the flow, Congress passed the Bankruptcy Abuse Prevention and Consumer Protection Act (BAPCPA) in 2005, prompting a flood of filings that topped out at over 2 million as debtors raced to file before the new law went into effect.

A simple answer to the question of what causes bankruptcy is consumer debt. A strong correlation exists between rising consumer debt and bankruptcy filings (Tabb, 2006). The number of credit cards and credit card debt increased from 661 million cards and $181 billion in debt in 1991 to 1,136 million cards and $645 billion in debt by 2004 (Board of Governors, 2006). Tabb (2007) explored the relationship between 10 measures of consumer credit and bankruptcy filing rates; statistically significant relationships existed for all measures except credit card delinquencies. Although bankruptcy and debt are highly correlated, correlation alone does not prove causation. The link between credit card debt and bankruptcy rates suggests that making the bankruptcy law more punitive is unlikely to decrease the filing rate (Tabb, 2007).

What is the face of the typical filer: someone down on their luck after getting sick, losing their job, and using credit cards to make ends meet and pay medical bills? Or is it the savvy consumer who abuses credit cards only to waltz into bankruptcy court to wipe out their debts and start afresh? Congress hotly debated these two faces of bankruptcy for eight years before finally passing a bankruptcy reform law.

J.M. Lown
Utah State University, FCHD, 2905 Old Main Hall, Logan, UT 84322, USA
e-mail: jean.lown@usu.edu

J.J. Xiao, (ed.), *Handbook of Consumer Finance Research,*
© Springer 2008

Americans look at bankruptcy through a "lens of fault" (Sullivan, Warren, & Westbrook, 1989, p. 8). The general public assumes that financial mismanagement is the main cause of bankruptcy while debtors report unanticipated trigger events such as job loss and/or medical problems (United Way of Salt Lake, 2006). Most of the debate and rhetoric accompanying BAPCPA, as well as the academic literature, approaches the topic from opposing perspectives.

The purpose of this chapter is to provide an overview of recent changes in consumer bankruptcy and current bankruptcy research and offer suggestions for research on the impact of the new law. The chapter will explain the basics of consumer bankruptcy and how chapters 7 and 13 differ. Two conceptual frameworks used to explain the increase in filings will be described. The main consumer provisions of the new law will be discussed along with some early assessments of the law, ending with recommendations for future research.

Consumer Bankruptcy Basics

Bankruptcy allows debtors, the individuals who file for debt relief, to discharge or wipe out most unsecured debts. Certain unsecured priority debts such as child support and alimony, student loans, and most tax debts cannot be discharged. Secured creditors can repossess or foreclose on collateral to enforce payment (Administrative Office of the United States Courts, 2006).

While bankruptcy is governed by federal law, title 11 of the United States Bankruptcy Code (The Code), there are many variations in how the law is implemented by federal judges. Consumer debtors can choose between chapters 7 and 13; the "chapter" refers to the sections of the federal bankruptcy code. Chapter 7 is the quick debt liquidation option, often referred to as straight bankruptcy (U.S. Trustee Program, 2005). While The Code provides for a court trustee to liquidate assets to repay creditors, most chapter 7 cases are no-asset cases. Within a few months of filing, unsecured debts are discharged. In contrast, a chapter 13 plan commits all of a debtor's disposable income to debt repayment for up to 5 years. Unlike chapter 7, chapter 13 can be used to prevent home foreclosure and vehicle repossession (U.S. Trustee Program, 2005).

Despite the law's promise of a "fresh start," more than two-thirds of chapter 13 repayment plans are dismissed, so the debtor does not receive a discharge of debt (Norberg, 2007). Porter and Thorne (2006) report that just one year after their debt discharge, chapter 7 debtors were in a similar or worse financial situation. For both chapters 7 and 13 debtors, excluding their debts, monthly expenses exceed income (Lown & Rowe, 2003).

Credit Expansion

A brief history of credit cards provides perspective on the growth in bankruptcy filings. Prior to deregulation of credit card interest rates resulting from the 1978 U.S. Supreme Court Marquette decision, lenders were very selective in issuing cards. Once interest ceilings were lifted, card issuers extended offers to marginal customers (Black & Morgan, 1999). The 1980s were the decade of "democratization of credit" when almost anyone could get a credit card (Black & Morgan, 1999, p. 1). Extending credit to riskier consumers is highly profitable because they accept offers with high interest rates and costly terms (Stavins, 2000). Although better known for the stock market boom, the 1990s were characterized by saturation marketing of credit cards and tremendous growth in debt burdens for most American families (Draut & Silva, 2003). So far the 2000s are characterized by tremendous increases in mortgage debt and explosive growth in predatory and subprime lending (Weller & Gino, 2005).

About 80 % of American households use credit cards, with 56 % of users carrying a balance (Board of Governors, 2006). Regions of the United States with high credit card debt burdens have higher bankruptcy rates (Stavins, 2000). Banks that lend to poor credit risks report high delinquency rates but also higher profits (Bird, Hagstrom, & Wild, 1999). Low minimum payments create perma-debt and universal default policies allow credit card issuers to raise the interest rate if a borrower pays late or misses a payment on another card (Public Broadcasting System, 2004). Looser credit standards resulted in higher bankruptcy rates, but with sophisticated computer algorithms, lenders make healthy profits (Stavins).

Conceptual Frameworks to Explain Bankruptcy

The dramatic growth in bankruptcy filings has been explained by two opposing camps: those who blame the reduction in stigma (cultural or economic incentives model) and advocates of a structural (financial distress) explanation who maintain that growing economic security and a fraying social safety net are to blame (Braucher, 2006).

Economic Incentives (Reduced Stigma) Model

According to the incentives model, the stigma associated with filing has diminished so that savvy consumers take advantage of the system by accumulating unsecured debt and then discharging it. Irresponsible debtors benefit from an overly generous bankruptcy system (White, 1998). White argues that state exemption levels affect bankruptcy decisions, yet very few debtors own sufficient assets to exceed these exemptions. "Current U.S. bankruptcy laws are so easily manipulated that almost any household can benefit financially from bankruptcy if it plans for bankruptcy in advance. Bankruptcy exemptions are in effect unlimited, which means that U.S. law gives too many households an incentive to file for bankruptcy rather than take responsibility for repaying their debts" (White, 1998, p. 685).

Much of the literature supporting the economic incentives perspective is based on opinion and economic modeling rather than on research on debtors. Among the leading advocates of the economic incentives perspective is law professor Todd Zywicki (2005), who argues that the growth in filings reflects moral decay among borrowers unwilling to fulfill their obligations. Zywicki argues that three factors have contributed to this growth: a shift in cost and benefits of filing to make bankruptcy more attractive, a reduction in personal shame and social stigma, and a shift toward a more impersonal relationship between debtor and creditor. Zywicki maintains that debtors who default are immoral and need to take personal responsibility for their choices and should be punished with a more punitive bankruptcy law.

Financial Distress/Structural Explanation

The opposing view (structural or financial distress model) contends that growing economic insecurity in a volatile economy, accompanied by aggressive extension of credit, has fueled the growth in bankruptcy. Using the Survey of Consumer Finances, Getter (2003) concluded that, faced with growing debt burdens and fewer societal support systems, an unanticipated trigger event is what sends consumers into bankruptcy. Deregulation of the credit industry has made consumer and mortgage credit too readily available to marginal borrowers (Black and Morgan, 1999) while predatory lending practices ensnare more consumers (Draut & Silva, 2003). Health care costs are rising faster than inflation, fewer workers are covered by health insurance, and larger deductible and coinsurance payments push families into bankruptcy (Himmelstein, Warren, Thorne, & Woolhandler, 2005). Athreya (2004) argues that stigma is not dead and offers an alternative explanation for rising rates, focusing on how computer technology has lowered transaction costs for lenders who market more credit to a wide range of consumers, including the highly risky.

The primary proponents of the structural explanation for the growth in bankruptcy are Sullivan, Warren, and Westbrook (1989, 2000), researchers who started collecting data for the Consumer Bankruptcy Project (CBP) in the late 1970s. The CBP relies on empirical data from bankruptcy files and interviews with debtors to explore the circumstances that drive them to file. The first phase of the CBP revealed that debtors are middle-class Americans who are drowning in debt due to "endless combinations of irresponsibility, misfortune, and fault" (Sullivan et al., 1989, p. 8). The two main factors fueling consumer bankruptcy are the growth in consumer credit and increasing economic volatility.

The CBP concluded that the bankruptcy laws were serving those for whom they were intended but in a less than satisfactory manner. Sullivan et al. (1989) concluded that proposals to make bankruptcy more bureaucratic and punitive in order to smoke out the abusers were not worth the time and money. They labeled the bankruptcy system as the social safety net of last resort in a country with a rapidly fraying support system (Sullivan et al., 2000).

A decade later, CBP phase II (Sullivan et al., 2000) found that the debt-to-income ratios of filers increased from 6 *weeks* worth of income in 1981 to 6 *months* worth in 1997. Because credit cards can be used to pay for almost any expense, it is impossible to determine from the bankruptcy files why expenses were incurred; thus they interviewed debtors to determine their reasons for filing. They concluded that many middle-class Americans were "economically fragile" and that this circumstance was much more widespread than indicated by bankruptcy statistics (p. xiv). CBP II identified five sources of financial stress: increased economic volatility, skyrocketing consumer debt levels, the economic impact of divorce and single-parent families, rising medical costs combined with reduced insurance coverage, and debtors' often unrealistic determination to hold on to unaffordable homes.

According to the CBP, increased debt, combined with uncertain jobs and incomes, translates into widespread financial distress for the middle class. "Bankruptcy is the ultimate free-market solution to bad debt" (Sullivan et al., 2000, p. 260). In a study of Utah filers, Lown and Rowe (2003) found debtors drowning in debt with no prospect of repaying. Confirming the CBP results, many Utah debtors reported very short job tenure, suggesting job loss contributed to the decision to file. Bermant and Flynn (1999) concluded that very few chapter 7 debtors had any prospect of repaying their unsecured debts. Weller and Gino (2005) attribute high bankruptcy rates among the middle class to a combination of living costs rising faster than incomes, job losses, health care costs, low savings, and unexpected expenses that trigger a filing.

Each side can produce data to support their view of why the U.S. bankruptcy rate increased dramatically in the past 25 years. According to Bermant and Flynn (2001),

> This is why studies about the causes of bankruptcy provide ambiguous or insufficient guidance for answering bankruptcy policy questions. The data always require interpretations that include a set of assumptions that go beyond the numbers themselves. Given different assumptions, the numbers will be interpreted differently. If we assume that there is less shame in society than there used to be, we are likely to interpret statistics regarding debt, divorce and bankruptcy differently than if we assume otherwise, but the current data don't prove the assumption either way. Our attitudes about debtors and about appropriate legal changes are, nevertheless, guided by our assumptions as well as our interpretations of the data (p. 4).

Braucher (2006) examined the interaction of consumer culture and structural economic arguments as explanations of overindebtedness. She analyzed the factors that are blamed for fueling the growth in bankruptcy and categorized them into economic factors driving the supply and demand for credit and cultural factors which affect both supply and demand. Braucher concluded that neither explanation is adequate by itself to explain the growth in bankruptcy.

Bankruptcy Reform

After eight years of lobbying by the credit industry, Congress passed the Bankruptcy Abuse Prevention and Consumer Protection Act of 2005. Consumers flooded the bankruptcy courts in the weeks leading up to implementation of the new rules to avoid the higher costs and restrictions of the new law (Truitt, 2007). The title of the law explains much of the rhetoric behind the legislation. With regard to preventing abuse, the rhetoric assumed that the main reason for filing is overspending by irresponsible debtors. Yet irresponsible "credit card junkies" accounted for only 2 % of the CBP sample (Sullivan et al., 1989, p. 178). A study of repeat filers in Utah (Llewellyn, 2005) found fewer than 10 % of debtors who may be abusing the system. According to one bankruptcy court official, perceived abuse was greater than any actual abuse (Truitt, 2007). It is a simple process for the court clerk to check a petitioner's social security number and report prior filings to the trustee for examination. Judges have always had the legal authority to deny a discharge to abusers.

Provisions of BAPCPA 2005

Under the means test, debtors with incomes exceeding their state's median for their family size can be required to file a chapter 13 repayment plan rather than a chapter 7 liquidation. Forcing debtors into a repayment plan is likely to result in lower discharge rates, with more debtors abandoning the system prior to completion. High chapter 13 filing rates result in repeat filings and thus higher overall numbers (Lown, 2006). Fewer than 10 % of debtors are likely to be affected by the means test since many have suffered a loss of income that contributed to filing.

Mandatory pre-filing counseling and pre-discharge financial education add costs. Time limits on filing after a prior discharge are extended from 6 to 8 years between chapter 7 discharges. Mandates for producing tax returns and other paperwork requirements add to the cost and stress of filing. Many general practice attorneys no longer take bankruptcy cases because of the additional paperwork. Chapter 13 debtors can no longer cram down vehicle debt to its current value. A concise summary of the law is available from the American Bankruptcy Institute (2005).

Impact of BAPCPA

Filings skyrocketed 30 % in 2005 to over 2 million cases (Administrative Office of the United States Courts, n.d.) with a massive spike in chapter 7 filings prior to the October implementation date as debtors rushed to file under the old law (Tabb, 2006). With so many cases pushed into 2005, it was no surprise that filings fell in 2006 to just over 600,000 (Administrative Office of the United States Courts, n.d.).

Due to the publicity surrounding BAPCPA, bankruptcy is now a more familiar concept to most Americans, which may increase filings (Mann, 2006). Based on the strong correlation between bankruptcy rates and both credit card and mortgage debt, Tabb (2007) predicts a quick return to pre-BAPCPA levels with rates leveling off at about 1.5 million cases. National Association of Consumer Bankruptcy Attorneys (2006) members expect that filings will rebound to pre-BAPCPA levels by mid-2007. According to these bankruptcy attorneys, the top reasons for filing include mortgage debt, unemployment, increase in credit card interest rates, and uninsured medical expenses. Survey respondents reported a major increase in time and paperwork devoted to each case as a result of BAPCPA. One undisputed fact is that filing for bankruptcy is more costly than in the past as both filing and attorney fees have increased (Truitt, 2007).

The National Foundation for Credit Counseling (NFCC) (2006) reports that providers are overwhelmed with requests for counseling and losing money on each session. NFCC-affiliated agencies are only able to meet the demand for services because of the dramatic drop in filings after the law took effect. While mandated counseling was designed to deter filings, NFCC reports that 97% of consumers seeking pre-bankruptcy counseling choose bankruptcy. Fees were waived for 16% of pre-filing counseling clients and 13% of pre-discharge education clients. "Based on current estimates of 600,000 bankruptcy filings in 2006 and assuming the same delivery mix, an annual funding shortfall of $7.52 million appears likely for pre-filing counseling services delivered by NFCC agencies" (p. 3).

BAPCPA is not likely to result in higher payments to credit cards issuers. Norberg (2007) reported that the median repayment to unsecured creditors prior to BAPCPA was $0. Of the 30% of debtors who promise to repay some unsecured debt in a chapter 13 plan, two-thirds to three-quarters of cases are dismissed (Evans, 2004; Norberg, 2007). Most chapter 7s (70% of all filings) are no asset cases with no repayment to unsecured creditors (Bermant and Flynn, 1999).

Nowhere in the reform debate was there acknowledgment that mental illness, low cognitive function, or addictions may play a role for some debtors. Perhaps these credit users will join the invisible, informal bankrupts who are too poor to file. Few observers believe that a 2- hour class will turn around the lives of many debtors.

Post BAPCPA, preliminary data suggest that about the same percentage of debtors qualify for chapter 7 as before the law went into effect; 94% of debtors earn less than their state's median income. Furthermore, only about 6/10 of 1% of filings are considered abusive (Truitt, 2007).

The consumer protection aspect of the bill came from the oft-cited claim that bankruptcy discharges cost each American family $400 in higher credit costs. If this were true, should not the cost of credit be lower now under BAPCPA? The regulations governing bankruptcy were changed by BAPCPA, but it is premature to draw conclusions regarding the impact of the legislation other than the fact that it has imposed considerable implementation costs, both time and money, on all parties involved (Thurston, 2007; Truitt, 2007).

Life After Bankruptcy

The Bankruptcy Code states that the purpose of bankruptcy is to provide debtors with a fresh start. Even after discharging their unsecured debts, most filers are barely making ends meet (Lown & Rowe, 2003; NFCC, 2006; Sullivan et al., 1989). "Most chapter 7 debtors have a substantial negative net worth at filing, but have a small positive net worth after discharge. Based on the information in their schedules, it appears that few affluent people file for chapter 7 bankruptcy, and few are made affluent by filing for bankruptcy" (Flynn and Bermant, 2001, p. 1).

Addressing the Bankruptcy Problem

The new law fails to address the underlying problems of abundant credit, weak usury laws, growing financial insecurity, reductions in health insurance and pensions, and creditors who have an incentive to troll the bottom for high risk–high profit borrowers. BAPCPA does not lock the courthouse doors but it raised the entry fee and level of punishment. While only the debtor files for bankruptcy, each case includes a cast of lenders who supplied the credit.

There has been no change in the underlying economic factors that contribute to consumer financial instability; in fact, the trend is strongly in the direction of the "you're on your own" economy with a fraying social safety net (Bernstein, 2006, p. 3). With adjustable mortgage rates adjusting upward, many homeowners who bought at the peak of the housing bubble in 2002 with non-traditional mortgages are facing foreclosure along with victims of predatory mortgage lending. Making it more costly to enter the bankruptcy system will only increase the total costs borne by debtors and society. The main factors that need to change in order to reduce the filing rate relate to credit supply and the underlying economy. Demos and The Center for Responsible Lending (2005) recommend policies to address the consumer debt crisis. On the demand side, increase savings and decrease debt, improve wages, provide universal medical insurance, and strengthen unemployment insurance. On the supply side, reform the credit card penalty pricing system of late payments and universal default, ban mandatory arbitration clauses, and require meaningful underwriting standards to ensure borrowers have the capacity to repay. Stronger regulation of predatory and subprime lending are needed to reign in the bankruptcy epidemic.

Sophisticated computer programs allow creditors to maximize profits by charging high rates to risky customers and to consumers who they think might become risky (Public Broadcasting System, 2004). With credit scoring models and credit reports, lenders control their rate of default (Mann, 2006). Lenders can turn off the credit spigot to borrowers at any time. The main reason for not tightening credit is that it would reduce profits. High delinquency rates mean more borrowers carrying balances at high interest rates. Lenders respond to these signs of borrower distress by raising interest rates and charging over-the-limit and late fees. Mann provides evidence that credit card charge-offs rose steadily over the past 10 years but, rather than cut back on lending, creditors opened the credit floodgates. Obviously borrowers, the target of a tighter bankruptcy law, are not the only parties with control over "social losses of financial distress" (Mann, 2006, p. 425).

Following the lead of Belgium, Mann (2006) advocates a lender tax on defaulted debt. While such a tax would likely reduce credit availability to marginal borrowers, and cause those on the way to bankruptcy to file earlier, filing sooner could reduce total losses and total costs. Mann also advocates analyzing and developing bankruptcy policy in relation to the much larger arena of the social safety net. Mann advocates reforms that would offer credit card companies incentives to limit lending to risky consumers.

While BAPCPA was financed by the credit card industry that spends millions on lobbying, it is unlikely to result in higher payments to credit card issuers because the repayment capacity simply does not exist. Over 90 % of chapter 7 filings are no asset cases with no repayment to creditors, and only one-third of chapter 13 debtors complete their repayment plan (Bermant, 2000). Forcing debtors into chapter 13 plans using the new means test will likely result in a further reduction in the completion rate.

Citing low financial literacy levels, Braucher (2006) argues for a comprehensive financial education program from kindergarten through high school to change the culture of low financial literacy as a prerequisite to reducing bankruptcy. The program could be modeled after homebuyer education programs and social marketing campaigns to change attitudes and behaviors related to smoking, racial tolerance, and safe sex. More alternatives to high cost emergency credit such as payday loans are needed as well (Braucher, 2006). As long as there are predatory lenders, there will be a need for the legal protection afforded by bankruptcy.

The Future of Bankruptcy

BACPCA places harsher burdens on debtors, shifting more of the cost of financial distress onto borrowers (Mann, 2006). The reforms are likely to encourage borrowers to delay filing, thus exacerbating the total financial cost to the debtor and to society. With no changes in the underlying causes, charging higher fees is unlikely to deter the crowds desperate for relief from overwhelming debts and relentless creditors. Locking the courthouse door will not result in higher debt repayment.

Based on the continued growth in mortgage and credit card debt, bankruptcy filings will soon reach pre-BAPCPA levels (National Association of Consumer Bankruptcy Attorneys, 2006; Tabb, 2007). Tabb concluded that "debtors file bankruptcy in very predictable numbers, depending not on what the bankruptcy law provides, but on how burdened they are with debt" (p. 104). BAPCPA is unlikely to reverse the upward trend in bankruptcy in light of growing economic insecurity and a meager social safety net. Tabb suggests that the only way to cut the filing rate is to reduce consumer debt levels, especially credit card and mortgage debt.

Research Needs

There are two general avenues for future research. One option is to replicate previous research using post-BAPCPA data to determine the impact of BAPCPA. Another avenue is to collect data from the bankruptcy files, both pre- and post-BAPCPA to determine what changes occur. There is a need to determine the pathways that lead to bankruptcy and how a filing might be averted. It would be valuable to compare similar debtors—those who filed for bankruptcy and those in similar trouble who managed to avoid filing. Which group of debtors is better off a few years later? Longitudinal research to follow debtors in the years after filing is needed. So far NFCC

(2006) data suggest that counseling does not deter filers. Does the new education mandate reduce repeat filings?

While chapters 7 and 13 debtors are assumed to represent personal bankruptcies, somewhere between 10 and 20% of these cases involved a small business. Sullivan et al. (1989) found that small business debtors owed far more than purely personal cases. Little research has been done to understand small business 7 and 13 cases. With more of U.S. job growth tied to small businesses, understanding the small business path to bankruptcy could provide useful information for entrepreneurs and educators. Do reasons for filing differ from one district to the next? Local legal practice influences the choice of chapter and thus the repeat filing rate. How quickly debtors are dismissed from chapter 13 for failure to make their monthly payment to the trustee varies among districts. An experimental design could be devised with some chapter 13 debtors receiving individual counseling to determine whether this improved completion (discharge) rates and whether the extra costs were justified.

Bankruptcy is supposed to provide a fresh start but most debtors are still in financial trouble even after discharge (Lown & Rowe, 2003). Would individual counseling and education help debtors improve their financial lives and avoid re-filing? What are the reasons behind serial filings? Is there a link between serial filings and mental health or addiction problems? Do financial institutions that provide counseling to customers with debt problems suffer fewer bankruptcies than similar financial institutions without counseling programs? What role can employers play in helping workers avoid bankruptcy? How important is financial literacy in deterring bankruptcy?

There is great interest in assessing the impact of financial counseling and education mandates of BAPCPA. Initial results from the NFCC suggest that virtually all their pre-filing counseling clients are drowning in debt and have no option other than bankruptcy. However, little is known about the long-term impact of the mandatory financial education class required of all debtors. Most of the education is being conducted by Internet or phone; is in-person education more effective? Does debtor education have any long-term impact? If unexpected trigger events are the main cause of bankruptcy (Getter, 2003), will debtor education help prevent repeat filings? The new law provides a wealth of research opportunities.

References

Administrative Office of the United States Courts. (2006, April). *Bankruptcy basics* (3rd ed.). Retrieved January 14, 2007, from http://www.uscourts.gov/bankruptcycourts/bankbasics04606.pdf.

Administrative Office of the United States Courts (n.d.). *Bankruptcy statistics.* Retrieved May 18, 2007, from http://www.uscourts.gov/bnkrpctystats/statistics.htm#calendar.

American Bankruptcy Institute. (2005). *Bankruptcy Abuse Prevention and Consumer Protection Act of 2005: 25 Changes to Personal Bankruptcy Law.* Retrieved January 17, 2007, from http://abiworld.net/bankbill/changes.html.

Athreya, K. (2004, Spring). Shame as it ever was: Stigma and personal bankruptcy. *Federal Reserve Bank of Richmond Economic Quarterly, 90*(2), 1–19.

Bermant, G., & Flynn, E. (1999, January). Incomes, debts, and repayment capacities of recently discharged chapter 7 debtors. *ABI Journal.* Retrieved January 15, 2007, from http://www.usdoj.gov/ust/eo/public_affairs/articles/docs/ch7trends-01.htm.

Bermant, G., & Flynn, E. (2000, July–August). Measuring performance in chapter 13: Comparisons across states. *ABI Journal, 19*(6). Retrieved January 15, 2007, from http://www.usdoj.gov/ust/eo/public_affairs/articles/docs/abi082000ch13.htm.

Bermant, G., & Flynn, E. (2001, September). Exploring the (complex) causes of bankruptcy. *ABI Journal, 21*(7). Retrieved January 15, 2007, from http://www.usdoj.gov/ust/eo/public_affairs/articles/docs/abi01sepnumbers.html.

Bernstein, J. 2006. *All together now: Common sense for a fair economy.* San Francisco: Berrett-Koehler.

Bird, E. J., Hagstrom, P. A., & Wild, R. (1999). Credit card debts of the poor: High and rising. *Journal of Policy Analysis and Management, 18*(1), 125–133.

Black, S. E., & Morgan, D. P. (1999, February). Meet the new borrowers. *Current Issues in Economics and Finance,* Federal Reserve Bank of New York.

Board of Governors of the Federal Reserve System. (2006, June). *Report to the Congress on Practices of the Consumer Credit Industry in Soliciting and Extending Credit and their Effects on Consumer Debt and Insolvency.* Washington, DC.

Braucher, J. (2006). Theories of overindebtedness: Interaction of structure and culture. *Theoretical Inquiries in Law, 7*(2), 321–346.

Demos & Center for Responsible Lending. (2005, October 12). *The plastic safety net: The reality behind debt in America.* New York: Author. Retrieved January 4, 2007, from http://www.demos.org/pubs/PSN_low.pdf.

Draut, T., & Silva, J. (2003, September). *Borrowing to make ends meet: The growth of credit card debt in the '90s.* New York: Demos. Retrieved January 4, 2007, from http://www.demos.org/pubs/borrowing_to_make_ends_meet.pdf.

Evans, D. A. (2004). *Predictors of 1997 Chapter 13 bankruptcy completion and dismissal rates in Utah.* Unpublished master's thesis, Utah State University, Logan.

Flynn, E., & Bermant, G. (2001, December–January). How fresh is the fresh start? *ABI Journal, 19*(10). Retrieved January 4, 2007, from http://www.usdoj.gov/ust/eo/ public_affairs/articles/docs/abi00decnumbers.html.

Getter, D. E. (2003). Contributing to the delinquency of borrowers. *Journal of Consumer Affairs, 37,* 86–100.

Himmelstein, D. U., Warren, E., Thorne, D., & Woolhandler, S. (2005). Illness and injury as contributors to bankruptcy. *Health Affairs, 24,* 63–73.

Llewellyn, B. (2005). *A profile and analysis of repeat bankruptcy petitioners in the district of Utah 1984–2004.* Unpublished master's thesis, Utah State University, Logan.

Lown, J. M. (2006). A question of abuse: Serial bankruptcy filers in Utah, 1984–2004. *American Bankruptcy Institute Journal, 25*(1), 24, 25, 68, 69.

Lown, J. M., & Rowe, B. R. (2003). A profile of Utah consumer bankruptcy petitioners. *Journal of Law and Family Studies, 5,* 113–130.

Mann, R. J. (2006). Optimizing consumer credit markets and bankruptcy policy. *Theoretical Inquiries in Law, 7*(2), 394–430.

National Association of Consumer Bankruptcy Attorneys. (2006). *Bankruptcy Law Anniversary Survey.* Retrieved January 15, 2007, from http://www.thehastingsgroup.com/ NACBASurvey/Summary.html#.

National Foundation for Credit Counseling. (2006, October 16). *Consumer counseling and education under BAPCPA: Year One.* Silver Spring, MD.

Norberg, S. F. (2007). Chapter 13 project: Little paid to unsecureds. *American Bankruptcy Institute Journal, 22*(2), 1, 54–56.

Porter, K., & Thorne, D. (2006). The failure of bankruptcy's fresh start. *Cornell Law Review, 92,* 67–128.

Public Broadcasting System. (2004). *Secret history of the credit card.* Retrieved January 17, 2007, from http://www.pbs.org/wgbh/pages/frontline/shows/credit/.

Stavins, J. (2000, July/August). Credit card borrowing, delinquency, and personal bankruptcy. Federal Reserve Bank of Boston. *New England Economic Review,* 15–30. Retrieved December 28, 2006, from http://www.bos.frb.org/economic/neer/neer2000/neer400b.pdf.

Sullivan, T. A., Warren, E., & Westbrook, J. L. (1989). *As we forgive our debtors: Bankruptcy and consumer credit in America.* New York: Oxford University Press.

Sullivan, T. A., Warren, E., & Westbrook, J. L. (2000). *The fragile middle class: Americans in debt.* New Haven, CT: Yale University Press.

Tabb, C. J. (2006). Consumer filings: Trends and indicators, Part I. *American Bankruptcy Institute Journal, 25*(9), 1, 58–61.

Tabb, C. J. (2007). Consumer filings: Trends and indicators, Part II. *American Bankruptcy Institute Journal, 25*(10), 42, 43, 100–105.

Thurston, S. M. (2007). Behind the numbers: The new workload of the U.S. bankruptcy courts. *American Bankruptcy Institute Journal, 26*(4), 42–43.

Truitt, J. D. (2007). The state of bankruptcy 18 months after BAPCPA. *American Bankruptcy Institute Journal, 25*(10), 52–53.

United Way of Salt Lake. (2006). *Living on the edge: Utahns' perspectives on bankruptcy and financial stability.* Retrieved January 17, 2007, from http://www.uw.org/Images/PDFs/UWBKReport.pdf.

U.S. Trustee Program. (2005, October). *Bankruptcy Information Sheet.* Retrieved May 18, 2007, from http://www.usdoj.gov/ust/eo/ust_org/bky-info/index.htm.

Weller, C. E., & Gino, A. (2005, February 18). *Rising personal bankruptcies: A sign of economic strains on American's middle class.* Washington, DC: Center for American Progress.

White, M. (1998). Why it pays to file for bankruptcy: A critical look at the incentives under U.S. personal bankruptcy law and a proposal for change. *University of Chicago Law Review, 4,* 685–732.

Zywicki, T. J. (2005). An economic analysis of the consumer bankruptcy crisis. *Northwestern University Law Review, 99, 4.* 1463–1542.

Chapter 23
Workplace Financial Education

Jinhee Kim

Abstract With the shift in retirement plans, workplace financial education has emerged as a key area of financial education. To date, more workers receive a variety of financial education program provided at workplaces than before. It has been assumed that workplace financial education influences participants' financial situation in a positive way. Although few conclusive studies about the effects of workplace financial education exist, a number of studies documented positive impacts of workplace financial education on financial knowledge, financial behaviors, retirement saving, and financial well-being. After existing literature is reviewed, conclusions and suggestions for future research are presented.

Workplace financial education has been a rising issue for the last two decades. Although workplace financial education—such as pre-retirement planning seminars—existed in the early 1980s, employers began to recognize the need to provide employer-sponsored education for employees as employee-directed retirement plans, such as 401(k)s, became more prevalent. There has been a remarkable shift away from traditional defined benefit plans and toward defined contribution plans. Currently, the participation rate for private industry workers in defined benefit plans is about 20 %, while participation in defined contribution plans is 43 % (Beckman, 2006). However, the composition was quite different in 1992–1993: 32 % of workers in private industry participated in a defined benefit plan and 35 % of workers participated in a defined contribution plan (Costo, 2006). This trend is expected to continue in the future and the era of the traditional defined benefit plan is largely behind us (Zelinsky, 2004).

With the shift of retirement plans, there is a growing concern about the adequacy of retirement saving. Researchers note that many Americans are not saving enough for their retirement (Lusardi, 2003; Lusardi & Mitchell, 2006) and/or investing properly (Lusardi, 2003). Financial literacy is associated with retirement planning (Lusardi, 2003, 2005; Lusardi, 2006) and further, planning has a positive

J. Kim
University of Maryland, 1204 Marie Mount Hall, College Park, MD 20742, USA
e-mail: jinkim@umd.edu

J.J. Xiao, (ed.), *Handbook of Consumer Finance Research,*
© Springer 2008

relationship with retirement savings (Lusardi, 2006). To help employees enhance their retirement security, some employers have provided financial education for employees to achieve their retirement savings goals. It is believed that workplace financial education could influence financial behaviors such as plan participation, contribution rate, and asset allocation, which are critical for employees' financial success.

Additionally, the Department of Labor issued guidelines under section 404(c) of the Employee Retirement Income Security Act (ERISA) of 1974. The guidelines encouraged plan providers to provide employees "sufficient information to make informed decisions with regard to investment alternatives under the plan" (Arnone, 2004). Under ERISA, an employer is a plan sponsor with fiduciary responsibility. It is assumed that the plan participant (employee) will make sound financial decisions when properly informed, educated, and given reasonable choices. Employers who recognize fiduciary liability issues imposed by ERISA and the Department of Labor have provided financial education and advice to their employees to help them make sound retirement decisions. Some employers offer investment advice while others are concerned about fiduciary liability associated with providing investment advice. The 2006 Pension Protection Act cleared up some fiduciary issues and allowed more employers to provide investment advice for employees. However, to date, employers that provide financial advice for their employees are the minority (Helman, Copeland, & Vanderhei, 2006).

Types of workplace financial education programs vary. Print materials, such as newsletters and retirement statements, are widespread. Some employers provide extensive year-around financial education programs that include personal counseling while others send only print materials to their employees. Generally, workplace financial education programs include retirement benefit statements, brochures, newsletters/magazines, seminars or workshops, workbooks or worksheets, face-to-face counseling, telephone counseling, web-based services, software programs, videos, and CD-ROMs (Kim, Kwon, & Anderson, 2005). Recently, some employers have started to provide employees with access to professional investment advice in-person or via the telephone or the Internet.

Although employer-provided financial education has become more prevalent, less than half of the employees in the United States benefit from such programs. It is estimated that only about 40 % of employees in the United States have received employer-provided financial education (Arnone, 2002). The 2006 Retirement Confidence Survey finds that 48 % of workers received employer-provided financial education and/or advice in the past 12 months and 27 % had access to professional financial advice offered by their employers (Helman et al., 2006). Another survey found that 22 % of employers report that they provide investment advice (Profit Sharing Council/401(k) Council of America, 2001).

The results of attending workshops on employees' financial behaviors vary. From the 2006 Retirement Confidence Survey, among the workers attending workshops, 3 in 10 reported modifying their retirement planning as a result of the material they received (29 %)—most frequently by saving more (48 % of those making modifications) or changing their investment mix (33 %). Among the 27 % of workers who had access to professional financial advice, 53 % received specific investment recommendations. However, 30 % never implement any of the recommendations, 57 % implement some, and 13 % implement all of the recommendations (Helman et al., 2006).

Although it has been assumed that workplace financial education influences financial behaviors in a positive way, research on the evaluation of such programs is not extensive. Arnone (2004) argues successful evaluation programs should define the objectives of programs and how to measure the goals. He continues that good evaluations should assess the changes in the actual impact of various educational programs over time, using both quantitative and qualitative measures. However, this level of evaluation has not been available. To date, most research has been limited to qualitative surveys with small samples or quantitative studies with cross-sectional data sets.

Effects of Workplace Financial Education

Researchers, financial professionals, policy makers, and employers have been interested in the effectiveness of workplace financial education. Many studies have used surveys to assess the effects of pre-retirement seminars on individuals' personal finances, such as financial knowledge, financial attitudes, financial behaviors, and financial satisfaction after the programs (Clark et al., 2003; Fletcher, Beebout, & Mendenhall, 1997; Garman, Kim, Kratzer, Brunson, & Joo, 1999; Hershey, Walsh, Brougham, Carter, & Farrell, 1998; Hira & Loibl, 2005; Kim, Bagwell, & Garman, 1998; Kim, Garman, & Quach, 2005; Taylor-Carter, Cook, & Weinberg, 1997).

A few studies have considered the impact of financial education offered at the workplace on retirement attitude and retirement preparedness (Hershey et al., 1998; Kim, Kwon, & Anderson, 2005; Taylor-Carter et al., 1997). Financial knowledge has a positive influence on retirement preparedness, and those who perceive that they know more about financial planning are more likely to be prepared for retirement financially (Hershey & Mowen, 2000). Additionally, those who attended financial planning seminars showed a more positive retirement attitude and financial expectations of retirement (Kim, Kwon, & Anderson, 2005; Joo & Pauwels, 2002; Taylor-Carter et al., 1997). Researchers suggest that pre-retirement training on financial planning could improve financial preparedness by triggering advanced financial activities (Hershey & Mowen, 2000; Kim, Garman, & Quach, 2005). Furthermore, these programs could stimulate individuals' savings activities and decision-making competencies (Bernheim & Garrett, 2003; Taylor-Carter et al., 1997).

Although these studies found positive relationships between financial planning seminars and retirement preparedness and retirement confidence, it is not clear how workplace financial education impacts individuals' activities. That said, it is assumed that financial planning seminars improve financial knowledge of participants. With increased financial knowledge, individuals become involved in more financial activities and in turn, become more financially prepared for retirement. However, studies have not specified how changes in financial knowledge and behaviors take place after the workplace financial education programs overtime. It is possible that behavioral changes take place in different time frame. It takes longer for some activities to take place than others. However, many studies assumed increased knowledge as a result of education program and have focused on changes in certain retirement planning behaviors of interest without this consideration. Employers are mostly concerned about employees' retirement behaviors such as participation and contribution rates, loans, and investment allocation and distribution (Arnone, 2004). In the past, plan providers often focused employee education on awareness of retirement plans and plan participation rates. Although participation rates alone do not reflect individuals' status of retirement planning, studies tend to focus on the participation rates. However, low rates of contribution, inappropriate asset allocation, high levels of loans from pension accounts, and lump sum distributions upon termination have become issues for many American workers.

Participation rates in employee-sponsored pension plans vary by types and sizes of industries. For defined contribution in 2006, the average participation rate for all workers, based on an estimate of the percentage of workers with access to a plan who participate in the plan, was 79 % (Beckmann, 2006). A number of studies found a significant relationship between workplace financial education and participation and contribution rates (Bernheim, 1998; Clark et al., 2003; Clark & Schieber, 1998). As individuals' financial knowledge is found to improve, retirement participation and planning horizons could be improved by the offering of information about the importance of planning for retirement (Bernheim, 1998) and planning horizons (Munnell, Sundén, & Taylor, 2001/2002).

Although participation rate and retirement account balance are important indicators of retirement behavior, there are a couple of other critical practices concerning retirement plan contributions, such as distributions after termination. Retirement plan distribution after termination creates a concern for employers (Arnone, 2004). There is an increasing trend of providing lump sum distributions of retirement plans as more workers have defined contribution plans and change their jobs more frequently than before. When workers leave their jobs, many workers cash out their funds to pay down debt or to use for living expenses, which often leads to a negative impact on retirement preparation. Although there is very limited research on workplace financial education and lump sum distribution, Muller (2001/2002) examined the relationship between workplace retirement education and the saving of lump sum distributions via the 1992 Health and Retirement Study. Retirement education itself did not increase the overall likelihood for savings of lump sum distributions. However, attending retirement meetings was associated with an increased likelihood of savings of lump sum distributions among persons aged 40 and under and a decreased probability of savings of lump sum distributions among college graduates and women. Still, these findings are not conclusive and call for additional research on this issue.

Often, studies that are conducted after the provision of workplace financial education seminars typically measure intention to change behaviors, rather than actual behavioral changes. With pre- and post-seminar surveys, Clark, d'Ambrosio, McDermed, and Sawant (2003) found that individuals reported that they are likely to change their retirement goals, which in most cases means increasing the expected age of retirement. They also found that women seem more responsive to financial education programs than men. For example, women were more likely to respond that they would increase their retirement saving and alter their investment choices in both basic and supplemental pension plans. Intention to change financial behavior is an indication of the effectiveness of workplace financial education programs despite the fact that not all intentions take place later.

Most studies used similar financial behaviors such as participation and contribution rates to measure impacts regardless of content, length, frequency, and intensity of workplace financial education programs. Yet, some studies compared different workplace financial education programs. Generally, findings from cross-sectional data reveal that workplace financial education programs take on many forms and improve retirement participation and savings rates. With data from 40,000 employees from 19 firms, Clark and Schieber (1998) found that enhancing the levels of plan communications improved participation rates. For example, general newsletters along with forms and statements increased the participation rate by 15 % while customized materials boosted the rate by 21 % compared to only providing forms and plan statements. In addition, frequency of education seems to affect plan participation as well. High-frequency education efforts improved participation rates more than low-frequency education programs (Bernheim, 1998).

Researchers also used the availability of workplace financial education programs instead of the actual attendance of such programs in studies. With panel data from an employer, Bayer, Bernheim, and Scholz (1996) found that workers who had access to workplace financial education programs showed higher participation and contribution rates for their retirement plan than others who did not have access to such programs. With a national household survey, Bernheim and Garrett (2003) examined workplace financial education and asset accumulation, including retirement participation, retirement saving, and total asset saving. In this study, instead of the attendance of workplace financial education seminars, the availability of workplace financial education was used to determine the impact on employees. Those with access to workplace financial education had higher 401(k) participation rates for themselves and their spouses. Workers at the 25th and 50th percentiles with workplace financial education offerings had higher retirement savings and general savings compared to those who did not have access to workplace financial education. Bernheim and Garrett's research focused on the impact of workplace financial education on not only retirement participation but general asset allocation. However, having an access to workplace financial education is not the same as attending workshops. Without a baseline study, the direct impact of workplace financial education on individuals cannot be assumed. Further, employees who work for employers offering workplace financial education might have different financial situations at the outset, compared to employees without access to workplace financial education.

A number of studies were conducted on financial literacy, planning, and savings of older Americans using the Health and Retirement Survey (Lusardi, 2003, 2004, 2005; Lusardi, 2006). Findings support relationships between financial literacy and wealth. Individual's financial literacy is strongly correlated to planning

(Lusardi, 2006). Also, retirement planning is associated with the size of wealth and investment portfolio (Lusardi, 2003; Lusardi, 2006). Notably, it was found that wealth is especially low for Blacks, Hispanics, and individuals with low education who exhibit high levels of financial illiteracy and lack of planning (Lusardi, 2005; Lusardi, 2006). As financial illiteracy is related to lack of planning and relationship between planning and wealth accumulation and investment remains strong, workplace financial education could improve financial literacy, planning, and ultimately wealth building. Workplace financial education seems to be especially important for those who have low financial literacy and low levels of wealth accumulation. Lusardi (2004) found that retirement seminars explain the variance in financial net worth and total net worth, especially for the least wealthy. This study does not prove the causal relationship between workplace financial education and wealth accumulation. However, it suggests that workplace financial education is associated with wealth and it could be an effective remedy especially for those with low levels of wealth.

As some researchers suggested that workplace financial education can enhance financial literacy and planning of individuals (Lusardi, 2004, Lusardi, 2006), a number of studies examined the effects of workplace financial education on general financial planning beyond retirement behaviors after the seminars were delivered (Clark et al., 2003; Garman et al., 1999; Hira & Loibl, 2005; Kim, 2007; Kim & Garman, 2003; Kim, Garman, et al., 2005; Loibl & Hira, 2005). Researchers (Garman et al., 1999; Kim & Garman, 2003) argue that workplace financial education should be comprehensive not limited to retirement plan or investment as many workers are struggling with budgeting and debt management. Such basic money management practices are prerequisite to retirement saving and wealth building. Findings of these studies revealed positive impacts of workplace financial education on financial knowledge and general financial behaviors.

Evidence shows that subjective rating of financial knowledge increases as a result of workplace financial education. Using a randomly selected national sample of employees from an insurance company, Hira and Loibl (2005) found that workers who participated in workplace financial education in the past 6 months had a better understanding of personal finances than others, leading to more positive expectations of their future financial situation and improved workplace satisfaction. With small samples, Kim and Garman (2003) and Kim (2007) found that self-reported financial knowledge has increased 3 months after the seminars. However, these studies did not test actual knowledge questions, rather they asked self-rating of financial knowledge.

Often, increased financial knowledge stimulates significant changes in general financial management practices beyond retirement planning. Loibl and Hira (2005) found that self-directed financial learning provided by employers facilitated positive financial management practices, such as making spending plans, saving for goals, evaluating spending, meeting large expenses, controlling finances, and estate planning. With data from chemical production company workers, Garman et al. (1999) found that workplace financial education improved personal financial behaviors of participants. With a post-workshop survey, Kim and Garman (2003) examined the impact of financial education and advice on workers' behaviors and found that a substantial number of employees reported increasing the amount of contributions to their employer's 401(k) plans, as well as increasing the amount of savings outside their 401(k) plans, due to the receipt of financial education in the workplace. In addition, workers had developed a plan for their financial future, developed a budget or spending plan, reduced some personal debts, and paid their credit card bills on time. With a pre-and post-survey design, Kim (2007) found participants improved their financial management, such as setting financial goals, evaluating risk management, following and reviewing a budget, and developing a financial plan, 3 months after they attended a series of workplace financial education workshops. That said, participants made only marginal improvements in general saving and no significant changes in saving for retirement. Another study shows more mixed results on behavioral changes. Clark et al. (2003) found a substantial disconnect between intention to change saving behavior at the end of the seminar and actual actions 3 months after the seminar. Participants noted an intention to change their behaviors but they do not always follow through this intention.

A couple of limitations are noted in these previous studies and suggestions for future studies can be made. First, most of the data in these studies came from employees' self-reported surveys. Some of the behavioral changes might be perceptive rather than actual. Retirement plan participation and contribution data from employers combined with self-reported data would be very helpful in determining if this is the case. Second, these studies did not employ an experimental design with random assignment and a control group. Without a control group, selection bias is a concern. Further, it is possible that employees in better financial situations and with better financial literacy seek out additional information about personal finances more frequently than those in poorer financial situations, Third, there are few studies with follow-up such as 1, 2, or 5 years after the receipt of education, to capture changes in financial management that may not take place within a couple of months, and to track whether participants sustain their changes in financial management. Further, the long-term effects of workplace financial education on employees' financial well-being such as financial security during retirement have not been documented due to the short history of the program. Research with longitudinal database could be helpful to understand these behavioral changes and long-term impacts. Fourth, many of the studies used small samples of white-collar workers and had different outcomes. As such, the results are not representative of other industries or workplaces. Workers from a variety of workplaces should be considered in future studies. Research should examine broader populations in order to expand current findings. Fifth, little is known about differences in effectiveness of workplace financial education programs. Although studies supported positive impacts of workplace financial education on financial behaviors, some studies found participants did not take actions as they intended as results of education. Further, many studies use similar questions to measure impacts although workplace financial education programs vary in content, time, and delivery. A one-time retirement seminar may not make a difference in wealth accumulation while it may increase the awareness of retirement planning for some participants. Impact of workplace financial education should be measured against the objectives of programs with appropriate methods.

Additional Benefits

A number of researchers assert that employee education programs are a win–win proposition. Workplace financial education could benefit employers as well as employees (Bernanke, 2006). Researchers have linked workers' personal finance and their work outcomes such as productivity and absenteeism (Garman et al., 1999; Hira & Loibl, 2005; Kim, 2000; Kim & Garman, 2003, 2004). Financial stress negatively impacts employees' absenteeism, pay satisfaction, organizational commitment, job performance rating, and productivity. Workplace financial education could improve the financial well-being of individuals and families by increasing financial literacy, financial management, and savings (Bernheim & Garrett, 2003; Hira & Loibl, 2005; Kim, 2007; Lusardi, 2004). Therefore, workplace financial education could increase employers' profitability by increasing productivity and reducing absenteeism of workers who take leave to deal with personal financial matters. Additionally, it could decrease overall absences from work due to financial troubles (Kim, 2000; Kim & Garman, 2003).

Based on previous literature about the relationship between personal finance and worker productivity, Kim (2000) developed an experimental model that depicts relationships among workplace financial education, financial well-being, and worker outcomes, and found that employees' financial well-being impacted personal finance conflicts at work, productivity, absenteeism, negative work time use, organizational commitment, and pay satisfaction. Additional studies have linked absenteeism and personal finance as well (Bagwell, 2001; Hendrix, Steel, & Shultz, 1987; Jackson, Iezzi, & Lafreniere, 1997; Joo, 1998). Workers with high levels of financial stress are more likely to experience higher levels of absenteeism, thus spending work hours handling personal finances, which decreases the time they are at work (Kim & Garman, 2003, 2004).

Using Kim's model, other studies found supportive evidence of the positive effects of personal finance on satisfaction at work (Hira & Loibl, 2005; Loibl & Hira, 2005). Self-directed financial learning stimulates good financial management practices, financial satisfaction, and career satisfaction (Loibl & Hira, 2005). Hira and Loibl (2005) found that attending workplace financial education seminars stimulated financial literacy, increased expectations for a better future financial situation, and resulted in greater financial satisfaction with their work. Moreover, it was found that workers' pay satisfaction is determined not only by actual salary but also by workers' characteristics such as the level of stress with their personal finances (Kim & Garman, 2004).

Researchers added that financial stress is associated with negative health consequences, in turn, affecting job performance. Often, stress-related depression impacts employers due to increased absenteeism and the presence of employers who may be at work but are mentally distracted (Weissman, 2002). Researchers have found that financial stress negatively impacts individual's health (Drentea, 2000; Drentea & Lavrakas, 2000; O'Neill, Sorhaindo, Xiao, & Garman, 2005; Weissman, 2002). Personal financial stress could have an impact on mental health in terms of increased anxiety, somatic problems (O'Neill et al., 2005; O'Neill, Prawitz, Sorhaindo, Kim, & Garman, 2006), and depression. Other studies have found that financial stress, such as consumer debt, was associated with negative physical health and health status (Drentea & Lavrakas, 2000). These studies suggest that stress-related symptoms and health outcomes could undermine employers' bottom lines by reducing productivity and increasing absenteeism at work. Therefore, workplace financial education could help employers as well as employees by decreasing employees' financial stress and employer's profitability. Further, such findings encourage more employers to provide financial education for their employees.

Conclusions and Recommendations for Future Research

The provision of workplace financial education has become a major trend in the United States. Although less than half of the workers benefit from such programs, a variety of programs including print materials, workshops, Internet, and personal counseling are being provided to employees at their workplace. While there is a growing national concern about retirement income security, workplace financial education, which is an effective tool to improve financial literacy, financial behavior, retirement savings, and financial well-being of employees, should be offered to more workers. Additional financial education would be especially beneficial for minorities, women, less-educated workers who often have high financial illiteracy, lack of planning, and low levels of savings. Moreover, these groups often do not have access to financial education at work. Researchers, practitioners, and policy makers should focus on the design and dissemination of critical financial information that could be delivered to more workers through the workplace. Also, such programs should be comprehensive, not limited to retirement planning or investment as many workers are in need of basic money management before they can benefit from retirement and investment.

The impact of workplace financial education has been documented in a number of ways, such as pre- and post-design studies, a cross-sectional national data set, and convenience sampled small data. Studies support the benefits of workplace financial education. Their findings suggest that workplace financial education improves financial literacy, increases confidence in financial management, increases retirement savings and general savings, and improves the overall financial well-being of recipient with some mixed findings on financial behavioral changes. However, few conclusive studies about the effectiveness of workplace financial education exist. Little is known about long-term effects of workplace financial education on participants' financial well-being such as wealth. Comprehensive research to assess the effectiveness of workplace education programs is needed in the future. Ideally, research would start with programs with measurable goals and objectives. Additionally, an experimental design including random assignment and a control group is recommended. Also, evaluations should assess changes in financial knowledge, behaviors, wealth, financial well-being, and possibly work outcomes as the result of various programs over time, using both quantitative and qualitative methods with longitudinal databases from employees' survey as well as employers'. Finally, a more diverse array of workforce populations should be included in the research.

References

Arnone, W. (2002). Financial planning for employees post-Enron. *Benefits Quarterly, 18*(4) 35–41.

Arnone, W. (2004). *Educating pension plan participants.* Pension Research Council Working Paper. PRC WP 2004-7. Retrieved December 20, 2006, from http://prc.wharton.upenn.edu/prc/prc.html.

Bagwell, D.C. (2001). Hierarchical regression analysis of work outcomes with personal and financial factors. *Writings of the Western Region Home Management Family Economics Educators,* 45–54.

Bayer, P. J., Bernheim, B.D., & Scholz, J. K. (1996). *The effects of financial education in the workplace: Evidence from a survey of employers* (Stanford Economics Working Paper # 96-007). Stanford, CA: Stanford University.

Beckmann, A. (2006). *Access, participation, and take-up rates in defined contribution retirement plans among workers in private industry.* Bureau of Labor Statistics. Retrieved January 18, 2007, from http://www.bls.gov/opub/cwc/print/cm20061213ar01p1.htm.

Bernanke, B. S. (2006). *Financial literacy.* Federal Reserve Board. Retrieved December 28, 2006, from http://www.federalreserve.gov/boarddocs/testimony/2006/20060523/default.htm.

Bernheim, B. D. (1998). Financial illiteracy, education, and retirement saving. In O. S. Mitchell and S. J. Schieber (Eds.). *Living with defined contributions* (pp. 38–68). Philadelphia, PA: Pension Research Council and the University of Pennsylvania Press.

Bernheim, B. D., & Garrett, D. M. (2003). The effects of financial education in the workplace evidence from a survey of households. *Journal of Public Economics, 87,* 1487–1519.

Clark, R. L., & d'Ambrosio, M.B. (2003). Ignorance is not bliss: The importance of financial education. *TIAA-CREF Research Dialogue, 78,* 1–14.

Clark, R. L., d'Ambrosio, M. B., McDermed, A. A., & Sawant, K. (2003). *Sex differences, financial education, and retirement goals.* Pension Research Council Working Paper. Retrieved December 20, 2006, from http://prc.wharton.upenn.edu/prc/prc.html.

Clark, R. L., & Schieber, S. (1998). Factors affecting participation rates and contribution levels in 401(k) plans. In O. Mitchell & S. Schieber (Eds.), *Living with defined contribution plans* (pp. 69–97). Philadelphia, PA: University of Pennsylvania Press.

Costo, S. L. (2006, February). Trends in retirement plan coverage over the last decade. *Monthly Labor Review, 58–64. Retrieved December 20, 2006, from http://www.bls.gov/opub/mlr/2006/02/art5exc.htm.

Drentea, P. (2000). Age, debt and anxiety. *Journal of Health and Social Behavior, 41,* 437–450.

Drentea, P., & Lavrakas, P. J. (2000). Over the limit: The association among health status, race and debt. *Social Science & Medicine, 50,* 517–529.

Fletcher, C. N., Beebout, G., & Mendenhall, S. (1997). Developing and evaluating personal finance education at the worksites. In E. T. Garman, J. E. Grable, & S. Joo (Eds.), *Proceedings of the Personal Finance Employee Education Best Practices and Collaborations Conference Vol. 1*(1), *Personal finances and worker productivity* (pp. 54–59). VirginiaTech Roanoke, VA.

Garman, E.T., Kim, J., Kratzer, C. Y., Brunson, B.H., & Joo, S. (1999). Workplace financial education improves personal financial wellness. *Financial Counseling and Planning, 10,* 79–88.

Helman, R., Copeland, C., & Vanderhei, J. (2006). *Will more of us be working forever? The 2006 Retirement Confidence Survey* (EBRI Issue Brief, No. 292). Washington DC: Employee Benefit Research Institute.

Hendrix, W. J., Steel, R. P., & Shultz, S. A. (1987). Job stress and life stress: Their causes and consequences. *Journal of Social Behavior and Personality, 2*(3), 291–302.

Hershey, D. A., & Mowen, J. C. (2000). Psychological determinants of financial preparedness for retirement. *The Gerontologist, 40*, 687–797.

Hershey, D. A., Walsh, D. A., Brougham, R., Carter, S., & Farrell, A. (1998). Challenges of training pre-retirees to make sound financial planning decisions. *Educational Gerontology, 24*, 447–470.

Hira, T. K., & Loibl, C. (2005). Understanding the impact of employer-provided financial education on workplace satisfaction. *Journal of Consumer Affairs, 39*, 173–194.

Jackson, T., Iezzi, A., & Lafreniere, K. (1997). The impact of psychosocial features of employment status on emotional distress in chronic pain and healthy comparison samples. *Journal of Behavioral Medicine, 20*(3), 241–256.

Joo, S. (1998). *Personal financial wellness and worker job productivity.* Unpublished doctoral dissertation, Virginia Polytechnic Institute and State University, Blacksburg, VA.

Joo, S., & Pauwels, V. W. (2002). Factors affecting workers' retirement confidence: A gender perspective. *Financial Counseling and Planning, 13*, 1–10.

Kim, J. (2000). *The effects of workplace financial education on personal finances and worker outcomes.* Unpublished doctoral dissertation, Virginia Polytechnic Institute and State University, Blacksburg, VA.

Kim, J. (2007). Workplace financial education program: Does it have an impact on employees' personal finances? *Journal of Family and Consumer Science, 99*(1), 43–47.

Kim, J., Bagwell, D. C., & Garman, E. T. (1998). Evaluation of workplace financial education. *Personal Finances and Worker Productivity, 2*, 187–192.

Kim, J., & Garman, E. T. (2003). Financial education and advice change worker attitudes and behaviors. *Journal of Compensation and Benefits, 19*, 7–13.

Kim, J., & Garman, E. T. (2004). Financial stress, pay satisfaction, and workplace performance. *Compensations and Benefits Review, 36*(1), 69–76.

Kim, J., Garman, E. T., & Quach, A. (2005). Workplace financial education participation and retirement savings by employees and their spouses. *Journal of Personal Finance, 4*, 92–108.

Kim, J., Kwon, J., & Anderson, E. (2005). Factors related to retirement confidence: Retirement preparation and workplace financial education. *Financial Counseling and Planning, 12*, 77–89.

Loibl, C., & Hira, T. K. (2005). Self-directed financial learning and financial satisfaction. *Financial Counseling and Planning, 16*(1), 11–21.

Lusardi, A. (2003). *Planning and saving for retirement.* Working Paper, Darthmouth College. Retrieved on May 1, 2007, from http://www.dartmouth.edu/~alusardi/Papers/Lusardi_pdf.pdf.

Lusardi, A. (2004). Saving and the effectiveness of financial education. In O. S. Mitchell & S. P. Utkus (Eds.), *Pension design and structure: New lessons from behavioral finance* (pp. 258–184). Oxford: Oxford University Press.

Lusardi, A. (2005). *Financial education and the saving behavior of African-American and Hispanic households.* Working Paper, Darthmouth College. Retrieved on May 1, 2007, from http://www.dartmouth.edu/~alusardi/Papers/Education_African&Hispanic.pdf.

Lusardi, A., & Mitchell, O. S. (2006). *Financial literacy and planning: Implications for retirement well-being.* Working Paper, Pension Research Council. Retrieved on May 1, 2007, from http://prc.wharton.upenn.edu/prc/prc.html.

Muller, L. A. (2001/2002). Does retirement education teach people to save pension distributions? *Social Security Bulletin, 64*, 48–64.

Munnell, A. H., Sundén, A., & Taylor (2001/2002). What determines 401K participation and contributions? *Social Security Bulletin, 64*(3), 64–75.

O'Neill, B., Prawitz, A. D., Sorhaindo, B., Kim, J., & Garman, E. T. (2006). Financial and health status of financially distressed consumers: A follow-up study. *Journal of Financial Counseling and Planning, 17*(2), 46–63.

O'Neill, B., Sorhaindo, B., Xiao, J. J., & Garman, E. T. (2005). Financially distressed consumers: Their financial practices, financial well-being, and health. *Financial Counseling and Planning, 16*(1), 73–87.

Profit Sharing/401(k) Council of America. (2001). *Investment advice survey 2001*. Retrieved January 8, 2007, from http://www.psca.org/data/advice2001.html.

Taylor-Carter, M.A., Cook, K., & Weinberg, C. (1997). Planning and expectations of the retirement experience. *Educational Gerontology, 13*, 143–156.

Weissman, R. (2002). Personal financial stress, depression, and workplace performance. In E. T. Garman, F. Williams, R. Weisman, H. Fried, W. A. Kelly, & W. W. Sayles (Eds.), *Financial stress and workplace performance: Developing employer-credit union partnerships* (pp. 51–65). Madison, WI: Center for Credit Union Innovation and Filene Research Institute.

Zelinsky, E. A. (2004). The defined contribution paradigm. *Yale Law Journal, 114*(3), 451–534.

Chapter 24
Regulating Consumer Lending

David A. Lander

Abstract In order to promulgate effective consumer credit regulation, policy makers must understand the supply and demand for consumer credit as well as the economic and sociological benefits and detriments. After an explanation of each of these factors, the article proposes legislation and regulation that will reduce the damage but allow nonsuspect transactions to continue to occur.

In 1978, the interest rate limitations that had applied to most consumer loans in the United States were dismantled. In 2003, economists at the Federal Deposit Insurance Corporation (hereinafter FDIC) declared a Consumer Lending Revolution (Burhouse, 2003), and in 2006, they declared a Consumer Mortgage Lending Revolution. The watchdog of the safety and soundness of the banking system proclaimed these "revolutions" in order to attract public attention because of their concern that the unparalleled explosion in the amount of consumer credit and the significant change in the terms on which that credit is extended had unleashed far reaching and potentially dangerous macroeconomic impacts. It is interesting to note that the bank regulators in South Korea had been blamed for the credit card debacle which had recently left South Korean households crippled with debt and its lenders mired in bad loans. Civic groups have blamed the regulators and the government for encouraging the use of credit cards to prop up economic growth in the wake of the 1997 financial crisis (Song, 2004).

There is dispute regarding the behavioral underpinnings of these revolutions. Have the increased costs of survival forced consumers to use increased access to credit to plug the holes in their safety net (Warren & Tyagi, 2003)? Or, are consumers choosing to purchase luxuries they cannot afford and ought not to buy (Schor, 1998)? Or, are they hyperbolic discounters who make a good faith decision to save tomorrow rather than today (Angeletos, Laibson, Repetto, Tobacman, & Weigberg, 2001)? Regardless, there is no dispute about increased pressure/desire to borrow, the qualitative increase in the amount borrowed (particularly the amount

D.A. Lander
St. Louis University School of Law School, 3700 Lindell Blvd., St. Louis, Missouri 63108, USA
e-mail: cdlander@charter.net

borrowed by those with the best chance of default), and the higher debt burdens being carried on the shoulders of low and moderate income Americans. If these liquidity constrained Americans happen to be homeowners, they have flocked to refinancers and home equity lenders to suck the equity out of their homes, often on terms that are likely to stab them in their backs (Hurst & Stafford, 2004). As consumers hit the credit card debt saturation point, their level of spending beyond their income has been sustained and increased through a series of specialty home mortgage products that sound like the furniture financing advertisements of another era. "No payments for six months, no interest payments (ever) (for two years)" or "two percent (or 0 %) interest for the first two years."

In the United States, we live in a different economy and society from those that existed 30 years ago. Growth in consumer credit in the United States has been staggering and changes in the nature of the borrowing vehicles has been striking. This explosive growth in consumer credit has had massive economic and sociological consequences on individual households, on the health of financial institutions, on the returns on investment capital, and on the American economy and society. These consequences are both micro and macro and range from extraordinarily positive to inordinately negative. They are both the cause and the result of structural change in our economic and social systems.

The elimination of price controls (a) created a profit opportunity for lenders and investors; (b) opened the door to allow millions of high-credit-risk Americans to become purchasers of credit; (c) allowed medium-risk Americans to borrow to the point that they become high-risk Americans; and (d) allowed Americans to purchase houses they thought were beyond their reach.

As more American consumers became homeowners and as the paper value of their homes increased, that paper equity became a port of entry into the world of home-equity extraction lending. All of this worked because lenders had been able to develop sophisticated methods of pricing credit and then selling that credit at a price that is profitable. This profit potential attracted the attention of the investment community that developed innovative methods of providing the capital to satisfy the advertising enhanced demands of borrowers. The pressure on the "sellers" of this credit accelerated to a frenzy. In this atmosphere, lenders are so anxious to lend to consumers that the pressure sometimes leads to dastardly results. In one early example that was a precursor of the subprime mortgage crisis, Green Tree Acceptance Corporation used an innovative accounting method to record the profit on the financing of a manufactured home at the time the loan was made. They made so many loans that additional manufacturing capacity had to be added, and they made those loans to so many people who clearly could not repay them that there were thousands of repossessions or foreclosures and an exceedingly high default rate. Some of the results: By the time all of this surfaced Green Tree had sold itself to Conseco which thereafter had to file a Chapter 11 bankruptcy; thousands of manufactured-home purchasers who had initially been surprised that they were granted credit to purchase these homes were surprised again as those same homes were repossessed or foreclosed when they were unable to service those loans; finally, there was such a glut of used repossessed manufactured homes that not only were the new manufacturing plants closed but some of the old ones had to close as well and lay off their employees. A spirited debate continues between those who favor usury or other antipredatory lending laws and those who oppose them. No one, however, disputes that the elimination of those price controls changed the nature of consumer lending and consumer borrowing by providing an extraordinary profit opportunity to financial institutions, as well as the investing public and also provides enhanced purchasing power to borrowers. Indeed, the declarations of the revolutions by the FDIC economists indicate that the regulators are wondering what all of this means for the banking system and its safekeeping. Stated another way, the United States economy is supported by a system of consumer lending that intentionally puts credit in the hands of large numbers of people who are certain to default, and many of the defaulted loans include the consumers' homes as collateral. That is a significant change from the system as it functioned 30 years ago. Is there a tipping point with regard to the number of defaults, bankruptcies, and foreclosures? Even in the light of the subprime mortgage crisis of 2007, although the mainstream business press and mainstream economists acknowledge the likelihood of increasing defaults, they assert we are well within the margin of safety. Others are less sanguine.

It is past time to reconsider the regulation of consumer protection in a world that has experienced the consumer lending revolution and the mortgage lending revolution. Although some state legislatures have worked to develop an appropriate statutory regime to deal with this new reality, most states, Congress, and the regulators have failed to respond to this crisis in a meaningful and effective manner.

The crucial question for those who set consumer regulatory policy is, if there is no limit on the cost of credit, if it is profitable to lend in ways that assure high rates of default, and if the societal message is to "borrow to meet your needs/wants," then what regulations, if any, should be imposed. For example, what information and education should be required and when should the credit user be required to listen and learn (the "financial literacy and disclosure rules"); should new limits be placed on the cost of borrowing (the "usury rules"); what specific practices and provisions should be outlawed or further restricted (the "predatory lending rules"), what non-bankruptcy limits should be put on enforcing consumer lending (the "enforcement restrictions"); and finally, where shall we set the barrier for a consumer bankruptcy discharge and what shall we extract from the consumer bankruptcy debtor for that discharge (the "discharge policy")? Policy makers must understand and consider the micro and macro economic and sociological benefits and detriments of the consumer lending explosion and then determine how to fashion rules and regulations in a manner that encourages the positive and discourages the negative economic and sociological effects of that credit.

Growth of Consumer Credit

The three primary stories of the growth of consumer debt in the 30 years since the dismantling of usury limits are the growth of third-party credit card debt, the emergence and ensuing explosion of subprime debt, some portion of which is referred to as predatory lending, and the huge growth in home mortgage debt, both purchase-money and nonpurchase-money, prime and subprime.

Credit Card Debt

Charge cards came into use around 1914 when Western Union and various department stores, hotels, and oil companies implemented their use. Credit cards evolved from charge cards when banks entered the industry as issuers in the late 1950s, issuing general purpose credit cards that allowed balances to be carried from month to month (Ellis, 1998; Mandell, 1990).

The growth of the industry was slowed for more than a decade because most merchants accepted only cards issued by local banks. The modern day credit card industry emerged in 1966 when Bank of America began licensing the BankAmericard credit card logo to other banks, and a national system to process credit card transactions began to develop. These participating banks later formed the entity known today as Visa. Another group of banks formed the MasterCard association in 1966 (Ellis, 1998). The mass mailings of cards and card applications led to a debacle or two, but the credit card lenders looked to have enough of a future that most banks stayed with it (Ellis, 1998; Manning, 2000).

The Visa and MasterCard associations developed the infrastructure for a nationwide credit card payment system and convinced merchants nationwide to accept their cards. However, state usury laws constituted practical prohibitions on the extension of credit to many higher risk borrowers (Ellis, 1998). Lenders were bound to the individual state limitations because of the way the federal banking law was interpreted at that time. Federal law subjects national banks to the rate ceiling imposed by the states. This law was originally interpreted as requiring the lender to charge no more than the limit prescribed by the state where the borrower resided (Ellis, 1998).

Partly in response to a U.S. Supreme Court case and the high inflation of the late 1970s, the legislative atmosphere at both the state and federal levels changed dramatically about the same time that President Carter was signing the Bankruptcy Reform Act into law, and in the span of the next decade, usury restrictions were rolled back and practically eliminated. As a result, it became profitable to lend to higher risk consumers (Ellis, 1998).

For many years, the credit card business was spread across a large number of local and regional competitors, but as volume exploded, costs of technology increased and costs of obtaining and keeping customers skyrocketed, consolidation and oligopolization occurred. From a market that had been richly diversified, by 2003 the top five credit card lenders had 50 % of a much larger market and the top 10 held over 83 % of that market.

This consolidation was both a cause and an effect of the enormous improvement in the sophistication of credit scoring techniques, which led to more profitable lending even to higher risk consumers. Lending to higher risk borrowers of course led to an increase in defaults, and higher costs and fees, and interest rates for the late-paying customer have grown in importance. For the lender, the most profitable customer is the one who pays but pays slowly (Pacelle, 2004). As consumer lending became more profitable during the 1990s, additional capital was increasingly drawn to the industry, and a secondary market began to function efficiently. As a result, there was an explosion in the dollars available to lend. Finally, the credit card behemoths were able to withstand the very high cost of sales through mass mailings to attract customers.

During the latter half of the 1990s, as the supply of credit card lending was increasing so significantly, demand for credit card borrowing exploded as well. One school of thought asserts that the increase in the cost of survival created this demand, while another school ascribes the increasing demand to the increasing desire to keep up with the Joneses and a third ascribes the problem to an inappropriate personal discount rate (Angeletos et al., 2001; Schor, 1998; Warren & Tyagi, 2003). Creative advertising of both credit and the items credit can buy likely contributed as well. Whatever the cause or causes, the result of all of this was the first stage of the Consumer Lending (or borrowing) Revolution that the FDIC has recently diagnosed and given a name.

As the volume of credit card debt increased, lenders worked hard to develop new customers. In 2006, approximately eight billion pieces of promotional mail were sent to prospective customers. Lenders developed innovative ways to convince customers to shift to their card or to refrain from shifting away from their card. At the same time, they implemented equally innovative methods of making the largest profit possible off of those consumers who paid but paid late. In early 2007, Congress held several hearings on outrageous techniques that credit card lenders use to increase their profits off the payments of consumers who pay late and who may be priced out of filing bankruptcy (or at least delayed) by the increased costs imposed on them by the Bankruptcy Abuse Prevention and Consumer Protection Act (BAPCPA). Just in response to these hearings, several large credit card lenders announced changes in some of the worst of these practices.

The Subprime Products Other than Mortgage Products

One school of thought asserts that the seemingly insatiable consumer appetite for credit was pent up demand created by the fact that so many people had previously been frozen out of the mainstream credit market. Americans who were deemed excessive credit risks by pre-1978 mainstream lending standards had always borrowed limited amounts from salary lenders, pawnbrokers, high finance furniture dealers, rent to own, street lenders, and family members. The elimination of usury legislation, however, and the development of sophisticated risk-scoring techniques made them desirable customers for mainstream lenders. With the development of capital sources, sophisticated pricing techniques, and sophisticated marketing mechanisms, mainstream lenders entered the field with both feet and immediately began to probe the outer limits of the profitability of this type of lending. They began to explore whether there was any upper limit on credit card interest rates, or on post-default interest rates and charges. So far, there appears to be no limit.

This lending might involve a credit card with a higher cost or a credit card secured by a car or other property; it might involve financing and sale of used cars at very high prices to poor credit risks or the "car title" method of lending which eases the rules for taking possession and taking title to the repossessed vehicle; it might include "payday loans" or other very short-term loans at very high rates that are often rolled over; and it might include renting to own at very high prices or tax refund anticipation loans.

Although these practices existed historically, they were outside the province of mainstream financial institutions and were limited by usury laws, by available capital, and by the capacity and infrastructure of the market that provided the funds. Mostly through acquisition of significant players in these markets, and through development of sophisticated secondary market mechanisms, mainstream financial institutions now provide a large and growing share of the credit in this subprime industry, and the investing community purchases a significant and growing amount of these subprime credit extensions through securitized vehicles. Consumer advocates have begun to have some limited success in publicizing, defining, and in some limited instances regulating practices that are deemed predatory, particularly for vulnerable and special populations such as the members of the military. Examples of recent laws that were developed in response to the predatory aspects of payday lending include the restrictions on small loans to those in the military as part of the Defense Department authorization legislation in 2006 and the fact that in 2007 22 state legislatures considered payday lending legislation, and it is conceivable that this process will put some limits on the costs of credit and outlaw the worst tactics and practices within the industry. Some states such as North Carolina have been serious about regulating subprime lending to ensure that it is not predatory. These efforts have begun to reverberate in the courts, the legislatures, financial regulatory agencies, and the court of public opinion. As quickly as they are enacted, lenders find new and innovative ways around them.

Mortgage Debt: Purchase-Money and Nonpurchase-Money

Home mortgage debt constitutes the overwhelming majority of all consumer debt. During the period from 2000 to 2006, seven factors combined to produce significant changes in the nature of mortgage debt, particularly among those homeowners with lower incomes and net worth. The impact of these developments on the liquidity-constrained homeowners (as one commentator has labeled them) cries out for both economic and sociological analysis (Hurst, 2004).

1. Home ownership increased, and 67 % of American households now own their own homes.
2. Home values rose. The price of the average house increased significantly faster than average disposable incomes every year between 2001 and 2006, a historically unusual event.

3. Interest rates were at out-of-market and historically low levels.
4. Americans refinanced over and over again at very low rates to reduce their monthly mortgage payments, putting large amounts of money in the hands of American homeowners (Brady, Canner, & Maki, 2002; Canner, Dynan, & Passmore, 2002; Krainer & Marquis, 2003; McConnell, Peach, & Al-Haschim, 2003).
5. The combination of low interest rates, rising home values, and the higher costs of other types of debt have also made withdrawal of equity immensely more popular than ever before (Canner et al., 2002).
6. As more and more home owning households sought to borrow beyond their historic credit limits, either to purchase a first home at increased prices or to shore up their financial condition, lenders found new ways to relax credit limits so that they could sell more and more of their products to a hungry buying public. Innovative products included teaser rates, interest only loans, special types of adjustable rate mortgages, all of this accompanied by no documentation or low documentation credit standards.
7. The investment community's search for ever higher returns continued to pour dollars into the system to provide the supply to meet the demand.

The equity in a person's home is the primary source of savings or reserve for most Americans. Between 2001 and 2006, so-called "cash-out refinancing"—taking out a new mortgage larger than the one being paid off and pocketing the difference— netted consumers about $250 billion per year of immediately available spending power. This was equivalent to about 3 % of the disposable income of all U.S. households in each year and, obviously, much more for those households doing the refinancing. Including all other forms of mortgage-related "home-equity withdrawal" during 2001–2006, U.S. households extracted cash equivalent to 8 % of disposable income on average in each year as a result of increased mortgage indebtedness. Net home equity extraction was equal to 6.9 % of disposable income and 5.1 % of GDP in 2004 (Greenspan & Kennedy, 2005). This was not entirely "free money" made possible by increasing house values, however. Mortgage borrowing grew faster than house prices throughout the period, so that the average ratio of mortgage debt to house value increased from 42 to 47 % between 2001 and 2006.

Twenty-five percent of the funds withdrawn were used for repayment of other debt, 35 % was used for home improvement and 16 % for consumer expenditures (Canner et al., 2002). Once refinancing homeowners had filled out the papers and paid the expenses necessary for that transaction, they could not resist reaching deeper and borrowing against the rising equity in their homes.

Mortgage debt increased from about 40 % of disposable income in 1970 to 60 % in 1990 to about 83 % as of 2003 and has exploded since then. The rise in home prices and the elimination of underwriting standards combined to allow consumers to borrow ever-increasing amounts. Teaser rates allowed most but not all consumer borrowers to make the first payments; when market rates became effective, it was clear to all that the borrowers would not be able to make the payments. So long as prices continued to rise, the borrower could refinance or sell the home. However, once the price escalation slowed down, massive defaults were inevitable.

One of the most remarkable developments in the mortgage market in recent decades has been the increasingly important role played by three federally related mortgage securitizers, Fannie Mae, Freddie Mac, and Ginnie Mae. Together, the pools of securitized mortgages that they create increased from practically nothing in 1970 to almost 50 % of all home mortgages outstanding by 2001. The so-called "private-label" mortgage securitizers of Wall Street took advantage of the corporate-governance problems uncovered at Fannie Mae and Freddie Mac to increase their share of the home-mortgage market from 8 to 18 % between 2003 and 2006. Federally related mortgage pools accounted for only about 38 % of the market in 2006. Wall Street seized on the opportunity to fill this void with private securitizations which insured higher fees than had been available when most of the sales were to Fannie, and without Fannie's credit standards, the amount lent and the number of loans and the loan terms were subject to greater creativity. Rating agencies lowered their standards to allow these factors to operate unimpaired.

Then, in late 2006 inevitably, the subprime market imploded, partly from its own weight and inevitability; partly because the rise in home values slowed and then stopped in many markets and the pressure cooker could not function without this safety valve; partly because investors began to be concerned about the rising number of defaults even when house prices were still rising.

The "cheerleaders" who write most of the business commentary are certain that the damage will be localized at subprime mortgage market. Others are concerned that it will broaden to the larger mortgage market but will be localized there, and still others are concerned that it will spread to the rest of the economy. Since much of our economic progress is based on overoptimism by the buying public, many commentators indicate that the only thing to fear is fear itself. Who knows.

Economic and Sociological Consequences

Economics

The short-term micro- and macroeconomic consequences of the consumer lending revolution are each readily apparent. Investors and investment banks have profited enormously by this increase. Financial institutions and other participants in the consumer lending stream have become more profitable and their share price has increased. The U.S. economy and the world economy are based, as never before, on consumers' spending considerably more than they have and considerably more than many of them will ever be able to repay (Burhouse, 2003). The portion of the national economy that is driven by consumer spending rather than business or government spending has increased to 77 % and spending by Americans is a primary support for the world economy. By comparison, 1960–1980 consumption held steady at 63 % of GNP, in 1980s rose to 66 % and was 66.5 % in 1997 (it was 65 % in 1950). In Japan, the comparable figure is 53 %.

Personal consumption as a percentage of GDP is at its highest level since WW2. Personal consumption increased has grown considerably in comparison to GDP growth since the late 1990s. Since 1950, virtually no period in which personal consumption growth has been larger than GDP growth in actual monetary terms except in 1953–1954.

A modern day Alexis de Tocqueville (a French political thinker, best known for his book *Democracy in America*) might note that if Americans ever begin spending within their incomes, our economy will collapse (de Tocqueville, 1835). The additional credit generated by the consumer lending revolution, in the form of credit card debt and home equity debt is the key underpinning of the U.S. economy. Whether this can sustain in the long run was a key dispute between former Federal Reserve Czar Greenspan and those who dared to challenge his assumptions. Only time will tell, but the importance of this additional spending generated by the additional debt is undisputed. Recent Federal Reserve data demonstrates the microeffects dramatically: Between 1994 and 2006, households' mortgage debt outstanding increased from 60 % of disposable income to 100 %. Nonmortgage consumer debt rose from 18 to 25 % of disposable income; so the average total household debt burden increased from 78 to 125 % of disposable income in a span of 12 years—the fastest such increase ever recorded. Household debt is up; mortgage debt is up; the ratio of income to debt is more troubling (Bucks, Kennickell, & Moore, 2006; Draut & Silva, 2003).

As consumer lending has become an extraordinarily profitable oligopoly, it has changed the face of financial institutions. Consumer and retail lending now have grown to constitute a crucial part of financial institution profitability. Perhaps no fact demonstrates this as sharply as the decision by these prestigious financial institutions to march into the areas of subprime lending. The facts are clear. Large financial institutions that dominate the consumer lending arena are extremely profitable; this profitability has helped to create the consumer lending revolution. Charges on consumers who pay the minimum payment and those who fall behind on their payments have grown to constitute the most profitable area of consumer lending. Not only do financial institutions rely on the profits from the astounding increase in consumer lending but so does the entire economy. More and more families are running harder and harder to stay in the same place or to reduce the amount that they are falling behind.

When consumers with too much debt marched in droves to the bankruptcy courts to discharge those debts, creditors marched to Congress to change the "too liberal" granting of that discharge. BAPCPA was enacted to force those consumers to use some of their future income to pay a portion of their debts in order to be able to discharge the rest of those debts and to otherwise make bankruptcy more expensive, inaccessible, and unattractive.

Beginning in 2006, there was a significant uptick in the default and foreclosure rate on mortgages, particularly subprime mortgages and particularly those with special interest features. There was significant fallout as Freddie Mac as well as the private securitization market closed the door to these products and even made recourse demands on their sellers, many of which threw up their hands in failure. The debate whether the number of defaults will have significant macroeconomic effects has been joined. At least one set of authors believes that Wall Street and the investing public bear some share of the responsibility for the excesses and deterioration of credit standards. Another interesting economic effect of the consumer lending revolution is that historical inclination of consumers to reduce spending has been considerably mitigated by the availability of credit.

Sociological Consequences

The key benefits of the various consumer credit vehicles are readily apparent; they provide a bridge to a better place. A person needs a car to be able to get to a new job but cannot afford the car until he/she has been working the new job and perhaps until after he/she obtains one or more promotions in that job. He/she buys the car on high-cost credit, takes the job, gets the promotion, and life is much better. Without credit he/she could not have bought the car and would remain without a job or in the former inferior job. Without installment lending, only people with enough in liquid reserves could purchase a car.

Credit provides a bridge toward greater upward mobility. A nicer car may provide enhanced status and self-esteem and provide tickets to a "better" life. A person wants more education or a computer or a new television and cannot afford them, but can obtain them through use of credit. Or, to shift from Julia Schor to Elizabeth Warren, a person needs housing in a safer neighborhood with better schools and cannot afford the move without the use of credit (Schor, 1998; Warren & Tyagi, 2003). Professor Warren demonstrates that in most households, all the adults who can work are working and their income is just enough to support the family. If they happen to encounter turbulence from loss of employment, health or family difficulties, there is little wiggle room. Her data supports the notion that people are spending beyond their income because that is what is required in order to have a safe and reasonable lifestyle. Lendol Calder goes a step further to say that the pressure that emanates from greater debt drives people to work harder and to be more productive (Calder, 1999).

Two prominent sociologists, George Ritzer and Robert Manning, say all of this is nonsense (Manning, 2000; Ritzer, 1995). They feel that inducing people to borrow more and then loading them down with deceptive and excess credit and then adding impossible default charges creates problems on both micro- and macrolevels. On the microlevel, credit defaults, repossessions, and foreclosures increase stress and create more mental health problems and family abuse. Debt is a primary contributing factor to family disharmony and divorce. Health suffers, employment suffers, and the reduction in happiness and life satisfaction cause a myriad of types of damage.

On a macrolevel, society must bear the consequences of more broken homes and dysfunctional families under the stress of debt, more jails, more people needing mental health services and more children and mothers needing shelter from abuse and rehabilitative services, and higher taxes to pay for all of this. Millions of

Americans labor under crushing debt loads that entrap them, shatter their dreams, and cripple their ability to save and increase assets. Fallout from the subprime mortgage crisis has demonstrated that multiple home foreclosures in a neighborhood have a negative and deteriorating effect on other homes and community institutions in the neighborhood.

Toward Understanding why the Demand Side is so High

It is important for policy makers to understand the nature of the demand side of this equation. As we have indicated, a debate rages regarding the uses of this credit and the behavior of the American consumer. Elizabeth Warren asserts that the increased cost of surviving in our society is the primary cause of increased credit and debt service obligations (Warren & Tyagi, 2003). Julia Schor says character flaws underlie this development (Schor, 1998). Angeletos et al. (2001) suggest that most consumers are hyperbolic discounters and honestly intend to save and pay tomorrow and to spend today. If Schor is right, then it is important to understand why so many people make choices that economists might see as irrational. If we assume that the consumer has real alternatives and is making choices that subject her to serious and unwarranted risks, then it is important to understand the behavior that leads people to make these unhealthy decisions. Many economists have shrugged their shoulders when asked why a significant number of consumers seem to act against their financial best interests. To fill the gap, a different breed of social scientists have stepped up to try to understand the ways that consumers use credit and make decisions regarding purchasing. Called behavioral economists in the United States (Angeletos et al., 2001) and economic psychologists in Europe (Lea, 1992), they have begun to explore the issues that Elizabeth Warren and Julia Schor have been debating. They have several theories. One is that human beings are acting in an irrational manner and therefore this spending and borrowing is not subject to classical economic analysis or explanation. A second theory is that people tend to be excessively optimistic regarding their long-term prospects and therefore make short-term decisions which are based upon false expectations over the long run. A third theory is that individuals simply have poor self-control in the short run, and a final theory is that people lack both the knowledge and information necessary to make a thoughtful rational analysis of the proposed borrowing or spending and that lack of information and knowledge interferes with their rational decision making. A combination of various human traits and conditions combine to render these motivations complex (Martin & Sweet, 2007). Hopefully, the work being done in these fields will shed light on consumer behavior in the years to come since those who believe overextended consumers are at fault would make them pay the price with limited opportunity to escape, while those who think overextended debtors are more sinned against than sinners feel they should be able to get out of debt more easily. These issues also affect the degree to which financial literacy programs can be effective.

Toward Understanding why the Supply Side is so High

It is also important for policy makers to understand the nature of the supply side of the equation. Once the rate caps evaporated, lenders began to probe the outer edge of profitability for lending. The investment community responded quickly and developed or modified existing vehicles to share in these attractive profit opportunities. Initially, these investments were in real estate mortgages and took the form of bonds and other forms of debt issued by Fannie Mae and similar private public secondary market players. As credit card debt exploded, card issuers needed additional liquidity and the securitization market for credit card receivables grew correspondingly. Most of it was prime credit card debt but the subprime credit card market provided both higher anticipated profits and higher risk.

As more and more consumers began to tap into their home equity and as more and more consumers needed to stretch further to purchase their first or next home, the subprime market began to take off, and by 2006, its share of all new mortgages went from 5 % in 2001 to 16 % in 2006. This occurred just as Fannie Mae was struggling with the aftereffects of perceived scandal and Wall Street seized upon the void to profitably substitute purely private securitization vehicles to purchase the subprime debt. This presented interesting opportunities for ignoring and eliminating the underwriting standards required by Fannie Mae. The result was that the ready supply of borrowers for these risky loans found a ready supply of capital. As of early 2007, mortgage-related activities at the major firms generate an estimated 15 % of total fixed-income revenue, according to Brad Hintz, an analyst at Sanford Bernstein reported in *New York Sun* on February 18, 2007.

Intervention

Intervention and Regulation of Consumer Credit

So, how do we decide whether to intervene in the consumer credit market; how do we decide whether and how to regulate or prohibit specific types of practices? Now that we understand the positive and negative micro- and macrosociological and economic considerations, we must design a regime that minimizes the negative effects of consumer lending and at the same time minimizes the destruction of the positive effects. Now that we understand how and why consumers make credit decisions that are likely to harm them, we must design a scheme that takes those harmful decisions into account and makes them less likely to occur and less likely to cause distress.

For example, intervention might be appropriate in order to ameliorate the negative consequences the credit revolution brings to individuals (i.e., undue strain, shattered dreams, domestic difficulty, homelessness, and mental illness) and to society (i.e., increased mental health costs and increased need for intervention in family disputes). If a certain type of credit device results in a default rate of 90 %, then there would likely be consensus that the distress and inefficiency of the credit device justified intervention, and likely prohibition. The negatively effected parties would be the lenders who were denied a profit opportunity, the investment community which is denied an opportunity for a rate of return based on this product; the 10 % of borrowers for whom this device is productive and who will not default; and finally, perhaps the other 90 % who default but who do not think they will default and who want the opportunity to try and succeed or try and fail.

The positively effected parties would be the 90 % who will be spared the consequences of default; the friends, family, and neighbors of that 90 % who are also spared the indirect consequences of those defaults and the public and private safety net which would have been required to provide help to the defaulters.

A prophetic article by George Wallace (Wallace, 1976) divides the people who will be regulated out of any particular market into three categories: those who would have chosen not to borrow even if they could and are therefore unaffected by the regulation; those who would have chosen to borrow and would have defaulted; and those who would have chosen to borrow and would not have defaulted. The philosophical question is whether to prohibit the third group from borrowing in order to protect the second group. Since the time that the Milton Friedman school of economics rose to supremacy, economists have scowled at efforts to protect consumers by interfering with the free market. It is conceivable that the next generation of economists will more fully understand the nature of consumers' behavior and on that basis will be more courageous and willing to deviate from a purely market-driven approach that is based upon the false notion that the consumer can be counted upon to act rationally. They may see the sense in a bit of protection, as paternalistic (or maternalistic) as it might be. So, if we decide it makes sense to intervene what might that intervention look like?

Disclosure and Financial Literacy

The first form of "intervention" is financial literacy education and disclosure of information regarding the credit extension. The decision to provide education and disclosure is based on the notion that the consumer would be more likely to act in her own self-interest if we could bridge the knowledge and information gap between her and the lender and if she understood both the degree to which and the reasons why she may choose to purchase more credit than she can likely repay.

The fundamental question is "what does she need to know and when does she need to know it." Over the past few years, the field of financial literacy has grown exponentially; there are programs in schools and there are programs aimed at adults. Little empirical work has been done to determine if these programs work (Braunstein & Welch, 2002); in fact, there is no consensus on what "work" means in this context. The key question for the curriculum drafters is "what are they trying to teach." Is the goal intellectual mastery of basic concepts of borrowing and interest rates which can be measured on a test? Is the lesson don't ever borrow? Is the purpose of the lesson to understand the costs of borrowing so that people will stay within certain limits? What about the person who is borrowing to pay her rent or put groceries on the table or obtain an education? What is the lesson for her? And what about the hyperbolic discounter?

Although sophisticated materials have been assembled by a number of sources to help teach the basic borrowing facts and concepts, very little has been developed that deal with behavior change. Several academicians have put forth counseling systems based on medical models. For example, in order to teach someone to change their behavior, there must be a "teachable" moment. Likewise, reduction in overspending may have similarities to reduction in smoking, drinking, gambling, or eating too much. The lessons of the behavioral economics movement may provide help in designing effective behavior change education (Martin & Sweet, 2007).

Education for people already in financial trouble has also gained great momentum. Recent bankruptcy legislation mandates such programs for bankruptcy debtors. The bankruptcy legislation requires that every consumer debtor obtain a briefing from a certified credit counseling agency in 6 months before filing and also receive an educational session after filing and before receiving a bankruptcy discharge. A study (Staten, Elliehausen, & Lundquist, 2006) has begun which will attempt to evaluate the effectiveness of these sessions. Recent calls have been made to require the prospective borrower to rely upon a trusted advisor before being able to engage in risky or complex borrowing.

For over 30 years, the consumer credit industry purports to have been "counseling" and "educating" the millions of people in financial trouble who have shown up on their doorstep rather than the doorstep of a bankruptcy lawyer (Lander, 1999). Over the past decade, the individual development account has been marketed as a way to induce low and moderate income consumers to save and to create a reserve for emergencies. A study of the value of these programs requires development of a consensus definition of "success." A recent survey on the value of credit counseling characterized "success" as not filing a bankruptcy petition within a specified period after a counseling session (National Foundation for Credit Counseling, 2002). A current assessment of the value of credit counseling is using credit scores as a measuring device (Staten et al., 2006).

Success for a consumer might be a lower income to debt–service ratio, whereas success to a creditor might mean greater profits with fewer ultimate write offs. We assume that creditors have developed mechanisms to measure the "success" of such programs but these measures are proprietary and little is publicly known about them.

Will financial literacy education before the transaction or after the default reduce the level of consumer borrowing? At this point, we have no idea. Although such programs have proliferated within schools, colleges, and adult education programs over the past half decade, standards have not yet been developed to test their effectiveness (Braunstein & Welch, 2002). It seems logical that such programs could promote better decision making for those borrowers who have choices, but not for consumers who are borrowing to "survive." They can also help potential borrowers who make more informed choices when the credit product is comprehensible.

Will behavior change counseling/education be effective? Many credit counseling agencies purport to include a behavior change element in their counseling but the quality and comprehensiveness of that counseling is problematic. As behavioral economists have begun to understand why consumers do not act more like purely rational automatons that economists have assumed them to be, this information may be translated into well-defined counseling sessions based on helping the consumer understand and modify her likely dangerously "irrational" behavior. There has been very limited investigation of this type of change in financial conduct.

The timing of any such financial literacy efforts may be crucial. There is current consensus that they should be integrated into the kindergarten through twelfth grade curriculum and more and more colleges are providing or requiring such courses. There are first-time homebuyer programs and there are programs for people already in financial trouble. One way of making sure that people are acting in a fully informed manner would be to require that overindebted consumers obtain a license to borrow before they could borrow additional money or before they could take a payday loan.

What About Disclosure?

In addition to literacy efforts, Congress and some states have passed various disclosure laws intended to help consumers make more informed decisions about credit. Truth-in-lending laws were enacted in the late 1960s to ensure that the consumer receives clear and conspicuous information regarding financing transactions. This legislation attempts to regulate advertising and consumer transactions so that the consumer may understand exactly what she is getting into and what the consequences of the transaction will be. Disclosure legislation has been a mixed bag. For example, we do know that many prospective borrowers use the standard information regarding the annual percentage rate to compare various lending products and various lenders, and that is a good thing. On the other hand, disclosures are often insufficiently clear and in 1980, in a law Congress rolled back many of the most important and effective provisions of the Truth in Lending Act. It would appear that consumers would benefit from fewer and clearer disclosure so that there would be a single easily comparable figure that describes the price a borrower will pay for the financing.

Other Possible Types of Intervention

Capping Interest and Fee

There was a time, not so long ago in the United States that the level of consumer debt was significantly less than it is today. One of the reasons was that it was not so profitable for lenders to lend to moderate or higher risk borrowers. It was not so profitable because nearly every state had a limit on the rate of interest that lenders could charge to consumers. These usury statutes were transported from England and

Western Europe and endured in the United States after most of those countries had largely abandoned them.

In spite of those general prohibitions, there were gaps in the usury wall, and states invented several convenient "fictions" to accommodate certain consumer lending transactions. For example, many states had small loan laws that allowed these lenders to charge more than the usury rate so long as they were registered and so long as the amount they lent was below a certain amount. Likewise, when consumers wanted to buy furniture "on time," the time price differential was invented to declare that the difference between what a consumer paid for an item of furniture over time rather than for cash was not "interest" which would be subject to the usury cap, but rather the time price differential. States did set limits on the "time price differential" but those limits were less restrictive than the usury rules would have been. States expanded time price differential to car lending and various other types of lending as well.

By the early 1970s, a number of studies were launched to determine the optimal interest rate zones. Inflation was out of control, and the prime interest rate was above 20 %. Congress, the Supreme Court, and the various state legislatures were all rolling back the usury laws that had protected a large segment of Americans from borrowing more than they could afford and bearing the consequences of their likely defaults, foreclosures, repossessions, and garnishments. In response to pressure from the home building industry, Congress had passed preemptive legislation that required a state to allow a floating cap for home mortgages.

Although the development of Visa and MasterCard associations had resulted in significant growth in outstanding credit card debt, not all consumers were granted access to credit cards. If lenders felt the applicable rate ceiling was too low to enable them to generate sufficient income to cover the losses incurred when lending to moderate or high-risk borrowers, lenders would deny that group access to credit. Therefore, in a regime of usury ceilings where the lenders' income potential was limited, lenders extended credit only to lower risk borrowers, and moderate or higher risk borrowers were shut out of the market. This situation resulted in less credit availability (Ellis, 1998).

Usury ceilings varied widely throughout the United States but at the end of the 1970s 37 states had interest rate ceilings on credit cards. Only three states had no limit and two states had limits that were above 18 % for a portion of the balance (Ellis, 1998). In the economic environment of the late 1970s, the general opinion on usury rates appeared to change. Part of the relaxation can be attributed to the high nominal interest rates for the time, which restricted credit availability and increased the range of potential borrowers for whom credit was not available (Ellis, 1998).

During the late 1970s, the Milton Friedman school of economics began its reign. Although they relied on most of Adam Smith's principles, they discarded Smith's support of usury laws in favor of a free-market economics that knew no bounds.

In 1978, the United States Supreme Court profoundly changed the framework/ foundation of usury laws with a ruling in the case of *Marquette National Bank of*

Minneapolis v. First Omaha Service Corporation. The Solicitor General of Minnesota was attempting to prevent First Omaha from soliciting credit card customers in Minnesota at the highest Nebraska interest rates by contending that the exportation of Nebraska's interest rate would make it difficult for states to enact effective usury laws. The Supreme Court agreed that such might be the case but it decided that the usury issue was a legislative problem to be handled by Congress. The Court held in *Marquette* that a section of the National Bank Act allowed a lender to charge the highest rate allowed in the lender's home state regardless of the lower rate limitation in the customer's state of residence.

The *Marquette* decision applied to all types of consumer loans but it had the greatest consequences for the credit card industry because credit card lending can be accomplished entirely by mail without the borrower and lender ever meeting. Credit card lenders headquartered in states with liberal usury ceilings can easily export those rates to borrowers residing in states with restrictive usury ceilings (Ellis, 1998). After the *Marquette* decision, liberalization of state usury ceilings occurred. Some states, such as South Dakota and Delaware quickly seized the opportunity to deregulate interest and other banking functions to attract banks and other consumer lenders. Citicorp was one of the first lenders to take advantage of the deregulation at the state level and established a new national bank and credit card center in Sioux Falls, South Dakota. The practical effect of *Marquette* was to force states to deregulate or face a loss of the credit card segment of the banking business. Major banks pressured state legislatures to relax limits on lending by threatening to move their businesses to states with more liberal ceilings. The four largest banks in Maryland moved their credit card opportunities to Delaware when the Maryland State Legislature refused to relax the state's usury law. Most leading banking states had relaxed or repealed their interest rate ceiling by 1982 (Ellis, 1998); therefore, the bank credit card market was effectively deregulated as the Bankruptcy Code was in its infancy.

In the 1980s, mainstream financial institutions realized that the death of usury laws combined with other developments provided them with an extraordinarily profitable opportunity if they would embrace the very customers they formerly shunned. Variously known as subprime, high-yield and predatory lending, this includes extending credit at high prices to customers who are shut out of the market for credit on more reasonable terms (Ellis, 1998). Many of the new borrowers would clearly benefit from this development although a certain percent would clearly suffer.

Interestingly, in 2006 as part of the military appropriations legislation, Congress imposed a usury rate of 18 % on payday loans to members of the military. Various states had sought to reimpose interest rate ceilings on payday lending and other various types of loans, and it is uncertain what the effect will be.

Although most economists continue to resist such restrictions insisting that the market should be left undisturbed so willing lenders and willing borrowers can make the music they wish to make, findings of behavioral economists that help explain "irrational" self-damaging consumer behavior is creating "chinks" in their armor. Since we know that consumers are not acting rationally and in their own best interests, that these transactions will cause harm based on that irrational behavior and that that harm will have both micro- and macroeconomic and sociological negative impacts, some economists agree that there is sufficient reason to reimpose these limits on the price lenders may charge for selling their credit. White (2007) suggests that in view of the prevalence of hyperbolic discounters, the only way to effect change is to modify the lenders' conduct. Since the hyperbolic discounter honestly believes that he/she will pay late and not need bankruptcy, making bankruptcy harder for his/her will have little effect on his/her conduct. Suggestions include: the French method of prioritizing the sharing of dollars by date of lending so that those who lent in the face of the most debt stand at the back of the line if there is money for the trustee to distribute, Oren Bar-Gill's suggestion (Bar-Gill, 2004) that credit card teaser rates and premiums be eliminated; as well as Ronald Mann's suggestions that creditors raise their minimum monthly payment. Professor Mann has also suggested a "distress" tax on profits of lenders that are earned on (Mann, 2006).

Outlawing or Restricting Offensive Practices or Products

Another way of regulating consumer credit is to identify offending types of transactions and prohibit or regulate those practices. For example, the combination of high interest rates and the practice of "flipping" may cause legislators to outlaw payday lending. Likewise, legislators might choose to prohibit lending products such as the tax refund anticipation loans or the title lending.

A variation is to identify and prohibit questionable practices such as cross defaulting a credit card to any other consumer obligation or the right of the lender to change the interest rate at any time. Other examples include teaser rates for credit card or home mortgages.

Another variation would be to require the lender to make an independent and rational determination that the credit transaction is "suitable" for the borrower. The Fed has listed three factors including suitability and cost and clarity of disclosure for determining if a transaction is predatory and therefore regulated or prohibited. For example, between 1999 and 2007, North Carolina enacted legislation to restrict payday loans, carefully license mortgage brokers, and defined and outlawed various predatory mortgage practices. Currently, many states are attempting to define "predatory lending" practices and to regulate or prohibit such practices. As this book went to press, Congress was seriously considering the "Mortgage Reform and Anti-Predatory Lending Act of 2007" which would increase regulation of questionable mortgage lending. The preamble to that legislation reads as follows:

> In order to increase uniformity, reduce regulatory burden, enhance consumer protection, and reduce fraud, the States, through the Conference of State Bank Supervisors and the American Association of Residential Mortgage Regulators, are hereby encouraged to establish a Nationwide Mortgage Licensing System and Registry for the residential mortgage industry that accomplishes all of the following objectives:
>
> (1)   Provides uniform license applications and reporting requirements for state-licensed loan originators.

(2)   Provides a comprehensive licensing and supervisory database.

(3)   Aggregates and improves the flow of information to and between regulators.

(4)   Provides increased accountability and tracking of loan originators.

(5)   Streamlines the licensing process and reduces the regulatory burden.

(6)   Enhances consumer protections and supports anti-fraud measures.

(7)   Provides consumers with easily accessible information regarding the employment history of, and publicly adjudicated disciplinary and enforcement actions against, loan originators.

To some degree, the growth of predatory lending has called upon regulators and lawmakers to substitute unconscionability and exemption and limits on enforcement. The first step is to identify the credit transactions we want to outlaw and the basis for that intrusion into the consumer credit market.

Nonbankruptcy Enforcement Restrictions

States have long had various kinds of laws to protect consumers who are at risk because of credit extensions. The most well known are the exemptions and redemption rights and limits on garnishments; other state laws require notice of default and right to cure. Such provisions vary greatly from state to state, and so far unsuccessful efforts have been made to provide a floor that would have the effect in bankruptcy of "guaranteeing" every debtor a minimum level of exempt property.

Bankruptcy Fresh Start as a Consumer Protection Device

In order to formulate effective bankruptcy policy after the Consumer Lending Revolution, it is necessary to acknowledge that seeds of the consumer lending revolution were sewn by the death of usury within weeks of the time the Bankruptcy Reform Act (BRA) came into existence. President Carter signed the Bankruptcy Reform Act on November 6, 1978, 6 days after *Marquette* was argued and 42 days before it was decided. For the following 25 years, consumer lending grew exponentially as did consumer bankruptcy filings under that law. Critics of the BRA blamed its liberal rules and "inexpensive" discharge rules for the enormous increase in the number of bankruptcies during the 1990s. Consumer advocates have countered that it was the enormous increase in borrowing and the expensive cost of credit to marginal borrowers that caused the increase. They asserted that in the face of the death of usury legislation, bankruptcy had combined with restrictions on predatory lending, truth-in-lending legislation, and financial literacy education to provide a substitute consumer protection rubric for consumer borrowers.

In response to the claims of creditors that the liberality of the BRA was inducing defaults and bankruptcies by those who could and should pay their debts, Congress passed BAPCPA in 2005 and significantly raised the costs of a bankruptcy discharge and made that more expensive discharge less valuable.

Among other changes, BAPCPA established a "means test" for determining if the debtor would be required to pay a portion of her debts in return for the discharge. This was intended to force more debtors into Chapter 13 and allow fewer opportunity to use Chapter 7. In order to decide where to set the bar and what price to exact for the bankruptcy discharge, we need to stand in the shoes of potential consumer bankruptcy debtors as they ponder their next move. Consumers consider filing for bankruptcy in order to receive a discharge of their unsecured debt and/or in order to keep their house, car, or furniture.

Thus, key policy issues involved in setting the parameters for bankruptcy relief are (1) the cost of the discharge, who is eligible, and to what extent must they pay a share of their future wages to obtain the discharge; and (2) to what extent should the bankruptcy discharge affect those creditors that have liens that are valid outside bankruptcy.

As we analyze these policy issues, we need to consider the decision stream of the population of people for whom bankruptcy seems a plausible option. For purposes of this consideration, we will ignore whether the problem is brought on by "illness, unemployment or divorce" or whether it is the conscious decision to "spend, spend and spend." At the first stages of financial distress, some consumers may have a relatively wide array of choices, but if the situation deteriorates that array narrows. Initial choices may include home equity loans either on the prime or on the subprime market, loans from family members and various other kinds of subprime loans. She may begin to "default" on selected bills, usually the ones with the least immediate impact. Collection efforts will intensify with telephone calls and letters; costs, fees, and charges will increase and will lead to an exponential increase in what she owes, all of which causes a downhill spiral. She may receive notice of lawsuits, repossession of the automobile, and foreclosure of the house. Her choices are to continue to pay, try to work out the bill with the creditor(s), go to a credit-counseling agency, file a Chapter 7 or Chapter 13 bankruptcy or bury her head in the sand.

The better credit-counseling agency will offer, for a reasonable price, diagnosis, counseling and education, and perhaps a debt management program which may include concessions by the creditor. The lowest quality providers will impose excessive charges and will provide no services (National Consumer Law Center & Consumer Federation of America, 2003). Home equity loans have the advantage of providing a tax benefit and perhaps a lower rate, but they often "mask" higher costs and, most importantly, subject the consumer to foreclosure and eviction.

The spate of home equity loans may well take many home owning consumers outside the ambit of Chapter 13 protection because the debt service requirement after interest rate increases will be beyond their means. If the costs of bankruptcy are set higher, the qualifications more stringent and the relief less effective, then marginal consumers may opt out of bankruptcy or delay bankruptcy rather than file earlier. During this period, collection efforts may intensify. If the debtor has no house and no car and is not subject to garnishment, then it is unlikely the creditor will receive much marginal value during this period. If the debtor has some assets and is either unable to obtain bankruptcy relief or disinclined to do so, then she may pay some marginal dollars to stop or delay the collection actions. She may also enter into a credit counseling debt management plan, which is intended to pay all of her unsecured debt on more favorable terms. She may jeopardize her home or car as a result of trying to pay her unsecured creditors in full.

Higher bankruptcy costs may lead some in this category to put off the filing and have a change in circumstances that will alleviate the situation and never file a bankruptcy. There will likely be a small uptick in collections and a significant increase in stress, family violence, mental illness, divorce, and suicide. If we assume that many borrowers are making unwise decisions, then it is possible that in the long run, in the face of a higher bankruptcy bar, with better education they will make wiser decisions and borrow less. If we assume that most consumers get in trouble without making unwise decisions, then they will continue to borrow at about the same rate.

If the bar is lowered, then marginal potential debtors will opt into bankruptcy and debts that may have been uncollectible as well as debts that might have been collectible will be written off officially. The set of those borrowers that would file if it were easier but not if it were harder are likely to be difficult candidates for collection even if they do not file. The battle between the most credit risky borrower and her creditors (or the purchasers of her debt) is a saga of calls, letters, and sometimes lawsuits, judgments, and collection efforts. The stronger the case for bankruptcy, the less leverage the collector has.

BAPCPA establishes a complex set of rules for determining whether the debtor has too much income for Chapter 7 but may only obtain a discharge by filing under Chapter 13 and pledging several years of future earning to the repayment of the debts to be discharged. Whereas BRA had allowed a Chapter 13 debtor to keep his or her car so long as he or she paid its value to the secured lender over the course of his or her plan, BAPCPA requires the debtor that wishes to keep the car to pay the entire debt rather than the value of the car. Among other changes, BAPCPA also imposes various additional duties on counsel for the debtor which has resulted in significantly higher attorneys and filing fees.

Conclusion

Is the system of consumer borrowing and lending in the United States working satisfactorily and if not, what might be done to improve the way the consumer lending and borrowing system works? The current system encourages consumers to borrow and to spend and encourages lenders to lend so that consumers and lenders and the economy may prosper. Some consumers use the borrowed money to improve their lives; others are burdened with the various kinds of distress and shattered dreams that accompany hopelessly high debt. Lenders seem to be able to lend profitably in the current environment and are unlikely to reduce such lending unless it is outlawed or becomes less profitable. Because even the most sophisticated credit-scoring devices have limitations, current practice and policy guarantee large numbers of defaults, large numbers of people going to credit counseling, large numbers of foreclosures, and large numbers of bankruptcies. This is the clear and currently inevitable effect of the Consumer Lending Revolution. The profitability of all lending, but particularly subprime lending provides an attractive investment opportunity and therefore there will be no shortage of dollars to lend on the subprime market.

Crafting effective policy and legislation is further complicated by the fact that those who pay late are among the most profitable individual customers; if lenders tighten their lending standards or if consumers reduce their borrowing, then financial institution profitability will fall and attract less capital, consumer spending will be reduced, and the economy will be less vigorous.

Positions on regulatory policies including bankruptcy and the effectiveness of education are related to opinions of whether Schor or Warren is correct. Those who make a negative value judgment on the people who borrow beyond their means would make them pay the price with limited opportunity for escape, as in the case of Dickens' Mr. Micawber (Dickens, 1850). Those who believe overextended consumers are not at fault feel overextended debtors should be able to get out of debt more easily. How then do we meet the goals of a vigorous economy, profitable and safe financial institutions, and consumers who are prosperous and relatively default free?

In the current political climate, it is extremely unlikely that income support programs (other than the Earned Income Credit) will be enacted or that the extraordinary inequality of income or wealth will otherwise be reduced. There are however, a number of steps that seem possible and may accomplish these more limited goals. For example, we should do the following:

1. Establish a suitability standard that places a burden on the lender to make a loan only when it is the suitable product and has a reasonable chance of being repaid.
2. Regulate subprime lending in order to establish an upper limit on the cost of credit and restrictions or prohibitions on the most nefarious lending products and practices; perhaps we could use the criteria established by the Federal Reserve Bank that the presence of very high pricing, lack of clarity, and failure to maintain reasonable underwriting standards as standards for defining predatory or regulable or prohibited conduct. We should carefully watch the states such as North Carolina that is leading the way in this field.
3. Reestablish usury rates for interest and fees.
4. Provide a reasonable floor on exemptions.
5. Implement and evaluate kindergarten through college and adult financial literacy programs, as well as savings incentive programs such as the individual development account;
6. Experiment with behavior change courses and counseling for those whose path to over indebtedness involved conduct susceptible to such counseling.
7. In light of the mass of home foreclosures caused by the subprime mortgage crisis, with regard to which the current bankruptcy law is of no help, amend the Bankruptcy Code to help forestall the tragedy caused by such massive foreclosures.

8. Repeal the BAPCPA changes to the consumer bankruptcy system.
9. Other methods of altering the conduct of the lenders would include the following:

- the French method of prioritizing the sharing of dollars by date of lending so that those who lent in the face of the most debt stand at the back of the line if there is money for the trustee to distribute;
- Oren Bar-Gill's suggestion that credit card teaser rates and premiums be eliminated; and
- Ronald Mann's suggestions that creditors raise their minimum monthly payment and impose a "distress" tax on profits of lenders that are earned on the backs of those with the highest chances of default.

References

Angeletos, G., Laibson, D., Repetto, A., Tobacman, J., & Weigberg, S. (2001). The hyperbolic consumption model: Calibration, simulation and empirical evaluation. *Journal of Economic Perspective*, *15*(3), 47–68.

Bar-Gill, O. (2004). Seduction by plastic. *Northwestern University Law Review*, *98*(4), 1373–1434.

Brady, P. J., Canner, G., & Maki, D. M. (2002). The effects of recent mortgage refinancing. *Federal Reserve Bulletin*, (July), 441–450.

Braunstein, S., & Welch, C. (2002). Financial literacy: An overview of practice, research, and policy. *Federal Reserve Bulletin*, (November), 445–457.

Bucks, B., Kennickell, A., & Moore, K. (2006). Recent changes in U.S. family finance: Evidence from the 2001 and 2004 survey of consumer finances. *Federal Reserve Bulletin*. Retrieved March 15, 2007, from http://www.federalreserve.gov/publs/bulletin/2006/financessurvey.pdf

Burhouse, S. (2003). Evaluating the consumer lending revolution. *FYI: An update on emerging issues*. Retrieved March 15, 2007, from http://www.fdic.gov/bank/analytical/fyi/2003/091703fyi.html

Calder, L. (1999). *Financing the American dream: A cultural history of consumer credit*. Princeton: Princeton University Press.

Canner, G., Dynan, K., & Passmore, W. (2002). Mortgage refinancing in 2001 and early 2002. *Federal Reserve Bulletin*, (December), 469–481.

de Tocqueville, A. (1835). *Democracy in America*. Paris, Charles Goesselin.

Dickens, C. (1850). *David Copperfield*. New York: Modern Library.

Draut, T., & Silva, J. (2003). *Borrowing to make ends meet: The growth of credit card debt in the 90's*. New York: Demos. Retrieved March 15, 2007, from http://www.demos-usa.org.

Ellis, D. (1998). The effect of consumer interest rate deregulation on credit card volumes, charge-offs, and the personal bankruptcy rate. *Bank Trends*, (March)(98-05), 1–11.

Greenspan, A., & Kennedy, J. (2005). Sources and uses of equity extracted from homes. (Federal Reserve Board Working Paper 2007–20). Retrieved August 23, 2007, from www.federalreserve.gov/pubs/feds/2007/200720/200720pap.pdf.

Hurst, E., & Stafford, F. (2004). Home is where the equity is: Mortgage refinancing and household consumption. *Journal of Money, Credit & Banking*, *36*(6), 985–1014.

Krainer, J., & Marquis, M. (2003, October 3). Mortgage refinancing. *FRBSF Economic Letter*, *2003–29*, 1–3.

Lander, D. A. (1999). A snapshot of two systems that are trying to help people in financial trouble. *American Bankruptcy Institute Law Review*, *7*(1), 161–191.

Lea, S. (1992). Assessing the psychology of economic behavior and cognition. In G. M. Breakwell (Ed.), *The social psychology of political and economic cognition* (pp. 161–183). London: Surrey University Press.

Mandell, L. (1990). *The credit card industry: A history.* Boston: Twayne Publishers.

Mann, R. (2006). *Charging ahead: The growth and regulation of payment card markets around the world.* Cambridge, MA: Cambridge University Press.

Manning, R. D. (2000). *Credit card nation: The consequences of America's addiction to credit.* New York, Basic Books.

Martin, N., & Sweet, T. (2007). Mind games: Rethinking BAPCPA's debtor education provisions. *Southern Illinois University Law Journal, 31*, 517–547.

McConnell, M. M., Peach, R. W., & Al-Haschim, A. (2003). After the refinancing boom: Will consumers scale back their spending? *Current Issues in Economics and Finance, 9*(12), 1–7.

National Consumer Law Center & Consumer Federation of America. (2003). Credit counseling in crisis. Retrieved April 7, 2006, from http://www.nclc.org.

National Foundation for Credit Counseling. (2002, March). *The impact of credit counseling and subsequent borrower credit counseling on subsequent borrower credit usage and payment behavior.* Retrieved October 10, 2005, from http://www.nfcc.org.

Pacelle, M. (2004, July 6). Growing profit source for banks: Fees from riskiest card holders, late payers and big borrowers are becoming cash cows. *Wall Street Journal.* Retrieved May 12, 2006, from http://www.WSJ.com.

Ritzer, G. (1995). *Expressing America: A critique of the global credit card society.* Thousand Oaks, CA: Pine Forge Press.

Schor, J. B. (1998). *The overspent American: Why we want what we don't need.* New York: Basic Books.

Song, J. (2004, July 19). Regulators blamed for South Korean credit card crisis. *Financial Times.* Retrieved July 19, 2004, from http://www.FT.com.

Staten, M. E., Elliehausen, G., & Lundquist, E. C. (2006). *The impact of counseling on subsequent borrower credit usage and payment behavior.* Credit Research Center Monographic #36, Georgetown University, Retrieved from http://www.msb.edu/crc/pdf/m36.pdf.

Wallace, G. (1976). The uses of low rate ceilings reexamined. *Boston University Law Review, 56*(3), 451–497.

Warren, E., & Tyagi, A. (2003). *The two-income trap: Why middle class mothers and fathers are going broke.* New York: Basic Books.

White, M. (2007) *Bankruptcy reform and credit cards.* (NBER Working Series Paper 13265). Available from http://www.nber.org/papers/w13265.

Chapter 25
Promoting Applied Research in Personal Finance

Sharon A. Burns

Abstract The purpose of this chapter is to briefly summarize the role that a national professional association plays in bringing quality research to professional financial counselors and educators. This chapter also includes a brief, non-exhaustive review of personal finance research. A research agenda from the perspective of financial counselors and educators is proffered.

Most national associations exist to assemble like-minded professionals who serve a similar population or provide the same or similar products or services in various geographic markets. Four national associations serve personal finance practitioners: the Association for Financial Counseling and Planning Education® (AFCPE®), the Financial Planning Association (FPA), the National Association of Personal Financial Advisors (NAPFA) and the CFP Board of Standards. The first three serve as professional associations for the purpose of enhancing the capacity of individual professionals to be successful. The purpose of the CFP Board of Standards is to develop and maintain the standards of the Certified Financial Planner designation. In the field of financial counseling, AFCPE serves the role of certifying body as well.

Other associations either serve professionals in smaller geographic markets, or personal finance is one of several components or topics addressed by the membership. Four associations are comprised primarily of researchers and academicians. These include the Financial Services Academy (FSA), American Council on Consumer Interests (ACCI), the Eastern Family Economics and Resource Management Association (EFERMA) and its sister organization, Western Family Economics Association (WFEA). Members of the FSA research financial services and personal finance topics. ACCI members primarily study consumer behavior and economic issues with some focus on personal finance topics. The latter two groups focus heavily on personal finance topics, and participants are primarily graduate students and university faculty. Two organizations of professional educators, the American

S.A. Burns
Association for Financial Counseling and Planning Education, 1500 West Third Avenue, Suite 223, Columbus, OH 43212, USA
e-mail: sburns@afcpe.org

J.J. Xiao, (ed.), *Handbook of Consumer Finance Research,*
© Springer 2008

Association of Family and Consumer Sciences (AAFCS) and the National Extension Association of Family & Consumer Sciences (NEAFCS), host national meetings, a portion of which are dedicated to addressing personal finance issues.

Many associations serve to address, in whole or in part, personal finance by enhancing the capacity of their members to provide counsel and advice to individuals and families, or research personal finance decisions. The Association for Financial Counseling and Planning Education (AFCPE) is unique because its membership rolls include both university academicians and researchers, educators and counselors, all of whom focus on improving the financial well-being of individuals and families. AFCPE serves as both a certifying body and a professional membership association.

History of the Association for Financial Counseling and Planning Education®

In early 1983, Tahira Hira and Jerry Mason, two faculty members from leading universities, discussed the need for an organization that "promoted the interests and supported the needs of financial counselors" (AFCPE, 2003). The faculty members' professional work focused on these issues and their instructional efforts aimed to prepare students to serve consumers as financial and credit counselors.

In the autumn of 1983, over 60 invited participants attended a conference in Provo, Utah, focusing on financial counseling. The conference agenda included discussions exploring the possibility of forming a new association of university faculty and cooperative extension educators. Additional talks centered on providing university students with curricula appropriate to serving as professional financial counselors. Out of this meeting, and during a subsequent conference in 1984, the Association for Financial Counseling and Planning Education (AFCPE®) was born.

It was not long before association leaders realized that the work of their members had more value in the larger context of increasing the financial well-being of consumers. This motivated association leaders to develop networks with professionals in a variety of occupations who helped individuals and families develop sound financial management practices. Members of the credit counseling industry and those counseling military members were specifically interested in the association because the synergy among academicians, researchers and practitioners could result in providing more successful programming and counseling to their clients.

During the early 1990s, association leaders identified the need to certify professionals who were providing one-to-one financial counseling or group financial education. Such a certification would (1) develop a corps of professionals to assist individuals and families with personal financial issues, (2) enhance and develop best practices, (3) encourage consistency across the range of financial counseling services and (4) signal to the public that an individual financial counseling professional met independently developed standards. A committee of academic researchers, university-based faculty, cooperative extension educators and credit counseling industry leaders convened to develop industry standards, curriculum and examination requirements. The work of researchers and academicians was particularly helpful in identifying the greatest personal financial obstacles and risks consumers faced and best practices in delivering educational programming and counseling to the individual client. The Accredited Financial Counselor^{SM} (AFC$^{®}$) certification program, resulting from the committee's efforts and association sanction, was made available to professionals late in 1993. Since that time, AFPCE has certified more than 2,000 professionals and as of this writing, AFCPE hosts over 2,000 members and certificants in good standing.

AFCPE's mission includes building the capacity of its practicing (counseling and educator) members to serve their clientele well. While the practitioners' work is very important to individuals and families, it is most likely to be successful when the practitioner employs strategies and practices confirmed through well-designed and implemented research programs. Conversely, researchers should look to practitioners to assist them in developing and prioritizing research questions and projects. An examination of research and its applicability to the provision of personal finance education and counseling programs to individuals and families is important in increasing the likelihood that programming will result in successful financial management practices.

Relating Research to Practice

Over the course of several years, it has become abundantly clear to AFCPE's staff and board of directors that the future of financial counseling and education depends upon the interdependency of research and practice. One current focus of the AFCPE strategic plan includes building this capacity and interweaving research programs and practice outcomes. In 2006, the association embarked on a "listening" tour of sorts. Several forums were used to gather information about the current state and future needs of financial education and counseling. These included a survey of members and a conference workshop.

In the 2006 survey, AFCPE members were asked to choose the "*one*" financial message consumers most need to hear from counselors and educators. The three most popular responses were (1) prepare a spending plan, (2) reduce debt and (3) save. During a workshop held at its annual conference in 2006 regarding the future of financial counseling and financial education, participants worked in teams to assemble "then" and "now" posters regarding financial messages, programs, research and program delivery. The topics that were repeated often on the "future" delivery posters included "online," "wherever you are," and "totally integrated." "Try something new," "innovative," "longitudinal," "decision making" and "integrated" were the words or phrases most often used on the "research—future" posters. "Financial freedom" was the overwhelming choice for the "one topic" programming needs to focus on in the future. "Wealth" and "nest egg," along with "truth" and "enlightenment," were highlighted often in the "message—future" posters.

The Current State of Personal Finance Research

The papers in this book provide a good synopsis of the history of research in the field of personal finance. They summarize or employ theories that form the basis for personal finance research, review data that has historically been available to or used by researchers, address Internet delivery of financial vehicles and services and examine consumer finance as it relates to specific populations or settings.

A perusal of research published in the past 5 years in six journals related to personal finance (*Financial Counseling and Planning, Journal of Personal Finance, Journal of Financial Planning, Financial Services Review, Journal of Consumer Affairs* and *Journal of Family and Economic Issues*) shows that the overwhelming majority of papers related to personal finance or financial counseling, and planning focused on (1) the relationship between specific demographic or social characteristics (e.g., life cycle stage, income) and a particular financial behavior (e.g., selecting a certain type of loan, saving money), (2) knowledge (e.g., about credit cards, savings, vehicles) and a particular financial behavior or (3) optimal behaviors (e.g., when to take Social Security benefits, assume investment risk or a particular mortgage). Israelsen and Hatch (2005) noted the lack of family financial management research in two leading family studies journals (*Family Relations* and *Journal of Marriage and the Family*).

Until recently, studies published in economics and finance journals focused heavily on the economic issues of the marketplace, individual decision making not directly related to financial decisions or corporate finance topics. Studies related to personal financial management behaviors are beginning to appear in these publications and other journals related to psychology and social work. The *Journal of Behavioral Economics* and *Journal of Economic Psychology* are dedicated to publishing research related to the interaction between economics and all types of behaviors and market choices.

Many of the studies published in journals regarding personal finance analyze data collected through large national surveys. The reliance on information from large data sets is practical for several reasons including availability, accessibility, cost and the opportunity to study large populations. Other projects employed localized surveys studying the choices of certain populations. Inherently, these are specific and not necessarily applicable to large populations. One common element in most of these works is a description of the behaviors of a particular group of respondents and an examination of the differences or similarities (often, demographic) betweens respondents who behaved one way rather than another.

Few published papers in personal finance research involve the collection and analysis of motivation data; satisfaction with and/or success of specific delivery methods of financial education, counseling or messages; or development of diagnostic tools for practitioner or educator use. However, the results of several research projects did provide results that could easily translate into useful information for a practitioner.

A good example of studies that provide results for use in research and practices include Lyons, Cude, Lawrence, and Gutter's (2005) project investigating online research methodologies, the results of which are useful in designing survey research programs. A paper written by Mayer, Huh, and Cude (2005) examined the role of cues in assessing web site credibility. The results offer direction in successfully providing financial information to consumers via the Internet. Two papers supported the use of one-to-one counseling. Collins (2007) studied the financial counseling process and its effects on mortgage default. Elliehausen, Lundquist, and Staten (2007) examined the impact of credit counseling on the subsequent behavior of borrowers. Three research papers considered the psychological and emotional aspects of financial management. The Clarke, Heaton, Israelsen, and Eggett (2005) and Pinto, Pacente, and Mansfield (2005) research examined how financial information, roles and responsibilities were passed from one generation to another and the effect on behavior. A paper studying the link between psychological type using a well-known personality profile scale and financial decision-making was presented by McKenna, Hyllegard, and Linder (2003). Two papers related to diagnosing financial distress and risk tolerance (Grable & Lytton, 1999; Prawitz et al., 2006) resulted in counseling tools that can be employed by practitioners to better serve their clients.

The Future of Personal Finance

The ultimate goal of a personal finance research program should be to enhance the long-term financial security and stability of all Americans. What the field of personal finance research neglects, and good practice requires, are studies related to the behavioral aspects of personal finance, the development of diagnostic and treatment tools and appropriate and useful delivery methods for financial counseling and education services. In addition, studies resulting in policy recommendations can enhance the awareness and importance of personal finance as a field of study. Such studies call for an interdisciplinary approach using the collaborative efforts of both researchers and practitioners.

Studies from the fields of behavioral economics and neurobehavioral sciences that may link the areas of personal finance and behavior change are emerging. In addition, evaluation experts are setting standards for developing and using both knowledge and outcome measures and reporting tools. Hopefully, personal finance researchers and practitioners will be involved with the design and implementation of such work.

Movements toward the understanding of decision-making, behavior change and program impact may require more research using scientific (as opposed to survey) observation and control group designs. Pilot studies may involve focus groups, case studies and observation research. Results of these more subjective research strategies can inform more in-depth control group and survey studies. And, a "wish list" of research would certainly include a longitudinal study of individual and family financial issues, motivations, decisions and outcomes of behavior change.

Below is a brief, non-exhaustive list of potential questions that a researcher interested in the practical use of his/her work might consider. The answers to these questions may vary by population, and practitioners would be grateful for those answers as well. In addition, most of the questions imply a subset of more detailed questions, answers to all of which would be of use to a financial educator or counselor. Note that none of the questions relate to knowledge gains unless that knowledge gain results in measurable behavior changes:

- Diagnostic and treatment tools:

  - What three (or five) measures can a counselor rely upon to diagnose financial trouble?
  - What budget planning tools result in reduced spending for consumers?
  - What roles do financial behavior rules (e.g., save 25 % of every raise) play in decreasing spending and increasing saving?
  - What roles do financial incentives play in decreasing spending and increasing saving?
  - Which treatment tools (e.g., counseling, cutting up credit cards) result in significantly reducing (1) an individual's propensity to consume and/or add to existing debt or (2) total outstanding debt load?
  - Which, if any, non-financial strategies or behaviors result in successful behavior changes such as reducing debt or increasing saving? For example, will an individual who watches fewer hours of television, does not carry credit cards in a wallet or shops only once a week decrease his spending?

- Messages and information presentation

  - What public financial messages result in a decrease in spending and debt and/or an increase in saving?
  - Which method(s) of presenting financial information to consumers is most likely to result in behavior change? For example, do consumers respond differently to financial information that is presented in dollars versus percentages or in prose versus graphs?
  - Are positive messages more successful than negative messages in inducing behavior change?

- Message, program and service delivery

  - Do behaviors differ when services are delivered via different media? For example, are consumers more likely to follow advice when given in person, through telephone, email or web-based counseling?
  - What counseling techniques are most successful in motivating a client to change his/her behavior for the better?
  - When is the best time in the decision-making process to provide education or counseling services?

Conclusion

During the past decade, for a variety of reasons, a marked increase in improving the financial literacy of Americans has developed. The media, policymakers and changing landscape of retirement plan programs have all contributed to the increased attention. Government entities, financial institutions and their foundations, community and social organizations and specialized financial education foundations serve the public interest through educational programming and research initiatives.

The field of personal finance research can play a significant role in fulfilling the needs of consumers, practitioners and policymakers. But, it is at crossroads. While it is interesting to know what people know and do, it is more important that practitioners understand what motivates a consumer to implement planned behaviors that increase the potential for long-term financial stability and security. In addition, studies that confirm best practices in terms of marketing and delivering financial education and counseling programs and common financial messages would be quite useful to practitioners. Policymakers rely on quality research to inform issues and outcomes.

The health care industry provides a suitable analogy for how the field of personal finance research needs to adapt to be more relevant. The counseling practitioner needs tools for diagnostic purposes and wants treatments that are effective in reducing financial distress and increasing a client's sense of financial well-being. Experts know what behaviors clients need to change to prevent financial instability and insecurity. But, counselors and educators will be more successful if they understand how to increase the likelihood that a family will accept and implement preventive practices.

Professional organizations, such as AFCPE, serve the personal finance profession best by uniting professionals with a diversity of perspectives to focus on common issues. Researchers, practitioners and educators, working together, can produce great outcomes from a well-designed national research program. The ultimate goal of a collaborative, interdisciplinary research program is to enhance the long-term financial security and stability of individuals and families.

References

AFCPE. (2003). The faces of history—the faces of the future. *AFCPE celebrates 20 years.* Columbus, OH: Association for Financial Counseling and Planning Education.

Clarke, M. C., Heaton, M. B., Israelsen, C. L., & Eggett, D. L. (2005). The acquisition of family financial roles and responsibilities. *Family and Consumer Sciences Research Journal, 33*(4), 321–340.

Collins, J. M. (2007). Exploring the design of financial counseling for mortgage borrowers in default. *Journal of Family and Economic Issues, 28*(2), 207–226.

Elliehausen, G., Lundquist, E. C., & Staten, M. E. (2007). The impact of credit counseling on subsequent borrower behavior. *Journal of Consumer Affairs, 41*(1), 1–28.

Grable, J. E., & Lytton, R.H. (1999). Risk tolerance quiz source: Financial risk tolerance revisited: The development of a risk assessment instrument. *Financial Services Review, 8*, 163–181.

Israelsen, C., & Hatch, S. (2005). Proactive research: Where art thou? *Financial Counseling and Planning, 16*(2), 91–96.

Lyons, A. C., Cude, B., Lawrence, F. C., & Gutter, M. (2005). Conducting research online: Challenges facing researchers in family and consumer sciences. *Family and Consumer Sciences Research Journal, 33*(4), 341–356.

Mayer, R. N., Huh, J., & Cude, B. J. (2005). Cues of credibility and price performance of life insurance comparison web sites. *Journal of Consumer Affairs, 39*(1), 71–94.

McKenna, J., Hyllegard, K., & Linder, R. (2003). Linking psychological type to financial decision-making. *Financial Counseling and Planning 14*(1), 19–30.

Pinto, M. B., Pacente, D. H., & Mansfield, P. M. (2005). Information learned from socialization agents: Its relationship to credit card use. *Family and Consumer Sciences Research Journal, 33*(4), 357–367.

Prawitz, A. D., Garman, E. T., Sorhaindo, B., O'Neill, B., Kim, J., & Drentea, P. (2006). InCharge Financial Distress/Financial Well-Being Scale: Development, administration, and score interpretation. *Financial Counseling and Planning, 17*(1), 34–50.

Index

Printed in the United States
100218LV00001B/12/A